Poison Blossoms from a Thicket of Thorn

Poison Blossoms
from a Thicket of Thorn

HAKUIN ZENJI

TRANSLATED BY

Norman Waddell

COUNTERPOINT · BERKELEY

Library of Congress Cataloging-in-Publication Data

Hakuin, 1686–1769, author.
  [Keiso dokuzui. English]
  Poison blossoms from a thicket of thorn / Hakuin Zenji ; translated by Norman Waddell.
    pages cm
  ISBN 978-1-61902-312-3 (hardback)
  1. Zen Buddhism—Early works to 1800. I. Title.
  BQ9399.E594K4513 2014
  294.3'927—dc23
                                        2013046383

Cover design and interior design by Gopa & Ted2

COUNTERPOINT
www.counterpointpress.com

Distributed by Publishers Group West
Printed in the United States of America

10 9 8 7 6 5 4 3 2 1

To the Memory of R. H. Blyth

. . . .

Contents

BOOK TWO: INSTRUCTIONS TO THE ASSEMBLY—GENERAL
DISCOURSES—VERSE COMMENTS ON OLD KOANS—
EXAMINING OLD KOANS

BOOK SEVEN: PREFACES (*JO*)—POSTSCRIPTS (*BATSU*)— INSCRIPTIONS (*MEI*)

Chronology of Hakuin's Life

1685	Born to the Nagasawa family of Hara, a village in Suruga province that served as a post station on the Tokaido Road linking Edo and Kyoto
1695–98	Performs austerities and sutra recitations to allay fears of hell
1699	Ordained by Tanrei Soden at the Rinzai temple Shōin-ji next to the family home, receiving name "Ekaku," "Wise Crane." Becomes student of Sokudō Fueki at Daishō-ji in Numazu
1703–1717	Extended Zen pilgrimage around the central and western Japanese provinces
1704	Studies literature with Priest Baō in Mino province
1705	Resumes pilgrimage; visits temples in western Japan and Shikoku
1707	Returns to Mino to nurse Baō, devoting nights to zazen. At Shōin-ji during catastrophic eruption of Mount Fuji
1708–10	Enlightenment at Eigan-ji in Echigo province. Deepens attainment with eight months study under Shōju Rōjin in Shinano province. Resumes pilgrimage; feeling "lack of freedom" in everyday life. Contracts "Zen sickness"; cures himself using Introspective Meditation learned from the hermit Hakuyū in Kyoto
1712	Nurses Sokudō, devotes spare moments to zazen and study of Zen records
1713–14	Visits Ōbaku priest Egoku; enters training hall of Inryō-ji, Sōtō temple in Izumi province
1715–16	Solitary practice at Mount Iwataki (Mino); returns at father's request to reside at Shōin-ji
1717	Installed as priest of Shōin-ji; continues post-satori training.
1718	Adopts name "Hakuin." Begins Zen to lecture on Zen texts

1726	Experiences decisive enlightenment while reading *Lotus Sutra*
1727–47	Instructs students at Shōin-ji. First large lecture meeting on *Record of Hsu-t'ang*, attended by four hundred people. Recognized as leading Zen teacher. First publication, *Sokkō-roku kaien-fusetsu*, appears
1747–ca.1760	Teaches at Shōin-ji; travels extensively to teach at other temples; publishes many works in Japanese and Chinese
1751	Lectures on *Blue Cliff Record* at Yōgen-in subtemple of Myōshin-ji headquarters temple in Kyoto
1758	Publishes *Gudō's (Precious Mirror's) Lingering Radiance.* Purchases Ryūtaku-ji site in Mishima
1759	*Poison Blossoms from a Thicket of Thorn* and *Supplement* published this year or next
1760	Appoints Tōrei abbot of newly built Ryūtaku-ji
1763	Physical debility gradually worsens
1764	Suiō Genro installed as successor at Shōin-ji
1766	Announces will no longer receive students. Autobiographical *Wild Ivy* published
1767	Lectures on *Poison Flowers from a Thicket of Thorn* at Ryūtaku-ji
1768	Lectures on *Supplement* to *Poison Flowers from a Thicket of Thorn.* Condition deteriorates; entrusts Suiō with personal affairs; dies on eleventh of the twelfth month

Introduction

*P*OISON BLOSSOMS FROM A THICKET OF THORN is a translation of selected works from *Keisō dokuzui*, a nine-volume compilation of Zen master Hakuin's (1685–1768) oral and written teachings. *Poison Blossoms* contains material spanning a period of roughly fifty years, from Hakuin's mid-twenties, when he was still engaged in Zen training, up until his early seventies, when the work was compiled. Also translated are two supplements, *Keisō dokuzui Shūi* (*Supplement to Poison Blossoms from a Thicket of Thorn*) and *Gudō's Lingering Radiance* (*Hōkan Ishō*), which were published around the same time as the main collection.

Iida Tōin (1863–1937), one of the most highly respected Japanese Zen masters of the modern period, with strong roots in both Sōtō and Rinzai traditions, had this to say about *Poison Blossoms*:

> Anyone who wants to understand Master Hakuin must read *Poison Blossoms from a Thicket of Thorn*. Half-baked Zen teachers who disparage Hakuin without having read it are like blind men groping at an elephant…. As the title indicates, it contains much material that is extremely difficult to grasp. Yet how can anyone claiming to be a descendant of Hakuin really know him unless he has read this work? I have always kept my own copy close at hand. It gives me the feeling that I am living together with the old master (*Zen'yū ni ataeru no sho* [*A Book for My Zen Friends*], pp. 305–6).

Besides being the longest of Hakuin's works, *Poison Blossoms* is also one of the most important. Statements in his letters—"Everyone is urging me to deliver lectures on my records in Kyoto [as soon as they are published]…. It will help to make them more widely known"—are an indication of the high expectations he and his followers had for it. The considerable effort he took to get it into print also reflects an awareness of its significance as a literary legacy: a sense that this would likely be the work by which later generations would judge him.

Like his contemporary Samuel Johnson, who opined that that every man's life can be best written by himself, Hakuin was apparently convinced that the surest way to guarantee that the publishing of his life records was done properly, was to do it himself. In contrast to most of his other writings, which are directed primarily at contemporary readers, *Poison Blossoms* and the *Chronological Biography of Zen Master Hakuin*, both compiled at about the same time, have their sights set on posterity.

Despite this, *Poison Blossoms* has remained largely unread to this day, even by priests of Hakuin's own Rinzai school, and in contrast to mainstays of Hakuin Zen such as *Yasenkanna* (*Idle Talk on a Night Boat*) and *Oradegama,* which have appeared in many editions over the years and attracted a wide variety of readers, it is virtually unknown. While the reason for such disregard is no doubt the formidable difficulties it presents to the reader, ironically, it is this very obstacle that has provided us with the keys to unlock its secrets.

When *Poison Blossoms* was finally published and Hakuin began lecturing and giving talks on it to students, his primary aim was of course a Zen-type exposition of its contents. Students who attended these gatherings inscribed the master's comments and explanations into their own copies of the book. Their transcriptions are often quotes of Hakuin's words verbatim, even to replicating the distinctive colloquialisms he used, giving readers the feeling of sitting in on one of the sessions. These annotated copies, especially those made by Hakuin's leading disciples, are extremely valuable to a reader of *Poison Blossoms*, for in inscribing their teacher's words for their own use, these young monks have enabled future readers to grasp the true meaning of a great many difficult passages.

Poison Blossoms belongs the *goroku* (Chinese, *yu-lu*) or "Zen records" genre, which for over a thousand years has been used in China, Korea, and Japan to preserve the words and deeds of eminent teachers for posterity. Compilations of these records, published individually, have accumulated over the centuries into a vast repository of teachings, dialogues, anecdotes, and writings, constituting by far the largest body of material in the Zen school's enormous literary canon.

The first of these Zen records appeared in the mid-T'ang dynasty. By the Sung dynasty, reflecting large institutional changes in Chinese Zen, a greater variety of material, genres such as religious verse, painting inscriptions, and letters were often included as well. Introduced into Japan along with the Zen teachings in the Kamakura period, these books became models for similar collections that the Japanese were soon compiling for their own priests. At their best, in the records of such priests as Lin-chi, Yun-men, and Hsu-t'ang, which are filled with inspiring Zen dialogue, vigorous encounters between master and disciple, and, in Hsu-t'ang's case, verse, they are among the most important works in the Zen literary tradition.

Poison Blossoms from a Thicket of Thorn, appearing in the Edo period near the tail end of this tradition, adheres to the same general format, containing talks and teachings in a wide variety of forms and styles: instructions delivered on various occasions; formal and informal talks; verse and prose comments on koans; cautions on practice for individual students; remarks uttered at anniversaries, funeral services, and other temple observances; essays, explanations of terms from Buddhist scripture; letters, prefaces, and epilogues; painting inscriptions, a great many religious verses, and extended commentaries on the *Heart Sutra* and Tung-shan's Five Ranks.

Yet *Poison Blossoms* also breaks with tradition in many ways, bearing like other aspects of Hakuin's teaching the unmistakable stamp of his unique Zen style. For example, although normally a Zen teacher's records are collected by his disciples after his death, in Hakuin's case not only was this done during his lifetime, but on his own initiative as well. Hakuin provided the manuscripts and pushed the project forward in the face of several serious setbacks. His disciples may have had roles in editing the collection, but I think we can safely assume that the master helped select the pieces and retained a strong hand in the editorial process. The title itself, *Poison Blossoms from a Thicket of Thorn*, is unusual; Zen records were invariably called simply, "The Recorded Sayings of Such-and-Such Priest." When *Poison Blossoms* was published, Hakuin began lecturing on it as though it was a classic Zen text, something that had never been done before either. No one had done it, that is, except Hakuin, who had already conducted lecture meetings on other of his works.

Hakuin's first title for the book seems to have been *Sendai dokuzui shū*, "A Collection of a Dharma Reprobate's Poison Flowers" ("Dharma Reprobate" is one of Hakuin's sobriquets). We know from his letters that he changed this to *Yōen dokuzui*, "Poison Blossoms From a Garden of Demons," before settling shortly before publication on *Keisō dokuzui*, "Poison Blossoms *from a Thicket of Thorn,"* a title apparently suggested to him by his student Daishū, who was editing the work.

Although the phrase "thicket of thorn" (*keisō*) occurs once in the *Chronological Biography* (*Precious Mirror Cave*, p. 196), the term *keisō dokuzui* does not appear anywhere else in Hakuin's writings. In the *Blue Cliff Record* and other classic Zen works, it is used to describe the venomous utterances—koans or words of a similar nature—that Zen teachers employ to spur students forward in their struggle to reach enlightenment.

THE PRINTING OF *POISON BLOSSOMS*

After publishing his first work in his late fifties, Hakuin wrote and printed more than thirty others over the final twenty-five years of his life. He was often able to finance the printing with money he received from friends and lay students, though when the donations were not sufficient, he was also obliged at times to contribute funds himself. Hakuin's entreaties to prospective donors reveal the various shifts he used as he struggled to line up donations, and are one of the hallmarks of his letters from this period. The letters also show him hounding disciples and urging publishers to get on with the printing process, sometimes before he has come up with the money, and sometimes even before he has begun writing the manuscript.

The first mention of Hakuin's Zen records is this not entirely accurate entry in the *Chronological Biography* (1756, age 71):

> A manuscript compilation of the master's writings and sayings made by his attendant Daishū was obtained by a layman from Osaka named Kida Ganshō [who had come to study at Hakuin's temple]. When Kida returned to Osaka he secretly took the manuscript with him and had it printed there (*Precious Mirror Cave*, p. 223).

Layman Kida (n.d.), after reading the work in manuscript, had evidently given Hakuin his promise that he would underwrite the cost of having it published. A colophon bearing Kida's name is attached to the printed edition of *Poison Blossoms*, giving what might be called the official account of the project:

> On my way through Suruga to the northeastern provinces in the winter of the sixth year of the Hōreki era (1756), I stopped at Shōin-ji to have an audience with Zen master Hakuin. He was

suffering from illness at the time, so I waited until his condition improved to receive his teaching. This gave me an opportunity to read a manuscript of his Zen records, compiled in nine fascicles by his student Daishū from Hōki province, which was kept in the attendants' quarters. In the work, master Hakuin vigorously attacks the sham Zen teachings that have appeared around the country with words and phrases of great power and penetrating insight. It was like hearing the howls of the lion king, or deep, ground-shaking thunder. At times the master points out errors in the *Blue Cliff Record*, at times he clarifies the meaning of Tung-shan's Five Ranks. Anyone who reads it is certain to cast false teachings aside and turn to the authentic path of Zen. In these pages, the guidance Hakuin gives to students negotiating the secret depths emerges with great strength and vigor. It is totally beyond ordinary, unenlightened understanding. If a work such as this did not exist, how could students become aware of the genuine path of Zen practice?

I thought that publishing this manuscript would help students to more readily penetrate the Zen source. When I mentioned this to Hakuin Rōshi, he replied, "No, don't do that. If the notions my mouth happens to mumble off when I am asleep are published, it will only steer future generations off course. Take the manuscript and burn it. I don't see any need to make a special effort to humiliate myself." Despite my most earnest attempts to make him change his mind, he remained adamantly opposed to the idea.

So when it came time for me to leave Shōin-ji, I bundled the manuscript secretly in with my belongings and took it back to Osaka with me. I began making arrangements for it be published as quickly as possible. There was no time for the text to undergo proper editing, so it is possible that some of the Chinese characters in the text may be mistaken. For that I must beg the reader's indulgence. It is nonetheless my hope and prayer that once these records are published, they will become a standard against which future generations of Zen students will measure themselves.

As we will see, however, Hakuin's letters tell a quite different story, showing clearly that he did everything in his power to get the work into print, and kept the project alive when circumstances threatened to sideline it.

Moreover, the content of Kida's colophon and style in which it is written so closely resemble Hakuin's own writings, that there seems little doubt it was not even written by Kida, but by Hakuin himself, who for some reason decided to compose it for him. Kida's colophon thus becomes, like Hakuin's story about learning techniques of meditation from the hermit Hakuyū in his cave in Kyoto, one of the "poetic fictions" one encounters from time to time in Hakuin's writings.

Poison Blossoms was printed in Kyoto, the center for Buddhist publishing at the time. Hakuin had sent his student Daishū Zenjo there to oversee the work and to act as a go-between in negotiations with the bookseller who had been commissioned to print the work. From the example of books such as *Idle Talk on a Night Boat* and *Gudō's Lingering Radiance*, which appeared at about the same time as *Poison Blossoms*, we know that when the printer already had payment in hand he could produce a single volume, writing a fair copy of the text, carving the blocks, and printing and binding the pages, in under a month. But given the size of *Poison Blossoms* and the great cost involved in producing it, the mere promise of payment was evidently not enough to induce the bookseller to start this process. So when Kida failed to produce the funds he had promised, work came to a standstill, delaying publication for well over a year.

Hakuin's attempts to persuade Kida to honor his commitment, and then to find some other means of covering the shortfall, are revealed in a series of six letters he sent Daishū in Kyoto as these events were unfolding. As I have already published translations of the letters in *Beating the Cloth Drum* (pp. 118–141), in recounting the story here I will merely summarize their contents.

The trouble that became the cause of all the printing delays had its source in a preface Hakuin had asked the Confucian teacher Yanada Zeigan (1672–1757) to write for *Poison Blossoms*. Zeigan, in the employ of the Daimyō of Akashi, a port city on the Inland Sea just west of modern Kobe, was one of the foremost Confucian scholars of the Edo period. Widely respected for his skill in composing Chinese poetry and prose, he also had a well-earned reputation for speaking his mind.

Hakuin first met Zeigan in 1750 when he was visiting Ryōkoku-ji in Akashi to conduct a large lecture meeting. In marked contrast to most Confucian teachers of the time, Zeigan had a genuine interest in Buddhism, especially Zen, and the two men seem to have quickly become good friends. Zeigan composed a verse praising Hakuin, thirteen years his junior, in glowing terms as a great figure of modern Japanese Zen.

Hakuin no doubt responded in kind; although his verse has not survived, we may assume that it was equally fair-spoken. In another verse, which is included in *Poison Blossoms*, Hakuin extolled Zeigan as "Deeply versed in Confucianism, Taoism, and Buddhism, / A great teacher who advocates the cardinal human virtues. / A great citizen of Akashi who follows in the illustrious footsteps of Hitomaro." There was a shrine to Kakinomoto Hitomaro, the ancient Japanese poet honored as the god of poetry, in Akashi, which was also the site of one of Hitomaro's most famous verses (see *Religious Art of Zen Master Hakuin*, p. 195).

That Zeigan was not merely praising Hakuin in his verse as a matter of literary convention is clear from a letter he wrote to one of his students in reply to a question about the "the grievous state of contemporary Buddhism." In his answer, Zeigan refers to his own interest in Zen as a young man, and though agreeing with the student's overall assessment, points out a few exceptions:

> The present generation of 'shavepates' are concerned mainly with fame and profit; they keep concubines and eat fish, and are unscrupulous in hoodwinking lay people into respecting them. Although priests in the Sōtō and Ōbaku schools still strictly uphold the precepts against sake and tobacco, many of the Rinzai priests you see make no attempt whatever to observe them. Nonetheless, genuine Zen priests such as Daigū, Gudō, Bankei, Tenkei, Kogetsu, and Hakuin have also appeared in the modern age. Their teaching styles may differ, but I believe that these men all attained the strength and capacity to pass on the transmission of the Zen lamp. (*Yanada Zeigan Zenshū*, p. 242)

Hakuin was no doubt pleased and gratified that his friend, a scholar whose erudition was unmatched at the time, had agreed to contribute a preface to this important publication. Unfortunately, their amicable relationship underwent an abrupt and irrevocable change when news reached Hakuin that Zeigan, after reading the manuscript of *Poison Blossoms*, had advised him to delete a piece titled "Reading *Jinja-kō Bengi*" (translated #161).

In this piece, Hakuin harshly attacked the anti-Buddhist views of Hayashi Razan (1583–1657), founder of the Hayashi School of Japanese Neo-Confucianism. As an advisor to the early Tokugawa shōguns, Razan was an iconic figure who had played a central role in establishing

Neo-Confucianism as the orthodox creed of Tokugawa governance, and he was still a powerful symbol of that policy. No doubt Zeigan was concerned that such an intemperate attack on Razan might attract the attention of government censors. His advice may also have been influenced by the knowledge that several years earlier Hakuin's *Snake Strawberries* had been put on the list of proscribed writings for breaking the taboo of mentioning Tokugawa Ieyasu, the first Tokugawa shōgun.

Zeigan's advice is the focus of the first of Hakuin's letters to Daishū, dated the fourth month of 1757. His reaction to Zeigan's well-intentioned suggestion is surprisingly harsh. He orders Daishū to "forget about Zeigan's preface," blustering that he no longer has any intention of using it. He also tells Daishū to inform Layman Kida of this decision.

In his second letter a little less than three months later, Hakuin tells Daishū that he has sent him funds to hire a scribe to write out a fair copy of the *Poison Blossoms* text for the woodblock engravers. This tells us that the work had still not gone beyond the editing stage. He has also apparently given more thought to Zeigan's advice, since he informs Daishū that he has decided "just in case" to move the piece on Razan from the main work to the end of the one-volume *Supplement*, where it would be easier to delete in the event trouble should arise. He also suggests that it might be a good idea to turn the book into a private, temple edition, presumably to protect the publisher and donors.

This second letter also contains the first intimation that Layman Kida is having second thoughts about providing the money to have the work printed. "Since Kida has still not made the donation," Hakuin tells Daishū, "you should discuss the matter with him very, very carefully, exercising the greatest prudence, but you should make known to him that I have been telling people about 'a praiseworthy layman' [Kida] who has volunteered to donate the funds for my Zen records." Kida should also be made aware that any mistakes Zeigan may have pointed out, miswritten Chinese characters, stylistic errors and the like, "are matters of no concern whatever in a book of Zen records." Finally, he reminds his student that "it would be an utter disgrace if the project had to be abandoned at this point."

But as the next letter shows, Kida's reason for dragging his feet on this matter apparently had less to do with the work's literary merits than it did with his reaction as a prudent Osaka merchant to the knowledge that as chief donor he might have to share some of the blame if government censors decided to bring action against the Razan piece.

This third letter, undated but obviously written a few weeks after the previous one, was sent from Kiso province, where Hakuin was traveling to conduct a round of lecture meetings (*Beating the Cloth Drum*, pp. 127–139). In it, Hakuin tells Daishū how pleased he was to receive copies of *Idle Talk on a Night Boat*, which had just been published in Kyoto under Daishū's supervision. But he notes with sadness the continued lack of progress on *Poison Blossoms*. His exasperation at learning that a fair copy has not even been completed leads him to deliver a further blast at Zeigan: "It was his advice [to scratch the Razan piece] that has caused Layman Kida to withhold the funds he had promised." While Hakuin admits that these "unexpected setbacks" have taken him "totally by surprise and thoroughly disappointed him," he can still refer to them as an "unavoidable set of circumstances that are due entirely to my own lack of virtue." Although he sounds as though he has still not entirely given up on Kida, one now senses a confidence that even without Kida's help he will be able to pony up the necessary donations from priests and laymen who have come to attend his meeting.

In his reply to Hakuin, Daishū seems to have referred once again to the errors Zeigan had pointed out in the work. "Those are the objections of a dull and ignorant scholar who lacks the eye of *kenshō*," barked Hakuin. "A man with no understanding of Zen, who just bandies words about while feeding on the dregs of the ancients. Even were a million like him to appear and voice similar objections, they would be equally worthless. Clear-eyed Zen masters who emerge in future from the ocean of the true Dharma, and truly superior students who have fought their way through the thicket of thorn and briar, will all admire and praise this work."

Ironically, on the seventeenth of the seventh month, only weeks after this letter was sent, the old scholar passed away at his home in Akashi at the age of eighty-five, perhaps not even having been apprised of Hakuin's displeasure.

There are no letters after this until the fourth month of 1758, almost eleven months later. Hakuin was now at Rurikō-ji in Mino province conducting a lecture meeting to commemorate the one hundredth anniversary of Gudō Tōshoku's (1579–1666) death. Hakuin deeply revered this eminent Myōshin-ji priest, regarding him as his great-grandfather in the Dharma. He proposed that an edition of Gudō's Zen records, which still remained in manuscript, be published. He tried to enlist the help of the participants at the lecture meeting, and he sent a letter to leading priests in Gudō's teaching line asking them to take part in the project as well.

Exasperated when the priests showed scant enthusiasm for the idea,

Hakuin immediately began composing a work in praise of Gudō and his achievements, pointing out the important role Gudō had played in keeping the traditions of koan Zen alive at a difficult point in its history. He also includes some harsh criticisms of his fellow priests for failing to understand the extent of their debt to Gudō.

Hakuin states that he had composed the work in the space of six or seven days, as he was jolted along in a palanquin between temples in Mino and Hida provinces, and that his real reason for writing it was the sadness he felt on witnessing the decline of the Zen school and the degeneration of authentic koan practice.

At Sōyū-ji in Takayama, Hida province, the next stop on Hakuin's teaching tour, members of the lay community pledged donations to cover the cost of printing the newly completed work, which he had now titled *Gudō's Lingering Radiance* (translated in Book Eleven). Hakuin's original intention may have been to publish *Lingering Radiance* as a supplement to the edition of Gudō's records he had proposed, but this plan had to be abandoned for lack of financial support, and Gudō's records were not published until 1797, twenty-nine years after Hakuin's death. Owing to the funds he received from the Sōyū-ji donors, however, Hakuin was able to send *Gudō's Lingering Radiance* to Daishū in Kyoto with directions that it be printed immediately. It appeared as a single, independent volume only a few months later, an inscription on its title page identifying it as a supplement to *Poison Blossoms*.

From the next letter, dated later the same month and written while Hakuin was still on the road, we learn that work on *Poison Blossoms* remained at a standstill ("The lack of progress is very discouraging"), but that yet another one-volume supplement, containing additional material that had been omitted from the original compilation, was in the works. The funds to publish it had been donated by Hakuin's longtime friend and lay student Shibata Gonzaemon. It probably appeared in 1759, at about the same time as *Poison Blossoms* itself (see *Beating the Cloth Drum*, p. 138).

The final letter in the series, posted three weeks later, contains nothing new on the publishing front, just continued expressions of disappointment at the lack of progress. Not too long after this, however, the logjam was somehow broken. There is nothing in the written record to explain how it happened. Layman Kida may have finally decided to donate the funds, or perhaps another of Hakuin's wealthy lay students came forward to help.

In any case, either at the end of 1758, or at some point in the following year, the book finally appeared, at about the same time as the one-volume *Supplement* and some months after *Gudō's Lingering Radiance.*

THE BOOK

The texts that were used to compile the original edition of *Poison Blossoms* were taken from two manuscript collections, both titled *Sendai dokugo shū,* "*A Collection of the Poison Words of a Dharma Reprobate,*" which were once preserved at Jishō-ji, the temple in Kyushu where the editor Daishū had served as head priest. One of these manuscripts, containing many passages in Hakuin's handwriting, apparently served as the basic sourcebook for *Poison Blossoms.* The other is an edited version of this text, presumably by Daishū, arranged under headings similar to those found in the final, printed version. It contains numerous corrections by various hands, including some by Hakuin.

Only one copy of the first printed edition of *Poison Blossoms* is known. Instead of the bookseller or publisher's name and device that is usually found on the final page, it bears the imprint Ganshō-tei. This name is found nowhere else in the records, and is probably one that Hakuin coined for the occasion. There is a preface by Sugawara Tameshige (n.d.), a Kyoto courtier whose connection to Hakuin is unknown. Sugawara was Hakuin's third choice. He initially asked Reizei Muneie (1701–69), another Kyoto courtier, and when Reizei declined, he asked Yanada Zeigan. When Zeigan fell into disfavor, he turned to Sugawara.

It is unclear when the second edition appeared, but it must have been during Hakuin's lifetime, since it was that edition in which Hakuin's disciples inscribed their annotations of Hakuin's talks. This second edition bears the joint imprint of booksellers Ogawa Gembei of Kyoto and Funatsu Shinuemon of Osaka, who evidently added their device after it became clear that no action would be taken against the book. Later imprints of this edition contain a second preface dated 1769, the year after Hakuin's death, in which it is stated that Empress Go-Sakuramachi had awarded Hakuin the posthumous *Zenshi* ("Zen master") title Shinki Dokumyō. With these exceptions, the text is unchanged from the first edition. This *rufu-bon,* or so-called "popular edition," is usually encountered in a uniform set including the *Supplement,* made up of ten fascicles (*kan*) in six volumes. The title on the inside front cover of volume one and the title strips on the covers of each of the individual volumes are printed in facsimile of calligraphy by the well-known Nanga painter Ike Taiga, who had studied Zen under Hakuin.

ANNOTATIONS

The annotations that students who attended Hakuin's talks on *Poison Blossoms* inscribed in their copies of the book, preserving Hakuin's explanations of his own words as well as additional remarks by close disciples such as Tōrei, not only give valuable insights into the passage in question, but often make it possible for us to read passages that would otherwise be extremely difficult to understand.

On a religious level, the annotations become in effect Hakuin's (or the annotator's) "capping words" (*jakugo*) on the text in question, acting as pointers to their true significance. On a more mundane level, they provide nearly flawless glosses on difficult terms and phrases and verbal allusions. They also identify people for whom Hakuin wrote the pieces, and the circumstances under which they were composed. Taken together, this wealth of information allows us to grasp Hakuin's utterances as he intended them to be understood, while at the same time giving them much greater interest.

Until recently, access to these annotated copies has been limited to the handful of Rinzai priests and laymen who owned them. Since over the past half-century most of these copies have found their way into library collections, future generations should eventually have access to them. The first critical edition of *Poison Blossoms,* based largely on the information in these annotated copies and containing glosses on all the difficult passages and cruxes, will soon be published in Japanese. Two hundred and fifty years after *Poison Blossoms* was published, the young student-annotators who transcribed their teacher's comments for their personal use have thus unwittingly made the contents of this vast storehouse of Hakuin Zen accessible to modern readers and enabled them to understand the meaning Hakuin intended when he wrote the pieces. The word "accessible" must of course be understood in a relative sense, since in the final and most important analysis, *Poison Blossoms* must always remain a singularly difficult, and unglossable, work.

THE TRANSLATION

The nine "books" and two supplements (here titled Books Ten and Eleven) that make up the *Poison Blossoms* collection are all composed in Chinese *kambun*. They consist of approximately four hundred and forty individual items, ranging in length from four-line verses to essays, discourses, and commentaries covering many pages of text. I have translated approximately two-fifths of the pieces, or a little over half in terms of total pages. I have translated all of the longer and most important pieces, and Book Six, containing the letters, and Book Eleven, *Gudō's Lingering Radiance*, in their entirety.

The translation is based on the text found in volume two of the *Hakuin Oshō Zenshū (Complete Works of Zen Master Hakuin)*. I was able to incorporate material found in Yoshizawa Katsuhiro's critical edition of *Poison Blossoms*, which is now the process of being published. I have made extensive use of his glosses on the text and in particular those containing the annotations described above, many of which I have incorporated into my own notes. When citing the annotations in the headnotes and afterwords to the individual pieces, I have set them in quotation marks, followed by (*annotation*), to distinguish them from my own remarks.

Items are numbered consecutively. I did not think it necessary to add the pages in the *Complete Works* since they are easy to find there. To avoid the inconvenience of endnotes, background material, explanations of terms, and other general information are contained in headnotes and afterwords to the individual pieces.

Dates are given as they appear in the Japanese text, according to the lunar calendar in use in Edo Japan. Years correspond en gros with their Western counterparts, but it means, for example, that Hakuin's birth is given as the twenty-fifth day of the twelfth month of 1685, not January 19, 1686, as it would be if converted to the Western calendar. I have, however, used the Western method of calculating age, subtracting one year from the ages found in the original texts, which follow the Japanese system of counting a person one year old at birth.

I would like to thank Nelson Foster for reading drafts of many of the pieces and offering encouragement and valuable suggestions. I would also like to express my gratitude to Yoshizawa Katsuhiro for generously allowing me to make use of the unpublished manuscript of his critical edition of *Poison Blossoms*. I also want to thank my wife for the many unselfish ways in which she helps to make these books possible.

BOOK ONE
Instructions to the Assembly (*Jishū*)

. . . .

Book One consists of ninety Jishū, "Instructions to the Assembly." These instructions, which Hakuin gave on various occasions to monks and lay students, appear here under four subheadings: Jōdō, formal talks delivered from the high seat in the Dharma Hall; Shōsan, informal talks; Nenkō, comments delivered on offering incense at death anniversaries and other commemorative events; and Ko, comments delivered while examining old koans.

In Book One, as elsewhere, the editor Daishū seems have attempted to arrange the pieces in chronological order.

1. Instructions to the Assembly from the High Seat at the Winter Solstice

Annual ceremonies are held in Zen temples to observe the beginning and end of the summer retreat, the winter and summer solstices, and anniversaries of prominent figures such as the Buddha and Bodhidharma. These first items, probably written in Hakuin's mid-thirties, give us glimpses of his teaching at a time when he was still engaged in post-satori training as head priest of Shōin-ji, his final decisive enlightenment still some years in the future.

In the tenth month, *yin* energy having reached its farthest point, *yang* energy begins again. Doesn't this express the propitious circumstances of Zen practicers who experience the great death and are then born again? It is a shame that wherever you go today you find people who have once experienced the bean bursting suddenly in the cold ashes turning into gimp-legged turtles, working themselves into a glass jar until they are unable to move. Unless they encounter the fangs and talons of the Dharma cave (koans), they will never gain their freedom until the day they die. Why is this?

When Liu Pang entered Han-chung, he signaled to his counselor Chang Liang to burn the plank road. How do you clarify this? The Chun Hexagram, Nine at the Beginning.

. . . .

The opening quotation is based on comments on the Fu (Return) Hexagram in the *Book of Changes.*

The tenth and eleventh months of the lunar calendar correspond approximately to December and January in the Western calendar.

The bean bursting suddenly open (reihai ichibaku) is descriptive of the sudden and unexpected way in which satori occurs.

When Liu Pang entered...burn the plank road. The statesman Chang Liang (262–189 BC) dedicated his life to overthrowing the Ch'in state that had annexed his country through war. Liu Pang, general of one of the rebel

armies attempting to regain the lost territory, took Chang Liang into his service. One of Chang Liang's counsels after Liu Pang succeeded in capturing
Han-chung in the Ch'in heartland, was to burn the plank road they had used
to reach Han-chung. This was a road constructed along a river gorge by setting wooden beams into holes cut in the cliff side. Burning this bridge, said
Chang Liang, would show Liu Pang's superior, who feared him as a rival, that
he had no intention of returning and was therefore not dangerous. Using this
and other strategies suggested by Chang Liang, Liu Pang went on to establish
himself as the first emperor of the Han dynasty. Here, Hakuin uses this saying
to indicate the wisdom of not attaching to a minor satori, once it is attained,
in order to achieve the final objective of great satori.

In the *Book of Changes*, the Chun ("Difficulty at the Beginning") Hexagram indicates the difficulties that arise when heaven and earth first meet
and all things are brought forth: "In the configuration Nine at the Beginning,
hesitation and hindrance still prevail, but it will benefit you to remain loyal
and constant, it will benefit you to give support to your lord." An ancient
commentary on this says: "Although experiencing hesitation and hindrance,
your aspiration is still to do what is right. When an eminent man subordi-
nates himself to those below him, he gains the hearts of all people" (The *I
Ching*, Cary Baynes, 2, p. 35).

Nine at the beginning. Hakuin uses these words as a koan: "This phrase is
a divine amulet that transforms your very bones. An indolent person could
never understand it." (annotation)

: 2. INFORMAL TALK (*SHŌSAN*) ON NEW YEAR'S EVE

*This Informal Talk is also an early one, probably written prior to
Hakuin's thirty-sixth year.*

*In contrast to Jōdō, which are formally delivered from the high
seat in the Dharma Hall, Shōsan are occasional teachings, that is,
not limited to a specific time or occasion. It should be noted, however, that terms such as these would be more appropriate in the
setting of a large monastery training hall. Hakuin, teaching in a tiny
country temple, did in any case not scruple over such fine distinctions. He is known to have delivered even the formal Jōdō lectures
in a quite informal manner on occasion, at times wearing ordinary
work attire.*

It is interesting to compare the comments Hakuin makes below on the New Year's preparations at Shōin-ji with a more detailed description in a verse comment he attaches to the word Emptiness in his commentary on the Heart Sutra (see Book Ten, pp. 377–385).

TONIGHT THE OLD YEAR ends. Tomorrow the new one begins. In houses everywhere in the land people will put on their best clothes to welcome it in. Placed over every door are pine saplings with roots, oranges with green leaves. However, even at such a time, isn't there a place of vital importance completely untouched by either new or old? *What is it?*

The air clears, wind combs through the young willow's hair,
The ice melts, ripples wash through wiry old beards of moss.

Where do you find proof of this vital place? Tapping the floor with my staff, I say: Confucius prayed for a very long time.

. . . .

A place of vital importance. "Our Zen school isn't ruled by 'new' or by 'old.' Didn't Yun-men and Lin-chi create their own springtime, making myriad flowers blossom?" (annotation).

The air clears...moss. Hakuin gives as his comment well-known lines of verse by the Heian scholar Miyako no Yoshika (824–859). They are quoted in early collections such as the *Wakan-rōei-shū* and in later Noh and Kyōgen plays, usually accompanied an account of their provenance: e.g., a man walking past the Rashōmon Gate in Kyoto on a moonlit night recites the lines. A demon inhabiting the gate is so moved by their beauty that he blurts out words of praise (*Wakan-rōei-shū*). In some versions the man recites the first line and the demon supplies the second.

Confucius prayed. Confucius said that because he always used the greatest prudence in conducting his affairs, for him everyday life had become a kind of prayer. There was thus no need for him to pray to the gods at special occasions. In describing this final comment, an annotation says, "He (Hakuin) has loosed a poison arrow."

: 3. Words on Offering Incense at the Anniversary of Bodhidharma's Death

The anniversary commemorating Bodhidharma's death is held annually on the fifth of the tenth month. Hakuin's verse is addressed to Emperor Wu of Liang, whose famous encounter with Bodhidharma in his palace at Chin-ling is the subject of Case 1 in the Blue Cliff Record.

> Do you sigh about the days before he arrived in your realm,
> As you sat waiting, gussied up like a widow on a green silk rug?
> But after he entered your palace, you failed to understand,
> A young crow, its mother lost, cries in the freezing mist.

THE EMPEROR ASKED, "What is the first principle of the sacred truth?" Bodhidharma replied, "Vast emptiness, nothing sacred about it." "Then who stands before me here?" he asked. "I don't know," said Bodhidharma. The emperor, unable to understand, allowed Bodhidharma to leave for the kingdom of Wei. Later the Emperor discussed the matter with Duke Chih, who told him that his visitor was in fact an incarnation of the Bodhisattva Kannon, who transmitted the mind seal of the Buddha himself. Regretting his mistake, the Emperor decided to send an emissary to invite Bodhidharma back. Duke Chih stopped him, saying, "He would never return, even were everyone in the country to go after him."

. . . .

"When Bodhidharma departed for Wei, the Emperor lost a person who could have filled all his needs. Now he can only sit and regret the lost opportunity" (annotation).

Young crow is literally *tz'u-wu,* "compassionate bird," so called from the belief that crows who have left the nest return to feed their mothers. "A young crow that wanted to repay its great debt to its mother now perches in the evening twilight emitting plaintive cries of regret" (annotation).

: 4. INSTRUCTIONS DELIVERED TO THE ASSEMBLY ON RECEIVING THE *RECORD OF BUKKŌ*

These instructions were inspired by the arrival at Shōin-ji of a newly printed copy of the Record of Bukkō. *Bukkō is the honorific Kokushi or "National Master" title of the Chinese priest Wu-hsueh Tsu-yuan (1226–1286; Japanese, Mugaku Sogen), who played an important role in the early transmission of Chinese Zen to Japan. A passage in one of Hakuin's surviving letters shows him ordering the work from the Edo temple where it had been published: "I would trouble you to send me two or three copies of Bukkō's records as quickly as possible. I will put them to use in these days of the degenerate Dharma as medicine for opening students' eyes"). This edition of Bukkō's* Record *was published in 1726, placing this piece in Hakuin's forty-first year—the same year he achieved his final decisive enlightenment—or shortly after.*

Some of the references in the following piece are based on a passage in The Record of Bukkō: *"When I [Wu-hsueh] was living in the land of great Sung China, before I came to this country, a divine being appeared to me while I was sitting in samadhi....He approached and said, 'In your compassion for the suffering of sentient beings, I ask you to visit my country'....The dream recurred several times, preceded each time by a golden dragon that came and entered my sleeve, and by the appearance of flocks of pigeons. Blue pigeons and white pigeons would fly about, pecking the ground, hopping onto my knees. At the time I didn't know what to make of it. However, not long afterwards a Japanese gentleman came and told me that the Japanese Shōgun wished to invite me to his country....In Kamakura, when I visited the [Tsurugaoka Hachiman] Shrine to offer incense to the Great Bodhisattva Hachiman [a Shintō deity, god of archery and war, enshrined at the Hachiman Shrine; also known in his Buddhist manifestation as "Dai-Bosatsu"], I noticed several wooden carvings of pigeons in the rafters above. I asked about them...and was told, 'They are messengers of the deity.' I knew then that Hachiman was the Bodhisattva who had visited me in China. I have heretofore been reluctant to speak about this matter....Should you, my disciples, decide to make a Zen portrait (chinsō) of me, you should have the artist record this experience of my former days by depicting a golden dragon and a pair of pigeons standing on my robe at my feet."*

As a young monk, National Master Bukkō plumbed the depths of Wu-chun's Dragon Pool, licked up large dollops of his poisonous slobber, then clambered up to the top of Hsu-t'ang's Eagle Peak, where he received some stiff kicks from a resting bull. A tall bamboo at the gate, reeking with stinking fumes, scared the demons off quicker than a peach-wood charm.

As Bukkō was sitting on his zazen cushion, a flock of celestial pigeons and a divine dragon sent by the great deity of the Hachiman Shrine found their way into his slumbering brain. As he meditated on his bamboo chair, this golden dragon disturbed dreams that were still unachieved. As for those dreams, even old Elephant Bone wouldn't have known what to make of them.

When Bukkō was conducting ceremonies opening Engaku-ji, a group of white deer raced through the temple, disrupting the event. *Too bad he didn't take an arrow and pot them all!* Once when he was giving *sanzen*, a black viper made its way into his chambers, causing great confusion. What a hateful old bonze, his life taken up with such things, causing terminal torment in a great many wise people.

His Zen records—vines and creepers whose snarls spread over the earth and curl up even into the heavens—have been out of print, so when I heard that the priest of Gekkei-ji had reissued them, I immediately wrote him a letter and ordered some copies. I burdened the priest at Funi-an with the onerous task of carrying my missive over the treacherous Hakone Pass to deliver to Gekkei-ji in Edo.

When the books arrived at Shōin-ji, I took one out. Even before I opened the cover, I could sense the National Master's poisonous milk welling forth beneath my eyes. At the same time, I also sensed the presence of his Dharma heir National Master Bukkoku, founder of Ungan-ji. I want Bukkō's *Record* to remain here in my temple, protecting it long into the future.

. . . .

Wu-hsueh achieved an initial enlightenment while practicing under Wu-chun Shih-fan (1177–1249). After Wu-chun's death, he studied with other teachers including Hsu-t'ang Chih-yu. In 1279, at the invitation of Regent Hōjō Tokimune (1125–84), de facto ruler of Japan, Wu-hsueh arrived in Japan and was appointed abbot at Kenchō-ji in Kamakura. Three years later, he was installed as abbot and founder of Engaku-ji, a temple that Tokimune, who had become his student, built for him adjacent to Kenchō-ji.

Here Hakuin plays on names associated with these teachers. *Dragon Pool* (Lung-yen) is the name of Wu-chun's chambers at the Hsing-sheng Wan-shou-ssu monastery on Mount Ching. *Eagle Peak* (Chiu-ling) is another name for Lung-yin-ssu, the temple where Wu-hsueh studied with Hsu-t'ang. *Resting bull* alludes to Hsu-t'ang's sobriquet Hsi-keng (Jap. *Sokkō*), literally "to rest from tilling the land," and *tall bamboo*, to well-known lines from one of Hsu-t'ang's verses: "A tall bamboo stands by the gate as we go to part; its leaves stir a pure breeze to bid you farewell." In China, peachwood charms inscribed with images and inscriptions were hung over gateways and doors to ward off evil spirits. Hsu-t'ang's utterances, Hakuin infers, have a similar power to keep evil demons at bay. *Fox slobber (koen)*, a virulent poison, is here a metaphor for Wu-chun's Zen teaching.

Bukkō's *Record* also tells of a herd of deer appearing at the opening of Engaku-ji to hear Wu-hsueh deliver his teaching. Hakuin's comment, "*Too bad he didn't take an arrow and pot them all,*" alludes to a well-known dialogue T'ang master Ma-tsu had with a hunter named Shih-kung, which resulted in the latter's becoming a Buddhist priest. As Shih-kung was out hunting he happened upon Ma-tsu's hermitage. "Who are you?" asked Ma-tsu. "A hunter," he said. "Do you know how to shoot?" asked Ma-tsu. "Of course," replied Shih-kung. "How many deer can you shoot with a single arrow?" "One arrow, one deer," replied Shih-kung. "Then you don't know how to shoot," said Ma-tsu. "Do you?" asked Shih-kung. "Of course." "How many can you get with one arrow?" "The entire herd," replied the master (*Records of the Lamp*, ch. 6).

Old Elephant Bone is the T'ang priest Hsueh-feng I-ts'un, although it is not clear why Hakuin singles him out here as a diviner of dreams. An annotation on this sentence cites the koan Hsueh-feng Sees a Snake, which begins, "There's a turtle-nosed snake in the mountains south of here" (*Book of Equanimity*, Case 24), and makes the comment: "Hsueh-feng made a koan out of seeing a turtle-nosed snake, but even he couldn't have divined [the meaning of] these golden dragons." Perhaps Hakuin cites Hsueh-feng merely as someone possessed of especially keen discernment.

A black viper would make its way into his chambers during sanzen. Apparently Wu-hsueh confronted students during *sanzen* interviews with a koan, or koans, in which a dead viper appears. These koans do not seem to have been committed to paper. The dead snake image appears in the *Blue Cliff Record*, Case 66: a student playing with a dead snake returns it to life and is bitten and slain, and then reborn, thanks to its deadly venom. In *Dream*

Words from a Land of Dreams, Hakuin uses the image with a more or less similar meaning twice in capping words, e.g., he comments, referring to a student's exchange with Zen Master Daitō, "The man was a dead snake, but Daitō's words brought him back to life" (*kan* 4, 396b).

Funi-an hermitage was in a small village near Numazu. The priest mentioned here is not identified, though the head priest at Funi-an at the time was Tetsuzui Genshō (1640–1744), who would have been eighty-six at the time.

National Master Bukkoku. Honorific title of Kōhō Kennichi (1241–1316), one of Wu-hsueh's most important Dharma heirs. Kōhō, the son of a Japanese emperor, founded Ungan-ji in Nasu (present Tochigi prefecture).

:5. INSTRUCTIONS TO THE ASSEMBLY AT THE ANNIVERSARY OF BUDDHA'S DEATH

Delivered at a Nehan-e, *an assembly to commemorate the Buddha's death, held on the fifteenth of the second month.*

> Two thousand years ago, the Golden Sage gave up the ghost,
> Leaving a rotten carcass that has stunk things up for untold ages.
> Now his descendants' foreheads are covered thick with sweat.
> After the rain, the pink peach blossoms are fringed in white
>   mist.

. . . .

Line 1: The "Golden Sage" is Shakamuni.

Line 3: Based on a passage in Mencius (III.2.4): "In ancient times, instead of burying their parents, people sometimes took their bodies and threw them into ditches or gullies. When they later saw that they had been eaten by foxes and sucked on by flies, sweat broke out on the foreheads of those unable to bear the sight. The sweat flowed from their inmost hearts; it was not something they wanted others to see."

Line 4: "The [true] whereabouts of the Buddha's golden body" (annotation).

:6. VERSE INSTRUCTIONS ON OFFERING INCENSE AT THE ANNIVERSARY OF BODHIDHARMA'S DEATH

> Poison milk spurting from the dugs on Big Teat mountain
> Has discombobulated hundreds of thousands of Buddhas,

Had proved fatal long before to the old Indian himself.
Now an inept father, my own boys stalwartly lap it up.

. . . .

Bodhidharma resided beneath Wu-ju feng (Five-Teat Pinnacle) on
Mount Sung.
The old Indian is Bodhidharma; the father is Hakuin himself.

:7. INSTRUCTIONS FROM THE HIGH SEAT DELIVERED AT A VEGETARIAN FEAST PROVIDED BY ZEN MAN MYŌSEKI ON BEHALF OF HIS MOTHER

Myōseki was a Zen priest from northern Honshu. His connection with Hakuin is unknown.

LONG AGO, AS ANANDA was sitting tranquilly in meditation, a hungry ghost appeared to him with fire blazing from its mouth. "You have only seven days to live," it declared. Ananda conferred with the Buddha, who gave him a dharani to recite and instructed him to hold a memorial service for beings trapped in the cycle of rebirth. The Buddha's disciple Maudgalyayana went to the Buddha after seeing his mother undergoing torments in hell and asked how he might save her. The Buddha taught him the Urabon service for the repose of the dead.

Now, Zen man Myōseki from Echigo, receiving news that his mother had passed away, has emulated Ch'en Mu-chou, and asked that a *suiriku* ceremony be conducted to provide sustenance for the brotherhood and requite his debt to his mother. After the sutras and dharani were recited, he asked me to deliver a Dharma teaching. I composed a verse:

Maudgalyayana performed the first Urabon ceremony,
Mu-chou wove straw sandals and left them at the roadside,
Eighty-year-old Ananda recited a dharani of divine power,
All to gain rebirth for their mothers in the heavenly realms.

. . . .

The story of *Maudgalyayana* making offerings to an assembly of monks to deliver his mother from the torments of the realm of hungry ghosts, said to be the origin of the annual Urabon observances performed for repose of the dead, appears in the *Ullambana Sutra (T.685)*. The *suiriku* ceremony, which originated in early Chinese Buddhism, is a form of the *segaki* ceremony.

The story about Ananda is based on the *Sutra of the Dharani for Delivering the Hungry Ghost Flaming Mouth* (Jap. *Kubatsu Enku Gaki Darani-kyō* T.1313.21); the offerings he made at this time are said to be the origin of the *segaki* ceremony, at which services are held and oblations of food and drink made to beings in the hungry ghost existence and those in the other realms of samsaric rebirth.

Ch'en Mu-chou (780–877?) wove straw sandals and left them by the road for travelers, supporting his mother with the donations they left behind.

:8. UNTITLED [EXAMINING A KOAN]

We know from an annotation that these comments were made when Hakuin offered incense at the memorial service for the mother of the monk Myōseki (see previous piece). Cheng-weng Ju-ching (1163–1228), under whom Eihei Dōgen, founder of the Japanese Sōtō sect, achieved enlightenment, and Hsu-t'ang Chih-yu, who is revered in Japanese Rinzai Zen as the teacher of Daiō Kokushi, founder of the lineage to which Hakuin belonged, were contemporaries, Ju-ching being senior by some twenty years.

I PUT THIS BEFORE YOU: When Zen master Hsu-t'ang met Head Priest Ju-ching of Ch'ing-tz'u temple, Ju-ching said, "Your parents' bodies are rotting away in a thicket of razor-sharp thorns. Did you know that?" "It's wonderful," replied Hsu-t'ang, "but it's not something to act rashly about."

The master (Hakuin) said: The means these two old veterans employ are exceedingly subtle and mysterious. Scrutinize them carefully and you will find that Ju-ching's question is as awesome as the great serpent that devours whole elephants and excretes their dry bones three years later. Hsu-t'ang's reply has the vehement purpose of the evil P'o-ching bird, which seeks to devour its mother as soon as it is born.

. . . .

This dialogue between Hsu-t'ang and Ju-ching occurs in the sketch of Hsu-t'ang's life that is appended to his Zen records. It took place at Ch'ing-tz'u monastery, where both Ju-ching and Hsu-t'ang served terms as head abbot.

Hakuin omits the final exchange: "Ju-ching gave Hsu-t'ang a slap. Hsu-t'ang extended his arms, saying, 'Let's take it slow and easy.'"

Hsu-t'ang and Ju-ching seem to have been friends as well as contemporaries. After Ju-ching's death, Hsu-t'ang wrote a colophon (dated 1265) for an edition of Dōgen's Zen records at the request of a Japanese priest who brought a manuscript of the work to him in China.

In the *Shan-hai ching (Classic of Mountains and Seas)*, an early work on Chinese geography, a huge serpent is described that "devours elephants and excretes their bones three years later. If a superior man partakes of its flesh, he will be protected from any illness." Although Hakuin may be comparing Ju-ching to the creature merely to stress his exceptional capacity, this same serpent sometimes appears in Zen literature as a symbol of someone of great ability who tries to consume something too large for him to digest, which may be the sense intended here.

P'o-ching ("mirror-breaker") bird. Mentioned in the *Heroic March Sutra* as an evil bird (perhaps an owl) that devours its own mother, the most heinous of all unfilial acts. Muchaku Dōchū, in explaining a reference in *Praise of the Five Houses of the True School* to "a bird with a compelling passion to eat its mother," writes: "Its poisonous heart is truly fearsome. When the time comes, it will not spare even its own teacher." In Zen texts the stress is generally on the bird's innate propensity to devour those it is closest and most indebted to, suggesting great capacity in a student that will enable him to surpass his teacher.

: 9. Verse Read on Offering Incense at the Thirteenth Anniversary of Priest Tanrei's Death

A wind gusting from India eastward to China and Japan
Has filled our branches with fine blossoms of every kind.
In each of their marvelous springtime shapes and colors
I clearly see the features of my late teacher's ugly face.

. . . .

According to the *Chronological Biography*, Hakuin wrote this verse during the New Year period of 1713, his twenty-eighth year, at memorial services commemorating the death of Tanrei Soden, the priest at Shōin-ji in Hara who in 1699 had ordained him into the priesthood. Hakuin had returned to

Shōin-ji from his peregrinations the previous summer, having heard of the death of his teacher Sokudō Fueki of Daishū-ji in Numazu (*Precious Mirror Cave*, p. 183).

:10. VERSE INSTRUCTIONS TO THE ASSEMBLY ON THE BUDDHA'S BIRTHDAY

Services in observance of the Buddha's Birthday are held on the eighth day of the fourth month.

> A birth unknown to either his father or his mother,
> A birth the sage Ashita could never have foreseen.
> Pines and cedars are heavy with last night's rain,
> The spating waters flow golden with their pollen.

. . . .

Ashita was a celebrated seer who foretold future greatness for Shakamuni at his birth.

Lines 3–4: "Last night's heavy rain has scattered all the pine and cedar flowers and everywhere is a bright golden color" (annotation). "Golden water—the Buddha's marvelously golden body—flows everywhere throughout the universe" (annotation).

:11. INFORMAL TALK ON THE EVE OF THE WINTER SOLSTICE

YIN ENERGY THAT BEGAN to strengthen in the fifth month has now reached its farthest point. There is nothing either up or down or in the four directions, and there is not the slightest sign of any warmth. When things advance to their farthest point, the change begins and *yang* energy starts to return. In the *Book of Changes* this is represented by a hexagram of six broken lines. It has long been the custom to put rush ashes into a bamboo pitch-pipe when the *yang* principle starts to return and observe the manner in which they float through the air as they emerge from the pipe. Here at Shōin-ji, I would take those ashes and use them to roast up the iron bull of Shan-fu. I'd take the bamboo pitch-pipe and blow down Kashapa's flagpole.

How to describe life at Shōin-ji as we reach the winter solstice? Poverty so dire even heroes like Meng Pen and Hsia Yu could do nothing to alleviate it. If it were possible for me to describe the actual conditions around here, I'm sure people would find them more ludicrous than the cack-handed bumblings of Cudapanthaka. The old woman who comes round to lend a hand became incensed when she saw my lice ridden robes. She immediately tossed them into a cauldron of water to boil the vermin out. My trusted servant just returned from the fields covered with dirt to announce that we can expect a fine crop of large daikon radishes this year. Brother Sa has set a trap for the tomcat who keeps sneaking in to harass my pet three-colored (*mikei*) cat. In the kitchen Brother Gaku is rapping on the kettle as he boils up a batch of rice gruel; it will be so thin we'll see our faces reflected in it.

None of the monks who have come here—men with eyes more rapacious than a crocodile's, barbs sharper than hedgehog quills—has the slightest concern for the descendants of Vulture Peak. With hawk-like claws and owl-like beaks, they have zero interest in temple rules or regulations like those established by Po-chang. Sleeping in decrepit shrines and deserted, broken-down halls they have managed to locate, they make their way here to study with me with their bodies wrapped in paper kimonos to ward off the cold, sipping water to relieve their hunger pangs.

When I teach them and talk to them about Zen, I sometimes employ snatches of country songs or some popular street jingles in the local Suruga dialect. Their only ration besides that is my harsh scolding outbursts and steady rain of abuse. Meals follow the tradition of P'u-hua—greens and more greens. As for supporting the fifty monks who've gathered here, I don't care a hoot in hell for that.

Long ago, Master Tung-shan delivered an Informal Talk to his monks as they were enjoying some seasonal fruit on the eve of the winter solstice. Recalling that, I decided to buy my monks some tangerines at the local market. I couldn't come up with the money. Still, don't be comparing my informal talk with Tung-shan's and concluding that mine has no redeeming merit. Tomorrow morning I'm going serve up a batch of fox slobber especially prepared just for you.

. . . .

At the winter solstice, there was a custom in ancient China of placing rush ashes into a bamboo pitch-pipe (a cylindrical tube used in woodwind musical instruments) and observing them as they emerged from the pipe. If they wafted through the air, it signified that the *yin* phase had ended and the *yang* phase had begun.

The iron bull of Shan-fu: when the people of Shan-fu put up a bridge, they propitiated the water gods by casting in iron the figure of an ox and launching it into the river. Hakuin uses these phrases in a Zen context twice in *Horse Thistles:* "A wren pecks the great Buddha of Chia-chou to smithereens, a mosquito jabs the iron bull of Shan-fu to pieces"; "Riding the iron bull of Shan-fu, chasing off the great Buddha of Chia-chou." The great Buddha of Chia-chou is a large stone Buddha, still extant, in Szechuan province.

Ananda said to Kashapa, "The World-Honored One passed on the brocade robe to you. What else did he transmit?" Kashapa called out, "Ananda!" Ananda replied, "Yes?" Kashapa said, "Take down the flagpole at the gate" (*Gateless Barrier,* Case 22).

Meng Pen and Hsia Yu are Chinese heroes of Herculean strength; the former could rip the horns from a living ox, the latter could tear off its tail.

Cudapanthaka was an extremely dim-witted disciple of the Buddha, unable even to remember his own name, who was always performing strange, inexplicable acts, yet who succeeded in attaining enlightenment.

Rice gruel: "eyeball gruel" (*medama-gayu*), also "ceiling gruel," was so thin that it was said one's eyes (or the ceiling) could be seen reflected in it.

Po-chang is credited with formulating the first set of rules and regulations for Zen training halls. P'u-hua is an eccentric T'ang monk who lived without any fixed abode; he appears in the *Record of Lin-chi.*

The reference to *Tung-shan Liang-chieh* is based on an account in his *Records:* "On the eve of the winter solstice, as the monks in his assembly were enjoying some fruit, Tung-shan said to Head Monk Tai, 'There is something as black as lacquer that supports the heavens above and the earth below. Although it is always active, activity cannot completely encompass its working. Tell me, where does it fall short?' 'It is in its activity that it falls short,' answered the head monk. Tung-shan gave a loud shout and ordered the fruit taken away." Hakuin alludes to this story again in another Informal Talk (below, #22).

Fox slobber, a deadly poison, is used here as a metaphor for the utterances of a Zen teacher, which can bring instant death (leading to rebirth).

:12. UNTITLED [EXAMINING A KOAN]

I PUT THIS BEFORE YOU: Priest Wu-tsu Fa-yen instructed the assembly, "Just eat the fruit, don't worry about the twists and crooks in the tree." Raising this koan with his assembly, Hsi-keng Rōshi said, "The useless old geezer, still clinging to life. He didn't even grasp what was going on. If it were me, I'd make everyone discover the worth of the fruit on their own. Is it rare and precious? Is it inferior and second rate?"

The master [Hakuin] said, "Those two cantankerous old gizzards. One resembles Wu-tsu taking a turn around a broken millstone, but he's different from Yen-t'ou whispering out the meaning. The other is like Chao-chou investigating the old woman, but he falls short of Hsueh-feng rolling out the wooden balls. Why is that? Close investigation shows that they didn't send offerings to the ministers of state."

. . . .

The Zen scholar Muchaku Dōchū said of this koan: "This is Master Ta-hui's 'Just study to become the Buddha, don't worry about trying to understand his words'"(Hsu-t'ang rikō, p. 102). The version of Wu-tsu's instructions in Records of the Old Worthies (Ku-tsun-su yu-lu, ch. 20), has him go on to say: "[But] if you don't know the tree's crooks and twists, how do you know how to partake of the fruit? If you don't pass through the patriarchs' barriers, how can you expect to grapple effectively with birth and death? What are the patriarchs' barriers? Tip Big Table Mountain over on its back." This latter emphasis is the one evident throughout Hakuin's writings: "At first, don't concern yourself with the teachings or anything else, just bore through into kenshō. But once you achieve kenshō, you can't attain great enlightenment without becoming fully conversant with the teachings."

Hakuin mentions four other koans in his own comments:

1. *Wu-tsu taking a turn around a broken millstone.* "When Wu-tsu was in charge of the mill, a monk pointed at the swiftly turning millstone and asked, 'Is that moving by supernatural means, or is it spontaneous and natural?' Wu-tsu hitched up his robe and made a circumambulation of the millstone" *(Ch'an-lin seng-pao ch'uan, appendix).*

2. *Yen-t'ou whispers out the meaning.* One day when Hsueh-feng was in charge of the kitchen at Te-shan's temple, the meal was late. Te-shan picked up his bowl and went into the Dharma Hall. When Hsueh-feng later asked him why he had left, Te-shan turned and went back to his chambers. On hearing about this, Yen-t'ou struck his fist in the palm

of his hand and said, "Just as I thought. Te-shan still hasn't grasped the final word." When news of Yen-t'ou's comment reached Te-shan, he summoned him to his chambers and said, "So you won't affirm this old monk?" Yen-t'ou whispered out his meaning to Te-shan. When Te-shan ascended the high seat and delivered his formal sermon the next day, it was somehow different than before. Yen-t'ou went to the monks' hall, smacked his fist into his hand, and burst into laughter. "How wonderful!" he said. "The old head priest grasped the final word. From now on, no one will be able to touch him" (*Records of the Lamp*, ch. 16).

3. *Chao-chou investigating the Old Woman.* One of Chao-chou's monks asked an old woman, "Which is the way to Mount T'ai?" "Go straight ahead!" she said. When the monk had taken a few steps, she remarked, "He looks like a proper monk, but he's just like all the rest." Hearing about this encounter, Chao-chou told his monks that he himself would go and check the old woman out. The next day he went and asked her the same question. She gave him the same answer. When he returned to his temple, he announced to the monk, "I've investigated the old woman for you" (*Gateless Barrier*, Case 31).

4. *Hsueh-feng rolling out the wooden balls.* In a formal talk from the high seat Hsueh-feng said, "Everywhere on earth is a gateway to freedom. You take someone's hand, try to make him enter, but he won't venture to pass through." A monk came forward. "You can't blame me," he said. Another monk said, "Once he enters, what happens then?" The master struck him. Hsuan-sha said to the master, "So-and-so employs his Zen activity with telling effect these days. How about you?" The master produced three wooden balls and rolled them out in front of Hsuan-sha (*Compendium of the Five Lamps*, ch. 7).

They didn't send offerings to the ministers of state. Allusion to an episode in the *Shih-chi* (*Records of the Grand Historian*). A chief minister, receiving a beautiful lady as tribute from a neighboring state, became so taken with her that for three days he neglected his official duties, even forgetting to send his subministers the ritual food offerings for the sacred altars. An annotation ventures the following comment: "Perhaps he means, 'I don't eat other people's leftovers. I don't feed others mine.'" In any case, Hakuin seems to indicate that the utterances given by Wu-tsu and Hsi-keng (Hsu-t'ang Chih-yu) both fail to pass his muster.

⋮ 13. Verse Instructing the Assembly During the *Rōhatsu* Training Session

This verse cannot be dated, but the descriptions of Shōin-ji in the accompanying annotations, made by people who seem to have taken part in the training session, suggest it was during the early years of Hakuin's incumbency, when the temple was in "an advanced state of disrepair."

A large number of Instructions to the Assembly (Jishū) delivered during the intensive rōhatsu *training periods are included in* Poison Blossoms. *Most, like this one, consist of four seven-character lines of Chinese verse.*

> A north wind assaults our small village with violent force;
> The old hall groans sullenly, as if ready to shatter and fly.
> The front well is buried in reeds shorn from the back roof.
> Old Chŏ's door is tearing apart the walls of Mr. Li's house.

. . . .

Although Suruga province where Shōin-ji is located is known for its temperate climate, in winter freezing winds can blow down from the heights of Mount Fuji and neighboring mountains. "It was freezing cold, and it penetrated the marrow of your bones. Typhoon force winds hammered the village, blowing things wildly about. The wind entered the hall through the broken ceiling and the cracks in the walls, throbbing and whirling around inside" (annotation). "It blew the wood shed and the privy askew, buried the well and the manure tank in debris. Gombei's house in front of the temple gate was lifted up and thrown against Hachibei's house, crushing its walls. It was like a strong typhoon" (annotation).

Old Chŏ, Mr. Li are common Tom, Dick, and Harry type names that appear frequently in Zen records. Here they stand for the Gombei and Hachibei mentioned in the above annotation, who it appears were neighbors of Shōin-ji.

：14. Verse on Offering Incense at the Anniversary of Bodhidharma's Death

Undated, but its place in Book One's roughly chronological sequence suggests the verse was composed in Hakuin's mid-fifties.

At my place I don't hang any likeness of the old Indian on
the wall,
Perhaps because I'm lazy; maybe because his Zen style is
too severe.
Raindrops pattering on fallen autumn leaves, though sobering to
the soul,
Cannot compare to sunset clouds glowing gloriously over fields
of yellowing grain.

. . . .

Lines 1–2: "Shōin-ji is so poor, if we hung his [Bodhidharma's] image, we wouldn't be able to place offerings before it" (annotation). Although not hanging his image makes us appear to be lax, in fact it means that our style of Zen is rigorous.

Lines 3–4: Favorite lines of Hakuin, the first line apparently alludes to the initial breakthrough known as *kenshō*, the second to the further deepening of that experience.

：15. Verse Instructing the Assembly During the *Rōhatsu* Training Session

This also probably dates from Hakuin's mid-fifties. The intensive rōhatsu training session is traditionally held at the beginning of the twelfth month in commemoration of the Buddha's enlightenment. According to traditional Zen accounts, Shakamuni entered the Snowy Mountains (the Himalayas) and engaged in arduous practice for six years, attaining enlightenment on the eighth day of the twelfth month when he looked up and saw the morning star in the sky.

Once he entered the mountains, he never left them.
He never bequeathed a single word to his fellow beings.

It was warm yesterday. I went out to gaze at the ocean.
Flying gulls, striped like tigers, filled the southern skies.

. . . .

"People say the Buddha left the mountains—an incredible lie! Enter the mountains and see for yourself—is there any entering or leaving? This is a matter about which neither father nor son has the slightest clue. No one has ever seen the Buddha do any such thing!" (annotation).

Shōin-ji was in a very picturesque location near Suruga Bay, with Mount Fuji towering up to the north, and the inlet and beach of Tagonoura, much beloved of Japanese poets, visible to the south.

:16. VERSE ON OFFERING INCENSE AT THE ANNIVERSARY OF BODHIDHARMA'S DEATH

This verse appears in the Chronological Biography *in the entry for 1736, age 51, occasioned by the completion of a new Monks' Hall at Shōin-ji* (Precious Mirror Cave, p. 203). *Its ultimate message: good monks are produced through arduous training, not by new buildings like this.*

Lacking enough room for our monks, we built a new hall,
Like beggars setting up tables to host a sumptuous feast.
North of the river, six men became great Dharma vessels;
Five fords and five bridges went up at Mount Shao-lin.

. . . .

"We built a new hall to house the monks, yet could no more provide for their needs than a beggar could" (annotation).

Six men. Master Fen-yang lived in a bitterly cold region of China "north of the river." At the urging of an Indian priest he met, Fen-yang compelled his monks to practice more assiduously; before three years were out, six men in his assembly attained great enlightenment *(Precious Lessons of the Zen School).*

Five fords and bridges are the five Chinese Zen schools, all stemming from First Patriarch Bodhidharma who taught at Mount Shao-lin. Thanks to them, the essential work of ferrying students across to the "other shore" of enlightenment was made possible.

:17. Verse Instructing the Assembly During the Rōhatsu Training Session

Having grasped the true secret of the Snowy Mountains,
I've kept it to myself, thinking no one would believe me.
I'm going to expound it for you as I teach this morning,
Guard it with utmost care, and don't pass it on to others.

. . . .

"What 'true inner secret' is he talking about? This old fellow's a downright menace" (annotation).

:18. Instructions to the Assembly Thanking Mr. Noda for Donating a Wooden Fish

Annotations identify this donor as Noda (Shigetsune) Jirōzaemon, (n.d.), a vassal of the Daimyō Ōkubo Norimasa, who had two fiefs in Suruga province. Noda served in the magistrate's office at clan headquarters in the village of Matsunaga, about three kilometers east of Hara. Mr. Noda also appears in the following piece (untranslated), a short address dated 1748 that Hakuin delivered from the teaching seat thanking Noda for donating a gift of noodles to the assembly of monks. These instructions probably date from the same general period.

Annotations also tell us that Noda purchased the wooden fish (gyoku, literally "fish drum": the mokugyo) in question for several gold pieces (ryō) from a Sōtō priest (referred to by his studio name Kasui-sai) in neighboring Tōtōmi province. A mokugyo is a hollowed-out wooden drum, carved in the stylized shape of two fish (or dragons), their tails in their mouths, contesting over the pearl of the Dharma shown lying between them. The drum is placed on a pillow and beaten rhythmically with a padded drumstick to accompany recitations of religious texts and to convene assemblies. It is said that beating on the mokugyo causes it to disgorge one's delusions; that, along with the belief that fish never close their eyes to sleep, made the instrument a symbol of concentration and wakefulness, qualities essential to students engaged in Zen training.

I N INDIA, AT THE time of the Buddha Kashapa, there was an evil priest who refused to heed either his parents' advice or his teachers' injunctions. After he died he was reborn in a hinterland far away as an enormous fish. It barked like the crocodiles that inhabit the southern seas, an evil tree grew out of its back, and its body was constantly buffeted by wind and waves.

One day it spied its former teacher passing in a boat. It rushed forward, emitting bloodcurdling roars, bitter resentment burning in its eyes, and threw itself headlong against the boat trying to overturn it. On seeing the piteous creature, the teacher was moved to offer it some Dharma teachings, and as a result the evil priest was able to eliminate his deeply rooted karma and regain human form. In thanking the teacher, he said, "Please use the wood from the tree that grew on my back and have it carved into a Dharma implement that can be used in your temple." The teacher entrusted the wood to a master craftsman, who from it created this hollow, strangely shaped percussion instrument. Students found it a constant aid in furthering their religious practice. It had two heads, whose two mouths held between them a wonderful gem; its entire body was like an enormous throat, which enabled it to pour forth an endless stream of noxious fumes that spread over vast areas.

With a single hand, patron Noda Shigetsune snatched the wooden fish from under the jaws of the black dragon. His follower Egaku of Sagami carried it here to Shōin-ji, where its booming voice now penetrates deep into the ears of Shōin-ji monks.

The wooden fish, bulbous in shape like an eggplant or gourd, its deep voice resonating like heavy thunder, distressed Zen master Shen-ting long ago, three thousand times in the morning, eight hundred times at night, greatly interfering with his dozes and naps. All twenty-eight Zen patriarchs in India and six patriarchs in China felt its steel fangs and razor teeth. It kept tune with Zen master Kuang-hui, robbing monks of their knowing and seeing. It blocked off the gates of enlightenment. It sat spinning out the inner secrets to Kasui-sai in Tōtōmi province for many years, revealing the subtle essence. It has now made its way into my inner chambers, where it devours Buddhas and treats with total contempt demons of every kind.

Just now I wrestled it to the floor and whispered into its ear, "I have a dharani—four five-character lines—that I want to dedicate to valiant Zen students throughout the universe. All who hear it will resolve steadfastly to attain the Way and be blessed with the fortune of eternal life. It goes [*Hakuin thereupon beats the wooden fish twenty times*]:

Poku poku poku poku poku
Poku poku poku poku poku
Poku poku poku poku poku
Poku poku poku poku poku"

. . . .

The source of the story about the evil priest is not known, though a somewhat similar account appears in the *Chiao-yuan ch'ing-kui,* a T'ien-t'ai work dealing with temple regulations, published in the Yuan dynasty (1347).

Asked, "What about before the wooden fish wumps?" Zen master Shenting said, "Looking at the sky, looking at the ground." "What about after it wumps?" "Ascending to the hall holding a begging bowl," he said (*Compendium of the Five Lamps,* ch. 11).

Kuang-hui Yuan-lien (n.d.) asked his teacher Nan-yuan, "What about before the wooden fish wumps?" "Looking at the sky, not seeing it," replied Nan-yuan. "What about after it wumps?" he asked. "Looking at the ground, not seeing it," said Nan-yuan (*Classified Collection of the Zen Forest,* ch. 16).

Poku poku. Larger *mokugyo* make a deep resonant sound—wump, wump— when struck. Hakuin's use of the onomatopoeic word *poku* (the Chinese character can also refer to a loud din, and to the attainment of selflessness) suggests he was beating a smaller variety.

:19. VERSE INSTRUCTING THE ASSEMBLY ON BUDDHA'S BIRTHDAY

On the Buddha's birthday, also called the Flower Festival, a small statue of the Buddha decked with colorful spring flowers is placed in the hall where the services take place.

"The Shōin-ji priest" refers to Hakuin, though neither the names of the unexpected "honored guests" nor the date of verse are known.

The Shōin-ji priest was suddenly thrown into a terrible fright,
Two eminent prelates came unannounced, took seats in the hall.
Unable for the life of him to produce a single decent verse,
He made a display of his ugliness before his honored guests.

:20. INSTRUCTIONS FROM THE HIGH SEAT, DURING A VISIT OF THE PRIEST OF KEIRIN-JI IN KAI PROVINCE

The Keirin-ji priest Ranshitsu Tōiku (d. 1743) visited Shōin-ji, probably in 1740, to formally invite Hakuin to conduct a lecture meeting on the Blue Cliff Record. *We know from the* Chronological Biography *that this large lecture meeting, attended by over two hundred people, took place in 1741, Hakuin's fifty-sixth year. It followed on the heels of the highly successful lecture meeting the previous year at Shōin-ji, even more heavily attended, on the* Record of Hsu-t'ang, *which Tōrei said "established Hakuin's reputation as the foremost Zen teacher in the land."*

Hakuin was no doubt prompted to use these particular words of Zen master Wu-tsu by the infestation of locusts that had devastated Suruga province that year.

I RAISE THIS BEFORE YOU: "Zen master Wu-tsu Fa-yen said in an address to his assembly, "The villages around here are suffering greatly from drought, but that is not what distresses me. What distresses me are Zen monks who lack the Dharma eye. Over a hundred men who came here for the summer retreat are practicing in this hall, but not a single one who has entered my chambers has been able to crack the koan of the dog and the Buddha-nature. That distresses me."

The Old Man of the Eastern Mountain [Wu-tsu] tossed a mass of flameless black fire into the pitch darkness, in hopes it would burn a great many monks to death. The words he spoke are truly formidable. However I would not have said what he did. I don't care whether any of you understands me or not, but this is how I would put it: "In this year of heavy locust damage, my only regret is that the seventy starveling monks who are studying at Shōin-ji return from their begging expeditions with empty bowls and must sit back on their heels, hugging their knees, issuing mournful sighs."

Hakuin tapped his staff on the floor and said, "Pleasure is the seed of suffering; suffering is the seed of pleasure. How glad I was to hear that the fields around Keirin-ji in Kai province were not harmed by the locust plague and are ripening to full maturity."

Striking the floor with his staff once again, he left the high seat.

. . . .

Wu-tsu Fa-yen's words appear in a letter he wrote that is included in *Ling-yuan pi-yu*, a collection of Zen master Ling-yuan's (d. 1117) letters of instruction to his students.

Black fire. Being flameless and undiscernible, black fire is impossible to escape. For Hakuin's description of black fire, see Book Four, #64.

Much of what we know about Ranshitsu, the priest who invited Hakuin to Keirin-ji, and his relationship with Hakuin is found in an encomium Hakuin delivered at ceremonies commemorating the third anniversary of his death (#28). It tells us that Ranshitsu served as head priest of Keirin-ji for twenty years, that he had an unflagging commitment to the Way that grew stronger with age, that he delivered Zen talks that were "steep and lofty," and that he was extremely severe in dealing with the many monks and lay students who came to him for instruction.

Crop damage in the home province of Suruga meant that monks at Shōin-ji were finding it difficult to obtain rice on their begging rounds. Hakuin's words seem to anticipate an easing of their straitened circumstances. At the upcoming Keirin-ji lectures, he intimates, their hunger would be relieved, giving them the opportunity to focus single-mindedly on their practice. "The farmers around Keirin-ji were looking forward to a bumper crop later that year, and Ranshitsu's compassion for the plight of the Shōin-ji monks prompted him to issue this invitation to Hakuin" (annotation). In addition to four senior Shōin-ji priests who accompanied Hakuin to supervise the Keirin-ji meeting *(Chronological Biography)*, we know from references in *Poison Blossoms* that many more monks, nuns, and lay followers studying at Shōin-ji made the trip to Kai province to take part as well.

The difficulties resulting from crop failure, which made it impossible for farmers to pay the onerous government land tax, or even to provide for their own needs, is a recurring theme in Hakuin's writings. Two works, *Snake Strawberries* and *Mutterings to the Wall*, are devoted almost entirely to this subject. A vivid firsthand account of the destruction locust infestations could cause, dating from autumn of the following year (1741), is found in the preface to *Sendai's Comments on the Poems of Han-shan*. Hakuin writes that he is quoting an account he heard from one of his students: "I've been living cramped up in a broken-down old room I found, sleeping on branches and twigs, surrounded by decay and dilapidation, leaky ceilings above me, sodden floors below....One morning I took my bowl and headed out into the balmy spring haze, bending my steps toward a nearby village where I hoped to obtain some alms. Suddenly, I found myself confronted by the headman of the village. He was blocking the way, looking like a half-crazed beggar, grasping a short club in his right hand and a shield of some sort in his left. "Locusts wiped us out this year," he shrieked. "There's not even a grain of rice to pay the government land tax. You beggars are as feared and loathed as the plague demon. If you try to pass, I'm going to give you a dose of this club!" His crazed eyes and high-pitched screaming were so intense I feared he might tear me limb from limb and devour me on the spot. I lowered my gaze, turned on my heels, and left. I tried some other villages, but it was the same everywhere I went. Finally I packed up my begging bowl and sheepishly returned in the growing darkness to my rundown shack. Sitting there, my head hunkered down, illusory thoughts flew through my mind. A constant growling came from my starved belly. Growl as it might, there wasn't so much as a twig within my gaze to use for a fire. Not a grain of rice to put in my mouth. Not a leftover weed to gnaw upon..."

An annotator adds to this: "Unless monks continue sitting until they are completely oblivious to sleeping and eating, they'll never find their way out of Hakuin's pit of black fire. Pleasure is the seed of suffering. Suffering is the seed of pleasure."

: 21. VERSE ON OFFERING INCENSE AT THE ANNIVERSARY OF SHAO-LIN'S [BODHIDHARMA'S] DEATH

This dates from 1747, the year Hara, where Shōin-ji is located, and other low-lying areas along Suruga Bay were struck by what appears to have been a tsunami. The intrusion of the saltwater contaminated the rice fields, resulting in a serious famine once again. Many of the monks studying at Shōin-ji, whose lodgings were in deserted shrines and temples spread over a wide area around Hara, with little hope of obtaining rice from begging expeditions, were obliged to disperse to other parts (Chronological Biography; Precious Mirror, p. 213).

Angry winds and waves have blasted fields and gardens,
Scattering my idle spirits and wild demons far and wide.
Twenty worthy monks, men with vitals sheathed in iron,
Gnaw on vegetable stalks, keenly savoring the adversity.

. . . .

Annotations provide details about this verse that we could not otherwise know: of seventy monks in training at this time, twenty stayed on and continued their practice—the "worthy monks with vitals sheathed in iron"—the other fifty, who left, are the "idle spirits and wild demons"—the average or mediocre students.

: 22. Informal Talk on a Winter Night

This account of Sōtō master Dōgen's study in China is dated by the annotations to the famine year of 1747. This no doubt explains Hakuin's comment about being unable to provide sufficient food for his monks. References to Dōgen in Hakuin's writings generally focus, as this one does, on his enlightenment experience and his commitment to "continuing practice" (gyōji), The high regard in which Hakuin held sect founder Dōgen contrasts sharply with the vigorous attacks he continually makes on contemporary Sōtō teachers for their "do-nothing" attitude toward training; for having students perform zazen but not forcing them, à la Hakuin, to strive with relentless urgency toward a kenshō *experience using koans.*

ON THE SECOND DAY of the seventh month in the first year of Pao-ch'ing (1227), Zen master Eihei Dōgen set out with his teacher Myōzen Hōshi in a trading vessel bound for distant Sung China. At the monastery on Mount T'ien-t'ung he requested and was granted an interview with Zen master Ju-ching. He made three bows to the master and said, "Although I am but an insignificant young monk from a far-off country, I rejoice that karma from my past lives has enabled me to be admitted into your Dharma assembly. Please, master, in your great pity and compassion, teach me the true essentials of the Way."

Ju-ching lit a stick of incense, placed his palms together in *gasshō*, and said, "Ever since our Zen school began the direct, undeviating transmission of the authentic Dharma from master to disciple, it has always had as its fundamental principle never leaving the training hall, and has had zazen alone (*shikan taza*) as the authentic way of practice. Today Zen students in temples throughout the land may sit many hours in meditation without lying down to sleep, but because they do not encounter an enlightened master, they never learn the way of entering true dhyana.

Because of that, the zazen they practice differs not in the least from that espoused by the heretical teachers. Even if they continued performing such practice until the end of time, they would never be able to enter the great dhyana of the Buddhas."

Dōgen performed three bows, and said, "In your great pity and compassion, please teach me the correct way to enter dhyana."

Ju-ching lit incense, performed *gasshō*, and said, "Brother Gen [Dōgen], when doing zazen, you should place your mind above the palm of your left hand."

Dōgen performed three bows and withdrew. Some days later he entered Ju-ching's chambers, made three bows, and said, "I placed my mind above the palm of my left hand as you instructed. Now, both my hands have totally disappeared. There is nowhere to place my mind."

Ju-ching lit incense, performed *gasshō*, and said, "Dōgen, you should make your mind fill your entire body. Make it reach each of your three hundred and sixty bones and joints, each of the eighty-four thousand pores of your skin, so that not a single place is left empty."

A few days later Dōgen entered Ju-ching's chambers, made three bows, and said, "I did as you instructed, placing my mind throughout my body. Now both my mind and body have fallen away. It is like a brilliant sun illuminating the vast heavens, although its round shape cannot be seen."

This time Ju-ching lit incense, performed *gasshō*, and said with a smile, "Brother Gen, for kalpas on end you have been revolving in the cycle of birth and death. Today you have entered the great and true dhyana where defilements do not arise. Preserve and protect this. Never let go of it."

Dōgen performed three bows, three additional bows, then withdrew with tears in his eyes.

This is one of the secret teachings of Sōtō Zen. I learned about it long ago from an old priest when I was staying at the Inryō-ji in Izumi province. I have obtained many good results from practicing it, but I have not readily taught it to others. I thought I would wait until I found monks whose minds were deeply committed to the Way. Every time I heard about how earnestly you men were practicing this winter in the face of arduous difficulties, gooseflesh would rise all over my body. I only regret that the kitchen larders are empty and I am unable to provide you with the proper sustenance for the cold winter nights. This is the reason I have been so talkative tonight, unconcerned about losing my eyebrows, and emulating Tung-shan with his tray of fruit.

People might call me an old Dharma reprobate, someone who having lost his nostrils has entered a dark cave to dip water that has been lying stagnant for a thousand years; they might say that my talking about Sōtō Zen has caused the drowning of many of the valiant heroes of Rinzai Zen. Having no way to rebut these charges, I can only clench my left hand into a fist and gnaw my fingertips. Why is that?

It is said that you should sell your bedding and buy a cow when the winter solstice falls at the beginning of the month, and sell your cow and buy bedding when it falls at the end of the month. But what about this year, when it falls right in the middle? What do you do then?

Hakuin gave the floor a thump with his staff and left.

. . . .

Dōgen arrived in China at the age of twenty-three, the first year of the Chinese Pao-ch'ing era (1223; pronounced Hōkyō in Japanese), accompanied by the Kennin-ji priest Myōzen (1185–1225), a disciple of Zen master Eisai, the man credited with introducing Chinese Rinzai teachings to Japan.

Hakuin strings together this account of the dialogues that passed between Dōgen and Ju-ching from material in *Hōkyō-ki* (*A Diary of the Hōkyō Era*), a practice journal Dōgen kept at the time, as well as from other traditional sources, and he seems also to have added a few touches of his own. Since *Hōkyō-ki* was not published until 1750, several years after this piece was written, he would have had to rely on a manuscript of the work.

The old priest that Hakuin visited at the Sōtō temple Inryō-ji while on the Zen pilgrimage he made in his twenties, the priest he refers to here, is identified in the annotations as Jukaku Dōnin. In *Wild Ivy*, written at the end of his life, Hakuin portrays Jukaku as a superior monk with a genuine aspiration for the Way, and describes a weeklong session of intensive practice they engaged in together. However in the *Chronological Biography*, compiled a decade or so earlier, Jukaku is described as "an old man who seemed half-demented, with an unsightly face and a robe hanging in tatters from his body…who ran off when he saw me coming," whom Hakuin finally cornered and persuaded to divulge the practice methods of his teacher Tesshin Dōin, the Sōtō priest who had founded Inryō-ji. One of these methods may have been the "secret meditation" described here.

In another Informal Talk delivered at the winter solstice, Hakuin refers to the "tray of fruit" master Tung-shan used in teaching his monks (see above, #11). He expresses sympathy for the difficulties monks practicing at Shōin-ji faced, and states that he would like to follow Tung-shan's example and treat his monks to some tangerines, but since there is no money to do that, he will instead personally dish them up some fox slobber (poisonous teachings) he has concocted specially for the occasion.

A teacher is said to be in danger of losing his eyebrows when compassion for his struggling students makes him resort to verbal explanations. Hakuin viewed doing this as one of the essential roles of a teacher.

Hakuin refers to himself here by the sobriquet Sendai, "Dharma Reprobate," which translates the Sanskrit *Icchantika*: a person unable to attain Buddhahood because he is completely devoid of merit. The term is also used, however, to refer to Bodhisattvas, who forgo final attainment of Buddhahood to remain behind in the world and help sentient beings.

Nostrils stand for the original face, something of most primary importance.

Making a fist and gnawing your fingertips. This phrase appears twice in Hakuin's writings. Here, as the annotations explain, it "describes [the frustration] of being unable to make any response." In *Oradegama,* "make a fist and bite your middle finger," is said to imply a feat that is impossible to perform, alluding to the circumstances of ultimate truth or reality that a student can clarify only by pursuing his practicing with unwavering resolve (*HHZ9*, p. 368).

Sell your bedding and buy a cow. At the winter solstice, occurring sometime during the eleventh month in the lunar calendar, the gradually shortening days and lengthening nights reach their farthest point and start to reverse course. A standard dictionary of Zen words and phrases give this explanation of the saying: "When the winter solstice falls at the beginning of the month, a good year is said to follow, so one will be able to keep a cow. If it falls at the end of the month, a lean year is expected, so the cow should be sold. The beginning of the month alludes to the time prior to satori, the end of the month to the post-satori period" (*Zengo Ji-i*, Nakagawa Shibuan). Another source has: "When the winter solstice falls at the beginning of the month, it indicates a warm winter, hence you can sell your bedding and buy a cow; when it falls at the end of the month, it means a cold winter, so you should sell the cow and buy warm bedding. The phrases indicate the two aspects of advancing and regressing in Buddhist practice" (*Daiō Kokushi goroku*, ed. Yanagida Seizan).

:23. VERSE INSTRUCTIONS TO THE ASSEMBLY DURING
THE *RŌHATSU* TRAINING PERIOD

The Snowy Mountains' forbidding scarps and peaks fill up
  the sky,
Bellowing roars from the great white ox resound like bolts of
  thunder.
You men, progeny of Hsu-t'ang, what have you got to show me?
Blowing on damp firewood doesn't make it burn, just covers
  you with ash.

. . . .

Lines 1–2: "The mountains of one's own mind soar high and sheer, but when
they are known, the great white ox roars out like thunder. This is not a place
easily approached" (annotation). The white ox of the enlightened mind,
from a parable in the *Lotus Sutra*, represents the supreme way of the Buddha or Bodhisattva that enables beings to liberate themselves from samsaric
suffering.

Progeny of Hsu-t'ang. Hakuin alludes to words that became known in
Japanese Rinzai Zen as "Hsu-t'ang's prophecy." When Nampo Jōmyō (Daiō
Kokushi, 1282–1334) was leaving to return home after studying with the
Chinese teacher Hsu-t'ang Chih-yu, Hsu-t'ang told him that in the future
authentic Zen students would "increase daily in the land beyond the eastern
sea [Japan]."

Damp firewood. This expression also appears in a verse in *Wild Ivy* (p. 3):
"What is earth's vilest thing? From which all men recoil? / Crumbly charcoal,
Damp firewood? Watery lamp oil? / A cartman? A boatman? A stepmother?
Skunks? / Mosquitoes? Lice? Blue flies? Rats? Brigand monks!" Hakuin goes
on to describe "brigand monks" as "the do-nothing silent illumination Zennists that now infest the land." This occurrence of the expression may also
allude to such priests, whose practices, according to Hakuin, prevent students from pursuing their practice with the determination needed to attain
the breakthrough *kenshō* experience, leaving them with a partial and incomplete realization. The last two lines would thus mean: "Are you really one of
the true Zen students Hsu-t'ang said would increase daily in Japan, or will
you become stuck in the partial attainment preached by bogus Zen teachers
of the present day?"

:24. Instructions from the High Seat During the Summer Retreat at Banshō-zan

This meeting took place in the summer of 1742, Hakuin's fifty-seventh year, conducted at the request of Priest Tokusō of Ryōtan-ji (full name, Banshō-zan Ryōtan-ji) near Hamamatsu, in neighboring Tōtōmi province. Hakuin's text for the lectures he delivered at this time was Precious Lessons of the Zen School *(Chronological Biography;* Precious Mirror Cave, *p. 207). The saying of Zen master Fa-yen that Hakuin cites here appeared before, #20.*

I RAISE THIS BEFORE YOU: "Zen master Wu-tsu Fa-yen said in an address to his assembly, "The villages around here are suffering greatly from drought, but that is not what distresses me. Over a hundred men who came here for the summer retreat are practicing in this hall, but not a single one grasps my teaching—that is what distresses me."

A hundred monks in tattered robes are attending the summer retreat this year. All of them are seasoned veterans, blind to the ways of the Buddha-patriarchs, and deaf to their words and phrases. They have the horse faces, magnificent swallow-like jaws, crocodile eyes, and tiger necks found in men of outstanding capacity. They asked me to say a few words today at the beginning of this sacred meeting. I searched my parched-up bowels high and low, not once but a hundred, a thousand times. I was still unable to come up with a single word worth smearing like warm shit over their young faces.

Why is that? Yesterday I went to Jissō-ji, accompanied by the priest of Ryōtan-ji and Goan Oshō of nearby Kōgan-ji. The head priest welcomed me as though I was an old friend. Ren and Min, senior monks at Jissō-ji, took extremely good care of me. They offered me rare delicacies with my meals, then urged me to spend the night at the temple. When I rose the next morning, a terrific downpour was pelting down. The spating torrents, howling angrily, rushed by with tremendous force, overflowing their banks and sweeping heavy oxcarts from the roads. Signs were up at all the fording places forbidding river crossings. I was obliged to wait until the rain let up and the swollen rivers subsided.

Later that evening when I returned to the Ryōtan-ji priest's quarters, I found seven or eight monks I knew sitting together engaged in pure talk about the Buddha Way that would continue long into the night. Others were doing zazen with their futons pulled over them. One of the attendants had set a tray of burning sawdust out to keep the mosquitoes at bay. The smoke was so thick it was difficult to breathe. To avoid suffocating, I pulled the bed covering over my head and slept, dead to the world, until the next morning.

But don't start saying that Hakuin is old and worthless, that he's lost his nostrils and isn't interested in giving Dharma talks. Have you not heard? "When walking at night, don't tread on anything white. If it's not water, it's usually a stone."

. . . .

Horse faces…tiger necks. Extraordinary attributes said to be found in superior Zen seekers. In the *Book of Han (Han-shu)*, outstanding warriors, described as having splendid jaws like swallows and necks like tigers, are said to move with incredible swiftness and freedom and to strike with great ferocity.

"*When walking at night…*" A caution for students to watch their step and be alert at all times, especially when they think they have reached some attainment. Hakuin uses these words in his commentary on the *Heart Sutra* as a capping phrase for the words "The Highest Mantra." A related injunction, "Look to what is right under your own feet!" stresses the urgent need to bore into one's own self-nature.

: 25. VERSE ON OFFERING INCENSE AT SERVICES COMMEMORATING BODHIDHARMA'S DEATH

I love drawing Darumas, done him thousands of times.
No wonder I'm having trouble painting his features now.
Soon as paper is put before me, his true face disappears.
Any of you monks acquainted with this unpaintable Daruma?

. . . .

This verse, probably from Hakuin's mid-fifties, contains a rare personal reference to his Zen painting. It reveals that he had already painted a surprising number of Darumas (the original says "several thousand"), and at a relatively early date, much earlier than art historians have suspected.

:26. Verse Instructions to the Assembly During the *Rōhatsu* Training Period

"This dates from the winter of 1739, Hakuin's fifty-fourth year. He lectured that winter on the Gateless Gate *collection" (annotation).*

> Breaching countless gateless gates, skinny elbows flying,
> He now returns, enters his native home in the mountains.
> What is it like, returning to one's old home in the hills?
> Like losing your human stripes, assuming those of a tiger.

. . . .

He is Shakamuni.
Tiger stripes are a sign of exceptional ability.

:27. Verse Instructions to the Assembly at Services Commemorating Buddha's Nirvana

Judging from the descriptions in the verse itself, as well as from the place the editor assigned them here in the ostensibly chronological sequence, it is probably safe to suppose that these instructions date from some time in Hakuin's fifties.

> All of you have made long trips to come here; I am deeply
>   ashamed
> We don't have enough space to put up more than one or
>   two men.
> Yesterday I heard some monks had to be turned away,
> They headed off in tears to find a broken-down shack.

. . . .

Providing for monks, including visitors, was part of a master's obligation. In *Idle Talk on a Night Boat*, Hakuin describes the conditions that monks who came to study at Shōin-ji had to face: "They were obliged to take up shelter in old houses and other abandoned dwellings, ancient temple halls, and ruined shrines. Their lodgings were spread over an area five or six *ri* around Shōin-ji. Hunger awaited them at daybreak. Freezing cold lurked after them at night. They sustained themselves on greens and wheat chaff" (*Precious Mirror Cave*, p. 90).

:28. Words Spoken on Offering Incense at Services Commemorating the Third Death Anniversary of Priest Ranshitsu of Keirin-ji

Ranshitsu Tōiku appeared before (#20). The services referred to here were held in 1745, in conjunction with a lecture meeting on the Vimalakirti Sutra *at Jitoku-ji, a branch temple of Keirin-ji, in eastern Kai province; three hundred people took part (Precious Mirror Cave, p. 210). Ranshitsu's Dharma heir, Rempō Chishō (d. 1770) the incumbent of Keirin-ji, who requested the lectures, was a longtime student of Hakuin.*

WE APPROACH THE TWENTY-NINTH day of the fourth month, the second year of Enkyō (1745), the third anniversary of Priest Ranshitsu's death. On the third day of the third month, Priest Rempō, his successor at Keirin-ji, opened a lecture meeting on the *Vimalakirti Sutra*. To fill the monks' bellies, Yun-men's sesame buns were turned out from the early hours of the morning. Choice delicacies like those Vimalakirti served Buddhas and Bodhisattvas at his assembly were also provided. At noon, Chin-niu came dancing out with his rice pail and treated the monks to a fine vegetarian repast. After the chanting of the sutras and dharanis, I was asked to offer incense and say a few words.

Old Ranshitsu resided at Keirin-ji for twenty years. He guided students who came under hammer with wonderful means and delivered superior utterances that were lofty and forbidding. Immense billows of virulent flame and smoke, shooting out from his forge, enveloped students and buried them under. In his inner chambers, he devoted himself with tremendous vigor and authority to the ageless work of turning the wheel of the vow. Eventually, he moved into a retirement temple, Fukuju-in, in the village beneath Keirin-ji. There his attainment, deeply grounded in the Bodhisattva vow, grew deeper and more powerful the older he became. Thanks to this man's dedication to the path of Zen, many priests, nuns, and lay followers in this part of Kai province are at this moment sincerely devoting themselves to the practice of the Buddha Way.

Head priest Rempō has now resided at Keirin-ji for ten years and has continued tirelessly to carry out the great aspirations of his teacher. He asked me to conduct a meeting and deliver lectures on the *Vimalakirti Sutra*. People from both far and near have come in large numbers to take part. They have devoted themselves earnestly to their practice, transforming the meeting into a great Dharma assembly. This is all owing to wind and waves that Priest Ranshitsu stirred up during his lifetime.

Offering incense and performing prostrations, I now hold up for praise the great virtues of the deceased.

I say: This soup of wood shavings is not the product of heaven and earth. Nor was it created by any human craft. It has emerged from the pitch-black ocean depths where it has been submerged for kalpas beyond time.

Forty years ago, I was doing zazen seated on a stinking, ragged old cushion inside the deep pit of black fire that is primal ignorance. I was groping around and suddenly I grasped it. Ever since that time, I have held it up and sported with it wherever I have gone, throwing inhabitants of Buddha lands into a panic fear, staggering denizens of Mara's court into quivering fits. No one could possibly discern its traces.

The fragrance from the incense that I now offer will reach the proud nostrils of old Ranshitsu seated in the tranquility of the great samadhi, and it will pierce his nostrils. It will drift on, permeating the entire universe, empowering with its blessings Buddhas, Dharma, and priests throughout the ten directions, the Naga deities who protect them, and beings, sentient and nonsentient, of every imaginable kind.

> This deadly perfume of mine will waft into the stinking orchid's chambers,
> The fragrance will linger on even in the dreams of folks in eastern Kai.
> After three years his words still shine with sparkling brilliance.
> Rising up within Amra's gardens, a single strand of incense smoke.

. . . .

Yun-men's sesame buns. "'What is the talk that transcends Buddhas and patriarchs?' Yun-men replied, 'A sesame bun.'" (*Blue Cliff Record,* Case 77).

Choice delicacies... A reference to passages in the "Fragrance Accumulated" chapter of the *Vimalakirti Sutra:* e.g., Vimalakirti tells Shariputra, who is worried about feeding the great multitude of Bodhisattvas who have assembled, "Why be distracted by thoughts of eating when you are listening to the Dharma? If you want something to eat, wait a moment. I will see that you get the sort of food you have never tasted before" (*The Vimalakirti Sutra,* p. 112).

Chin-niu came dancing out. "At mealtimes, Priest Chin-niu would carry the rice pail to the front of the monks' hall and dance around, laughing loudly and calling out, 'Grub for the Bodhisattvas!'" *(Blue Cliff Record,* Case 74).

Soup of wood shavings (bokusatsu-kō). "Master Tung-lin said to the assembly, 'I have nothing especially deep or subtle for you at this time. Just a soup of wood shavings and plate of iron spikes. It's up to you how to get them down'" (*Compendium of the Five Lamps*, ch. 20). Here the expression seems to allude to bits of incense wood, which in Hakuin's comments that follow become a metaphor for ultimate reality or Buddha-nature. In *Dream Words from a Land of Dreams*, the expression appears paired with "a plate of iron spikes" (*tetsutei-han*) to signify something impossible to get your teeth into.

Forty years ago. "He was in Echigo, sitting on an old stinking cushion not even a crow would take a second look at" (annotation). The reference is to Hakuin's initial breakthrough into enlightenment, which he experienced at the age of twenty-three during a practice session at Eigan-ji in Echigo province.

Deep pit of black fire. "He is probably referring to the bottomless depths of his cinnabar field (*tanden*)" (annotation).

Verse, lines 1–2: Ranshitsu's name is literally "orchid chamber." "The fragrant incense I [Hakuin] have secretly had in my possession these forty years is no different from Orchid Chamber's smell. Thanks to Orchid Chamber's virtue, people in eastern Kai province that he has guided and taught will remember his outstanding accomplishments even in their dreams" (annotation).

Lines 3–4: "This is because on arriving at this third anniversary, Master Ranshitsu's exemplary influence continues to grow stronger. Hence this meeting on the *Vimalakirti Sutra* and Ranshitsu himself represent the totally emancipated Dharma-body—it all came about from this single strand of incense smoke" (annotation). *Amra's gardens.* The park on the outskirts of Vaishali where the *Vimalakirti Sutra* was preached.

: 29. Verse Instructions During the *Rōhatsu* Training Period

According to Zen tradition, Shakamuni achieved great enlightenment while practicing in the Snowy Mountains (Himalayas).

> Don't say two-year-olds have no trouble understanding it,
> When even we eighty-year-olds can't put it into practice!
> Wise prelates Matanga and Gobharana both botched it up.
> Endless barriers block the way into the Snowy Mountains.

. . . .

The T'ang poet and Zen layman Po Chu-i asked master Tao-lin, "What is the essential meaning of the Buddha Dharma?" "Do no wrong. Do only good," he replied. "Even a two-year-old child could say that," said Po. "Yes," said the master, "But an eighty year-old man can't put it into practice" (*Compendium of the Five Lamps*, ch. 2).

  [Kashapa-] Matanga and Gobharana. Translators of the *Sutra of Forty-two Sections*, they are regarded as the first Buddhist monks to arrive in China.

: 30. INSTRUCTIONS FROM THE TEACHING SEAT AT
A VEGETARIAN FEAST SENIOR MONK YAKU
HELD FOR HIS DECEASED FATHER

Senior Monk Yaku (Yaku Jōza), full name Donsen Gen'yaku (n.d.), from Bungo province (present-day Oita prefecture on the island of Kyushu), arrived at Shōin-ji after having experienced a strong satori. Hakuin soon disabused him of the notion that his training was over, and he stayed on to engage in post-satori training. He took up residence in Kannon-ji on the eastern outskirts of Hara and com-muted to Shōin-ji for sanzen with the master. Yaku later became head priest at Chūshō-ji in Kawachi province, south of Osaka. The deceased father on whose behalf he provided the vegetarian feast is referred to by his posthumous name, Teian Sempo Jōza. The suffix Jōza (Senior Priest), though usually reserved for clerics' posthumous titles, was on occasion given to lay followers as well, sometimes in conjunction with a deathbed ordination. The piece is dated 1745, Hakuin's sixtieth year.

  Yaku appears three times in Hakuin's Chronological Biography: *in the capacity of a temple steward during lectures on the* Record of Hsu-t'ang, *as a supervising priest at a lecture meeting on the* Vimal-akirti Sutra, *and in an episode in which he submits an enlighten-ment verse to Hakuin, which is alluded to below. Hakuin apparently thought highly of Yaku's literary skills, since he entrusted him with the editing of his lectures on the* Record of Hsu-t'ang (Sokkō-roku kaien-fusetsu), *his first publication, and also had him write the pref-ace for it (*Essential Teachings of Zen Master Hakuin, *pp. 1–7).*

DON'T GO HANGING OUT any calabashes. People will only laugh if you do. When the yellow dragon's blind eyes opened for the first time and he peered dimly around, wasn't he met with howling laughter?

Don't go making impressions with a phony gourd seal either. It will only make your own hackles rise if you do. Tse Wei-na attained satori, but when his teacher rashly confirmed it, didn't he burn with anger and resentment long afterwards?

Senior Monk Yaku from Bungo province began his religious training at a certain temple, achieving a significant breakthrough that filled him with strength. He was all ready to cease his training and begin sweeping the Zen world clean from top to bottom. In spring of the fifth year of Gembun (1740), Yaku strode into my Dharma precincts with a cocky, self-confident air. He wore a battered sedge hat and was dragging a large staff he'd wrenched off a wisteria bush somewhere. He looked like an old crane stalking through a flock of chickens. My monks rubbed their eyes and stared enviously.

I took a quick glance at him and tested him with a line of ordinary dialogue. It knocked him right back. His Zen function was dull and sluggish, incapable of turning and responding freely and easily. This was completely contrary to the reports I had been getting about him. I told him: "Now that I see you face to face, you're not quite what I'd been led to expect." From that time on I assaulted him with endless sallies of stinging invective, assailed him with deafening shouts. I was merciless. I didn't let up on him for a second.

Yaku decided to hang up his traveling staff for good and stay on at Shōin-ji as my student. He would come to me for *sanzen* mornings and evenings, his head lowered in shame. He would run off afterwards, his bugged-out eyes filled with tears. But he bore down, spurred on by the burning indignation he felt toward priests like Ch'eng San-sheng and Ching-feng, men who had prematurely confirmed their students' enlightenment. Before long he gave up both eating and sleeping, was oblivious to hunger and cold.

In autumn of the second year of Kampō (1742), I went in response to a request from Ryōtan-ji in Tōtōmi province to conduct a Dharma meeting. All the Shōin-ji monks except Yaku accompanied me on the trip. He was in too sorry a state to travel. During the month we were away, Yaku continued to bore his way into the story of Chien-feng's Three Kinds of Infirmity. Suddenly, the prison walls fell away and he was free. Knowing that I was on my way back from Ryōtan-ji, he set out from Shōin-ji and made his way down the Tōkaidō to meet my palanquin. He waylaid me on the road, holding out a verse he had written expressing the understanding he had achieved. I took one glance at it and began assailing him angrily, using even stronger abuse than before. As Yaku walked back to Shōin-ji with us, he kept scratching his head. Deep creases lined his brow.

Three years later, Yaku achieved another sudden breakthrough. This time, he had managed to stumble up into the foothills to the left of Eastern Mountain. But I still wasn't happy, and he wasn't really satisfied either. He was fired by a burning aspiration that could not be held back. This was of vital importance to the assembly, firing up the younger monks around him and spurring them to greater effort.

This year, the second of Enkyō (1745), is the seventh anniversary of his father Teian Sempo Jōza's death. Senior Monk Yaku emptied his purse of the few coins it contained and said, "I would like you to hold a ceremony for my deceased father. There is no need to chant sutras or dharanis. What I want is for you, in your great compassion, to raise up the Zen teachings, to utter a phrase or two, one of those impenetrable adamantine cages or prickly chestnut burrs, for the sake of the many cold, starving monks practicing here at Shōin-ji."

I thought of Kuang Tao-che penetrating the koan about Hsing-hua striking Supervisor Monk K'o-pin and dreaming that very night of his mother, who told him that owing to his attainment she had gained rebirth in the deva realms where she could hear the compassionate teachings of the Bodhisattvas. Master Ta-hui of the Ching-shan monastery was deeply moved by this story. "When accumulation of merit from deep faith and devotion to practice results in the attainment of *prajna* wisdom," he said, "it is something truly beyond our comprehension."

How can there be a single doubt that Teian Sempo Jōza will be delighted beyond measure in the other world to learn what his son Senior Monk Yaku has achieved? It is because of this that I agreed to the senior priest's request and offered these words. Will it perhaps be a case of offering a great reward and waiting for a valiant man to appear?

. . . .

Hanging out a calabash. Merchants did this to advertise they had vinegar on sale. Here the expression cautions students against mistaking an initial, partial attainment for genuine enlightenment, as Yaku did when he arrived at Shōin-ji. There is a saying, "even though he doesn't hang out a calabash, his vinegar is perfectly mature" (*Record of Hsu-t'ang*, ch. 8).

The blind yellow dragon is Huang-lung ("Yellow Dragon") Hui-nan. Hui-nan's enlightenment was sanctioned by Ch'eng San-sheng (Le-t'an Huai-ch'eng), but he was later humbled in an encounter with master Tz'u-ming. Hakuin deals with Huang-lung's study under Tz'u-ming in *Talks Introductory to Lectures on the Record of Hsu-t'ang* (*Essential Teachings*, pp. 83–6).

A gourd (or melon) seal. A sham seal carved from the firm flesh of the fruit, which will yield impressions resembling that of a genuine seal; here it indicates the fraudulency of Ch'eng San-sheng's certification.

Tse Wei-na, better known by the name Pao-en Hsuan-tse, lived in Fa-yen's assembly for many years. He was entrusted with the position of *wei-na,* in charge of supervising other monks, but he never once attended Master Fa-yen's lectures or talks. When Fa-yen asked him why he never had any questions about his Zen practice, Tse explained that he had already finished his training under master Ching-feng. Fa-yen asked how he had achieved his realization. "I asked Ching-feng," Tse replied, "What is the self of the person who studies Zen?" and he replied, 'Ping-ting t'ung-tzu comes for fire.'" "Those are fine words," replied Fa-yen. "But I doubt that you understood them." "Since Ping-ting is associated with fire," replied Tse, "looking for fire with fire would be like looking for the self with the self." Fa-yen burst into laughter. "Tse Wei-na, now I can assure you that you didn't grasp Ching-feng's meaning." Tse indignantly stalked out of the monastery. Some days later he reconsidered his action: "Fa-yen is a great teacher with five hundred monks studying under him. There must be something in what he says." When he returned to the monastery, Fa-yen said, "Why don't you ask me that question?" "What is the self of the person who studies Zen?" said Tse. Raising his voice, Fa-yen answered, "Ping-ting t'ung-tzu comes for fire." At that instant, Tse entered great enlightenment.

Chien-feng's Three Infirmities. Book of Equanimity, Case 11. Hakuin deals with this koan at some length in *Essential Teachings,* pp. 19–23.

Entering the foothills…Mountain. Tung-shan, Eastern Mountain, refers to Master Wu-tsu Fa-yen, who called himself "the fellow who lives in the foothills to the left of Tung-shan," and to the style of Zen taught in his lineage. According to an annotation, it signifies "Yaku had grasped the true meaning of constantly striving forward [in post-satori training]."

Chestnut burrs (rikkyoku-hō) indicate matters, usually koans, that are impossible to swallow.

Adamantine cages (kongō-ken), enclosures made of a diamond-hard substance from which it is impossible to escape. Often used to describe the formidable difficulties of *nantō* (hard-to-pass koans).

The story of Kuang Tao-che (n.d.) appears in *Ta-hui's General Discourses* (*Ta-hui p'u-shuo,* ch. 3): "Kuang Tao-che was a Dharma heir of Master Chen-ching, who prized his simplicity and honesty and appointed him head priest at Chiu-feng. When Kuang was on his first Zen pilgrimage, he always told his companions, 'Because I hated to part from my mother, I wasn't eager to leave on a pilgrimage. I must study very hard and turn any merit I acquire to her benefit.' He formulated a set question and posed it to priests wherever he went: What is the meaning of Hsing-hua striking supervisor monk K'o-pin? [see following note]. One teacher responded to the question by getting down from his chair, extending his arms, and sticking out his tongue. Kuang struck his zazen mat and left….He next took the question to Priest Lin of Shih-shuang, who said, 'What about your own meaning?' Kuang struck his zazen mat. 'A fine zazen mat,' said Lin, 'but you don't know where this ends.' Kuang then took the question to Master Chen-ching, whose response was also, 'What about your own meaning?' Kuang struck his zazen mat. "Others hit things, so you hit things too!" shouted Chen-ching. At that, Kuang entered great enlightenment, grasping the inner meaning of the koan. That night his mother appeared to him in a dream and said, 'Because my son achieved enlightenment, I have been reborn into the deva realms and am able to receive the compassionate instruction of the Bodhisattvas.'" Ta-hui's comment: "When faith and devotion to practice achieves merit like this that results in Buddha wisdom, it is truly beyond our comprehension."

Hsing-hua striking K'o-pin. After a dialogue between these two monks, Hsing-hua struck K'o-pin, telling him that because he has lost their Dharma battle he must pay a penalty of five taels and treat the entire assembly to a vegetarian feast, which he himself will not be allowed to attend. K'o-pin quit the temple in a huff, but some years later he became Hsing-hua's Dharma heir and successor (*Transmission of the Lamp,* ch. 12). Commenting on this encounter, Sung master Po-yun Shou-tuan said, "K'o-pin later completed his religious quest and greatly venerated Hsing-hua. Throughout the centuries K'o-pin has been held up in Zen temples as a monk who realized his great debt to his teacher and went on to repay it in full" (*Extensive Records of Zen Priest Po-yun,* ch. 2). This story, in stressing the need for continued practice following satori, reinforces an essential theme of Hakuin's Zen.

Offering a great reward…a valiant man to appear? Hakuin's final comment is originally from *San Lueh ("The Three Strategies"),* an early Chinese treatise on war: "Beneath a great reward valiant men are sure to gather." It is used as a capping phrase in the *Blue Cliff Record,* Case 26; *Book of Equanimity,* Case 13, and other Zen works.

: 31. VERSE ON OFFERING INCENSE AT THE ANNIVERSARY OF BODHIDHARMA'S DEATH

> Kitchen piled with vegetables, the chopping blade wears thin,
> Stoking the stove with maple leaves, the fire tongs kept busy.
> We'll lay out a memorial offering he'll be unable to touch;
> For the blue-eyed Indian's belly, truly gut-wrenching news.

. . . .

An annotation explains the sense of the first two lines: "Because we consume large amounts of carrots and burdock root at Shōin-ji, the blade on the vegetable chopper was worn thin. Because we lacked firewood, we used autumn leaves instead, so the kitchen fire had to be constantly stoked." Hakuin used the first two lines of this verse in his autobiography *Wild Ivy* (p. 40) to express his state of mind as a young monk when he took leave of his teacher Shōju Rōjin, apparently signifying that although he has tried diligently in many ways to bring his training to completion, he still feels the need to continue.

Line 3–4: "A feast that no one knows how to take a bite of" (annotation). The words "he" and "blue-eyed Indian" both refer to Bodhidharma.

: 32. VERSE ON OFFERING INCENSE AT THE ANNIVERSARY OF BODHIDHARMA'S DEATH

This is dated the fifth of the tenth month, 1746, and was probably written while Hakuin was visiting Hōrin-ji in Kai province to deliver lectures.

> Yesterday news arrived of the Ryūun-ji priest's death.
> Today we hung up the portrait of the old Indian monk.
> Both transmit the meaning of coming from the West.
> When you finish your rice, wait until the tea is served.

. . . .

Ryūun-ji was located in Numazu. The head priest was Taidō Zekan (d. 1746), who was succeeded by Settan Ehatsu, a close friend of Hakuin's, whom he had known from the days when they were young acolytes at Daishū-ji in Numazu. In 1717, the year Hakuin became head priest of Shōin-ji, Settan began serving as his attendant.

The old Indian monk is Bodhidharma (the text has "Bear's Ears Peak," the site of Bodhidharma's tomb in eastern I-yang province).

What is the meaning of Daruma's coming from the West? [to China] is one of the most common Zen questions.

: 33. INSTRUCTIONS TO THE ASSEMBLY AT THE OPENING OF A MEETING ON THE *LOTUS SUTRA*

Hakuin read out this long verse at Sekirin-ji in Kai province in the spring of 1746, his sixty-first year. He was conducting a lecture meeting there at the temple's request.

> Anyone who seeks to master the Buddha's Way
> Must begin by attaining a *kenshō* of total clarity.
> When it's as clear as if it's lying in your hand,
> Crack the secret ciphers of Eastern Mountain:
> How did Chao-chou see through the old woman?
> Why did Master Hsing-hua strike duty monk K'o?
> Chen Ts'ao's sizing up Zen monks from the railing.
> Huang-lung's growing vegetables by the zazen seat.
> Chien-feng's three kinds of deep-rooted infirmity.
> Yun-men's Barrier liberating groups of blind men.
> What's it like rubbing shoulders with him all day?
> A band of brigands dozing under an old oak tree.
> When you've bored through each of these koans,
> You may turn to the *Lotus* and *Vimalakirti* sutras.
> Unless you grasp their meaning, even with *kenshō*
> You'll fall unawares into the abyss of emptiness,
> The two fearful voids of the self and the Dharma,
> Entrapped inside half-baked Two Vehicle Zen.
> Men today think it's enough to experience *kenshō*,
> A great fraud perpetuated by the Lesser Vehicle.
> They are always quick to ridicule the Two Vehicles,
> Never suspecting they're as good as dead themselves.
> Venerable disciples Purna, Shariputra, Kapphina,
> Ananda and Mahakashapa, and Subhuti as well
> Had far deeper attainment than priests of today,
> They were heroes who could swallow all India whole.

But to stop them from nesting within their satori,
The Mahayana sutras condemn such attachment.
Angulimalya scorned it as a worm-like wisdom,
Buddha dismissed its adherents as scabby foxes.
Old layman Vimalakirti strongly denounced them
As charred seeds from which no life could emerge.
Shravakas, Solitary Buddhas, and Bodhisattvas
Were as fervorless as flies caught in hot soup.
Wise ones, they lamented, cried sorrowful tears,
Were possessed of attainment, yet dismal and sad.
But hearing the Buddha expound his third teaching,
Concerning faith and reason, their eyes finally cleared.
I have always rued my school's ignorance of the sutras,
Like blind donkeys they just wander aimlessly on.
Even with *kenshō,* if the Buddha's words are unknown,
You're like a cart that's only fitted with a single wheel.
And if you read the scriptures without having *kenshō,*
You're no better than a parrot, imitating others' words.
I want you men to keep the ancients' practice in mind,
And spur the vow-wheel forward to save living beings.
Never forget how Hui-chung achieved his attainment,
Always remember National Master Daitō's broken pot.

. . . .

Eastern Mountain. (Tung-shan) refers to Fa-yen Wen-i (885–958), who lived there. Regarded as founder of the Fa-yen school of Chinese Zen, Fa-yen is known for the marvelous efficacy of his Zen utterances.

Secret ciphers or passwords (*angō-rei*), originally secret passwords used in wartime by soldiers, refers here to efficacious koans generally, such as those Hakuin enumerates in the following lines:

1. Chao-chou Sees Through the Old Woman. (*Gateless Barrier,* Case 31).
2. Hsing-hua Strikes Supervisor K'o-pin. (*Compendium of the Five Lamps,* ch. 11). Temple Supervisor (Wei-na) K'o-pin leaves the temple after being struck by Master Hsing-hua but later attains great enlightenment and becomes Hsing-hua's successor.
3. *Ch'en Ts'ao Sizes Up Zen Monks.* Standing high on the upper story of a pavilion, Layman Ch'en Ts'ao correctly discerns the character of some traveling monks passing below. (*Compendium of the Five Lamps,* ch. 4; also *Blue Cliff Record,* Case 33).
4. Huang-lung Hui-nan said to monks who came to him for instruction,

"Reciting sutras in the bell tower. Growing vegetables by the zazen seat."
When head monk Sheng offered a good turning phrase: "A ferocious
tiger sits blocking the road," Huang-lung retired, turning his position
over to Sheng.

5. *Chien-feng's Three Infirmities* appears in a dialogue between Chien-feng
   and Yun-men (*Essentials of Successive Records of the Lamp*, ch. 33). See
   Essential Teachings, pp. 19–20.

6. *Yun-men's Barrier* appears in the koan Ts'ui-yen's Eyebrows (*Blue Cliff
   Record*, Case 8).

7. "In the morning our eyebrows entangle, in the evening our shoulders
   rub. Who is it? All day long the pillar goes back and forth. Why am I
   unable to move? If you can penetrate these two turning phrases, your
   lifetime of practice is complete." Daitō Kokushi's Final Admonitions to
   his Monks *(Daitō Yuikai)*.

8. Kanzan Egen (1277–1360), founder of Myōshin-ji, is known for his saying, "[The koan] Chao-chou's Oak Tree works like a brigand."

Venerable disciples...Subhuti. Priests who are numbered among the Buddha's
ten great disciples.

Angulimalya. In *Oradegama*, Hakuin comments on students who instead
of engaging in koan practice directed toward *kenshō*, follow the teachings of
"do-nothing Zen": "Even the Buddhas cannot cure an understanding such
as this...Even if they continue in this way for endless kalpas, they will still
be nothing more than dead dogs....The Buddha has compared them to sca-
brous foxes. Angulimalya has scorned them as having the intelligence of
earthworms. Vimalakirti has placed them in the category of scorched buds
and rotten seeds" (Adapted from *Selected Writings*, p. 115).

Wise ones: those who have attained the three stages (*san-ken*) of the
Bodhisattva's career and the three fruits (*shi-ka*) or stages of sainthood in
the Lesser Vehicle teaching.

Faith and reason. The Buddha is said to have preached the *Lotus Sutra* in
three different ways to accord with the capacities—superior, average, and
inferior—of Shravaka disciples, so they would all be able to grasp his meaning. The chapters on faith and reason (or study) belong to the third preaching, in which he explained that with faith and study it was possible for all his
disciples to attain Buddhahood.

Hui-chung. After receiving his teacher's Dharma transmission, Hui-chung
went to live on Mount Po-ya in Nan-yang and did not leave his mountain
hermitage for over forty years *(Records of the Lamp,* ch. 5).

Daitō's broken pot. "If only one person concentrates his practice on investigating his self, he may be living in the wilderness in a hut thatched with a single bundle of straw and spending his days eating the roots of wild herbs cooked in a pot with broken legs, but it is he who is face to face with me every day, and it is he who requites his debt to me. Who should ever despise such a one? O monks, be diligent, be diligent" (Daitō Kokushi's *Final Admonitions*).

:34. Verse Instructions to the Assembly During the *Rōhatsu* Training Period

> This noise and bustle, giving talks, chatting with guests,
> Grabbing some sleep, are all forms of zazen practice.
> When offering incense this morning, I forgot the verse,
> After the meal I recited *Namu Myōhō-renge-kyō* instead.

. . . .

Probably written in 1746, Hakuin's sixty-first year. According to the *Chronological Biography*, he was busy teaching this year in various temples in Suruga and neighboring provinces, and when winter came he was completing lectures he had started previously on the *Lotus Sutra*. While the exact circumstances surrounding this verse are unclear, it seems Hakuin was caught up in various other affairs when the *rōhatsu* training period arrived.

This noise and bustle… zazen practice. "Zazen that continues in one's daily activities" (annotation).

Lines 3–4: "I forgot to read the verse, but I couldn't do anything about that, so I recited the Daimoku several times instead" (annotation). The Daimoku is the invocation "*Namu Myōhō-renge-kyō*," literally, "I place my trust in the *Lotus Sutra*."

:35. Teaching Delivered from the High Seat at the Opening of a Meeting on the *Wisdom Sutra* at Seibon-ji

Seibon-ji is a Zen temple a few hundred yards east of Shōin-ji along the Tōkaidō. The text itself dates the teaching to a lecture meeting held during the New Year period of 1747. This would place it at a time of severe famine, and apparently also in the aftermath of a fire that caused great destruction in Hara village. This may be the con-

flagration described in Hakuin's essay on "Black Fire" (Book Four, #64), which ravaged Hara when he was in his mid-fifties. These fires were not uncommon. In a section titled "Kyūshinbō encounters a devastating fire" in Dharma Words in Japanese on Cause and Effect, Hakuin vividly narrates his memories of another conflagration he had witnessed as a four-year-old in 1690. This is probably the same one mentioned in the travel diary of the German physician Kaempfer, which he heard about when he passed through Hara on his way to Edo in 1691.

Lecture meetings on the six-hundred fascicle Wisdom Sutra, the Daihannya Haramitta Sutra (Sanskrit, Mahāprajnā-paramita-sūtra) were sometimes conducted to obtain protection from fire and sickness, as well as to ensure good harvests. Because of the sutra's enormous size, it was usually recited by the tendoku method in which only a few lines of each chapter are read and the rest omitted.

Seibon-ji still houses one of Hakuin's largest paintings, depicting Emma, the King of Hell and the realm of the dead. It is hung at annual gatherings to worship Jizō, the "Bodhisattva of Hell." For a reproduction, see The Religious Art of Zen Master Hakuin, p. 233.

THE VIRTUOUS POWER OF the gods is perfectly clear, yet if a person does not revere the gods, its light cannot shine with full and radiant effect. The misfortunes people suffer are many and various, yet with the gods' help and protection their troubles can be eliminated. Hence it is said: "It is owing to people's devotion that the gods' divine power gains in strength; it is owing to the gods' divine power that people's good fortune increases."

My home village Ukishima-ga-Hara is located not far from the ocean, and is subjected to strong winds that have in the past been the cause of catastrophic conflagrations. These fires occur about every five to ten years, causing the villagers great distress. They have in some cases obliged family members to disperse and move to other parts. An idle old priest like me, living in relative ease in a temple, is able to exist only because of the villagers' support. They supply the food that I eat. Whenever they experience distress, it cannot help but wring my heart. These recurring fires have long troubled me, but since I lack the secret arts that Luan Pa possessed to prevent them, not to mention the illustrious virtue of National Master Shōichi, my only recourse is to rely on the six hundred fascicles of the

Great Wisdom Sutra. I feel sure that if we offer a recitation of the sutra to the gods, they will take pity on the villagers and exempt them from the calamity of fire long into the future. In any case, I could not just sit by in my temple and watch them suffering such grievous losses.

This year, spring of the fourth year of Enkyō [1747], I privately informed senior priests in the surrounding areas of my intention to hold this meeting. All gave their wholehearted support. "It will be an excellent source of good karma in this life and the next," they said. We borrowed a set of the *Great Wisdom Sutra* from Tokugen-ji next door and we are now assembled here for this splendid Dharma meeting. I pray most humbly that all Buddhas throughout the ten directions, the various gods who protect the Dharma—devas, dragon kings, and the other guardian gods, and especially our great and august ancestral Japanese *kami* Amaterasu-ō-mikami, and the sacred deities enshrined at Mount Fuji, Mount Ashitaka, Mount Akiba, and Kitano—will muster all their radiant illumination and bestow its virtues on this meeting, so that our village will be forever free of the calamity of fire. If the villagers understand this aspiration of ours, and from now on assemble regularly on the 24th of the first month each year to chant this sutra, it will be an outcome for which I have long fervently wished.

The senior priests at Seibon-ji issued me solemn orders: "You must take advantage of this rare opportunity to deliver formal Zen lectures on a koan story that will serve as an offering to men and devas and promote the teachings of our Zen school." Unable to refuse them, I have taken these moments to babble off a word or two to the brotherhood. Don't say Seibon-ji doesn't show concern for its weary monks.

. . . .

"It is owing to people's devotion...good fortune increases." The source of this saying, which Hakuin also uses in *The Tale of Yūkichi of Takayama (Precious Mirror Cave*, p. 47*)*, is unknown. "If a person has a firm belief in the Way, whoever he is, he will enjoy good fortune" (annotation).

Luan Pa. Governor of an ancient Chinese province, Luan Pa was known for his knowledge of occult arts. He once spat out a mouthful of wine in a southwesterly direction, saying it would help put out a fire raging in a neighboring province. It was later learned that a fire in a large city to the southwest had been extinguished by a sudden rainsquall from the northeast that smelled strongly of wine (*Biographies of Divine Sages*, ch. 5).

Shōichi Kokushi is the posthumous "National Master" title of Enni Ben'en (1202–1280). From Hakuin's native Suruga province, Enni studied in

Sung China, receiving the Dharma transmission from Master Wu-chun at the Mount Ching monastery, then he returned to Japan and founded the Tōfuku-ji in Kyoto. "There is a legend that when a great fire was raging at the Mount Ching monastery, Enni helped put it out using water from the stream that runs under the Tsūten Bridge at Tōfuku-ji" (annotation). Charms offering protection against fire are still produced and distributed at Tōfuku-ji.

Hakuin says that this large sutra was recited by the *tendoku* method, in which the recitation is divided among the monks, with each monk reading two or three pages at the beginning and end of each fascicle of the sutra; the portion in between is "read" by shuffling the pages a few times.

:36. Untitled [Examining a Koan]

I PUT THIS BEFORE YOU: Once an old woman asked someone to take a donation to master Chao-chou and request that he revolve the sutra repository for her. Upon receiving the donation Chao-chou got down from his seat, turned the sutra repository one revolution, and said, "Tell the woman I have revolved the sutra repository." When the person reported this, the woman said, "I asked him to revolve the sutra repository. Why did he only turn it half way?"

"In closely investigating this story, Chao-chou is like a venerable dragon lying hidden inside an old well, the woman is like a half-starved hawk peering down at a lump of fresh meat. Why is this?"

> Peach flowers aspire of themselves to ripen into fruit,
> People should not be resentful of the predawn winds.

. . . .

The sutra repository rests on a central axis that allows it to be turned. Devotees who revolve it are thought to gain the same merit as reading the works in the Buddhist canon. The story of Chao-chou and the old woman is found in *Compendium of the Five Lamps*, ch. 4 (it appears again below, #68). In *Essentials of Successive Records of the Lamp*, ch. 10, the priest who receives the request is Ta-sui Fa-hsin, not Chao-chou. Daisetz Suzuki translates Zen master Ta-hui's comments on this koan in *The Training of the Zen Buddhist Monk*, p. 78.

An annotation attached to Hakuin's comments reads: "Chao-chou (the dragon) purposely concealed his ability to fly freely through the air. The old woman is out to swallow Chao-chou whole."

Hakuin concludes with a couplet by T'ang poet Wang-chien. It is included in *San-t'i-shih*, a thirteenth-century collection of mid- and later T'ang poetry that was closely studied in Japanese Zen circles. The following explanation of the couplet appears in a Japanese commentary on *San-t'i-shih*: "Fresh spring colors have faded, the few remaining peach flowers rapidly fall and scatter away. Since they do this because they themselves want to ripen into fruit, we should not resent the wind for scattering them. The peach flowers are like a lovely court lady who having lost her youthful beauty and her lord's favor is obliged to give up her position at court. She cannot blame her lord, or others, for her sorrow. It is her own fault. She could have avoided this fate if she had not sought such a life in the first place" *(Soin-shō).*

: 37. Words on Offering Incense at the Ceremony Commemorating the Thirty-fifth Day of Shintatsu-myōsō-shinnyo's Death

Shintatsu-myōsō-shinnyo *is the posthumous name of the wife of Furugōri Tsūgen (n.d.), the eldest son of a prominent samurai family of Suruga province with close ties to Hakuin. Hakuin uses the term* shoshi *to describe Tsūgen, a designation signifying that he had not yet been appointed to an official position, so he and his wife were apparently still young, probably in their twenties or thirties. The memorial service referred to here was the fifth in a series of weekly observances held over a forty-nine-day period following a person's death, normally held on the seventh, fourteenth, twenty-first, twenty-eighth, thirty-fifth, forty-second, and forty-ninth days.*

Tsūgen's father Furugōri Kentsū (1695–1746), a retainer of Inaba Tango-no-kami, the lord of Odawara castle, was a fervent Nichiren Buddhist who lived in Hina village not far from Hara. After beginning koan study under Hakuin in his mid-thirties, Kentsū became a patron of Shōin-ji. An enlightenment verse he presented to Hakuin is recorded in the Chronological Biography *(Precious Mirror Cave, p. 200).*

In the present piece, dating from 1747, the year after Kentsū's death, Tsūgen and his wife appear as Hakuin's students as well. Tsūgen may also be the physician Furugōri that the Chronological Biography *mentions having attended Hakuin in his final days (ibid., p. 234).*

THERE IS A COUNTRY gentleman named Tsūgen living in Fuji county in Suruga province. He was married to a fine lady who was adorned by the chaste virtues she had cultivated in the fine robes of great honesty and simplicity. I once painted an image of Kannon Bodhisattva at her request, which she revered and worshipped for many years. Together with her husband she probed the depths of Chao-chou's Mu, engaging it constantly through hidden practice and unobserved activity. This year, the fourth of the Enkyō era (1747), she contracted a serious illness, and it was not long afterwards that the mirror on her dressing chamber was covered over for good.

It is now the thirty-fifth day since her passing. To commemorate the occasion Tsūgen has provided a vegetarian meal, and I have been asked to lecture on the *Lotus Sutra*. I earnestly hope that the services we conduct today will further the cause of Zen.

I put this before you: Tao-wu and Chien-yuan went to a household to offer condolences to a bereaved family. Chien-yuan struck the coffin and said, "Alive or dead?" Tao-wu said, "I won't say alive. I won't say dead." "Why won't you say?" Chien-yuan asked. Tao-wu said, "I won't say." On their way back to the temple, Chien-yuan said, "Say it right now! If you don't, I'm going to hit you." "If you want to do that, go ahead," said Tao-wu. "I'm not going to say." Chien-yuan struck him.

In the bargaining between these two old veterans, one of them is like Yen-t'ou's laughter, the other like Hsuan-sha's utterance. Why is that? Carefully scrutinize their words.

> When Wen-chun passed away, she left behind an empty bed,
> And a weeping husband, Hsiang-ju, to raise two children alone.
> As I try to imagine the profound grief of such a bereavement,
> The image of a lady's sickbed devotion remains etched in
>   my mind.

. . . .

Chao-chou's Mu, Case 1 in the *Gateless Barrier* collection, is often the first koan given to Zen students. Hakuin used it as such for many years until changing to the sound of one hand koan in his final decades.

The episode involving Tao-wu Yuan-chih (739–835) and his student Chien-yuan (768–835) appears in somewhat different form in Case 55 of the *Blue Cliff Record*.

Yen-t'ou's laughter alludes to a Zen dialogue (*Compendium of the Five Lamps*, ch. 7; *Blue Cliff Record*, Case 66) that requires some knowledge of Chinese history unfolding at the time the dialogue took place. The rebel leader Huang Ch'ao (d. 884) led an uprising against the ruling T'ang dynasty and after many bloody campaigns finally succeeded in capturing the capital Ch'ang-an. Putting large numbers of its inhabitants to the sword, Huang Ch'ao proclaimed himself emperor of a new dynasty, only to be overthrown several years later and forced to commit suicide. The dialogue: Yen-t'ou asked a monk, "Where have you come from?" "From Ch'ang-an," he replied. "That would be after Huang Ch'ao passed through. Did you pick up his sword?" Yen-t'ou asked. "Yes I have it right here with me," said the monk. Yen-t'ou thrust his neck forward, and shouted, "Ka!" "Master," said the monk. "Your head has fallen." Yen-t'ou roared with laughter. Later, the monk went to visit Hsueh-feng. "Where have you come from?" asked Hsueh-feng. "From Yen-t'ou," he said. "What's he telling people these days?" said Hsueh-feng. The monk told of his encounter with Yen-t'ou. Hsueh-feng gave him thirty blows with his staff and chased him from the room. The Sung master Hsu-t'ang, commenting on this, said, "If that monk had grasped the vital Zen function in Yen-t'ou's laughter, even if Hsueh-feng's staff had been a great deal longer, it could never have touched him" (*Record of Hsu-t'ang*, ch. 1).

Hsuan-sha's utterance: This refers to a comment Hsuan-sha Shih-pei made on hearing that Ling-yun had experienced enlightenment when he saw peach blossoms in flower: "It is all fine and good, fine and good, but I guarantee you brother monk Ling-yun still hadn't got it all." The phrase "Hsuan-sha's utterance" appears with various meanings in Zen literature. Hakuin often uses it when stressing the necessity of continuing post-satori training. He even had it carved as a motto on a seal that he impressed on his paintings, in a no doubt self-depreciatory sense: "I tried to depict the truth in this painting, but was unable to get it all." Here it apparently alludes to something not fully achieved.

Verse: The famous Chinese poet Ssu-ma Hsiang-ju (d. BCE 117), left penniless by a series of misfortunes, fell in love with the young widow Wen-chun, the daughter of a wealthy man. They eloped, but indigence forced them to open a small wine shop, where Wen-chun served the customers and Hsiang-ju, dressed only in a loincloth, did the rest. Wen-chun's father, unable to bear the shame of having his daughter working in a wine shop, made them a large gift of money. Hsiang-ju later tried to introduce a concubine into their marriage but gave up the idea when Wen-chun wrote a poem expressing her intention of divorcing him.

Hakuin draws a parallel between this legendary couple and Tsūgen and his wife. It cannot be known with certainty how far the similarity extended, but Shintatsu-myōsō-shinnyo was young like Wen-chun, and may also have been a beautiful widow when she married Tsūgen. An annotation also states that like the Chinese couple, they had two children.

BOOK TWO
Instructions to the Assembly–
General Discourses—Verse Comments on
Old Koans—Examining Old Koans

. . . .

*Book Two consists of fifty-four pieces, fifteen more Instructions
to the Assembly (Jishū), eleven Prose Comments on Koans
(Nenkō), and two Addresses from the High Seat (Jōdō).
In addition there are five General Discourses (Fusetsu); twelve
Verse Comments on Koans (Juko); and nine Comments
on Koans (Koko), in which the remarks focus on errors in comments or capping words others have made on koans, or points
they have overlooked. Of these thirteen are translated.*

I. Instructions to the Assembly (Continued)

:38. Verse Instructions to the Assembly at the Opening of a Meeting on the Four Part Record

The Four Part Record *(Shibu-roku) is a compilation published in Japan made up of four short Chinese works:* Verses on Belief in Mind *(Hsin-hsin-ming),* Verses on Realizing the Way *(Cheng-tao ke),* The Ten Ox-herding Pictures *(Shih-niu t'u), and* The Principles of Zazen *(Tso-ch'an i). This verse dates from 1751, Hakuin's sixty-sixth year. He delivered it while on a teaching trip to western Honshū (Chronological Biography, Precious Mirror Cave, 217–18), prior to a lecture meeting on the* Four Part Record *he conducted at Hōfuku-ji in Iyama, Bizen province. He spent three weeks at Hōfuku-ji, which was the home temple of his student Daikyū Ebō (1715–74). Daikyū later served as head priest of Hōfuku-ji, and became one of Hakuin's most important Dharma heirs. The Senjaku (Thousand-Foot-Deep) Well referred to in the opening line is located within Hōfuku-ji's precincts.*

> The springs of the Senjaku Well are infused with deadly poison,
> Spewing cold fumes, they strike pilgrims down with blighting
>   force,
> They wither Buddhas' and demons' vitals before they even drink.
> Have any of the disciples here made these springs their own?

. . . .

As the "disciples" in the final line (*shibu-shu*) refer to the four kinds of Buddhist disciple—monks, nuns, laymen and -women—we know that all of them were in attendance at this meeting.

:39. On Offering Incense at a *Suiriku* Ceremony Sponsored by Mr. Yoda

At the Suiriku *ceremony (Suiriku-e), food and drink is offered for the repose of the dead and for the liberation of all beings, in the water (sui) and on land (riku), suffering in the realms of transmigration, especially those trapped in the realm of hungry ghosts (gaki).*

This Suiriku *ceremony apparently took place at Gyokurin-ji in Matsuzaki village, on the western coast of the Izu peninsula, in 1752. Sixty-seven-year-old Hakuin traveled to Izu to deliver lectures at Kiichi-ji, located just east of Matsuzaki. The sponsor of the lecture meeting, Yoda Takanaga (also Sajiemon), head of one of Izu's wealthiest and most important families, resided near Matsuzaki, and Gyokurin-ji had been built as their family temple. The Yodas were also important patrons of Kiichi-ji, and helped Hakuin on more than one occasion in his building and publishing projects. Another piece Hakuin wrote some twenty years earlier (1734) praises Takanaga for a donation he made that enabled a new bell tower to be constructed at Kiichi-ji (#68). The closeness of Hakuin's association with the Yoda family is further seen in a long letter he wrote Takanaga in 1755 attempting to resolve a family dispute; the letter is translated in* Beating the Cloth Drum, *pp. 99–109.*

O N THE FIFTH DAY of the tenth month of 1752, a *Suiriku* ceremony was held under the sponsorship of Yoda Sajiemon, the chief patron of Kiichi-ji. Offerings were made to Kannon Bodhisattva, the central image enshrined at the temple, and to Jizō Bodhisattva, and a vegetarian feast was provided for five hundred people who had gathered for the services. Mr. Yoda requested that a memorial service be conducted for the late Tengan Zenkei Zogen, former head priest at Gyokurin-ji, now dwelling in the great tranquility of eternal samadhi, to benefit him in his final attainment of wisdom. Mr. Yoda asked me to offer a pinch of incense and add a few appropriate words. As the purpose was a truly commendable one, I made the following verse.

> The three worlds are the exquisite golden form of Buddha,
> The six ways of karmic rebirth are his body in its entirety.
> Within this there is no birth and death, there is no Nirvana,
> No enmity exists for this, and no partiality for that either.

Tengan Zenkei Zogen, your aspiration was as deep as the ocean, your self-nature as vast and clear as the heavens above. The merit that accrues to you from this meeting and vegetarian feast should enable you to waken promptly from your thirty-year dream. The merit from the sutras and dharani recited here should enable you to eliminate the fundamental ground of samsaric delusion and the twelve links that create the condition of samsaric suffering. You will then dwell in the groves of Zen, enjoying the Dharma's joyful compensations, sporting freely and endlessly in the ocean of the Bodhisattvas' vow; you will fully attain the three Buddha bodies and four wisdoms, raising up the great Dharma standard of the Buddhas and patriarchs and delivering beings of every kind in all the realms of existence.

The ceremony we hold today is the result of the deeply rooted faith that donor Yoda has acquired over the course of many lives. I have no doubt whatever that the Bodhisattvas Kannon and Jizō will look with favor upon Mr. Yoda's sincere aspiration and bestow their protection not only on his own family but on the families, children, and grandchildren of others as well, guarding them from illness far into the future and extending to them the blessing of long and fortunate lives.

. . . .

Nothing is known about Tengan Zenkei, who according to this had died thirty years before. The term Zogen, literally Senior Priest or First Monk, is a suffix also commonly used in posthumous names.

:40. VERSE INSTRUCTIONS DURING THE *RŌHATSU* TRAINING PERIOD

> Snowy mountains, crags, and summits loom before him,
> His world frozen hard and solid, free of all defilement.
> Yet the golden Indian's mind still hasn't yet succumbed,
> Any talk of leaving would be like a boozer's final sip.

. . . .

"The great snowy mountains [the Himalayas] in Shakamuni's (the golden Indian's) belly pierce right through the abode of non-thought" (the fourth and highest of the four abodes in the realm of nonform, where only the barest traces of discriminative thought remain) (annotation).

"His mind is not completely dead, his attainment is still not fully mature, so he shouldn't be talking about leaving the mountains. Since he's not ready to return to the world just yet, rattling on about it is like a drunk taking just one more cup—something best avoided" (annotation).

:41. VERSE INSTRUCTIONS ON OFFERING INCENSE AT THE ANNIVERSARY OF BODHIDHARMA'S DEATH

This was written on the fifth of the tenth month (Bodhidharma's Death Anniversary), 1754, when Hakuin, sixty-nine years old, was visiting Tōgen-ji ("Peach Blossom Temple") at the Yui post station west of Hara for lectures on the Records of Sung-yuan.

> One balmy fall day I entered the Peach Blossom Spring,
> Encountered Bodhidharma returning home with his boot.
> A horse leech baring its fangs snarls up at the Big Dipper.
> A dew worm takes the bit in its mouth and fords the river.

. . . .

Peach Blossom Spring (*Tōgen* in Japanese). A utopia of great beauty, based on a fable written in 421 by the poet Tao Yuan-ming about the chance discovery of an ideal realm where the people lead an ideal existence, completely isolated from the outside world. The Peach Blossom Temple in the fishing village of Yui, three stops west of Hara, was regarded as one of the most beautiful spots on the Tōkaidō.

The final two lines, typical Zen *impossibilia*, "describe the state of things in Peach Blossom country, Hakuin's encounter with Bodhidharma" (annotation).

:42. VERSE INSTRUCTIONS DURING THE *RŌHATSU* TRAINING PERIOD

> Long ago Buddha sat doing zazen in the Snowy Mountains,
> Lightning split the great cosmos, rivers turned in their courses.
> When he left samadhi, folks nearby began dashing wildly about,
> A white ox was reported trembling fearfully from head to foot.

. . . .

"When the World-Honored One left samadhi, lightning began flashing out and striking the ground. Everyone scattered and began dashing wildly about" (annotation). "The bullock is the white ox of the *Lotus Sutra*, a metaphor for mind; it is the white ox Shakamuni had been disciplining in the Snowy Mountains" (annotation).

Hakuin used this verse for an inscription on a painting of *Shakamuni Leaving the Mountain*. The painting was destroyed in the war, but was reproduced as a frontispiece in the second volume of the *Hakuin Kōroku* (1902).

II. General Discourses (*Fusetsu*)

General Discourses (Fusetsu). Oral teachings given in relatively informal circumstances. Fusetsu are thus contrasted with the personal, one-on-one teaching that takes place in the master's room during dokusan, and also with the more formal Jōdō, which the teacher delivers from the high seat, wearing a Dharma robe, after offering incense at the altar. The teacher may deliver a General Discourse from the high seat, but without offering incense or wearing the Dharma robe. It should perhaps be noted that Hakuin does not seem to have always observed the fine distinctions of temple discourse. He is said, for example, to have on occasion delivered Jōdō wearing his everyday robe while seated on the floor, with his kiseru pipe in hand.

:43. General Discourse Given During a Lecture Meeting on *Ta-hui's Arsenal*

This meeting was held at Shōin-ji in 1743, Hakuin's fifty-eighth year. Ta-hui's Arsenal (Ta-hui wu-k'u; 1186) consists of anecdotes about contemporary and near-contemporary Rinzai priests that Ta-hui Tsung-kao related to his students. The first two paragraphs of the dialogue between Hakuin and a monk questioner appear in

Hakuin's Chronological Biography *in the entry for 1743* (Precious Mirror Cave, p.208).

IN SPRING OF THE third year of Kampō (1743), on the day master Hakuin began lecturing on *Ta-hui's Arsenal,* a monk who had come to attend the meeting asked, "It is said 'an enlightened person does not peck. The moment there is any pecking, it is lost.' What does it mean?" Master Hakuin replied, "When the chick wants to get out of the egg but has not yet begun pecking at the shell, the mother hen must not peck at it from outside. You must be able to discern whether the time is right for the student or not."

The monk bowed before the master. The master said, "Peck!" The monk immediately emitted a shout. The master said, "Awakened!"

Another monk asked, "What does 'arsenal' mean here? I can understand that a granary stores grain and an arsenal stores weapons, and that during a crop failure when the people don't have enough to eat the emperor orders the granaries opened to provide food and alleviate suffering; to suppress uprisings he musters his armies and orders the arsenals opened and armor and weapons supplied so the troops can subdue the malefactors. But surely such weapons are useless to a Zen monk. If he is authentic, the kind of person who can take life without even blinking an eye, he will be able to get the job done even with the stub of a worn-out old broom. What good would it do him to arm himself with a lot of useless blunt swords and broken lances? Didn't Lao Tzu say that 'weapons are ill-omened tools, to be used only as the very last resort'? Aren't everyone's eyes horizontal and their noses up-and-down? When a manservant is summoned, he doesn't change into a maid, does he? Don't your hands grasp and feet move perfectly well? What possible need is there for such useless tools? Not to mention lecturing and explaining the idle verbal dregs left by the ancients, smearing students' faces in it? Doesn't this suggest these stories of Ta-hui are highly questionable?"

[Hakuin:] Come closer and listen to what I say. If a person possesses the heroic spirit of a Han Hsin or P'eng Yueh and the ability of a Kuan Yu and Chang Fei [four legendary military heroes of ancient China], and acquires their wonderful skill with sword and lance, then I would agree that he could dispatch someone with a stubby old broom. It's no different for those patricians who plumb Zen's secret depths. Those who have toppled the hard-to-pass barriers of the patriarchal teachers one by one, spending their sleeping and waking hours inside the thicket of thorn and briar, plunging and sporting in seas of virulent poison, could take a person's life with a stubby broom. But a cough or a clearing of the throat could also serve as a death-dealing weapon. A fried bun or a sesame rice cake could be a weapon of choice, or it could even serve as a whole arsenal.

But to come here as you do with a totally lifeless understanding of "eyes horizontal, nose vertical," prattling about killing people with broom stubs is absurd. You will end up falling straight into hell when you die, into the merciless clutches of denizens who will cut you in two or chop off your legs. So don't be asserting that the whole world is as smooth and calm as the surface of a mirror. When you babble about a manservant not changing into a maid, you turn those words into a sharp lance that will lay the gardens of the patriarchs to waste. When you spout off about hands grasping and feet walking with perfect freedom, it becomes a razor-edged weapon that can destroy time-honored Zen traditions. Nothing more ominous could occur in a training hall, where students pass through the forge to be singled out as future Buddhas.

If you don't believe what I am saying, then try to clarify the vital function at work in the words, 'A chick inside the shell pecks. The mother hen doesn't.' You won't be able to. You will just stand there speechless and bug-eyed. Those hands which you claimed could freely grasp won't be able to grasp it. Those feet you say move freely will be paralyzed. Or do you still insist your activity is perfectly free and unrestricted? This is the most shameful thing that can occur within the halls of Zen, and also the most unfortunate. It was to save students from such pernicious evil that Zen master Ta-hui collected these divine life-taking amulets. This is why he bequeathed these claws and fangs of the Dharma cave to us.

Over seventy monks are now assembled at my temple. They have turned their backs on more comfortable, well-appointed training halls elsewhere in the country, showing no concern for their splendid buildings. Instead, they have elected to come here to Shōin-ji, to hole up within these tumbledown old walls and steadily refine their realization in hard-fought and unwavering pursuit of the Way.

It is because I realize how deeply devoted they are that I come out like this and subject them to my speechifying, bandying about these verbal complications. I'm like a person who tries to relieve his great privation and suffering by warming someone else's hands. But when the most vital point is reached, when you come up against words and phrases altogether impossible to penetrate, I will show you no mercy whatever. Not a single drop. Those of you who have not yet penetrated those barriers must therefore be prepared to steel your hearts and fire yourselves with an indomitable spirit of determination.

There will be some among you who will sit atop peaks where no one has yet set foot, who will descend into secret valleys that are completely cut off from the world. There, forgetting both sleep and food, cold and privation, moaning pitifully, they will press on in pursuit of the Way.

Anyone who joins the ranks of those teachers who lecture on Zen records today, who make everything crystal-clear to their students, obstructing them from entering the gates of enlightenment with their kindhearted, unstinting efforts to have them understand the meaning of the texts, is helping to perpetuate a chain of transgressions so boundless and far-reaching in extent that it will be utterly impossible to atone for them.

Look at the way a fisherman works. He gathers a suitable quantity of shellfish or shrimps to use as bait, attaches them to his hook, and casts his line into the vast flood. But once a large fish has been caught, he discards the bait. I work in the same way. I let out a thousand yards or so of line, spread some verbal decoys around, make sure the koan bait is set. Then I wait for a giant fish to show up, the kind of behemoth who could swallow the boat. I bait all my hooks with such virulent poison that all who see them are flabbergasted, all who hear them go limp and crumple to the ground. In this I outdo even Prince Jen, who baited his hook with fifty bullocks. When a golden-tailed carp of the eastern seas rises and swallows my bait, I first make sure he has given up the ghost—body and life together—and then I discard the bait.

The dim-witted priests you find everywhere you go today who deride the use of words and letters and ridicule them as unnecessary verbal entanglements, are totally mistaken. Totally. They are hunkering over a stagnant pool at midnight groping blindly for dragons.

To the Zen patricians engaged in plumbing the secret depths, I humbly say: "You who have yet to penetrate the matter should put aside entangling words and letters and just bore into this single koan: "An adept Zen teacher does not peck. The moment he does, all is lost."

Thank you. Be sure you all stay healthy.

. . . .

It is said an enlightened person does not peck... "This exchange cannot be explained in words. Each student must discern it through hard practice" (annotation).

You will end up falling straight into hell... chop off your legs. These were two methods of execution in ancient China. Hakuin means that a monk like this will undergo such punishments when he falls into hell.

Here Hakuin uses words from the *Latter Han History* (ch. 8) to describe the danger of a Zen teacher being too obliging and kindhearted (using "grandmotherly kindness") when instructing students: "For men he likes, he will rip off his own skin to provide them with beautifying plumes" (the quotation continues: "For those he dislikes, he will wash off all the dirt to find some scar or imperfection").

Verbal decoys. The "decoys" in this case are grass and leaves that fishermen would float on the water, knowing that fish will be attracted and gather beneath them. "A metaphor for a Zen teacher uttering a word to test a student. The significance is in the testing, not in the words he utters" (annotation).

"Prince Jen made an enormous fishhook with a huge line, baited it with fifty bullocks...and cast with his pole into the eastern sea....[After a year], a huge fish finally swallowed the bait....When Prince Jen had landed the fish, he cut it up and dried it...and there was no one in the country who did not get his fill" (*Complete Works of Chuang Tzu*, p. 296).

When a golden-tailed carp. Vigorous carp able to swim beyond the Dragon Gate (a three-tiered waterfall in the Yellow River that cut through the mountains) were said to transform into dragons. A metaphor for authentic Zen students.

They are hunkering... pool. Allusion to lines in Hsueh-tou's *Verse Comments on One Hundred Old Koans* (*Hsueh-tsu po-tse sung-ku*), ch. 7: "The fish have already ascended Lung-men's three-tiered sluices and transformed into dragons, but the fool still gropes for them at midnight in a stagnant pool."

44. General Discourse Introductory to a Lecture Meeting on the *Lotus Sutra*

Hakuin's statement here that this series of lectures took place in 1746 is substantiated in Tōrei's draft Chronological Biography (age 61). Tōrei goes on to state that this was the first time Hakuin lectured on the Lotus Sutra, and that it took place in the second lunar month at Genryū-ji, a Rinzai temple in Tadehara west of Shōin-ji overlooking the swiftly flowing Fuji River.

Hakuin delivered many of the General Discourses at the beginning of such lecture meetings, using them to set the tone for the session and inspire students to greater effort in their practice. He

commonly incorporates words and phrases from the lecture text into
the discourse, and no doubt they would have been recognized as
such by his audience. I have confined myself in the notes to indicat-
ing only two or three of these allusions. The Lotus Sutra *is known*
for its many parables; a large portion of Hakuin's discourse is given
over to a parable of his own.

I N SPRING OF THE third year of Enkyō (1746) Kairyū Oshō, incumbent
at Genryū-ji, a priest who has always desired to promote the Zen teachings, made arrangements for a lecture and practice session to be held that
would be open to all students. He asked me to discourse on the fundamental aspiration for which Buddhas have appeared in the world.

I have a certain affinity with the *Lotus Sutra*. Some twenty years ago
I obtained the hidden secret, so difficult to grasp, that lies concealed
within it. One night, as I was reading the Parables chapter by candlelight,
suddenly I penetrated through and grasped this hidden meaning, and
as I did I found that my entire body was bathed in a nervous sweat. For
many years I remained silent about the realization I had experienced,
not wanting to explain it with undue haste. But today, even at the risk
of losing my eyebrows, I am going to a turn it into a Dharma gift by
divulging it to you.

This is something students of the Lesser Vehicle can never grasp. It
strikes them completely deaf and dumb, and they run off quivering in
consternation. Students of deep insight and attainment might hear it and
come to believe in it unquestioningly, but they still would be unable to
penetrate to a full and clear understanding. That is reserved exclusively
for Bodhisattvas of the highest stages, those who have achieved full attainment. They will drink it up as though it was a heavenly nectar, rejoicing
that the wealthy man's treasure has suddenly fallen unsought into their
hands.

Now I am going to tell you something that happened at the beginning
of the Kampō era (1741–44). A samurai retainer of the Hikone clan of Ōmi
province, Mr. Fujiwara something-or-other, was entrusted with the great
sum of five hundred *ryō* and told to deliver it to Edo. He set out accompanied by four or five other men. On the road between Mino and Owari
provinces, a man they encountered began walking and running beside
them. When they reached the post station inn, they shared lodgings with
him. He was very polite and extremely well-mannered, and the samurai

took a liking to him. One day, the fellow produced five *ryō* in gold coins and said to the samurai, "Because you have allowed me to accompany you, I have come this far without incident. I am the son of a poor farmer of Mino province. I have an elder brother in Edo who has been seriously ill for many months and my parents want me to use this money to bring him back home. I am on my way there now, but I am worried about carrying such a large sum on my person. If you would be so kind as to let me place it in your traveling pouch, I would be able to get a good night's sleep, which I am in need of. I will get it back from you when we reach Edo." Mr. Fujiwara accepted the money with a smile on his face. He put it into his leather pouch, and the party resumed their trip. He had it with him when they set out in the morning, kept it close at hand when they stopped for the night. When Mr. Fujiwara got into his palanquin, the man would ask, "Is the money bag all right?" When Mr. Fujiwara got out of the palanquin, he would ask, "Is the money bag all right?"

One morning when they woke up, the man was nowhere to be seen. The leather pouch had disappeared at well. Mr. Fujiwara's companions were all cock-a-hoop, not knowing what to do, but he remained perfectly calm. As they resumed their journey, he was even seen to smile. After walking three or four leagues, they encountered a man on horseback coming from the opposite direction. He had a letter for Mr. Fujiwara. After opening it and glancing at it, Mr. Fujiwara broke into a wide grin. When they arrived at the next post station, they saw the leather money pouch hanging from a pillar. Paying a small reward, Mr. Fujiwara retrieved the pouch and set out for Edo once again, smiling all the while. His companions, unable to fathom what had taken place, wondered at his strange behavior. When they stopped for the night and the pouch was opened, they found nothing inside but a collection of rocks. Upon pressing Mr. Fujiwara to explain what had happened, he produced from his kimono the letter that had been delivered to him on the road and showed it to them. It read:

> I am known as Oshio So-and-so of Mino province. I am a thief by trade, and am most certainly destined to end my life under the executioner's blade. Bowing low before his excellence Mr. Fujiwara, I take the liberty of addressing this letter to him.
>
> I was born to a very poor family. I was nurtured in poverty by my mother and raised at the hands of my ignorant father. Despite that, my mother never despised our fare of bean curd

lees and rice bran, and she never took anything that belonged
to others. Although father couldn't even make out the *kana*
syllabary, he too never swerved from the path of honesty. I was
blessed with a fine physique and grew to be over six feet tall,
with powers of observation in no way inferior to my fellows.
Unfortunately, there seems to have been a larcenous streak
ingrained in me from the start. I despised people like Po Yi
and Shu Ch'i for their stupidity. I belittled the talents of celebrated brigands like Tao Chih and Chuang Yu. I fell in with
Hou Pai, forged a close friendship with Hou Pei. The past ten
years I have been pretty much on the run. I didn't even know
whether my parents were alive or dead. I tunneled into store-
houses, broke into rice sheds, bored through gates and doors,
stole livestock. Everything I ate, everything I wore, was produced by other people's sweat and blood. I have lived in constant fear of being caught and dragged to a place of execution.
I have kept the dogs and crows waiting a long time to sink their
teeth into my remains. I have so far narrowly escaped that fate,
always expecting death to come tomorrow, or perhaps tonight.
But as I can't avoid being caught much longer, I have become
extremely cold-blooded. Not even a speck of mercy remains
in my heart. Although in robbing people I sometimes burned
their homes, taking their children's lives, the money it got me
never lasted even a fortnight. There is no doubt whatever that
I am destined for hell.

When I discovered that you were on your way to Edo with
a large sum of money, I carefully searched through my book
of tricks and finally came up with a ruse I could use to take it
from you. How was I to know that it would be I who would
fall victim to the clever strategy you had devised? On stealing
someone's money, my general rule is: if the mark goes east, you
go west; if he goes west, you head east. This time, however,
when I saw your palanquin heading east, I had no choice but
to follow you eastward as well. After I had run along beside you
for eight or nine leagues, my mind was made up. "If my plan
succeeds, the money will be mine. If it fails, I will give myself
up and throw myself once again on Mr. Fujiwara's mercy." I felt
that way because I now realized you were no ordinary man.

So I was forced to continue eastward with you and your party. In the end, things turned out as I had feared. To this point in my career no one, from the far north of Honshu to Kyushu in the far west, had ever escaped the snares I laid, but in this case, things fell out in a completely different way. When I realized you had turned the tables on me, that I had been caught in your trap, I was flummoxed. My liver froze. My knees shook uncontrollably. It would probably have been best if I had done away with myself then and there. I regret that I was not able to throw my villainous carcass in front of your Excellency's horse and let him stamp the life from me. What have I to live for now? Even to think of it overwhelms me with shame.

In any case, I will return the money pouch to you. You will find it hanging on a pillar at the next post station. I ask that you please return the small amount I entrusted to you for safekeeping. It is stolen money. If you kept it, it would only tarnish your virtuous reputation.

Praying for his excellence Mr. Fujiwara's continued long life and prosperity, and hoping he enjoys even greater success in the future, Oshio bows down with the deepest respect and offers him this letter.

Old Hakuin, half-dead, gasping out his final breaths, has once again pounded the great Dharma drum and ascended the Dharma seat to mumble out yet one more long and prolix discourse. But somewhere within those words of his is a secret key for breaking through the Barrier. Don't complain that the old man has gone senile on you, that you can no longer make head or tail of what he is trying to say. This old gizzard's primary concern is to set forth, in the Buddha's place, his fundamental reason for appearing in the world, which was to promulgate the path of liberation. If a person can discern this reason, he will surely also grasp the essential meaning the Buddha revealed when he preached the *Lotus Sutra* on Vulture Peak. Hence an old poem states, "Yesterday, in wind and rain, my old friend set out from here on a journey." How can we clarify this? The *Lotus Sutra* says, "A being who slanders this sutra shall receive the following punishments."

All the best to you all. Please take care of your health.

A final verse:

A blind old duffer squats in a cave wrapped in an endless tangle
of vines.
Unfazed by the difficulty, he takes them in his hands and plays
with them,
Tripping up eighty-four thousand men and gods, sending them
sprawling to earth.
The *Lotus* is a truly formidable barrier, prowled by hungry
wolves and tigers.

. . . .

Open to all students. This was an unrestricted assembly (*musha no hōe*),
"open to all those who aspire to the Way, adherents of all Buddhist sects,
clerics and laity, men and women" (annotation).

Nervous sweat. Literally, "white sweat," that is, one not caused by physical
exertion but by psychological stress. Hakuin tells the story of the enlightenment he attained at this time in the *Chronological Biography*, p. 198.

Not wanting to explain in undue haste. Words from the *Lotus Sutra*, Parable of the Medicinal Herbs chapter.

Losing my eyebrows. It is said that the eyebrows of a teacher who explains
the Dharma will fall off.

The wealthy man's treasure. A reference to the famous story in the Parables chapter of the *Lotus Sutra*. The young son of a wealthy man runs away
from home and for the next fifty years wanders from place to place in abject
poverty. Finally, by chance, he returns to the gate of his father's residence,
is immediately recognized and invited inside. The son is terrified, over-
whelmed by the splendor of the estate, and runs away. The father entices
him back by offering him work drawing night soil from the privies. After a
series of gradual promotions the son finally becomes supervisor of the rich
man's affairs. Just before his death, the rich man publicly acknowledges his
son and transfers to him the whole of his estate.

Po Yi and *Shu Ch'i* were princes of the ancient state of Ku-chu who
renounced their birthright and wandered into the mountains, living on roots
and berries until they finally perished from cold and hunger.

Tao Chih and *Chuang Yu* were famous brigands of the Robin Hood type
in ancient China. The brothers Hou Pai and Hou Pei were celebrated thieves
of the ordinary mercenary type, their names becoming synonymous with
their trade.

Yesterday, in wind and rain... These words appear in the following poem
found in the *Ku-shih yuan* collection (ch. 4): "Walking out the east gate of the

city, I gaze down the road toward far-off Chiang-nan. Yesterday, in wind and rain, my old friend set out from here on a journey. I want to cross the wide river, but it is deep and has no fords. I wish we were a pair of yellow cranes and we could soar off back to our native place." Hakuin uses the verse as a capping phrase in *Dream Words from a Land of Dreams*.

The Lotus Sutra *says...* In the Parables chapter, these punishments are specified: "If he should become a human being, his faculties will be blighted and dull, he will be puny, vile, bent, crippled, blind, deaf, hunchbacked. The things he says people will not believe..." (pp. 75–6).

:45. GENERAL DISCOURSE INTRODUCTORY TO A LECTURE MEETING ON THE *FOUR PART RECORD*

Hakuin lectured on the Four Part Record *on numerous occasions. It is not known where he delivered this General Discourse.*

SENG-TS'AN'S *Verses on Belief in Mind* and Yung-chia's *Verses on Realizing the Way* work like invincible diamond-pounders, like drums smeared with virulent poison, like the vicious fangs of a marauding tiger, like the *pa*-serpent's terrifying maw. Even if a person possessed learning that rendered him conversant with all the works in the Buddhist canon, native ability that enabled him to swallow up every manner of things in the eight directions, he would still be unable to fathom the unbounded vastness of these Zen poems. Among the four works in this collection, the secret harmonies of *Verses on Realizing the Way*, are particularly hard to grasp, though in recent times teachers who peddle harebrained notions of them are more numerous than rice grains in a bulging storehouse.

These smelly, shriveled-up old farts ensconce themselves atop the teaching seat and try to surround themselves with large assemblies. If they can get ten or twenty of their shiftless followers to show up, they begin jabbering off things like this:

"I have nothing further to do; my study is complete. You have nothing further to do; your study is complete too. 'Having nothing further to do' means I no longer rely on words or letters, do not get tangled up in words, have no need to penetrate koan barriers or understand Zen's essential principle, and can just spend my time in lumpish stupidity. That is what I mean by 'having nothing further to do.' 'My study is complete' means I have no concern whatsoever with worldly and unworldly affairs. I put aside good and evil, picking and choosing, and engage in no religious practice whatever. That's what I mean by 'my study is complete.'"

Don't you know that the nature inherent in each and every person is not something obtained through practice and realization? It is perfectly bright and clear from the start, utterly free and untrammeled, without need of any "marvelous enlightenment." It is just a matter of drinking tea and eating rice, relieving your bowels and bladder. What need is there to seek anything beyond that? This is Zen's "direct pointing," its "perfect way that is not difficult." It also agrees with the words, "Only you must avoid picking and choosing." This is what is meant by 'a person whose study is utterly complete and has absolutely nothing further to do.'"

With teachers like this, it is no wonder that the true traditions of Zen have fallen into the dust, its gardens shriveled to the roots. He is wrong! Preposterously wrong! The great earth itself could not contain an error of such magnitude. Men like him could not see Yung-chia even in their dreams. They should be looked on as shaven-headed heretics, regarded as devils clothed in Buddhist surplices. If any of you here harbors a single notion that bears any resemblance to this, you will never be able to break free of Mara's entangling nets and will remain permanently confined within the cycle of birth and death, sinking eternally into the pitch blackness of a bottomless abyss.

It is therefore with profoundest respect that I offer the following words to superior seekers of the hidden depths.

"Why do Seng-ts'an's verses resemble the fangs of a ferocious man-eating tiger? How is Yung-chia's poem like the *pa*-serpent's maw?" Take these and gnaw at them. From the front, from the rear. Gnaw at them wherever you can. Once you are drenched in the muck sweat experienced by those who die the great death, you will know for the first time that old Kokurin (Hakuin) did not give you a bum steer.

. . . .

Diamond-pounder (kongō no sho). A pronged iron or brass instrument used especially in esoteric Buddhist ritual, said to represent firmness of spirit that overcomes delusions. Hakuin compares it to the way the enlightened utterances of these two poems destroy evil passions. The poison-smeared drum (*zudokku*) kills all who hear its sound. In ancient Chinese bestiaries the *pa*-serpent (Japanese, *hada*) is described as an immense snake that seizes elephants and swallows them whole, excreting their bones three years later (*Shan-hai-ching; Classic of Mountains and Seas,* ch. 10). The *Classic of Mountains and*

Seas also tells us that the elephants sought help from human beings for protection against the serpents. Mounted on the elephants' backs, men succeeded in killing the serpents with their arrows and amassed great fortunes by selling the mountains of elephant bones they discovered in the serpents' caves.

"The perfect way is not difficult" and "Only you must avoid picking and choosing" are the opening lines of *Verses on Belief in Mind.* "A person whose study is complete and has nothing further to do" is from *Verses on Realizing the Way.*

46. GENERAL DISCOURSE INTRODUCTORY TO A LECTURE MEETING ON *THE POISONOUS SEAS OF MOUNT CHING*

Here Hakuin uses the title The Poisonous Seas of Mount Ching *(Ching-shan tsa-tu-hai) for Ta-hui's Arsenal, which has appeared before (#43); "Mount Ching" refers to the monastery on Mount Ching where Ta-hui served for a time as head priest.*

The lecture meeting at which this talk was given was held at the Jiju-in in Izu province in autumn of the sixth year of Hōreki (1756). It was a busy year for Hakuin, now seventy-one years old. In spring he conducted lecture meetings on the Heroic March Sutra, *and during the summer on the* Record of Daiō, *the* Precious Mirror Samadhi, *and his own commentary on the* Heart Sutra. *We further learn from the* Chronological Biography *that while Hakuin was delivering this General Discourse, he was greatly troubled by an inflamed carbuncle. The inflammation subsided several days later after being treated by his physician, who had also treated Hakuin for a carbuncle in 1751, his sixty-sixth year, during a lecture meeting he was conducting at a nearby temple.*

THESE CLAWS AND FANGS of the Dharma cave, these divine amulets that divest you of your life, are the greatest assets in the Buddhas' wonderful storehouse. Average students never see them even in their dreams. These are reserved solely for the person who commits himself to the daunting hardships of genuine Zen training.

Zen master Ta-hui was a Dharma grandson of the Master of the Eastern Mountain [Wu-tsu Fa-yen]; from his chambers emerged Wan-an Tao-yen. Ta-hui's Dharma struggle began in the training hall of Zen master Chan-t'ang Wen-chun (1061–1115). He underwent austere discipline in a hundred forms and suffered a thousand trials until with his haggard face he looked like a son who had just lost his parents. Later, he entered the chambers of Zen master Yuan-wu, and there his search came to an end as all his many efforts reached fruition. He was like a dragon that had entered its native element of clouds and rain.

Don't let anyone tell you that the head of Miao-hsi Hermitage [Ta-hui] was a reincarnation of Yun-feng Yen-yueh (1131–1162). His sagacity in devising stratagems would put Chang Liang and Ch'en P'ing to shame. It would quiver the livers of a million valiant iron knights, making their knees shake and rattle. In employing ploys and devices he forced all the stalwart heroes within the four seas to show white flags of surrender, made even Sun Tzu's tactics seem lame in comparison. Thirteen men who practiced under him at Yang-yu reached enlightenment after applying themselves with the singlemindedness of a child bent on avenging his parents' murder. Ta-hui awarded the robe of transmission to his Dharma heir Ying-an T'an-hua. Seventeen years of untold difficulty at Heng-yang and Mei-yang allowed his realization to mature fully, and enabled him to say, "I'd sooner throw a dipper of warm shit over you than try to teach you Zen."

In autumn of the sixth year of Hōreki (1756), the old priest of Jiju-in in Mishima, who for many years willingly lapped up the venomous slobber of past sages and has ceaselessly lamented the sad decline of Zen's true traditions, invited me to deliver some comments on the koans in Ta-hui's *Poison Sea Collection*. The Kyōgen performer Gihan paid me a visit and tenaciously implored me to accept. The priest at Rinsen-an pledged his wholehearted support. I myself gradually warmed to the idea, and now I have taken up my *hossu* and seated myself here on the Dharma chair to speak, humbly and respectfully, to elder priests who have assembled from the surrounding areas, and to valiant patricians of the secret depths who have filled the hall. I ask you all to pledge that you will push forward the wheel of the great vow and raise up the fortunes of our school. I request as well that you kindly refrain from rejecting as worthless these clumsy ruminations of mine!

. . . .

Reincarnation of Yun-feng. From *Stories Recorded at Yun-wo Hermitage* (Yun-wo chi-t'an), anecdotes of Zen priests compiled by Ta-hui's student Chung-yun (1116?–?): "In the first year of Ta-kuan (1107), Ta-hui, after engaging in practice in quiet retreats, went at the age of nineteen with two other monks to Pei-tu Hermitage. A large dog that had been let loose barked angrily as they approached. While the other two monks beat a fearful retreat, Ta-hui went striding boldly ahead. The animal suddenly began wagging its tail, greeting Ta-hui as though he were an old and trusted friend. The head priest at the hermitage gave Ta-hui permission to stay, and accorded him the greatest courtesy. 'I'm only a young monk,' said Ta-hui. 'I'm unworthy of such consideration.' Glancing at a clay statue that stood in the hermitage, the head priest said, 'At around midnight last night I had a dream. A person appeared and told me that Zen master Yun-feng would arrive at the hermitage today. He said I should do all I could for him while he was here.' Ta-hui, though still feeling unworthy of the attention, thanked the head priest. After he left for other parts to continue his practice, he asked elder priests that he met about Zen master Yun-feng. One of the priests, to help explain Yun-feng's teaching, showed him Yun-feng's *Records*. Ta-hui opened the book and read it avidly. After reading it just once, he had it by heart and never forgot it. From that time on, word passed through the monasteries that Ta-hui was a reincarnation of master Yun-feng."

Chang Liang and Ch'en P'ing are known for their skill in devising (often devious) strategies to advance their ruler's aims. Sun Tzu (sixth century BCE), is author of *The Art of War*.

Kyōgen performer Gihan. An annotation tells us that Gihan was a *sarugaku (kyōgen)* performer from Edo who sometimes stayed in a hermitage at Jiju-in, presumably to engage in Zen practice. Nothing else is known of him. Rinsen-an is in the present-day city of Numazu.

: 47. GENERAL DISCOURSE GIVEN DURING ZEN LECTURES ON THE RECORDS OF NATIONAL MASTER RYŪHŌ

The lectures Hakuin refers to here were given at the age of seventy-two, in the seventh year of Hōreki (1757), at a practice meeting held at Nanshō-in in Minobu, Kai province. National Master Ryūhō is properly Daitō Kokushi, National Master Daitō, the honorific title of Shūhō Myōchō (1282–1338), founder of the Daitoku-ji in Kyoto, and the Japanese Zen priest Hakuin revered above all others. We know from an annotation that Hakuin was lecturing not on Daitō's records themselves, but on Dream Words from a Land of Dreams (Kaian-kokugo), *his Zen commentary (teishō) on Daitō's Zen records, which had been published seven years earlier.*

Worthy of note is Hakuin's mention of his famous Sound of One Hand koan, which the priest of Nanshō-in, Hakuin's long-time friend Senyū Chiei (1688–1763), had, at the age of sixty-eight, recently passed. In the verse couplet attached at the end of the talk, Hakuin alludes to Nanshō-in's location overlooking the swiftly flowing Fuji River as it rushes down from the Mount Fuji highlands to empty into Suruga Bay.

ANYONE WHO WANTS TO understand the *Records* of National Master Daitō first of all must penetrate the koan Su-shan's Memorial Tower. There are greater and lesser Dharmas, there is genuine and false fortune. Even if someone rises to the heights of worldly success and is blessed with carriages, or a crown, and more wealth than Shih Ch'ung, if within he has no links to *prajna* wisdom, if he lacks the guidance of a good friend and teacher and merely abandons himself with prideful self-indulgence to his passions and desires, after he dies he is destined to descend into the endless suffering of one of the three evil destinations. It is for this reason that worldly fortune is said to be a curse in the three worlds.

If, however, a person is possessed of true mettle and pursues his training diligently heedless of his own well-being, he will one morning kick over the roiling karmic seas of birth and death and achieve a *kenshō* as clear and unmistakable as if seen in the palm of his hand. His penetration will extend from the highest heavens all the way to the Yellow Springs, and he will experience a tremendous joy and perfect, untrammeled freedom. In all the human world and deva realms, there is nothing to compare with it. He will not rest satisfied with this, however, but will continue to push forward, never retreating, chewing to pieces and swallowing down all the claws and fangs of the Dharma cave, ripping to shreds the divine life-destroying talismans, constantly carrying out the great practice of the Bodhisattva, assembling great Dharma assets, and attending to the great Dharma giving that brings immeasurable benefit to men and devas. He is a person of truly inestimable worth, a man of genuine good fortune and virtue.

The priest of Shōfuku-zan Nanshō-in is one who has attained this good fortune by engaging in secret practice and hidden activity, unbeknown to others. Recently, he suddenly stomped the birthless sound of my One Hand koan into the ground. Then he totally silenced the ocean of words and phrases. And he didn't stop there, either. He came and asked me to hold a lecture meeting that would elevate the path of Zen and promote its regimen for liberation.

One of the ancients said that when a false person preaches the true Dharma, the true Dharma becomes a false Dharma, and when a true person preaches a false Dharma, the false Dharma becomes a true Dharma. Tell me—are these lectures a true Dharma or false one?

> After the morning meal I walk slowly down the temple corridor.
> Below, endless small boats move swiftly down the Fuji River.

. . . .

There are greater and lesser... false fortune. "Those with great resolve achieve a great satori; those with small determination achieve a small satori. Without the Bodhi-mind, any fortune achieved is bad fortune, self-centered and self-seeking. With the Bodhi-mind, it becomes good fortune, work that imparts the Dharma gift to others" (annotation).

Shih Ch'ung. An immensely wealthy man of the Chin dynasty known for his ostentatious life style.

One Hand Koan. Hakuin's Sound of One Hand koan came in two steps: First hear the sound of one hand, then put a stop to all sounds.

When a false person preaches the true Dharma. Attributed to Zen master Chao-chou in the *Compendium of the Five Lamps,* (ch. 4).

Verse couplet. "When you can wring these lines by the neck, you will know if Hakuin's Zen lectures are true or false" (annotation).

III. Verse Comments on Old Koans (Juko)

Juko (Chinese, sung-ku) is a form of Zen discourse in which a teacher takes a koan and elucidates it with verse comments in the Zen manner. In the nenko (nien-kung) form these comments are in prose.

:48. "The practicer who observes all the precepts does not enter Nirvana."

> Competing ants, pulling at a May fly's stiff dead wings.
> Two young swallows perched to rest on a willow branch.
> Silkworm girls carry baskets, their faces pale and drawn,
> Village boys stealing bamboo shoots vanish through a hedge

. . . .

An annotation to this verse, by someone obviously close to Hakuin, describes how it came to be written: "In composing the verse, the master did not open his books and consult any of the ancients' verses. 'I will compose the verse first,' he thought, 'then see how it measures up against the exalted productions of the old teachers.' Leaving Ryōsen-ji in Tokura where he was visiting at the time, he stopped to rest as he was passing through Numazu. It was then that the first line of the verse came to him. The second line was conceived when he reached Kawabe village, and the third as he was passing through some open fields. Then suddenly, as he was entering another village, he had the final lines as well. By the time he arrived back at Shōin-ji, he had a complete verse, and it was one that possessed merit even when compared against those of the ancients" (See *HZB*, plates 75–6).

The ultimate source for the words of the koan to which this verse comment is attached appear in *Manjusri's Preaching of the Great Wisdom Sutra* (*Monjushiri-shosetsu maka-hannya-haramitta-kyō*, ch.1, T.23): "Not one of the five grave transgressions is inborn, is reborn in the deva realms, falls into hell, or enters Nirvana. Why is that? Karmic causes and conditions always operate within the realm of ultimate reality, neither coming nor going, neither a cause nor a result. This is because the Dharma universe is boundless and has no before or after. As a consequence, Shariputra, we can see by considering that monks who commit the gravest transgressions do not fall into hell and that monks who maintain the precepts in perfect purity do not enter

Nirvana, that such monks are not Arhats and they are not not Arhats; they have not exhausted delusions and they have not not exhausted delusions. Why is this? Because such monks maintain perfect equanimity in the midst of all things."

Zen master Ta-hui, no doubt one of the "ancient teachers" whose verses Hakuin may have considered consulting, commented on this koan: "Place a saucer of oil in the lamp on the wall. Set some wine on the altar before the hall. If you feel sad or depressed, drink three cups of wine. Whence can trouble approach you then?" (*Record of Ta-hui*, ch. 10.)

A sidelight on this verse is provided in the records of Daikyū Ebō, one of Hakuin's most important Dharma heirs. Daikyū first arrived at Hakuin's temple at the age of twenty-six having already studied with Kogetsu Zenzai in Kyushu and received his confirmation. On leaving Kogetsu's temple, he and his brother monk Kaigan Kotetsu (who also became a Hakuin heir) traveled to the mountains of Kumano for a prolonged practice retreat to mature their attainment. At a temple on the way, they chanced to see an inscription hanging on the wall. It was a verse comment in Chinese on the koan, "Precept-breaking monks do not fall into hell; monks who rigorously uphold them do not enter Nirvana." They were unable to make any sense of the verse at all, and decided it must be gibberish some foreigner had scribbled down. On learning it was the work of a priest named Hakuin, they changed their plans and proceeded directly to Shōin-ji. After personal interviews with Hakuin convinced them that they were no match for him, they decided to stay on, pledging that they would not leave until they had completed the great matter of Zen practice. Later in life, Kaigan wrote that Daikyū was much superior to him in capacity. "Daikyū knew after once crossing lances with the master that he had lost. I was unaware that he had taken me alive until my bow was broken and I'd used up all my arrows" (*Stories from a Thicket of Thorn and Briar*, pp. 125–31).

IV. Examining Old Koans (*Koko*)

Koko (literally, "I put this old koan before you"), like the previous Juko, are concerned with elucidating koans. In the Koko form, the teacher focuses on points that he deems have been overlooked or are in error in the original koan or capping words.

:49. UNTITLED [TE-SHAN CARRYING HIS BUNDLE]

This koan, together with Hsueh-tou's comments, appears in the Blue Cliff Record, *Case 4.*

I PUT THIS BEFORE YOU. When Te-shan arrived at Kuei-shan, he carried his bundle with him into the teaching hall. He paced from east to west and from west to east. He looked around and said, "Nothing. Nothing. [Mu, Mu]." Then he went out.

Hsueh-tou commented: "I've got him pegged."

It would be a mistake to interpret Hsueh-tou's "I've got him pegged" to mean he had discerned that Te-shan, in uttering the words "Nothing. Nothing" in the Dharma hall, was sitting in the enlightened realm of his original nature. Hidden within Hsueh-tou's "I've got him pegged" is a very important matter of the Yun-men school. It is extremely difficult.

Years ago I added a capping phrase to Hsueh-tou's comment: "A cry from a cat in a Pure Land of mice." I see now that they are far off the mark—as remote as heaven from earth—and find that my body has become drenched with sweat. Unless you men devote yourself to your practice with tireless effort, you will never be able to savor these words of Hsueh-tou.

. . . .

The following series of notations, by different hands, on Hakuin's capping words, "A cry from a cat in a Pure Land of mice," were entered into a copy of *Poison Blossoms.* They have an interest rivaling that of the text itself.

"This comment, 'A cry from a cat in a Pure Land of mice,' was added to *Poison Blossoms* based on oral teachings heard by the master's attendants and other monks in the brotherhood. They were later noted down by Layman Tsūgen of Mino province, who read them in some borrowed transcripts. Comments our late master originally delivered on this koan differ greatly from those he gave in his later years."

"These capping words are based on a parable: A poor man encountered a foreigner on the road. The foreigner produced a letter and told the poor man, 'In this county, at such and such a tree, if you clap your hands three times, a man will appear. You should give this letter to him.' The poor man came to a place such as the foreigner had described and did as instructed. Entering a large gate, he saw a great hall covered with silver and gold and embellished with precious gems. He saw young boys and temple maidens dancing to sacred music, and rare and delicious foods. On announcing that he had a letter to deliver, the poor man discovered that he had entered a Pure Land of mice and rats that was adorned with countless rare and precious jewels. This aroused his cupidity and he decided to steal some of the jewels. Pinching his nose with his fingers, he imitated the sound of a cat screeching. Suddenly everything around him became impenetrably dark, then dazzling bright by turns. He found that he was underground, in a small, hole-like space. Just then, a man who lived nearby heard sounds in the earth beneath him. Taking them to be mice trying to gnaw their way out, he grabbed a mattock and began striking down into the earth with it. The poor man, though injured by the blows, crawled slowly out, feeling very foolish."

"These capping words [attributed to] our late teacher are based only on hearsay reports. Hsueh-tou's phrase contains within it the vital function of master Lin-chi. It conceals Yun-men's very essence. Coming up against such a phrase, even someone who has bored through to the wondrous meaning of the Buddha-patriarchs and attained a state of perfect freedom will be like the man imitating a cat scream in the Pure Land of mice. Because of that, even monks who have served as the master's secretary, or as his personal attendants, hold differing views as to the authenticity of these capping words. Among the comments that have been recorded as those of the master on the *Blue Cliff Record*, I have found numerous mistakes as well. I have corrected them, since they will be passed on to future generations."

Inscribed after these comments is a notation by Tōrei's disciple Karin: "These are Tōrei's notes."

Following this is annotation inscribed by Tōrei himself: "Layman Tsūgen saw only the surface of the matter and could not discern its full, inner meaning. In his old age my teacher became forgetful, and cases of this kind were not infrequent."

:50. Untitled [Yun-men's Every Day Is a Good Day]

This is the final part in a series of comments by Hakuin that focus on Master Hsueh-tou's verses on the koan, "Every day is a good day" (Blue Cliff Record, Case 6). Only Hakuin's opening statement and his comments on the eighth and final part of Hsueh-tou's verse are translated here.

I PUT THIS BEFORE YOU: Yun-men said, "I don't ask about before the fifteenth day. Try to say something about after the fifteenth day." Yun-men himself then answered in their place: "Every day is a good day."

These words are extremely difficult to pass through. Be aware that they have arms and legs capable of forging genuine people, and also wondrous means to bring them to full enlightenment. Which is why Hsueh-tou said, "I love the fresh devices Yun-men came up with. He spent his entire life pulling out nails and wrenching out wedges for people."

Now where in this koan are the "wondrous means" that produce these genuine people? I want you to deeply savor the verses Hsueh-tou has bequeathed us.

. . . .

Hsueh-tou's complete verse commentary on Yun-men's koan reads:

> Throwing away one, he picks up seven.
> Nothing is comparable above, below, in any direction.
> Sauntering on, treading the sound of the flowing stream underfoot,
> His tranquil gaze spots the tracks of flying birds.
> Grass is thick and wild, mist hangs all around.
> The flowers on Subhuti's cliff are a terrible eyesore.
> I snap my fingers; how lamentable Emptiness is.
> Don't do anything. If you do, it's thirty blows.

Hakuin comments on the final line, "Don't do anything. If you do, it's thirty blows:

"This is like a spoiled little child who won't stop crying. His mother does her best, soothing and cajoling him to make him stop, but he refuses to listen to her. Finally, she says, 'All right, cry all you want. Cry all day. Cry from morning until night. But if you stop crying, for even a second, there'll be no dinner, and I'll put you out of the house.'

"If you want to know the meaning of Hsueh-tou's thirty blows, you should go and ask the spoiled little brat's mother. Ha Ha."

BOOK THREE
Oral Secrets of the Sōtō School's Five Ranks—Dharma Words—Words at Minor Buddhist Observances

· · · ·

Book Three consists of two lengthy commentaries, one on Tung-shan's Five Ranks, the other on Tung-shan's Verses on the Five Ranks, two Dharma Words (Hōgo), and twelve Comments at Minor Buddhist Observances (Shōbutsuji), and remarks he delivered at funeral services and at consecration ceremonies for Buddhist images.

I. Oral Secrets of the Sōtō School's Five Ranks

:51. The Five Ranks of Phenomenal and Universal, a Secret Oral Transmission of the Sōtō Tradition

The Five Ranks (Go-i in Japanese) are stages or ranks of realization attained in Zen practice. Hakuin's comments on the Five Ranks are followed by a commentary that deals with lines in the Precious Mirror Samadhi (Pao-ching san-mei, #52), *a long poem on the doctrine of the Five Ranks, and the five verses Tung-shan wrote on them attempting to elucidate their essential meaning. Exemplary translations of both these pieces appeared in* Zen Dust, *though in the first one (#52), the part where Hakuin interprets the Five Ranks in terms of hexagrams in the* Book of Changes (I Ching) *is omitted, no doubt because they are among the most difficult passages to understand, much less to translate, in all of Hakuin's writings. I can claim little merit for my own attempt except that it is complete.*

The Book of Changes, *perhaps the most important of China's classic texts, is based on the universal principles (ranks) of yin and yang—the former passive and female, the latter active and male— that underlie all existence. In the* Book of Changes *the basic ideas are framed on the principle that the universe is in a condition of constant change and transformation, all things being produced by the Tao through the interaction of these universal principles of passivity and activity. In Hakuin's day, as in Tung-shan's, these ideas were a standard element in the intellectual apparatus of well-educated Chinese and Japanese, and quotations from the* Book of

Changes *appear frequently in the classical Zen texts of China and Japan.*

Hakuin's *use of the hexagrams in the* Book of Changes *is confined for the most part to this treatise on Tung-shan's Five Ranks, in which they play a key role. His own long struggle with the Five Ranks continued well into his teaching career. Later, he apparently transmitted its secrets working with advanced students in his private chambers, though as we see here, and in* Gudō's (Precious Mirror's) Lingering Radiance *(below, pp. 458-61), he also made it part a part of his published legacy as well.*

The Five Ranks are: 1. Phenomenal within Universal *(Shōchūhen)*, 2. Universal within Phenomenal *(Henchūshō)*, 3. Coming from within the Universal *(Shōchūrai)*, 4. Arriving at Mutual Integration *(Kenchūshi) and 5.* Mutual Integration Attained *(Kenchūtō)*. *The first two Ranks show the relation between the perspectives of sameness or identity (Shō; Universal) and difference (Hen; Phenomenal), Universality Within Phenomenal, and Sameness within Difference. The third, fourth, and fifth Ranks clarify their essential oneness.*

This is how a modern-day Rinzai Zen teacher has described the Five Ranks: "The Five Ranks has sometimes been called the philosophy of Zen. Intellectual ability has no part in the comprehension of the wisdom of the patriarchs. The study of the Five Ranks is more nearly like a severe and final examination, for he who undertakes this study will be called upon not only to review all that he has previously come to understand, but to clarify, correlate, and deepen still further the insight he has attained. He will have to polish again each facet of his spiritual jewel, which he has cut so laboriously and painstakingly. But, in doing so, he will see for the first time the total inclusiveness, perfect symmetry, and matchless beauty to which it has been brought under the training devised by the old masters" *(Miura Isshū,* Zen Dust, *pp. 62-3).*

The term "precious mirror" (Japanese hōkyō) appears here as a metaphor for the pure and clear mind or self-nature inherent in sentient beings, with Precious Mirror Samadhi *referring to the highest stage of samadhi achieved in the practice of the Bodhisattva path. Hakuin explains it as follows in his work* Horse Thistles: *"On entering this samadhi the student, while constantly living and comporting himself within the realm of differentiation, sees phenomenal existence with all its myriad differences appear before his eyes—the old and the young, the high and low, halls and pavilions, verandas and corridors, grasses and plants, mountains and rivers, hillocks and worthless rubble—and he realizes that they are all the pure self-nature inherent within himself. It seems to him as though he is regarding his face reflected in a bright mirror. If over a period of months and years his mind continues at all times to reflect things in this same way, the things reflected of themselves become the precious mirror of his own house; and the student, being reflected in them, becomes the precious mirror of their houses as well. It is like two mirrors each constantly reflecting each other, reciprocally interpenetrating each other, yet not a single image is reflected on either of the mirrors. When a thing reflects on my mirror, both myself and the thing reflected immediately vanish—like snowflakes disappearing into a red-hot furnace— leaving nothing but a vast open void of perfect serenity—the perfect serenity of nonduality"* (HHZ2, pp. 300–1).

The most complete account of Hakuin's personal struggle to grasp the Teachings of the Five Ranks is in the Chronological Biography. *It states that he began to study them under his teacher Shōju in 1708, at the age of twenty-three (See* Precious Mirror Cave, *172–77). Writing of the present piece in* A Detailed Study of the Fundamental Principles of the Five Houses, *Tōrei says: "In spring of the third year of the Kan'en era (1750), my late master Hakuin delivered formal lectures on the* Blue Cliff Record *at Daijō-ji at Ihara in Suruga province. He summoned me one morning during the meeting and said, 'The farther you penetrate into the Dharma, the deeper it becomes. I spent a lot of time studying it long ago in Shōju's chambers. I asked my fellow monk Sōkaku to thoroughly investigate under Shōju the important matter of [the Five Ranks']* "when their permutations end, they are five." *But after that, for over thirty years, whether I was active or at rest, I was unable to feel truly at ease. Today, I have for the first time penetrated its secret mysteries completely. In comparison to this, everything I previously understood was no more than a shadow or an echo. I intend to write this down and present it to the assembly'"* (Goke sanyō yōro-mon, *ch. 3).*

THE PRECIOUS MIRROR SAMADHI states,

> In the six lines of the Double Li hexagram
> Phenomenal and Universal are interdependent.
> When folded, they become three,
> When their permutations end, they are five.

The author of the *Precious Mirror Samadhi* is unknown. The work was transmitted from Shih-t'ou to Yueh-shan, and then to Yun-yen. It has been handed down in the inner room from one master to another, and to this day it has never been readily divulged to others. The Five Ranks were first clearly formulated when the transmission reached Priest Tung-shan, who composed for each of the Ranks a verse to elucidate its fundamental working. The Five Ranks are truly like a bright torch obtained on a midnight path, like a ferry encountered when lost at a difficult river crossing.

Sad to say, the Zen gardens have gone to seed in recent times and have now become utterly barren. Today, many Zen people refer to a state of half-witted ignorance as the "ultimate Zen of direct pointing," regarding such supreme Dharma assets as the *Precious Mirror Samadhi* and the Five Ranks of Phenomenal and Universal as outworn, unnecessary tools. They give them no more notice than they would a shard lying forgotten in the back room of a dilapidated old house. They are like blind men who fling away their walking sticks, thinking they no longer need them. But because of that they are destined to stumble and fall into the deep muck of the Two Vehicles' partial attainment, from which until their dying day they will be unable to get free. They are above all ignorant of the fact that the Five Ranks is a vessel that can carry them across the poisonous seas to enlightenment, a precious Dharma wheel that can crush to smithereens the indestructible prison house of the two voids. Ignorant of this vital means of practice that can take them steadily deeper into enlightenment, they end up drowning in the stagnant waters of the Shravaka and Pratyeka-buddhas, perishing down in a black pit with other blasted sprouts and dried-up seeds.* In the end, not even the hand of a Buddha can save them.

I was entrusted with a matter forty years ago in Shōju Rōjin's chambers

---

*By remaining attached to emptiness (the two voids: emptiness of self and emptiness of the Dharma), a student fails to go forward and practice the vital Bodhisattva path in which he works to complete his own training while teaching others, and because of that Buddhahood can never germinate within him.

that I now want to give you as a Dharma offering. It can only be transmitted secretly from master to student, and only to students of superior capacity, those true patricians of the secret depths who have once experienced the Great Death and been reborn into life anew. It is not for students of lesser or mediocre ability. It must be treated with great care, and its importance must never be underestimated.

The ocean of the Buddhist teaching is limitlessly vast, with Dharma gates beyond count. There are secret oral transmissions that have been passed down in each of the Five Houses and Seven Schools of Chinese Zen. Yet for sheer perversity and complexity, I have never yet come across any teaching comparable to the Five Ranks. Perplexing comments about the Double Li hexagram, torturous interpretations of "Folding and Transforming." One branch is attached to another branch, one entanglement piled on the other. If there was some Dharma principle from which they had been propounded, I was unable to discern it. It seemed to me that such a teaching could only mislead Zen students and compound the difficulty of their quest. How could even a Shariputra or an Ananda possibly grasp them? I couldn't for the life of me understand how patriarchs of the Zen school could propagate irresponsible nonsense of this kind and recklessly perplex later generations of students. These doubts stayed with me for a long time.

However, once I went to Iiyama and began practicing under Shōju Rōjin, the rhinoceros of these doubts suddenly fell down dead. I now know with certainty that if a student continues his practice using these Five Ranks, he will achieve favorable results. You need have no reservations about using the Five Ranks because Shōju did not receive them in oral transmission from a Sōtō teacher. Shōju clarified the Five Ranks on his own, through intense, singleminded effort that enabled him to penetrate the verses Tung-shan composed on the Five Ranks. Do not despise or belittle his teaching because he did not receive it from a Sōtō priest.

Various interpretations have been proposed about the meaning of "reciprocal interpenetration, folding and transforming." Two that are often cited are those by the Ming teacher Yung-chueh and the Ching teacher Hsing-ts'e:* Doubling the Li trigram (unbroken, broken, unbroken

---

*Yung-chueh Yuan-hsien, a famous Ts'ao-tung (Sōtō) master at the end of the Ming dynasty, wrote about the *Precious Mirror Samadhi* and the Five Ranks in the *Tung-shan Ku-che*. The Ching dynasty priest Hsing-ts'e evaluates traditional interpretations of the Five Ranks, including Yung-chueh's, in the *Pao-ching san-mei pen-i*, first published in Japan in 1698.

lines) produces the Double Li hexagram. Taking the second, third, and fourth lines of the Double Li hexagram—the *Hsun* trigram (broken, unbroken, unbroken lines)*—produces the Rank of Phenomenal within Universal (*Shōchūhen*). Taking the third, fourth, and fifth lines, the *Tui* trigram (unbroken, unbroken, broken lines), produces the Rank of Universal within Phenomenal (*Henchūshō*). Combining these two configurations—the *Tui* and *Hsun* trigrams—produces the *Ta Kuo* hexagram. Taking the second, third, and fourth lines of the *Ta Kuo* hexagram—the *Ch'ien* trigram—produces the Rank of Coming from within the Universal (*Shōchūrai*).

These explanations enabled me to grasp the idea of "folding, they become three," the "folding" of the lines of the Double Li hexagram to obtain the Ranks of Phenomenal within Universal, Universal within Phenomenal, and Coming from within the Universal. But their explanation of "Reaching completion, it becomes five" was not at all convincing. I was not able to understand that to my satisfaction until I began my study under Shōju Rōjin. Even then, "the interpenetration of Phenomenal and Universal" remained frustratingly unclear. It was as if the word "interpenetration" had been completely ignored. The rhinoceros of doubt raised its head once again.

Then, in the summer of the first year of the Kan'en era (1748), while I was doing zazen, the hidden secret of the reciprocal interpenetration of Phenomenal and Universal suddenly became perfectly clear. It was as though I was looking at it in the palm of my hand. The rhinoceros of doubt instantly fell down dead. Beside myself with joy, I wanted to take the understanding I had grasped and immediately pass it on to others. I am ashamed to say that I even considered defiling my monks' mouths by squeezing that stinking milk out for them from my old teats—however, I held back from doing that.

Young men, if you want to penetrate this deep and fundamental source, you must investigate it in secret with your whole body. I myself have worked at it laboriously for some thirty years now, so you should not think it will be an easy matter! Never suppose that it will be enough for you just to "break up the family and scatter the household."† You must vow to bore

---

*The lines of trigrams and hexagrams are always counted from the bottom up.
†A phrase connoting the attainment of enlightenment. "Chao-chou said, 'Since I was eighteen I've been able to break up the family and scatter the household'" (*Blue Cliff Record*, Case 80).

your way through seven, eight, even nine thickets of thorn and briar, and still you must not think that is enough, for now you must vow to penetrate the secrets of the Five Ranks.

For the past eight or nine years I have been encouraging you men who share the daily gruel with me to investigate the secrets of the Five Ranks, but you have turned your backs on it as the doctrine of a different school of Zen. I am deeply saddened that so few of you have undertaken to investigate the Five Ranks. Recall your Bodhisattva vows: "the Dharma gates are endless, I vow to study them all." And this Dharma gate is one that leads to the fundamental source of the Buddha Way, the vital path of Zen practice.

Shōju Rōjin said: "The teaching of the Five Ranks derives from the great compassion of the Zen patriarchs, who devised it by skillfully employing their superior expedient means. Their main purpose in doing this was to provide a method that would enable students to directly realize the Four Wisdoms." This is altogether different from the debates and contentions found in the Teaching Schools. By Four Wisdoms is meant the Great Perfect Mirror Wisdom, the Wisdom of Sameness, the Wisdom of Marvelous Observation, and the Wisdom of Benefiting Others.

Followers of the Way, even though you continue to refine your study of the three learnings [precepts, meditation, and *prajna*] for endless kalpas, if you have not realized the Four Wisdoms you cannot consider yourself true sons of Buddha. Followers of the Way, if engaging in genuine practice you bore through and smash open the dark cave of the eighth, or *alaya*, consciousness, at that moment the precious radiance of the Great Perfect Mirror Wisdom will suddenly shine forth. When that happens, you will think it strange that the light of the Great Perfect Mirror Wisdom is pitch black, like lacquer. This is called the rank of "Phenomenal within Universal."

Once you clarify the Great Perfect Mirror Wisdom, you will enter the rank of "Universal within Phenomenal" and begin devoting yourself to the practice of the *Precious Mirror Samadhi*. Then, by clarifying the Wisdom of Sameness, you will be capable for the first time of entering to some extent the realm in which unobstructed interpenetration of ultimate principle and phenomena obtains. You must not remain satisfied with that, however. You will then enter into the rank of "Coming from within Universality," and after that, by means of the rank of "Arriving at Mutual Integration," you will clarify the Wisdom of Marvelous Observation and the Wisdom of Benefiting Others. You will in this way clarify all four Wisdoms. When you finally reach the rank of "Unity Attained," you will have returned home, "sitting among the coals and ashes." What does that mean?

It is said that once pure gold is produced after endless smelting, it can-not become ore once again. Your greatest fear should be the satisfaction of achieving a minor attainment. How priceless the merit gained through the practice of the Five Ranks of Phenomenal and Universal! It allows you not only to realize the Four Wisdoms but also bring to perfection the Three Buddha-bodies within you. Does it not say in the preface to the *Treatise on the Adornments of the Mahayana*: "The eight consciousnesses inverted become the Four Wisdoms; when the four Wisdoms are brought together, they are attended by the Three Buddha-bodies"? Hence this verse by the Sixth Patriarch Hui-neng:

> Self-nature is possessed of the three Buddha-bodies;
> When it shines forth, the four Buddha-wisdoms are yours.

Hui-neng also said: "The pure Dharma-body is your own nature; the per-fect reward-body is your wisdom; the untold millions of transformation-bodies are your activities."

52. PRIEST TUNG-SHAN LIANG-CHIEH'S VERSES ON THE FIVE RANKS

1. PHENOMENAL WITHIN UNIVERSAL

Tung-shan's Verse:

> At the third watch of the night, before the moon comes up,
> Don't wonder if we don't know each other when we meet;
> Old suspicions still remain hidden deep within our hearts.

THE RANK OF PHENOMENAL [within Universal] is the Great Death, the shout of *Ka!** It indicates that you have entered the profound prin-ciple and discerned the Way. When a genuine student, one whose accu-mulated achievements have filled him with the strength that is gained through hidden practice, suddenly bursts forth into enlightenment, the empty sky disappears and the iron mountains crumble. Above there is not a tile to cover his head, below he has not an inch of ground to stand on.

---

*The spontaneous cry said to emerge at the attainment of enlightenment.

There are neither delusive passions nor enlightenment, neither samsara nor Nirvana. Everything is a single, solid mass of emptiness, lacking any sound or odor. It is like a clear pool that has no bottom, like a boundless sky free of even a trace of cloud.

A student who experiences an initial attainment often tends to believe that he has concluded the great matter, that he has mastered the Buddha Way. He clings fast to his attainment with a death-like grip, refusing to let go. This is called "stagnant pool Zen" and its followers, "spirits who stand guard over a corpse in a coffin." But even if the student clings to his attainment steadfastly for thirty or even forty years, he will never be able to emerge from the cave of the Pratyeka-buddhas' small and self-confirmed attainment. Hence it is said, "a person whose Zen activity is not free of attachment to enlightenment will sink back into the poisonous seas." These are what the Buddha referred to as "great fools, doggedly attached to their first realization." Even though the student may have clearly grasped the genuine wisdom of absolute identity, he is still unable to fully manifest the marvelous wisdom in which all things are perfectly free and unrestricted. So long as he remains seated quietly, passively ensconced within this state of emptiness, all things within and without are utterly transparent and his understanding is perfectly and unmistakably clear. But with the wisdom he has attained, the moment his mind comes into the slightest contact with the world of differentiation with its defiled circumstances of turmoil and confusion, agitation and vexation, love and hate, he finds himself utterly helpless, and all the miseries of existence press in upon him. It was in order to save students from this serious illness that the rank of Universal within Phenomenal was provisionally established.

2. UNIVERSAL WITHIN PHENOMENAL*

Tung-shan's Verse:

> A bleary old granny chanced upon an ancient mirror,
> She peered straight into it, but she saw no likeness at all.
> Pity such a muddlehead would try to find an image there.

If the student remains ensconced in the rank of Phenomenal within Universal, the wisdom that transcends likes and dislikes will always be hidden

---

*"It does no good only to realize that all phenomena exist within enlightenment, You must also know that enlightenment exists within all phenomena" (annotation).

from him, and all his views will be distorted and sterile. Hence Bodhi-sattvas of superior capacity dwell in the dusty realm of differentiation, constantly carrying out their activity amid distinctions in endless variety. They grasp all the myriad phenomena before their eyes—the old and the young, exalted and lowly, halls and pavilions, corridors and verandas, plants and trees, mountains and rivers—as the true and pure face of their original self. It is just as though they are seeing their faces in a bright mirror. As they continue to experience things in this way over the months and years, at all times and in all places, they naturally become the precious mirror of the Bodhisattvas' house, and the Bodhisattvas become the precious mirror of their houses as well.

Zen master Dōgen wrote: "For the self to contrive to realize the myriad dharmas is delusion; for the myriad dharmas to come forward and realize the self is satori."* This is precisely what I have been saying. It is Dōgen's "mind and body fallen away, fallen away mind and body." It is like two mirrors reflecting one another, without there being even the shadow of an image between them. Mind and surrounding environment are one and the same; things and oneself are not two. "A white horse enters the reed flowers." "Snow piled up in a silver bowl." This is the *Precious Mirror Samadhi*. It is what the *Nirvana Sutra* means when it says: "The Buddha sees Buddha-nature with his own eyes."

Once you have entered this samadhi, however much you push and shove the great white ox, he does not go away. The wisdom of your true nature reveals itself before your very eyes. Such is also the meaning of the expressions, "There exists only one Vehicle," "the Middle Path," "the True Form," and "the Supreme Truth."

But if the student on reaching this ground takes it into his head that he has achieved full attainment, he will fall, as before, into the deep pit of attachment to partially achieved Bodhisattvahood. Why does this happen? Because the student is ignorant of the practice Bodhisattvas carry out and because he is not aware of the causal conditions for creating a Buddha-land on earth. It was in order to save him from this misfortune that the patriarchs devised the rank of "Coming from within Universality."

---

*Words from the *Genjōkōan* fascicle of Dōgen's *Shōbōgenzō*. Dōgen uttered the following "mind and body falling off…" on attaining enlightenment as a young monk in China (*Hōkyō-ki*).

3. Coming from within the Universal

Tung-shan's Verse:

> Within nothingness exists a way beyond the worldly dust.
> Don't break the taboo of using names that cannot be spoken,*
> Your eloquence will surpass that of the man whose father
>   pierced his tongue.†

In this rank, the Mahayana Bodhisattva does not dwell within the realization he has attained. His great compassion shines forth unconditionally as he is carried forward by the four great and pure vows into an ocean of free and unrestricted activity, whipping the Dharma wheel forward, seeking deeper attainment above for himself while helping other sentient beings below. This is what is called the return that is at the same time a going forward; a going forward that is at the same time a return. You must know, moreover, that the moment will come when bright and dark meet. It is for that purpose that the expedient of the rank of Arriving at Mutual Integration has been devised.

4. Arriving at Mutual Integration‡

Tung-shan's Verse:

> The two blades cross, no need for either to draw back.
> Experts here are rarer than a lotus blooming amid fire.
> Their *ki* soars upward, mounting to the heavens.

---

*These are *imina,* the personal names of a respected person such as the emperor, or one's father, the use of which was taboo and scrupulously avoided. The annotations stress that "Dharma," "mind," and all words relating to the true self, are to be carefully avoided as well.

†He-ruo pi (544–607), a general who helped the Emperor of Sui unify the country. Pi's father, a high official in the emperor's service, was sentenced to death for using a taboo name. His final words to his son were, "You must fulfill my aspirations. My tongue has cost me my life. You must remember that." To reinforce his stern warning, the father took an awl and stuck it into his son's tongue, drawing blood" (*Sui Shu,* ch. 52).

‡Arriving at Mutual Integration, the dark integrates into the light, the light into the dark; silence integrates into speech, and speech into silence...As in this rank total ripeness is not yet achieved, the word 'arriving' is used" (annotation).

In this rank, a Bodhisattva of great capacity turns forward the wheel of Dharma where bright and dark are not-two. Buried in the world's defilements, his head is covered with dust, his face streaked with dirt; within a welter of sounds and sensory perceptions, buffeted this way and that, he is like a lotus flower blossoming amid a blazing fire, its color and fragrance growing fresher and brighter as it encounters the flames. He enters the marketplace with empty hands and benefits others with free and unrestricted activity, always on the road yet without leaving home, leaving home yet always on the road.* Is such a person an ordinary man? Is he a sage? The evil ones and heretics could not possibly discern him. Even Buddhas and Patriarchs cannot lay a hand on him. Were you to attempt to indicate his mind, the rabbit horns and tortoise hair would shoot immediately beyond the farthest mountains.† Nor is he allowed to make this his final place of rest. Which is why it is said, "His *ki* soars up as before to ascend the very heavens." What, after all, is he to do? He is to know there is one more rank, "Mutual Integration Attained."

. . . .

Line 1: "Self and others benefit equally. Neither advance or retreat. Two experts in martial arts face each other. If either makes the slightest move, he forfeits his head" (annotation).

Line 3: "He doesn't accept even this as sufficient, but continues to strive forward" (annotation).

5. Mutual Integration Attained‡

Tung-shan's Verse:

> Who dares become one with being and nonbeing without falling
>   into them?
> Everyone wants to pass beyond the four ordinary Ranks,
> To return and sit down inside the coal and ashes.

---

*"On the road = working to save others. At home = pursuing deeper realization within himself" (annotation).

†"If you try to see this fellow and your mind moves even the slightest, he is no longer there" (annotation). Rabbit horns and tortoise hair, things that do not exist, are used here as metaphors for attachment to the Buddha-nature's ungraspable reality.

‡"Now mutual integration is perfectly achieved, with no opposition between Phenomenal and Universal" (annotation).

. . . .

Line 3: "Bundling up the four previous Ranks, he tosses them in the fire and takes a good firm seat" (annotation). "A place of absolute darkness where neither light nor darkness, being nor emptiness obtains, a place where you know absolutely nothing" (annotation).

Hakuin's verse comment:

> How many times has the idle old gimlet Te-yun
> Come down from Marvelous Peak!
> Getting other foolish saints to help,
> They keep filling the well with snow.

A student who wishes to penetrate Tung-shan's rank of "Mutual Integration Attained" should start by tackling this verse.

. . . .

Hakuin uses for his final comment a verse by Hsueh-tou Ch'ung-hsien (*Ancestral Heroes Collection*). Te-yun appears in the *Flower Garland Sutra* as one of teachers the student Sudhana visits on his pilgrimage. Long years of rigorous practice have made him like a gimlet whose sharp point is rounded through constant use. Living atop the peak of supreme enlightenment, he descends into the world and working together with others attempts "to fill the well with snow"—a metaphor for the Bodhisattva's unending and purposeless activity of teaching others.

II. DHARMA WORDS (*HŌGO*)

Hōgo are instructions for religious practice, generally written and given to a particular student.

:53. FOR SENIOR MONK SŌJITSU (SŌJITSU SHUSO)

Not much is known about this monk. Akiyama Kanji identifies him as Genshitsu Sōjitsu (d. 1782), a student and successor of Nanryō

Jiban (n.d.) of Daijō-ji in Ihara village, some miles west of Hara
(Buddhist Monk Hakuin, p. 220).

IN ACCORDANCE with instructions left by Nanyrō Oshō of Daijō-ji, my longtime student Sōjitsu Shuso was installed there as his successor. His brother monk Chūi Shuso has assisted him from the start, serving him as devotedly as he would his own parents. When the two men visited my temple yesterday to pay their respects, I joyfully congratulated Sōjitsu on the appointment.

However, my attendant Eisan was not pleased. He voiced the following complaint.

"Sōjitsu Shuso is a true Zen hero. Everyone in the brotherhood at Shōin-ji was sure that before long he would receive a post at some great monastery and make his mark in the world, greatly benefiting the Zen school. How disappointed we all were to learn that he was going to take up residence in that old temple. It is so impoverished it would pinch Fan Jan's forehead in dismay, bow Yuan Hsien's head in dejection. What a waste it is to throw a man of such talent into a weed patch like that. It's like sending an innocent man into exile on a remote island. It will bring tears to the eyes of all who hear about it; it will furrow the brows of all who see it take place. It has greatly dispirited the monks in the brotherhood. 'The master is wasting this monk's talents,' they are saying. 'Worse than tossing him onto a rubbish pile.' Some are angry. Some saddened. Master, you alone seem to rejoice in this appointment. I cannot for the life of me understand why. Do you really think it is a good thing?"

I replied, "Ah, I wasn't aware you all felt that way. The happiness I feel is totally unconnected with any of the reasons you mentioned. When Nanryō Oshō passed away last summer, he left final instructions that Sōjitsu was to succeed him at Daijō-ji. He asked me to see that they were carried out. I sensed from the start that there might be problems. If Sōjitsu refused to go along with the plan, I would be unable to carry out Nanryō's dying wishes, and the Dharma lineage at the temple would be in jeopardy.

"It was with some apprehension that I brought the matter up with Sōjitsu. His reply was: 'I have always given the deepest consideration to the debt I owe for the great compassion and kindness my teacher bestowed on me. If he had told me to go live among the barbarous tribes beyond the southern ocean, even to reside in the land of the cannibal *raksha* demons, how could I have refused him? And this is merely a question of serving in the nearby Daijō-ji." Involuntarily, my palms pressed themselves together in *gasshō*.

"You see, that is the reason for my great happiness. How could considerations of prestige or lack of it, wealth or poverty, have any place in such a matter?"

Long ago, at his teacher Ma tsu's bidding, Zen master Ling-yu went to Mount Ta-kuei. He lived there for thirty years. Conditions were so difficult, the temple so poor, it was said no smoke was seen from the cooking fire for days on end. In time, however, a large brotherhood, some fifteen hundred monks, gathered there to receive Ling-yu's instruction.

After the death of his teacher Shih-shuang, Zen master Fang-hui went to Mount Yang-ch'i and lived there alone for twenty years. He said, "Living at Mount Yang-ch'i, my dwelling is of the poorest sort. The floor is constantly scattered with pearls of snow. As I sit sighing in the frigid darkness with the collar of my thin robe pulled up around my neck, I recall the ancient teachers who lived out in the open, with nothing but trees for shelter." In time, the Dharma flourished greatly at Mount Yang-ch'i.

While I certainly do not mean to compare myself to these ancient worthies, Shōin-ji, when I first came to reside here, was in an advanced state of ruin. We endured great privation for almost twenty years. The roofs leaked constantly. The flooring was sodden. At night the gods of poverty howled away. Starving temple rats were reduced to gnawing at their entrails. My liver quails even now when I recall those years.

The great teacher Bodhidharma, who had been a royal prince in the land of Kōshi in India, journeyed all the way to China and took up residence at Mount Shao-shih. He had a mere handful of disciples. It is not hard to imagine the hunger and cold they experienced there. In later years Bodhidharma is said to have traveled all the way to Japan, secluding himself on Mount Kataoka in Yamato province. Prince Shōtoku went there visit him. He found Bodhidharma living as a beggar in a state of near starvation, clothed in a ragged old straw raincoat and battered rush hat.

It is for this reason that Zen master Hsi-sou praised Bodhidharma as a "model for all the Zen students of India and China." It was no doubt the extreme poverty of his life, the cold and hunger he endured, that made Hsi-sou hold him up as an example like this.

Everyone hankers after wealth and prestige and very often because of that they bring ruin on themselves, destroying their virtue in the bargain. But there are people even among the lay community who take no notice of such things. For this reason, I have drawn a picture showing Bodhidharma at Mount Kataoka to celebrate Sōjitsu Shuso's installment as head priest at Daijō-ji.

. . . .

Fan Jan (Fan Tan; d. 185) rose from the humblest circumstances to become a minister of state; Yuan Hsien was a disciple of Confucius. Both were remarkable for overcoming obstacles of poverty and privation.

Zen master Fang-hui...lived alone on Mount Yang-ch'i for twenty years. Wu-tsu said, "When my teacher Fang-hui first began living at Mount Yang-ch'i, the old buildings had broken beams and afforded him little shelter from the wind and rain. One night when winter was approaching and the bench was covered with snow and sleet, the master could find no place to sit. The monks begged him to allow them to make repairs, but Fang-hu'i put them off. 'Buddha said, "at a time when the Dharma is in decline and even the high cliffs and deep valleys are changing and inconstant, how can I expect to find satisfaction for myself and have everything just as I wish?...." You are already in your forties and fifties—how can you waste your time with concerns about comfortable room furnishings?' Still refusing their request, he ascended to the hall the following day and said, 'I live in a room with gaps in the walls and benches covered with pearls of snow. Sighing in the darkness, I just hunch my neck down into my robe and recall the ancients who spent their lives living outdoors under the trees'" (*Precious Lessons of the Zen School*, ch. 1).

Hakuin wrote a *waka* describing Fang-hui's life at Mount Yang-ch'i that appears in his writings.

> Forget the thought
> "How cold it is!"
> There once was a man
> too busy to sweep
> the snow from the floor.

In *Moshio*, the following headnote is attached to the verse: "Snow fell constantly, blowing into my room. Cold winds from the mountain peaks also found their way through chinks made in the reed fence to let moonlight in, chilling me to the bone. I shrunk down inside my paper robe, pulling the thin lapels up around my eyes (*Moshio-shū, HHZ* 13, p. 324).

Bodhidharma on Mount Kataoka. A story in *Genkō Shakusho (Chronicle of*

Buddhism of the Genkō era), the earliest comprehensive history of Japanese Buddhism, compiled by the Rinzai priest Kokan Shiren and published in 1322, describes Bodhidharma as leaving China after teaching there for some years and returning to his home in Kōshi (Orissa in eastern India?), and then, at the age of eighty-six, visiting Japan: "Prince Shōtoku, entrusted by Empress Suiko with the reins of government, encountered Bodhidharma as he was riding past Mount Kataoka in Yamato province...Bodhidharma was living in the guise of a beggar, clad in tattered rags and lying at the side of the road. There was an uncanny glint in his eyes and a rare fragrance emanated from his body. Bodhidharma made no reply when Prince Shōtoku asked his name, but when he put his question in a Japanese verse, Bodhidharma responded with one of his own."

"A model for all Zen students." A saying by Hsi-sou Shao-t'an (n.d.), author of *Praise of the Five Houses of the True School.* It is said to have been a favorite of Shōju Rōjin.

Mount Kataoka. Two of Hakuin's paintings of this subject are reproduced in *HZB Zenga-hen,* #236–7.

:54. IN RESPONSE TO A REQUEST FROM TENRYŪ CHŌRŌ

Although nothing is known about Tenryū Chōrō (Chōrō is a term of respect used for a senior priest), not even his dates, an annotation identifies his temple as Saihō-ji, which was apparently located near the tip of the Izu province in Matsuzaki, a village Hakuin visited on a number of occasions. This undated piece can probably be regarded as more or less typical of inscriptions Hakuin was writing in response to the many requests he was receiving.

ALL THINGS HAVE A beginning and an end, but few of them in the end are truly achieved or fulfilled. Students of Zen begin with an aspiration we cannot but love and cherish, a spirit and enthusiasm we can only honor. However, once they take their places in the world as temple priests, where they are free to deal with the heat and the cold according to their own personal whims, fame and profit become sweeter to them than sugar candy, and Zen practice becomes more distasteful to them than medicine from the most bitter of roots. Their life becomes more relaxed by the day, they weaken and degenerate by the month, but eventually they are teachers, with an assembly of students of their own to guide. As the years pass, they are beset by growing fears and worries. I myself am one who belongs to this fraternity.

Becoming a temple priest is indeed a most formidable, most perilous, undertaking, something one must approach with the greatest care and circumspection. Ticking them off on my fingers, I recall at most only five of my students who have ended their careers satisfactorily.

When I heard recently that you had returned to become a temple priest in Matsuzaki, I was pleased, but my pleasure was mixed with an equal measure of regret. The necessity for training does not cease once satori is attained. That is not the moment to relax your efforts. The more you attain, the greater you must strive. The deeper you enter, the greater must be your devotion to your practice. Such is the meaning of "the koan that is never completed" (*miryō kōan*).

Do not allow your quest to falter or cease because you get caught up in the endless entanglements of secular affairs. Nor should you acquire a liking for quiet spots where you can retire to sit until you shrivel away. You must apply yourself steadily and singlemindedly, whether you are walking, sitting, standing, or lying down, whether you are in a place bustling with activity or a place of great tranquility. Keep asking yourself, "Where have I made mistakes? Where have I not made mistakes?" Such is the example we see in the lives of our illustrious Zen predecessors.

In speaking to you in this way, I am like a defeated general exhorting his troops, a person who should feel a certain shame. Yet it is said, is it not, that when you see the carriage in front of you overturn, you are able to avoid the same mistake yourself?

. . . .

"Everything has a beginning . . . fulfilled." A well-known phrase from *The Book of Odes* (*Shih-ching*).

Beset by growing fears and worries. That is, "the possibility they might fall into Hell" (annotation).

Where have I made mistakes. "If you mean to concentrate on your training, you must constantly explore and examine yourself from hour to hour as you spur yourself forward. 'Where was it I was able to gain spiritual strength?' 'Where was it I failed to gain strength?' 'Where was it I made mistakes?' 'Where was it I made no mistakes?'" Found in "Zen Master Fa-yen's Instructions For Students Leaving on Pilgrimage," in *Spurring Students Through the Zen Barriers* (*Zenkan-sakushin*, pp. 42–4).

See the carriage in front overturn. Hakuin refers to a proverb, *Zensha no kutsugaeru wa kōsha no imashime,* "The overturning of the carriage in front serves as a warning to the carriage that follows behind," from *The Book of Han (Han-shu).*

¦55. Dharma Words Written for Bonji

These Dharma Words (Hōgo) were omitted for reasons unknown from the printed edition of Poison Blossoms. *They are translated from the manuscript texts.*

In the Chronological Biography *for 1742, Hakuin's fifty-seventh year, we read: "In spring a Zen monk named Bonji came and requested an interview. He asked the master for a religious name and underwent the ceremony making him a disciple"* (Precious Mirror Cave, p. 207). *Nothing more is said about this monk, who does not appear anywhere else in Hakuin's records, leaving readers somewhat puzzled as to why he is mentioned at all. I think the information provided in this piece helps explain why the editor (Tōrei), or perhaps Hakuin, wanted this included in the records.*

Hakuin used a text similar to these Dharma words in Sendai's Comments on the Poems of Han-shan, *as an extended comment on a poem by Han-shan's companion Shih-te: "I sigh when I see the know-it-alls / Exercising their minds uselessly all day long, / Standing at the crossroads spouting plausible words, / Confusing and deceiving people of all kinds. / They create only bad karma for themselves—tickets to hell, / Never acts of the kind that would bring them favorable rebirths. / Should the demon of impermanence suddenly appear, / Their minds will surely be at sixes and sevens"* (Kanzan-shi Sendai-kimon, 1746 woodblock edition, vol. 3.59r).

ZEN MAN BONJI BEGAN his Buddhist training by practicing the Tendai sect's threefold contemplation* and studying the scriptures. Becoming dissatisfied with this, one morning he got up and left. He plunged immediately into the stormy seas of the Zen ocean. Not long after, when he began encountering Zen's difficulties and experiencing some of their bitter taste, a feeling of pride and arrogance emerged within him, welling up

---

*Threefold Contemplation (*Sangan*). Contemplation on the emptiness of existence, the temporariness of all things, and the truth of the middle way.

like an incoming tide, rising up like a towering peak. He put on a ragged sedge hat, grabbed his walking stick, and set out on a hunt through the patriarch's tiger caves, an exploration of the demon's palaces. He combed the western provinces of Chōshū, Iwami, Hizen, and Chikuzen, and the northern provinces of Shinano, Echizen, Nōtō, and Kaga as well, visiting every Zen teacher he could find. Barging into their temples, he conducted himself in a totally ungoverned manner, spouting scurrilous abuse, committing outrageous acts, insulting veteran senior priests, treating younger monks with contempt, slandering and reviling teachers and patriarchs of the past. The Zen teachers at the temples he visited, knowing they would be unable to control him, adopted a wise and safe course. They just let him vent all his spleen, doing and saying what he pleased, and then sent him on his way.

He went around telling his friends, "I used to spend my time in Tendai temples, until I realized how worthless those people are. I entered the poisonous groves of Zen, thinking that by nourishing myself on its bitter leaves and villainous fruits I could become a celebrated teacher. I traveled all over the country looking for a genuine master, but since I never found a single one worth his salt, I just went around exposing their incompetence. I was even ready to buy a boat and sail to China so I could look for someone there. But I gave that up when I realized the Chinese priests would be no different from the ones I encountered here."

Bonji's travels brought him here to Suruga. He tramped all through the province, passing Shōin-ji's gates on more than one occasion, completely ignoring us as beneath his notice. When someone mentioned my teaching, Bonji dismissed me with a few choice verbal assaults.

In spring of this year [1742], karmic winds blew Bonji my way again, and he strayed by mistake into the Dharma Reprobate's Cave [Sendai-kutsu; one of Hakuin's sobriquets]. Holding a steel rod in one hand and a colorfully decorated fan in the other, he looked like a ferocious tiger peering down a fox's den, or a hungry falcon taking a bead on a limping hare. He eyed me like someone who had just murdered his parents. It was obvious that he was all fired up, ready to start as much commotion as he could.

There was no way to confront a fiery spirit like that head-on, so I started out easily. By engaging him in one or two Zen exchanges, I was able to drive him into some tight corners. I deflated his overweening pride with some stiff doses of my staff. In further encounters, including some vigorous give and take, I was able to test his mettle more thoroughly. Finally, Bonji ran out of arguments and exhausted all his verbal resources. His pride was completely crushed. He thereupon knocked his head to the floor, performing the bows that made my disciple. He requested a Zen name, which I gave him: Bonji.

Bonji, I said, you are going to have to be extremely careful. Someone with a mind as prideful as yours can never complete Zen training. His resolve to pursue the Way will weaken. He will engage in all sorts of ugly behavior, commit cruel, inhuman acts. Such a person may even beat his parents or violate his sister. I suspect that those Zen teachers you reviled and humiliated around the country had a hard time suppressing the delusory thoughts arising in their minds. They probably lost their appetites and had difficulty eating for days on end. Their followers were also surely saddened, and are still seething with resentment. For those evil acts, who is responsible? Men who harm people with weapons injure their bodies. Those who harm them with words usually not only forfeit any reputation they may have acquired, they also incur the wrath of the gods of heaven and earth and are shunned with loathing by other human beings.

There was an evil demon many years ago that possessed a glittering golden body and yet lived in a state of great and perpetual hunger. Loathsome maggots constantly poured from its mouth, creating a terrible stench. The demon was originally a Buddhist priest who had rigorously observed the precepts. According to the Buddha, he had become a demon because he was unable to refrain from speaking ill of others.*

Another monk fell into hell for reviling and insulting an elder priest. He was later reborn into a family of the lowest *candala* caste, but while he was still in his mother's womb he emitted a foul odor that filled the entire room. He was committing various small, disgusting acts as soon as he was born, not to mention startling people with the terrible stench he emitted. He was constantly going to the privy, scooping up handfuls of dung and wolfing them down with relish. The virtuous priest who related his story also explained the evil karma that had brought about such a retribution.

Attendant P'ing of Mount Ta-yang, a leading student of Zen Master Ming-an, mastered the inner secrets of the Sōtō school, its Five Ranks and Three Fundamentals,† and was regarded as the finest of the monks at Ta-yang. He became one of the foremost Sōtō priests of his time, later

---

*Based on the story in *Fa-yuan chu-lin*, ch. 76. The source of the next story is unknown.
†The Three Fundamentals of Tung-shan's Zen (*Tōzan sanshō kōyō*): 1. Perfect unity between teacher and student 2. Not attaching even to enlightenment 3. Not falling into dualistic views.

residing at the Mount Ta-yang monastery, but he was never able to over-come a propensity to be prideful and arrogant. He could never tolerate having others surpass him in any way.

Before Zen master Ming-an passed away, he announced to his followers, "Leave my tomb undisturbed for ten years. Then I want you to open it and perform services for me once again." Attendant P'ing, feeling envious of his teacher's final words, opened the tomb after only three years. He found Ming-an's body completely unchanged, just as it had been in life. This angered him. He gathered some brushwood, placed his teacher's corpse on it, and set fire to it. After three days, the corpse remained completely unscathed by the flames. Ming-an's followers prostrated themselves before it in reverence. Some of them sat before the pyre wailing in grief. This further enraged Attendant P'ing, who grabbed a mattock and with loud shouts began striking furiously at the corpse, chopping it into small pieces. He then poured oil over the remains and set fire to them again.

When government officials learned of P'ing's actions, they divested him of his priest's robe and begging bowl and made him return to lay status. P'ing started calling himself by the secular name Huang Hsiu-ts'ai, but no matter where he went people would drive him away. Not even his former friends would have anything to do with him. He ended up living as a beggar until one day he was attacked and mauled to death by wild dogs.*

Ah, do you see what pride can do to a man's life? Here was a valiant hero, an imposing presence in the groves of Zen, but his mind became so crippled by pride that he ended up without a single place in all the vast universe to rest his head. It was all the result of his self-pride. This is a demon that is always seeking out those who are clever and sagacious. He enters them through any one of a thousand openings, finally insinuating himself deep into their vitals. You should emulate the great ocean, which is superior to the tributary streams that flow into it because it remains beneath them.† Students engaged in religious training must likewise main-tain an attitude of humility.

Long ago a priest of the Onjō-ji in Ōmi province encountered the god of plague and pestilence. He asked the god, "Which do you fear most, dharanis and secret charms, monks and diviners, weapons, or fragrant incense?" The god replied, "We spread disease at Heaven's command, so we have nothing whatever to fear. Yet, when we come upon a humble and

---

*The story is found in *Ta-hui's Arsenal*, ch. 2.
†Allusion to a passage in the *Tao-te ching*.

compassionate man, someone always surrounded by numberless guardian gods, there is no opening where we can enter and perform our work. A humble person who always keeps his thoughts under control has greater merit and good fortune than the earth itself. We can do nothing against him. The virtue of his compassion is vaster than the sky. Minor gods can find nowhere to attach to him.

"Now a prideful person, someone whose self-esteem makes him contemptuous of other people, is always surrounded by great hordes of demons and devils spurring him on to ever greater acts of arrogance. Taking hold of a person like that is as easy as entering our own home. The demons and devils that surround him will even lend us a hand and help us to achieve our ends. So the arrogant and prideful all fall into our clutches. Since we are now in the latter day with the Dharma growing steadily weaker, more and more people are relying on their own feeble understanding, pride and arrogance flourish. Pride appears from a lack of wisdom. No wonder we are so busy these days! Even I find it truly frightening."

There was a monk of this type named Batsu Jōza at Eigan-ji in Echigo province when I was staying there many years ago.* When he referred to Zen masters around the country and to his comrades as well, he wouldn't even accord them the respect of using their full names.† Once he starting off criticizing people, he never stopped. At the time, I thought to myself, "Someone like this will sooner or later lose his appetite for the Way."

Three or four years later I was in retreat on Mount Iwataki in eastern Mino province. The spring rains had continued for days on end, so I had secured the door and settled down to some concentrated practice. Someone rapped at the door. When I didn't respond, he rapped again. I opened the door a crack and asked who it was. He said he was a monk on his way from Owari province to northern Mino, and he begged a night's lodging at my hut. I opened the door and let him in. I gave him some tea and food, which he immediately devoured on his hands and knees like a dog. He was unimaginably filthy and gave off a terrible stink. He had a long scar that extended from his brow all the way to his ear, and clots of fresh blood remained on his face. On examining him more closely, I realized that he was Batsu Jōza! But he was a miserable outcast, a mere shadow of his

---

*Hakuin attained an initial enlightenment at the age of twenty-three while he was attending a retreat at Eigan-ji (see *Precious Mirror Cave*, pp. 165–67).
†Literally, "he would refer to them using only two characters of the masters' (four-character) names, and only one character of his fellow monks' (two-character) names."

former self. There was no trace of the former spiritual resolve. What had happened to all that knowledge and eloquence? He had been reduced to the level of an out-and-out beggar. Feeling pity for him, I said, "I allowed you in because I thought you were a traveling monk. Now I see that you are seriously wounded and your life may be in danger. If you died here, people might think I was the one who gave you that sword cut. There's a shrine building at the foot of the mountain. Go and sleep there. I'll bring you more food tomorrow."

I took off my monk's robe and put it around him. Batsu left in tears. I was weeping too.

A month or so later, I heard that three bandits apprehended in northern Mino had been executed at Kahara village, one of whom was a priest from Owari province. What a sad and miserable end.

Batsu had a friend from Shimotsuke province named Mō Jōza. Mō Jōza had a sharp and nasty tongue in no way inferior to Batsu's own. He too had committed some serious transgression and been returned to lay status. He worked as a sweeper and dishwasher at a small theater in Edo, but I heard that he too ended up as a beggar, and that he died in the streets like a dog.

In Harima province there was once a priest gifted with such great intelligence and insight that people stood in awe of him. He made a trip to Kyoto to procure a large donation to replace an image in the main hall of his temple. He also acquired a beautiful woman while he was there. He dressed her as a nun and brought her back to Harima with him, where they set up house just like a married couple.

The priest placed a large closed wooden case on the altar of the main hall. "Before long," he announced, "we will have a wonderful new image to put here, and we will conduct a splendid enshrinement ceremony for it." He had in fact already sold the Buddhist image that had originally been enshrined in the hall. No one knew that inside the wooden case he had placed a cheap, gaudy-colored clay image.

One morning eruptions began appearing all over the priest's body. They festered, and he became so foul and filthy that he was forced to sleep in the stable with the horses. Mosquitoes and horseflies swarmed over him, and he was blanketed by a thick black covering of flies. Before long, he ceased to respond to people, and finally, weeping sorrowfully, passed away.

Then there was a veteran Sōtō Zen teacher in Dairyū-ji in Shimofusa province. He was another one given to expounding his half-baked views unreservedly as though he was the wisest of men. Late one night in the winter of 1672, he had a score of the hundred monks in his assembly in to share tea and cakes. They talked deep into the night. The priest was holding forth on the Zen teaching, appraising the merits of teachers past and present and uttering criticisms and disparagements of various kinds, when suddenly he began screaming.

"All of you, look at my face. The trees and plants around this temple all belong to my brothers the tengu demons. They are waving their feathered fans and summoning me. How can I refuse to go? Do not weep or feel sad when I have gone. I will return before long and invite you all to join us." With a final shriek, "Farewell!" he got up and started to dash out of the hall. His mouth was gaping from ear to ear, his eyeballs were streaming blood and goggling from their sockets.

Seven or eight of the strongest monks grabbed him and tried to hold him down. A pitched battle ensued. He dragged young monks around the room, fighting with the strength of a bull elephant, and lunging out with the ferocity of a hungry tiger. The members of the brotherhood gathered, formed a ring around him, and began chanting sutras and dharanis. They continued with great concentration until they were all drenched with sweat. The priest cursed and reviled them and kept trying to tear the sutras from their hands.

Then an elderly priest took a volume of the *Rishubon* and forced it into the teacher's mouth to silence him.* The teacher, no longer able to cry out, continued to issue muffled groans. Just at that moment there was a deafening noise and the surrounding forests and hills began to quake and shudder.

From the forest a loud voice was heard. "Is he in there? Is he in there? We were not able to get him tonight, but we will come again. We will surely take him with us." The voice then called out all their names, gave an angry shout, and vanished.

Soon after, priests and lay people came hurrying from villages all around, filling the temple precincts. On someone asking why they had come, they shouted, "A great fire is raging in the hills, everywhere is bright red with flames! We have come to fight it."

For seven straight days, the monks in the assembly continued to recite the sutra singlemindedly, and the crazed priest returned to normal. If it hadn't been for the great power of the Buddha's sutras, how could he ever have regained his former self?

---

*The *Hannya rishubon* is the 578th section of the *Great Wisdom Sutra*. Apparently the old priest shoved an entire volume of the sutra into the teacher's mouth.

Another priest in north-central Wakasa province also strayed from the Buddha Way as a result of his superior intellect. Although he raised his younger brother's daughter, when she came of age they began sharing the same bed. The priest already had a "hidden wife," and when she saw how infatuated he was with the young girl, she became insanely jealous. Because of this, the priest ended up killing her and throwing her body into a nearby lake. The woman's children went to the magistrate's office and filed a complaint against the priest. He was arrested, lashed to a roadside post, and then executed with a lance thrust.

A person named Bunshū, who lived years ago in a small hermitage at Ikeda in Mino province, is yet another priest who lost his desire to pursue the Way. He invoked a magic charm against a man and woman who had revealed a secret he had entrusted to them, and within a week they were both dead. Not long after, the priest became deranged. Everything he saw seemed to be a razor-sharp leaf—the kind that grows on the trees in hell. He died an agonizing death, wailing and moaning to the end.

There are countless other examples I could give you—a senior priest who incurred divine wrath by killing a horse; a priest who was executed for killing an elder monk who had criticized him; a Zen priest who fell seriously ill after throwing out a Buddhist image. There are dozens of these examples I could cite, but there are circumstances that do not allow me to speak of them. They were all like you, Bonji. They were wise and learned, but prideful and arrogant.

It is indeed unfortunate that these people forfeited their lives because of a single mistaken thought and fell into hell's eternal torments. A great pity, since they had no doubt endured many privations at the beginning of their religious training. They had probably peered through the fences into the patriarchal gardens, and they may have had talent of the kind that could serve as a foundation to turn them into the ridgepoles of our school. There were men and women who respected them, who feared them, who followed them, and who loved them. They could have been heroes of the Zen groves, superior teachers of the Dharma caves. Who could have foreseen that because they were unable to control their prideful thoughts they would die more miserable deaths than dogs or wild beasts? Careful examination shows that their downfall began by disparaging and reviling others in order to gain greater reputation for themselves. What a grave mistake that was! Not only did they lose the human body on which they had hung their Buddhist surplice, but they fell into hell and its tortures for endless kalpas.

(A passage in which Hakuin relates the story of Gedatsu Shōnin is omitted here. It is given below, Book Eleven, pp. 464-66. See also Wild Ivy, *pp. 43-5).*

When I entered the realm of enlightenment for the first time, I myself became prideful, more arrogant than you are, Bonji. Then I heard an old, true story from a venerable priest which drenched me in a thick and shameful sweat and etched itself deep in my vitals. My pride and arrogance melted completely away. If I hadn't heard that story, I would no doubt have ended up like one of the evil priests I've been telling you about—more miserable than either Batsu Jōza or Mō Jōza. I have little wisdom that I can use to help others. No virtue for them to place their trust in. But because that old priest reproached me for my arrogance, I am able to doze away peacefully in this tiny temple of mine.

Bonji, pledge to me that from now you will undertake the practice of never disparaging others.* In doing that you will cancel out all the bad karma you have piled up so far. When the World-Honored One walked along a path, it is said that the trees and plants all bent down to honor him, that everyone he passed prostrated themselves in reverence, and everyone he approached welcomed him in a similar manner. When Ananda asked the Buddha about this, he replied, "Ultimately, it is because I have never disparaged anyone."

Someone once asked Soshō Hosshi, "Why is it that everyone feels happy gazing at your face? Whether lay or cleric, young or old, they all feel as though they are looking at their father or mother," Soshō replied, "Whenever I look at people, I feel deep in my heart that they are to be revered and respected as Buddhas and Bodhisattvas. How could they feel enmity towards me?"

A person whose benevolence makes people yield to him with respect is like the phoenix among birds. A person whose august bearing makes people yield to him is like a tiger or wolf in the animal world. When the phoenix soars up into the heavens, the other birds all look up to him with reverence. But when the tiger or wolf emerges from the forest, the other animals cringe with fear and flee, bitter and resentful. An arrogant person who behaves in a haughty manner will have no friends; neither the king and his ministers, nor any other upstanding person. Not even his family or acquaintances in his native place will associate with him. His friends

---

*Hakuin alludes to the Bodhisattva Never Disparaging, who appears in a chapter of that name in the *Lotus Sutra*.

will not love him, and the gods and demons will have no sympathy for him either. People who pride themselves on being clever are usually regarded by others as lacking in intelligence and common sense. An arrogant man, though certain that he is competent in all things and is being held back by others, usually ends up losing everything he has. Hence it is said that arrogance is a storehouse of calamities; humility a storehouse of good fortune.

Bonji, so far you have spoken and acted as you pleased. You have run roughshod over the whole world, your strong spirit refusing to yield to anyone. Your sharp tongue has enabled you to better others in argument. But don't say, "I have never even caught a cold. Why should I circumscribe my behavior?" This is like felling one of the giants of the forest. The task isn't accomplished with one stroke of the axe. But keep chopping away, steadily and without stopping, and the tree will eventually topple over. When the time comes for it to fall, it will fall no matter how many people try to prevent it. Committing a single bad act will not destroy you. But if you keep on committing them, you will one day, suddenly, be destroyed. When that happens, no matter how fervently you pray to the gods or Buddhas, it will do you no good. As the *Book of Changes* says, "Unless you perform repeated acts of benevolence, you will be unable to make a name for yourself; unless you perform repeated acts of evil, you will not be ruined."

It is a truly perilous position that you are in. Observing your antics yesterday, I felt as though I was watching a small child toddling towards an open well. You seem at least to have understood to some extent the error of your ways. I am very pleased that a monk with true Zen mettle has returned to life. This is no doubt the result of wisdom you acquired through practice in your former lives, which you have not yet completely exhausted. If you were not a true Dharma vessel and I did not admire your discernment, do you suppose that I would take the time to go on scribbling down page after page like this, using up good ink and paper, and rubbing my tired old eyes? There is an old saying, "A woman paints herself for those who love her; a samurai dies for someone who understands his worth." I am not asking you to die for someone who admires you, only to change your mistaken ways.

Be very careful and prudent in your conduct, Bonji. For the next twenty or thirty years you should become an ignorant dolt, a blockheaded simpleton, nourishing your virtue and avoiding all trouble and misfortune. Remaining in such a state of mind will enable you to put an end to your bad behavior just as surely as water slakes thirst. After a tree receives good nourishment for many years, it can serve as a ridgepole. When water is preserved carefully in coffered ponds, it can save farmers from the misfortune of drought. Didn't National Master Hui-chung of Nan-yang stay quietly at his mountain temple doing zazen for forty years? Didn't National Master Daitō live with beggars under the Gojō Bridge for twenty years? Their Zen has been passed down by their descendants and it now has spread beyond the seas and to the ends of the universe.

It is because of this that Ming-chiao Ta-shih said, "Students, you should worry about your lack of virtue. You shouldn't be concerned about not receiving a position of authority."* These words are a model to be held up for all time. You should use them as a mirror to examine yourself. If rice plants do not mature into ripeness, they are no different from barnyard grass. Pine trees can be used for ridgepoles, but until they have grown and matured a great many years, they will be of no more use than an ordinary twig or branch.

Observing your arrogant behavior yesterday, Bonji, I couldn't help recalling Batsu Jōza and Mō Jōza. As the karmic winds have blown us together and placed us, if even for a few days, in a position of teacher and student, I cannot just watch you act this way and do nothing. I spoke a few words to you yesterday, but afterwards it seemed to me that they were insufficient. So when night came, I hung up the lamp and with tears in my eyes began writing this down. Then I waited for you to come around again. Still, I didn't write it for your eyes alone. I want other students engaged in Zen practice to read it as well.

I recalled various times in my own life when I had committed acts of arrogance, so I wrote them down too in hopes they might serve as a caution to younger students. I am embarrassed to say that even now, gasping out my final breaths and for all intents as good as dead, I still not only lack the requisite inner virtues, but I have not engaged in much "secret application, private diligence" type of Zen practice either. The reason my students have not cast my unworthiness aside and have come to regard me as a teacher or parent can only be the consequence of some measure of favorable karma lingering from the past.

However, even someone as ignoble as me is not entirely devoid of parental affection, the kind that makes me want to pass some sweets along to you. Do you find these words of mine sweet? Or are they bitter? If you find among them something you think is worth keeping, then roll it up, stick it into your robe, and read it from time to time. If you decide that it

---

*Words quoted at the opening of *Precious Lessons of the Zen School.*

is a tissue of nonsense not worth your consideration, then you have my permission to toss it into the fire. But the stories I have related here are all of them true. I have not made them up.

III. WORDS AT MINOR BUDDHIST OBSERVANCES (SHŌBUTSUJI)

The items in this section are remarks Hakuin delivered at funeral services and consecration ceremonies for Buddhist images.

:56. SPOKEN AT AN EYE-OPENING CEREMONY FOR THE BODHISATTVA KANNON

This is an early piece, written when Hakuin was thirty-two. The "eye-opening" (tengan) ceremony a Buddhist priest conducts to consecrate a carved or painted Buddhist image is also said to impart life to it. The rites have been compared to an artist bringing a figure he has painted to life by dotting in the pupils of its eyes with a final touch of his brush.

TEMPLE PATRON YAGI MATAZAEMON Mitsusuke is an amiable man whose religious aspiration is pure and unadorned. He treats his family and relations with affection, and he has formed an excellent relationship with the villagers around him.

During a trip Yagi made in autumn of this year, 1717, he stopped at the Okabe post station at the house of a gentleman named Furui. There were enshrined in Furui's residence two statues of Kannon Bodhisattva, both exquisitely carved, with unusually beautiful features. Yagi regarded them with great veneration. He worshipped them over and over, unable to take his mind off them.

Mr. Furui said, "I see many people travel along the Tōkaidō. Although most of them set out early in the morning, even if they walk at a constant pace they do not reach the next stopover until darkness has set in. They are so intent on reaching their destination that they fail to take notice of the great scenic spots they pass—the pine forest on Miho peninsula, even Mount Fuji itself, not to mention temples and shrines and other places of lesser interest. How unusual it is to find someone such as you who amid the dust of this mundane world possesses such deep faith in the Three Treasures (Buddha, Dharma, and Sangha)."

Mitsusuke said, "I'm only an ignorant countryman. I do not possess the inner wisdom that would enable me to grasp the Buddhist teachings, and few relationships in the outside world that might bring me closer to them. Still I would, if possible, like to have one of your images. I could pick it up on my return trip. I would promise to treat it with the greatest reverence, to hold regular services for it, provide offerings, and have religious verses written to praise its virtues. It would help later generations turn to the path of Buddha and keep them from falling into the terrible ways of suffering that otherwise lie waiting for them."

Mr. Furui said, "I will give it to you. I have heard that it is only when devotions such as you have proposed are made before an image that it truly becomes a Bodhisattva possessed of all the countless virtues. Now it is enshrined like a figurine at a gravesite, just standing there enduring the stares of the vulgar, no different from a useless stick of old wood. Isn't it said, 'There are not two suns in the universe?' Why should there be two Bodhisattvas standing side by side?" He thereupon took one of the images and gave it to Mitsusuke. Mitsusuke was dancing with joy, just like a person who had obtained the precious night-shining gem or wrested the priceless pearl from under the dragon's jaws.

Mitsusuke came to me and asked that I perform an enshrinement ceremony for it and open its eyes. Offering incense and making my bows before this truly beautiful image of Kannon, I then read out the following verse of praise to celebrate the Bodhisattva's lofty, far-reaching vows:

> What need is there for me to "open" the Great Being's thousand
> eyes?
> Outside the hall, a misty rain; beyond the lattice, a plum tree
> blossoms in the cold.

. . . .

There are not two suns. "There are not two suns in the universe; there is only one man in heaven and earth" (*Zenrinkushū*). "One moon and one sun are enough" (annotation).

Two Bodhisattvas standing side by side. "Manjusri said, 'When I desire to manifest the Buddha-body, I don't manifest two of them side by side'" (annotation). "A world where there are two kings or two generals will know no peace" (annotation).

The precious night-shining gem. A fabulous pearl said to glow in the dark (*T'ai-p'ing Kuang-chi,* ch. 494). A priceless pearl that had to be procured from under the jaws of a dragon at the bottom of the sea appears in the *Chuang Tzu.*

Thousand Eyes. One of Kannon's countless manifestations is the Thousand-Armed, Thousand-Eyed Kannon of Great Compassion (*Daihi Senju Sengan Kannon*); there is an eye in the palm of the hand of each of its thousand arms.

:57. Spoken at an Eye-Opening Ceremony for Shakamuni Buddha

Hakuin delivered this piece at a lecture meeting at the age of fifty-four, one year before the great lecture meeting on the Record of Hsi-keng *that established his reputation throughout the country. The lecture meeting described here is mentioned in the* Chronological Biography: *"Autumn. In the eighth month of 1739, the master acceded to a request from his lay student Akiyama Yashitomo and gave talks at the Akiyama residence on the* Letters of Ta-hui. *Tetsu of Kai, Jun of Izumo, and Kō of Bitchū served as attendants at the meeting, and Kyū of Rinsen-an, Chū of Bizen, Sha of Bungo, Ro of Kai, Totsu, and other monks arrived to take part. More than thirty people attended the meeting, which continued for over a month"* (Precious Mirror Cave, *p. 204). Ta-hui's* Letters, *one of Hakuin's favorite texts, which he had used for his first lecture meeting as a young priest at Shōin-ji, contains detailed instructions for Zen practice. Ta-hui wrote them specifically for lay followers such as those who were attending this meeting at the Akiyama residence.*

Akiyama Yashitomo (1682–1750; also Michitomo) was a long-time Hakuin student and a great patron of Shōin-ji. A lengthy piece Hakuin wrote on awarding Akiyama a lay Buddhist name is translated below (Book Five, #77).

Hakuin first explains how the meeting came about, then he delivers a long verse that he wrote for a ceremony, held during the meeting, to enshrine a statue of Shakamuni Buddha, probably in the shrine room of Mr. Akiyama's home.

IN SPRING OF THE second year of the Gembun era (1737), after responding to a teaching request at Rinzai-ji in Itadori village in southern Izu province, I stopped in northern Izu on my way home to spend the night at the residence of Mr. Akiyama Yashitomo in Yasuhisa village. Mr. Aki-yama and his family received me with the warmest cordiality, and asked me with great earnestness to conduct a Buddhist meeting at his home. As I was exhausted from all the traveling I had been doing, I had to refuse his request. Although sympathetic to my condition, Mr. Akiyama was not ready to take that for a final answer, so I made him a promise. "I will return for an extended stay this coming autumn or winter, and then I will do my best to fulfill the wishes of you and your friends."

After that, between autumn and winter of 1737 and the beginning of autumn of 1739, letters and emissaries arrived from Mr. Akiyama urging me to carry out my promise. On the fifteenth day of the eighth month, Mr. Akiyama's son Tomoshige came to my temple in person and repeated his father's invitation three times. No longer able to shirk my responsibility, at midnight I climbed into a bamboo palanquin and slipped quietly away from Shōin-ji, heading southeast. I traveled at night to avoid a hot and onerous daytime journey. Three monks accompanied me, Brother Tetsu, who trotted along in the vanguard, and Brothers Jun and Kō, who took up the rear.* They hurried right along with their bowl pouches clutched tightly to their chests. After a journey of three or four leagues, I got down from the palanquin and walked through the gate of Mr. Akiyama's residence. The topmost branches of the trees were tinged with the first rays of dawn.

The entire family had been awaiting my arrival. They immediately rushed out and greeted me with faces wreathed in joyous smiles. Brother Kyū, who had been engaged in a retreat at a spot about a league distant, was also there, though no one had been sent to tell him about the meet-ing. Other unbidden participants who were waiting for us were monks Chū, Sha, Ro, and Totsu.† They were standing around calling out to one another, creating a commotion. By the time the morning meal was ready, the number of visiting monks had increased to a dozen or so. They stood around laughing together with Mr. Akiyama's children. Finally, they lined up in front of me, performed deep bows, and formally asked me to deliver Zen lectures (teishō) on the Letters of Zen Master Ta-hui.

Once again I was unable to refuse. I proceeded to jabber away at them twice each day, morning and night. The rest of my time I spent in my bed,

---

*Tetsu: Kaigan Chitetsu; Jun: Enkei Sojun; Kō: Daikyū Ebō.
†Brother Kyū is Ekyū (n.d.), who was with Ryōsai one of the senior priests in the early period of Hakuin's residence at Shōin-ji. The other monks were all students of Hakuin who were, or had formerly been, studying at Shōin-ji.

sleeping soundly, snorting out volleys of thundering snores that reverberated through the house.

Each day Yashitomo would quietly practice zazen with the monks and engage them in pure talk about the Way. He was so unobtrusive that he almost seemed not to be there. His son Tomoshige, at his father's wish, assumed command of the family servants during the serving of the morning rice gruel and midday meals. Relatives and friends supplied the kitchen with the fruits of earth, stream, and ocean. Voices both young and old praised the assembly; their sighs of admiration echoed throughout the room. The meeting was an unexpectedly great success, of the kind that is rarely to be encountered in this defiled latter day world. Without my even realizing it, the meeting continued for an entire month. As the final day approached, Tomoshige produced a beautifully adorned golden statue of Shakamuni Buddha. At the final vegetarian feast, he asked me to "open its eyes." I placed my palms together in *gasshō*, and composed this verse:

> I arrived here on the fifteenth of the eighth month, fourth year
> of Gembun
> In response to a teaching request I received from Akiyama
> Yashitomo.
> Many Zen monks also came, wielding great iron traveling staffs,
> Stealing stealthily in, all silently sworn to guard the Dharma
> fortress.
> "There are some letters by the master of Yun-men yuan," they
> said,*
> Bowing twice; then they formally requested my detailed
> comments.
> Mustering my strength, for three or four sessions I prattled at
> them.
> Clerics and laymen who filled the room hung intently on every
> word.
> Such earnest faces, I could hardly declaim in a slapdash manner.
> Extending my stay, I continued lecturing for an entire month.
> Many friends and relations came, bamboo mats under their arms.
> High and low, young and old crowded in together, sitting and
> standing.
> Akiyama's mother and wife ran cheerfully about, toiling
> tirelessly,

---

*Yun-men yuan: one of the temples where Ta-hui, the author of the *Letters*, resided.

Eldest son Tomoshige nimbly carried out his father's wishes.
One day the host appeared clutching a gilt figure of Shakamuni.
Bowing before it, I noted its fine features and exquisite form.
He asked me to conduct an eye-opening ceremony for the
 Buddha.
Which I did, but not by painting in eyes or by reciting any
 sutras,
But by chanting out a splendid dharani, powerful and profound,
Directly to the Buddha's face, offered for the benefit of all beings:
"A cool, refreshing breeze arises, passing gently through the
 room,
After autumn rain, the water in the pond is pure and clear."*

The overwhelming kindness since I arrived and disturbed the
 household—
Is that not itself the true opening of Shakamuni's Dharma eyes?†
I earnestly hope the Buddha's profound merit and endless virtue
Makes this family, branches and leaves, prosper long into the
 future.

IIIB. *HINKO*

Included under the *Shōbutsuji* rubric are five *hinko*, literally, "grasping the torch [that lights the funeral pyre]," words Hakuin spoke as officiating priest at funeral services. Most of them were for monks who had trained at Shōin-ji. The cemetery at Shōin-ji is filled with gravestones of young monks who died while training there under conditions of great privation; these first two examples are no doubt typical of many such obsequies Hakuin must have been obliged to conduct.

*Based on lines by Yuan-wu, which are said to have brought his student Ta-hui to achieve a satori (*Compendium of the Five Lamps*, ch. 19). See below, #81, Supplementary Note 2.
†"The priests and lay people gathered here are Shakamuni's eye. It is also no other than the Pure Land, the self-nature of not only the Buddha but of each person in this room" (annotation).

:58. VERSE AT THE FUNERAL OF SENIOR MONK GENSHITSU SOMON

Although Genshitsu Somon (n.d.) was presumably a monk in train-ing at Shōin-ji, and judging from the final two lines of Hakuin's verse, a quite advanced student, nothing else is known about him. An annotation says he came to Shōin-ji from a temple named Dairyū-ji in nearby Yanagisawa.

Brother So, has your brushwood gate now shut for good?
This old priest's bowels have been secretly rent to pieces.
That lock on the great matter is pitilessly hard to pry open,
You showed you were a true son of the Buddha-patriarchs.

:59. VERSE AT THE FUNERAL OF SENIOR MONK SHIGAN SŌKATSU

Senior Monk Shigan Sōkatsu (Shigan Sōkatsu Jōza, n.d.) was from Sōgen-ji, an important provincial Zen temple in Harima (part of present Hyōgo prefecture). Sōkatsu was one of several monks from that temple who studied with Hakuin, most prominent among them being Kōsei Egyō (d. 1776), who became an important Dharma heir.

After swallowing up the deadly springs at the Zen source,
You came here and began gnawing on my old green rug.
Shoved out of your cave, tumbling over and born anew,
You manifested a million lion hairs, lacking half a pound.

. . . .

Lines 1–2: As is usual in these addresses, Hakuin plays on the Chinese char-acters of the monk's name and home temple, not all of which are explained or reflected in the translation. The name Shigan Sōkatsu is literally, "lion cliff that gives life to the Zen source." Sōgen-ji, where he served, is "temple of the Sixth Patriarch's fountain source," or more simply, "the Zen source." "Green rug" is a metaphor for Hakuin's Zen essence, his most treasured possession (see explanation, p. 245).

Lines 3–4: A lion is said to test the mettle of its cubs by pushing them off the cliff where they were raised; those that have what it takes to be proper lions perform a somersault in midair and fly back to the cave. One hair of the lion king is said to manifest a hundred million hairs. There are references in Hua-yen literature to hundreds and millions of golden lions appearing in each of the hairs of the lion king, each of which manifests countless lions in their turn, in a neverending progression, like Indra's Net. Hakuin also uses this expression in *Dream Words from a Land of Dreams*, ch. 4.

The final "lacking half a pound" is unclear, though it seems to allude to the need for continued post-satori training. Tōrei, setting the expression beyond the reach of intellectual discrimination, links it to Case 45 of the *Blue Cliff Record* ("A monk asked Chao-chou, 'All things return to the One. Where does the One return to?' Chao-chou said, 'When I was in Ch'ing-chou, I made a shirt that weighed seven pounds'") by saying, "What does this mean? Unless you grasp Chao-chou's seven-pound shirt, how can you hope to grasp this half pound?" (annotation).

:60. Verse at the Funeral of Jissai Eishin Daishi

Jissai Eishin Daishi is the posthumous name of the wife of Watanabe Heizaemon (n.d.), the proprietor of the main honjin *inn at the Hara post station,* honjin *being inns of the highest class, used by Daimyō and ranking government officials. Watanabe's son Sukefusa (n.d.) was a childhood friend of Hakuin.*

Jissai Eishin appears in Book Five, in inscriptions (untranslated here) Hakuin wrote bestowing Dharma names on her and her husband. In those pieces Hakuin describes her as a devout Buddhist who performed her devotions with great diligence, and a fine mother who raised her son to be a splendid gentleman. As heads of the wealthy Watanabe family, both Heizaemon and Sukefusa were important patrons of Shōin-ji. When young Hakuin was engaged in his Zen peregrinations around the country, Watanabe Heizaemon wrote and asked him to remonstrate with Sukefusa, who he said had committed unfilial acts of some kind. An account of these events, and the letter Hakuin wrote Sukefusa, can be found in Beating the Cloth Drum, *pp. 1–14.*

Dewdrops under a sickle moon, a million points of light.
Camellia petals dropping like soft voices from the window.

Your splendid life of eighty years, brief as a night dream.
While listening to the shrilling crickets, dawn has come.

. . . .

The difference between this verse and the ones Hakuin delivered at funeral services for his monks is striking. Whereas the latter are written in the style of his teaching verses, the former, even while conveying implications of Zen doctrine, seems very direct and poignant.

BOOK FOUR
Explications (*Ben*)

. . . .

*In this literary form, the writer assesses a matter to determine
its authenticity, validity, or true meaning. Although the
Explications included may originally have been delivered orally,
in their transcribed form most of them read rather like essays.
In dealing with terms and passages from sutras and Zen texts
that he had questioned, Hakuin explains how he resolved his
doubts and clarified his understanding of them in the course of
his practice. Four of the ten pieces in this section are translated.*

: 61. Entering Inside a Lotus Thread

Here Hakuin takes up a passage from the Record of Lin-chi: *"Followers of the Way, make no mistake. When the Asuras fight against the god Indra and are defeated in battle, they lead their host of eighty-four-thousand followers and all of them hide in a hollow filament of a lotus. Is this not miraculous?" (*Zen Teachings of Master Lin-chi, *pp. 48–9). A similar passage appears in the* Flower Garland Sutra, Fugen Bodhisattva *chapter.*

It should be noted that the final sentence of the passage Hakuin quotes here, "Indra, unable to attack them there, withdrew," differs from that found in most editions of the Record of Lin-chi. *He may be quoting from memory, but he may also have simply added the additional words himself.*

Lotus threads are very fine, delicate filaments produced from viscous fluid that exudes from the root of the lotus plant when it is cut. These filaments were dried and woven into a cloth that was used for garments and as canvas for religious paintings. They appear in Buddhist literature as a metaphor for something extremely small and fine.

This piece also appears in Sendai's Comments on the Poems of Han-shan, *kan 2, which he compiled in 1741, during his mid-fifties, and probably dates from around the same time.*

ZEN MASTER LIN-CHI said, "When the Asuras fought against the god Indra and were defeated in battle, they led their host of eighty-four-thousand followers and hid together with them in a hollow lotus filament. Indra, unable to attack them there, withdrew." His words are based on a passage in the *Flower Garland Sutra*.

I always found it strange that after their defeat the Asuras chose to conceal themselves inside a lotus filament. Asuras possess extraordinary supernatural powers. They could have have easily crowded their evil host of eighty-four thousand inside an infinitely smaller place—in the eye of a mite that makes its nest in the eyebrow of a mosquito, in a mosquito's nose, in a mote of dust, or on the tip of a needle. Why did they choose a lotus filament as a place of concealment?

On achieving victory over the Asuras, Indra and the Four Guardian Gods under his command would have moved with the fleetness of the wind. In no time at all they would have searched the lotus ponds, found the lotus stalks, and extracted the lotus filaments. The Asura forces would have little hope of escaping them. Even if they were able to hide, Indra and the other gods all possess the Heavenly Eye, which takes in at a single glance all existence without exception as though gazing at a crystal in the palm of the hand. They would have immediately discovered the Asura forces. If it was winter or early spring, when the buds had not yet appeared on the lotus roots and everything is bare, they would have apprehended them with even greater ease.

My doubts about this remained with me for many years. Then recently while I was doing zazen, it all suddenly became clear to me. Elated, I have written down here what I discovered for some of my Zen students. It is a subtle example of the manner in which sutras employ metaphor, and I think it can be of great use to someone engaged in practicing the Way. Let me now try to explain it for you.

Suppose a superior religious seeker engaged in practicing the Way continues to sit quietly with his backbone perfectly straight until body and mind disappear and he becomes one with all things, as tranquil as a perfectly clear body of water, or a portion of the vast empty sky. If even a slight flicker of thought arises, though, the firmament fills with cloud and fog, waves swell up that can swallow ranges upon ranges of towering peaks. Valleys and mountains howl in raging fury, noisome vapors spit forth ice and hail, and lightning and thunder dart from the deadly encompassing clouds.

Such circumstances as these describe the time when the Asuras, enjoying a great victory, reveal the immensity of their bodies, making vast oceans seem shallow, boundless skies seem narrow, and they shake the sacred halls and pavilions with their horrendous roaring. The human mind quails before this; even the cinnabar field may break and crumble.

But if at such a time the student bores into his koan, or concentrates single-mindedly on his own original self, then everything—the ocean of the Dharmakaya and the fundamental source of his own mind—will suddenly become calm and tranquil, just as when a great dipper of cold water is poured into a seething cauldron. This is descriptive of the conditions that prevailed when Indra achieved his great victory.

Each of the Four Guardian Gods has now secured his position; the other heavenly deities are rejoicing and congratulating one another. In the

Dharma Hall, each of the mani gems in Indra's Net is reflecting a million other mani gems, endlessly manifesting a realm where all phenomenal existences, in an ever-changing lord-and-vassal relation, are interfused while at the same time remaining mutually unhindered.

At such a time, the devil legions, eighty-four-thousand strong, without a single place to hide, vanish without leaving a single trace behind. No matter where you search in any of the ten directions, no matter what means you use, you cannot discover a single one.

At this point, the practicer is waltzing about in a rapture of delight, thinking, "Everything has now been settled!" But he must wait, for he is unaware that those devil legions are at that very moment insinuating their way into those subtle thoughts of joy, and will lie waiting, hidden, inside them.

What do I mean by subtle thoughts of joy? Minute flows of delusive thought that are difficult to completely cut off and are constantly trickling out, like water, from the eighth consciousness. Is this not the meaning of those hosts of afflicting demons—delusive thoughts that are difficult to cut off—concealing themselves inside a lotus root? Once they have insinuated themselves with great subtlety into the holes in the lotus root, where it is impossible to attack them, one has no recourse but to retreat.

Yang-shan asked Kuei-shan, "Those subtle flowings from the mind—how many years since you've been rid of them?" "Seven years," replied Kuei-shan.* This too refers to rooting out the devil hosts hidden inside the hollow filaments of the lotus root. How do you accomplish it? The patriarchal teachers contrived an expedient device for severing, as if with a fine sword, the fundamental source of delusive thoughts. It is far more effective than trying to smash the thoughts themselves—even if you took a ten-thousand-ton hammer to them!

A monk asked Chao-chou, "Does a dog have the Buddha-nature, or not?" Chao-chou said, "Mu."

If you concentrate on this koan, you will find that it has extraordinary efficacy. If you really want to attain a realm of peace and repose, you should work on this koan. If you continue attacking it from the top, from the bottom, and from every other possible angle, and you suddenly die the great death and are born anew, you will find that you will blush as you recall all these stories.

Strive hard. Do it now, don't wait until you've grown old and find tears running down your withered cheeks. Then it will be too late! It is my sincerest hope that you will succeed!

*Record of Hsu-t'ang, ch. 1.

: 62. THE TATHAGATA SUMERU LAMP KING

Here Hakuin explains the alaya, *or eighth, consciousness (ālaya-vijnāna), also called the storehouse consciousness, a key concept in the Mahayana Yogacara tradition that often appears in his writings.*

The Tathagata Sumeru Lamp King, a Buddha who appears in the Vimalakirti Sutra, *dwells in the universe called Merudhvaja located northwest of Mount Sumeru.*

I N THE BEYOND COMPREHENSION chapter of the *Vimalakirti Sutra* it says:

> At that time Vimalakirti said to Manjusri, "You have visited countless thousands, ten thousands, billions of *asamkhyas* [an uncountably large number] of countries. What Buddha lands have the best lion thrones endowed with the finest qualities?"
>
> Manjusri replied, "Layman, to the east, beyond countries numerous as the sands of thirty-six Ganges, lies a universe called Merudhvaja (Sumeru Shape). Its Buddha is called Sumeru Lamp King, and he is there now. This Buddha's body is eighty-four-thousand *yojanas* in height and the lion throne he sits on is eighty-four-thousand *yojanas* high and adorned in the finest fashion."*

This passage contains the finest parable in the *Vimalakirti Sutra*, one that expresses its deep and boundless meaning. One can understand why teachers in the past in commenting on it have sometimes been mistaken. Here we encounter not only the marrow of the *Vimalakirti Sutra* but the very core of the ancients' teaching. It expresses the profound truth of non-duality, which transcends by far the realm of human comprehension. A practicer of Zen who reads this sutra and continues to study it with care will before long suddenly open the true eye of ultimate nondiscriminatory wisdom.

When I first read the *Vimalakirti Sutra* in my youth, I had considerable doubts about it. Where it said, "to the east, beyond countries numerous as the sands of thirty-six Ganges, lies a universe called Sumeru Shape," I thought to myself, "That sounds strange. It would be billions upon billions

---

*Vimalakirti Sutra, pp. 76–77. A *yojana* was a unit of measurement in ancient India, equal to the distance the royal army could march in a day.

of countries. I've read that the Ganges River is huge, over forty leagues across. Who could determine how many particles of sand it contains? Each particle is no larger than a grain of finest wheat flour. Even if you put a few liters of them into a container, it would still be exceedingly difficult to count them all. And the sutra speaks of the sand in a river forty leagues in width! Not even the gods and demons would be able to count it. Moreover, we are talking not of one or two Ganges, but of thirty-six! It stands to reason that no one could count all that sand. No doubt it is to be understood as an amount totally beyond calculation. But if that is so, why use a fantastic number like thirty-six Ganges in the first place? Could it be designed to confuse students engaged in Buddhist practice? The Bodhisattva Manjusri was the teacher of all seven Buddhas of the past; surely he would not want to befuddle people like me with such senseless numbers. Doesn't the irresponsible use of fantastically large numbers invite criticism from Neo-Confucians like Chu Hsi who disparaged Buddhism for "teaching ideas that sound loftier than the *Great Learning* but are in fact groundless illusions?"* Or could it be there is a profound principle at work here? But if that is the case, why has no one ever pointed it out?

Ever since the *Vimalakirti Sutra* arrived in China it has been read by many people of great wisdom. The men who translated sutras into Chinese were extraordinarily talented scholars too—Yen-fo Cheng in the Latter Han Dynasty, Chih-ch'ien in the Wu dynasty, Shu Fa-hu and Shu Shu-lan in the western Chin, and Hsuan-chuang in the T'ang. In the Sui dynasty the great teacher T'ien-t'ai Chih-i lectured on the *Vimalakirti Sutra* each year during the summer retreat, inspiring the Indian priests who heard him. In the eastern Chin dynasty there was a priest named Gitamitra. In the Latter Chin there were eight hundred outstanding scholars working at Kumarajiva's translation center in the Hsiao-yao Gardens. Kumarajiva's vast learning enabled him to penetrate the works of all three divisions of the Tripitaka—sutras, precepts, and commentaries—with a discernment that was acclaimed throughout India. Among his students were men of superior wisdom such as Tao-sheng and Seng-chao, men of great erudition such as Seng-jui and Seng-jung. These people investigated in minute detail not only all the major doctrinal points set forth in the sutra, but minor points, even down to the most insignificant, as well. They left virtually nothing untouched.

---

*In Chu Hsi's (1130–1200) preface to his edition of the *Great Learning*, *Ta-hsueh chang-chu*.

Then why on earth have all these men remained completely silent about the sutra's most essential teaching? Ch'ang-shui Tzu-hsuan of the Sung dynasty is the only person who has ventured an opinion on this point.* In his *General Commentary* on the sutra, he wrote, "The Buddha-body's height of eighty-four-thousand *yojanas* expresses the perfect and complete Recompense Body he attained by means of the eighty-four-thousand paramitas. The lion seat, eighty-four-thousand *yojanas* high, expresses his utter fearlessness amid the eighty-four thousand forms of absolute emptiness."

However, I do not think his comments are sufficient to explain the matter. The *Vimalakirti Sutra's* fundamental principle is set forth in the "Beyond Comprehension" chapter. Its very life and essence is revealed in this phrase about the sands in thirty-six Ganges.

The deep doubts this raised in my mind remained with me for many years—it felt as though I always had something lodged between my teeth. Then one night recently when I was doing zazen, the sutra's subtle and profound meaning suddenly became clear to me. There it was, revealed right before my eyes! Overjoyed, I waited until dawn and then I called you all into my chambers to tell you about it. I am writing it down as well, because some of you seemed to respond to my oral teaching as though you were deaf and dumb.

My sole wish is for you to experience a joy equal to my own. If you closely peruse the idle thoughts I have set forth here, I have no doubt whatever that you will share my joy. If you experience it just once, all the inner subtleties of the sutra will suddenly appear to you as clearly and distinctly as a fruit lying in the palm of your hand. While I am the first to admit that my ideas lack depth and discernment, I beg you not to fling them aside with contempt. I wrote them down reluctantly, against my better judgment. But it makes no difference to me if people want to say that old Hakuin in his dotage has begun chewing the food up soft before he gives it to his children.

If a student wants to fully grasp my meaning, he must first plunge his mattock down squarely into the field of the eighth consciousness. If he does that, he will encounter the Buddha Sumeru Lamp King face to face. If he doesn't, he will never, until the day he dies, achieve any true resolution.

The words "pass beyond" in the sentence "passing beyond countries

---

* *Wei-mo ching lueh-su.* Chang-shui Tzu-hsuan (965–1038) was a priest of the Hua-yen school.

as numerous as the sands of thirty-six Ganges," is similar to the "passing across" of the six paramitas. It means emancipation, "reaching the opposite shore [of enlightenment]." "Thirty-six" [written with the numbers "three-six" in Chinese] refers to the three subtle and six coarse mental states.* What are the three subtle mental states? Ignorance (the unenlightened condition), the perceptive faculty, and the objects perceived. They express the Dharma of the eighth, or storehouse, consciousness. Once you fully grasp this, you know it for what it is, no more than a flower in the air. What are the six coarse states? Consciousness of likes and dislikes, consciousness of pleasure and pain, attachment resulting from such consciousness, assigning names to things, karmic acts resulting from the previous states, and suffering resulting from those acts. These are dependent on the seventh consciousness. Once you fully grasp it, you know that it too is a flower in the air.

As a practicer intent on pursuing the Way continues to perform zazen assiduously, he finds that delusive thoughts gradually diminish as he returns deeper into the fundamental source of his mind. This is what the sutra refers to as "passing to the east." It corresponds to the Thunder trigram (two broken lines over one unbroken) in the *Book of Changes*, and to the element Wood. In seasonal terms it is spring, the time when all things begin to emerge. As such, it is the fundamental source of all phenomena.

It is clear from this that the sixth and seventh consciousnesses are both embraced within their fundamental source in the eighth consciousness. Once the sixth consciousness returns to its basic ground in the eighth consciousness, it abruptly transcends the confines of the evil passions as found in the three subtle and six coarse mental states; delusions vanish, passion-ridden thoughts subside, and emptiness and tranquility free of all illusion emerge.

---

*Three subtle mental states (*sansai*) and six stronger, less subtle ones (*rokuso*) produced from them are posited in *Awakening of Faith in the Mahayana*. The subtle states, produced from the unenlightened condition of primal ignorance (*avidya*), are extremely weak and indistinct mental functions in which no difference yet exists between subjective mind and objective phenomena, whereas the less refined, robust mental states occur in the interaction between mind and objective phenomena. Together the nine mental states describe the processes of unenlightened existence. To reach enlightenment one must proceed from the coarser states (corresponding to the first six consciousnesses) involving various levels of interaction with the objective world, to the final, most subtle state, corresponding to the eighth, or storehouse, consciousness, where no such interaction occurs.

This, in itself, is the return to the matrix of Buddhahood that is within you, to the tranquility of the immoveable and unwavering source of mind; it is crossing worlds as numerous as the sand in thirty-six Ganges and reaching the universe where the Buddha Sumeru Lamp King dwells. People today often refer to this mistakenly as the dwelling place of the self's original part, thinking that it is perfect realization of the universally endowed Buddha-mind. Ch'ang-sha called this the great and unmistakable sign that you are still enmeshed in the endless cycle of transmigration. Lin-chi called it a pit of abyssal darkness that is beyond all knowing.

If upon reaching this point, superior seekers engaged in the authentic practice of the Way do not become content with it and regard it as final satori, and if they keep boring on straight ahead without backsliding, they will before long experience a sudden and profound insight. This is the moment described above when the mattock strikes down into the field of the eighth consciousness, the moment the eighth, or storehouse, consciousness, without design or plan, suddenly inverts, transforming into the Great Perfect Mirror Wisdom, the seventh consciousness transforming into the Wisdom of Sameness, the sixth consciousness into the Wisdom of Marvelous Perception, and the first five consciousnesses—seeing, hearing, smelling, feeling, thinking—into the Wisdom of Benefiting Others. You are then for the first time able to believe without any doubt that the three Buddha bodies are intrinsically embodied in utter perfection within the Four Wisdoms. For a being blessed with the great good fortune of being reborn in the human or deva realms there is nothing to surpass this, for at that moment trees and grasses, countries and lands, sentient and nonsentient beings, heavens and hells, Buddha-realms and demon-realms, all become a single mass of ineffable divine light within the Great and Perfect Mirror Wisdom. It is this, in and of itself, that is the Buddha Sumeru Lamp King.

In the radiance of the Buddha Lamp King's illumination, the karmic suffering caused by the eighty-four-thousand passions becomes at once the Buddha Lamp King's marvelously subtle form. He and his precious throne rise up eighty-four-thousand *yojanas*, as does his universe, the white hair between his eyebrows, and the offerings that are made to him.

Question: You say that within the Great Perfect Mirror Wisdom the afflicting passions and the Bodhisattvas, the Pure Land and impure world all achieve oneness with the Buddha body. Having actually experienced this for myself, I have no doubt it is true. Still, what reason can you give for holding up the eighty-four-thousand evil passions alone as the Buddha body?

Reply: The Buddha's body is the ultimate in beauty, the evil passions the ultimate in wretched ugliness. The *Vimalakirti Sutra* sets forth nondiscriminatory Buddha wisdom as the fundamental principle of nonduality. The lowest and most despicable evil passions are viewed as manifestations of the highest, most sublime Buddha body. The sutra says, "Shariputra declared to Vimalakirti, 'The Buddha's precious throne is so wide and lofty, I am unable to ascend it.'" Once Shravakas and Pratyeka-buddhas of the Two Vehicles have extinguished their evil passions, they attempt to see the Buddha's body. How can they know that the eighty-four-thousand evil passions themselves are, in their entirety, the true purplish-gold body of the Buddhas; that these passions are the Buddhas' "precious thrones adorned in the finest fashion"? Since those of limited attainment cannot know this, it is quite understandable that Shariputra was unable to climb upon the throne.

Vimalakirti said, "Yes, yes, Shariputra. I understand very well. If one pays obeisance to the Buddha King Sumeru Lamp, he will be able to ascend the Buddha's throne." Does not the sutra also say that the Buddha is manifesting himself right now? If so, where is he at this very moment? You must not make the mistake of setting out to the east to look for him, thus cutting yourself off from him by thirty-six *yojanas* of Buddha-lands. He is the Buddha-mind itself, possessed from birth in all its perfection by each and every person; he is the completely emancipated wayfarer listening right at this very moment to the Dharma. In other words, the Buddha that Manjusri is referring to is present right here at this very moment.

If you can catch even a single glance of him, you will also be able to grasp his countless millions of Dharma thrones, even if they were to manifest themselves in a single mote of dust. You yourself would be able to take them and put them inside a mote of dust as well.

Whether the practicer believes in this or not is determined solely by the weakness or strength of his attainment and the shallowness or depth of his wisdom. When the Buddha is distant, he is all too distant and the practicer, his vigor exhausted, becomes drained of spirit and resolve. When the Buddha is close, he is exceedingly close, and duality of subject and object ceases to exist.

The *Lotus Sutra* says, "Buddhas take their seat within the Dharma's absolute emptiness." In the *Treatise on the Perfection of Great Wisdom* it is said, "Wherever a Buddha sits, whether on a chair or on the ground, is called his lion throne....It is like the lion, king of four-legged beasts, who fearlessly stalks the world alone, making all other beasts submit to him."

The Buddha-lands chapter of the *Vimalakirti Sutra* has, "The Buddhas' various countries are like empty space." In other words, these thrones exist within the absolute emptiness of all things. How can they be compared to thrones in the worldly realm, prized for their carved and polished gems? The sutra states, "Bodhisattvas immediately change their shape and seat themselves on a lion throne forty-two-thousand *yojanas* high." The *General Commentary* comments, "This clarifies the height, eighty-four-thousand *yojanas*, of Buddha's body. At this point Bodhisattvas are at the stage of practice, having deferred their final attainment. They are thus diminished to half the size of a Buddha."

I do not believe this explains the sutra's meaning satisfactorily either. The eighty-four-thousand passions that afflict sentient beings are in and of themselves the Buddhas' true and real Dharma-body. Well aware of this, Bodhisattvas place their trust for the time being in the practice of the four universal vows, the twofold process of benefiting themselves and benefiting others. This is why the sutra says they are forty-two-thousand *yojanas* in height.*

I have not set my worthless views before you like this because of a fondness for idle speculation. The great master Hui-neng stated long ago, "Amida's Pure Land lies one hundred and eight thousand leagues from here, a distance created by the ten evils and eight false practices in ourselves."† Lin-chi explained the phrase in the *Lotus Sutra* "sitting for ten kalpas in a place of practice" as an allusion to the ten perfections or paramitas.‡ Another of the ancient Zen worthies explained a statement in the *Nirvana Sutra* about carrying a load of cooking oil to a person twenty-five leagues distant, as a reference to the twenty-five states of unenlightened existence.§ Now I have no intention of assuming a sober, wrinkle-browed countenance and emulating any of these great sages. I am merely offering

---

*Four and two are taken from the number forty-two thousand.

†Ten and eight from the number one-hundred-and-eight thousand. The quotation is from the *Platform Sutra*. (See *Essential Teachings*, p. 47.)

‡Lin-chi quotes a passage in the Phantom City chapter of the *Lotus Sutra*: "'The Great Universal Wisdom Excellence Buddha sat in the place of practice for ten kalpas' refers to the practice of the ten perfections or paramitas" (See *Zen Teachings of Master Lin-chi*, p. 71).

§This appears in *Ta-pan nieh-p'an ching shu*, Kuan-ting's commentary on the *Nirvana Sutra*, ch. 21.

a suggestion or two that I think may help explain some of the deficiencies in the *General Commentary*.

Question: Wouldn't what you have been saying imply arbitrary attachment to the ultimate principle alone, which would negate phenomenal existence altogether?

Reply: No, it would not. Apart from the fundamental principle there are no phenomena. Apart from phenomena there is no fundamental principle. Remember what Eshin Sōzu said*: "Nondiscrimination without discrimination is not in conformity with the Buddhist teaching. It is evil and pernicious nondiscrimination. Discrimination alone without nondiscrimination is not in conformity with the Buddhist teaching either. It is evil and pernicious discrimination."

Although you may wonder why this is so, you should rather experience for yourselves the great joy I have described to you. Since I have that joy right here within me now, it is impossible for me to resist offering it to you.

: 63. THE EIGHTH CONSCIOUSNESS

EACH PERSON IS ENDOWED with eight consciousnesses. The first five consciousnesses, the so-called five roots or sense organs (eyes, ears, nose, tongue, and body as the organ of touch) are those that receive stimuli—form and color, sound, smells, and so forth—from the external world. But they unable to distinguish good and bad, beauty and ugliness in people and things.

The sixth consciousness is also called the samsaric consciousness. Whenever it appears, it is always in the vanguard. Whenever it leaves, it always takes up the rear. Because of this, its arising invariably occurs in consort with the three subtle mental states and together with the six coarse mental states.† It moves in and out of the first five consciousnesses and it hides inside the eighth consciousness. The sixth consciousness moves in all ways and directions, sometimes concealed and sometimes manifested, entering and exiting, extending and drawing back. Not even a Buddha's hand can control it. Hence it is said that being reborn as

---

*Otherwise known as Genshin (942–1017). The quotation is from *The Essentials for Rebirth* (*Ōjōyōshū*).
†See above, p. 147.

an animal and attaining Buddhahood are both contingent on the sixth consciousness.

The seventh, "thought-transmitting" consciousness lies hidden in the dark areas between the sixth and eighth consciousnesses.

The eighth, *alaya*, or storehouse consciousness, also called the nondiscriminating consciousness, exists in a passive state, blurred and indistinct. It is an utter blankness, as dull and unknowing as a vast pool of still, clear water with no trace of movement whatever. Within it is stored each of the passions you have experienced in the past—sadness and compassion, love and hate—without exception. Joy and anger, suffering and pleasure, purities and impurities of various kinds are all stored here, never to be lost.

If a Zen student who keeps pressing steadily forward in his practice suddenly smashes open this dark cavern, the light of the Great Perfect Mirror immediately shines forth with blinding brilliance. At that instant he realizes the four Buddha wisdoms and makes the three Buddha bodies his own. For this reason the eighth consciousness is sometimes called the Buddha-store consciousness. In King Emma's court in the realm of the dead, it is called the Pure Crystal Mirror.*

On entering this nondiscriminatory consciousness. the Zen student must not retreat even a hairsbreadth, but bore steadily on seeking the great transformation. Arousing a great mass of doubt, he must probe the question: at this very moment, having become one with the nondiscriminating *alaya* consciousness utterly free of thought and emotion, where does life come from, where does death go? If an illusory thought should suddenly appear, he must take it and proceed straightaway to determine the place whence it arose. Or he can take up Chao-chou's Mu and work on it, or Tung-shan's Three Pounds of Hemp,† or some other koan, and concentrate on boring assiduously into it. As his concentration gradually begins to mature, he will find that when he walks he is unaware he is walking, when he sits he is unaware he is sitting. It will seem to him as though he is in the midst of a vast emptiness, perfectly clear and open; that he is encased in a thick sheet of ice extending out for ten thousand leagues; or as though he is sitting inside a perfectly transparent jar of immaculate crystal. If he keeps pressing forward without fear or hesitation, he will before long find

---

*Also called the Mirror of Karma. It hangs in Emma's court in Hell, and a person is made to stand before it and see reflected in it all the sins he has committed in his life.
†Both koans are included in the *Gateless Barrier* collection: Chao-chou's Mu, Case 1; Tung-shan's Three Pounds of Hemp, Case 18.

that the ice sheet suddenly shatters into oblivion, that the great pavilion towering above him topples over. The entire universe in all ten directions and all the heavens and hells will become one with his mind and body, and will then all at once disappear without a trace.

This is the occasion that I mentioned when the student strikes his mattock down into the ground of the eighth consciousness. At that moment, no empty space exists in the ten directions; not an inch of ground exists anywhere on earth. The radiant light of his Great Perfect Mirror will suddenly shine forth with such purity and clarity and brightness that there is absolutely nothing whatever to compare it to. This state of attainment is sometimes referred to as the ninth, or immaculate, consciousness.*

If the student clings doggedly to this state, thinking it is sufficient, his attainment will always remain small and partial like those of the Two Vehicles, the Shravakas and Pratyeka-buddhas. The old den they nestle comfortably down into is a truly terrifying place. It is an empty, incomplete Nirvana.†

But the student who refuses to accept this as an ultimate attainment and goes on whipping forward the wheel of the four universal vows for endless kalpas without ever backsliding, bringing benefit to countless sentient beings, confirming the four Buddha wisdoms and cultivating the three Buddha bodies, until he finally clarifies the one great matter of human life—such a person is a fully realized Bodhisattva, a true and authentic child of the Buddha.

:64. BLACK FIRE

This piece was written between Hakuin's fifty-first and fifty-fifth years.

DURING THE GEMBUN ERA (1736–40), a fire broke out at the neighboring Numazu post station. I sent two of my monks and our old

*A ninth consciousness (*amala*), lying below the eighth consciousness, is postulated in some Buddhist schools.
†Hinayana Buddhism holds that though an Arhat enters into Nirvana after death, while living he is in a state of "limited Nirvana." According to the Mahayana, Nirvana is attained completely the moment the ties to karmic existence are severed and Buddhahood obtained. An Arhat would thus still have residues of illusion, karma, and suffering.

servant Kakuzaemon to find out what was happening. Kakuzaemon came running back, gasping for breath, and made the following report.

"Ahh, there is nothing as terrifying or as hateful as fire! Eight hundred dwellings, suddenly reduced to ash. How damaging and destructive it is! And yet it also has a trait that I admire."

"What would that be?" I asked.

"It occurred to me, on considering how rapidly fire spreads in the darkness, that if it burned with a black flame it would destroy many more human lives, and I probably wouldn't have returned here alive. It is fortunate that its flames burn so brightly. Even tiny fires, small as a bean or grain of wheat, flicker like stars, almost as though they had a consciousness of their own."

Kakuzaemon's words set me to thinking. I turned them over and over in my mind. The black fire of impermanence—birth-and-death—moves with wind-like speed, never ceasing day or night, and consumes us all. Not a single person, young or old, exalted or lowly, priest or layman, wise or foolish, can escape its destruction. Yet no shouts of "Fire!" "Fire!" are ever heard. Moreover, the principle of karmic retribution—cause and effect—works with perfect clarity right before our eyes. Even the smallest, most minor evils are consumed in this fire, burning like dim stars in the night. The most frightening thing is that most people remain unaware of this, until sooner and later they are completely enveloped in the flames. It is truly sad.

I shouted, "Kakuza!" Kakuzaemon looked up. "Don't say that you returned here alive and unharmed. Don't you know that you've been burned to a crisp? You're a lump of charcoal!"

Kakuzaemon sat with a blank look on his face. I gave a loud shout. His blankness only deepened.

. . . .

Tōrei's *Draft Biography* of Hakuin (entry for age thirty-two, the year Hakuin became head priest at Shōin-ji) identifies Kakuzaemon as an elderly servant who performed chores around the temple, "working from morning to night gathering fuel and tending the vegetable gardens." The mental blankness of Kakuzaemon in the final paragraph is explained in the following annotation: "Master Hakuin wants to show that most people are like Kakuzaemon, immersed this very moment in the midst of this raging fire. Because it consumes everyone, religious-minded and Bodhisattvas alike, the master was always teaching people, "Watch out! Be careful what you do!" but most, like

Kakuza, remain completely unconcerned, their minds empty of religious aspirations, intending to live to be a hundred or two hundred years old.... Nonetheless, when the day arrives that they must face death, they suddenly act as though their heads were on fire—too late, too late."

BOOK FIVE
Records (*Ki*)—Explanations (*Setsu*)

. . . .

Book Five is comprised of ten ki *and six* setsu. *The* ki *consist of accounts of the origin and background of temples, Buddhist images, a sutra repository, Buddhist relics, spirit stones, and people Hakuin deemed worthy of note. Eight of the* Ki *are translated here, and four of the* Setsu, *all but one of which are explanations of Dharma names that Hakuin awarded students.*

I. RECORDS (*KI*)

65. RECORD OF THE HERMITAGE AT MOUNT IWATAKI

This is one of the earliest of Hakuin's surviving inscriptions, having been composed at the age of thirty-one. He signs it with his ordination name, Ekaku; he would not adopt the name Hakuin until two years after this. He was nearing the end of an extended period of pilgrimage that began at the age of eighteen, during which he had experienced several deep enlightenments. He was trying to locate an isolated spot where he could engage in solitary practice, and he learned by chance of just such a sanctuary in the mountains of Mino province, where a layman named Shikano Tokugen had constructed a small hermitage and was looking for a priest to occupy it. There Hakuin undertook the severe regimen of zazen, subsisting on one bowl of gruel each day, which is described in his autobiography Wild Ivy *(pp. 54–64), and in the* Chronological Biography *(Precious Mirror Cave, pp. 287–91). To these accounts can be added a brief description by Tōrei, in his* Commentary on the Daruma Zen-kyō: *"The master, by pushing himself mercilessly, finally succeeding in breaking free from the illness (Zen sickness) that had for so long impeded his practice. Entering the Kokūzō Hall on Mount Iwataki, he devoted himself to zazen for over twenty months. He was forced to leave when an old family servant came and escorted him back to Shōin-ji, where not soon after he was installed as head priest"* (Daruma Zen-kyō settsū kōsho). *The Record of the Hermitage at Mount Iwataki was apparently composed at the request of Layman Shikano. A draft copy of the inscription in Hakuin's hand is still extant. It is reproduced in HZB #193.*

The hermitage at Mount Iwataki was built by Layman Shikano Tokugen of Yamanoue village. Mr. Shikano is a simple, honest man, a devout follower of Buddhism, who is always kind and generous in his dealings with the villagers. His two sons, wealthy men like their father, have inherited his modesty and humility.

Upon falling ill this spring, Layman Shikano told his sons, "I'll soon be one hundred years old. I don't have much time left. When I die, I want you to take a portion of your inheritance and have my mortuary tablet enshrined on Mount Kōya."*

"We will do that," said the sons, "but we would like to do something more."

"Invite some monks from a large temple to conduct Buddhist rites, and provide a vegetarian feast for them," said the father.

"We will do that," they said, "but it is still not enough."

"What do you propose?" asked the father.

They lowered their heads.

"You are dutiful sons. You have never done anything counter to my wishes. The gods and Buddhas are witness to that. You shouldn't hesitate to speak."

They said, "You have built and repaired many shrines and temples, among them the Kokuzō Hall on Mount Iwataki.† It is a place of great sanctity, in a setting of unmatched natural beauty. When it fell into disrepair in the past and became the haunt of monkeys, deteriorating to the point that its walls began rolling away, you rebuilt it, and it once again became a well-known pilgrimage site. However, there is no guarantee that it will not suffer the same fate in the future. What we would like to do is to build a hermitage at the site and have a priest reside there, so that your mortuary tablet can be enshrined in the hall. We can endow the hermitage with paddies that will yield two *koku* of rice. This will be of benefit to you in your future life as well, so it will be like killing two birds with one stone. We will take care of everything."

The layman was extremely pleased. "Thank you for giving such great consideration to my welfare," he said. He told them to begin work without delay.

Such is the story of how the hermitage on Mount Iwataki came to be built.

---

*A mortuary tablet (*ihai*) with the deceased's posthumous Dharma name inscribed on it was normally enshrined in the family temple, where it received the benefit of the services performed daily by the temple priests. Those who could afford it might also have a tablet enshrined in a larger, famous temple as well, such as the one mentioned here on Mount Kōya, in present Nara prefecture.

†Kokuzō (Sanskrit, *Ākāshagarbha*), a Bodhisattva whose name, literally "Sky Repository," signifies that his wisdom and merit are as boundlessly vast as the sky.

• 66. RECORD OF MOUNT FUJI IN MINO PROVINCE

*The colophon attached to this piece is dated 1716, placing it around
the same year as the previous one, at the time Hakuin was practicing at the Iwataki hermitage. It was written at Layman Shikano's
request, probably using information supplied by him. Shikano is
said to have been a follower of the Nembutsu teaching, hence the
frequent references to Amida and the Pure Land faith.*

*The "Mount Fuji" of Mino Province (Mino Fuji) referred to here
rises to a height of approximately one thousand feet to the north of
the present city of Mino-kamo in Gifu prefecture.*

Hakuin's colophon is not found in the Poison Blossoms *version of
the piece; it has been added from a holograph draft included in the
recently published* Hakuin's Zen Painting and Calligraphy *(#191).*

AT ITS ULTIMATE SOURCE, the Perfect Way is ineffably silent and mysterious, its essence dark and deeply hidden.* When the slightest stirring occurs within this mysterious darkness, the two principles (*yin* and
yang) come into existence. The pure and empty is called heaven; the rigid
and unmoving is called earth. There is an immense, solid mass of this earth
known as Mount Fuji, whose splendid form dominates the surrounding
provinces of Suruga, Tōtōmi, and Kai. Its incalculable virtue has a pro-
tective influence that extends over the entire country of Japan. Soaring
majestically many miles into the sky, its rugged slopes of eternal snow are
like enormous, wonderfully carved walls of pristine whiteness. Spreading
out from its clear, cloud-piercing cone are seven or eight brilliant silver
petals, making it resemble a finely sculpted lotus flower. The tutelary god
of the peak, Sengen Daiji, is a manifestation of Amida Buddha. Majestic
and august in appearance, he works in sincere and intimate ways.†

A person wishing to climb to the summit of Mount Fuji must choose
the warmest days of midsummer for the ascent. Even then he must clothe
himself as heavily as for the coldest winter months, and make sure he is
supplied with enough food for a journey of a hundred leagues. Before

*The first part of this paragraph echoes passages from a number of ancient Chinese
works, including the *Chuang Tzu* and the *Book of Changes*.
†Sengen Daiji (also called Sengen Bodhisattva, Senkan Daimyōjin, and Fuji Gongen)
is enshrined in the Fuji Shrine, an inner shrine at the mountain's summit that forms
part of the larger Sengen Shrine.

attempting the climb he must first undergo ritual purgation—ten days of fasting and ablutions. If even the slightest defilement remains, earth-shaking roars are heard deep in the mountain's hidden grottoes, sounds of profound resentment immediately reverberate from its peaks, poisonous mists spew forth from empty caverns, noxious fumes spit out from precipitous cliffs, whirlwinds throw storms of solid sleet and hail, producing angry, bellowing thunder. Many climbers vanish without a trace, never to be seen again. For reasons like these, few people climb to the top of Mount Fuji even once in their lives. Those who do it three times, or nine times, are virtually nonexistent.

Here in the village of Yamakami in Kamo county, Mino province, lives a gentleman named Shikano Yoshibei. Shikano is benevolent and generous, and is well known for his strong religious faith. One of his ancestors six or seven generations back climbed Mount Fuji annually for almost fifty consecutive years. On his final climb, as he was fighting off the frigid night cold, he made a silent vow to the god of the mountain: "I have grown old. I am feeble in mind and body. I deeply regret that I will be unable to continue my pilgrimages to this holy peak. If it is possible, I would like to take a sapling from one of the pine trees at the foot of the mountain, carry it to my home province, and replant it there. If it does not wither, I will take it as a sign that the god has not forsaken me."

With his thoughts moving between sadness at leaving the mountain and the prospect of obtaining a pine sapling, he drifted off to sleep. A sacred monk appeared to him, forbidding in appearance, his demeanor stern and severe. Standing there sublimely, he suddenly proclaimed, "No one before has ever climbed this mountain with such sincere devotion. I know that old age has made you infirm so that you will not be able to come here again. Nonetheless, you must not just throw aside the deep resolve that has inspired you all these years. If a mind of great sincerity drops its guard even the slightest bit, all the merits it has achieved will be lost.

"When you return to your native Mino province, this is what you should do. To the northeast of your house you will find a mountain that resembles Mount Fuji. I will give you a sacred image of Amida Buddha, which I want you to take and enshrine on that mountain together with the pine sapling. If you worship it with unflagging devotion, you will assure peace and tranquility to your descendants and receive the love and respect of your neighbors." The monk then gave Yoshibei the sacred image.

When Yoshibei awoke, he found a small golden image of Amida Buddha, about an inch and a half high, glittering brilliantly in his hand. He returned to his village in extremely high spirits and upon seeking the sacred mountain, found it exactly where the monk said it would be. He erected a shrine on the mountain, naming it Mount Fuji as the monk had instructed, and enshrined the statue of Amida Buddha inside it. He planted the pine sapling at the summit. Now brilliant green trees hundreds of feet high soar quietly into the moonlit clouds, all of them descendants of the original pine sapling.

From all around villagers came to marvel at the shrine and to worship the image of Amida. In the following decades many marvelous events occurred in the surrounding area, like shadows being cast from the Buddha, or miraculous echoes from his sacred presence.

As the years went by, however, the number of worshippers dwindled, and the shrine was gradually forgotten. A brush fire swept the mountain, destroying both the shrine and the image.

As the Buddha's body is formless, it should undergo no change whatever, and yet Shakamuni Buddha's birth at Lumbini, and entrance into Nirvana under the Sala trees, is the norm for all the great sages who appear in the world in their compassion to teach others. In view of that, can we not say that losing the sacred golden figure of Amida Buddha in Mino that Yoshibei had received long ago on Mount Fuji in Suruga is also a case of the Buddha's sacred teaching in response to the needs of sentient beings?

This year, the summer of the sixth year of Shōtoku (1716), a guest came to visit Layman Shikano Tokugen. "How long since has it been," he asked, "since the fire destroyed all trace of the shrine on Mount Fuji? You now have two fine sons, and both of them enjoy prosperity and health. Does this not accord with the divine revelation you received on Mount Fuji long ago? If so, why have you failed to carry on the fine and noble aspiration that generations of your ancestors have cherished? Why have you made no effort to rebuild the shrine?"

In deep appreciation the layman replied, "You are perfectly right. Thank you for showing me the error of my ways." Working together with his son and grandson, the layman had the shrine rebuilt and a new image enshrined inside it. People came from all around to worship in silence before it. The sounds from the mountain torrents and the colors and forms of the mountain all seemed to take part in the rejoicing.

Someone said, "Mount Fuji is the world's most sacred mountain, its size and towering height are unmatched. There is nothing to which it can be compared, which is why it is known as the *Fu-ji* or 'one and only' mountain.* Aren't you belittling the great peak by giving its name to our small mountain in Mino province?"

I [Ekaku] replied, "You are viewing these peaks merely in terms of their size and height. If you see them and worship them as Amida Buddha's boundless vow that is as deep as the ocean, as Amida's radiant light that illuminates all things universally, you will also regard them as manifestations of Universal Compassion (*Fu-ji*). People in the past, with their deep faith, could not have been worshipping Suruga Fuji and Mino Fuji as two separate mountains so I can see no reason whatever why this mountain Fuji can't also be named Fuji."

Without uttering a word, the man left. I thereupon wrote all this down and presented it to Layman Shikano.

. . . .

The following colophon is found in what is apparently the original manuscript of this piece in Hakuin's handwriting; it is not included in the *Poison Blossoms* version of the text (*Hakuin*, Takeuchi Naotsugi, plate 466): "I respectfully proclaim the following to Shikano Yoshibei, Layman Tokugen, a patron of endless good works: Ekaku, an insignificant teacher from Shōin-ji in Suruga province, a carp hidden in the depths of the Ocean of True Dharma, performed nine bows and inscribed this with his knees shaking in fear.

Autumn, the eighth month of the sixth year of Shōtoku (1716)."

:67. Record of the Obitoke Jizō (Girdle Unfastening Jizō) at Nanaoyama in Mino Province

Jizō Bodhisattva, who like other Bodhisattvas works to save sentient beings suffering in the six paths of karmic existence, is popularly venerated in Japan as the guardian of young children and the patron saint of safe childbirth, appearing in many different forms in response to supplicants' needs. One of these forms is the Obitoke Jizō. Temples around the country became centers for the worship of

---

*The Chinese characters *fu-ji*, "not-two," are sometimes used for Mount Fuji to express its incomparable beauty; from a Buddhist standpoint they would indicate Mount Fuji as a symbol of the truth of nonduality.

this Jizō, whose name, Obitoke, literally "girdle unfastening," derives from the practice of binding a woman's abdomen during her pregnancy, with the unfastening denoting a safe childbirth. The temple or shrine referred to here has vanished from history, although the image of Obitoke Jizō it enshrined is now in Myōchi-ji, a Zen temple in Mino province.

Hakuin's own encounters with the Bodhisattva are recorded in the Chronological Biography. *In his thirty-eighth year (1723), a bit later than the events recorded in this inscription, we read of Jizō appearing to Hakuin in a dream: "His body was of infinite magnitude, filling all space. The master, sitting in attendance at the Bodhisattva's side, asked him, 'How do I incorporate the attainment I've achieved into my everyday life?' The Bodhisattva looked around at him and said, 'As if sitting inside a thicket of razor-sharp thorns and briars.' Cold shivers passed up and down the master's spine." Some of Hakuin's most powerful calligraphies, ones he began writing in his eighties, are inscribed: "I place my trust in [Jizō,] the Bodhisattva of Hell" (see* Religious Art of Zen Master Hakuin, *pp. 244–45).*

A H, HOW MARVELOUS ARE the great Bodhisattvas! With boundless compassion, they declare a universal vow to save all sentient beings from suffering, assuming infinite manifestations in response to beings' different needs, apportioning themselves throughout the six ways of existence so they can lead the suffering multitudes to liberation.

The Tōmyō-in at Nanaoyama, a site sacred to Jizō Bodhisattva, is a temple situated in a setting of unsurpassed natural beauty. A legend passed down in this part of Mino province credits the founding of Tōmyō-in to Lord Oda Nobunaga.

In the first year of the Kyōhō era (1716), when I was engaged in a pilgrimage in search of the Way, I paid a visit to Rōdō Rōshi in eastern Mino province.* Rōdō was a descendant of National Master Kanzan in the seventeenth generation of his Myōshin-ji lineage. A priest to whom virtuous conduct came simply and naturally, Rōdō scrupulously observed the Buddhist precepts, he engaged in hidden practice, never fal-

---

*Hakuin was thirty-one this year and, according to his life records, was engaged in solitary practice on Mount Iwataki in Mino province. Rōdō Gidon (n.d.), head priest at Yōsen-ji in present-day Mino-kamo, later founded Dairyū-ji in nearby Kaji. Nothing else is known about him.

tering even during the summer heat or winter cold. Anyone who aspired to match Rōdō Rōshi as a teacher would need to possess a will of metal or stone.

Rōdō told me the following story: "One day in the ninth month of this year, while I was immersed in samadhi, it suddenly seemed that I was visiting a mountain of marvelous beauty. It towered up into seven separate peaks, which shone like gold pieces in the autumn sun. Isolated on a plateau halfway up the mountain, I saw an ancient hall, and inside it, standing firm and upright, was an image of Jizō Bodhisattva. Set before him in a clay saucer about eight inches in diameter was a solitary lamp. I prostrated myself before the figure, my gratitude so profound that I found my entire body covered with sweat. I was awakened from my dream by a knocking outside my chambers. I got up and opened the door. It was Kaji Kohei Tamesada from Murohara south of the village.

'You woke me from an auspicious dream,' I said.

'Would you tell me what it was?' he asked.

"When I described to Kaji what I had seen, he clapped his hands together in astonishment. 'Amazing! Absolutely amazing!' he exclaimed. 'It's as though I had been summoned here today because I had foreseen you would have such a dream.'

When Rōdō asked him to explain, Kaji related the following story. "The place you visited in your dream is Mount Nanao, southeast of Murohara. There used to be a temple there, sacred to the Bodhisattva Jizō, which had been constructed by Oda Nobunaga.* After extending his control over Ise and Ōmi provinces to the west and Suruga and Tōtōmi provinces to the east, and gaining control of the rich plains of Mino province, Lord Nobunaga ruled the country from Gifu Castle on Mount Kinka. His powerful spirit prevailed through the eight directions, his vigorous determination consuming all who opposed him. He was truly the hero of his age.

"It happened that one of his wives experienced a pregnancy that was so difficult even the most skillful physicians could do nothing but look on with wrinkled brows. A diviner they summoned said, 'Not even the gods can do anything for her. Unless you enlist the compassionate assistance

---

*Oda Nobunaga (1534–82), a lord of Owari province whose military successes enabled him to bring large areas of the country under his rule. His successors Hideyoshi and Ieyasu carried this unification process to completion, leading to the founding of the Tokugawa Shōgunate. Not known for the sensitivity and devotion he displays in this narrative, Nobunaga was notorious for his ruthless suppression of Buddhism.

of Jizō Bodhisattva, mother and child have little chance of surviving. Jizō saves all beings suffering in the six paths of existence. His spiritual power can bring truly miraculous results. Ten leagues to the east of this castle is a mountain with seven peaks. It is a site sacred to the Bodhisattva. If you erect a temple there and declare a vow before the Bodhisattva, none of the women in the villages surrounding the mountain will ever experience a difficult childbirth, not only now but in the future as well. What you must do before anything else is make supplications to the Bodhisattva.'

"Lord Nobunaga gladly agreed. No sooner had he performed his devotions to the Bodhisattva than the abnormal twisting in his wife's placenta disappeared, and with it the suffering she and the child had experienced vanished. Everyone in the castle began chanting the name of Jizō Bodhisattva with their palms pressed together in *gasshō*, marveling at this manifestation of the Bodhisattva's power. Lord Nobunaga wept tears of joy.

"Nobunaga immediately dispatched a horseman ten leagues eastward to locate Nanaoyama [Seven-Ridge Mountain] near our village. It was not long before an image of Jizō Bodhisattva was shining forth from a splendid temple he had constructed there. People came to worship it and ever since that time many wonderful miracles have occurred in the area.

"With the passage of many years, however, the temple fell into disrepair, and the Bodhisattva disappeared. Ruins were all that remained. Yet the miraculous power of the Bodhisattva continued unchanged, and to this day no case of difficult childbirth is ever heard of in the surrounding villages. Women living in villages several leagues distant have shared in this benefit—they have not been plagued by difficult childbirth either.

"After a meeting we held recently in our village, the headman said, 'Village elders support the idea of rebuilding the temple. To be favored with this sacred site sanctified by the Bodhisattva's divine power, is as difficult as carrying Mount T'ai under one's arm.* To construct a hall and enshrine a Buddhist image in it would be as easy as breaking a branch off a tree.'

"I (Rōdō) told them, 'To cast a fine bell you must employ a skilled metalsmith. Establishing a proper temple is no different. Unfortunately, these days a truly enlightened priest is not easy to find.'

'As a result of our discussion,' Kaji replied. 'A decision was made to ask you, Master Rōdō, to assume that role. It is for that purpose I have come here today. You might refuse our earnest request, but what about the

---

*The sayings, "To clasp Mount T'ai under the arm and step over the Northern Sea" (an impossibility), and "breaking a branch from a tree" appear in *Mencius*, I.i.vii.

Bodhisattva who appeared to instruct you when you were doing zazen?'
There was no way that Rōdō Rōshi could refuse. "You are right," he said.
"Let's go and have a look at this sacred site. After the temple is rebuilt,
perhaps I'll decide to live out the rest of my days there."

Kaji joyfully prostrated himself before the Rōshi, and then left. I was
staying with the Rōshi at the time. He told me to write a detailed record
of everything that had transpired. I have thus composed this inscription,
and I now await the completion of the Jizō Hall.

:68. A RECORD OF THE SUTRA REPOSITORY AT KIICHIZEN-JI

*This inscription written during Hakuin's forty-eighth year (1733)
relates circumstances involved in the construction of a sutra
repository to house a set of Buddhist scriptures at the Zen temple
Kiichi-ji in Izu province. Much of the focus is on the role Layman
Yoda Takanaga (d. 1739), the temple's chief patron, played in bringing the project to completion.*

*Manpō-zan Kiichizen-ji, to use Kiichi-ji's full and official name,
is located near the small town of Matsuzaki in a particularly
remote area of the Izu peninsula a few miles inland from its southern extremity. The temple is nestled in a beautiful setting on the
southern slope of a hill overlooking a small river valley. This part
of western Izu is even today one of the least accessible areas of the
peninsula. In premodern times, its craggy, deeply indented coasts
and rugged mountainous terrain, relatively easy to cordon off with
barriers at key points, were made to order for feudal authorities
seeking a place to isolate criminals and other undesirables.*

*One of those sent there was the Chinese Zen monk I-shan I-ning
(1247–1317), who had been dispatched to Japan as an emissary of
the Yuan government, but was confined for a time at the spot where
Kiichi-ji now stands on the suspicion that he was a spy for Mongol
forces then menacing the country. When his bona fides as a Zen mis-
sionary were later established, he was installed as abbot at Kenchō-ji
and Engaku-ji in Kamakura, and later at Nanzen-ji in Kyoto, where
he taught many promising young monks in this early period of Japanese Zen. He later founded Kiichi-ji.*

The sutra repository (Kyōzō) is a building housing a large sutra storage case equipped with shelves of special containers filled with Buddhist scriptures. The revolving storage case (Rinzō), whose invention is attributed to Fu Ta-shih (497–569), a famous layman of early Chinese Buddhism, is a large, cylindrical cabinet with eight sides, each side containing tiers of shelves filled with scriptures, set on a central pivot that is revolved to allow access to all scriptures on the shelves. By revolving the cabinet one turn, a person is said to acquire the same merit as reading the entire Buddhist canon.

The temple patrons mentioned in the text, Ōishi Shigemichi and Yoda Takanaga, were wealthy landowners and Zen laymen who lived in Ōsawa, a small village adjacent to Kiichi-ji. The Yodas, one of the richest and most important families in all of Izu province, had close ties to Hakuin. Several letters Hakuin addressed to the Yoda family are extant, one of them a lengthy text he sent to Takanaga's eldest son, which is dated twenty-two years after this piece was written (see Beating the Cloth Drum, pp. 99–109). An inscription Hakuin wrote for a Suiriku-e ceremony that he conducted in Matsuzaki at the Yoda's request, dated the second year of Hōreki (1752), is also included in Poison Blossoms, #39.

THE FORTY-NINE YEARS the old Indian (Shakamuni) spent teaching sentient beings is ultimately summed up in a single instant of thought.* What need is there to understand how to split open a particle of dust?† The lofty words preached in countless numbers by generations of sages can be disposed of by simply raising a single finger.‡ Why bother walking around a rope seat?§ Cakravartin, King of the golden wheel, vanquishes all foes throughout the world, even the most perverse and intractable. Shakamuni's treasure of the great Dharma wheel crushes the thieves of delusion that afflict sentient beings.

Manpō-zan Kiichizen-ji in Naga county, southern Izu, is a sacred temple founded by Zen master I-shan I-ning from the land of the Sung. Wise sages

---

*Shakamuni is reported to have said, "In forty-nine years (from his enlightenent until his Nirvana), I have never preached a single word."

†Hakuin writes: "When the mind of a person absorbed in samadhi suddenly opens up in perfect clarity and the light of wisdom shines forth, it is like splitting open a particle of dust and seeing within it the entire body of Vairocana Buddha" (Poison Blossoms, Book Four; untranslated).

‡Allusion to Chu-chih's "One Finger Zen" (Gateless Barrier, Case 3).

§The allusion is explained below.

have invested the old mountain with an auspicious haze of immeasurable heights. Dragon Kings and devas protecting the precincts have imbued the ancient pines with a marvelous redolence of timeless age.

In winter of this year, the eighteenth of Kyōhō (1733), six thousand and seven hundred volumes of Buddhist scripture had been assembled and an octagonal sutra repository in which to house them was completed. A project of such magnitude was not realized overnight, and it was possible only through the combined efforts of temple patrons Ōishi Shichiroemon Shigemichi, who initiated the project, and Yoda Sajibei Takanaga, who brought it to completion.

Shigemichi was born in the neighboring village of Minewa. He was a fine, benevolent gentleman of unpretentious demeanor. As he gazed at the falling flowers in springtime, thoughts of the frailty and uncertainty of worldly success saddened him. As he trod over the fallen autumn leaves, he felt keenly the brevity of human life. "Izu province may be small and insignificant," he thought to himself, "but it is not poor in Buddhist temples, and it possesses a goodly share of Shintō shrines as well. Old Layman P'ang cast his entire wealth into a lake.* I will cast my wealth into the building of a repository for the Buddhist sutras."

One night a venerable figure with a dignified presence suggestive of ages past appeared to him in a dream. Slowly and quietly, the figure said, "If you visit the temple at Mount Fukino, you will find a person there who will help you."† On visiting the temple, Shigemichi did indeed encounter such a man. He was the priest of the temple. When Shigemichi told his story, the priest was deeply impressed, and decided to join forces with Shigemichi. The two men then set about to make their aspiration a reality. They solicited throughout the province and in time succeeded in assembling four thousand Buddhist sutra scrolls, which they donated to Kiichi-ji. This donation took place in the fourth year of Kyōhō (1719). It was indeed a formidable achievement. The name of the priest was Tetsugai, who now serves at Fumon-in in Dōyama.‡ Shigemichi took the tonsure, receiving the Dharma name Layman Mumon Chōjin, and soon after that, he passed away.

Twelve years slipped past. In autumn of the seventeenth year of Kyōhō

*The legend that P'ang Yun, a famous Zen layman, cast his fortune into Tung-t'ing Lake is found in the preface to the *Recorded Sayings of Layman P'ang*, p. 40.
†Fukino-zan Hōzō-in, a Sōtō temple in Matsuzaki.
‡Fumon-in was a Sōtō temple in Kawazu village on the eastern coast of Izu peninsula. Although nothing is known of Tetsugai, an annotation states that he accompanied Hakuin on some of his early Zen pilgrimages.

(1732), Mr. Yoda sighed to himself, "Mr. Ōishi passed away before a complete set of the Buddhist scriptures could be collected. I'm going to carry on his splendid project and bring to completion."

As the head of one of the wealthiest families in southern Izu, Takanaga lived in affluent circumstances. By donating a small fraction of his wealth, a complete set of sutras and commentaries was soon procured and the construction of the sutra repository completed as well. In order to maintain the gift, he also donated some rich rice fields with a yield of several *koku*. The Buddha said, "There are twenty things of great difficulty for human beings. [One of them is] for a man of great wealth and position to develop an aspiration for the Way."* It would seem that Takanaga is someone who has been exempted from this prophecy from the golden mouth of the Buddha himself! It is a rare occurrence and one of truly incalculable worth!

Sōzaemon Mitsuyu, a farmer in neighboring Michibu village, was inspired by the benevolence and generosity of these two men to donate a statue of the deity Benzaiten carved by Prince Shōtoku for enshrinement in the sutra repository. Extraordinary! Benzaiten is one of many forms assumed by the Bodhisattva Kannon, who includes among his infinite manifestations the celebrated laymen Fu Ta-shih and Vimalakirti. Such a deity is to be deeply venerated.†

On the day long ago when the great teacher Fu Ta-shih conceived the idea of the revolving sutra repository, he is said to have pledged: "It is my deepest wish that all those who enter this hall will be reborn in the human realm for many future lives and arouse the Bodhi-mind, and that all those who come and turn this repository one revolution will derive exactly the same merit they would receive from reciting and holding in mind all the sutras and commentaries."

How can one doubt, in view of this, that the men whose donations made the construction of this repository possible, as well as the clerics and laity who engaged in the actual work, will all be blessed with good fortune in their future existence? Eidō Oshō, the abbot of Kiichi-ji,‡ sent a letter to Shōin-ji asking me to compose an inscription that would set forth this series of events.

---

*From the *Sutra of Forty-two Sections*.
†Benzaiten (Sanskrit, Sarasvati). A goddess of music and wisdom, possessed of perfect and unbounded eloquence that helps her spread the Buddhist teachings.
‡Eidō Eibō (d. 1778).

So intense was my joy on hearing the wonderful news about the sutra repository that I set to work, without even considering my limitations. I composed this inscription, though I was only able to cover a mere tenth or so of what actually occurred. In addition to the matters requested by Eidō Oshō, I have included several stories of my own as well, which I committed to paper in hopes that good and right-minded people might read them.

One of them took place in the Tenna period (1681–84). It about a mendicant monk of Settsu province who wandered from village to village to assemble donations for a great collection of the Buddhist sutras. One night a white horse appeared to him in a dream. It was weeping. "Please, priest," it said, "have compassion on me and add me to your list of donors." The monk laughed and said, "You seem to be covered all over with hair. I don't suppose you'd have even a scrap of paper to your name. What on earth could you donate to me?" The horse replied, "I usually travel twice daily between Nose and Ikeda. I'll make the trip three times a day, and donate the proceeds of the extra trip to you." The owner of the horse saw the same dream, and immediately began looking for the monk. When he finally found him, the two men grabbed hands with tears in their eyes. The man ended up giving the horse to the monk as a donation.*

There is another other story about a young wife who lived long ago in Wakasa province. While visiting one of the ancient temples in the area she entered the sutra repository and turned the revolving sutra case one revolution, repeating as she did the posthumous name of her deceased mother. She fell into a trance, in which she saw a heavenly being riding through the sky on a five-colored cloud surrounded by blinding purple light and casting an exquisite fragrance over the fields below. The woman cowered in fear, her hands pressed together in *gasshō*. "How wonderful that an ordinary countrywoman like me should be allowed to worship such a being," she marveled. Addressing her, the being said, "Don't you recognize me? I am your mother. Thanks to the merit you just gained by reciting my name with singleness of mind when you revolved the sutra repository, I have in spite my of unworthiness attained rebirth in the Heaven of the Thirty-three Gods. I only regret that I was unable to be reborn into the Tushita

---

*The monk is Tetsugen Dōkō (1630–1682) of the Ōbaku school, who traveled around the country collecting donations to finance the printing of the first complete woodblock edition of the Chinese Buddhist canon in Japan. Known as the "Tetsugen edition," it was finally completed in 1678. The story is found in Gettan Dōchō's *Gasan-kō* (1698).

Heaven and join the assembly of the Compassionate One, Maitreya Buddha. During my life on earth I kept twenty pieces of gold hidden beneath the pillar at the northeast corner of your room. I want you to use that money to have the broken tiles on the roof of the sutra repository repaired. If you do, I will surely be reborn in the Tushita Heaven."*

When Zen master Yueh-t'ang Shao was abbot at Mount A-yu-wang, a group of bandits broke into the temple to steal the Buddha-relics.† While all the monks dispersed in terror, Yueh-t'ang grabbed the Buddha-relics and fled into the mountains behind the temple. He dug a deep hole and hid himself inside it, clutching the relics to his bosom. The bandits searched high and low for the relics, and failing to find them became incensed and decided to burn down the main gate. When they began to set fire to it, however, the sutra repository suddenly began to revolve with a heavy thundering sound, causing the badly frightened bandits to flee. Ahh! Sutra repositories are always surrounded by wise and sacred beings, and they are under the protection of the king of the Naga gods. That is why a miracle like this occurred. It is a truly admirable story.

A woman once sent the priest Chao-chou some money and asked him to revolve the sutra repository for her. After receiving the donation, Chao-chou rose from his Zen chair and made one circumambulation of it. When the woman learned of it, she said, "I asked you to turn the repository one revolution. What do mean by turning it only halfway?"‡

Let me [Hakuin] ask you: "What is the complete turning of the sutra repository? If your discernment can fully penetrate this, you have achieved the great matter, you have bored through all the six roots and six dusts. If, on the other hand, you are still unsure about the black and the white, come here to the temple and give the sutra repository a turn."

With this, I joyfully performed *gasshō* and said:

---

*The Heaven of the Thirty-three Gods (Sk. *Trayastrimsha*). One of the heavens in the realm of desire, located atop Mount Sumeru. According to the *Lotus Sutra*, rebirth in this heaven is possible to whose who perform good works, such as transcribing sutras. The Tushita Heaven, the fourth of the six heavens in the realm of desire, is the dwelling place of Maitreya Bodhisattva, the future Buddha. According to the *Flower Garland Sutra* (*Maitreya*, ch. 19), rebirth there is possible to those who receive Shakamuni's teachings and strive to attain enlightenment.
†Yueh-t'ang Tao-shao (n.d.). This story appears in *Chronicles of the Buddha-patriarchs*, ch. 47.
‡*Compendium of the Five Lamps*, ch. 4.

I pledge to turn the merit of such virtue as I attain to keeping the country at peace, the people happy and prosperous, its temples pure and good, and its temple patrons prosperous and healthy; I pledge together with all suffering sentient beings throughout the universe to realize the supreme Buddha Way and the wheel of the true Dharma.

All Buddhas and all Bodhisattvas in the three worlds and throughout the ten directions, *Maha Prajna Paramita.*

:69. Record of the Founding of Muryōjuzen-ji

This is the first of two pieces on Muryōjuzen-ji (usually referred to by the shortened form Muryō-ji), the small temple in Hina village six miles west of the Hara post station that Hakuin reestablished in his sixties. Muryō-ji, together with Shōin-ji, where Hakuin resided as head priest, and Ryūtaku-ji, the large practice temple he founded in Mishima in his final years, is one of three temples most closely associated with his religious career. It was to graves erected in these temples that Hakuin's ashes were divided and interred after his death. The story of Hakuin's determined attempts to convince his student Tōrei to become the first head priest when Muryō-ji was rebuilt, told in the correspondence that passed between the two men at the time, can be found in Beating the Cloth Drum, *pp. 142–177. The local historian Akiyama Kanji's research on Hakuin and his relation to Muryō-ji is found in* Buddhist Monk Hakuin *(pp. 184–206).*

THIS TEMPLE HAS BEEN given the name Ummon, or "Cloud Gate." It is located near the miraculous spot where Kaguya-hime, "the moon princess," was born and raised, and where the old bamboo cutter lived who appears in the tale of the princess. The temple, whose mountain name is Shinkō, is sacred to Sengen, the great Bodhisattva of Mount Fuji. Built on the site of an old temple of the same name, Muryō-ji is situated in a most beautiful natural setting, and people throughout the country regard it as a sacred place.

Long ago in the time of Emperor Keikō (71–130), an old bamboo cutter saw a strange light glowing every night from a stalk of bamboo. When he cut the bamboo, he discovered an infant girl inside. He and his wife were overjoyed and raised the girl as their own daughter. She had a natural beauty, with skin that seemed to glow with radiance. She grew into a beautiful young woman, bewitching all who saw her. An endless procession of suitors arrived to seek her hand. Officials of high rank came, saying they would give their lives to obtain the priceless pearl beneath the jaws of the dragon. Princes came, saying they were eager to attain the fabulous nine-holed shell found high in the cliff swallow's perilous hillside nest. Her reputation eventually reached the ears of the emperor. He dispatched an emissary from the capital to pay her a visit. The emissary approached the house in wonderment and disbelief, discovering an ethereal light surrounding it and a divine fragrance emanating from the young girl's room. When he returned to Kyoto and reported this, the emperor made the long and difficult trip to Suruga to see her. Hearing of his coming, the parents were afraid. They took the princess with them and hid inside a stone cave north of their home. They burned cottonseed and gizzard shad to make it seem as if a cremation had been performed. When the emperor smelled the smoke, he believed the young girl had died, and was beside himself with grief. Not long after that, the girl disappeared into the rocky grottoes beneath Mount Fuji and was never seen again. Local people regarded her as an incarnation of Sengen Bodhisattva. The girl's father was fond of hawking. She herself had a pet white dog. His favorite hawk and the dog are now enshrined as gods in the Ashitaka and Kushi Shrines on the slopes of Mount Fuji. This story has been passed down from ancient times.

A small, white stone stupa was recently unearthed in the area. It revealed that a temple named Muryōju-ji had formerly existed at the site. Surely the discovery was due to the secret working of Sengen Bodhisattva. We call the new temple we have built at this spot Muryōju Ummon-an. Although my disciples and I belong to the Rinzai lineage of National Master Daitō, our strength, sad to say, is meager when compared with the vast scope of Daitō's vow and aspiration. Although the time to revive the traditions of this great Zen master is now at hand, the vigor with which we pursue this effort is also unfortunately inadequate.

At the beginning of the Genroku era (1688–1704), at this site in Hina village the elderly priest Dokuon Genri restored Ummon-an, and at the end of the Enkyō era (1744–48), Master Kairyū gathered donations and made three attempts to reconstruct the temple. [After Dokuon's death,] Layman Ishii Gentoku of Hina village was entrusted with the funds and began laying plans to bring Dokuon's plan to fruition. Before his death, Layman Ishii entrusted the project to his friends and fellow laymen, Mr.

Furugōri and Mr. Sugisawa. They have succeeded admirably in carrying it through to completion.

Today, on the eighth of the fourth month, the second year of Hōreki (1752), the rebuilding of the Ummon-an hermitage has finally been completed. It has been furnished with a well, a kitchen, and all the proper temple fittings. The new head priest of Ummon-an [Tōrei] has been placed in charge of the opening ceremony. I herewith place my palms together in *gasshō*, and say:

> It is my fervent prayer that the foundation of imperial rule may grow ever stronger, the sun of Buddhism may shine ever more brightly, and this temple may be protected against fire and calamities of every kind. I also pray that in the future all those who reside in this temple will whip forward with steadfast determination the great wheel of the Bodhisattva Vow, and while sporting on their sleeves the sacred amulet that divests people of their lives and polishing the keen claws and fangs of the Dharma cave will strive to lead sentient beings to deliverance. As we gather here to celebrate the completion of this new temple, do you know the person we can count on to assure that this is carried out? He is none other than the new head priest, Tōrei Enji Anju.

. . . .

Hakuin devotes the first half of this account to the *Taketori Monogatari, The Tale of the Bamboo Cutter,* a well-known fairy tale that according to local legend took place near the Muryō-ji site. *Taketori Monogatari* is one of the oldest extant Japanese narrative tales, dating from the tenth century and perhaps earlier. The most commonly told version of the story is quite different from the one Hakuin relates here, which may represent an early, oral form of the tale. In the more widely known version, an old bamboo cutter sees a strange light glowing from a stalk of bamboo, cuts the bamboo open, and discovers a tiny infant girl the size of a thumb inside it. He and his wife raise the girl as their own, naming her Kaguya-hime, Princess Kaguya. Thereafter, whenever the old bamboo cutter cuts down a bamboo, he finds a nugget of gold inside, and the family becomes wealthy. The infant grows into a young girl of ordinary size and extraordinary beauty. Five princes come seeking her hand in marriage, and the old bamboocutter persuades his daughter to accept one of them for her husband. She asks the princes to bring various articles, promising to marry the first one who does. All the articles, however, are things impossible to obtain, so none of the men are successful. The girl's reputation reaches the ears of the emperor, who travels to Suruga, falls in love with her, and asks her to marry him. She rejects the offer, saying that she has come from another country, far away. Finally she reveals to her foster parents that she has come from the moon, and must now return. A heavenly entourage appears and she is conveyed back to the capital of the moon. The emperor, saddened to lose her, learns that Mount Fuji is the place closest to heaven and has his soldiers carry a letter for the princess up to the summit and burn in hopes it will reach her. The men are also ordered to burn an elixir of immortality (*fushi*), which becomes the name of the mountain. It is said that the Japanese characters for the mountain, "mountain abounding with warriors," derive from the sight of the Emperor's men ascending the slopes to carry out his orders, and the smoke that issues to this day from the summit of Mount Fuji comes from the burning letter and elixir.

:70. Record of the Relics at Muryōjuzen-ji

The second of two pieces on Muryō-ji (see #69) is an account of Buddha relics that were donated to the temple. Hakuin dwells briefly on the history of such relics and lavishes praise on his lay student Yotsugi Masayuki for his generosity in offering them. According to the entry in the Chronological Biography *for 1752 (when Hakuin was sixty-seven, the same year this account was written), "In winter, to celebrate the completion of the Muryō-ji, Layman Chikan (Yotsugi Masayuki) gave Tōrei seven Buddha relics for enshrinement in the temple and requested that Hakuin deliver lectures there on the* Sutra of the Bequeathed Teaching." *The entry for the following year has, "Hakuin went in the spring to view the relics that had been enshrined at Muryō-ji"* (Precious Mirror Cave, pp. 220–21). *Tōrei wrote two accounts of the relics, and the Confucian teacher Yanada Zeigan, a friend of both Hakuin and Yotsugi, also wrote one. The ones by Tōrei, which are still in manuscript, supply additional particulars concerning his friend Yotsugi's gift.*

Yotsugi Masayuki (n.d.), who also went by the sobriquet Gifu-ya (after the name of his establishment), was a wealthy Kyoto merchant who lived at the corner of Sanjō and Takakura streets near the heart of the city. He was an ardent Zen student from his youth, and gave donations on numerous occasions to help Hakuin carry out building and publishing projects. Yotsugi hailed from the same small village in Ōmi province as Tōrei, whom he helped during his early years of training by lending him hermitages in the eastern hills of Kyoto for his solitary retreats. After being introduced to Hakuin by Tōrei, Yotsugi became a devoted student of the master. His name appears in the letters of Hakuin's final decades.

"Relics" (Skt. sharira*) are tiny, gemlike fragments that are found among the ashes of people possessed of exceptional spiritual attainment after their cremation. Enshrined in stupas and beautifully fashioned reliquaries, these relics were greatly prized and worshipped as objects of great sanctity and believed to possess miraculous powers. Although Hakuin's* Account of the Relics at Muryōjuzen-ji *is in keeping with the veneration Buddhist followers generally show towards such relics, in another work he demonstrated a more typically Zen perspective: "A monk who was studying under Zen master Yun-chu refused a pair of trousers the master had sent to him, saying, 'I already have the ones I was born with,' but when Yun-chu asked him, 'What did you wear prior to your birth?' the monk was unable to answer. Later, when the monk died and his body was cremated, relics were found among his ashes. When these were shown to Yun-chu, he said, 'I'd much rather have had one phrase from him in response to the question I asked when he was alive than ten bushels of relics from a dead man"* (Essential Teachings, p. 77).

It should also be mentioned that when Hakuin's own body was cremated, a great many relics were found among the ashes. "They resembled particles of sand or tiny pebbles, and were the color of precious blue gems. The true fruits of the master's meditation and wisdom...they were divided into three lots and interred in stupas erected at the master's three temples, Shōin-ji, Muryō-ji, and Ryūtaku-ji" (Chronological Biography, Precious Mirror Cave, p. 234).

YOTSUGI MASAYUKI, WHO LIVES at Takakura in Kyoto, is a man of natural grace and courtesy. He possesses firm resolve and fine aspiration. He has devoted himself to Zen study, displaying both courage and keen discernment, and has taken pleasure in putting the Bodhisattva Way into practice. He devoted himself with great perseverance over a period of many years to assembling a collection of genuine relics of Shakamuni

Buddha, which had been preserved over the centuries at seven different sites in our country. In winter of this year, the second of Hōreki (1752), he took particles from each of these relics and donated them to Ummon-zan Muryōzen-ji. They will guard and protect the temple long into the future. Nothing could give this old priest any greater pleasure.

Now, five days after the winter solstice, I came to the temple and opened the doors of the reliquary that houses the relics. Clerics and lay people assembled from far and near, gazing at them and making bows of veneration. For three days I conducted a lecture meeting on the *Sutra of the Bequeathed Teaching*. I read out a verse to open the meeting:

> Seven tiny crystal beads, the true relics of the Buddha's body,
> Their quiet radiance illuminating and benefiting sentient beings,
> Now are safely enshrined upon the summit of Mount Ummon,
> Guarded over, and jealously preserved, by five temple gods.

Relics of the Buddha's adamantine Dharma-body have the power to permeate all realms of existence, a radiance that can swallow up the causes and conditions of karmic existence. Long ago, when Shakamuni entered Nirvana under the Sala tree, his Dharma heir, the Venerable Mahakashapa, obtained from his breast the wonderfully auspicious swastika that is deemed to be the Buddha's mind seal. On the day Buddha relics first entered our own country, the great *kami* Amaterasu personally entrusted them to a shrine maiden, declaring, "I myself will always pay reverence to them." The auspicious light that hovers constantly over Kongōshō-ji at the Ise Shrine and the perpetual sacred mist that forever envelops Cockleg Mountain in India are emanations from the sacred relics preserved at those sites.

Once when a fleet-footed demon stole and ran off with one of the Buddha's teeth, the guardian deity Idaten crossed the heavens with great speed and recovered it. When Mongol troops broke down the gates of Mount T'ien-t'ung to steal the Buddha relics in the monastery, Priest Yueh-t'ang saved them by digging a hole in the cliff behind the temple and crawling inside with the relics clutched to his breast. These events show that even barbarians from far-off foreign lands know that the Buddha's relics are more precious than a bright torch on a moonless night road; that even gods and outlandish demons regard them with the reverence and gratitude they would feel for a seaworthy ship in a perilous ocean storm.

Long ago in India, King Ashoka divided the Buddha's relics into eight lots, and further parceled them into smaller fragments, which he had interred in eighty-four-thousand stupas erected throughout the country. In China, Emperor Yang of the Sui dynasty in China constructed thirty-six Buddhist temples, placing a relic stupa in each one, and entrusted their protection to the gods and demon hosts.

In our own land, Prince Shōtoku, a reincarnation of the great Chinese priest Nan-yueh Hui-ssu, also venerated relics of the Buddha. Shōgun Minamoto Sanetomo dispatched Adachi Morinaga to Sung China to obtain Buddha relics, and though the relics Morinaga procured were almost taken from him at the court of the Chinese emperor, he eventually succeeded in returning with them safely to Japan.

In such ways as these, fragments of the Buddha's relics have come to be enshrined at seven different locations in Japan. Pieces taken from them have now been donated to Muryō-ji, where their radiance will forever illuminate the surrounding mountains and valleys. Truly they are a treasure beyond price! Painted on the reliquary that holds the relics are images of the Four Heavenly Kings who guard the Dharma. Because of this gracious gift, our tiny temple has become one of most noted Buddhist establishments in the eastern provinces. It has all been made possible thanks to the devotion and benevolence of Layman Yotsugi Masayuki of Kyoto.

. . . .

Guarded...by five temple gods. Statues of the gods of the Asama, Ashitaka, Inukai, Akiba, and Kitano Shintō shrines, enshrined at Muryō-ji.

The swastika, formed of spiraled hair on the Buddha's breast, is among the auspicious attributes possessed by a Buddha, said to symbolize the mind seal that is the mark of enlightenment.

Amaterasu ōmikami, important Shintō deity of the Ise Shrine, is portrayed as entrusting Buddha relics to the shrine in the *Genkō Shakusho,* without, however, mentioning the words attributed to him here.

Kongōshō-ji, a Rinzai temple on Mount Asama to the northeast of the Ise Shrine; it has a well-known relic pagoda.

Cockleg Hill. The Buddha's Dharma heir Mahakashapa went to Cockleg Hill in India at the end of his life hoping to transmit the golden robe he had received from the Buddha signifying the Dharma transmission to Maitreya, the Buddha of the Future.

Fleet-footed demon (shōshitsu-ki). Story from the *Nirvana Sutra.*

Yueh-t'ang Tao-shao. The story appeared before, p. 173.

Nan-yueh Hui-ssu (515–577). A Chinese T'ien-t'ai priest whose incarnation in Japan as Prince Shōtoku (572–622) is found in the *Records of Seven Generations (Shichidaiki).*

Adachi Morinaga (1135–1200). Follower of Minamoto Sanetomo. A portion of the Buddha's tooth Adachi is said to have obtained in China was enshrined at Daiji-ji in Kamakura.

:71. AN HONORABLE MAN AT THE ABE RIVER CROSSING

This story, still told in the Suruga area, concerns an incident that took place at one of the dangerous river crossings on the Tōkaidō not far from Hakuin's temple. In 1929, Furukawa Taikō Rōshi, then head priest at Seiken-ji, a large and important Zen temple near Shizuoka, had a commemorative stele describing the incident erected at the site. From it, we learn that the honorable man's name was Yoshibei.

Hakuin wrote this piece in 1738, his fifty-third year, not long after the event. The German physician Kaempfer, who made two trips from Nagasaki to Edo and back, left an informative firsthand description of the circumstances at these river fords some forty years earlier.

Several of the rivers we cross over, chiefly upon Tookaido, run with so impetuous a rapidity towards the sea that they will bear no bridge nor boat, and this by reason partly of the neighboring snow mountains, where they arise, partly of the frequent great rains, which will swell them to such a degree as to make them overflow their banks. These must be forded thro' in shallow places. Men, horses, and baggage are deliver'd up to the care of certain people, bred up to this business, who are well acquainted with the bed of the river, and the places which are the most proper for fording. These people, as they are made answerable for their passengers' lives, and all accidents that might befall them in the passage, exert all their strength, care, and dexterity to support them with their arms against the impetuosity of the river, and the stones rolling down from the mountains where the rivers arise. Norimons [palanquins] are carried over by the same people upon their arms.

(*History of Japan*, Vol. II, pp. 294–5. Glasgow: MacLehose and Sons, 1906).

The cheapest way of crossing the river was by riding piggyback on one of the porters' shoulders; at high water a pair of carriers were required. People of means could make crossings in litters or palanquins, four porters for a single passenger, six for two.

This piece, showing Hakuin celebrating good character with reference only to the Chinese classics, without any explicit connection to Zen, also manifests the respect he felt for people of low social rank, whom he holds up implicitly as models of conduct for his own followers and for those of high status.

Poison Blossoms (#94) contains a preface Hakuin wrote for a roster of donors for a project he had initiated to build a bridge over a difficult river crossing in Tōtōmi province.

I N THE THIRD YEAR of the Gembun era (1738) autumn rains continuing for days on end raised river levels throughout Suruga province. Officials closed the river crossings, and travelers on the Tōkaidō, people of all social ranks, were greatly inconvenienced. Some were stranded for five days, some even for ten. At the Abe River, about a league west of the town of Sumpu [present day Shizuoka], several thousand people who had been waiting for the water to subside were busily struggling to make their way across the river now that daybreak had arrived. Some were sitting astride the neck of one of the hardy river porters, hanging on for dear life to their sturdy arms. All were having a difficult time negotiating the still swiftly flowing water. Old and young were crying out to one another; rich and poor were floundering side by side in the rapids.

One man, with a threadbare old pouch hanging from his waist and the look of someone who had fallen on hard times, was bargaining with a porter for a reduced fee. Suddenly, with a show of anger he unfastened the pouch from his waist and took off his kimono. He bundled them up together, putting them on top of his head, and waded into the river, obviously intending to ford it on his own. Once or twice in the midst of the treacherous stream he slipped and nearly fell and was almost swept away, but finally succeeded in reaching the western bank.

Soon after that, as the porter was returning to the place where they had argued over the fee, he spied in a hollow place on the riverbank a leather bag filled with what seemed to be four or five strings of coins.* On picking it up, he found it was surprisingly heavy. When he looked inside, he found

---

*Literally, "five strings of hundred-*mon* coins." Four strings equaled one *ryō*.

it was filled with large gold coins. He thought, "That fellow who just went across must have dropped it. He grudged me a mere five *mon* carrying fee, and then put his life at risk by crossing on his own. If it belongs to him, he'll be out of his mind when he discovers it is missing. The poor fellow might even keel over and die right there on the roadside."

He immediately crossed the river again and began hurrying after the man. When he had gone several leagues, reaching the bottom of Utsunoya Pass, he caught up with him. The man was naked to the waist, his right hand grasping a walking staff, hurrying precipitately down from the pass on the stone steps set in the mountainside. He was weeping miserably.

The porter said, "Aren't you the person who made the crossing this morning on your own?"

"Yes," he replied.

"Why are you going back?"

"I dropped something," the man replied, "and I'm in a hurry." He turned to run off.

Grabbing the man's robe to stop him, the porter said, "Just what I thought. What did you lose? Describe it to me. If it's what I think it is, I'll return it to you."

"I lost a bag of coins," he said.

"What was inside it?"

"One hundred and fifty *ryō* in one *ryō* gold coins. Fifty *ryō* were wrapped in a piece of yellow-bordered green silk—about a foot square. The other hundred *ryō* were in another, smaller bag; it was tied with a yellow cord. There were also seven or eight letters I'd received from home."

"You needn't worry any longer. I found the pouch," said the porter. "I brought it to return to you." He produced the pouch and handed it to the man. The man took it with tears cascading down his cheeks, raising it above his head in thanks.

"Even when you lose something inside your own home, it's difficult to find it," the man said. "But here on the Tōkaidō, with its heavy traffic? Men and horses coming and going all day long? No matter how quickly I could have returned to the spot and looked for the pouch, there wasn't much chance I'd ever see it again. Yet I couldn't just forget about it. If I hadn't found it back at the river, I would have had no choice but to drown myself. I couldn't have faced my wife and children after something like that. So while I was determined to return and look for it, I had no idea I'd encounter a person of your upright character who would return the money to me. You've not only given my money back to me but my life itself. You've saved my life. Please accept half of the money in the pouch. It can't repay even a tenth of the kindness you've shown me."

"I can't accept any money," said the porter. "If I had wanted your money, why would I have run after you? Now I must get back to the ford. I have a job to do carrying people across the river. I have a wife and children to support. Please continue on your journey, sir."

As the porter started to leave, the man grabbed his hand and, with tears rolling down his cheeks, said, "Please listen to my story. I am a poor man from Kii province. I left home to work the fishing nets in Awa province. The money in that pouch represents the wages that I and thirty of my fellow workers earned through hard work. They entrusted their money to me to take back to their families in Kii province. The fifty *ryō* wrapped in yellow silk belongs to our master in Awa. He asked me to take it to Kii for him as well. He is a splendid person, quite well off too, so if I explained to him what happened, I am sure he would understand. Please accept the fifty *ryō*. It would make me feel much easier. I must also ask you your name. To help repay the debt of gratitude we owe you, my wife and children will surely want to chant your name mornings and evenings as a mantra of gratitude."

"If I agreed to accept the money," the porter replied, "how could I ever have an easy conscience? If I act against what I feel to be right, my heart would never feel at ease—it is not made of stone. I am a poor, half-starved river porter. I work at the Tōkaidō river crossing and I live in an impoverished village. I'm not the kind of person who announces his name when he meets people. I have a father approaching seventy, a wife who is now over thirty years old, and a four-year-old son. I rent out my shoulders to people who need to ford the river. It is very hard, working at full tilt from morning till night without a moment's rest. I can't be sure from day to day that my family will have enough to eat. Yet I have borne the cold and hunger, and I believe that I have lived an honest life. If it meant I must starve by the roadside, I would never accept money from a traveler that I wasn't entitled to. Any food that I bought with it would only defile my wife and children. Not to mention the heavenly gods, who see everything as clearly as a fruit held in the palm of their hands. They would surely not let such a transgression go unpunished. It is your money. All I did was glimpse it. If people had to give part of their money to others just because they happened to see it, wouldn't they have to parcel out their fields and gardens, villages, mountains, forests and trees, to others as well?" Without another word, he departed.

The man, his eyes still filled with tears, immediately set out after the porter. Recrossing the Abe River, he proceeded to the castle town on the other side and located the porter's dwelling. Entering the door, he saw the old father, sitting under a window that had been rudely cut in one of the walls. He was plaiting straw sandals, working with his legs stretched straight out and straw cords hooked between his toes. A woman was seated beside a stove, sewing some tattered garments. Placing his hands before him on the ground, the man prostrated himself, then explained what had taken place and begged them to accept a reward. The old father, after a giving him a brief glance, returned to his sandal making, which he seemed to enjoy immensely. It was as though they hadn't even heard what he said. The woman got up and with a knitted brow took the man's hands and pushed him out the front door.

The man stood in front of the door weeping pitifully. Neighbors and passersby had tears in their eyes as well. Finally, he left and went to the local magistrate's office to tell his story. The magistrate summoned the old man and the wife. To soothe their feelings, he said, "People such as you are indeed praiseworthy. Like subjects of the Emperors Yao and Shun.* If everyone was like you, the world would be a perfect place."

To the traveler, the magistrate said, "You may leave now. Go and tell your comrades that everything will be taken care of satisfactorily." He produced five *ryō* that he said would be used to reward the porter.

Ahh! When I heard this story, I thought of the saying: "Until a person is confronted with great difficulty, you cannot discern his true mettle; until he is confronted with great wealth, you cannot know if his heart is true and just."† How true it is!

:72. A STARVING MAN AT THE BUN SHOP

Hakuin's Chronological Biography *tells us that "In the winter of 1744, his fifty-ninth year, while the master was visiting Jishō-ji in Kai province, donations were gathered and a printing was made of*

---

*Two legendary emperors of ancient China known for their moral uprightness and wisdom, and as rulers of an ideal society.
†Based on a saying from the *Book of Rites*: "Confronting wealth, [the sage] does not attempt to acquire it. Confronting a calamity, he does not attempt to avoid it" (*Li Chi*, I. 1–4).

the Heart Sutra *using movable type. On the way home he lectured at Rinsen-an in Shimizu on* Ch'uan-lao's Comments on the Diamond Sutra. *Since the hall was extremely small, with room for only six students, it was not possible for a large number of people to participate. During the meeting the master taught using the story of a man at a tea shop"* (Precious Mirror Cave, p. 209).

In some brief Words of Instruction to the Assembly that Hakuin delivered at the meeting (Poison Blossoms Book 1; *untranslated*), *he states that "several tens" of people had been accepted for the meeting and that over a hundred people actually attended, so that a temporary shed-like building had to be constructed to accommodate them all. He also points out Rinsen-an's connection with the well-known Sōtō teacher Suzuki Shōsan (1579–1655). Shōsan's memorial stupa was erected at Rinsen-an, and the head priest Ekyū (n.d.), who was a student of Hakuin, was in the fourth generation of Shōsan's lineage.*

I N WINTER OF THE first year of Enkyō (1744), as I was returning from a trip to northern Izu, several priests and former students of mine who had been lying in wait for me among the shady bowers of Rinsen-an in Nagasawa, suddenly attacked from ambush. They had secretly hatched a plan to have me deliver Zen lectures at the temple. Quietly ensconced at Akiyama Kokan's residence in Yasuhisa village at the time,[*] I was not interested in embarking on any Dharma engagements.

Head priest Ekyū led the first assault, surrounded by a cohort of green troops waving Dharma banners and urging me to accede to the request. I held firm against them. A second wave, led by Layman Kōrin, including foot soldiers of all ages, young and old, stormed in, pressing me to comply. I valiantly fought them off. Deeming their numbers insufficient, they called in reinforcements. Jun and Ka came in the vanguard, forces under Yu and Kan took up the rear, and they ultimately succeeded in overwhelming Rinsen. Kyū was in the main party, supported by Tetsu and Chō, with Ji and Rin held in reserve. Outside, troopers Chū, Yaku, Betsu, Daku, Rin, and Ki awaited yet another group advancing from the north.

---

[*]Akiyama Kokan is Akiyama Yohei Michitomo, a wealthy farmer and landowner of Yasuhisa village in northern Izu (now incorporated into the city of Numazu), who appears several times in *Poison Blossoms*, most prominently in the long inscription Hakuin wrote awarding him the name Ittsui (below #77).

Finally, totally surrounded, unable to advance or retreat, no further resistance possible, I surrendered and was taken by Layman Kōrin.*

The layman carried me off to his country retreat. A sumptuous banquet of the choicest delicacies was set before me. I was accorded the greatest courtesy, as though I was a guest of the highest rank. They then produced a copy of *Ch'uan-lao's Comments on the Diamond Sutra* and asked me to deliver some comments on it.† I declined. "A vanquished general does not talk of war,"‡ I said. But they refused to listen to my objections. My fate was sealed. I was finally forced to deliver my confession.§

During the meeting a man came forward, greeted me, and said, "Priests and laity who came from far and near to hear these talks must feel like a farmer who has been blessed by a heavy rainfall after a long and severe drought. However I am unable to openly take part in the meeting as I would like to. Some of my unworthy acquaintances would surely criticize me if I did. To avoid their censure, I decided to participate in secret."¶

"I understand your position," I replied. "Whatever one does, it is important it be done prudently, with due consideration to the circumstances involved as well as to the consequences.

"Just yesterday a fellow walked into the village from the east. He had the despondent look of a man who had fallen on very hard times. His wildly disheveled hair was like a lump of mugwort that had been blown around by the wind, his haggard brown face like a cabbage leaf withered by the frost. A tattered old robe clung to his skeletal frame, leaving his thighs and elbows exposed and making him look like a molting quail. His sedge hat was so broken it didn't even cover his ears. And yet hanging from his shoulder was a pouch that from the looks of it contained several strings of coins.

"Taking off his hat, and loosening the string on his money pouch, he

---

*Hakuin refers to these senior monks by the shortened names he used for the men in his assembly. Those about which something is known are: Jun, Enkei Sojun, age twenty-nine at the time; Ka, Tōrei Enji, twenty-three; Tetsu, Kaigan Kotetsu (n.d.); Chō, Bunchō (n.d.); Yaku, Donsen Gen'yaku (n.d.): and Daku, Sōkei Ichidaku (n.d.). Layman Kōrin cannot be identified.

†*Ch'uan-lao's Comments on the Diamond Sutra*, containing Zen comments in prose and verse by the Sung dynasty priest Ch'uan-lao Chih-fu (n.d.). Hakuin lectured on this work a number of times.

‡*Shih-chi*, ch. 92.

§That is, the lectures on *Ch'uan-lao's Comments*.

¶"Perhaps this man was a follower of Nichiren Buddhism" (annotation). Followers of Nichiren had a reputation for hostility toward other Buddhist traditions.

declared to the young girl at the teahouse, 'I'll have twenty or thirty of your best fried buns.' Although wary of the beggarly looking stranger, she was reassured by the plump money pouch he held in his hand, and she put twenty or so of the five *mon* buns on a tray and handed them to the man. He grabbed them and immediately wolfed them down. Looking as though he wanted still more, he suddenly fastened his money pouch and lit out like a rabbit escaping from its pen.

"The girl ran after him, yelling, 'Cheat! Thief! He ran off without paying!' Several men happened to be nearby and joined in the chase. They soon caught up with the man, surrounded him, and began pressing him for the money. He refused to part with the battered old pouch, but they finally forced it from his grasp. When they opened the pouch, they found that it was filled with pebbles. Enraged, they began reviling the man and beating him mercilessly. It was as if a hungry ghost had chanced upon a scrap of food and had suddenly tumbled back into hell.*

"Weeping, the man raised himself up and placed both hands on the ground before him in a deep bow. 'Please, I beg you,' he said, 'stop beating me for a moment and hear me out. It is said that when cornered or pressed to extreme, birds will peck at you, beasts will grab for you, and men will tell you lies.† Having experienced such extremity, I know how true that is!

"'Despite my appearance, I am the son of a wealthy Kyoto family. I never learned the proper way to conduct myself, did not accept advice from my elders or my brothers, and spent all my time in the pleasure quarters, drinking and indulging my sexual appetites. I regarded my parents as deadly enemies, my relations as menial servants. I used money as though it was water; fine silken garments were of no more consequence to me than mud or sand.

"'I brought the large and splendid family business to the brink of collapse. My parents, no longer able to deal with me, went to the magistrate's office and officially disowned me. People say that the universe is boundless. I now found myself alone in that boundlessness, with no place I could go for shelter. How many times during that period I contemplated suicide. A sharp sword. Drowning. But life is not so easily cast away, death not so

---

*The realm of hungry ghosts (*preta*), whose beings are condemned to constant, unappeasable hunger and thirst, is the second lowest of the ten realms of living beings, the lowest being hell.
† *Hsun Tzu.*

readily embraced. Swallowing my pride, I resolved to travel to Edo and brazenly throw myself on the mercy of an acquaintance I had there.

"'I set out for the city, a hundred leagues distant, without a coin in my pocket. On the way, sleeping in the open, I experienced in full measure the severity of the elements. So painful did I find it to contemplate my present situation that I thought my heart would rend into pieces. And, as it turned out, the man I had counted on for help knew all about my past behavior and refused to have anything to do with me. He didn't even offer me a lukewarm cup of tea. It was the same wherever I turned.

"'Having reached the end of my tether, there was nothing I could do but head back to Kyoto. Again I suffered greatly from hunger and cold, dying nine times over, feeling as though I shouldered the misfortunes of Confucius's men in Ch'en and the privations of Po I and Shu Ch'i all in one.[*] For three days I had nothing to eat, and could barely keep from tumbling over and falling to my death in the valley below. Without the slightest idea how to save myself, I made up my mind after some deep soul-searching that my living or dying would be decided at that roadside teashop. If I ate without paying, I would be severely beaten. If I didn't eat something, I would surely die of starvation. Rather than perish unbeaten, I resolved to extend my life by enduring the punishment.

"'That is my story. Who could have imagined things would end up this way? A twenty-four-year-old man, flesh and blood, the son of a father and mother, destined to be beaten severely, flogged to death for his crimes, and not even the most benevolent person would raise a finger to help. I was rejected by everyone I counted on, turned away everywhere I sought support. When you think about it, my life was given cheaply. Only thirty fried buns!'"

"When the man finished speaking, he fell back to the ground weeping. The villagers who had gathered around him had tears in their eyes as well. Scratching their heads, they turned away and left him lying in the dust." That young man endured a severe beating in order to preserve his life. You young monks studying here also endure great suffering in order to gain the life of wisdom found in the eternal Dharma-body. In both cases, considerable endurance is required, but the result is as different as the moon is from a snapping turtle.

---

[*]"When Confucius was in Ch'en, he ran out of provisions and his followers became so weak that none of them could stand up" (*Analects*, Duke Ling of Wei).

It is written in the *Ch'en Kui*:[*]

> A carpenter shows courage by climbing fearlessly onto the roofs of high buildings and towers. A fisherman shows courage by plunging into the water and seizing large creatures of the deep. A warrior shows courage by rushing straight into the jaws of the enemy, heedless of the danger. A faithful minister is one who shows courage by speaking out to his master at the risk of displeasing him, unmoved by any previous rewards he has received and without fear of possible torture and death.

What I want to say is that a Buddhist monk shows his courage by severing all the attachments to family that are so difficult to sever, renouncing wealth and profit so difficult to renounce, forsaking fame and reputation that are so difficult to forsake, forgetting old customs and practices that are so difficult to forget. He throws aside his myriad connections with worldly life and devotes himself singlemindedly to negotiating the Way. He strives to bore through the old stories in the koan barriers that are so difficult to bore through, penetrate the patriarch's barriers that are so difficult to penetrate, enduring privations that are so difficult to endure, contenting himself until his death with a life of spartan simplicity. Maturing into a great Dharma vessel, he proceeds to help others by constantly imparting the Dharma teachings to them, raising up the auspicious sun of the Buddha Dharma so it will shine brightly amid the eternal darkness. He never wavers or falls back from this mission. Such is the courage of Zen monks who negotiate the hidden depths.

Truly, there is no matter on earth that is greater than birth and death and no achievement that is richer and fuller than leaving birth and death behind and entering enlightenment. We do not know whence life comes, thus it is called the great matter of life; we do not know where we go when we die, thus it is called the great matter of death.[†] If a person is able to penetrate to an understanding of life, he will also understand death; if he penetrates to an understanding of death, he will understand life. The great matter of life is like a great mass of raging fire, the great matter of death like

---

[*] *Ch'en Kui*. which takes its title from a famous minister of that name who served during the Three Kingdoms period (3rd century) sets forth a vassal's proper role in serving his master.

[†] This recasts a passage in *The Record of Ta-hui*, ch. 20.

an adamantine cage from which there is no escape.* Hence it is said, "birth and death is the great matter, death arrives with great speed." Those words are extremely difficult to believe, extremely difficult to grasp. They deal with a matter of greatest importance that is impossible to breach through ordinary reflection or cogitation.

You followers of the Way, do not despair if your progress toward enlightenment is slow. You should despair if you have trouble achieving pure singlemindedness in your practice. Do not despair if you find it difficult to enter enlightenment. Just press forward and seek it through continuous and unbroken application.

Confucius said,† "The superior man has his mind fixed on penalties; the petty man has his mind fixed on profit." The superior man is circumspect and thorough in serving his master, rising early in the morning and retiring late at night, and regretting his insufficient ability. Fearing the punishment meted out to unworthy vassals, his mind is fixed on penalties. Because of this, the rewards that Heaven bestows are never far away. It is the opposite with a petty man. He fawns and flatters, works when his master is watching and takes it easy when his back is turned. He expects to be amply rewarded immediately upon performing some trifling act, and if he is not he is quick to anger and resents his master. Because of that, misery and self-created woes are never far away.

It is the same for the patricians of Buddhism who follow the path of Zen. They engage in secret practice and hidden activity, reflecting on the privations and suffering of their Zen predecessors. Ashamed that Zen study has become slack in the present day, they devote themselves to their training unflaggingly day and night. Not expecting quick results, they proceed steadily forward, with far-reaching aspirations. Because of that, attainment is not far away. With mediocre monks, it is the opposite. After sitting idly in zazen for three or four months, they start to grumble, complaining about the lack of results. They go around moaning and scratching their heads, deeply troubled. Why does this happen? It is because enlightenment, breaking free of birth and death, is extremely difficult to achieve, and the temptation to beat a hasty retreat is always close at hand.

*"You can't lay a hand or foot on this great mass of fire; if you [are in the adamantine cage, a place from which it is impossible to escape, and] try gnawing your way out, it will only shatter your teeth and destroy your mouth" (annotation).
†The Master said, "A superior man has his mind fixed on virtue; a petty man's mind is fixed on other men. A superior man has his mind fixed on the sanctions of the law: a petty man has his mind fixed on the favors he may receive" (Analects, IV).

Sentient beings move endlessly through the cycle of birth and death, enduring interminable suffering. Inhabitants of the heavenly realms, who live in a state of continuous pleasure, never have a chance to seek enlightenment. Both pleasure and pain, both happiness and unhappiness exist only in this human world. Whether you devote your time on earth to serious religious practice or idle it away depends on you alone. The time to gain release from that endless suffering is now. What are you waiting for?

You, my friend, are worried that your companions might criticize you for attending this meeting. If you give consideration to such matters, you will never be able to forge a true link to *prajna* wisdom. The important thing for you is to forget such things, see their criticism for what it is worth, and devote your attention solely to resolving the great matter of human life.

In one of his previous existences, Shakamuni Buddha was a young boy named Sessen Dōji. In order to hear the second half of a gatha on impermanence, Sessen threw himself into the jaws of a Yaksha demon. In another existence, Shakamuni placed himself between the jaws of a starving tiger. Reborn as a Deer King, he rescued a herd of deer from a raging wildfire; reborn as a doe, he sacrificed himself to protect the fawn he was carrying from the hunter's trap.* Are you so timid as to shrink from mere words someone might say about you?

Nagarjuna's *Treatise on the Perfection of Great Wisdom* states, "Although five hundred people harshly reviled the Buddha, he would not be in the least perturbed; although five hundred people praised him, he would not show signs of pleasure."† The criticism of such people is of no more consequence than a tiny scab on the skin. What will you do about the truly serious illness that afflicts you—the eternal night that is birth and death? Will you ignore this grave malady and worry about the tiny scab? Devote yourself diligently to your practice. If you do, you will surely experience good results. Doesn't Lieh Tzu say, "Those who achieve great things do not

---

*The first story in this paragraph is from the *Nirvana Sutra*, ch. 14, Noble Practice chapter: Sessen Dōji heard the first half of a verse on impermanence by a Buddha of the past: "All things are impermanent, such is the law of birth and death," and sacrificed himself to a Yaksha demon in order to hear the remaining two lines: "Once birth and death disappears, the happy state of tranquility and nirvana prevails." The following three stories are from the *Konkōmyōō-kyō* (*The Golden Splendor Sutra; Suvarnaprabhāsa-sūtra*), ch. 10; *Ching-lu yi-hsiang* (*Different Aspects of Sutras and Vinaya* ; a Buddhist encyclopedia), ch. 47, and *Lui-tu-chi ching* T 152 (by K'ang Seng-hui, a Chinese collection of Jataka tales), ch. 3.
† *Treatise on the Perfection of Great Wisdom*, ch. 27.

worry about trifles"?* Such is the path young monks destined to become men of truly great stature should take.

:73. MR. GOTŌ'S TAKING OF LIFE

This piece is not found in the printed edition of Poison Blossoms. *It is translated from a manuscript preserved at the Matsugaoka Library of Kamakura. An accompanying annotation tells us it was deleted from the final manuscript when government censors (whose offices were located in Kyoto's Nijō Castle) let it be known unofficially that they would be unable to pass it for publication, citing "certain objectionable material" it contained. We are not told what this material is. Although with a talking turtle making an appearance, the tale certainly seems fanciful enough to avoid being associated with contemporary events, the problem may have been the identifying by name of a provincial Daimyō and one of his retainers.*

"Mr. Gotō's Taking of Life" resembles one or two other pieces in the Poison Blossoms *collection that seem at first sight somewhat out of place among these Zen records. In content and style they strongly resemble stories in* Accounts of the Miraculous Effects of the Ten Phrase Kannon Sutra for Prolonging Life, *or in some of the narratives I translated in* Beating The Cloth Drum. *These are designed to highlight the perils of ignoring the fundamental Buddhist principle of cause and effect, and a number of them end, like this one, with the guilty party getting his due deserts, reduced to beggary, then torn to bits by wild dogs.*

It seems likely that Hakuin heard of the Gotō story soon after it is purported to have happened. The Chronological Biography *has young Hakuin visiting a temple in Fukuyama, a castle town on the Inland Sea near the city of Hiroshima where the story allegedly took place, in 1707, during the pilgrimage he made around the country in his twenties (*Precious Mirror Cave*, p. 161).*

AROUND THE BEGINNING OF the Genroku era (1688–1704), there was a retainer named Gotō in the service of Mizuno Sakushū, the Lord of Fukuyama Castle in Bingo province. Giving no credence to the Buddhist

*"One who sets out on a great enterprise does not concern himself with trifles; one who achieves great successes does not achieve small ones." The *Book of Lieh-tzu*, p. 152.

teaching of cause and effect, Mr. Gotō indulged in the taking of life, building a small pond behind his house and filling it with several hundred turtles, which he took great pleasure in eating. One day he invited some friends for a turtle dinner. He went out to the pond, grabbed a large turtle, and placed it on the chopping block. As he was about to deliver the *coup de grâce*, the turtle's frantic struggling knocked the knife from his grip. It sank to the bottom of the pond. Cursing his luck, Gotō said to the turtle, "Swim down and find my knife. If you bring it back to me, your life will be spared." Released into the pond, the turtle soon reappeared with the knife gripped in its mouth. Taking it, Gotō then reached into the pond and grabbed the turtle. He returned it to the chopping block and promptly killed it.

That night, the guests assembled and to their delight the turtle was brought to the table. They were still eating it with great relish when Gotō related the story of how he had tricked the turtle. They suddenly lost all interest in the food, excused themselves, and left. Gotō laughed to himself. "Acting like bunch of women," he said, ridiculing them. "Well, let them go. Good riddance!" He took his seat at the table and consumed all the food and drink by himself. Soon he began to feel feverish all over, and that night he was plagued by bad dreams. His eyebrows and hair fell out, and ulcers appeared on all his fingers. A physician came and prescribed him some medicine, but it had no effect. Someone said, "You could cure yourself if you drank a potion of Chinese medicine mixed with raw liver taken from a young girl." Gotō had a search made throughout the province for a suitable young girl, but he was unable to find a single one who suited his needs.

There was a fine-looking young servant in the Gotō household named Kiyo. Gotō decided to use her liver for his potion. When he was unable to get his wife to go along with his plan, he enlisted the help of a butcher who had a shop north of the castle. He told Kiyo to carry a box filled with leather handballs to the butcher's house. On her way there she happened to meet her uncle. "It will be dark by the time you return," he told her as they parted. "Make sure you let my wife know when you get back."

That night, a priest came and rapped at the uncle's door. "Kiyo is in great danger. You must hurry and save her," he said. The uncle, greatly alarmed, ran to the Gotō residence and asked to see his niece. "Kiyo is sick," he was told, but when he refused to be denied, a retainer came out and said, "To tell the truth, we haven't seen Kiyo for several days. We have people out looking everywhere for her. I'm sure we will find her before long. I will inform you right away if she doesn't turn up. Until then, please don't tell her family about her disappearance."

The uncle left, his suspicions deepening, and on returning home he set out again to visit the butcher. On the way, he met up with the man. He was carrying a box of leather handballs. The uncle grabbed hold of the butcher and said, "Last night when I saw Kiyo, she was taking that box to your house. What are you doing with it? Where is she?"

"Mr. Gotō has been trying to obtain the liver of a female fox. I got one today, so I am on my way to his house to deliver it to him. I don't know anything about Kiyo," he replied.

The enraged uncle took the butcher, lashed him to a willow tree at the roadside, broke a thick branch from the tree and began beating him with it. The uncle delivered countless blows until the man's body was lacerated and covered with blood. "I'll give you a lot worse than that unless you tell the truth. I'll break every bone in your body!" he cried, giving him a score or so more furious blows with the club.

"Stop! Stop! I'll tell you!" the butcher screamed. Weeping bitter tears he said, "The liver in this box is Kiyo's. I tried to refuse, but Mr. Gotō would not listen, and I was sure he would have taken his sword to me if I hadn't carried out his orders. I decided it would be best for me to do as he said and receive payment for it. Not only did I never get the money, I ended up being beaten within an inch of my life."

The uncle was so distraught his baleful cries could be heard throughout the nearby village. From Kiyo's house family members came running, having been deeply worried ever since the priest had come and told them of the danger she was in. When they heard what had happened, they too fell to the ground weeping. All they could do now was to gather Kiyo's remains and take them home. The butcher confessed that he had disposed of Kiyo's body in a reed thicket on the banks of the river.

The uncle handed the butcher over to the local magistrate, who ordered Gotō to be arrested and his household placed under close confinement. Together with the other family members the uncle proceeded to the reed bank to look for Kiyo's body. They found her lying peacefully on a bed of broken reeds. Shedding tears of gratitude, they gathered around her, overjoyed to find her alive.

"How glad I am to see you all again," she said. "Yesterday, Mr. Gotō sent me out on an errand. Suppressing certain fears I had, I made my way to the butcher's house. He led me into a dark shed behind his house and tied me to a post. He stabbed me in the chest several times. I was scared to death. He took out a sword and put it against my chest. But then a wonderful thing happened. The Abuto Kannon suddenly appeared amid a radiant light. I don't know what happened after that, because I fainted away."

Her uncle, weeping with joy, opened Kiyo's robe. He discovered a lacerated brocade pouch, which was found to contain one half of a small scroll of the *Kannon Sutra*. It was the same scroll on which Kiyo's mother had inscribed the sutra when she had visited the Abuto Kannon to pray for the Bodhisattva's help in conceiving a child. She had performed three prostrations before inscribing each of the Chinese characters of the text.

This discovery greatly affected everyone, and they proceeded to the Abuto Kannon Shrine to offer thanks. The uncle went to inspect the box. On opening it he found that it contained the other half of the *Kannon Sutra*. It emitted a strange radiance and an ineffable fragrance that further astonished everyone.

Since Kiyo had been saved, Gotō was spared the executioner's blade, but all his worldly goods were confiscated. He was banished from the province and ended up a beggar. He wandered tearfully from village to village until one day he was attacked and torn to pieces by wild dogs.

II. Explanations (*Setsu*)

:74. Explanation of the Dharma Name Daiin ("Great Recluse")

Hakuin apparently wrote this undated piece to explain to an unidentified layman the significance of the Dharma name Daiin, "Great Recluse," which he had conferred upon him.

The recluse, who withdraws from the world for various reasons to live in solitude and seclusion, appears very early in Chinese literature in the poem "Summoning the Recluse," attributed to Ch'u Yuan (fourth century BCE). In a poem by the Chin dynasty (265–420) poet Wang K'ang-min, the small recluse and the great recluse are contrasted, apparently for the first time: "Small hermits conceal themselves in the hills and marshes, / Great hermits hide themselves in the capital." Later writers offered many different twists on this theme, reflecting sundry biases and backgrounds. One well-known example is Po Chu-i's "The Half Recluse," written in the mid-T'ang, which endorses a position somewhere between the two extremes as the most likely to bring happiness. Although Confucianism was essentially opposed to any turning from the world, and Taoism wholeheartedly in support of it, Buddhism has generally taken a positive attitude.

Hakuin, whose interest in reclusion turns, predictably, on the way in which he can relate it to Zen training, identifies the great recluse with someone who has "realized formlessness" (that is, true enlightenment), and the small recluse with someone of only partial attainment. In this sense, he can hold up his version of the "great recluse" as infinitely superior to even the most celebrated hermits of Chinese legend, men who had renounced the world but who never got around to the more important business of renouncing them- selves. He constantly warns students of the danger of falling into the "dark pit of partial attainment," where they will no longer have the gumption to carry their practice through to completion. This outcome cannot be avoided, he says, unless their initial attainment (kenshō) is followed by post-satori training—vigorous application to advanced, difficult-to-pass koans under a qualified teacher— which will allow them to deepen their realization and finally enable them to lead others to the goal of enlightenment as well. As bent as he was on working in all quarters to get his message across, it cer- tainly follows that Hakuin would interpret the recluse's "traceless- ness" in terms of inscrutability of mind rather than public obscurity.

I T WAS SAID IN ancient times that "small recluses hide themselves in the mountains and great recluses hide themselves in the city." After having given the matter considerable thought, I have come to regard this saying as shallow and commonplace, and not altogether accurate at that.

Ahh! Recluses, recluses. How difficult it is to become one, and how difficult to discuss them. A figure with a goosefoot staff clutched in his hand and a gourd dipper slung over his shoulder, standing on a precipice motionless as a stack of firewood, or sitting under a tree humming sweet songs. But if he has no inner virtue worth your praise and no outward charm worth your emulation, such a person is merely a ignorant fool, someone who has hoodwinked his fellow men with pointless displays of his reclusive habits. He thinks that shouldering a mattock and going around with bracken roots in his hand makes him a recluse, but no matter where he goes to live, in the mountains or in the marketplace, he is just a poor, cold, hungry little man—totally ridiculous. He certainly doesn't deserve to be called a recluse. It is said that a recluse is a person who conceals his virtue and hides his radiance. What I want to know is what virtue he has to conceal, what radiance he has to hide.

I have heard that genuine recluses are found in the southern lands* who don't hide themselves either in the mountains or in the city. They make the formless hills their home, conceal themselves in echoless valleys, take refuge in undying forests, and make nonabiding their abode. They are found hurrying through city streets beyond comprehension, selling firewood at a place nowhere to be found. As recluses, not even Ch'ao Fu or Hsu Yu could lay a hand on them.† Not even Po I or Shu Ch'i would be able to flush them out. Why is this? Because they never manifest emotion, thought, or perception in any of the three realms, and because in whatever they do, they never leave the samadhi of complete cessation.‡ It is people such as this that we can speak of as great recluses.

. . . .

A version of this inscription that appears in *Sendai's Comments on the Poems of Han-shan* (*kan* 1) ends with the additional sentences: "Is not Han-shan with his mugwort hair, dirty face, and ragged robe engaging in the dignified conduct [of the Bodhisattva] within the samadhi of complete cessation? Perhaps he is such a [genuine] recluse—perhaps he is not."

---

*"Southern lands" (*Nanpō*) is apparently a reference to India.

†Ch'ao Fu, "old nest-elder," so called because of his habit of sleeping in trees to avoid contact with the world, was offered the throne by Emperor Yao, but refused it. When Emperor Yao offered the throne to Hsu Yu, Hsu not only declined but immediately washed out his ears to cleanse them from the defilement. He drank stream water from the hollow of his hand, and when someone gave him a gourd for a dipper, he hung it on a tree and later threw it away because the noise it made rattling against the tree disturbed him.

‡Shariputra was sitting in quiet meditation under a tree in the forest. Layman Vimalakirti approached him and said: "Ah, Shariputra, you should not assume that this sort of sitting is true quiet sitting! Quiet sitting means that in this threefold world you manifest neither body nor will. This is quiet sitting. Not rising out of the samadhi of complete cessation and yet showing yourself in the ceremonies of daily life—this is quiet sitting. Not abandoning the principles of the Way and yet showing yourself in the activities of a common mortal—this is quiet sitting. Your mind not fixed on internal things and yet not engaged with externals either—this is quiet sitting. Unmoved by sundry theories, but practicing the thirty-seven elements of the Way—this is quiet sitting. Entering nirvana without having put an end to earthly desires—this is quiet sitting. If you can do this kind of sitting, you will merit the Buddha's seal of approval" (*The Vimalakirti Sutra*, p. 37).

:75. On the Dharma Name Rōsen ("Old Sage")

*Hakuin wrote this inscription at the request of "Zen man Chū,"
a Zen monk about whom nothing else is known. The first line of
Hakuin's verse below alludes to the word "old," the second line to the
word "sage" in the name Rōsen. Feathers of the Chen bird were a
deadly poison. Clubs made from the wolf-fang bush were used as
weapons in ancient China.*

IN THE EIGHTEENTH YEAR of the Kyōhō era (1733), on a day western
breezes were filling peoples' hearts with thoughts of home, Zen man
Chū from Shimōsa province came and announced that he would be
returning to his home temple. He also asked me to write a verse on the
theme of *Rōsen* ("Old Sage"), his teacher's Dharma name. As his teacher
is an old friend of mine, I was unable to refuse. When I was remiss in
carrying out my promise, brother Chū came pestering me about it like a
little child trying to wheedle something out of its mother. So I wrote out
this verse for him:

> His temples snow white even before the great beginning,
> His face unknown even to the ancient emperor sages.
> With a *Chen*-feather robe, a wolf-fang mace in his hand,
> He's much keener on killing you than on giving you life.

Just then a visitor came. When he read the verse, he was amazed. "Does
such a person actually exist in this day and age?" he asked. "He does
indeed," I replied, "Rōsen is just such a fellow.

"Every word that comes from a Zen teacher must accord with ultimate
truth. Every syllable that spews from his mouth has to be perfectly genuine. If they aren't, his teachings become wild, reckless talk, acts of dishon-
esty and deceit. You could write his words on a rice cracker and throw it
to the dogs, but even they wouldn't touch it.

"You should turn and examine within your own original self: What
does old in 'Old Sage' mean? What does 'sage' mean? Bore through them,
all the way through to the bottom! You'll understand that they are not in
the least bit different from what I have been affirming to you. You will
experience a marvelous joy and wonderful clarity that you will be unable
to express in word or thought.

"But between affirming it and not affirming it, there is a difference of a thousand leagues. If you direct your light within, and examine your own self, you will discover that this is how your mind is—it is an 'Old Sage.' There is no use going and asking someone else about him."

Again the visitor was flabbergasted.

"Next time you come," I told him, "I'll have to write a verse and award you a name. I'll call you *Layman Flabbergasted*."

The visitor dropped his head and laughed. I wrote this for him as well, in hopes that he will make his way to the farthest reaches of the Buddha Way.

. . . .

Thoughts of home. The original is literally "water shield (*junsai*; a perennial water grass used in soups) and sea bass." Based on a story told about the poet Chang Han (3rd century BCE), who served the Prince of Ch'i but resigned his post because he could not go without the water shield soup and pickled sea bass of his native Sung-chiang in Kiangsu province. The term is often used for someone unable to resist thinking of his home province, his mother's cooking, etc. Hakuin is alluding to thoughts of the true self-nature, one's "native place."

:76. EXPLANATION OF THE DHARMA NAME LAYMAN DAIKŌ KOGAN

Akiyama Sōzaemon (n.d.), the recipient of this Dharma name, who appears elsewhere in Poison Blossoms, *was the head of the Aki-yama family of Yasuhisa village in northern Izu province and one of the most prosperous landowners in the Izu-Suruga area. A draft of the inscription, composed in the form of a letter and dated, is extant, allowing us to place the piece in the fourth month of 1725, Hakuin's fortieth year.*

It has been suggested that Hakuin's association with the Akiyama family began as a result of the marriage of Sōzaemon's daughter Chika into the Watanabe family of Hara, an event that took place before Hakuin was installed as head priest at Shōin-ji. Heads of the Watanabe clan ran one of the main (honjin) inns at the Hara post station, which catered to Daimyō and others of high rank. Sōzae-mon and his son Michitomo were both important patrons of Shōin-ji during Hakuin's tenure there. Information about the Akiyama clan is found in Shamon Hakuin, *by the local historian Akiyama Kanji.*

Sōzaemon's son Michitomo was also a Hakuin student, and received a Buddhist name from him as well. The inscription Hakuin wrote explaining his name is translated in the following piece, #77.

Hakuin wrote this inscription the year before his final decisive enlightenment, at a time when he was engaged in intense zazen practice (Precious Mirror Cave, p. 197).

AKIYAMA SŌZAEMON SHIGEMASA IS a reclusive gentleman of Yasuhisa village in northern Izu province. He has a sincere, upright character that is distinguished by a refined elegance and quiet determination. He comes from a long line of wealthy landowners in Suruga and Izu province that has flourished unabated for several hundred years, rising like an immense tree above the other giants of the forest, with magnificent twisting branches curling outward from its majestic, dragon-like trunk. Coming from such stock, Sōzaemon's mind was bound to turn toward the Way. He began his Zen study with Ho Oshō of Enjō-zan Ryōsen-ji. Later, he came to pay me a visit. It was as though karmic influences had ordained our meeting. I now regard him as an elder brother. Three years ago he invited me to his home, but since at the time I was intent on devoting myself quietly to my zazen practice, I was unable to accept his offer.

In the spring of this year, the tenth of Kyōhō (1725), having viewed the scattering springtime flowers and falling autumn leaves and become deeply aware of the transience of human life, Sōzaemon came to my temple and asked me repeatedly for a Dharma name. Once again, however, I was unable to respond to his request. His second son, Tsunehide, came and appealed earnestly on his father's behalf. Realizing the depth of his sincerity, I was unable to let matters slide any longer. I wrote out the name Daikō Kogan Koji [Layman Great Light of the Other Shore]. It is based on the Sanskrit words *Maka-hannya-haramitta*, which may be rendered as "Reaching the Great Wisdom of the Other Shore."

One day, the layman came into my chambers, made two bows, and said, "I'm ashamed to have a name like 'Reaching the Great Wisdom of the Other Shore.' I'm just a slow-witted country farmer. I lack the karmic seeds within that would connect me to Buddha wisdom. I don't do the kind of hidden practice that would convey me to the other shore. There is such a great disparity between the meaning of my name and the actual reality."

"I am glad you asked me that question," I said. "The mind that seeks to answer it is the very marrow of the Buddhas, the life-root of the ancestral teachers. People call it 'the great and important cause for which Buddhas have appeared in the world.' Also 'the treasury of the true Dharma eye.' It is the direct path that will convey you swiftly and suddenly to the other shore. It is the inner sanctum of the celestial treasure trove.

"Layman Daikō, I want you to investigate over and over: What is the mind that produced that doubt? Bore into it when you are doing zazen. Bore into it when you are standing and moving about. Bore into it when you are immersed in everyday activities and when you are in places of tranquility, whether moving, sitting, or lying down. Bore from the front. Bore in from the sides. Bore into it until there is nothing left to bore into, and mind, thought, perceptions, and emotions all become suspended. Your body and mind will be as though seated inside a glass jar of clearest crystal. With knower and known forgotten, you will become one with the seeking mind and everything will abruptly cease to exist. At that moment, if you just keep pushing fearlessly ahead, you will find that it is like a vast sheet of ice suddenly shattering, like shoving over a jade tower. Everything in the ten directions will suddenly vanish without a trace. It will be a vast emptiness within and without. Whatever you do, whether active or at rest, will be perfectly clear and true. The joy you will experience will be far greater than anything you have seen or heard in all your seventy years.

"At that point, if you fire your spirit with even more resolve and continue to bore in with great care and assiduity, you will realize in yourself the nonduality of fundamental truth and changing phenomena, the oneness of enlightenment and illusion. There will be no shore for you to leave, no yonder shore to seek, no dhyana or wisdom to practice, and there will be no contradiction whatever between the name you bear and the reality you live. You will still be the same old useless duffer you are now, with nothing to do, your eyes horizontal, your nose up-and-down, but even the Buddhas and patriarchs will be unable to lay a hand on you. When that time comes, this screed I've written out will be an embarrassment to you. You will feel nothing but shame for your speculations about name and reality, and shame as well to be called Daikō Kogan, Reaching the Great Wisdom of the Other Shore. Ah, what a glorious moment it would be!"

The layman bowed and departed. I then wrote this down and sent it to him—creating yet another reason to hang my head in shame.

. . . .

Ho Oshō. The annotations identify this priest as Kenryū Sōho (n. d.) of Enjō-zan Ryōsen-ji in eastern Suruga province.

I was unable to accept his offer. This is apparently the period of intense zazen practice described in Hakuin's *Chronological Biography* (fortieth year).

:77. EXPLANATION OF THE DHARMA NAME LAYMAN ITTSUI KOKAN (ONE MALLET, OLD MIRROR)

Akiyama Michitomo (1682–1750) was the son of Akiyama Sōzae-mon, who appeared in the previous piece (#76). A student of Hakuin like his father, Michitomo received this lay Buddhist name in 1743.

Four years earlier, in autumn of 1739, Hakuin had conducted the monthlong series of talks at Michitomo's residence (Precious Mirror Cave, p. 204) described in some detail in #57. Over thirty people attended to hear him deliver Zen comments on the Letters of Ta-hui, *a collection of letters the Sung priest Ta-hui sent his lay students which Hakuin held in high regard.*

Ittsui, "One Mallet," is a wooden hammer used in Zen temples. It has an octagonal head that is struck against a wooden block to announce the start of ceremonies and other proceedings. The word Ittsui might also be translated "one blow from the mallet," as in the Zen phrase ittsui sentō, *"one blow from the mallet, a thousand hits." Kokan, "Old Mirror," is a metaphor for the Zen mind or intrinsic Buddha-nature. Michitomo's name may thus be rendered as "One blow of the mallet shatters the old mirror."*

IN YASUHISA VILLAGE OF northern Izu province lives a country gentle-man named Akiyama Yohei Michitomo. He has always greatly valued the Buddha-mind school [Zen] and placed his trust in its teachings. He has been visiting my small temple for almost thirty years now. He is deeply devoted to Zen practice, and though he has not fully penetrated its secrets, his efforts have never slackened. He is a gentleman of the old school, with a quiet and lofty manner. Though buffeted by the eight winds or seven mis-fortunes, he never allows himself to stray into perverse thoughts of good fortune, reputation, or prestige. Even amid the privileged circumstances of his everyday life, his pure and lofty nature does not change.

On a trip he made with me for a ninety-day meeting at Rinzai-ji in southern Izu, he maintained this same quiet, lofty bearing throughout the entire retreat. Later, when he accompanied me to the Keirin-ji training hall in Ujō, Kai province for another ninety-day retreat, and he shared the same adversities as the training monks, he always maintained that same quiet dignity and demeanor of times past, as though he was indifferent to thoughts of profit and loss, right and wrong. Not even veteran Rinzai monks, men who had embraced the Way and devoted themselves to zazen and koan practice for twenty or thirty years, could measure up to him.

In spring of this year, the third of the Kampō era (1743), he came to me and requested a lay Buddhist name (dōgō). I gave him the sobriquet Ittsui Kokan. He asked me what it signified, so I explained it to him carefully, step by step.

"All sentient beings possessed of consciousness and born in one of the four ways [from the womb, an egg, moisture, or by metamorphosis] possess an old mirror that always reflects unerringly the five colors and the myriad things in their suchness. The hills and streams, the entire earth in all its endless shapes and forms, the heavens and hells, the pure and impure lands, the realms of Buddhas and demons, samsara and Nirvana— they are all reflected in the mirror of this Buddha-mind, with not even a single hair left out. Hence the old mirror is also referred to as the store-house consciousness. When enlightenment is attained, it then is called the Great Mirror Wisdom.

"There are those who devote their entire lives to constantly wiping and polishing this mirror, enduring untold suffering over three lives, for over sixty long kalpas. They belong to the path of the Shravakas.

"However, there are those who take a mallet to the mirror and are able to smash it, enabling them to penetrate it all the way to its source. They are then able to use the brilliant light of the Great Mirror Wisdom at will, to take it up and put it down freely, liberating the vast multitude of sentient beings reflected in the mirror, never slackening or falling back from this work even with the passage of endless time. They are the great Mahayana Bodhisattvas, beings who have reached sudden and complete attainment. You must become one of them. You must not end up a Shravaka!"

"What about the one mallet?" asked the layman.

Placing my palms together in gasshō, I said, "A monk asked master Chao-chou, 'The myriad things return to the one. Where does the one return?' Chao-chou said, 'When I was in Ch'ing-chou, I made a shirt that weighed seven pounds.' Those words function with exceeding efficacy to sever the root source of birth and death. They work like a sword whose great blade, extending into the heavens, completely demolishes the ancient den of primal ignorance, and they fall with greater force than a five-ton mace.

"If a student takes up such a mallet and strikes down at the surface of the mirror three thousand times in the morning and eight hundred times in the evening, and then, mustering all his strength, goes on to strike it a thousand, ten thousand, a million more times, never once turning from the work or shrinking from the hardship, he will see results before a week is out. Samsara. Nirvana. Afflicting passions. Enlightenment. The mallet smashes them all into oblivion. Empty space disappears completely and iron mountains crumble, producing in the student a most profound and intense joy. These are all auspicious portents of the rebirth that comes in the wake of this destruction.

"And when rebirth suddenly occurs, Dharma gates beyond number and their boundless meaning are now all embodied in the head of that mallet, and the Bodhisattva proceeds to use it with complete and utter freedom, strolling at his ease through countless lands and countries to help the multitudes of beings. When you reach that point, Layman Ittsui Kokan, even if the Buddhas and patriarchs got together and marshalled all their efforts, there is no way they would be able to touch you. What a splendid moment it will be!"

A faint smile appeared on the layman's lips. I then wrote this explanation out and gave to him.

. . . .

Eight winds are causes that incite the evil passions—gain, loss, slander, eulogy, praise, ridicule, pain, pleasure. The *seven misfortunes* are joy, anger, grief, pleasure, love, hate, desire.

Ninety-day meeting. This was a lecture meeting on the *Blue Cliff Record* held in 1737 at Rinzai-ji, in the Kamo district (*Chronological Biography; Precious Mirror Cave*, p. 204). The Keirin-ji meeting referred to in the following sentence, also on the *Blue Cliff Record*, took place in 1741, two years before this inscription was written.

BOOK SIX
Letters (*Sho*)

. . . .

The fifteen letters in this Book have all been translated.
They constitute the only group of Hakuin's shorter, personal
letters (as opposed to long, book-length epistles such as
Oradegama) *published until the twentieth century.*

78. To the Head Priest of Gekkei-ji

Hakuin wrote this letter to a priest named Shundō Sekiryū (n.d.), incumbent of Gekkei-ji, a temple in the Ichigaya district of Edo, to order some copies of the Bukkō-roku, *the recorded sayings of Wu-hsueh Tsu-yuan (1226–1286), which had been published by Gekkei-ji in the ninth month of 1726. Two Instructions to the Assembly (Jishū) on the* Bukkō-roku *are found in* Poison Blossoms, *the earliest (#4) dating from that same year, suggesting the letter was written in autumn of 1726.*

Bukkō is the Kokushi *or National Master title the Japanese emperor bestowed on Wu-hsueh, an eminent Chinese priest who came to Japan by imperial invitation to serve as head of the Kenchō-ji monastery in Kamakura, and later at Engaku-ji, constructed for him nearby. Gekkei-ji belonged to the Engaku-ji line.*

This letter, which reveals the great respect Hakuin had for Zen master Wu-hsueh, also contributes nicely to our feeling for how he related to contemporary Zen masters. His letter begins, unusually, with a poem.

> Branches, fields, feathered with white frost.
> Mikan trees, heavy with bright orange fruit.
> Piercing cold, biting through my thin black robe.
> Ripening chestnuts, turning deep rich purple.

I TRUST THAT YOUR TEACHING banners are raised up high and that marvelous new products are issuing from your Dharma forge. Although I have not yet had the good fortune of making your acquaintance, news of your virtuous activity has long filled my ears, and been a source of great pleasure to me.

I recently learned of the remarkable deed you have performed in republishing National Master Bukkō's Zen records. It is surely a result of your deep vow and boundless compassion. Such a truly great accomplishment will benefit the Zen school for thousands of years. It is like handing a compass to someone on a fogbound sea, or a flaming torch on a dark night road.

A Zen monk who stopped over here recently on his way to Kyoto was carrying a copy of your new publication. I made him stay here a while so I would have an opportunity to read it through. As I did, it seemed as though the vital essence of Nan-yueh's Zen had suddenly come to life, as though the genuine traditions of Eastern Mountain shone radiantly from my desktop. One look at the National Master's words abruptly resolved doubts that had long remained in my mind. I felt a deep admiration that swept clear years of plaguing obstructions. I was so overcome with joy and appreciation, I found tears rolling down my old cheeks. How could I have known that such a great treasure would suddenly appear like this in our own country, and at a time when the Dharma is in such a perilous and degenerate state!

I would respectfully like to request two or three copies of the work, to be sent to me here at Shōin-ji as quickly as possible. I want to preserve them in my temple to serve as "eye-opening medicine" for future generations of students. I am sending Sochō, one of my young monks, to your temple. He will explain matters to you in more detail.

Place take good care of yourself as the weather grows colder.

Most humbly and sincerely, [Hakuin]

. . . .

Nan-yueh's Zen. Nan-yueh Huai-jang (667–744), an heir of Sixth Patriarch Hui-neng, was founder of one the three main lines of Chinese Zen, one of which later evolved into the Lin-chi (J. Rinzai) school. Eastern Mountain (Tung-shan) refers to Wu-tsu Fa-yen's (1024?–1104) style of Zen. The Yang-ch'i line of Lin-chi to which Hakuin belonged was a later offshoot of the Nan-yueh branch.

⁝79. To Layman Ishii

This relatively early letter, dating from Hakuin's forty-ninth year, is addressed to the physician Ishii Gentoku (1671–1751), his close friend and lay pupil. Fifteen years older than Hakuin, Layman Ishii resided in Hina village, six miles west of the Hara post station. He began practicing at Shōin-ji in 1728, eight years after Hakuin was installed as abbot, a little over a year after his decisive enlighten-

ment at the age of forty-one. A number of miscellaneous pieces Hakuin wrote for or about Layman Ishii that are included in Poison Blossoms *confirm that Ishii was considerably advanced in his Zen study. This is further substantiated by the difficulty of the teaching Hakuin addresses to him here.*

A long verse Hakuin sent Ishii to express his thanks for two large boulders Ishii had donated to the Shōin-ji gardens, filled with vivid images describing the progress of the unwieldy objects as they are rafted down from the foothills of Mount Fuji, landed on the coast near Hara village, then manhandled overland to Shōin-ji, is one of more memorable pieces in the Poison Blossoms *collection (translated below, #130).*

An earlier, more fully annotated version of this letter was published in Beating the Cloth Drum.

M Y ATTENDANT BOKU, WHILE on a trip to his native province, stopped by the residence of Layman Ishii. Claiming to be indisposed, he threw himself at the Layman's feet and implored him for his help. He borrowed the Layman's private chambers and for ten days devoted himself assiduously to zazen.*

I overheard a discussion several of Boku's comrades were having about him. "Boku hit on a truly splendid plan," they decided. "He is sure to return with a much deeper attainment." I wasn't so sure. "Boku," I said to myself, "This was not a good idea. Being a kind and deeply compassionate man, when the Layman sees how troubled you are, he is sure to be greatly concerned and want to help you. But whatever help you receive now, even the deeper attainment that may result, it is going to stick to your bones and cling to your hide, and will prevent you from experiencing the intense joy that should accompany the sudden entrance into satori. You will remain a half-assed little stable boy the rest of your life, your wisdom never completely clear, your attainment never truly alive and vital. A most regrettable outcome indeed!" Yesterday, the evening of the twelfth, Boku returned to Shōin-ji. I sat in wait for him with a black snake up my sleeve.†

---

*The word *chambers* (*hōjō*), normally used for the quarters of a teacher or head priest, also alludes to the room where the great Layman Vimalakirti taught. An annotation says that the room was Ishii's teahouse.

†Hakuin alludes to his *shippei*, a black-lacquered bamboo stick.

By and by, an unkempt and disheveled Boku entered the temple gates. His face was no different from when he had left.

"What words did the Layman have for you? I asked.

"He didn't utter a single word to help me," Boku said with tears raining down his face.

Unable to keep from bursting into laughter, I cried out, "How wonderful! If you had come back here with even a grain of Zen understanding, I would have snatched your robe and begging bowl from you, given you thirty blows with my staff, and chased you out the gate. You had a very close shave! You might have ended up achieving nothing but to get the Layman entangled in your personal troubles. I had no idea he would be so rigorous in dealing with you!

"Boku, the great and essential matter is like partaking of a peach. You mustn't be hasty. You have to wait patiently until the fruit is fully ripe. Then, when the soft, pink fruit is cut in two, the kernel falls out of itself, and the flesh, with its wonderful configurations, can be enjoyed in all its marvelous fragrance and delicious flavors. How marvelously edifying it is to watch this happen!

"Watch the way a mother hen warms an egg. When she has warmed the egg sufficiently so that conditions are ripe for hatching, instead of pecking the egg, the mother hen waits, holds back, until she hears the faint pecking sounds inside the shell. She gives the shell a single peck, and the baby chick emerges. It is truly heartwarming to watch her forthrightly attending to her task, cocking her head this way and that, up and down, as she restrains herself from pecking. Yet if she did not hold back, if she pecked the shell too early, she would have ruined everything, producing a sight too terrible to behold.

"Or consider the case of a pregnant woman. Although her time has not yet arrived, she and her husband have taken every possible precaution and secured in advance the services of a physician. Now, a physician of only middling talents, who is eager to achieve results and hasten the delivery, may decide to force the birth prematurely or to attempt a perilous breech delivery, gravely imperiling the lives of both mother and child.

"Or take the example of a man who comes down with the ague and suffers periodic bouts of convulsive shivering. If the physician attempts to cure the man quickly after he has suffered only one or two paroxysms, the infection will remain in his system, only to recur later in more virulent form. Hence the saying, 'A mediocre physician neither helps nor harms. A poor physician harms without helping. It is wisest not to send for either.'

"One day when I was in Mino province, I observed a cicada casting its skin in the shade. It managed to get its head free, and then its hands and feet emerged one after the other. Only its left wing remained inside, adhering to the old skin. It didn't look as though the cicada would ever get that wing unstuck. Watching it struggling to free itself, I was moved by feelings of pity to assist it with my fingernail. 'Excellent,' I thought, 'Now you are free to go your way.' But the wing I had touched remained shut and would not open. The cicada never was able to fly around the way it should have. Watching it, I felt ashamed of myself, regretting deeply what I had done.

"When you consider it, present-day Zen teachers act in much the same way in guiding their students. I've seen and heard how they take young people of exceptional talent—those destined to become the very pillars and ridgepoles of our school—and with their extremely ill-advised and inopportune methods end up turning them into something half-baked and unachieved. This is the primary cause for the decline of our Zen school, the reason the Zen groves wither away.

"Now and again you come across superior seekers of genuine quality who are devoting themselves to hidden application and secret practice. As they continue steadily forward, accumulating merit until their efforts achieve a purity that infuses them with strength, their emotions gradually cease to arise altogether, and they find themselves at an impasse, unable to move forward despite the most strenuous application. It is as if they are trapped inside invincible enclosures of adamantine strength, or are sitting in bottles of purest crystal, unable to move forward, unable to retreat—becoming blockheads, utter dunces.

"Suddenly the moment arrives when they become one with their questing mind. Mind and koan both disappear. Breathing itself seems to cease. This, although they are not aware of it, is the moment when the tortoise shell cracks and fissures, when the Luan-bird emerges from its egg. They are experiencing the auspicious signs that appear when a person is about to attain the Buddha Way.

"What a shame if at such a critical moment, someone who is supposed to be their good friend and teacher succumbs to tender emotions, indulges them in grandmotherly tenderness, and serves them up various intellectual explanations that knock them back into the old familiar nest of conceptual understanding, that drag them down into the cavernous old den of darkness and delusion. That, however, is not the end of the damage teachers do them, for they then bring out a phony winter-melon seal,* impress

* A false makeshift seal carved from melon rind.

it on a piece of paper, and award it to the student: 'You are like this,' they say. 'I am like this, too. Preserve and protect it with care.' The trouble is, the roots binding the students to life are still not severed. The gardens of the patriarchs still lie beyond their farthest horizons. Any teacher who does this, though he may love his student dearly, causes him irreparable harm. For their part, the students start dancing around, rolling their heads this way and that way, wagging their tails joyfully, eagerly lapping away at the fox slobber doled out to them, completely unaware it is a virulent poison.* They waste their entire lives stuck in a half-drunken, half-sober state of delusion. Not even the hand of a Buddha can cure them.

"A foolish man long ago heard that if you put a leech out under the sun in very hot weather, it would transform into a dragonfly and soar into the sky. One summer day, he decided to put it to the test. Wading into a marsh, he poked around until he found a particularly large old leech. Throwing it on the hot ground, he watched very carefully as the worm squirmed and writhed in agony. Suddenly, it flipped over on its back, split in two, and transformed into a ugly creature with a hundred legs like a centipede. It scowled furiously at him, snapping its fangs in anger. Ahh! This creature that was supposed to soar freely through the skies had turned into a repulsive worm that could do nothing but crawl miserably over the ground. A truly terrifying turn of events!

"There was a servant in ancient China who worked in the kitchen of a temple in the far western regions of the country. The temple was filled with monks engaged in the rigors of training. All the time the servant wasn't engaged in his main job preparing meals for the brotherhood, he spent doing zazen. One day, he suddenly entered a profound samadhi, and since he showed no sign of coming out of it, the head priest of the temple directed the senior monk in charge of the training hall to keep an eye on him. When the servant finally got up from his zazen cushion three days later, he had penetrated the heart and marrow of the Dharma, and had attained an ability to clearly see the karma of his previous lives. He went to the head priest and began setting forth the realization he had attained, but before he had finished, the head priest suddenly put his hands over his ears. 'Stop! Stop!' he said. 'The rest is something I have yet to experience. If you explain it to me, I'm afraid it might obstruct my own entrance into enlightenment.'

*Wild fox slobber is a highly poisonous substance, generally used by Hakuin with a positive connotation for the "turning words" used by Zen teachers.

"How invaluable that story is! There was nothing halfhearted about the ancients' practice of the Way; it was difficult in the extreme. One of them said, 'It is like passing through a region infested with venomous insects. You must pass through with all possible haste, not stopping to accept even a single drop of water from someone you meet.'* The great master Yun-men said, 'While you are engaged in practice, if anyone comes up and tries to teach you Zen, I want you to take a dipper of warm shit and throw it over him.'

"That is why to outstanding students who are engaged in negotiating the hidden depths I say, 'I would rather you sink into the sea of birth-and-death and remain there until the skin on your body is covered all over with festering sores, than for you ever to go to others for your strength.'"

Before I had even finished speaking, Boku performed two prostrations. "Master," he said, "thank you for the great compassion you have shown in giving me this teaching. Although I cannot hope to comprehend it all, and do not doubt it in the least, I do have a few questions about it.

"In the past when teachers dealt with their students, there was no room for any hesitation—it was as if they had a naked sword blade raised in their hands. They were like the giant golden-winged Garuda, monarch of the feathered kingdom, cleaving through the whale-backed seas and deftly seizing live dragons beneath the waves. Zen monks are like vigorous red-finned carp when the peach trees are in blossom, butting their way upstream straight into the tremendous current, braving the perilous forked lightning of the Dragon Gate.† At the utterance of a single word, they enter realization. At the sound of a single shout, they attain cessation. If those who call themselves teachers all behave like dead otters and those who call themselves their followers all behave like dumb sheep,‡ the halls of Zen throughout the land, training grounds where Buddhas are singled out, will be rendered utterly useless—no better than coffins for the dead—and the assertions of the perverse silent-illumination Zen teachers with their box-shrub Zen will carry the day.§ If that happens, the supreme teaching of the Buddha-mind school will plunge to earth

---

*The story on which this is based is given in Supplementary Note 1 following this letter.
†The Dragon Gate (Lung-men) is a three-tiered waterfall cut through the mountains to open up a passage for the Yellow River. It was said that on the third day of the third month, when peach trees are in flower, carp that succeeded in scaling this waterfall turned into dragons.
‡See Supplementary Note 2 following this letter.
§See Supplementary Note 3 following this letter.

forever, and its true and rigorous traditions will disappear forever from the ancestral groves."

I gave a sigh, and said, "Boku, come over here. I want you to listen to what I say. In studying Zen, it is necessary to pierce completely through when you penetrate to the source. It is the same with all the workings of heaven and earth. The wonderful transformation of springtime does not take place without the winter's severity, the intense cold that makes the hundred plants and grasses fade and shrivel, the bamboo split and shatter. But with the advent of spring, the ten thousand buds and blossoms emerge, rivaling one another with their charms and beauties. Hence the saying, 'to make something grow and develop, you must cut it back. To make something flourish, you must check its progress.'

"Long ago, when the First Patriarch Bodhidharma was living in seclusion doing zazen at Shao-shih, he had a student named Hui-k'o. Hui-k'o possessed outstanding talent and learning, and a dauntless and heroic spirit. For three years he continued to refine his attainment while serving as Bodhidharma's attendant, with untold hardship and suffering his constant companions.

"Today's students practice the Way clothed in warm garments, they get plenty to eat, and they are as soft and weak as the eldest sons of a wealthy family. Could any of them venture to stand stalwart and resolute in a courtyard on a bitter cold night like Hui-k'o, buried up to the waist in icy snow like a stack of firewood?* Suffering of this intensity cannot be endured unless one is made of stone or metal or has the wooden legs of a statue. The marrow-chilling cold of the Northern Wei winter constantly penetrated the thin cotton robe he wore. He stood resolutely and silently through that adversity until dawn, never relaxing his efforts for a second, or weeping a single tear. Bodhidharma never offered him the slightest help whatever. Finally, Hui-k'o took a knife and cut off his left arm. Hsi-sou was perfectly justified in holding Bodhidharma up as a model for Zen monks throughout the world.†

"When the Sixth Patriarch Hui-neng raised the Dharma standard at Ts'ao-ch'i, the priest Nan-yueh came to study with him. Hui-neng asked, 'What is this that thus comes?' Nan-yueh stood in a daze, unable to respond. Hui-neng did not utter a single word to relieve his confusion, and it was not until Nan-yueh had practiced arduously for eight more years that the

---

*The story is found in *Compendium of the Five Lamps*, ch. 1; *Gateless Barrier*, Case 4.
†Hsi-sou Shao-t'an (n.d.), in his *Praise of the Five Houses of the True School*.

patriarch finally offered him a turning word.* Ahh! This good teacher, who had accumulated great merit over eighty rebirths,† now, when the time was ripe, employed his marvelous means with incomparable skill to bring about Nan-yueh's liberation. Why didn't he employ them at the start, and simply lead Nan-yueh to the immense joy of liberation? You do not get the incandescent fire to forge fine Pin-chou steel by stoking the furnace with kindling. The oranges of Chiang-nan do not assume their delicious sweet flavor until they have passed through the bitter frosts. Any honest farmer would be ashamed to cook unripened grain for his meals, would he not?

"Students who have not yet penetrated the source should not be troubled if their entrance into enlightenment is slow in coming, but they should worry if their practice is not pure and genuine. Students who have already penetrated to attainment should not be troubled if people fail to revere them, but they should be concerned about the difficulty of achieving a pure and genuine practice.

"Long ago, when Lin-chi practiced for three years at Huang-po's temple, he received words of sanction from Huang-po's disciple Ch'en Tsun-su: 'Someone whose practice is this pure and genuine is certain to become a great shade tree [for all the beings of the world].'‡ Lin-chi was by that time extensively versed in the sutras and commentaries, and he had exhaustively investigated the precepts as well. Today's students lack this extensive knowledge of the scriptures or precepts. Because of that, they confound their own feelings, perceptions, and understanding for absolute truth, go around shooting off their mouths and peddling their half-baked ideas to others, and end up making a total waste of their lives.

"Observe the manner in which a clear-eyed teacher like Mu-chou [Ch'en Tsun-su] was able unequivocally to affirm Lin-chi: 'Your practice is pure and genuine!' That purity and that genuineness of practice is extremely difficult to attain, even if a student devotes an entire lifetime to Zen training. However, once you attain it, you are without doubt a tiger with wings. Boku, there is no reason you cannot become a man of such capacity.

*Compendium of the Five Lamps, ch. 3.
†Based on lines by Yuan-wu K'o-ch'in: "I venerate the Sixth Patriarch, an authentic old Buddha who manifested himself in the human world as a good teacher for eighty lifetimes in order to help others" (cited in Tōrei's Snake Legs for Kaien-fusetsu, 21v).
‡The head monk in Huang-po's assembly at this time is unidentified in standard accounts of this episode in Record of Lin-chi and Records of the Lamp; in others he is given as Ch'en Tsun-su (Mu-chou Tao-tsung, n.d.). In none of the versions does he utter such words directly to Lin-chi.

"Yet Lin-chi went three times to ask Huang-po about the cardinal meaning of the Buddha Dharma. Each time he received painful blows from Huang-po's stick and withdrew in tears. But he was still not liberated, so he set out to see Master Ta-yu. Huang-po gave him not the least bit of help. After experiencing a significant understanding at Ta-yu's, Lin-chi returned to Huang-po and reported what Ta-yu had told him. Huang-po said, 'If that blabbermouth dares show his face around here, I'll give him thirty blows with this stick of mine!'*

"An authentic Zen teacher like Huang-po is like a solitary peak towering forbiddingly into the sky. Today, you could comb the entire earth and not come up with a single person like him.

"The great teacher Hsuan-sha practiced arduously at Hsueh-feng's mountain hermitage, forgetting both food and sleep, but was unable to achieve a breakthrough of any kind. He left the temple with tears in his eyes, yet Hsueh-feng did not utter a single word to help him. At this point, you can be sure that one of today's teachers would have burdened him with a copious load of warm shit. As it turned out, when he reached the foot of the mountain, Hsuan-sha tripped and fell, and experienced a sudden realization.†

"It is like a melon grower harvesting his crop. He waits until their fragrance and flavor are at their peak before he goes into the melon patch. When he does, he has no need to carry a knife with him, only a bamboo basket. As the melons are fully ripe, the roots and tendrils and stems don't have to be cut; they have fallen away of themselves, leaving the fruit lying there on the ground. All he has to do is to go and pick them up.

"Don't you see? Hsuan-sha's enlightenment had fully matured just like those melons. It was a stinking fruit whose smell has wafted down through the centuries and taken the lives of countless pilgrims who partook of it. Yet if Hsuan-sha's teacher Hsueh-feng had taken out his knife at the critical moment, stepped in and cut the stem, Hsuan-sha's teaching would never have been transmitted to future generations.

"Hsiang-yen trained at his teacher Kuei-shan's temple for many years without attaining even a glimpse of realization. Making up his mind to leave, he went to inform Kuei-shan with tears in his eyes. Kuei-shan was

---

*See Supplementary Note 4 following this letter.

†"One day Hsuan-sha took up a traveling pouch and left his temple to visit other teachers around the country. On his way down the mountain he struck his toe hard on a rock, drawing blood, but amid the intense pain he had an abrupt self-realization...and promptly returned to Hsueh-feng" (*Essentials of Successive Records of the Lamp*, ch. 23).

completely unsympathetic. He didn't even look at him. After traveling around, Hsiang-yen took up residence in a solitary hermitage. One day as he was sweeping, his broom threw a fragment of tile against a bamboo trunk. When the sound it made reached his ears, all the barriers suddenly fell away. He bathed and put on a clean robe. Facing in the direction of the Kuei-shan's temple, he offered some incense, performed three prostrations, and said, 'It is not my late teacher's religious virtue I revere. I revere the fact that he never once explained everything to me.'*

"The following story is told about a monk who visited a Zen teacher and begged insistently for the principles of Zen. The teacher never paid him the least attention. The monk waited for a chance, then one day suddenly grabbed the master and hurried him to a secluded spot at the rear of the temple. He seated the master on the ground, spread out his prostration cloth before him, and performed three bows. 'I appeal to your great mercy and compassion,' he said. 'Please teach me the principles of Zen. Guide me to sudden enlightenment.' The master ignored him. Enraged, the monk flew into a fit of passion, sprang to his feet and, eyes red with anger, broke off a large branch from a nearby tree. Brandishing it, he stood in front of the master glaring scornfully at him. 'Priest!' he cried. 'If you don't tell me what you know, I am going to club you to death, cast your body down the cliff, and leave this place for good.' 'If you want to beat me to death, go ahead,' replied the master. 'I'm not going to teach you any Zen.' What a pity. This monk was obviously gifted with special capacity and spiritual strength and had what it takes to penetrate the truth and perish into the great death. But notice what great caution and infinite care these ancient teachers exercised when leading students to self-awakening.

"Zen Master Tao-wu responded to a monk with the words, 'I won't say living. I won't say dead.' 'Why is that?' asked the monk. 'I won't say. I won't say,' replied Tao-wu.† Tao-wu did not refuse to speak because he was reluctant to teach the monk. He was trying to protect him. If he had tried to teach him something, it would only have harmed him. In fact, there is no way a teacher can teach the Buddha-patriarchs' marvelous, untransmittable Dharma to others. If a priest tells you he has liberated students by teaching them the Dharma, you can be sure of two things: he has not penetrated the source, and he is not a genuine Zen teacher. But for you, what is essential is not whether he is genuine or not. What is essential is

*Hakuin paraphrases an account in *Compendium of the Five Lamps,* ch. 9.
†See Supplementary Note 5 at the end of this letter.

to pledge that you will never have anything to do with false teachers like him. The Zen you practice must be true and authentic, and it must be practiced under a true and authentic teacher. Would you call Zen sages like Bodhidharma, Hui-neng, Huang-po, Hsueh-feng, and Tao-wu dead otters? Would you characterize venerable teachers like Hui-k'o, Nan-yueh, Lin-chi, Hsuan-sha, and Hsiang-yen as dumb sheep?

"The exchanges that took place when teachers and students faced each other in the past did not always dispense with words, and when the students asked questions, they were generally for the purpose of seeking instruction, receiving appraisal of their own views, probing the master's insight, resolving a troubling problem, or making a personal assertion.* They were nothing like the half-baked encounters carried out by the pseudo-Zennists of today, with teachers who can't tell the difference between fine and coarse, between rock and precious jade, wading in from the outset, doing what they can to free up the cicada's wings,† spewing out great quantities of the worst imaginable filth, leaving their students' faces lacquered over with the stuff."

Boku said: "But there are students who reach satori by studying the words and teachings of the Buddha-patriarchs, and there are students who achieve great and final cessation by following a teacher's advice. By comparing them to inhabitants of Uttarakuru, or to people addicted to worldly wisdom and skillful words, to lump them with the dried buds and dead seeds of the Two Vehicles—wouldn't that mean they have no hope of ever attaining the Buddha's Dharma?‡ Surely the Dharma should have some expedient means that could be used to help them?"

---

*These are among eighteen types of questions Zen students are said to ask their teachers, as formulated by Fen-yang Shan-chao (947–1024) in *The Eye of Men and Gods*. A complete listing and explanation is found in D. T. Suzuki's *Essays in Zen Buddhism, 2nd Series* (Rider, London, 1950), pp. 80–82.

†*Free up the cicada's wings*. A similar expression appears in the *Book of Latter Han*, to describe a lord showing great partiality to a favorite; here it refers to the statement made earlier about a teacher ruining a student's chances for enlightenment by stepping in prematurely to help him achieve a breakthrough.

‡Two of eight difficult situations (*hachinan*) in which it is difficult for people to encounter a Buddha, hear him preach, and attain liberation: being in Uttarakuru, the continent to the north of Mount Sumeru, where inhabitants enjoy lives of interminable pleasure; and being enthralled by the worldly wisdom and skillful words of secular life. *Dried buds and dead seeds* (*shōge haishu*) is a term of reproach often directed at followers of the Two Vehicles, who are said to have no possibility for attaining complete enlightenment.

I sighed and replied, "The ocean of true reality is boundless and profoundly deep. The Buddha Way is immeasurably vast. Some people do nothing but seek fame and success until their dying day, never showing the slightest interest in the path of Zen or the Buddha's Dharma. Others become engrossed in literary pursuits or become addicted to sake or women, oblivious to the hell fires flaming up under their very noses. Some, relying on insignificant bits of knowledge they pick up, shamelessly deny the law of cause and effect, woefully lacking any true grasp of its working. Some find ways to attract large numbers of people to their temples, believing to the end of their days that this is proof of a successful teaching career. Now it is true that compared to fellows of that stamp, students who reach satori thanks to teachings they hear, or arrive at cessation thanks to advice they receive from a teacher, are indeed wonderful occurrences—as rare as lotus flowers blossoming amid raging fire. The attainment they achieve is due to large stores of karmic merit accumulated in previous existences. It is not easy to achieve, it is not insignificant, and it must be valued and deeply respected.

"But for all that, there is still no getting around the fact that genuine practicers of Zen must once achieve *kenshō* (see their true nature), and then bring the one great matter of their life to final cessation. Satori and cessation are one thing, they are not two. But differences inevitably appear in the profundity of the satori and the strength or power that results from it. Let me try to describe this to you by explaining how progress toward final cessation, and lack of progress as well, appears in four types of students following their initial *kenshō*.

"First you have the students who engage in genuine Zen practice for a long time until principles and wisdom are gradually exhausted, emotions and views eliminated, techniques and verbal resources all used up. They wither into a perfect and unflappable serenity, their bodies and minds completely dispassionate. Suddenly, satori comes. They are liberated, like the phoenix that soars up from its golden cage, like the crane that breaks free of its pen. Releasing their hands from the cliffside, they die the great death and are reborn into life anew. These are students who have thoroughly penetrated, who have bored through all forms and penetrated all sounds and can see their self-nature as clearly as if it was in the palm of their hand. After painstakingly working their way through into the final barrier koans set up by the patriarchal teachers, their minds, in one single vigorous burst of effort, abruptly transform. Such students possess deep discernment and the innate ability that enables them to enter liberation at a single blow from the iron hammer. They are foremost among all the outstanding seeds and buds of our school. The only thing they still lack is the personal confirmation of a genuine teacher.

"Next there are students who move forward in their koan practice until they gain strength that is almost mature. Thanks to a word or phrase of the Buddha-patriarchs or perhaps some advice from a good friend, they suddenly break through into satori. Let us call them initial penetrators. Their penetration is complete in some areas, but not in others. They have a sure grasp of Dharma utterances of the *hosshin* type, words such as 'White waves rise on the mountain peak. Red dust dances at the bottom of a well.'* But when they come up against the important matter of the more advanced koans, they are as the deaf and dumb. As long as they are sitting quietly doing zazen, the principle of true reality is perfectly clear and the true form of things immediately manifested, but the minute they return into the everyday world and begin dealing with some troublesome matter or other, this serenity instantly disappears. It withers away amid the constant disparity between their meditative and quotidian life, their inner wisdom and daily activity.

"There are also students who spend much time and effort tenaciously engaging in hidden practice and secret activity until, one day, owing to the guidance of a teacher, they finally are able to reach a state of firm belief. We can call them the believers. They understand without any doubt whatsoever about principles such as self-nature being apart from birth-and-death and the true body transcending past and present. But the great and essential matter of the Zen school is beyond them. They can't even see it dimly in their dreams. They are not only powerless to save others, they are unable to bring their own liberation to completion either.

"It was for students of the second and third type, who are engaged in the practice that one of the ancients described as gradual practice followed

---

*In the system of Zen study developed in later Hakuin Zen, *hosshin* or Dharmakaya koans are used in the beginning stages of koan practice (see *Zen Dust*, 46–50). The lines Hakuin quotes here are not found in the *Poems of Cold Mountain (Han-shan shih)*, but are attributed to him in *Compendium of the Five Lamps* (ch. 15, chapter on Tung-shan Mu-ts'ung), and are included in a Japanese edition of Han-shan's poems published during Hakuin's lifetime. "The master ascended the teaching seat and said, 'Han-shan said, "Red dust dances at the bottom of the well. / White waves rise on the mountain peaks. / The stone woman gives birth to a stone child. / Fur on the tortoise grows longer by the day." If you want to know the Bodhi-mind, all you have to do is to behold these sights (annotation).'"

by sudden realization, that the step-by-step practice set forth in the *Ten Ox-herding Pictures* and the precious norms laid out in the Five Ranks were devised.* If they continue to practice assiduously, it is possible for them to advance into the ranks of those who have fully penetrated.

"Finally, there are students who come to believe in a teaching they hear, accepting it as true even though it has no more substance than a shadow, and cling tightly to it until the day they die. These are the self-deceivers. They have been bamboozled by words, yet continue to follow them scrupulously. They have neither penetrated the wondrous and perfect self-nature that exists within their own minds, nor are they able to understand the true reality of the external world. Following arbitrarily the movements of their own minds and perceptions, confounding them for manifestations of truth, they pick up various plausible notions and spout them to everyone they meet: 'It's like a precious mirror that reflects unerringly a Chinese or a foreigner in all their perfections and imperfections when they come before it; like a mani gem set out on a tray reflecting all shapes and all colors without a single trace remaining behind. Intrinsically, your mind is like that. There is no need to refine it. No need to attain it through practice.' Having no doubt that they themselves belong to the ranks of the genuine priests who have achieved final cessation, if they hear of someone engaging in secret training and hidden practice, they fall about clutching their bellies in paroxysms of laughter.

"Ahh, They are plausible, all too plausible. The trouble is, they haven't yet broken free of the indestructible adamantine cage, they are wandering ever deeper into the forest of thorn, and they have recognized a thief as their own son. It is because of this that the great master Ch'ang-sha said, 'The reason practicers fail to attain the Way is because they confound the ordinary working of their minds for truth. Although *that* has been the source of birth and death from the beginning of time, the fools insist on calling it their 'original self.' They are like Temple Supervisor Tse before he visited master Fa-yen, like Chen Tien-hsiung before his encounter with Huang-lung.†

"We might compare the ones who have fully penetrated this matter to

---

*The Ten Ox-Herding Pictures are a series of pictures and verses that illustrate the Zen student's progress to final enlightenment. The Five Ranks, comprising five Ranks of the Particular and Universal, are a teaching device formulated by Tung-shan of the Ts'ao-tung (J. Sōtō) tradition.
†See Supplementary Note 6 at the end of this letter.

a prince of royal blood who is heir apparent to the throne. Born of noble stock, with intrinsic nobility that has no need of the benefits others must obtain through practice, he is universally acclaimed in all lands, and brings peace and prosperity to the world. The entrants (those who attain an initial realization) and the convinced (those who achieve a firm belief) are like the Chinese Emperors Liu Hsiu and Su Tsung, who strove to establish their authority,* but being surrounded on all sides by rebellious tribes who refused to bring them tribute, could never afford to neglect thoughts of armament and defense. Those I termed "the hoodwinked" resemble rebels like Wang Mang and An Lu-shan, both of whom proclaimed themselves emperor but were unable to maintain their grip on wealth and power.†

"As the priest Nan-t'ang declared, 'You must see your self-nature as clearly as if you are looking at it in the palm of your hand, so that each and every thing becomes perfectly and unmistakably your own wondrously profound field of Dharma truth.'‡ This is a matter demanding the greatest caution. Because of this, the Zen school declares: 'Clarifying your self but not the things before your eyes gets you only half, and clarifying the things before your eyes but not your self gets you only half as well. You must know that if you press on, the time will come when it will all be yours.'§ It is also said, 'If students of the Way want to confirm whether they have truly entered realization, they must examine their mind thoroughly both in the activities of everyday life and amid the tranquility of zazen. Is the mind in the realm of active life different from the way it is during meditation? Do they hesitate or have any trouble in penetrating the various mean-

---

*Liu Hsiu (first century) was a royal descendant of the Western Han who defeated the usurper Wang Mang and established the Eastern Han dynasty. Emperor Su Tsung (8th century) regained the throne that had been usurped from his father.

†Wang Mang (c. 45 BCE–23 AD), a powerful official of the Western Han dynasty and rebellious T'ang general, and An Lu-shan (c. 703–757) both attempted to usurp the throne and declare themselves emperor.

‡Nan-t'ang is Ta-sui Yuan-ching (1065–1135), an heir of Fa-yen Wen-i. The quotation appears in *Eye of Men and Gods*, ch. 1. Hakuin cites it frequently and includes it in *Redolence from the Cold Forest*, a selection of quotations he made for students that was first published in 1769.

§In *Detailed Study of the Fundamental Principles of the Five Houses of Zen* (*Goke sanshō yōro mon*) Tōrei explains the Zen terms "gains you half" (literally, "raise it up halfway") and "gaining it all" as follows: "'Raising it totally up' refers to grasping the treasury of the Buddha's true Dharma eye and making it one's own activity. 'Raising it partially up' refers to not yet having achieved this total attainment; to having achieved only half, or only one tenth" (*HOZ* 7:157–58).

ings of the words of the Buddha-patriarchs? How could someone who has thoroughly grasped the marrow of the Buddha-patriarchs possibly fail to understand their words and sayings?"*

"Therefore to patricians engaged in boring into the secret depths, I say: 'Those of you who have already achieved *kenshō* should place your-selves in the hands of a genuine teacher and follow and seek occasional advice from seasoned monks with deep experience as you continue the day-to-day practice of refining your attainment, concentrating yourself singlemindedly on fully exhausting the secret mysteries and penetrat-ing completely through the bottomless source. Those who have not yet achieved *kenshō* should be grappling with one of those meaningless koans. You might concentrate on Lin-chi's "person who is standing right here listening to me preach."† Bore into him at all times, whether you are in a quiet place doing zazen or actively engaged in the activities of everyday life. Grasp the person who is engaged in this nonstop seeking. Where is he? What is the mind that at this very moment seeks him? Entering ever deeper into these matters, and when mind ceases to function, when words and phrases are exhausted, attack it from the sides, attack it from the front and from the rear, keep gnawing away at it, gnawing, gnawing, until there is no place left to gnaw.'

"You may feel as though you are clinging perilously to a steel barrier towering before you, as though you are gagging while trying to down a soup of wood shavings,‡ as though you are grasping about at clouds of green smoke or probing through a sea of red mist. When all your skills have been used up, all your verbal resources and reason utterly exhausted, if you do not falter or attempt to understand and just keep boring steadily inward, you will experience the profound joy of knowing for yourself whether the water is cold or warm. The practice of Zen requires you to just press forward with continuous, unwavering effort. If you only exert yourself every other day, like a person experiencing a periodic fit of malar-ial fever, you will never reach enlightenment, not even with the passage of endless kalpas.

"There is a sea beach only several hundred paces from my native village

---

*No source has been found for these words; perhaps they are Hakuin's own.

†"If you cease your mind from its constant striving, you are no different from the Bud-dhas and patriarchs. You want to grasp the Buddhas and patriarchs, but you who are listening to my teaching at this very moment, you yourself are the Buddha-patriarch" (*Record of Lin-chi*, p. 23).

‡ For this saying, see above, #28, p. 52.

of Hara. Suppose someone is troubled because he doesn't know the taste of seawater and decides to sample some. He sets out down to the ocean beach, but stops and comes back before he has gone even a hundred steps. He starts out again, this time returning after taking only ten steps. He will never get to know the taste of seawater that way, will he? Yet if he keeps going straight ahead and he doesn't turn back, even if he lives far inland in a landlocked province such as Shinano, Kai, Hida, or Mino, he will eventually reach the ocean. By dipping his finger in the ocean and licking it, he will know instantly the taste of seawater the world over because it has the same taste everywhere, in India, in China, or in the southern or northern seas.

"It is the same for the Dharma patricians who explore the secret depths. Proceeding straight ahead, pushing steadily forward, they bore into their minds with unbroken effort, never slackening or regressing. When the breakthrough suddenly arrives, they penetrate their own nature, the nature of others, the nature of sentient beings, the nature of evil passions and enlightenment, the nature of the Buddha-nature, the nature of the gods, the Bodhisattva-nature, the nature of sentient and nonsentient beings, the craving-ghost nature, the contentious spirit nature, the beast nature—they are all of them grasped in a single instant of thought. The great matter of their religious quest is completely and utterly resolved, and there is nothing left for them to do. They are freed from birth and death. What a thrilling moment it is!

"But a matter of particularly bowel-wrenching intensity still remains, and that is the very heart of the matter that has been personally transmitted from one Zen patriarch to another and carefully maintained without alteration or diminution to the present day. Even students who have succeeded in breaking free of the adamantine cage and negotiated their way through the thicket of razor-edged briars, unless they also encounter a genuine teacher along the way and receive his personal instruction, they will be unable to grasp this matter, even in their dreams. Why? Because from the very beginning, the sage teachers have been like celestial dragons grasping the precious night-shining pearl tightly in their claws, not allowing turtles, sea urchins, fish, or other inhabitants of the deep to observe it. They are like venerable dragons, masters of the clouds and rain, whose essential role is totally beyond the ken of frogs and earthworms and others that inhabit the waters. I speak of Zen masters like Nan-ch'uan, Ch'ang-sha, Huang-po, Su-shan, Tz'u-ming, Shao-shih, Chen-ching, Hsi-keng, Daiō, and Wu-hsueh.

"Now, I don't want you to think I've been spinning out these stories just to impress you with my insights and learning. I heard them thirty years ago from my teacher Shōju Rōjin. He was always lamenting the fading Zen transmission, which he said now hung by a few thin strands. These concerns of his became deeply engrained in my bones and marrow. They have been forever etched in my liver and bowels. But being afraid that if I spoke out I would have trouble making people believe what I said, I have for a long time kept my silence. I have constantly regretted that you, Mr. Ishii, and the two or three other laymen who study here with you were never able to meet Master Shōju. For that reason I have taken up my brush and rashly scribbled down all these verbal complications on paper. Having finished, I now find my entire back bathed in a profuse sweat, partly in shame, partly in gratitude. My only request is that after reading this letter, you will pass it on to the Fire God with instructions to consign it to his eternal storehouse. *Hahahah.*"

. . . .

Supplementary Notes
Supplementary Note 1. The following story appears in *Records of the Lamp*, ch. 17: "Asked by a monk, 'How should a monk comport himself throughout the twenty-four hours?' Ts'ao-shan replied, 'As if passing through a region filled with poisonous insects (*ku*), not letting a single drop of water pass his lips.'" Understanding of this dialogue requires an explanation of the meanings attached to the word *ku* (translated "poisonous insects"). In *Tso-chuan (Tso's Narrative)*, the oldest of the Chinese narrative histories, we read: "Chao-meng asked, 'What is the meaning of the word *ku*?' The physician answered, 'It refers to anything that causes excess, agitation, delusion, or trouble. The ideograph *ku* represents a jar filled with insects. The grub that insinuates its way into grain stock is also a destructive *ku* insect. In the *Book of Changes*, women who seduce men and the wind that topples trees in the mountains are also described as *ku*.'" The word also occurs in the records of the Sung master Hsu-t'ang: "There was a custom in the Fu-chien District prevalent since the T'ang dynasty of throwing various insects such as venomous snakes, lizards, and spiders together, waiting until only one of them remained alive, and then mixing its venom and blood into a potion to ward off evil spirits or to kill people by a casting magic spell on them." In the Yuan dynasty medical treatise *I-fang tai ch'eng lun*: "It is said that people living deep in the mountains of Min-kuang put three kinds of poisonous insects into a container and bury it in the ground

on the fifth day of the fifth month. They allow the insects to devour each other until only one remains, called a *ku*. They extract the poison from this insect, and when they want to harm someone, they put it into their food or drink."

Supplementary Note 2. *Dead otter (shi-katsudatsu)* Zen. According to a glossary of Zen terms dating from shortly after Hakuin's time, this refers to the quietistic practices of "silent illumination" *(mokushō)* Zen employed in the Sōtō school. The Sung master Ta-hui speaks of "bands of miscreant shave-pates who have not yet opened their own eyes but who nonetheless strive to lead others into a state of quietistic stagnation in the realm of the blind otters" (*Ta-hui's Letters*; Third Letter to Cheng Shih-lang). In his work *Kōrōju*, the Tokugawa scholar-priest Muchaku Dōchū concludes that the term does not refer to an otter (he suggests instead a red-haired, wolf-like animal): "Although I have been unable to discover precisely what this creature is, it is said to 'play possum,' pretending to be dead, in order to draw people near so it can seize and devour them."

Dumb sheep Zen is said to refer to monks who are unable to tell good from bad and lack the sense to correct their mistakes. Hakuin generally applies the term to "do-nothing" Zennists: i.e., those who do not actively seek *kenshō* through koan study.

Supplementary Note 3. *Box-shrub* Zen. The growth of the box tree or shrub (*tsuge no ki*) is so slow that it was said to sometimes cease growing altogether and, during intercalary years, even to shrink in size. Ta-hui uses the term to describe students who not only cease making headway in their practice, but by attaching to satori actually backslide (*Ta-hui's General Discourses*, ch. 2). *Carry the day* roughly paraphrases the expression "bare the left arm," referring to a gesture that is made to show one has been won over and will support another's cause. "Marquis Chou Po, before setting out to subjugate the Lu family, issued an order to his army, saying, 'Those who are for the Lu family bare their right arms, those for the Liu family bare their left arms!' They all bared their left arms, and he was able to launch an attack and gain the upper hand" (*Records of the Grand Historian*, p. 280).

Supplementary Note 4. In the *Record of Lin-chi* account (also *Blue Cliff Record*, Case 11), the head monk in Huang-po's assembly tells Lin-chi to ask Huang-po about the essential meaning of the Buddha Dharma. He goes to Huang-po three times, each time receiving blows, and decides to leave the temple. The head monk tells Huang-po, "That young monk who's been com-ing to you [Lin-chi] is a genuine vessel for the Dharma. If he comes and tells you he's going to leave, please use your expedient means in dealing with him. If he continues to bore his way through, I'm sure that he will become a great tree and provide cool shade to all the world." Huang-po suggests to Lin-chi that he might visit Ta-yu. At Ta-yu's temple, Lin-chi explains why he left Huang-po, adding that he wasn't sure whether he was at fault or not. Ta-yu says, "Huang-po spared no effort. He treated you with utmost tenderness and grandmotherly kindness. Why do you talk about fault and no fault?" Lin-chi experienced a sudden enlightenment, and said, "There's not much to Huang-po's Dharma." Lin-chi returned to Huang-po and related what had happened at Ta-yu's place. Huang-po said, "I'd like to get hold of that fellow and give him a good dose of my stick!"

Supplementary Note 5. Once Tao-wu Yuan-chih (769–835) and his student Chien-yuan went to pay their respects to a man who had passed away. Chien-yuan rapped on the coffin and said, "Living or dead?" Tao-wu replied, "Won't say living. Won't say dead." "Why won't you say?" asked Chien-yuan. "Won't say," replied Tao-wu. On their way back to the temple, Chien-yuan declared, "If you don't say it right now, I'm going to hit you." "Go ahead and hit me if you want. Won't say living. Won't say dead," replied Tao-wu. Chien-yuan struck him. When they were back at the temple, Tao-wu told Chien-yuan that if the temple supervisor found out what he had done he would surely give him a beating, and suggested that Chien-yuan go away for a while. Chien-yuan left and, while studying under Shih-shuang, attained a realization upon hearing Shih-shuang repeat the words, "Won't say, Won't say" (Records of the Lamp, ch. 15. Also Blue Cliff Record, Case 55).

Supplementary Note 6. A monk named Hsuan-tse was supervisor monk in the brotherhood of Zen Master Fa-yen Wen-i. The master said, "How long have you been here with me?" "It's been three years now," he replied. "As a member of the younger generation that is responsible for carrying on the transmission, why haven't you ever asked me about the Dharma?" "To tell the truth," Tse replied, "I already entered the Dharma realm of peace and com-fort when I was studying with Zen Master Ch'ing-feng." "By what words did you attain that realm?" Fa-yen asked. Tse replied, "I once asked Ch'ing-feng, 'What is the self of a Buddhist monk?' He answered, 'Ping-ting t'ung-tzu [the fire god] comes for fire.'" "Those are fine words," said Fa-yen. "But you probably didn't understand them." Tse said, "I understand them to mean that since Ping-ting is a fire deity, looking for fire with fire would be like looking for the self with the self." "Just as I thought," said Fa-yen. "You didn't understand. If that were the extent of the Buddha Dharma, the transmission could not have lasted down to the present day." Indignant, Hsuan-tse left the monastery, but on his way down the mountain he reflected, "The master is known throughout the land as a great teacher. He has over five hundred disciples. There must be some merit to his words." Returning penitently to the monastery, he performed his bows before Fa-yen, and asked, "What is the self of a Buddhist monk?" "Pin-ting t'ung-tzu comes for fire," the master replied. At the words, Hsuan-tse attained great enlightenment (*Records of the Lamp*, ch. 17).

Chen Tien-hsiung is Ts'ui-yen K'o-chen (n.d.), a Dharma heir of Tz'u-ming (Shih-shuang Ch'u-yuan, 986–1039); he acquired the nickname "Breast-beater Chen" because on attaining enlightenment he began elatedly pummeling his chest. "As a student living on intimate terms with Tz'u-ming, Chen grew convinced of his superior talents. But while accompanying Chen on a summer practice retreat, Tz'u-ming's senior disciple Attendant Shan [later Huang-lung Hui-nan, 1002–69], soon saw that Chen's attainment was incomplete. One day, when they were walking in the mountain, he picked up a pebble, put it on top of a large boulder, and said, "If you come up with a good turning word for this, I'll believe that you truly understand Master Tz'u-ming." Glancing to his left and right, Chen seemed on the verge of replying, but Shan gave a loud shout. "You haven't even overcome mental discrimination yet! You hesitate and lack resolution! How can you ever hope to grasp Tz'u-ming's inner meaning?" Realizing the truth of Shan's words, Chen was thoroughly ashamed. He immediately returned and resumed his practice with Tz'u-ming, and was finally able to achieve complete enlightenment (*Compendium of the Five Lamps*, ch. 12).

: 80. TO THE PRIEST OF EIGAN-JI

This letter dates from 1727, Hakuin's forty-third year. Although the recipient cannot be identified, Eigan-ji, the temple where he served, was the site of one of the more dramatic episodes in Hakuin's religious career. It was at Eigan-ji, located in Takada in Echigo province, that twenty-three-year-old Hakuin achieved his first significant breakthrough into enlightenment. According to Hakuin's narration of the event in his autobiographies Wild Ivy *(pp. 22–26) and* Tale of

My Childhood, *the experience was so powerful that he was sure he had attained the final, decisive awakening he had been seeking. He went to the head priest Santetsu Soran (d. 1727)—the person whose death prompted the present letter—and set forth his understanding, but neither Santetsu nor Buttō, the senior priest at Eigan-ji, would give him the confirmation he was expecting. It was after this practice meeting ended that Hakuin went to neighboring Shinano province and encountered Shōju Rōjin, the man he came to regard as his true teacher.*

*Santetsu is referred to in this letter as the priest of Hōsen-ji, a temple in eastern Suruga province near Hakuin's Shōin-ji that Santetsu had established in 1709, while still head priest of Eigan-ji, as a place of retirement. When he had served at Eigan-ji for thirty years, Santetsu turned the temple over to his Dharma heir Buttō and retired to Hōsen-ji, though apparently he continued to teach there as well. When Buttō died in 1726, Santetsu was obliged to return to Eigan-ji, which had in the meantime been moved to Utsunomiya in Shimofusa province (present Tochigi prefecture), where he passed away several years later.**

The praise Hakuin lavishes on Santetsu in this letter written in his forties, is in marked contrast to the harsh portrait he paints of him in the autobiographies he wrote in the final decade of his life (see Precious Mirror Cave, *pp. 25–7; pp. 165–6).*

A T SHAKAMUNI'S BIRTH, AN auspicious ray of light appeared that was still seen far away in China a thousand years later. It is said that when the World-Honored One entered Nirvana, the rainbow of white light that appeared reached to China as well. When First Patriarch Bodhidharma left one of his boots behind in Northern Wei and set out to return to India, the lapels of Emperor Liang's robes were soaked with tears.

When word came that the great priest of Hōsen-ji (Santetsu) had passed away at Eigan-ji in Utsunomiya, priests and monks from dozens of temples in western Suruga province gathered at Hōsen-ji to express their deep sadness and regret. The virtue of the man was such that people felt the same kind of grief that was experienced at the death of Shakamuni

---

* It was thought until recently that the Chinese characters for Santetsu's name were pronounced Shōtetsu, however *furigana* attached to the name in one of Hakuin's printed works shows the correct reading to be Santetsu.

Buddha or Bodhidharma.

When Santetsu left Hōsen-ji and went back to his home temple Eigan-ji in Utsunomiya, we waited three years for him to return to Hōsen-ji. How could we have expected that this shattering news would come instead? A great ridgepole has suddenly broken in the house of Zen. A towering Dharma shade tree has fallen. The leaves and moss in Eigan-ji's gardens have been drained of all their color. Zen groves throughout the country wither and fade. Santetsu possessed a lofty Zen spirit that had been refined to the utmost purity. He possessed a mind so trenchant that it could cut through steel. Losing such a teacher has made us all deeply sad and despondent.

Utsunomiya is such a great distance from here, we were not able to go to Eigan-ji and take part in the sutra recitations for him. We can do no more than face toward the temple, gaze up into the clouds and mist, and express our feelings of deep sorrow. Santetsu Oshō was a great Dharma vessel, a man whose Dharma eye was fully open. After teaching at Eigan-ji for ten years, he succeeded in producing a genuine Dharma heir. Thanks to that he was able to retire to Hōsen-ji here in Suruga. Students from all over the province hastened there to study under him; and many lay parishioners became his devout followers as well.

We are now entering the eleventh month. It becomes colder by the day. We hope that you will all take good care of yourselves.

⦂ 81. Reply to Priest Rempō of Keirin-ji

Rempō Chishō (d. 1770), a Dharma heir of Ranshitsu Tōiku (d. 1743; see #28), was the head priest of Keirin-ji in Kai province, a temple Hakuin visited frequently to conduct practice meetings. An annotation tells us that Rempō "studied with the master for many years, even after becoming head priest at Keirin-ji." He was thus one of a number of Zen teachers in Suruga and the surrounding provinces of Kai, Tōtōmi, and Izu who continued their post-satori training under Hakuin while training students in their own temples. According to Tōrei, Rempō applied himself to koan study under Hakuin "with the greatest determination" (Draft Biography).

Since it is known that Rempō succeeded Ranshitsu at Keirin-ji on the latter's death, this letter can date no earlier than Hakuin's

late fifties, and, given Hakuin's reference to "enjoying the years left
to him," possibly even a decade or so later.

YOUR LETTER OF THE twelfth of the fourth month reached my desk
on the twelfth of the fifth month. Reading it over several times, I
felt as though you were actually here conversing with me. Wonderful.
Wonderful.

I was concerned that you may have wondered why I had not replied to
your letter. It was not due to conscious neglect on my part. The letter you
sent took an entire month to reach me.

I fear that I didn't treat you with proper hospitality when you visited
Shōin-ji at the end of the third month. Now whenever I sit in my room and
think about how impolite I was, the shame makes beads of perspiration
trickle down my spine.

I was very glad to hear that your health has been good since your return.
For myself, I am still enjoying the years left to me, living like a simpleton,
without care or trouble. I potter around the temple gardens to check how
my eggplants are doing. I am happy to be able to tell you that you need not
be concerned about me.

You said you are boring into the impassable koan I gave you day and
night, putting it right down inside you and attacking it as relentlessly as
you would a mortal enemy, not even stopping to eat. Splendid! Bravo! This
is the incomparable joy of the Zen Dharma!

These days, people in temples throughout the country have submerged
themselves in the dead, stagnant water of quiescent, silent illumination
Zen. They make no headway whatever, achieve nothing at all. They just
dilly-dally their lives away in that half-alive, half-dead state. They reject
the essential matter of koan study, shoving it aside without a thought,
having no more use for it than a merchant would for a mattock or plow.
One of their teachers says things like this: "Don't look at the koan stories;
that is a muddy quagmire that will only suck your self-nature under. Don't
look at words or letters; that is a dense thicket filled with entangling vines
that will strangle the life from your Zen spirit. Your self-nature has no
love for words and letters. It has no fondness for koans. It wants simply to
retain an easy tranquility, a free and unrestricted state of mind. That is the
true and authentic meaning of Zen's direct pointing. The self-nature that
is inborn in each and every person is originally perfectly clear, free, and
unrestricted. It doesn't mistake a heron for a crow. It doesn't mistake the

sky for the earth. It feels fire as hot and water as cold. It works perfectly well, with no lack whatsoever, without recourse to Shakamuni's teachings, without borrowings from Bodhidharma's Zen. Why would you want to go seeking anything beyond that?"*

He certainly sounds plausible, all too plausible. The trouble is, following such a path means you are mistaking the workings of your mind for ultimate truth and turning yourself into a piddling little imp. The patriarchs characterized such a person as the Great King Stuck-in-the-Mud, slumbering away all by himself at the rear of a deserted old shrine."† The ancients—people who rejected fame and profit and without a thought to their own well-being devoted themselves singlemindedly to the pursuit of the Way—are as different from such priests as cloud is from mud.

But at some future date a monk will come along, so bold and shameless he won't even acknowledge his own teacher. He will grab one of those koans, the kind that resembles a stick of flaming hot steel or a deadly poisonous chestnut burr, and thrust it under this fellow's nose, demanding, "What is the principle of this!" It will be like a dauntless warrior rushing headlong at him flourishing an enormous sword over his head, intent on cleaving his head in two. At that moment, not a word or phrase will issue from his lips. He won't be able to grunt even a simple sound like "*gu.*" There is nowhere he can escape. The slightest hesitation means certain death. This is something he can't swallow down and can't spit out either. He won't have the strength to muster any anger or summon up any tears. He'll just stand there with glazed and goggling eyes, his mouth turned down in a frown. There won't be even a spark of life. He won't be able to raise his head. All that talk, all the big sermons he'd been making to people in the hinterlands won't do him a bit of good now. He'll be like a sick horse under a heavy load stumbling down an endless road on a scorching

---

*Similar formulations are found almost verbatim among the teachings of Bankei Yōtaku, whose Unborn (*fushō*) Zen was extremely popular in Rinzai circles in the decades prior to Hakuin's appearance as a teacher. See *Unborn: The Life and Teachings of Zen Master Bankei.*

†"There is a type of priest whose understanding consists in remaining deaf and dumb, doing nothing whatever. He lives in a temple, gobbles down rice, and clings to this inert and lifeless state like a dead otter, in expectation that enlightenment will come to him. He is called the Great King Stuck-in-Satori, a clod of mud lying forgotten in the corner of a broken down house in a vast swamp somewhere deep in the mountains. He does nothing but consume the rice he undeservedly receives as alms" (*Record of Yun-an*, ch. 7).

day—his whole body will be bathed in heavy, shame-induced sweat. Can someone like that be called a descendant of the Zen patriarchs? Later on, when he is charged with training a group of monks, heroes who have come to him from all over the land, how can he possibly deal with them and provide the guidance they need?

The reason he finds himself in this predicament is simply because he has mistaken the unmoving stillness of the storehouse consciousness for his original face. If he had genuinely clarified the heart and mind of the Buddha-patriarchs, how could he fear the old koans that transmit their sayings and doings? In the past, a Zen teacher of the true stripe did not trouble students with the ramifications of Buddhist doctrine or with the study of words and phrases. He just gave them a short and venomous koan and had them bore steadily into it. If a student commits himself to authentic Zen practice, throwing his entire being into a koan with single-minded focus that does not allow previous notions, views, or emotions to intrude, and he keeps boring into it—gnawing from the top, gnawing from the bottom, and from all sides—he will reach a point when words and logic are totally exhausted. All at once, everything will suddenly fall away, and he will then have "words and letters" truly in his grasp. Strutting through the world with the complete and utter freedom of the lion king, whenever he encounters someone he responds with the speed and force of lightning. This is a level of attainment those idle, disembodied spirits [of silent illumination Zen], lying open-eyed like zombies in their coffins, could not even glimpse in their dreams.

After hearing only a single word, worthy teachers of the past would set out on a journey of ten thousand leagues in order to pay respects to the person who uttered it, prostrating themselves before him and offering incense to him. Students thought nothing of traveling a thousand leagues and enduring untold hardships to visit a true teacher. Hence the saying, "The single phrase, 'Together with it' made a Zen monk walk through a thousand mountains."* Yet the sightless shavepates of today regard the old koan stories as no more than needless words, unnecessary entanglements.

---

* A monk asked Ta-sui, "It's said that the whole universe will be destroyed in the world-ending kalpa fire. I want to know whether 'this' [the eternal Buddha-nature] is destroyed along with it." "Destroyed," replied Ta-sui. The monk said, "It disappears together with the universe?" "Together with it," said Ta-sui. Yuan-wu, in his commentary on this koan, quotes a verse by T'ang priest Ching-tsun that begins: "Clearly no other Dharma exists. Who said it was transmitted to Hui-neng? One phrase, 'Together with it,' made one monk walk through a thousand mountains" (*Blue Cliff Record*, Case 29).

What runs through those minds of theirs? How sad that the groves of Zen have been reduced to such unprecedented decay.

Rempō Oshō, how truly praiseworthy that in the midst of this sorry situation you alone have girded up your spirit, set your jaw, and vowed to penetrate the great matter that furrows such deep creases in Zen monks' brows. Ahh! It is as rare as an Udumbara flower blossoming amid the flames! Your effort is certain to be rewarded with a marvelous result. Your attainment of the claws and fangs of the Dharma cave is near at hand. This is my earnest prayer, my earnest prayer.

The great matter is achieved in the same way that a red-finned carp butts its way upstream, plunging through the hundred leagues of black-cloud barriers blocking off the Dragon Gate to become a dragon; in the same way that the golden garuda plummets into the vast sea to seize its dragon prey beneath the waves. It is an altogether formidable undertaking, possible only for someone of genuinely great stature. Students of middling talent cannot hope even to attempt it.

Long ago, Chen of Ts'ui-yen and Supervisor Monk Hsuan-tse* contracted difficult maladies similar to the one we see in today's priests. Finding themselves unable either to die or to stay alive, they visited the great priests Fa-yen and Tz'u-ming. When those teachers pointed out their errors, they were like sick monkeys breaking free of their golden chains.† Su-shan was another monk who toppled back down into the comfortable old nest he had created for himself. He remained lodged inside it for a long time, rising and falling like a drowning man, until Lan-an's old wisteria vines encircled him, squeezed the life from him, and freed him of all his shackles.‡

At the beginning of his career, Master Kao of Mount Ching, "the Reviler of Heaven," was content to remain within an initial, rudimentary understanding. He later engaged in extremely difficult practice for several years, until one morning he was bowled over by a lethal wind sweeping in from the south and all obstructing and impeding spikes and wedges finally vanished.§

At the beginning of Hsu-t'ang Chih-yu's career, when he was a monk

---

*Chen Tien-hsiung (n.d.) and Supervisor Monk Hsuan-tse (n.d.), judging themselves to be fully enlightened, left their teachers early. When they discovered their mistake, they returned and completed their training. Their stories are found in *Beating the Cloth Drum*, pp. 44–5.

† The golden chain is a metaphor for attachment to satori.

‡See Supplementary Note 1 at the end of this letter.

§See Supplementary Note 2 at the end of this letter.

in the assembly under Zen master Yun-an, he was given the story Nan-ch'uan Kills the Cat. He offered the turning words, "Not even the great earth could hold it." Yun-an acknowledged the words with a faint smile. Hsu-t'ang was still not satisfied, however, and spent the next four years working on the story of Su-shan's Memorial Tower. One day he blundered into a poisonous flame that issued from the old Buddha of Ta-ling, and he lost both home and country. Now when he reexamined the koan stories he had penetrated before, he found his understanding of them was altogether different.*

Hsu-t'ang's example is an invaluable one. He went on to serve as the head priest at ten leading Zen temples, although while residing in them he comported himself as though he were dwelling alone in a small grass hut. The least syllable that spilled from his lips was like the deadly milk of the lion king, the tail feathers of the *Chen* bird.†

Driving off students with his deafening roars, he was like a ferocious tiger eyeing a lame sheep, like a starving falcon drawing a bead on a limping hare. But if he had stopped and remained like a dead man, fastened to the words, "Even the great earth cannot hold it," none of these remarkable achievements would have been possible. How grateful we should be that our Zen school is possessed of these marvelous prescriptions [koans] that can transform your very bone and marrow. At the same time, there were also among the followers of Zen those who were never able to cure themselves completely until the day they died—examples are Master Tun of Lung-ya and Master I of T'ien-p'ing.‡

You wrote in your letter that if I had some shortcut for penetrating koans you would like me to send it to you as quickly as possible. I have no shortcuts or other expedients I would consider smearing over your face. If I agreed to your request and doused you with a dipper of such vile ordure, you would revile me mightily for it later on. And, Rempō Oshō, if you possess any such shortcuts yourself, I want you to bundle them right up and toss them into another world.

I look forward with eager anticipation to hearing a *Ka!* [the shout emitted at the moment of enlightenment] from you that will rattle the walls

---

*See Supplementary Note 3 at the end of this letter.

†"A single drop of lion milk from the Tathagata's enlightened mind, put into a sea filled with boundless delusions, will destroy them all" (*Flower Garland Sutra*, ch. 78).

‡Chu-tun of Lung-ya's story is told in Case 20 of the *Blue Cliff Record*; Tsung-i of T'ien-p'ing's in Case 98.

of my ramshackle little hermitage. I stand on tiptoe, waiting for that with pricked ears.

All my best wishes to you, and please, for the Dharma's sake, take care of yourself during these noxious rainy months.

. . . .

Supplementary Notes

Supplementary Note 1. Su-shan Kuang-jen (837–909) had an initial attainment that made him overly self-confident. On hearing that master Kuei-shan Lan-an had said that being and nonbeing are like a vine clinging to a tree, he immediately set out and visited him. "Where do being and nonbeing go if the tree suddenly falls down and the vine withers?" he asked. Without answering, Kuei-shan gave a loud laugh and started for his quarters. Su-shan said, "I sold my belongings and traveled over three thousand leagues to ask you this question. Won't you at least give me an answer?" Kuei-shan told his attendant to give Su-shan two hundred coins. "Later on," he told Su-shan, "you'll meet a one-eyed dragon who will rid you of your problem." Later, when Su-shan heard about a teacher named Te-ch'ien, who was blind in one eye, he immediately set out to visit him. He told Te-ch'ien about his encounter with Kuei-shan, and then asked him, "If the tree falls and the vines wither, where do being and nonbeing go?" "You're only going to make Kuei-shan laugh even harder," Te-ch'ien said. At those words, Su-shan attained great enlightenment. "Kuei-shan's laugh had a dagger in it all along," he said, regretting his mistake, and performed a bow in the direction of Kuei-shan's temple far away (abridged from the account in *Compendium of the Five Lamps*, ch. 13).

Supplementary Note 2. One day when Ta-hui was studying at Yuan-wu's temple, Yuan-wu ascended to the teaching seat and said: "A monk asked Yun-men, 'From whence come all the Buddhas?' Yun-men said, 'The eastern mountain walks over the water.' If it were me, I wouldn't say that. If someone asked me, 'From whence come all the Buddhas?' I would say to him, 'A fragrant breeze sweeps in from the south, a refreshing coolness pervades the halls and pavilions.'" When Ta-hui heard those words, he was suddenly severed from before and after. Yuan-wu said, "It's not easy, is it? You've reached the fundamental ground, but unfortunately, though you've succeeded in dying, you're unable to get reborn. Not being able to doubt words and phrases is a grave illness. Don't you know the saying, 'Release your hands from the edge of the precipice and affirm it in enlightenment. Once you come back to life after you die, I won't be able to deceive you again.' You must believe that such a principle exists." He put Ta-hui in the hall where the prominent lay visitors lodged, appointing him an attendant at large. He was allowed to enter Yuan-wu's quarters daily, as freely as the great laymen did.

Yuan-wu brought up the phrase, "Being and nonbeing are like a vine clinging to a tree," and asked him about it. As Ta-hui was about to open his mouth to speak, Yuan-wu said, "That's not it! That's not it!" After six months passed, Ta-hui finally decided to ask Yuan-wu about his enlightenment. "I've heard that you asked about that phrase when you were studying with master Wu-tsu. I want to know how Wu-tsu answered your question." Yuan-wu smiled but did not answer. Ta-hui continued to press him. Finally, Yuan-wu reluctantly answered, "I asked him the meaning of 'being and nonbeing are like clinging like a vine to a tree.' He said, 'Try to draw it and you'll fail. Try to paint it and you'll fail.' Then I asked him, 'What about when the tree falls and the vine withers?' He said, 'It follows the form.'" At those words, Ta-hui [interrupted him and] said, "I understand." When Yuan-wu gave him some koans to test him, he responded to them without any hesitation whatever. "Now you know," said Yuan-wu, "that I was not deceiving you" (adapted from *Compendium of the Five Lamps*, ch. 19, section on Ta-hui).

Supplementary Note 3. Hsu-t'ang said, "I chanced to meet some of Yun-an Rōshi's followers as I was passing through Cha-shang, and they asked me to join their assembly. I was allowed to enter the master's chambers, but was not able to make any comments or capping words. Whenever I tried to say something, he would say, 'Take it easy, just remain mindless and unfettered by words.' In his chambers he invariably brought up the koan The Old Sail Not Yet Raised, but the moment I opened my mouth, he would begin reviling me. One day when I was in the attendants' quarters, it occurred to me: 'The Old Sail Not Yet Raised is not all that difficult to grasp. It refers to what is prior to the formation of the bubble, prior to the arising of thought. The Rōshi is just being arbitrary in his behavior. I'm going to lay a trap and turn the tables on him. Master Yen-t'ou sized a person up just seeing him approach and then launched an attack that left the person wordless. It was like the saying, "receiving a cow and giving a horse in return." [i.e., returning a great favor with an even greater one.] Why won't this priest allow me to utter even a single word?'

"Bearing my understanding in mind, I went to Yun-an's quarters and presented it to him. Before I had finished asking my question, he said, 'Why can't you just keep your mouth shut and find a quiet place and reflect privately on your own self? Spending day after day debating in your mind the pros and cons of the old teachers—where is that going to get you?'

"I left. By the time I returned to my quarters I was feeling extremely uneasy. Then, suddenly, I understood the words in The Old Sail Not Yet Raised, 'A monk who lives a life of purity does not enter Nirvana.' I also felt that I had finally penetrated the other, easier koans as well. The next day, at the first beat of the drum announcing *sanzen*, I entered Yun-an's chambers. He saw at a glance something different about me, so he didn't mention The Old Sail Not Yet Raised. He asked instead about the story of Nan-ch'uan killing the cat. I offered the capping words, 'Even the great earth cannot hold it.' He lowered his head with a faint smile [acknowledging it]. Half a year later, however, my mind was as uneasy and unsettled as before. When people greeted me, I could no longer respond as I previously had. For the next three or four years I worked steadily on Su-shan's Memorial Tower. One day, in a state of no-mind, I suddenly grasped the meaning of the old Buddha of Ta-ling's emitting a shaft of light, and I achieved a totally unrestricted freedom. From that time on, I was not deceived by others. When I took up koans I had previously penetrated and examined them again, I realized at once that my understanding was now completely different. I also knew with certainty that the great matter was something that had nothing to do with words or letters" (*Hsu-t'ang yu-lu*, ch. 4).

: 82. REPLY TO PRIEST REMPŌ OF KEIRIN-JI

Another letter to Rempō Chishō of Keirin-ji in Kai province (see above, #81). This one can be dated to 1741, Hakuin's fifty-eighth year. It seems that a monk named Zen Zennin (n.d.; Zennin = "Zen man") had brought a set of three-scroll paintings depicting "Three Buddhas" (san Sonbutsu) to Shōin-ji to have Hakuin write an inscription for them. Later in the Poison Blossoms *collection (#103), Hakuin describes these same scrolls in a verse titled "On Creating Images of Three Buddhas with the Sacred Names of Three Thousand Buddhas," which he says he saw for the first time on the wall of the Keirin-ji during a visit he made to the temple in 1741. The images of the three Buddhas depicted on the scrolls done in the* moji-e, "*calligraphic picture*," *style, in which the figures are produced by inscribing various words and phrases instead of the usual lines and washes. In this case, the figures of the Buddhas would have been created entirely using the sacred names (myōgō) of the three thousand Buddhas of past, present, and future written in minute Chinese characters.*

ZEN ZENNIN ARRIVED HERE after a long trip in the sweltering summer heat, bringing your letter and the two gifts you sent, which I accepted with deep gratitude. I don't know how to thank you. I am extremely glad to hear that you are healthy and that nothing is changed at your temple. Fortunately, I too am in fine fettle, no physical complaints whatever, so please don't waste time worrying about me.

I have finished inscribing the words you requested on the scrolls. I am afraid it is a very sorry performance indeed. I hummed the verse that you sent me on the fifth of the fifth month over and over, then I tried my hand at matching it, using your rhymes, but again the result was so poor I'd rather you did not even see it.

I was so moved by the genuine sincerity I felt from your letter that even after reading and rereading it several times, I was reluctant to put it down. When I came to the part about Hsueh-feng investigating the senior monk,* I was pleasantly surprised. But I was not without some sense of doubt as well.† I regret that this is a matter that cannot be expressed adequately in a word or two in a letter. Let us open our minds to each other when we meet this autumn and thrash it out together then.

You find a great many so-called Zen teachers these days who say whatever pops into their heads, spouting irresponsible nonsense about Zen. This pernicious custom began appearing thirty or forty years ago. A man of your natural modesty and sincerity bears them little resemblance. Nonetheless, the matter in question here is difficult in the extreme. Hsuan-sha, when he heard that Ling-yun had attained satori on seeing some peach blossoms, said, "He hadn't fully penetrated it." Yuan-wu was very slow in acknowledging Fo-teng's satori.‡ Such examples show how careful and circumspect the ancient teachers were when it came to confirming the great and essential matter.

I will entrust a few additional thoughts to Zen Zennin to pass along to

---

*"Hsueh-feng asked the senior monk, 'The two words you have spoken are both subordinate words. What is the essential word?' The monk could make no reply." (*Compendium of the Five Lamps*, ch. 7). "Rempō had apparently given his own answer in place of the monk" (annotation).

†"I am pleased that you have been so diligent in your practice but am dubious about your satori" (annotation).

‡See the supplementary note following this letter.

you. For the Dharma's sake, I want you to take good care of yourself in this terrific heat.

Yours, [Hakuin]

. . . .

Supplementary Note. Hsuan-sha said, "It is all perfectly true, totally proper and good, but I guarantee you the elder brother still hadn't got it all" (See p. 69, note on Hsuan-sha's utterance, for the dialogue). "Fo-teng studied with Kuang-chien Ying, but he left without achieving a satori and entered the brotherhood under Zen master Fo-chien to avail himself of that master's guidance. Still failing to gain entrance into satori, he left the assembly, saying, 'Even if I do not break through into satori until the end of my life, I vow that I will never stop trying.' With that, he began doing zazen throughout the days and nights. He carried out his practice with the diligence he would have shown in mourning his deceased parents. He continued for forty-nine days. Fo-chien addressed the assembly and said [quoting words from the *Dhammapada*]: 'Everything in the universe, every one of the myriad phenomena, are imprinted with the seal of the One Dharma.' Hearing them, Fo-teng attained sudden enlightenment. He went to Fo-chien for an interview. Fo-chien said, 'A pity to have the one bright pearl picked up by this madman!' He then proceeded to check Fo-teng's attainment. 'Ling-yun said, "From the time I saw those peach blossoms right up until the present, I've had not a single doubt." What about that "having no doubts"'? Fo-teng replied, 'How could I possibly grasp Ling-yun's nondoubting now, not to mention understanding all its particulars?' Fo-chien then asked, 'Hsuan-sha said, "It is all perfectly true, totally proper and good, but I guarantee you the elder brother still hadn't got it all."' Fo-teng said, 'You must deeply understand the extent of Hsuan-sha's grandmotherly kindness.' Fo-chien approved his understanding. Fo-teng bowed, got up, and presented a verse: 'All day gazing at the sky, his face did not look up. / Not until the heavens filled with peach blossoms did he lift his gaze. / Even if he had a net that encompassed the whole sky, / Once he'd burst from the cage, he should cease.' After exhorting Fo-teng to keep and protect his attainment, Fo-chien that night addressed the assembly and said in a loud voice, 'Senior Monk is sleeping easy now.' Yuan-wu, hearing about this, suspected that Fo-teng's attainment was not yet complete. 'I won't acknowledge it until I've investigated him myself,' he said. Yuan-wu sent someone to bring Fo-teng to his temple. One day they happened to be walking around the monastery precincts together, and they approached the edge of a pond. Yuan-wu suddenly pushed Fo-teng into the water. 'What about when Niu-t'ou had not yet seen the Fourth Patriarch?' he asked. 'When the pond is deep, fish gather,' replied Fo-teng. 'What about after he saw the Patriarch?' asked Yuan-wu. 'When the tree is tall, the breeze is summoned,' said Fo-teng. 'What about the time of seeing and nonseeing?' asked Yuan-wu. 'When you stretch your leg, it contracts and shortens,' replied Fo-teng. Yuan-wu extended great praise to Fo-teng's reply" (*Compendium of the Five Lamps*, ch. 19, section on Fo-teng).

:83. TO ATTENDANT KŌ

In this letter, Hakuin urges a monk named Kō, who had recently served as his personal attendant, to return to Shōin-ji so Hakuin could help him bring his training to a successful conclusion. Attendant Kō is identified in an annotation as Daikyū Ebō (1715–74), who became one of Hakuin's most important Dharma heirs. For a biographical sketch of Daikyū, see afternote below. This letter is no doubt typical of the correspondence Hakuin kept up with senior students around the country, some of whom had left at the finish of their training, and some of whom had been obliged by circumstances to cut short their training and return to their home temples.

Typically, Hakuin would offer these students words of encouragement and keep them up to date on the latest doings at Shōin-ji. But his primary concern, seen throughout the letters, seems to have been keeping tabs on his students' progress. He often issued warnings to those who had achieved an initial kenshō, cautioning them to be aware of the dangers of lapsing into the "do-nothing" passivity of "silent illumination Zen," which would occur if they did not continue to devote themselves to their koan practice.

THE NEW PRIEST AT Daikei-ji dropped your two letters off when he passed through here. I read them through several times. I was glad to learn you are in good health and earnestly engaged in your practice. Life here at Shōin-ji is poor and simple as always, but not one of my veteran monks has left for other parts. There are now nearly seventy men in the assembly. Monks Chū, Yaku, Gu, Goku, Tetsu, Sha, Rin and Ro, Chō and Tō, are still here. Mon and Shō are intermittently in attendance, and Ryō and Soku continue to bore steadily onward.* Everyone is resolutely bent on refining and polishing their attainment. They endure the bitter cold and other privations without complaint, never slackening their efforts at all.

At the beginning of spring, seven or eight seasoned monks of superior ability arrived. We accepted them into the brotherhood, and everyone gathered together and engaged in "pure talk" about the Way. I found them to be splendid religious seekers of the greatest ability, sincere and generous, humble and compassionate, possessed of strength, courage, and wisdom. For a doddery old monk like me, it was a joy that would be hard to match. You were the only one missing. When you finish your lectures on *Treatise to Assist the Teachings*,† be sure that you bend your steps back here and lend some help to your decrepit old teacher.

I never could understand why you had to run off by yourself to a remote province thousands of leagues from here. You never tied up with a single good companion or teacher. Never acquired the slightest spiritual benefit from leaving here whatsoever. You've just wasted your time—your most precious asset—and for what? People tell me, "He shifts from one beautiful spot to another." "He's well settled, has plenty of food and good lodgings." "He's looking for a place where he can live out the rest of his days." "He goes and performs devotions at temples and shrines." If that is indeed the extent of your religious aspiration, you are a truly doubtful sort of monk. They also say that what you really want is to spend three, five, maybe seven years ensconced quietly in some solitary retreat where you can devote yourself without interruption to nurturing and maturing your attainment. If that is your intention, it is equally misguided. For someone in your present situation, now is the time to make certain that the seedling is nurtured and brought into full flower. Why would you want to cling mulishly to this "withered sitting" style of Zen, hunkered dubiously down in some hinterland, turning your mind to ash, extinguishing thoughts and feelings, blinding your wisdom, blundering your life away? Time, you will find, passes by at great speed. You go on inanely wasting your time, like a young girl sewing up piles of diapers and buying mortars and pestles

---

*The only monks in this list about whom anything significant is known are *Chō*: Bunchō (n.d.); *Yaku*: Gen'yaku (n.d); *Tō*: Reigen Etō (1721–85); and *Ryō*: Ishin Eryō (1720–69). They appear in the *Chronological Biography (Precious Mirror Cave*, pp.142–240).

† *Fu-chiao pien*, a work by the Rinzai teacher Fo-jih Ch'i-sung (1007–72) criticizing the anti-Buddhist thought of Han Yu and others, and attempting to show the harmony of Confucian and Buddhist teachings.

and other kitchen equipment before she's even found a husband. What a terrible, shameful waste!

It's said you should acquire friends who are superior to yourself. The outstanding seekers of the past were determined from the moment they took up their traveling staffs and set out on pilgrimage to locate a teacher of superior attainment, someone who would be able to help them bring their training to completion. Once that teacher was found, they invariably remained with him to receive the benefits of his personal influence.

Today's students are not like that. Lacking the clear eye of wisdom, they linger about, worshipping the dust of some worthless, toothless old bonze. They dawdle aimlessly over here, poke blindly around over there, roaming this way and then that way, not stopping for a moment. They are ridiculous. In the past, Bodhidharma, a man possessed of profound innate wisdom, stayed with his teacher for forty years. Wise priests like the Ferryman Monk and Yang-ch'i stayed and served Yueh-shan and Tz'u-ming up until the day those teachers passed away. Only then did they leave and engage in solitary retreats by themselves. The same was true of Ma-tsu's eighty Dharma heirs, and of superior priests like the "three Buddhas"—Fo-kuo, Fo-chien, and Fo-yen—who studied under Wu-tsu Fa-yen. They all stayed with their teacher until they had completed their training.

The priest Chueh-fan Hui-hung left his teacher Chen-ching too soon, thinking to himself, "I've made off with Chen-ching's precious green rug." Ta-hui later rebuked him for those words. "Chueh-fan attained something," he wrote, "but there was also something he didn't attain."* Tou-shuai Ts'ung-yueh also left Chen-ching too soon, thinking, "I've smashed to dust the secret jewel Chen-ching received from his teacher Huang-lung." Only later, when Senior Monk Ch'ing-su took him to task for those words, did he finally understand that the temple hall also has an inner

---

*Chueh-fan Hui-hung (1071–1128). Ta-hui's comments are quoted in the *Record of Hsu-t'ang*, ch. 4: "Chueh-fan had a satori while he was with Chen-ching (K'o-wen), but soon after circumstances arose that obliged him to leave. He left Chen-ching much too soon and because of that, although he attained something, there was also something he did not attain." In Zen records, *precious green rug* appears as a metaphor for one's most treasured possession: the Buddha-mind. It is based on a story in the *Annals of the Chin State*: "Thieves entered the study where a scholar was sleeping. As they were about to make off with all his belongings, he called out from a corner of the dark room, 'Burglars, please do not take the green rug. It is an old and precious family heirloom.' The burglars were so startled that they bolted out the door" (*Chin-shu*, ch. 80).

sanctum. "It must be," he realized, "that I am still unaware that I have contracted an illness from my teachers. Why is that? Because as I try to work for the sake of others, I find I am unable to pour forth everything I have inside me."*

Genuine patricians of the secret depths, in order to be able to undertake the teaching of the true Dharma, enter the training hall, mingle with the brotherhood, sit silently at the rear of the hall, work on koans they haven't yet passed, engage in practice sessions with their comrades, and in this way gradually accumulate Dharma assets and mature into great Dharma vessels. They are then able to uplift the great teaching, raise the Dharma torch, and lead others to liberation, sustaining the life-thread of wisdom and requiting the enormous debt they owe the Buddhas and patriarchs. Such is the ancient, time-honored reality in the groves of Zen.

Think about it. You will have plenty of time later to hide yourself in the boondocks and investigate the matter of your self, but only limited time remains to me in which to sit in these broken-down old chambers laughing and chatting with my monks. I just wait, counting the days and nights off on my fingers, until you return. After I leave on my final pilgrimage, you will be free to go anywhere you want, hide yourself from the world, if that is what you desire. It won't be too late then.

On the other hand, if you want to forget your fundamental purpose, turn your back on your old teacher's wishes, and follow in the footsteps of failures like Shan-hsien of Hsueh-tou or Sheng-chiao of Tung-shan,† even if you bury yourself in some mountain fastness, deserted moorland, or empty valley, or hide away inside a cave and remain there for three, five, or even ten years refining and maturing your attainment, you will never acquire the ability to teach even a poor sort of dunce.

Recently word reached me that the Kyoto priest who ordained you has been seriously ill for some time now and may die at any moment. This is another matter of great importance that you cannot ignore.

When this letter reaches you, don't waste any more time. Hang up your traveling staff that keeps taking you farther and farther away from here. I look forward with keen anticipation to seeing you again. I have entrusted the rest of what I want to say to the Daikei-ji priest, who will transmit it

---

*Tou-shuai Ts'ung-yueh (1044–91). Hakuin relates this story in *Talks Introductory to Lectures on the Record of Hsu-t'ang* (*Essential Teachings of Zen Master Hakuin*, pp. 95–6).
†Anecdotes in *Ta-hui's Arsenal* about these two priests have them leaving their teachers after an initial realization and failing to complete their training.

in person to you.

My best wishes, [Hakuin]

. . . .

Like Tōrei and many of Hakuin's other leading students, Attendant Kō (Dai-kyū Ebō) came to Hakuin after first studying with Kogetsu Zenzai. Kogetsu, a highly regarded Rinzai teacher in Hyūga Province on the southern island of Kyushu, was about ten years older than Hakuin.

According to the entry for Daikyū in *Biographies of Zen Priests of Modern Times*, he was born in Iwakura village north of Kyoto and ordained at the age of five by a priest named Jikuden Denʾō (n.d.) at Shōfuku-an in the neighboring village of Kino. At fifteen he was made an attendant of Zōkai Etan at Tōfuku-ji in Kyoto, and when Zōkai died the following year, Daikyū moved to Hōfuku-ji in Bitchū Province (modern-day Okayama Prefecture), an important temple in the Tōfuku-ji branch of Rinzai Zen. At twenty-two he traveled to Hyūga to study with Kogetsu, then set out several years later (exactly when is unclear) on a pilgrimage to eastern Japan that led him to Hakuin at Shōin-ji. (For an anecdote describing Daikyū's first meeting with Hakuin, see *Precious Mirror Cave*, pp. xxiv–xxv).

Although in Hakuin's *Chronological Biography* there is a reference to Dai-kyū as Hakuin's attendant as early as 1739, according to the account in *Biographies of Zen Priests of Modern Times*, Daikyū first arrived at Shōin-ji in 1742. This account also has Daikyū being appointed an attendant, achieving a decisive enlightenment the next year (which was confirmed by Hakuin), and then leaving Hakuin not long after the enlightenment to return to Hōfuku-ji.

Since the letter addresses Daikyū as "Attendant Kō" (a title Hakuin could have used until 1755 when Daikyū was installed as abbot at Hōfuku-ji) and was sent when Daikyū was no longer at Shōin-ji, we may tentatively suppose that following confirmation of his satori, Daikyū left the temple to engage in further practice on his own. This was the course Tōrei and Suiō adopted as well, also in the face of Hakuin's opposition. If so, the writing of this letter can be narrowed down to between 1743 (or 1739) when Daikyū was appointed Hakuin's attendant and achieved his enlightenment, and 1747, which is the year that the monk named Tō (later Reigen Etō), who is mentioned in the letter as studying at Shōin-ji, is known to have returned to his home temple. Hakuin's comments about Daikyū having been away for a long time seems to suggest a date closer to 1747.

In any event, despite the fears Hakuin expresses in the letter, Daikyū seems to have fulfilled his promise and developed into a powerful teacher. In his spiritual autobiography *Wild Ivy* (p. 58), Hakuin describes attending a large lecture meeting that Daikyū conducted at the great Tōfuku-ji in Kyoto. According to *The Annals of Tōfuku-ji*, eight hundred and thirteen priests and monks, including Tōrei and other students of Hakuin, participated in the meeting. Through meetings such as this one at Tōfuku-ji, Daikyū is credited with having introduced Hakuin-style Zen to the large Gozan monasteries in the capital.

Modern Rinzai historians have ranked Daikyū with Tōrei and Suiō as one of Hakuin's three chief disciples. Suiō, who succeeded Hakuin at Shōin-ji, is reported to have said, "Among the students that came under old Hakuin's hammer, Tōrei alone was able to enter his chambers and make off with all his Dharma assets; and only Daikyū penetrated deeply to his Dharma source" (Katō Shōshun, *Chronological Biography*, p. 32). After Daikyū's death, he was awarded the Zen master title Daihi Myōgyō Zenshi.

: 84. To the Head Priest at Zuihō-ji

Zuihō-ji was a Zen temple in the city of Sendai in northeastern Honshū that was supported by the ruling Date clan. Nothing more is known about its head priest, not even his name, nor about Hakuin's connection with him. The content suggests that Hakuin wrote the letter in the latter part of his life.

A T THE BEGINNING OF spring, Seki Zensha of Kai delivered the letter and the other two articles that you most graciously sent me.* Reading the letter over, I was very pleased to learn that you are vigorously engaged in your teaching efforts and enjoying good health. I can happily report that I too am in fine fettle. I spend my hours whiling away the time remaining to me chatting and laughing with one or two friends.

Word has reached me here in faraway Suruga province of the Dharma meeting you have planned next spring on *Treatise to Assist the Teachings*. It is said that the guardian Naga deities have joined forces and helped you to complete your preparations for the assembly. It will be an achievement of great importance for modern-day Zen to have the Buddha Sun brightly illuminating the northern lands and dispelling all the clouds and mist.[†]

At night no doubt there will be many offering incense and standing,

---

*An annotation identifies Seki Zensha (Zensha means "Zen man") as Daiun Zenkō (n.d.) of Hōseki-ji in Kai province.
†Hakuin is playing on the name Fo-jih ("Buddha Sun"), author of *Treatise to Assist the Teachings*.

staring eastward like stacks of brushwood as they dream of traveling to Sendai. I am only sorry that I will not be able to attend the meeting and hear your Dharma teaching. A two-week trip all the way to Sendai is a bit too much for me now. I detest having become so fat and useless. I rage at the towering mountains that lie between us.

Fortunately, the newly named head priest at Daikei-ji, who will be leaving for home shortly to take up his new post, has said that he will visit you next spring.* I am going to give him two gold *ryō* for you, to convey in some small measure the joy and admiration that your undertaking has given me. Please accept them.

And, for the sake of men and devas alike, please take good care of yourself in the severe winter that lies ahead.

For now, [Hakuin]

85. TO THE RETIRED RŌSHI AT RYŌSEN-JI THANKING HIM FOR A STONE OX

The retired Rōshi is Rokuin Etsū (1685–1756), who was born the same year as Hakuin and accompanied him on some of his early travels. This led to what was apparently a lifelong friendship. Ryōsen-ji is located in Shimizu, a village just east of Numazu, about eight miles from Hakuin's temple. Since Rokuin died in 1756, and we can assume that he had retired not too many years before that, we can tentatively date Hakuin's letter to his sixties.

The ox, white ox, and water buffalo appear frequently in Zen literature as a symbol of the ultimate principle, supreme Buddhahood itself. Although the famous Ten Ox-herding Pictures is the example that first comes to mind (and this letter contains several allusions to that work), in the Classified Collection of the Zen Forest *more koans are listed for the ox or water buffalo (including some stone oxen) than for any other animal.*

A STONE OX HAS MADE his appearance at Shōin-ji. A burly water buffalo, flapping his tail. He's pushed himself forward till he's right under my nose. He won't be wandering off into the winds and mists anymore,

---

*This Daikei-ji priest, also referred to in the Letter to Senior Monk Kō (above, #83) cannot be identified.

entering other people's fields to nibble their fragrant grasses. He is a loyal, gentle beast. But give him the whip, he won't budge. Call out to him, his head won't turn. His horns are small, still pushing their way up, but his nostrils proclaim a proudness of spirit that reaches to the heavens. He is perfectly straight and true, utterly distinct, completely open and unbared. Even the most experienced herdsman could find nowhere to apply his whip, the most skilled butcher nowhere to insert his knife. A water buffalo that would shock Nan-ch'uan into silence, that would set Kuei-shan's teeth rattling with fear. Rumor has it that he bolted away from one of the temple patrons down at the foot of the mountain. Chinese characters can be discerned on his lower left flank. What could they be? No one's going to put a cord through this fellow's nose. I'll see his full, round perfection every day, his majestic, solitary dignity. As a splendid example of the Zen groves, he could have no equal.

I do not know how to thank you for such a kind gift—it transcends all worldly measurements. I find myself dancing joyfully about, humming one of those songs the young village oxherders sing.

I have much more to say, but for now . . . [Hakuin]

. . . .

Hakuin alludes to an address Ch'ang-ch'ing Ta-an made to his assembly: "I lived with my teacher Kuei-shan over thirty years, eating his food, passing his excrement—but I didn't study his Zen. All my time I was looking after an ox. Whenever he left the path and got into the tall grass, I would pull him back. If I caught him trampling people's rice fields, I would flog him with my whip to make him stop. Things continued for a long time like this. It was a pitiful existence for him, always being ordered about. But now he has transformed into the White Ox on the Open Ground [Lotus Sutra]. Now, all day long he is utterly unbared beneath my very nose. He doesn't budge an inch, even if I try to chase him off" (Records of the Lamp, ch. 9).

Other allusions are to Nan-ch'uan and Kuei-shan, who appear in well-known koans on the ox theme. "Chao-chou asked Nan-ch'uan, 'When a person has grasped the Way, where should he go?' 'He should become a water buffalo at the layman's place down the hill,' replied Nan-ch'uan" (Compendium of the Five Lamps, ch. 4).

:86. Reply to the Two Monks Kin and Koku

Here Hakuin declines an invitation by two unidentified monks
known only as Kin and Koku to lecture on the Vimalakirti Sutra.
This is one of only a handful of early letters that afford valuable
glimpses into Hakuin's early years as head priest of Shōin-ji (he was
installed in 1717). He describes the period as one of great privation
and impoverishment, with the temple "in an incredible state of dis-
repair." During these early years, as he was still focused on his own
religious quest, a few students, mostly lay people, were coming for
instruction. In autumn of 1726, amid this practice-oriented life, he
finally achieved his decisive enlightenment. As he says that he has
been at Shōin-ji for twelve years, the present letter must date from
his forty-third year, 1729, a little over two years after the enlighten-
ment experience.

It is interesting in view of the frenetic round of teaching Hakuin
engaged in later in life, and especially during his sixties and seven-
ties, to find him at forty-three, at the start of his teaching career,
reluctant to take on such a lecture assignment. According to the
records, his first such lectures, on the Blue Cliff Record, *took place*
eight years after this.

M Y HUMBLEST APPRECIATION FOR the letter Brother Rai recently
brought me containing your request for me to conduct a lecture
meeting on the *Vimalakirti Sutra,** together with a list of expected participants. While I seriously doubt you can rely on a shuffling jackass like me
to perform like a thoroughbred stallion, or hope for an old crow to start
caroling like a celestial phoenix, I am nonetheless sincerely grateful that
you even remembered this boorish rustic and thought it worthwhile to
make a sincere effort to assist in his upbringing. I have no doubt that you
were inspired by a deep aspiration to advance the teaching of the Dharma.

I, alas, am not a superior man. I have neither wisdom nor virtue. I am
sure you have heard about the adversities we've been experiencing here at
Shōin-ji. After my first eight years here as head priest, and a great deal of
trouble, we finally succeeded in striking a vein of water and reviving the
dried-up old well. Now four years and much additional hardship later,

---

*Hakuin refers to the sutra as *Beyond Comprehension Sutra,* using the name of one of
its central chapters.

we have managed to finish rethatching the leaky roofs. I still do not have a student who is capable of helping me run the affairs of the temple, and there are no parishioners to turn to for financial help.

More to the point, even after scrutinizing my heart from corner to corner, I am unable to come up with a single notion that I could communicate to the participants at such a lecture meeting, much less hold forth on the *Vimalakirti Sutra's* wonderful teaching of nonduality. In view of this, after repeated and agonizing self-examination, I am afraid I have no choice but to decline the high honor you have sought to bestow upon me. Even as I write this, my eyes are wet with tears and my body is drenched in a thick, shame-induced sweat. Certainly there is no lack of veteran priests in your own area, any one of whom I am sure would be capable of carrying out the task you propose.

Asking your deepest forgiveness in this matter, I am, yours truly, [Hakuin]

:87. To the Priest of Seitai-ji from Monks Assembled for a Meeting on the *Blue Cliff Record* at Hōtai-ji, Requesting Zen Lectures on the *Record of Hsu-T'ang*

*The next four letters (#87–90) all date from Hakuin's mid-twenties, making them the earliest-known examples of his writing that have survived.** He was at this time midway through the fifteen-year pilgrimage around the country that began when he was eighteen. He had achieved an initial satori, which he had succeeded in deepening and clarifying a year later while practicing with Shōju Rōjin in Shinano province. Hakuin was now continuing his training more or less on his own, focused on what he would later call the "post-satori" phase of Zen practice.*

These letters provide a perspective of the latter years of Hakuin's pilgrimage that is somewhat different from that gained from the autobiographical writings and Chronological Biography. *Here he appears as the leader of a company of young monks who were engaged in ferreting out teachers who could help them in their study of Zen texts, and attempting to test the teachers' mettle in the process.*

---

*I must therefore amend a statement I made in *Beating the Cloth Drum* when I said that a letter Hakuin wrote at twenty-nine was his earliest.

The first two letters, which Hakuin wrote on behalf of his fellow monks, are addressed to the same person, referred to only as the head priest of Seitai-ji in Mino province. It is probably Gugaku Fukaku (d. 1723), who was head priest at Seitai-ji (located in present city of Mino) at the time and seems to have had a reputation for his formal lectures (teisho) on Zen texts. He had several years earlier conducted meetings at Seitai-ji on the Record of Lin-chi *and the* Blue Cliff Record *(Biographies of Zen Priests of Modern Times, section on Jakuji Jōsan).*

Hakuin sent the letters from Hōtai-ji (the temple name is also given as Hōdai-ji) in Suruga province where he had gone with the group of monks to take part in a lecture meeting. The account in the Chronological Biography *for 1710 has: "Hakuin traveled in the spring with monks Daigi, Shōgan, and Rokuin to attend Jōsui's lectures on the* Blue Cliff Record *at Hōtai-ji in Sumpu, Suruga province" (Precious Mirror Cave, p. 176). A priest named Jōsui Tōju (1653–1720) was head of Hōtai-ji at the time. The mention of pomegranate blossoms in the first letter suggests a date in late spring or early summer.*

Hakuin requests lectures on the Record of Hsu-t'ang, *a ten-fascicle collection containing the Zen records of the important Chinese Lin-chi teacher Hsu-t'ang Chih-yu (1185–1269). As the teacher of Nampo Jōmyō (Daiō Kokushi), Hsu-t'ang assumed great importance in the Japanese Rinzai school, especially in the Yang-ch'i line to which Hakuin belonged. When Hakuin decided to conduct his own first full-scale lecture meeting at Shōin-ji in his mid-fifties, the* Record of Hsu-t'ang *was the text he chose (see* Essential Teachings of Zen Master Hakuin*).*

THE RECORD OF HSU-T'ANG is an old mirror that distinguishes the true from the false, a precious sword that cuts and slashes Buddha-patriarchs to death. It has a devilish, bloodthirsty purpose that thrusts and strikes directly out at students. It possesses a marvelous illuminative power that never fails to reveal a person's vitals. In the vast storehouse of the Dharma King, it is a truly great treasure. Contained within it are the "Comments on One Hundred Koans,"* which are especially esteemed for their power to take veteran monks by the nose and drag them off to feed

* *Hsu-t'ang po-tse sung-ku.* A collection included in the *Record of Hsu-t'ang* containing Hsu-t'ang's verse comments to one hundred koans.

in the weeds. Their standard of wisdom is solemn and awe-inspiring, their meaning dark and profound. Trying to grasp them is like clawing your way up a wall of solid steel ten thousand feet high. Zen practicers today who work on them find it is like dangling a short rope down a thousand-foot well. They are never able to moisten their throats and their thirst becomes increasingly unbearable. This priceless gem has thus been left untouched and forgotten,* buried away among common stones and pebbles.

Master, we know that you stand shoulder to shoulder with the Buddha-patriarchs, a true model for our Zen school. There is absolutely no reason to hold back, not to use all the power at your command in dealing with young monks like us. You must be aware of the desolation that prevails in present-day Zen. Why have you remained silent? We fervently hope that you will bless us with a lavish Dharma rain, one that will return the school once again to the splendid springtime that was seen in Hsu-t'ang's time, and fix for all time the teaching that emanated from the ten temples where he resided. You should not be concerned about losing your eyebrows.† You should not abandon over a hundred young monks who are thirsting for your teaching. The destiny of the Zen school rests in your hands alone. We beg you to sympathize with our plight and to send us a favorable reply. If you do, we will immediately dispatch ten of our number to you. They will work under the guidance of your temple supervisor to help prepare for the meeting. Do not be concerned about a lack of space in your residence hall. If necessary, we will quarter ourselves in cowsheds or in the nooks and crannies of your bathhouse.‡ If there are not enough hands in the kitchen, our assistance, humble as it is, we offer there as well. We implore you to understand. If this meeting takes place and one lamp transfers its light to ten thousand others, what could be more wonderful than that?§

We enter a wonderful time of year. Rain has brought out the pomegranate's flaming red blossoms and turned the wheat shoots a lovely green. We fervently hope for the Dharma's sake that you will take good care of your health.

---

*Hakuin alludes to a famous jadestone that Pien Ho discovered in the mountains. The story is told below, p. 366.

†It is said that if a teacher descends to using explanations to teach students, his eyebrows will fall off.

‡In the *Record of Hsu-t'ang* (ch. 4) there is a reference to monks causing trouble for farmers by entering their farm buildings to practice zazen.

§An image from the *Vimalakirti Sutra*.

With deepest respect and greatest reverence, very sincerely yours, [the monks at Hōtai-ji]

:88. Second Letter to the Priest of Seitai-ji from Monks Assembled for a Meeting on the *Blue Cliff Record* at Hōtai-ji, Requesting Zen lectures on the *Record of Hsu-T'ang*

We may assume that this second letter was written the same year as the previous one, in summer or perhaps autumn of 1710. There is no evidence that Hakuin and his colleagues were able to reverse the Seitai-ji priest's decision, mentioned here, to reject their proposal.

Y OUR LETTER ARRIVED YESTERDAY, the evening of the sixth. We assembled, offered incense, and opened it with reverence. Unable to find a single word in it that would suggest you had accepted our request, we were so astonished that we could only let our tongues pop out.* We were, however, able to talk with the messenger who delivered the letter and are extremely glad to learn of your continued good health.

Why has a person of such compassion and benevolence spurned the sincere aspirations of a hundred young monks, throwing them aside like clods of dirt? In casting about for a reason, we decided that it was because a teacher with your severe teaching style did not want to "ride his cloud down to earth"† and undertake expedient teachings for a group of such callow young monks. This has made us thirst even more for your teaching.

We also received a letter from a monk in the attendants' quarters of Seitai-ji addressed to Tōya, an attendant at our temple.‡ It says, "Because our teacher is elderly, he is unable to agree to your request." But each and every word in Zen master Hsu-t'ang's records transmits the bone and marrow of successive generations of Zen patriarchs. How can anyone but a great and veteran teacher, someone with a vast and deep store of experience, hope to deal with its profound meaning? That is why we addressed our request to

---

*An expression of self-reproach for a shortcoming or failure.
†This phrase alludes to a teacher descending, like a Taoist sage on a white cloud, from the realm of the absolute, the so-called "first principle," where verbal explanations are impossible, to the level of the relative, everyday world and employing expedient means to explain using verbal means.
‡Nothing is known of this monk.

you. Why would we go to an ordinary priest, the kind you find everywhere these days, who spends his life pounding and eating green rice?*

The Zen school is on the verge of total collapse. If you refuse us because of your age, would that not be the same as a faithful minister ignoring a great and imminent peril he knows is threatening his country? We are convinced that by grasping a single *shippei* in your hand, you could deliver talks that would have the power to subjugate even Buddhas and Zen patriarchs.

Please, master, for our sakes, strike with your uplifting mallet and smash the entangling words and phrases that fill Hsu-t'ang's Dharma cave.

Even if we do not receive a positive reply, on the day the present lecture meeting on the *Ch'in-tou Sutra* is completed,† we intend to set out and seek the Dharma banners that fly over Seitai-ji. Once there, we have resolved to burn our sedge hats, leggings and other travel gear and settle down for good.

Our feelings cannot be fully explained in a letter, not even a long screed like this one that extends a whole yard in length! We respectfully appeal to the supervisor monk and guestmaster at Seitai-ji to exert every effort on our behalf.

With deepest respect and greatest reverence,
Very sincerely yours, [the monks at Hōtai-ji]

: 89. To the Priest of Hōun-ji from Participants Assembled at Hōtai-ji for a Meeting on the *Blue Cliff Record*

This and the following letter (#90), like the previous two (see introduction to #87), were apparently written in 1710, Hakuin's twenty-fifth year. He had traveled to Hōun-ji in Suruga the previous winter to help head priest Keirin Eden instruct students and stayed over until the following spring. He then set out with fellow monks

---

*A priest whose understanding is still immature. "Hsu-t'ang poured abuse on [bogus] priests around the country for merely pounding and eating green rice" (*Record of Hsu-t'ang*, ch. 1).

† A reference to the *Blue Cliff Record*. Hakuin creates this tongue-in-cheek title by drawing a character from the names of each of the two authors, Yuan-wu K'o-ch'in and Hsueh-tou Ch'ung-hsien.

Daigi, Shōgan, and Rokuin to attend the lecture meeting on the Blue Cliff Record *at Hōtai-ji in Sumpu mentioned in the previous letters (Chronological Biography; Precious Mirror Cave, p. 176). During this meeting, Hakuin and his fellow monks must have hatched a plan to ask Keirin to deliver lectures on the* Record of Lin-chi *at Hōun-ji. As Hakuin had just come from a fairly long stay at Hōun-ji, it seems likely that the idea originated with him. In any case, as the other monks were no doubt aware of Hakuin's literary talent and probably also considered him their de facto leader, he was delegated to compose these two letters to Keirin.*

AFTER LIN-CHI ROARED a final shout seated astride a blind donkey, his comings and goings ceased forever. Ma-tsu's splendid Zen style was on the verge of a total eclipse. Ahh! What a truly splendid feat old San-sheng performed when he gathered up his teacher's fox slobber and put it together in a book! The resolute determination he demonstrated, issuing from his Bodhisattva vow, came to take on truly vital importance!

But Lin-chi's records are filled with words and phrases so steep and forbidding, it is altogether impossible for us to get our teeth into them! Each time we open it and start to read, we immediately find ourselves thrown into the most desperate straits, uncertain and confused. We are then left with no recourse whatever, master, but to run to you for help. Now is just such a moment. We beg you fervently to let us hear your great lion roar. In the coming days, when we visit your temple, we hope you won't drench us with freezing water like Yeh-hsien.

. . . .

San-sheng Hui-jan (n.d.) was a disciple of Lin-chi and is credited with compiling the *Record of Lin-chi*. According to that record, Lin-chi's final words before dying came in a famous exchange with San-sheng: "When the master was about to pass away, he seated himself and said, 'After I die, do not let my True Dharma Eye disappear.... Later on, when someone asks you about it, what will you say?' San-sheng gave a loud shout. 'Who would have thought that my True Dharma Eye would disappear when it reached this blind donkey!' said Lin-chi. After speaking these words, the master, sitting erect, entered Nirvana."

Ma-tsu Tao-i (709–788) was an important teacher three generations earlier than Lin-chi in the same Nan-yueh line and is regarded as the first in that line who used the teaching methods that later came to be associated with the

Lin-chi school. (Wild) fox slobber (*koen*, or *yako-enda*) is a virulent poison, used metaphorically for the poisonous words used by Zen teachers.

Yeh-hsien Kuei-hsing (n.d.) is reputed to have been an extremely strict teacher, much feared by monks. Once, at the coldest time of the year, Yuan of Ching-shan and Huai of T'ien-i came to stay at his temple and went to his room to pay him a formal visit. Yeh-hsien reviled them and drove them away, and kept dousing them with water until they were back in the guest quarters, their robes drenched through. All the other monks, angered at this behavior, left the temple. Yuan and Huai, however, put their robes in order and began doing zazen. Yeh-hsien came and reviled them. "I'm going to give you a beating if you stay around here!" he said. Yuan approached him. "We've traveled several thousand leagues to come here and study Zen under you," he said. "Do you think we'd leave just because you threw a dipper of water over us? Beat us to death if you like, but we're not going anywhere else." Yeh-hsien laughed and said, "If you two are really that committed to studying Zen, you might as well stay here a while." He made Yuan head of the kitchen (*Ta-hui's Arsenal*).

:90. A Second Letter Addressed to the Priest of Hōun-ji from Participants Assembled at Hōtai-ji for a Meeting on the *Blue Cliff Record*

In this letter, Hakuin reiterates the request he made for lectures on the Record of Lin-chi *in the previous letter. He pulls out all the rhetorical stops as he insists that whether Keirin agrees to their proposal or not, he and his fellow monks are going to visit his temple and stay there, permanently if necessary, until Keirin relents. It is not known if they followed through on this threat or if Keirin finally agreed to do the lectures. The records show, however, that a few years later Hakuin got his lectures on the* Record of Lin-chi; *they were delivered at Shōin-ji by another priest, Setsu Jōza, from nearby Ketsujō-ji (Chronological Biography, 1711; Precious Mirror Cave, p. 181).*

SOON AFTER WE SENT our letter, we received your reply. It arrived with unexpected dispatch. When we humbly and respectfully broke the seal and read the letter, the deep kindness of your words made us feel as if we had been granted a personal audience and were hearing them directly from your own lips. It has increased the deep reverence and admiration we feel toward you.

With unassuming modesty you cite "a lack of virtue or wisdom" as reasons for refusing our request. Surely that reflects a larger, more far-reaching vision, a desire to yield to priests of the younger generation in the performance of such duties. How wonderful when the aspiration to promote and uplift the Zen teaching rises to such heights! It is yet one more reason to increase our reverence and admiration for you.

The spring sun is extending its rays over the southern fields; in the western quarter, planting is about to begin. In declining our request you mentioned how busy you were readying the temple fields and gardens for planting. When veteran Zen teachers of the past like Po-chang and Ti-tsang went into the fields with plows and rakes in their hands and labored side by side with their monks, oblivious of the frigid cold of winter or blistering summer heat, they set sterling examples for the students who gathered to their temples from around the country.* We will gladly assume responsibility for any work that needs to be done at your temple. I myself am determined to exert all my meager efforts, to work like a blind donkey to that end. But we can no longer just remain languishing here in the visitors' quarters awaiting a reply.

Master, there is not a Zen monk in the country who does not know your name. You are an example to us all. If you refuse us, saying you want to attend to your fields and gardens, where else can we go for help? We beg you to consider that. Excusing yourself by saying that you are only a drowsy tiger like Hu-ch'iu, or by feigning illness like Vimalakirti†, just gives us more cause to revere you.

You are a dragon king, with power to control the movement of the rains and mists. Would not refusing our request mean that you are unwilling to allow the Dharma rain and mist to fall?‡ Why will you not consider the predicament of budding young Zen saplings that wish to flower and bear

---

*Po-chang Huai-hai (749–814) is known for his saying, "A day without work is a day without food." Several anecdotes depict Ti-tsang Kuei-ch'en (867–928) working in the fields together with his monks.

†Apparently a reference to Hu-ch'iu Shao-lung (1077–1136); the name Hu-ch'iu means "Tiger Hill," and his teacher referred to him as "Drowsy Tiger." Layman Vimalakirti used his skillful means to make it appear that he was sick so that people would come to inquire about his health, enabling him to teach them.

‡ That is, to bestow beneficial teachings on students.

fruit? We beg you to act as a bright mirror to us, a flaming torch in the paths of darkness.

Whether we hear some word of agreement from you or not, we are resolved to visit your temple, break our traveling staffs, and stay there for good. Please show compassion for our plight.

It is difficult with brush and paper to truly and fully express our most earnest thoughts to you. When we sit poised to write, our features grow rigid and solemn.

Spring is near, but the days alternate between warm and cold. For the Dharma's sake, please take good care of your health.

:91. REPLY TO GIN AND NYŪ, IMBIBERS OF BUDDHA'S AMBROSIA, AT A MEETING CONDUCTED AT SHŌJU-JI

Shōju-ji is a Zen temple in Morioka, in the then-remote northern area of the main Japanese island. Nothing is known about priests Gin and Nyū. References in the letter suggest a relatively early date in Hakuin's teaching career, perhaps his late forties or early fifties. As there is no record of any meeting on the Heroic March Sutra *(Shuramgama Sutra) at that time, it is possible that the plan never materialized.*

"Imbibers of Buddha's Ambrosia" (kanro-mon) is an elegant way of describing especially capable priests.

I RECEIVED YOUR LETTER ON the sixth of the ninth month. I am grateful to you for proposing that I conduct a lecture meeting. But the text you suggest, the *Heroic March Sutra*, contains the supreme secrets of the Buddhas. Only a priest who has grasped the essential core of the Zen school and has the capacity to preach it as well could even hope to get his teeth into it. A callow bonze of my meager abilities would be incapable of carrying out such an important mission. Besides that, Shōin-ji is an extremely poor temple, with no space or other means of taking in a large number of visiting monks.

Because of these reasons, I had decided to refuse your proposal, but some of the temple priests in the neighborhood came around and began urging me to accept. Considering that you have resolved to come here all the way from Morioka, and since temples in this area have promised to give their help, I have no choice, unworthy as I am, but to humbly accept

your request. Though an ignorant priest of lazy habits, I vow to do everything in my power to make the lecture meeting a success. Overcome with
emotion as I write this down, I am yours truly, [Hakuin]

:92. ADDRESSED TO THE PRIEST OF RINZAI-JI,
WELCOMING THE APPOINTMENT OF SENIOR PRIEST
EDAN AS HEAD PRIEST OF MYŌŌ-JI

*As this letter dates from Hakuin's thirties, when the head priest of
Rinzai-ji was Yōzen Soin, we may assume that he is the recipient.
Details of Yōzen's life and relationship with Senior Priest Edan are
not known. Senior Priest Edan, Kyōsui Edan (d. 1743), who had
studied with Kogetsu Zenzai and later with Shōju Rōjin, whose
Dharma transmission he is reported to have received, was apparently quite a bit older than Hakuin. He accompanied him on many
of his youthful peregrinations around the country, and the two men
became lifelong friends. Kyōsui was with Hakuin at Eigan-ji in 1708
when Hakuin achieved his first enlightenment. Kyōsui served at
Myōō-ji in Chiyoda village (incorporated into present-day Shizuoka
city), and in 1723 was installed as head of Rinzai-ji.*

SUMMER IS BEGINNING, WISTERIAS are offering their beautiful purple flowers, pomegranate trees are bursting into scarlet bloom. I am
extremely glad to hear that you are in good health, and that everything is
running smoothly at your temple. Nothing is more important than a vigorously prospering Dharma teaching. Things are pretty much unchanged
around my little hermitage too. I take things easy. I enjoy going out and
walking through the vegetable garden and surveying the wheat field.

When I met the retired Rōshi of Myōō-ji recently,* I learned that Senior
Priest Edan is to be installed as head of the temple. It made me very, very
happy. It is entirely due to your benevolence and the special efforts you
have made on his behalf. Nothing can compare with such generosity and
compassion. My only regret is that I am unable to cross the pass and visit
Rinzai-ji to thank you in person. For the sake of men and gods alike, I ask
that you take very good care of your health.

---

*This priest has not been identified.

: 93. To the Newly Appointed Head Priest of Reishō-ji in Mino Province

An annotation identifies the recipient of this letter as Mugoku Shusui (n.d.), a grandson in the Dharma of Reishō-ji head priest Bankyū Echō (d.1719), who makes a number of appearances in Hakuin's autobiographies. Since Hakuin mentions here that Bankyū had died the previous year, this letter dates from 1720, Hakuin's thirty-fifth year, not long after he had returned from his pilgrimage to become head priest at Shōin-ji. Nothing is known about Mugoku or his relationship with Hakuin, though since Hakuin suggests that Mugoku had been a student of Bankyū, it is possible that the two men met in the Reishō-ji training hall during one of Hakuin's sojourns there in his twenties.

Hakuin first met Bankyū in 1705 when he visited Reishō-ji (also referred to as Reishō-in) in Mino province during the first years of his pilgrimage around central and western Honshu. Later, in autumn of 1714, toward the end of the pilgrimage, he revisited the temple, staying on into the winter. He took part in the rōhatsu *training session, during which he achieved satoris that "deepened his understanding" (*Precious Mirror Cave, *p. 183).*

It is interesting that in Wild Ivy, *the spiritual autobiography Hakuin wrote in his eighties, he is critical of Bankyū and the method of Zen training at his temple: "When I took up residence in the Monks' Hall of the Reishō-in in Iwasaki there was a large contingent of more than fifty monks in training. Sad to say, they were all pursuing the dry and lifeless methods of 'Unborn Zen' that had taken such a hold on people's minds in those days. Old monks and young monks alike did an admirable job on their morning and midday meals, but aside from that they spent all their time seated like lumps in long, lifeless ranks, nodding away like oarsmen. At night, they waited, listening with pricked ears for the bell to announce the end of the sitting period. Then they lined their pillows up in long rows and laid themselves down to sleep, chanting loudly back and forth, 'Great happiness and peace. Great happiness and peace.' I alone mustered a dauntless spirit, swearing with great resolve that I would not lie down even to rest....Looking back, I can see now that those nightly choruses of 'Great happiness and peace' worked to excellent advantage by increasing my determination to forgo all sleep or rest. [When*

I took these things up with Head Priest Bankyū.] he told me that this was all 'unwanted meddling' on my part: that poking my nose into others' affairs would only distract me from my own practice, and I should stop it" (Wild Ivy, p. 47).

WHEN CONFUCIUS DIED, THREE thousand of his heroic admirers were stricken with grief. When Shakamuni passed away, eighty thousand saints and sages wailed in lamentation. With the death of Bankyū Oshō on the nineteenth of the sixth month last summer, a bright torch was extinguished that had illuminated the paths of darkness, a ferryboat vanished that had been a boon to those stranded on the shores of delusion. I myself have a longstanding debt to your teacher's kindness and compassion. I should like to be able to travel to Mino and join you and the other mourners at his funeral rites, but the distances are so great, the mountain trails so steep and perilous, I am unable to do more than sit here grieving and lamenting, gazing futilely eastward at the evening clouds. I beg your forgiveness. A thousand apologies.

I can imagine the deep sorrow even a person of your determination and ability and finely tempered Zen mind must feel at this time.* That said, I cannot express how happy I am to hear that you have kept the Dharma banners flying steadfastly and are using the same wondrous means and the same severe manner—a hundred rules, a hundred regulations—in teaching your monks as before.

Zen monk Nin was on his way home,† so I am entrusting him with a small consideration to give you as an offering for the deceased. We are now enjoying balmy autumn weather, the chrysanthemums are fragrant, the buds are swelling on plum trees. For the Dharma's sake, please take good care of yourself.

---

*"This because your sorrow is different from that of people in the ordinary world, arising from the fact that Bankyū's Dharma teaching has now been lost" (annotation).
†Zen monk Nin (Nin Zenkaku) cannot be identified. The term *Zenkaku* normally refers to a monk in training.

BOOK SEVEN
Prefaces (*Jo*)—Postscripts (*Batsu*)—
Inscriptions (*Mei*)

. . . .

I. Prefaces (*Jo*)

As a literary term, Jo includes inscriptions affixed to documents and collections of various kinds in addition to prefaces and introductions in the Western sense.

:94. Preface Written for a Roster Listing Donors for the Construction of a New Bridge at Yatsuyahata, Composed at a Lecture Meeting on *Precious Lessons of the Zen School*

In 1742, at the age of fifty-seven, Hakuin traveled to Ryōtan-ji in Tōtōmi province to conduct a lecture meeting on Precious Lessons of the Zen School (Chronological Biography). *Tōrei's Draft Biography elaborates on this by telling us that the lectures were occasioned by services commemorating the six-hundred-and-fiftieth anniversary of the death of Fujiwara Sadasato, a local ruler who had established Ryōtan-ji, and that the head priest at Ryōtan-ji at this time was Dokusō Hōun (n.d.).*

Ryōtan-ji, also referred to here by its "mountain" name Banshō-zan, was located on the eastern side of Lake Hamana, seventeen stops west on the Tōkaidō from the Hara post station. Hakuin's trip there would have necessitated a number of river crossings, including one over the particularly hazardous Ōi River, as well as a steep climb over the Satta Pass.

As Precious Lessons of the Zen School, *unlike most Zen texts, is concerned largely with practical virtues, Hakuin's decision to use it is in keeping with the assembly he would address, and with the bridge fund he started.*

I N AUTUMN OF THE second year of Kampō (1742), I set out for Banshō-zan Ryōtan-ji in Iinoya, Tōtōmi province, in response to an invitation I had received from the temple to conduct a lecture meeting. After a journey of three days, covering forty leagues [approximately one hundred miles], we finally arrived at our lodgings at Hōju-ji in Rokutō. We set out the next morning, proceeding at a leisurely pace, and arrived at the plain of Mikatagahara.* A teahouse under an ancient pine tree provides a shady place of rest for weary travelers.† The Ryōtan-ji priest [Dokusō] was waiting for us with food, tea, and cakes. He had come all the way there to welcome me with undeserved hospitality.

In due course, our palanquins set out in a northwesterly direction. We came to the banks of the Yahata River, which flows southeast from the foothills of the high mountains. Eight sturdy porters, four to a side, lifted the palanquins onto their shoulders to carry us over the river. Monks and laymen came wading out to greet us from the far bank, their robes hiked up round their waists. As they entered the swiftly rushing river, which now reached to their thighs, I noticed that their jaws were firmly set and their brows furrowed apprehensively. *Why isn't there a bridge over this river?* I thought to myself.

When I visited Jissō-ji in Tōrin three or four days later, we had to cross the river again. The porters said, "It's a dangerous crossing. The river often overflows two or three times in a single month. People are carried away and sometimes drown." Again I thought, *Putting up a bridge here would be a deed of great virtue and essential importance. If lay people and priests from this area were to combine their efforts, such a project should not be too difficult to accomplish. If it is done little by little, in small steps, it should not take too long to complete. An undertaking such as this, which would provide great relief to people, can also be seen as a kind of skillful means, promoting the salvation of sentient beings.*

With that, I made up a small booklet to serve as a roster in which to list the names of people who contributed donations to the project. As a start, I donated the four strings of coins I had received for the lectures.‡ I composed a verse, which I inscribed on the roster as a preface. I made copies to give to the priests of four of Ryōtan-ji's subtemples: Daitsū-an, Jikō-an, Genkai-an, and Entsū-an.§ A small start, the first step in a journey

---

*The site of a famous series of battles in 1573 between Takeda Shingen and Tokugawa Ieyasu.

†An annotation supplies a sidelight: "An elderly couple was there selling rice cakes."

‡Each string of coins was made up of a thousand *mon*; four thousand *mon* made up one *ryō*.

§For Daitsū-an and Genkai-an, see below, #96.

of a thousand leagues, but my hope is that the project will eventually grow and assume mountainous proportions. The verse:

> Erecting a bamboo bridge over a surging mountain torrent
> Far excels the merit of erecting pagodas throughout the land.
> Hearing of the flooding during the spring and autumn rains,
> How could I just sit idly by and let people come to harm?

:95. Preface for a Booklet (*Kakuchō*) Containing Names of the Deceased

Kakuchō *are notebooks containing the posthumous names and dates of death of family members, friends, and acquaintances. Priests and lay followers use them to keep track of the correct dates for commemorating deaths at daily sutra recitations or other services. This particular* kakuchō, *still preserved in a private family collection in Numazu, is described as a small pocket-sized booklet.*

Mr. Ayabe, the layman who asked Hakuin to write the preface, was from Ōhira village in eastern Suruga province. An advanced Zen student who earned Hakuin's praise for the attainment he had achieved, he is identified in an unpublished inscription Hakuin wrote awarding him a posthumous Dharma name as Ayabe Den'uemon (d. 1764).

ON AN AUTUMN DAY in the twentieth year of Kyōhō [1735], the recluse Ayabe came to me with a small booklet and asked if I would write a preface for it. It was a so-called "ghost roster," a list of the posthumous names of family members and friends, people with whom he had been on intimate terms, that he had compiled to remind him when to offer morning and evening sutra recitations on their behalf. He had conversed intimately with these people in small rooms, he had eaten and drunk with them on festive occasions, and had formed friendships as strong as those of Chen-tsung and Lei-i or Kuan-chung and Pao Shu-ya.* When close relatives and friends are taken from us and we begin to lament them, our grief and sorrow knows no bounds. Yet as time passes the memories dim,

---

*Two celebrated friendships, one appearing in *The Book of Lieh Tzu*, the other in *Book of the Latter Han*.

and even their death anniversaries and memorial days tend to be forgotten. This holds true even of one's own flesh and blood, one's parents and brothers and sisters. It is in the nature of things.

It is indeed commendable that Mr. Ayabe made such a request to me, but I thought to myself that as praiseworthy as his act is, it is not good enough. It is good but still insufficient. Why do I say this?

Each human being has direct links to the four Buddha wisdoms; he is endowed with the Mirror Wisdom that provides three kinds of transcendental knowledge.* This is called the "matter of great importance," for which Buddhas appear in the world. It is called the treasure of the true Dharma eye. Grasp it and you are a Buddha-patriarch, possessed of boundless virtue. Lose it and you are immersed in the suffering of birth and death. In all the infinite lands in the universe, nothing is so wonderful and precious as this. This, in itself, is the mind that at this moment cherishes the memory of one's family members and friends. It is a precious thing that each of us is born with. To understand this precious matter and discern its true sublimity, you must exert yourself and examine with singleminded diligence, in whatever you do, throughout the twelve hours of the day, the questions: What is this activity I am undertaking? What is this discussion I am engaged in? Is it my spleen and stomach, liver and gallbladder? Is it blue, or yellow, or red, or white? You must seek it incessantly, seek it throughout your life, sure in the knowledge that you will grasp it.†

If you continue in this way to investigate it here, there, and everywhere, you will in one or two days, whether you give up sleeping and eating or not, find arising within you a spirit of dauntless inquiry that will without fail break through into satori. Once this intense spirit of inquiry takes even slight hold in your mind, before many days are out the breakthrough into satori will occur.

---

* *Sanmyō*: three kinds of knowledge attained by Buddhas, Bodhisattvas, and Arhats that enables them to understand and remove the evil passions that cause suffering and to know the former lives and future destinies of themselves and others.

†Presumably a reference to a passage in the *Record of Lin-chi*: "Your physical body is made up of the four great elements, spleen and stomach, liver and gallbladder, empty space—none of these are able to preach the Dharma or hear the Dharma. What is it, then, that knows how to preach the Dharma and hear the Dharma? It is you who are right here before my eyes; this solitary brightness without shape or form. If you can see it in this way, then you are no different from the Buddhas and patriarchs" (adapted from *Zen Teachings of Master Lin-chi*, p. 25).

Once the breakthrough occurs, you see at a single glance, without any doubts or uncertainties, your own mind, others' minds, the Buddha-mind, the mind of gods, and the mind of sentient beings. This is what is called "the pure mind knowing the minds of others."* Once you see others' minds, you realize beyond doubt that the mind inherent in us all is infinitely vast, perfectly clear, lofty, as tranquil as a piece of pure incarnate emptiness, without a trace of birth-and-death or illusion, subject or object, or any vestige of passion or delusive thought. This is called "the pure mind freely destroying all evil passions."† Once this capability to destroy the passions is realized, you discern at a glance your own world, the world of others, the worlds of Buddhas and of devils, Pure Lands in all directions, and all the impure lands of the six paths of samsaric existence as though you are looking down at them in the palm of your hand. This is called "the pure heavenly eye that discerns all things everywhere."‡

When the heavenly eye opens, you see all beings throughout the past and future being born and reborn in the endless cycle of birth and rebirth with perfect clarity as though reflected on a precious mirror. This is called "pure knowledge of the lives of oneself and others."§ When past, present, and future are perceived in this way, you hear, freely and instantaneously and without any lack, the voices of Shravakas, Bodhisattvas, Buddhas, and gods, the voices of the Devil King, sentient and nonsentient beings, the voices of hungry ghosts, fighting spirits, beasts, and the voices, both high-pitched and low, of the human world—tearful, lamenting, joyful, wrathful, abusive, and praising. This is called "the pure heavenly ear that hears all sounds."¶ Once this heavenly ear opens, you will know that everything you do—eating rice and rice gruel, or any other activity—is something that is neither acquired through practice nor learned. It all takes place within the samadhi of free and unrestricted activity that is inherent in us all. This is called "the pure ability to transform oneself or objects at will."**

When that moment arrives, the infinite Buddhist teachings, their boundless and ineffable meaning, and all the world's accumulated merit,

---

Tajinzū, fourth of the six supranormal powers (*rokujinzū*) Buddhas and Bodhisattvas are said to possess.
†Sixth of the six supranormal powers, *rōjinzū.*
‡Second of the six supranormal powers, *tengenzū.*
§Fifth of the six supranormal powers, *shukumyōzū.*
¶Third of the six supranormal powers, *tennizū.*
**First of the six supranormal powers, *jinkyōzū* (also *jinsokuzū*).

all its precious Dharma adornments—they are all of them complete in your mind, not a single one lacking. Is this not what Yung-chia meant when he wrote, "The six paramitas and myriad good deeds are all complete and perfect within you yourself"?* What reward in either the human or heavenly realms can exceed this! Not even the joy of obtaining the three vehicles or four fruits is greater.†

Ah, how difficult it is to acquire human form. How difficult to encounter and hear the Buddha's teaching. And once a person has acquired human form and heard his teaching, because of the difficulty in believing in it, he yearns after illusory fame and profit, he frets and suffers amid the realm of delusion, and in his careless stupidity he ends up returning once again to his former abode in one of the three unfortunate ways of existence.‡ What a terrible pity, and how terribly sad it is. Belief and nonbelief, though separated by only a single thought, are as different as cloud and mud. It is the vast difference between rising up and falling down.

Long ago, the great teacher Shakamuni gave up a throne and a home in imperial palaces to enter the priesthood and live a life of poverty and privation. Why should we, so greatly inferior in our capabilities, attach so doggedly to the world? What reason can we give? Some of the ancient sages managed to live tens of thousands years, yet even such long lives are like illusory flowers that appear in the air, more fleeting than a galloping horse glimpsed through a chink in a wall. Compared to their lives, ours are as brief as a mayfly's, ephemeral as a fleck of foam on the water. Buddhism teaches us that wisdom is to believe in cause and effect and fear the suffering of karmic retribution, that a wise person is someone who sees into his self-nature by grasping his own mind. These are not words to deceive us, nor are they illusory teachings. They are the absolute truth, genuine and unadorned.

I certainly do not mean to suggest that you have to discontinue the meritorious practices you have been engaged in. I mean that even as you devote yourself to cherishing and caring for your grandchildren and children, you should engage in continuous self-examination and once every morning read these words I have written. If doing this enables you to establish a firmly rooted faith, it will be better than eighty thousand individual good deeds of whatever kind. How wonderful that would be!

---

*Yung-chia Hsuan-chueh (d. 713), in *Verses on Realizing the Way.*
†The three vehicles (*sanjō*) are those of the Bodhisattva, Pratyeka-buddha, and Shravaka; the four fruits (*shika*) refer to four stages of sainthood in the Hinayana tradition.
‡Hell, the realm of hungry ghosts, and the realm of animals.

I did not take up my writing brush merely to show off my literary skills. I did it because when I saw faith beginning to send out its roots in your mind, I was so overjoyed that without realizing it I just started scribbling away. My scribbling was solely to nurture those roots and make them grow deeper and stronger. I want you to reflect on that.

:96. PREFACE ON SENDING OFF MITANI SOCHIZUMI TO EDO

The piece, like #94, was written in Hakuin's fifty-seventh year, at the time of the lecture meeting on the Precious Lessons of the Zen School *held at Ryōtan-ji. Although it was presumably written as a preface for a work or collection of some kind, we are not informed of its origins. Perhaps it was a collection of verses friends had written for the recipient. In any case, this piece is characteristic of inscriptions Hakuin wrote on various occasions for and about Daimyō and lesser officials in his native Suruga and the surrounding provinces, and is interesting in revealing the close relationships he had with these important figures.*

Mitani Sochizumi (n.d.) was apparently the Karō, or Chief Councilor, of Kondō Chikazumi (1694–1788), the Daimyō of Iinoya Castle in Tōtōmi province (a site now incorporated into the city of Hamamatsu). Chikazumi's grandfather Kondō Hidechika (also Yasumochi), was celebrated as one of the "Three Stalwarts of Iinoya" for the role he played in helping Tokugawa Ieyasu achieve his conquest of Tōtōmi province in the second half of the sixteenth century on his way to founding the Tokugawa Shōgunate in 1600.

KONDŌ CHIKAZUMI OF IINOYA Castle in Tōtōmi province is a descendant of Kondō Iwami-no-kami Hidechika, a military retainer of the first Tokugawa Shōgun Ieyasu. He uses the sobriquet Genkai-sai. A man of inherently noble character, Chikazumi has for many years been a devoted follower of the Buddha Way. He constructed two hermitages, Genkai-an and Daitsū-an, at sites of great scenic beauty located about several miles to the east and to the west of Iinoya. In each of the hermitages he enshrined a statue of the Bodhisattva Kannon. His vassal Mitani Sochizumi assisted him in carrying out these projects.

In autumn of the second year of Kampō (1742), when I was at Ryōtan-ji to conduct a large Dharma meeting, Mr. Mitani invited me to one of these hermitages, and I was able to spend several days amid its beautiful natural surroundings. He told me, "My lord did not build these hermitages because he hoped they would someday become large and splendid temples. His true purpose was simply to provide a place where people sincerely interested in Zen practice—even one person, or two—could stay in order to concentrate on investigating the matter of their self."

I responded to this with a sigh of admiration, saying, "Lord Chikazumi is a truly wise man. With his inherent capacity for pursuing the way of Zen, he may be the person with the deep aspiration needed to raise up the fortunes of our school. If this aspiration arouses a Zen stalwart to come here dragging his battered old cooking pot, and he stays here, chewing on nothing but vegetable stalks, and he proceeds to quietly and rigorously engage in hidden practice and thoroughly investigate the great matter, then you mustn't speak of this hermitage as if it were a crude hut made from a few handfuls of reeds. It would then surpass a thousand million times any great monastery with splendid golden halls. I well know that his vision is one that far transcends the ideas others in his position have. I have also heard that Lord Chikazumi's everyday behavior is straight and true, that he upholds the precepts, performs zazen, and recites sutras with rarely seen devotion and vigor. It is as rare as a lotus flowering amidst the flames. My only wish is that he takes his practice just one step further."

Mr. Mitani said, "What would that be? Please tell me."

"In the *Sutra of the Bequeathed Teaching*, the Buddha enumerated twenty difficulties humans must overcome if they are to reach attainment. One of them is the difficulty for wealthy and famous people to develop a liking for the Way. Everyone is inherently capable of directly attaining the four Buddha wisdoms. Who is there that does not have a liking for the Way? But to enter that Way is extremely difficult. Unless a person enters the Way and experiences oneness with all things for himself, even though he takes only one meal each morning and spends his days and nights engaged in a life of rigorous practice, and even though that becomes known to the heavenly gods and they shower him with flowers and make the air fill with the scent of marvelous incense, it is all meaningless, nothing more than an indication that he is mired within birth-and-death on a grand scale. But there is a single word or phrase that can sever even the finest, most minute roots of delusion. It is like a fine sword of enormous length that stands leaning against the sky, always ready to destroy the old nests of illusion, or like an iron hammer of untold weight that will smash illusory thoughts to finest powder.

"A monk asked Chao-chou, 'All things return to the One. Where does the One return to?' Chao-chou replied, 'When I was in Ch'ing-chou, I made a cloth coat. It weighed seven pounds.'* These words can work with marvelous effectiveness. If you take them and apply yourself to them in your practice, if you bore into them when you are meditating and when you are engaged in daily activities, whether you are walking, standing, sitting, or lying down, bore into them from the sides and from the front and from the rear, and continue boring into them until there is no place left to bore, no place to put either a hand or foot, nothing whatever you can apply thought or understanding to—at that time, if you keep pushing steadily forward without faltering, the time will come when everything will suddenly fall away and satori will open up. The joy you will experience then will be something you have never seen or experienced before. No beneficial act you could perform could produce a result of this magnitude. How could anyone who aspires to become a person of great stature think it worth his while to engage in any good or beneficent acts apart from this?"

Mr. Mitani said, "I would like you to write this down and give it to me as a parting gift before I leave for Edo." I did as he requested.

:97. Preface Congratulating Layman Kubota Sōun on his Seventieth Birthday

Nothing whatever is known of Layman Kubota. Ba Shigesada, who appears in the piece, is also difficult to identify, since Hakuin uses a short form of his surname. He could be Mr. Ōba or Mr. Baba, both of whom were government officials in Suruga province who appear elsewhere in Hakuin's records.

Layman Kubota Sōun, who lives by the old marketplace in the southern foothills of Mount Fuji, is a man of noble character and aspirations. He is truly one of the finest gentlemen in the entire county. This year, the sixth of the Gembun era (1741), he reached the ripe old age of seventy. To celebrate this, his many friends got together and presented him with a handscroll containing a collection of verses and other writings. Some of the words were divinely inspired; others demonstrated amazing turns of

*Blue Cliff Record, Case 45.

phrase. The scroll was already inscribed with a large assortment of verses. "Hakuin alone has not made a contribution," they said, so they asked Ba Shigesada, an elder from a neighboring village, to come here and request a piece from me.

I said to Mr. Ba, "Do you suppose that after Layman Sōun receives these congratulatory verses, he will take care of his health and live to be eighty?"

"Entirely possible, if he keeps taking good care of himself," he said.

"If he keeps on doing that, do you think he can he reach the age of ninety?"

"That would be much more difficult—maybe only one or two chances out of ten."

"How about a hundred. Do you think he could reach that?"

"Even reaching ninety is extremely difficult, so the chances of him reaching a hundred are not very good," said Mr. Ba.

"Precisely," I said. "But even if he did, even if he lived for eight hundred years like P'eng Tsu, or for a thousand like the sages Chih-sung and Huang-shih, he would eventually die. His life would still be as transient as the shadow from a lightning flash, or a fleck of foam on the vast sea. Even if your life does happen to extend for a long period of time, it is not something you want to place your trust in.

"But there is one man who does exist even before the creation of heaven and earth, his beginnings completely unknown. When the universe is destroyed, he will continue on. He is always there with the utmost clarity right before your eyes. His vast immensity is inexhaustible. He has been called the fundamental principle of all existence, what Lao Tzu called 'Tao.' He has been named the True Man who is timeless. Even the gods of heaven and earth do not fail to worship him.

"Layman Kubota's mind at this moment, as he is busy greeting and seeing off guests, thanking them for congratulations and compliments received, holding and playing with his grandchildren, is just like this. If he fully grasps that mind and the eye of wisdom opens wide in him just as he is, he is a timeless, undying sage. If he does not grasp it, he remains an ignorant, deluded man, and however long he lives, he will one day ultimately perish."

Layman Kubota, seek out the whereabouts of this mind. What is the true substance of the person who is now seeing and hearing and perceiving? If you continue to bore into this constantly, you will one day experience a joy much greater than any you have ever known. This is the marvelous Dharma that Zen says "transforms your bones." It is the "wondrous art that the father cannot transmit to the son."

It is this that I offer you in response to your request for some words to celebrate your seventieth birthday.

98 Preface for a Collection of Verses on a *Bonseki* Written at Daichū-ji

In addition to this early piece dating from Hakuin's thirty-seventh year, an annotation informs us of a verse, "Words for a Bonseki," which he contributed to this collection of verses. It is also included in Poison Blossoms *(#147).*

Bonsan ("tray mountains") and Bonseki ("tray stones"), miniature landscapes of stones, sand, or flowers, evolved as part of the culture that developed in Japanese Zen monasteries during the Muromachi period. The priests cultivated them with a special zeal, and they appear as a recurring theme in the literature of the Five Mountains. For a discussion of the Zen school's connection with the pastime, see Religious Art of Zen Master Hakuin, *Chapter Three, "Rocks, Pumpkinhead, Toys, and Birds."*

The identities of "Not Come" (Burai) Sensei and the Master of "Not Reside" (Fujū) Hermitage, assuming they are based even loosely on actual persons, are unknown.

NOT COME SENSEI BROUGHT a rock to the Master of Not Reside Hermitage. "Mount T'ai is a larger version of this One Fist Rock," he said. "This One Fist Rock is a smaller version of Mount T'ai. Although there is fundamentally no difference between them in size, people deludedly see one as large and one as small. The names One Fist Rock and Mount T'ai are themselves only provisional ones. As both One Fist Rock and Mount T'ai are nonsentient, why should anyone give rise to false, deluded notions about them? Therefore, One Fist Rock must have a hidden teaching which is totally inexpressible."

The Master of Fujū Hermitage showed no sign of being pleased. Not Come Sensei tried to draw him out using other means. The Master of Fujū Hermitage took One Fist Rock, placed it in the middle of the tray, and sat straight and erect, facing it without uttering a word. Not Come Sensei nodded his head. One Fist Rock nodded its head as well. With that, the Master of Fujū Hermitage danced the "dance of long life." Not Come Sensei is essentially not going or coming, and the Master of Fujū Hermitage is essentially never residing anywhere. This rock alone remains on its tray throughout past and present, serene and brilliantly vivid, beloved and cherished by all.

I thus told my monks to compose verses on the *Bonseki*. I joined them by adding a verse of my own:

> After Empress Nu Kua created heaven and earth,*
> And shooting stars metamorphosed into mountains,
> I rolled down winding valleys looking for my home,
> Tumbled from rugged peaks, and clambered up again.
> I found this small scrap of land, a sage-like realm,
> Evoking times when things first came into being.
> Sitting mindlessly across from two gaping men,
> Clouds rising at the alcove come sailing my way.

In summer of the seventh year of Kyōhō (1722) Tetsu, the temple steward at Daichū-ji, brought a scroll to my temple. "The Rōshi had the monks compose verses on *Bonseki*," he said. "He wants you to evaluate them."

"Is that so?" I replied. "Come nearer and listen closely. In forests where the phoenix roosts, lesser fowl swallow their cries and peeps. On the savanna where the lion dwells, the other animals crouch down in fear. Now, Daichū-ji is a wealthy temple with a fine crop of 'good fields' [monks], many of them ripened and ready for the harvest. Why come to a lazy good-for-nothing like me, who spends all his time dozing off as if his eyelids had become glued shut, who doesn't read a single word, who has forgotten nine-tenths of everything he was ever taught or learned? Compared to those 'good fields' of yours, I am no more than a weed or tare. You must winnow out the worthless, ill-formed grains and select only those that have ripened to maturity. I am completely unqualified to judge the quality of your verses, so please don't ask me."

But Tetsu persisted. "I don't mean that our own roost is lacking in phoenix monks. How could the lion's den be devoid of lions? No, the idea to ask you was mine. Didn't even the quail, a bird unable to fly even eight feet, approach the great roc that can soar a hundred thousand *ri*?† Why do you insist on refusing me?"

---

*The sister and successor to the legendary Fu Hsi, Nu Kua is said to have created the earth when it first emerged from chaos.

†"The little quail laughs at the P'eng bird [which has a back like Mount T'ai, wings like clouds filling the sky...and can soar ninety thousand *li*], saying, 'Where does he think

"Ah! I can see that you are resolved to force a dog to roar like a lion, to compel a butcher bird to warble like a phoenix."

And so I drafted this short piece containing the attempts I made to evaluate the verses—no doubt it will provide some good laughs for the monks at Daichū-ji.

II. POSTSCRIPTS; COLOPHONS (*BATSU*)

:99. POSTSCRIPT FOR VERSES ON A *BONSEKI* WRITTEN BY THE MONKS AT DAICHŪ-JI

This postscript was written for the same collection of verses as the preface in the previous #98.

THIS SCROLL CONTAINS VERSES with qualities seen in the ancient poetry of the Han and Wei dynasties, the elegance of compositions from the T'ang and Sung. It is invested with the hidden mysteries of the mountains and forests, and splendid flavor of the rocks and springs. Here are the secret arts of Wang Ch'ang-ling; the wonderful realm of Chia Tao.* I found myself unable to put these verses down. I hummed them over and over, roaming slowly through them while taking my midday nap.

In my dreams I saw a Taoist priest. He was standing there casually with spiky hedgehog hair and a reptilian snout. He was clad in rags, looking altogether broken and beaten. With an insistent voice that seemed tinged with anger and resentment, he said, "A monk can kill a rock, or he can give it life."

"Please tell me what you mean," I asked.

Pointing to a small stone on a desk, he said, "This miniature mountain has untold grace and beauty. Long ago I transformed myself into the consort Pao Ssu, the favorite of Emperor Yu of the Chou dynasty. I rode in a

---

he's going? I give a great leap and fly up, but I never get more than ten or twelve yards before I come down fluttering among the weeds and brambles. That's the best kind of flying anyway.' Such is the difference between big and little." *Chuang Tzu*, p. 31.
*Celebrated T'ang poets.

palanquin around the country with his majesty, visiting all the great and celebrated mountains. I saw the rugged beauties of Mount Tai-hua, the incomparable Mount Chiu-i, the splendors of Mount Li, and the wonderful peaks of Mount Lu. But this little piece of stone right here possesses all their virtues. Not even the gods and demons could create such a miraculous shape.

"If a group of monks were to wrinkle their brows and expend a little effort, they could surely produce wonderful verses of purest gold that would give this stone a brilliant radiance that would increase its fame tenfold. Although it is only an ordinary insentient lump of stone, it can, if it encounters a good man, acquire greater and more auspicious virtues.

"Once when I was sojourning your country I congealed myself into a huge boulder. I was a solid piece of resentment and anger, truly murderous in my purpose. I rose up more than twenty or thirty feet in height. I killed indiscriminately, dispatching those of both high and low estate, killing birds and animals and humans. I continued killing, over and over, until the entire landscape was covered with rotting corpses. I was sure that not even the demons and gods could oppose me. How was I to know that I would encounter an old priest's staff and be broken to pieces, smashed so completely that not even a small particle would be left? Although a rock or stone is inanimate, when it brings harm to humans and other beings, it becomes evil and accursed.

"I was referring to myself when I said that 'a priest can kill a rock, and a priest can give it life.' A priest appreciates that his debt extends even to the earth and its rocks, and he is unable to ignore them and pay them no heed. That is the reason I want you to add a verse of your own to this collection, one which will bestow its luster on me."

"Ahh," I said, "Now I understand. It was you who received the arrow from Miura's bow long ago in the Genryaku era [1184–5]."

The Taoist priest dipped his head and smiled. When I had finished writing my verse, I looked around. He was nowhere to be seen.

. . . .

The final part of the story is based on an account in the *Honchō Kōsō-den* (*Lives of Eminent Japanese Priests*), #36: "In Nasu county in Shimotsuke province there was an evil rock. Any man or beast that incurred its enmity died. People called it the Life-taking Rock. One day, the Sōtō priest Genō Genmyō went up to the rock and said, 'You are originally a solid lump of stone. Where does your fundamental nature come from? Whence does your spirit arise?'

He rapped the stone three times with his staff. The stone is said to have ceased its evil deeds from that time forth."

In the Noh play *Sesshōseki* (*The Life-taking Rock*), which is based on this story, Gen'ō is passing through Nasu no Hara (the Field of Nasu) and sees a bird fall dead from the sky as it flies over a large and strange-looking rock. A woman appears and tells him that the rock is called the "Life taker" because it kills all living beings that approach it. She further explains that at the time of the Emperor Toba-no-in, there was a lady of great beauty and talent at the imperial court who won the emperor's affection, but who was revealed by a diviner to be an evil fox demon in disguise. She ran off and hid in the field of Nasu in the northern provinces but was hunted down and killed by a band of men led by Miura-no-suke Tsunetane, an archer of great skill. Her spirit took possession of the gigantic rock where she died, which came to be known as the Life-taker. The woman who tells Gen'ō the story disappears, but not before revealing to him that she is the spirit of the rock. When Gen'ō performs Buddhist rites on behalf of the spirit to lead it to the Buddha Way, the boulder splits apart, revealing the fox spirit in its true form, which promises the priest it will do no more harm.

:100. POSTSCRIPT WRITTEN FOR A COLLECTION OF LINKED VERSES

This postscript dates from Hakuin's thirty-sixth year, several years after he was installed at Shōin-ji, during a period when he was striving to complete his own training while at the same time taking his first steps as a Zen teacher.

Linked poetry (renku) was a popular form of collaborative Chinese verse (kanshi) in which two or more poets composed a poem by writing alternating lines or couplets of verse.

Of the three people who appear in the inscription, the priest of Daichū-ji, the "master of Jōsetsu-an," and Attendant Kin, only the first can be identified. He is Kōga Chidan (n.d.), the head priest of the Rinzai temple Daichū-ji, located near the city of Numazu.

O N A BEAUTIFUL MOONLIT night in the sixth year of Kyōhō (1721), the master of Jōsetsu-an and the old priest of Daichū-ji sat bathed in the radiance of the autumn moon, reflecting each other's light like two bright gems. They composed a series of splendid linked verses. Attendant

Kin was there jotting them down. He brought the verses to my temple and showed them to me in private.

As I began reading them, I felt like the morning sun had swept away the mist, like the autumn moon had burst from behind the clouds. Such matchless elegance! Such singular genius! It was as though I was browsing through the halls of the imperial library itself, or gazing at the precious boughs in a grove of red coral. The surprising shifts they took, their sudden changes, brought to mind a tiger that transformed instantaneously into a dragon and soared abruptly up into the heavens. A powerful beauty. Untrammeled freedom from start to finish. It was dazzling to my eyes and invigorating my heart, completely enthralling me. I thumped my knees over and over in admiration.

Attendant Kin produced a small sheet of writing paper. "I am on orders from the two priests to receive your appraisal of their verses," he said.

With deepest respect for their worthy presence, quaking before their stern severity, I replied, "Ahh! Such earnest men. Such ardent men. It is they who bear the destiny of our school upon their shoulders. Theirs are the hands that will wave high the great Dharma standards. I will revere them to the end of the world. I will love and respect them until my final breath.

"But (ahh!) how could the great and special favor I have always received from them have led me to this embarrassing situation? I have heard it said that when a clumsy person tries to do a carpenter's work he is certain to cut his hands. It is best that I emulate disciple Min and respectfully refuse your request."*

Attendant Kin bowed his head and said, "Do not refuse. Do not refuse. Do not be like the donkey of Ch'ien-chou. Be like a tiger cub at the foot of the cliff." Thereupon I made two bows and proceeded to mark up the manuscript with notations. In making red check marks above the verses, I am like a rootless vine twining around an old and venerable pine tree.† In scribbling clumsy comments underneath the verses, I am guilty of offering a common shell as if it were a precious jewel.

---

*The reference to a clumsy person doing a carpenter's work is from *Lao Tzu*. Min Tzu-ch'ien was a disciple of Confucius: when someone wanted to appoint him to a high position, he said, "Will someone kindly refuse this offer for me? If they continue to press me, I will have to retire to the banks of the Wen River." (*Analects of Confucius*, p. 43).
†"Rootless vine," *nenashi-kuzura*, is the dodder. Hakuin compares the markings he makes with his notations on the verses to this wiry, twining vine that is parasitic on other plants. The precious jewel is the fabulous jewel of Lu, which appears in the *Spring and Autumn Annals*.

. . . .

The final paragraph alludes to a story told by the T'ang poet Liu Tsung-yuan. A donkey was taken to Ch'ien-chou, where donkeys were unknown. A tiger who chanced to see it was frightened by its size; hearing it bray, the tiger ran off and hid in the forest. After observing the donkey for many days from concealment and growing used to its braying, the tiger came out of hiding and approached the donkey. The donkey kicked angrily out at him, and the tiger, rejoicing to know that this was the extent of the donkey's power, promptly devoured it. Attendant Kin is telling Hakuin not to worry about being like the donkey of Ch'ien-chou that was thought to have a capacity that it didn't really have. He does have the capacity, and should act instead like a fearless young tiger.

III. Inscriptions (*Mei*)

The term Mei *was originally applied to inscriptions containing succinct formulations of some fundamental principle or rule of conduct that were composed to be engraved on stone, metal, or wooden surfaces. In time, it came to refer to maxims or other similar elegant compositions in general. Four of those included in the* Poison Blossoms *collection were composed for temple bells, four for memorial stupa towers and grave tablets, and a few for various commemorative occasions. Only two of them are translated here.*

:101. Inscription for a Temple Bell at Ketsujō-ji

Ketsujō-ji is a Rinzai temple in the hills west of Sumpu (present-day Shizuoka). Hakuin's words about the "soundless sound" of the temple bell parallel those he used when exhorting students "to hear the sound of the single hand."

> The preaching from your gaping golden mouth,
> Transcends the vast ocean of Buddhist scripture,
> It booms the darkness from sentient beings' minds,
> Producing "fields of merit" of infinite virtue.

But if the ear discerns even the faintest sound,
You fall into the endless abyss of false appearances.
Turn within and penetrate the sound's true source,
And you are one with the immensity of the great void.
Buddha preached the Dharma with a single voice,
But what about the screeching of a snowy egret?
One hundred and eight tunes, all are uncreated,
But can you exclude the croakings of a crow?
[All who hear your marvelous soundless sound]
Are eternally protected by countless demon legions,
Are extolled and praised by the thousand Buddhas.
It shakes apart the caves where demon cohorts lurk,
Blasts dens of deluded thinking into oblivion,
It once cautioned a recluse from drinking wine,
It once saved a fish tortured by a ring of swords.
In people, it perfects good deeds and conduct,
Dispels illness and infirmity in all their forms.
It swallows the cold, chaste moon on the right,
And spits out the bright shining sun on the left.
Mind and Buddha and sentient beings are one,
Just so this unity of gold and silver and copper.
All the merits and virtues I have described above
Are merely your golden lingering reverberations.

. . . .

Golden mouth. The Buddha's teaching is said to issue from his "golden mouth." "Fields of merit" *(fukuden)* refers to people whose attainment, like a fertile field, produces an endless yield of merit and virtue.

If the ear discerns. Instead of being deluded by sensory perceptions, investigate their fundamental source in your own mind.

Buddha preaches…single voice. "Although the Buddha preaches the Dharma with a single voice, sentient beings hear it differently" (*Vimalakirti Sutra*). But on achieving oneness with the bell's sound in the attainment of satori, all sounds, egret cries included, are the Buddha's golden voice preaching the Dharma.

One hundred and eight tunes. The bells that are rung in Buddhist temples at the year's end are said to dispel human illusions. When the sound of this bell is truly heard, i.e., through attainment of satori, one knows that illusions are no different from enlightenment, that all things are constantly preaching the Dharma.

Cautioned a recluse. The recluse is the famous poet and wine bibber Tao Yuan-ming (365–427), whose friendship with Hui-yuan (334–416), a famous priest of early Chinese Buddhism, is referred to in several Buddhist collections. According to an account in *Yao-shan t'ang wai-chi*, ch. 12, when Hui-yuan and his fellow devotees formed the White Lotus Society, Tao was not invited to join. One day Tao set out to pay Hui-yuan a visit. As he was passing a large temple, he heard the temple bell boom out. His brow knitted into a frown as he realized he would not be able to imbibe in the temple's sacred precincts. Being confirmed in his habit, he immediately ordered the litter bearers to turn around.

Ring of swords. Allusion to a story involving Candakaniska, a famous Scythian king, who in the course of conquering northern India is said to have massacred millions of its inhabitants. Evil deeds of such magnitude destined him for the depths of hell, but thanks to the teachings he received from the Bodhisattva Asvaghosa, this fate was meliorated to rebirth as a fish. It was, however, a fish with a thousand heads, which suffered the endless torment of having a wheel of swords growing from its body constantly swirling about and severing the heads, which were then immediately replaced by new ones. An Arhat who appeared to him in the guise of a Buddhist monk, by ringing a small temple bell, saved him from this misery (*Fu-fa tsang-chuan*, ch. 5).

Are merely your. "To begin, you must turn within and investigate and fully grasp the source of the bell's sound" (annotation).

:102. INSCRIPTION FOR A SMALL TEMPLE BELL

This inscription dating from 1724, Hakuin's thirty-ninth year, is for a small temple bell (hanshō; literally, "half bell") that hung in the Main Hall at Shōin-ji.

THIS IS NOT MIND. It is not a thing or object either. It is created neither by causes and conditions nor by human handiwork. Even Li Lou would be unable to discern its true shape.* Shih K'uang would be unable to hear its voice.† Such is this small "half" bell.

Investigate the meaning of the word "half" and you will find that its body encompasses the entire immensity of empty space throughout the

---

*Li Lou lived at the time of the Yellow Emperor. His sight was so acute he could see the filament at the tip of a stalk of autumn grass at a distance of a hundred paces.
†A celebrated court musician of Duke P'ing of Chin.

ten directions of the universe. Investigate this immensity and you will find that it is devoid of sound or smell, yet leaves absolutely no aftertraces whatever. Truly it is the greatest tool in the Dharma King's storehouse.

In spring of the ninth year of Kyōhō (1724), a foundry was commissioned to cast the new bell. It is now finished and hangs in a corner of our Main Hall. Whenever you strike it, a vast and marvelous sound rings out with utter freedom. Pressing my palms together in celebration, I say,

Before you were cast	*Gon gon gon gonnn*
After you were cast	*Gon gon gon gonnn*
Yet hardest of all is this	*Gon gon gon gonnn.**

---

*"Although its marvelous sound exists both before and after it is created, I want to ask my monks: 'Where do you suppose this *Gon gon gonnn* comes from?'" (annotation).

BOOK EIGHT
Inscriptions for Paintings (*San*)

. . . .

Book Eight, one of the shortest in the Poison Blossoms
*collection, consists of texts in verse and prose that Hakuin
inscribed on his paintings. In view of the great number of those
paintings that have survived, it is surprising to find how few
of the ones bearing the inscriptions included here are known
to exist. Because of this, sometimes our only clue to what a
painting was like is the information found in the inscriptions
themselves, and in the annotations attached to it.*

Hakuin inscribed these three verses on a set of three paintings, each one containing an image of a Buddha, together representing the three Buddhas of the three kalpas of past, present, and future. The artist, instead of painting the Buddhas in the usual manner, delineated them by using the names of Buddhas, a thousand for each Buddha, written in very small Chinese characters.

This inscription, from the beginning of the Kampō era, which began in 1741, places it in Hakuin's late fifties. The present whereabouts of the paintings are unknown.

I T IS WRITTEN IN the *Sutra on Creating Images of Buddha*,* "The Buddha said to the King of Khotan, 'If in the past, present, or future a person creates an image of Buddha, the boundless merit and virtue of such an act is beyond calculation. He will be reborn in the heavenly realms, where he will enjoy pleasures of every kind, and his body will assume the purplish golden color of a Buddha. If he happens to be reborn in the human realm, it will be into the household of a king, prime minister, or a man of great wealth or great wisdom and benevolence.'" The Buddha also states in a verse in the *Lotus Sutra*, "All persons who draw or paint, or have others draw or paint, an image of the Buddha adorned with myriad blessings and virtues, will all attain the Buddha Way. This is so even if it is the doodling of young boys, painted using a stalk of grass or a finger nail. These persons will gradually accumulate merit, and all of them will attain the Way."† Both of these statements are spoken from the long, broad tongue of the Buddha himself, so they are true beyond any possibility of doubt.

When I was invited to Keirin-ji in Kai province at the beginning of the

* *Tso-fo hsing-hsiang ching*, T 692.
†Cf. *The Lotus Sutra*, p. 39.

Kampō era (1741), I saw drawings of three Buddhas hanging on a wall of the temple. It appeared at first as though the painter had skillfully depicted the Buddhas in an antique style using thin black ink. On closer inspection, however, I realized that the figures were not painted in the ordinary manner, but were made up of inscriptions of the sacred names of the three thousand Buddhas, written in very small Chinese characters. One thousand Buddhas' names were used for each of the three Buddhas.

Ah! Such elaborate, painstaking workmanship! Such skillful art! I was filled with admiration for the artist, who had carried out his task with reverence and devotion. My palms spontaneously came together in *gasshō*, and I bowed my head.

The head priest of Keirin-ji told me, "These are recent works by Zensui Rōjin of Myōraku-ji. He produced them in the midst of a 'sportive samadhi,' in the time he had left over from his zazen. He sent them here about ten days prior to your arrival so they would be here waiting for you to inscribe some words on them."

I readily agreed to play my part in the undertaking. However, the whole time I was at Keirin-ji I was so busy conducting the lecture meeting and attending to visitors and taking students' *sanzen*, that I didn't even have time to pare my nails. When the meeting ended, I had to leave to return to Shōin-ji, so I could do no more than bow my head as I passed the paintings hanging on the wall.

Yesterday, an attendant monk whom the Keirin-ji priest had dispatched arrived at Shōin-ji to extend the Rōshi's summer greetings to me. After the monk had introduced himself, he produced the three scrolls. "In coming here, I followed the three Buddhas through the torrid summer heat, crossing many precipitous mountain peaks. Master, do not say that you are too busy, that 'you don't even have time to pare your nails.' Please write the inscriptions and allow me to return with the scrolls tomorrow."

I hung up the night lamp and set to work inscribing the verses, battling the sweltering heat, my back bathed in sweat. When I finished, I stepped back and read them over. The Chinese characters were rough and shabby looking. The verses themselves were clumsy and shameful. Another torrent of sweat began pouring down, bathing my body from head to foot. One might call it the muck sweat of the guilty.

[My verses for the three paintings:]

Three thousand Buddha names, all meticulously inscribed,
Have indeed been converted into three Buddha images.

They are ungraspable through past, present, and future.
Wake the Buddha within. Get him out of those weeds!

How noble, a person who depicts a thousand Buddhas.
Far nobler than attaining their three Buddha-bodies.
Yet even a hundred thousand names won't be enough.
Unless he wakens the true Person, he's not even close.

They have thousands of names, but are just one Buddha,
Right now, where is he working to save sentient beings?
After Ts'ui Hao's poem, Yellow Crane Pagoda declined.
My thoughts often turn to that tiger-priest Ch'ang-sha.

. . . .

Wake the Buddha within. "Vairocana Buddha appears in you yourself, from within the Three Poisons" (annotation). The "weeds" refer to dwelling in the three poisons—covetousness, anger, and ignorance—the source of passions and delusions.

Where is he working to save sentient beings? In answer to this question, an annotator (perhaps quoting Hakuin) writes: "He [the one Buddha] is right here in this room, but no one knows it."

Yellow Crane Pagoda. A large and imposing tower in Wu-chang, celebrated in a famous verse by the eighth-century poet Ts'ui Hao: "Long ago a man sailed off on a yellow crane, / Now all that remains is the Yellow Crane Pagoda. / Once the crane left, it never returned, / For a thousand years clouds wandered aimlessly by. / The clear river reflects the trees of Hanyang, / Fragrant grasses flourish on Parrot Island. / Beneath the sunset, where is my native place? / Mists mantling the river bring feelings of regret." It was said that the excellence of Ts'ui Hao's verse kept later poets from attempting their own poems on the pagoda; even the great Li Po is said to have written, "My fist can smash the Yellow Crane Terrace, / My foot can kick over Parrot Island./ Their loveliness only leaves me wordless, / Having Ts'ui Hao's poem over my head." As a result of this poetic neglect, the site, with all its splendid poetic possibilities, was forgotten and fell into ruin.

The allusion to "the tiger priest" Ch'ang-sha in the final line is linked to the three previous lines. In a dialogue between Zen master Ch'ang-sha Ching-ts'en and a bright young man who had read the *Sutra of the Thousand Buddhas' Names,* the young man said, "All these thousands of Buddhas are merely names. Where could all the lands be where they reside? And where are they working to save sentient beings?" Ch'ang-sha said, "After Ts'ui Hao wrote his poem on the Yellow Crane Pagoda, did you compose a verse on it, young man?" "No I didn't," he replied. "You should take the time to write one," said Ch'ang-sha (*Compendium of the Five Lamps*, ch. 4). "There was no one to write on the subject. Everything was falling into ruin. A good thing Ch'ang-sha came along when he did" (annotation).

:104. Verse Inscribed on a Painting of Manjusri Bodhisattva

Hakuin painted a great many images of Buddhas and Bodhisat-tvas. His earliest-known painting in this genre, a depiction of the Bodhisattva Manjusri, dates from his thirty-fourth year (following inscription, #105). An annotation one of Hakuin's students inscribed in Sendai's Comments on the Poems of Han-shan *says: "From his youth the Rōshi [Hakuin] had a great fondness for painting Bud-dhist images. The first ones he painted were of Manjusri, the Bodhi-sattva of Wisdom."*

A detailed commentary on the following verse is found in Religious Art of Zen Master Hakuin, *pp. 216–18.*

I bow deeply before the Great Sage Manjusri
Whose pure, clear Dharma-body is painted here.
If you see him there on the surface of the paper,
You are digging a well in pursuit of white cloud;
But if you seek him apart from his painted image,
You are traveling eastward in pursuit of the sun.
Do you see!!
I bow deeply before the Great Sage Manjusri.

. . . .

If you see him there… "Laymen! Don't think the real Manjusri is found in this picture! Seeking him there is like looking for fire at the bottom of a well. You won't find him on that piece of paper. Yet if you seek him somewhere else, somewhere outside the picture, you won't find him there either. That would be like facing east to view the setting sun" (annotation).

:105. Verse Inscribed on a Painting
of Manjusri Bodhisattva Riding a Lion

Manjusri, the embodiment of prajna *wisdom and teacher of the Buddhas of the past, is one of the most important figures in the Mahayana pantheon. He is often depicted riding on a lion, the king of animals, whose roar represents the invincible working of* prajna *wisdom. Manjusri is often paired with the Bodhisattva Samant-abhadra, the embodiment of love and compassion, who rides an elephant. The painting and inscription are reproduced in HZB #203, with a date corresponding to Hakuin's thirty-fourth year.*

> He is sits all alone on top of Mount Wu-t'ai,
> His crazy pranks were seen around Kuo-ch'ing.
> Though finding him is a totally impossible feat,
> To deal with that difficulty a few sleights exist:
> *"Split open a poppy seed and get some white rock!"*
> *"Scoop up some cold frost on the ocean floor!"*
> It is said he summers at three different spots,
> In fact, the great void all around is his bed.
> If you want to pay him your respects in person,
> Your only way is to cast delusive thinking aside.
> When your mind is empty of such discrimination,
> His marvelous features are all seen plain as day.
> The eye cannot discern those awesome attributes—
> This not-seeing is just where he makes his abode.
> *Look! The dog licks oil from a sizzling plate.*

. . . .

Mount Wu-t'ai. Manjusri is said to dwell on this sacred mountain in Shan-hsi. The poet and Zen eccentric Han-shan, said to be a manifestation of Manjusri, lived in the mountains of T'ien-t'ai in eastern China, paying frequent visits to Kuo-ch'ing temple, where his sidekick Shih-te worked in the kitchen.

   "Split open poppy seeds and get some white rock! / Scoop up some cold frost on the ocean floor!" No source has been found for these phrases, and it is possible they were coined by Hakuin. Penetrating them is the "sleight" Hakuin referred to above.

Three different spots. "Mahakashapa asked Manjusri where he spent his summer retreats. He replied, 'I spend one month at the Jetavana monastery, one month with my young attendants, and one month in whorehouses and bars'" (*Ch'an-lin lei-chu*, ch. 14).

The great void... is his bed. "Because the whole universe in the ten directions is where Manjusri resides" (annotation).

The dog licks oil from a sizzling plate. A phrase used to describe earnest endeavor that cannot achieve its purpose. Here it presumably refers to effort spent trying to see Manjusri's formless form. Two annotations are attached to the final comment: (1) "He's put his mouth in a cauldron of boiling water, he'll burn his nose bad!" (2) "Useless effort."

:106. Verse Inscribed on a Painting of Kannon Bodhisattva, the Sixteen Arhats, and Various Devas

No painting of Kannon inscribed with this verse has been discovered among Hakuin's countless depictions of the Bodhisattva, and although some of his Kannon paintings show her together with sixteen Arhats, and others with deva beings, no known paintings depict her together with both the sixteen Arhats and devas.

In some paintings Kannon is shown surrounded by worshipping devotees sporting turtles, octopus, squid, shrimp, and fish of various kinds on their heads, probably the "sea dwellers" (gunrin) mentioned in the verse:

> To the twenty-eight Arhats sitting here
> Venerating the Body of total freedom,
> To deva hosts of the heavenly realms,
> To various supplicating sea dwellers,
> The Great Being preached this verse,
> Personally turning the Dharma wheel:
> "You beings who have assembled here
> Are no different whatsoever from me.
> But you lose the gem in your hand
> Looking up and away at the moon:
> The moon is the gem in your hand,
> The gem in your hand is the moon.

I earnestly hope those who see this
Enter together the Buddha-nature sea.
The Kannon painted on this paper
Is the same Kannon within each of you.

. . . .

The twenty-eight Arhats are among the endless forms Kannon manifests to teach sentient beings. "Kannon is venerating Kannon!" (annotation).

Great Being. Kannon Bodhisattva. "It is because you always seek it without that you neglect what is within, and fail to worship the Kannon in yourself" (annotation).

The moon is the gem... is the moon. "Originally it is neither within nor without. Our true, nondual relation with Kannon exists in such a negation..... If you call this nonbeing, you fall into the heretical view that death ends all. If you call it being, you fall into the heresy of eternal changelessness. What then can you do? You must hear the sound of One Hand" (annotation).

:107. Verse Inscribed on a Painting of Kannon Seated on the Grass

Although no painting fitting this description or bearing this inscription has been discovered, judging from the verse and accompanying annotations, we know that it depicted Kannon in one of his endless manifestations as a young boy seated on a bed of grasses. The grass seat is made of the kusha *grass that the Buddha is said to have received from Brahman priests; when he sat upon it, this grass seat miraculously transformed into an invincible Diamond Throne.*

He sits there on a cushion of green grass,
Holding a vase with a green willow slip.
Whose little boy are you?
Whose little boy are you?
Sunlight glints from the bamboo stirring in the cool breeze,
Under a horned moon, the dew gleams faintly from the pines.

. . . .

Whose little boy. "My goodness, what a wonderful lad! And he's right there within us all!" (annotation).

Sunlight glints…pines. "This is the Buddha's Dharma-body revealed in primal suchness. It is extremely difficult to penetrate here, but if you grasp it, you are face to face with the living Kannon" (annotation).

:108. VERSE INSCRIBED ON A PAINTING OF MR. MA'S WIFE

Mr. Ma's Wife Kannon (Japanese, Merofu Kannon), sometimes also referred to as Fish Basket Kannon (Japanese, Gyoran Kannon), is one of thirty-three manifestations the Bodhisattva is said to assume. It is based on a tale found in several Sung dynasty Zen works such as the Pien-nien t'ung-lun, *ch. 22, and* Hu-fa lun, *ch. 9.*

Hakuin's four-line verse is prefaced by a long headnote in which he relates his version of the story.

THERE WAS A HAMLET on an island in the sea called Golden Sand Shoal. None of its inhabitants, young or old, had any knowledge of the Buddha's Dharma, nor did they believe in the working of cause and effect, not to mention the sufferings that awaited them in the afterlife. One day an old woman arrived in the village accompanied by a beautiful young girl. The girl carried herself with extraordinary grace and her face was as fair as a peach flower. Although no one knew where the old woman had come from, it was said that she was interested in finding a husband for the young girl. Immediately the youths of the village began vying passionately for the girl's hand.

The old woman brought them to their senses by saying, "Why are you making such a fuss about this? There is after all only one girl, and there are more of you than I can count. She could not possibly accept all of your offers unless she manifested thousands of bodies like the Bodhisattva Kannon. Now I have a Buddhist scripture called the *Kannon Sutra.* If someone is able to memorize this sutra by tomorrow morning, that person will have my consent to marry the girl." She produced copies of the sutra, passed them out to the men, and showed them how to read it. They strove with all their effort, competing against one another to commit the sutra to memory. By the next morning ten of them had succeeded in doing so. The old woman next distributed copies of the *Diamond Sutra,* with the same conditions as before. Seven or eight men were able to memorize it. She then gave them the *Lotus Sutra,* a much longer text, saying she would choose for a husband the man who memorized it all. The men found it an extremely difficult task. Try as they might, one by one they reluctantly abandoned the attempt. One went away shaking his head, yawning wearily. One rolled up the sutra scroll with a deep sigh. Another took the sutra and tearfully threw it aside. Another, on finding his hopes dashed, just bolted off. The only one able to accomplish the difficult task was a son of the Ma family.

He took the young girl as his wife and their marriage took place amid great rejoicing. But the young woman fell ill and before long died. All the villagers on the island were deeply saddened by her death. They were thus brought to appreciate the transience of human life, and began the practice of reciting Buddhist sutras.

One day, an Indian priest carrying a long staff descended from the sky and proceeded to the young woman's grave. Poking in the earth with the staff, he uncovered a set of bones that glittered with a radiant light, illuminating everything around it. "These are the sacred bones of the Bodhisattva of Great Compassion," he pronounced in a loud voice. "You must revere them and strive to free yourselves from the karmic obstacles now hindering you." He then vanished into the sky.

> Using skillful means, the Great Compassionate One
> Manifests thirty-two forms according to arising needs.
> He appeared and saved beings as a pretty young girl,
> Manifesting himself in the form of Mr. Ma's wife.

. . . .

The following account of the story, from *Hu-fa lun*, a Sung dynasty work, will give a better idea of how Hakuin has souped it up.

"In the twelfth year of the Yuan-ho era of the T'ang (817), there was a young girl of great beauty at Golden Sand Shoal in Shan-yu [Shan-tung province] who sold fish from a basket she carried. All the young men competed to make her their wife. The young girl said, 'I will teach you a text called the *Kannon Sutra*. If you recite it all through the night, I will become your wife.' At dawn the next day, twenty men had performed the feat. She said, 'I am only one woman, so it is not possible for me to marry you all. Why don't you recite the *Diamond Sutra* in the same way?' About half the men were able to accomplish this, so next she asked them to recite the *Lotus Sutra* for a period of three days. Only one man, a son of the Ma family, was able to do it, and he and the young woman, in conformance with all the established proprieties, were married. But no sooner had she entered his house than she fell ill and died. Her corpse, swiftly decomposing, soon almost completely disappeared, and the remains were quickly buried. The next day, a Buddhist priest came. Together with the woman's husband, he opened the casket. They found nothing but a set of golden bones. The priest said, 'Your wife was an incarnation of Kannon Bodhisattva. She desired only for you to gain salvation.' Then he disappeared into the sky. From that time forth many people began reciting sutras in Shan-yu."

109. Verse Inscribed on a Painting of Fudō Myō-ō

Fudō, the "Immovable" (Sk. Acalanātha) is the central figure of the fierce Myō-ō class of deities that protect Buddhism and its adherents from harm. Fudō Myō-ō assumes a fearsome appearance, holding a rope in his left hand and a sword in his right, which he uses to destroy evil passions.

> From a mass of fiercely burning flames
> He manifests a body of unbridled wrath,
> Running roughshod over Buddha realms,
> Kicking over the nests of Mara's demons.
> He eliminates all suffering and calamity
> Just as the bright sun dissipates the mist.
> Both gods and demons bow before him
> Like grasses bending before the wind.
> Uniting precepts, meditation, and wisdom,
> Fusing mind, Buddha, and sentient beings,
> His wondrous power works sudden miracles
> Like flames flaring from a lattice window.
> Flowers fall and scatter, small birds twitter,
> Wherever you encounter them, he is there,
> His virtuous shape as majestic as a mountain,
> As boundlessly vast as the great sky above.

. . . .

Fudō Myō-ō often appears as the central figure in a grouping of five esoteric Buddhist images, surrounded by four other Myō-ō—Gōzanze, Gundari, Daiitoku, and Kongōyasha—who are sometimes regarded as manifestations of various aspects of Fudō's power. Hakuin records a youthful encounter he had with these five Myō-ō in his work *Horse Thistles:* "When I was a young boy, I went to a temple of the Shingon sect. There I saw for the first time images of the Five Great Myō-ō. I must say they seemed extremely strange to me. I found it hard to believe Buddhist images could have such absurd appearances. Could they be guardian deities of those street performers who engage in one-man sumo [*hitori-zumo*]? Or perhaps images worshipped by practicers of jujitsu? Anyway, I thought, smiling to myself, they were certainly an unseemly group. Recently, however, I have come to regard their appearances as manifestations of something of truly inestimable value. They indicate the spirit of fierce, indomitable courage a Buddhist practicer must possess if he is to successfully negotiate the Buddha Way. The great sage Fudō Myō-ō stands sternly at the center of the group, protected by the other four Myō-ō, who personify his fierce spiritual powers. Their wrathful appearance…expresses the inner secret of the great matter of Buddhist practice, the maintaining of private application and hidden practice that has been called 'the essence within the essence.' I believe that these images of the Five Great Myō-ō are the very ones to enshrine in Zen training halls, where the mistaken teaching of 'withered sitting' has held sway in recent times" *(HHZ2,* pp. 245–6).

: 110. Verse Inscribed on a Painting of Feng-kan

Feng-kan (literally "Big Stick") is usually shown in Zen painting and sculpture together with the Zen eccentrics Han-shan and Shih-te and his pet tiger as one of the Four Sleepers (Ssu-shui). An anecdote recorded in the Poems of Han-shan (Han-shan shih) *tells of this legendary priest "riding out of the pine trees on the back of a tiger, entering Kuo-ch'ing Temple and causing great consternation in the brotherhood by roaming through the corridors calling out for people to 'get out of the way.'"*

We learn from an annotation that this and the following two verses (#111–12) were inscribed over a set of three scroll paintings that depicted Feng-kan, Han-shan, and Shih-te. In Han-shan's poetry collection we read that Feng-kan was an incarnation of Amida Buddha (The Buddha of Boundless Life), and Han-shan and Shih-te incarnations of the Bodhisattvas Manjusri and Samantabhadra.

Feng-kan sleeps, his arm slung around the tiger,
An incarnation of the Buddha of Boundless Life.
But what about this Buddha of Boundless Life?
I want you to tell me: Whose incarnation is he?

. . . .

I want you to tell me. "He's incarnated in every one of you" (annotation).

:111. VERSE INSCRIBED ON A PAINTING OF HAN-SHAN

This painting was one of a set of three depicting Feng-kan, Han-shan, and Shih-te (see #110).

Someone asked me to inscribe a Han-shan painting,
Heedlessly, without thinking, I agreed to do it.
Now time has come for me to return the painting.
I sit with glazed eyes, chewing my writing brush.

:112. VERSE INSCRIBED ON A PAINTING OF SHIH-TE

This painting was one of a set of three depicting Feng-kan, Han-shan, and Shih-te. The Poems of Han-shan *(Han-shan shih) contain a section of fifty-five verses attributed to this boon companion of Han-shan. In his preface to the poems, the official Lu Ch'iu-yin describes Shih-te as working in the kitchens of Kuo-ch'ing temple and slipping leftovers to Han-shan, who lived in the mountains surrounding the temple. There are references in the same collection to Shih-te as an incarnation of both Samantabhadra Bodhisattva and of Manjusri.*

He sits facing the Buddha, he gobbles up his offerings.
He flies at the temple's guardian deities, whip in hand.
What gives this fellow such a free, untrammeled spirit?
His mind has not even the slightest flicker of thought.

. . . .

He sits...in hand. Allusions to Shih-te's eccentric behavior. He is said to have grabbed the offerings set before the statue of the Bodhisattva Manjusri in the temple refectory and eaten them himself. He would suddenly take a seat before the statue and remain there all day long. When birds came and ate the offerings set out before the statues of the temple's guardian deities, he took a stick and beat the images, saying, "You can't even protect your food from birds, how can you expect to protect the temple?" *Records of the Lamp*, ch. 27.

The final line of the verse is difficult to construe; I have paraphrased it based on a similar verse Hakuin inscribed on another painting of Manjusri.

:113. Verse Inscribed on a Painting of Daruma

In Hakuin's fifties, when he was beginning to extend his teaching activity beyond the confines of Shōin-ji, he commented that he had already painted thousands of portraits of sect founder Daruma (Bodhidharma). Nonetheless, although he painted Daruma far more than any other subject, with the possible exception of Hotei, surviving examples from Hakuin's forties and fifties are relatively few. This verse was inscribed on one of the earliest-known examples of the theme, bearing a date of Kyōhō 4 (1719), his thirty-fourth year (HZB, #54).

> An Indian chap, his self magnificently revealed,
> A clear mass of emptiness vast beyond measure.
> Many have endeavored to confront this old bugger,
> Moaning through the long nights on a zazen seat.
> Some even say they've got him, "He's in my hands!"
> Trouble is, Daruma is really several hedges away.
> You can't paint him, can't get him down in verse either—
> You don't find a phoenix poking in rotten mouse guts.

:114. Verse Inscribed on a Painting of Daruma

As another Daruma painting with the same inscription is dated the fifth of the tenth month, 1726 (HZB #53), we may tentatively place this verse around the same year, when Hakuin at forty-one was only months away from his final decisive enlightenment.

> Bulging blue eyes whose purity shames the sky itself,
> A purple beard whose slightest touch swallows the sun.

But we don't waste time with reveries like that around here,
We're busy mending paper robes with starch from leftover yams.

. . . .

We don't waste our time. "A Zen monk doesn't pay attention to such things. If he does, difficulties arise. He's better off taking some leftover yams and concentrating his efforts on using them to patch up his paper robe" (annotation). "The paste made from baked yams is good for that" (annotation). There is probably also an allusion here to the uncompromising Zen style of the master known as "Lazy" Ts'an, who lived alone in a cave subsisting on yams baked in ox dung, and adamantly refused all offers of advancement, even from the emperor himself (*Blue Cliff Record*, Case 34).

:115. VERSE INSCRIBED ON A PAINTING OF DARUMA

A follower of the Nichiren sect
Wanted to honor the old Indian.
Mount Shao-lin, Mount Minobe.
Same autumn colors, the same sun.

. . . .

"Probably done at the request of a Nichiren Buddhist" (annotation).
Bodhidharma lived at Mount Shao-lin. The headquarters temple of the Nichiren sect is at Mount Minobe, just west of Mount Fuji.

:116. VERSE INSCRIBED ON A PAINTING OF DARUMA

Two bulging blue eyes, round as horse bells,
Jowls rimmed with a jet-black scimitar beard.
He's not a Buddha. He's not a patriarch either.
He's not a deity, nor one of the immortal sages.
Still he confounded the thinkers of six schools,
And produced five lines of wise Zen patriarchs.

. . . .

The six schools are those whose teachings Daruma is said to have refuted in India before travelling to China.

Five lines. The main schools of Chinese Zen—Lin-chi, Ts'ao-tung, Yun-men, Kuei-yang, and Fa-yen—that derive from Daruma, the First Patriarch.

: 117. Verse Inscribed on a Painting of Lin-chi

Lin-chi I-hsuan (d. 866) is the founder of the Zen lineage to which Hakuin belonged. Examples of his use of the shout and clenched fist appear in the Record of Lin-chi, *and in Japan, at least, this fierce teaching style became one of the hallmarks of his line of Zen.*

> As a son he wasn't filial.
> As a monk he broke the precepts.
> He threw punches at everyone he met,
> He shouted thunder at anyone he saw.
> A presence as pitiless as autumn frost,
> A shame such a man had so many bad habits.

. . . .

He wasn't filial. Allusion to the story of Lin-chi as a young monk striking his teacher Huang-po.

: 118. Inscribed on a Painting of Priest Baō of Zuiun-ji

We know little about the Rinzai priest Baō Sōchiku (1629–1711) apart from what we can glean from Hakuin's writings. The name Baō means literally 'Old Horse.' Hakuin first encountered Baō in his nineteenth year, when he was on his pilgrimage around the country. At the time he entered Baō's temple, Zuiun-ji in Mino province, Hakuin had become disenchanted with Zen practice and was considering giving it up for a career in writing or painting.

Writing of his experiences at Baō's impoverished temple in his autobiographies Wild Ivy *(pp. 16–17) and* A Tale of My Childhood *(Precious Mirror Cave, pp. 18–20), and also in his* Chronological

Biography, *works all dating from his final decades, Hakuin dwells on Baō's literary gifts (he was apparently known as a writer of Chinese verse and prose) and also on his eccentricities and severity, describing him as "hard and sharp as flint, ruthless to the core, venomous as they come, almost impossible for monks to endure." Hakuin ended up staying at Baō's temple a whole year, in the course of which he decided to rededicate his life to Zen study. A little over a year after leaving, Hakuin heard reports that Baō was gravely ill and discontinued his pilgrimage to return to Zuiun-ji and care for the old priest.*

In this inscription, which can be dated from a surviving holograph to 1739, much earlier than the accounts of Baō in the autobiographies, Hakuin emphasizes Baō's ability as a religious teacher.

The most detailed modern study of Hakuin's relationship with Baō is found in HOS, pp. 29–36.

THIS ISN'T A PAINTING of Old Sai's horse. It isn't one of Ch'ao Fu's cows, either. But for over forty years, this man trampled over monks throughout the country. This isn't the lion of Fen-yang or the tiger of Shaolung. But he was a terrifying presence who knocked Zen seekers back thousands of leagues.

He reached his maturity grazing in the uplands of Ashikaga in Shimotsuke province, and lapping the sweet waters of Mino province. When I was a young monk, I took my whip in my hand and for several years tried to break this wild bronco. I never even got a glimpse of him. Three or four other monks were with me at the time, attending to the old courser's feed and water, but none of them was ever able to measure up to his Zen working either. But don't say he had no outstanding disciples. The great earth and its mountains and rivers themselves are old Baō's angry glare.

. . . .

Old Sai's Horse. A shortened form of the saying *ningen banji Saiō ga uma,* "for human beings all things are like Old Sai's horse," meaning that the ways of Heaven are inscrutable; that a setback may turn out to be a blessing in disguise. When Old Sai's horse ran off, people tried to sympathize with him. He replied that his fortune would change before long. When the horse returned, bringing another fine riding horse with it, people congratulated him on his good luck. He replied that this would only bring him bad luck. When his son fell from the horse and broke his leg and people commiserated with him, he replied that it would surely be a source of good fortune. An army from a neighboring state invaded his homeland, and all the young men were conscripted and killed in the fighting that ensued. But the son, whose disability kept him at home, survived *(Huai-nan tzu)*.

Ch'ao Fu's cows. "Emperor Yao summoned Hsu Yu, who was tilling his fields, and offered to make him ruler of the entire country. Not wanting even to hear such words, Hsu Yu went and washed his ears out at the riverside. Ch'ao Fu happened along with a herd of calves. He was about to let them drink at the river, but he stopped them when he saw Hsu Yu washing out his ears. "I can't contaminate their mouths with that," he said, and took his calves farther upstream" *(Kao-shih chuan)*. Presumably, Hakuin uses this phrase to assert that Baō was no recluse. This point is verified by a humorous account told in the *Draft Biography* of nocturnal visits Baō made to a nun who lived in the town.

Disciples of the Sung priest Fen-yang Shan-chao were known as the "four lions of Hsi-he." Hu-ch'iu ("Tiger Hill") Shao-lung's benign appearance and tremendous inner strength earned him the sobriquet "sleeping tiger."

119. PRIEST UNZAN OF BUTSUJITSU-AN

Although it is unclear from the title, we learn from the piece itself that Hakuin inscribed these words on a portrait of his close friend Unzan Sotai (1685–1747), who had passed away on the second of the fifth month of 1747. This inscription is dated the twenty-second of the seventh month, less than three months later.

A native of Suruga province, and born the same year as Hakuin, Unzan began his study under Kogetsu Zenzai in Kyushu. He achieved an initial satori, then returned to Suruga and became a disciple of Tessen Genteki of Butsujitsu-zan Kongō-ji in Kadoma village, about four miles east of Shōin-ji. After later succeeding Tessen as head priest of Kongō-ji, he continued koan work under Hakuin.

An annotation quotes Hakuin saying, "We were close friends from the time I was a young monk. We practiced very hard together." When Hakuin left Shōin-ji on trips, Unzan is said to have always accompanied him. The closeness of their friendship is illustrated by an anecdote in Hakuin's Chronological Biography, which describes Unzan reclining on the floor behind Hakuin as Hakuin was giv-

ing a Zen interview (sanzen) to his lay follower O-Satsu (Precious Mirror Cave, p. 201). Unzan appears in Book Nine, #126 and #127.

AN INSPIRING SPIRIT THAT was vast and pure. A presence that shone like a beacon pointing to the ancient and lofty Zen traditions. He sailed across the western sea and threw himself under the black radiance of an old moon [*Kogetsu*], crushing the Buddha mind-seal to dust. Returning to his home in the eastern provinces, he passed beyond Hsuan-sha's utterance, shattering the sharp fangs and talons of the Dharma cave. From then on, he greatly discommoded withered-sitting Zennists wherever he found them. On occasion he would draw portraits of elder priests in the neighborhood seated on their Dharma chairs.

I knew him well for forty years. Now the tears well up and will not cease. Several of his students came asking me to inscribe some words on a portrait the priest of Fukō-ji had painted of him. It was done in a free and untrammeled style, the true product of enlightened 'sportive' samadhi. The words I inscribed are no more than delusions I babbled off in a dream at the foot of the Sala tree. Before I was able to complete the inscription, however, my chin dropped to my chest and I dozed off. I encountered Priest Unzan in a dream. We were both wreathed in broad smiles. When I woke up, I found that the tears rolling down my old cheeks had drenched my robes. It is now midday, the twenty-second day of the seventh month.

. . . .

Hsuan-sha's utterance (Gensha dōtei). In Hakuin Zen, this phrase is invariably used to indicate that an attainment is still incomplete. It appears in a comment Hsuan-sha Shih-pei made when he heard that the priest Ling-yun had experienced enlightenment on seeing some peach flowers in bloom: "It is all good and proper, very proper and good, but I guarantee you that elder brother [Ling-yun] still hadn't got it all" (See p. 69).

Hakuin often used the phrase to emphasize the need for continued post-satori training. He even had it engraved on a stone seal, which he impressed on some of his paintings, perhaps to indicate that although he had tried to depict the truth of his subject, the painting still "hadn't got it all."

An annotation attached to the phrase "He passed beyond Hsuan-sha's utterance," states, "This is also something I got him to do." This annotation, presumably quoting Hakuin's own words, indicates that after Unzan returned to Suruga province he was able, thanks to Hakuin's guidance, to deepen the initial attainment he had achieved under Kogetsu.

He drew the portraits. Not much is known about this side of Unzan's talents, though a few of his surviving works, bearing inscriptions by Hakuin, are preserved in temples in the Numazu area.

I knew him well for forty years. That is, beginning in their early twenties; the *Chronological Biography* states "they were friends from the age of seven or eight."

Head priest of Fukō-ji. Kokuzen Hōkin (n.d.). Fukō-ji was a Zen temple in the village of Tokura.

At the foot of the Sala Tree (Sara juge). This is abbreviated from the sobriquet *Sara juge sendai rōnō,* "the old reprobate monk seated under the Sala Tree," which Hakuin often used in signing his paintings and writings. "Reprobate" (*J. sendai*) refers to an *icchantika,* one who has no possibility of attaining Buddhahood, either because he is evil-minded or because, out of compassion, he chooses not to enter Nirvana but to remain in the world and carry out the Bodhisattva's mission of helping sentient beings.

:120. Verse Inscribed on a Painting of Shōju Rōjin

Hakuin wrote this inscription for a portrait of his teacher Shōju Rōjin. He had painted the portrait at the request of his disciple Dōka (later Tōrei Enji). Tōrei explains the circumstances in a long annotation that also gives a brief a summary of his practice under Hakuin:

In the third month of the first year of Enkyō (1744), having already had my satori confirmed (*inka*) once or twice, I entered a small hall at Shōin-ji and began to practice the Lotus samadhi. The master gave a loud shout as he scolded me about the Old Woman Burns Down the Hut, his voice penetrating deep into my marrow. I was in agony for many days after that. [I returned home] that winter to care for my sick mother. In the tenth month of the next year (1745), now twenty-four years old, I shut myself up for an extended retreat in the Higashiyama area of Kyoto, pushing myself as relentlessly as I could physically endure. In the first month of the next year I sent a letter to Shōin-ji. The master [Hakuin] replied with a verse praising a realization I had achieved. That summer, the fifth month, my mother passed away. In autumn I ordained my younger brother into the priesthood. That winter, I moved to Kōin-an in Higashiyama. . . . In spring of 1748 [my brother] Fumō, now my disciple, requested a meeting. When he came I gave him a copy of *Records of the Authentic Lamp (Shōtō-roku)*, a biography of Shōju Rōjin, and an inscription written by master Hakuin. I traveled to Shinano province where I succeeded in collecting material about Shōju's life. When I presented the biography of Shōju I had compiled to master Hakuin, asking him to revise my work, I requested a portrait of Shōju. Fumō went to Sekigahara in Mino province to visit the Miwa family [the family of Shōju's teacher Shidō Munan] to see if he could find a portrait of Zen master Munan. He then proceeded to Shinano province to try to verify some of the dates in Shōju's career, and to locate, if possible, some of his books or manuscripts. On Fumō's return, he went directly to the master and informed him of the details he had discovered. The master was extremely pleased, and painted a portrait of Shōju. He inscribed this verse on the back of the painting. He wrote to me, saying, "You yourself should write a colophon over this portrait." Such is the record of how this verse came to be written.

Dōka came to me and personally requested a portrait of Shōju.
I tried over and over; not one painting resembled him in the
    least.
I could keep doing it forever, my efforts would still fall short.
A broken kettle puts on straw sandals and fords at Meng
    Crossing.

. . . .

Younger brother. Known only by his Buddhist name Fumō (d. 1794), which he received from Tōrei.

Records of the Authentic Lamp (Shōtō-roku). A compilation by the Japanese priest Tōyō Eichō (1429–1504) first published at the beginning of the sixteenth century, consisting of the records of eminent priests, Chinese and Japanese, in Tōyō's Myōshin-ji lineage. Tōrei held it in great esteem and used it throughout his career. The biography of Shōju that Tōrei compiled is probably the *Shōju Dōkyō Etan Anju Anroku*, a short work first published in 1931 in Abe Hōshun's *Shōju Rōjin* (Gagetsu-an, Nagano). Tōrei, who has been called the historian of Hakuin's line, also compiled a spiritual biography of Shōju's teacher, Shidō Munan (1603–1676).

Dōka. Tōrei's name as a young monk.

Lines 3–4: "Unable to paint Shōju's original face or true Dharma-body in ink, Hakuin ends by making a final, verbal attempt to depict it [in a koan of his own making]" (annotation).

The Meng Crossing. A strategic river crossing in Henan province.

:121. Verse Inscribed on a Painting Showing Mr. Yotsugi Relieving Villagers in Distress

Yotsugi Masayuki was a wealthy Kyoto layman who after becoming a student of Hakuin aided him in a number of his publishing projects. Yotsugi was from the same village in Ōmi province as Tōrei, and provided hermitages for young Tōrei in eastern Kyoto when he was in the capital for practice retreats. It was probably Tōrei who first introduced Yotsugi to Hakuin.

This piece was written in 1752 at Kiichi-ji in southern Izu. "The master received a request from Kiichi-ji and went there in the autumn to lecture on the Record of Bukkō. *Tsutsumi Yukimori came all the way from Kyoto to attend. He told Hakuin how Yotsugi Masayuki had relieved villagers in northern Kyoto who were in great distress. The master made a painting depicting the events and added an inscription to it" (Precious Mirror Cave, p. 220). Although Katō Shōshun states in his edition of Hakuin's* Chronological Biography *(p. 241) that the painting is extant, it remains unpublished and its whereabouts are unknown. Yotsugi also appears in one of the letters included in* Beating the Cloth Drum *(p. 133).*

Tsutsumi Yukimori (n.d.), also known as Nara-ya Kichibei, was related to Yotsugi and may also have served as his head clerk (bantō) at his business in Kyoto.

Mr. Yotsugi (his first name is Masayuki)
Vigorously pursues the study of Zen
While carrying out his Bodhisattva vow,
Tirelessly working for his fellow men.
At a meeting I held in Akashi last year
He passed my first two koan barriers,
Hearing the sound of the single hand,
Then putting a stop to sound altogether,

Though he hasn't reached my inner sanctum,
And many tough barriers still lie ahead.
Yotsugi procured seven Buddha relics,
Which he placed in a jeweled reliquary.
Tōrei brought this treasure to Suruga,
And enshrined it in his temple there.
Folks from all over come to worship it,
Filing in and out like lines of red ants.
In spring of the second year of Hōreki
A blizzard left snow over twenty feet deep,
Isolated villagers in Kyoto's northern hills.
Thirty hamlets from Kurama to Ōhara
Had no fire in their hearths for over a week,
And the villagers were hungry and cold.
Yotsugi, grieved to hear of their plight,
Was moved to utter the following vow:
"Even should it take everything I own,
Leave me penniless till the day I die,
I must save them from certain death.
How can I just sit by idly and watch?"
A relative named Tsutsumi Yukimori,
Who fully supported Mr. Yotsugi's plans,
Trekked nine leagues through deep snow
To tell villagers help was on the way,
Fortifying them with hope and courage,
Inspiring them with a will to survive.
Tsutsumi then returned to the villages,
Leading pack horses loaded with rice.
Two men like Yotsugi and Tsutsumi
Are rarely found in this dusty world.
Without a stalwart such as Tsutsumi
Yotsugi couldn't have achieved his goal
Without donations Yotsugi provided
Tsutsumi could not have performed his deeds.
It is said that a diviner long ago, reading
Death in the face of an acolyte monk
Sadly informed the poor young fellow
He only had seven more days to live.
The weeping boy, overcome by despair,

Went sadly to bid his parents farewell.
On his way home he passed a tiny rivulet,
Where a line of ants was being carried away.
Seeing their plight, he broke off a reed
And used it to make a bridge for them.
The diviner, meeting the boy again, said,
"You must have performed some splendid deed,
I now see signs of long and prosperous life.
I am sure you will save a great many lives."
When the boy told how he rescued the ants,
Even his teacher was pleased and impressed.
He lived to become a priest of great virtue,
Dying when well over ninety years old.
If saving the lives of those small insects
Could change a boy's fate to such an extent,
Just imagine the futures of these two men,
Who saved many people from certain death!
Their exploits inspire the most earnest prayer:
"May we all attain perfection of wisdom together."
Unable to suppress my admiration for these men
I painted this so people will know what they did.

. . . .

Two koan barriers. Yotsugi had passed Hakuin's koans while taking part in the lecture meeting Hakuin held on the *Record of Hsu-t'ang* in the winter of 1750 at Ryōkoku-ji in Akashi, Harima province, located on the coast of the Inland Sea just west of the modern city of Kobe (*Precious Mirror Cave,* p. 217).

On his way back from teaching in western Japan, Hakuin stopped over in Kyoto for lectures on the *Blue Cliff Record* at the Yōgen-in subtemple of Myōshin-ji. Tōrei was with him as an attendant and later accompanied him back to Suruga. The Buddha relics Yotsugi donated to the newly rebuilt Muryō-ji, where Tōrei had been appointed head priest, were officially enshrined in the eleventh month of 1752 (see #70).

Kurama and Ōhara. Villages in the hills several miles north of Kyoto, an area that normally receives heavier snowfall than Kyoto itself, though a depth of twenty feet would be unusual.

:122. Verse Inscribed on a Painting of a Boy Riding a Water Buffalo

> Where'd you get your hands on that buffalo,
> Young fellow? And whose little boy are you?
> Such a skinny rider, and such a sturdy beast,
> Nasty customer even with a ring in his nose.
> I can tell you some things about taming an ox:
> Attempt to catch him, he'll surely slip away;
> Give him his head, he snuggles right up close.
> *Booieee Booieee*

:123. Inscribed on a Painting of a Crab

Hakuin did several paintings of a crab and frog, but no painting of a crab answering this description is known.

BOTH ARMS RAISED UP high, both eyes staring like stalks at the blue sky, this tiny riverside creature scrabbles its way into the reeds. On looking more closely, I discovered that it was Crab Sensei. I addressed him:

"Ah! How strong and brave you are, even as you humble yourself before all things for your peace and security. The trouble comes when someone gets puffed up and arrogant. You always gaze upward as though worshipping the Buddha's blue eyes, like you were one of the host of eighty thousand who attended the preaching at Vulture Peak. It is a gaze that takes everything in, like the usurper Wang Mang, whose loathing enemies would even today devour him alive. It is the gaze of a cat who pretends to doze under a peony in the warm spring sun, and suddenly leaps to catch a butterfly. It is the gaze of a Zen monk steadily scanning the distant heavens and aspiring to the freedom to transcend those heights (though this is a perilous trap for him).

"But what is your real intent in assuming that brave and manly attitude with your six legs and two pincers and revering Heaven like that?"

Crab Sensei replied, "I have my reasons for scuttling sideways the way I do. I'm not just indulging in some cheeky sport. I must also point out that I am different from the four examples you just gave."

With deepest respect I then said to him, "I was sure that was the case. Would you please tell me about your needs?"

Shuffling and scuttling around, Crab Sensei whispered in a tiny voice,

"To tell the truth, I'm quite an ignorant fellow. I'm not sure myself. I've just always acted like this."

"Could it be your original nature?" I asked.

Edging sideways, Crab Sensei said, "I don't know. I don't know," and disappeared into the reeds.

. . . .

Wang Mang (1st century BCE). After marrying his daughter to the Han emperor P'ing Ti, Wang Mang poisoned him, had his daughter name her infant son as emperor and appoint himself Regent. He later declared himself emperor. When he was overthrown by his own army, his soldiers tore his corpse into pieces.

The gaze of a Zen monk. "This is where a great many monks stumble to their ruin....[They shouldn't] seek Buddhahood above or try to save sentient beings below. They should swallow up [negate] all Buddhas of the three worlds" (annotation). "This is the real meaning of these words of master Hakuin" (annotation).

I don't know. I don't know.... "Tōrei: 'Although this inscription seems to espouse the Taoist doctrines of Lao Tzu and Chuang Tzu, at a deeper level it is urging people to turn to the Buddha Way. Lao and Chuang teach spontaneity and naturalness, that all things derive from Heaven. Buddha teaches that the three worlds (past, present, and future) exist, and that within them cause and effect hold sway, that good and evil are both produced by the mind. In the pieces that follow, the master's verses about a hungry ghost thrashing a skeleton [#124, #125] teach that good and evil is all produced by the mind'" (annotation).

:124. Verse for a Drawing of a Hungry Ghost Thrashing a Skeleton

> Instead of thrashing the bones of his former self,
> Why not just grasp the mind that is beating them?
> How priceless is the mind that does the thrashing,
> It is itself the mind of the ancient Buddhas.

:125. VERSE FOR A DRAWING OF A HUNGRY GHOST THRASHING A SKELETON

This long verse was inscribed, like the one in the previous piece, on a drawing of a hungry ghost (Sanskrit, preta; Japanese, gaki). From other similar works Hakuin painted, we can assume the drawings depicted a skeletal figure with a skull-like head and a grossly distended stomach thrashing with a bamboo rod at the scattered remains of a disinterred corpse. The story that inspired the image and verses appears in a number of Chinese collections of Buddhist tales. The version found in a work titled Divergent Concepts in Sutra and Vinaya Texts *is as follows:*

> "Long ago in a foreign land there was a man who beat his corpse after he died. When onlookers said, 'You are dead. Why are you beating your corpse?' he explained, 'When I was alive, this was my body. I committed a great many bad deeds because of it. When I saw sutras or precepts, I didn't read them. I stole, I deceived people, I raped women. I was unkind to my parents, I used my wealth selfishly only on myself, and never donated alms. Because of this body you see here, I fell into the evil realms of existence when I died, and underwent punishments and suffering impossible to describe. That is why I beat my corpse'" (Ching-lu I-hsiang, *ch. 46*).

Hakuin's own interpretation of the story, which unfolds as he retells it, is given a typical Zen twist at the end. The much shorter inscription on the same theme that appeared in the previous piece (#124) can be said to encapsulate both the tale and Hakuin's underlying message.

Hungry ghosts, who inhabit the second lowest of the six realms (roku-dō) in which unenlightened beings are reborn, live in a state of perpetual, insatiable thirst and hunger. Occupying the top rung on the ladder of rebirth in the six realms are heavenly beings (devas) such as the one that appears in the second half of Hakuin's verse. These godlike beings, because they experience unremitting pleasure, lack any incentive to cultivate wisdom or compassion. Devas are beings of great power, wealth, and longevity, and they are normally invisible to human and other beings on lower levels of existence, but in time even they grow old, manifesting the five signs of decay (ten-nin no gosui)—dirty clothing, withering of garlands in their hair, unpleasant odors, sweaty armpits, and uneasiness of mind—and when they die, they are reborn into a lower, less fortunate realm of existence. Among the six realms of existence—deva, human, Asura, beast, hungry ghost, and hell—it is in the human realm alone that realization of the truth of Buddha's teaching and escape from the suffering of the six ways are possible.

Long ago, a Zen priest did zazen in a graveyard
Bathed in the pale moonlight of a lonely moor.
At midnight, feeling a mournful breeze stir up,
He looked and saw a hungry ghost beating a corpse,
Pummeling it violently with raging, wolfish passion,
Its hawk-like eyes glaring with fierce burning hate.
What had whipped it into such a wrathful state,
Kept it thrashing ceaselessly all through the night?
Quaking with fear, the priest approached and said,
"Who were you? What house or family were you from?
What grave injustice do you feel you must avenge?
What has fired your anger to this towering height?"
Glowering darkly but with signs of shame as well,
The ghost broke into tears, and told the priest his tale:
"I was a man of great wealth and high position,
A womanizer addicted to the pleasures of the flesh.
I showed no kindness or compassion to my parents,
Cared no more for others than for a stump or stake.
Disbelieving in life after death or the future world,
My mind just thirsted onward like a ravenous beast,
Thinking only of itself and its own immediate needs.
When I died, I fell into the hellish form you now see,
Doomed to walk forever through razor-leaf trees,
To suffer unspeakable torments in cave-like darkness,
All a result of the hateful bones you see rotting there.
They gave me greater pain than the broad-headed axe.
My hatred for them never ceases and never abates,
So I come here each night and thrash at them like this."
He then stopped speaking, flushed with bloody tears,
Choking with bitterness, emitting heartrending cries.

The priest, his own eyes glistening, turned and left.
When he had gone no more than a hundred steps,
Chance led him to the edge of another graveyard,
Where he saw a deva praying at a pile of bones.
It wore a crown of jewels, slippers of silk brocade;
Tinkling in gems, it exuded rare, sweet fragrance.
Auspicious five-colored clouds floated overhead,
Celestial light shone from the surrounding trees.
Drawing near, the priest addressed him with awe:
"I feel privileged to gaze on your exalted form,
But why have you appeared in this graveyard,
And why do you bow before a pile of stinking bones
More wretched and worthless than chips of wood?"
"Come closer and I will answer you," the deva said.
"I have good reason to bow before these bones.
I was born to a poor family, poorest of the poor,
Not even enough rice bran for our starving bellies.
By the gradual accumulation of various good acts,
I was reborn in the palace of the Thirty-three Gods.
When I lived in the human world, this was my body;
I came to repay a small part of the debt I owe it."
Then he suddenly vanished into the clouds and mist,
Only the plaintive cries of autumn insects remained.
What a shame that the priest, on meeting those beings,
Was remiss in his duty to confront them as he should.
Even if the ghost thrashed the bones into fine powder,
It wouldn't free him from the seas of birth and death.
Even devas reborn into the initial meditation heavens
Grow old and die, and revert to less fortunate births.
But if you grasp the mind that thrashes those bones,
The four Buddha wisdoms will suddenly blaze forth.
The deep mind-source within you is a precious thing,
Can become a raft to ferry you beyond the world.
Even someone burdened by deep obstructing karma
Will find it suddenly vanish upon grasping this mind.
It is not a teaching to delude or deceive you,
It is eternal truth, unchanging till the end of time.

. . . .

In the latter parts of the verse Hakuin employs terminology from ancient Buddhist cosmology. The Triple World, the locus of illusion or unenlightened being, is comprised of (1) the World of Desire, the dwelling place of all those in the six paths, including six kinds of heavenly beings; (2) the World of Form, whose inhabitants are less captive to desire but still attached to form; and (3) the World of Formlessness, whose occupants are free from both desire and form. *The palace of the Thirty-three Gods* is in the second-lowest heaven in the World of Desire, while the *initial meditation heavens*—Hakuin specifies Daibonten (Skt., *Mahā-brahma*) and Bonpoten (Skt., *Brahma-purohita*)—are the second and third lowest stages in the first meditation heaven of the World of Form.

BOOK NINE
Religious Verses (*Geju*)

. . . .

The word geju, *derived from the Sanskrit* gatha, *verses or versified discourse in Buddhist scripture, came to be used in later Chinese and Japanese Zen in a looser sense for Buddhist verse in general. While the many* geju *Hakuin composed as Instructions to the Assembly and for temple observances such as Buddha's Birthday appear elsewhere in* Poison Blossoms, *most of those in Book Nine are unrelated to any specific teaching category, being written for individual priests and laymen, or as occasional verses.*

:126. WRITTEN WHILE STAYING AT RYŪUN-JI

Ryūun-ji is located a little over a mile east of Hara in what is now the city of Numazu. Its head priest at this time was Settan Ehatsu (also Ehotsu; n.d.), one of Hakuin's oldest friends. Slightly older than Hakuin, in his teens Ehatsu was a novice under Sokudō Rōshi at Daishū-ji in Numazu at the same time as Hakuin, whom he accompanied on a number of his early travels and apparently came to recognize as his teacher. After Hakuin was installed as head priest at Shōin-ji, Ehatsu came to assist him whenever extra help was needed. Despite this close relationship, Ehatsu appears in Hakuin's records only once, and that in passing, in Wild Ivy *(p.49).* Hakuin *is recorded as saying during his Zen lectures on* Poison Blossoms, *"This took place forty years ago" (annotation), which would place the verse no later than his early to mid-forties, a period during which he was engaged in a regimen of particularly intense practice* (Chronological Biography)*.*

The following two verses, #127 and #128, written for Unzan and Senior Priest Jun, were also composed during this stay at Ryūun-ji. The three men had probably gathered at Ryūun-ji for the rōhatsu sesshin *held in the twelfth month. If written at the end of this intense period of practice, all three verses can be said to express Hakuin's state of mind at the time.*

> Poking about in the predawn light for his broken-legged pot,
> The old priest wants to simmer up some Sleeping Dragon tea.
> Wumps from the wooden fish resound from the recitation hall,
> A crow flaps by, crossing through the mist of the old village.
> Although the cold is ten times more intense than at Shōin-ji,
> For peacefulness and tranquility, Ryūun-ji cannot be matched.
> Head priest Settan, attending scrupulously to his guests' needs,
> Has the senior monk bring glowing coals to keep me warm.

. . . .

The "old priest" is Settan, head priest of Ryūun-ji. "Sleeping Dragon tea" is apparently an herbal decoction Settan was using for an indisposition of some kind, or perhaps he was preparing it for the monks. In the hall, the monks are beating loudly and rhythmically on the "wooden fish" (*mokugyo*) as they perform the morning sutra chanting.

A crow flies by. Hakuin used the fourth line of the verse as an inscription on a number of his paintings: as a comment on a picture of two flying crows, on portraits of Bodhidharma, and most often on paintings of Shakamuni Leaving the Mountain (*HZB* #573, 44, 144, 155, 160, 161), a theme that would tie in with the supposition that Hakuin wrote the verse at the conclusion of the rigorous winter training period.

Although the cold: "Ryūun-ji, located in the foothills below Mount Fuji, is much colder than Shōin-ji, and also much quieter, since it is not situated right by the busy Tōkaidō Road like Shōin-ji is" (annotation).

: 127. For Unzan Oshō, Using the Same Rhymes as the Previous Verse

Unzan Oshō, Unzan Sotai (1685–1747), was head priest of Kongō-ji in Kadoma, Suruga province, which was located about four miles east of Shōin-ji. Apparently he was also staying at Ryūun-ji when Hakuin wrote this set of verses.

Unzan achieved an initial satori while studying under Kogetsu Zenzai in Kyushu. After receiving Kogetsu's confirmation, he returned to his native Suruga province where he was installed as head priest of Kongō-ji. The Chronological Biography *(1719, age 34) tells us, "Unzan of Kongō-ji and the master were close long-time friends, having known each other since they were six or seven years old. Unzan visited Hakuin at Shōin-ji regularly to continue his study, later achieving a satori. Whenever Hakuin left Shōin-ji to travel, Unzan always accompanied him" (Precious Mirror Cave, pp. 194–5).*

> *Naikan* meditation excels the finest herbal potions known,
> I recently threw out the clay pot I'd been using to brew them up.
> Our constitutions are different, one of us weak, one strong,
> But the hair on both our heads is grizzled equally with snow.
> No one knows how many more such meetings we will have,

Yet we have each discovered pleasure in this illusory world.
Neither of us has found it through seeking or chasing,
Only by exchanging phoenix flights in verses like these.

. . . .

Naikan ("Introspective Meditation") is the therapeutic meditation Hakuin used to cure himself of the "Zen sickness" he contracted in his late twenties. The story of how he acquired this method from the hermit Hakuyū in the mountains east of Kyoto is told in *Idle Talk on a Night Boat* (*Precious Mirror Cave*, pp. 83–115).

Our constitutions different. "You (Unzan) are weak; I (Hakuin) am strong." In fact, Unzan died more than twenty years before Hakuin.

Yet we have each discovered. "Within this delusory world of dreams we have both discovered how to enjoy the pleasures of the Dharma."

Neither of us. "Once you grow old, there's nothing left to do but drink tea and recite the Nembutsu." "We did not go out to seek fame or profit in the world" (annotations).

An annotation by Tōrei adds, "He [Hakuin] was devoting himself assiduously to the study of painting and calligraphy [at this time]." Another unidentified, annotator, whose comments seem to convey Hakuin's own words, has: "It took place forty years ago, when I painted a picture of a celestial phoenix. I was working very hard on my painting and calligraphy at the time." These comments, telling us that Hakuin devoted a great deal of time and effort to painting and calligraphy during his forties, are a valuable contribution regarding a matter that has long puzzled students of Hakuin's life.

Only by exchanging alludes to the pastime of exchanging verses like these.

:128. THANKING SENIOR PRIEST JUN FOR SPONSORING A VEGETARIAN FEAST, USING THE SAME RHYMES AS BEFORE

Senior Priest Jun has not been identified, though we know from the context and the annotations that he was a priest residing at Ryūun-ji who had requested a memorial service for a deceased, and unnamed, teacher.

You rose early, boiled up water for the tea,
Hurried to the kitchen to wash out the pots,
Hurried to the hall and set out the candles,

Chopped greens and roots from the frost-covered fields.
Offering a meager feast for a shiftless guest,
You mourn your teacher in the Great Silence.
A mind like yours is surely to be cherished,
You didn't get it from the bull-headed shrike!

. . . .

Hakuin is offering a backhanded compliment. The bull-headed shrike or butcher-bird *(mozu)*, said to eat its mother, represents the ultimate in unfilial behavior, whereas Jun, by his conduct, shows his devotion to both his late teacher and to Hakuin.

:129. THREE VERSES INSTRUCTING SENIOR MONK TETSU WHO RETURNED FOR MORE STUDY

Senior monk Tetsu, later Kanjū Sōtetsu (d. 1770), served as head priest of Rinzai-ji in the castle town of Sumpu (present Shizuoka City), where he had succeeded Hakuin's friend Kyōsui Edan. He studied with Hakuin at Shōin-ji, appearing in the records, as he does here, as Senior Monk Tetsu. Tetsu had apparently left Shōin-ji after an initial satori but before his training was complete and returned to his home temple Rinzai-ji.

In 1748, at Kanjū's request, Hakuin conducted a lecture meeting at Rinzai-ji to commemorate the two-hundredth anniversary of temple founder Daikyū Sōkyū's death (below #156; Precious Mirror Cave, pp. 213–14).

I.

You've stayed away, keeping your distance from me these
    ten years.
Did you often feel you were scratching an itch through a shoe?
You ran off happy with your partial gain, buried yourself in
    the city,
But the evil storms of the poison sea now drench you once
    again.

. . . .

Scratching an itch through a shoe. An idiom used here to describe Tetsu's unavailing efforts to get at the basic source of his problem.

Evil storms refers to the difficult koan work Tetsu was now engaged in under Hakuin's tutelage. "Tetsu was struggling with 'What is the color of the wind?'" (annotation). This was a koan Hakuin devised for advanced students.

II.

I always loved that pure steel I saw in you, Master Tetsu,
But more than kindling is needed to get a red-hot fire.
Throw yourself back into my inferno of eternal darkness,
Once you're burned to cinders, good results will appear.

. . . .

Pure Steel. Hakuin is playing on the name Tetsu—"steel"—referring specifically to the steel of Pin-chou in China, whose legendary purity was attained by using an extremely hot furnace.

Eternal darkness. Primal ignorance (*avidyā*).

Once you're burned. "Because of being bruised and battered by the merciless tempering and refining he undergoes at Hakuin's forge, working on koans such as Nan-ch'uan's Death and The Buffalo Comes Through the Window" (annotation).

III.

At Great Plum Peak your flower was only half open,
Illusory flowers can hardly be harbingers of spring.
Luckily, the cold this year will penetrate your marrow,
We can expect the plum flowers' pure scent before long.

. . . .

Great Plum Peak, Daibai-zan, is the mountain name of Hōjō-ji, a temple in the remote mountains of Tamba province west of Kyoto where Tetsu had studied under head priest Daidō Bunka (1680–1752). In Chinese, and to a lesser extent Japanese literature and art, the plum blossom with its exquisite scent, appearing during the depths of winter, symbolizes winter's end and the imminence of spring. Hakuin exploits the temple's mountain name to allude to a "partial attainment" Tetsu had achieved at Hōjō-ji.

Two annotations make clear that Hakuin was urging Tetsu to surpass this initial experience: "'Half-open blossoms' is the breakthrough Tetsu achieved under Daidō Oshō." "The satori he experienced at Daidō's temple was like a 'flower in the air' (*kūge*), that is, illusory and totally useless."

:130. VERSE THANKING GENTOKU RŌJIN FOR A GIFT OF REMARKABLE SPIRIT ROCKS

As a lover of rocks, Hakuin can have had few equals. The "spirit rocks" (kiseki) mentioned here were actually boulders that had been transported from Hina, Ishii Gentoku's (Rōjin means "Venerable Old Man") home village in the mountains below Mount Fuji, to Hara on the coast. It would have been a major undertaking, requiring the assistance of large numbers of men. After being hauled to the river and put onto rafts, the rocks were floated down to the ocean; there the rafts were met by boats that towed them along the coast to the beach near Hara, where they were unloaded. Hakuin's firsthand account conveys in vivid terms his exuberance and state of excitement to the reader. The verse opens with Hakuin awaiting the arrival of the rocks with keen anticipation.

> I rose before dawn, went and prodded the cooks to hurry
>   the rice,
> Sent men into the dark to round up monks with special
>   strength.
> I feared for the raftsmen struggling in the swift mountain
>   torrent,
> For the spirit rocks they had on board were no ordinary stones.
> I knew the river gods would try to snatch them for themselves,
> They would surely covet such rarities for their watery dwellings.
> I told the men who fashioned the bamboo ropes to stand ready,
> Told everyone I met to call me as soon as the raft was in sight,
> Stationed lookouts—like a commander leading men into battle.
> All of a sudden we heard the lookout's cry, "the raft is coming!"
> A wave of joyous commotion passed quickly through the crowd.
> Nimble-footed men began hurrying about, calling to one
>   another.
> Forgetting the raftsmen's safety, I yelled, "Are the rocks secure?"

The heavily burdened rafts came into view—we gaped in
  wonder.
There was a tall rock with a sage-like dignity, yet not overawing,
A flat one crouched like a tiger or panther, but was full and
  plump.
They were covered with emerald moss like two ancient dragons,
And had distinctive markings which declared them to be
  siblings.
A thousand men shining with sweat strove against unyielding
  stone,
Battling with heroic courage against the frosty guardians of the
  peaks.
Fresh blood was mustered; vigorous youths, seven or eight
  strong
Spit in their fists, flexed their arms, and tried to work their will.
The beach gave way, the raft tipped, casting many into the sand;
Drained and dispirited, they were unable to get the rocks ashore.
Mr. Shōji appeared leading a large contingent of men and boys,
Old Kokan came running with a troop of neighborhood youths.
One final great united effort—and the rocks were on the beach!
Once again they dug in, refusing to budge a single hairsbreadth,
Much less agree to be carried off to Shōin-ji's temple garden.
But, thanks to the efforts of a benevolent master of many arts,
The rocks were coaxed forward, herded along like cows or sheep.
A poem accompanied these gifts, more splendid than brocade.
Humming it quietly to myself as I sat amid the frenzy of activity,
I felt a profound purity penetrating deep into my bones.
No gift of precious jewels could have brought me such great joy.
My infatuation for the streams and rocks is truly beyond cure,
Treasures like these mean more to me than a dozen walled
  castles.

:131. FOR KI ZENNIN ON HIS RETURN TO MINO PROVINCE

*All that is known about Ki Zennin (Zennin="Zen man") is provided
in an annotation to this undated verse: "He was a monk named
Zenki from Tsūgen-ji in Mino province."*

328 : POISON BLOSSOMS FROM A THICKET OF THORN

On leaving us to return to his home in Mino, Ki Zennin
Took out a sheet of paper, asked me to write something.
I have a poem for him. I've had it ready for many years,
It strips the wise of their wisdom, fools of their follies.
It makes gods and demons flee, wailing and lamenting,
Secretly creases deep furrows in my Zen monks' brows.
It takes the lives of Buddhas and lives of hungry ghosts
Quicker than sparks can fly off a flintstone.
It is said: "A pillow at the mountains, at the river, shoes,
Go carefully, and hurry, but do not stumble in your haste."
In the morning, your robe will be laden heavily with frost,
In the evening, your steps weighed down by frozen cloud.

. . . .

I have a poem. Hakuin's Sound of One Hand koan, which he began using in
his sixty-second or sixty-third year. This provides the letter with a *terminus
ad quo*, and, since he says he's already been using the koan a long time, it was
probably written considerably later than that.

"*A pillow at the mountains, at the river, shoes.*" The annotations agree that
these are cautions for traveling monks. One says: "If you're heading east on
the Tōkaidō, you should stop in Numazu for the night and cross the mountains of the Hakone barrier in the morning. If you're heading west, don't stop
until you cross the Fuji River; then rising water won't trouble you." Another
says: "'A pillow at the mountains' means you should stop over when you
come to the high mountains and cross them the following day. 'At the river,
shoes' means if you stop after a difficult river crossing, your journey will be
trouble-free." Yet another says, "Mountains should be crossed in the morning; rivers should be forded in the evening," tying these two directives to the
poem's final two lines: "When you cross the mountains in the morning, your
robe will be heavy with frost. When you cross the river before stopping for
the night, you will be enveloped in frozen clouds."

:132. RESPONDING IN VERSE TO A REQUEST
FROM KAISHUN RŌJIN

*An annotation attached to this piece states, "Kaishun was a priest of
the Shingon sect. He reached a certain degree of understanding." Kaishun (n.d.) was apparently acquainted with Hakuin's friend Yōshun*

Shudaku, the head priest of Seiken-ji in nearby Okitsu. A meeting Kaishun had with Hakuin is recorded in the Chronological Biography *for 1733: "In spring a priest named Kaishun of the Shingon sect came to Shōin-ji for an interview with Hakuin. The master took a fire iron and held it up in front of Kaishun's face. 'If you feel the slightest hesitation before this piece of iron, you are not yet truly enlightened.' Kaishun was dumbfounded"* (Precious Mirror Cave, p. 202).

Kaishun Rōjin is a priest of many accomplishments,
A patriarch whose lineage traces back to Kōbō Daishi.
Having mastered the secrets of the three mystic acts,
He recently began a study of the Five Houses of Zen.
He made repeated forays into the Green Dragon's den,
Experiencing the dire perils that lie beneath its jaws.
He showed up here yesterday, knocking at my gate,
Pressed me for a verse I had promised to write for him.
Pondering it, I knew this would be no ordinary poem,
It had taken over three kalpas of most diligent work.
Any demons that read it will bolt like terrified hares;
Any gods that read it will flee begging for their lives.
Sometimes it's no different from granny Chang's ears,
Sometimes it's the same as mother Li's arched eyebrows.
But as soon as I tried to write it down for you,
My brush tip froze harder than a steel spike.

. . . .

Kōbō Daishi (Kūkai) is the founder of Japanese Shingon Buddhism. In esoteric Buddhism, the "three mystic acts" (*san-mitsu*) of body, speech, and thought enable the practicer to attain unity with a divinity.

Pondering it. An annotation, apparently conveying Hakuin's own words, has: "This entire room I'm sitting in is my verse. It has taken over three infinite kalpas of time to produce it."

Granny Chang's ears. These two lines epitomize the essential import of the verse, which, as the final two lines also suggest, utterly transcends verbal expression.

:133. FOR BANSUI OSHŌ'S SEVENTH MEMORIAL ANNIVERSARY, USING MATCHING RHYMES

Bansui Soboku (n.d.) was the priest of Chōgetsu-ji, a temple in Magomi village now incorporated into the city of Numazu on the western slope of Washizu-yama, a distinctly shaped mountain Hakuin depicts in several of his paintings.

An annotation informs us that Hakuin composed this verse for Bansui's memorial service as he was being sculled across Suruga Bay to Chōgetsu-ji ("Fishing for the Moon Temple") in a small boat. Chōgetsu-ji is about six kilometers east of Hara along the shore of Suruga Bay. He would have boarded a small boat, propelled from the stern by a single sculling oar, at the pine-forested shore near Hara. The annotation adds, in what sounds like a transcript of Hakuin's own words: "On the way, the boat passed over the reflection of snow-covered Mount Fuji on the water. A delightful sensation!"

> Emperors Shun and Yu attained it, achieving the Mean,
> Chin and Ch'u with all their wealth could not approach it.
> Chōgetsu-ji's gate looms into view, my verse finally finished.
> The oarsman sculls us slantwise over a solitary white peak.

. . . .

Emperors Shun and Yu... Mean. Allusion to words Emperor Shun spoke to Emperor Yu, "The mind of man is uncertain; the mind in accord with the Way is difficult to clarify. Devote your effort to following and fostering the way of the Mean" (*Book of Documents*).

"What does it mean, 'attained it'? It means hearing the Sound of One Hand" (annotation).

Chin and Ch'u. Allusion to a passage in *Mencius:* "The philosopher Tseng Tzu said, 'The wealth of the states of Chin and Ch'u cannot be rivaled. Their rulers may have their wealth, but I have my benevolence. They have their exalted ranks, but I have my integrity" (II.2.ii).

:134. On the Thirteenth of the Ninth Month, An Evening at Mr. Shōji's Residence

Hakuin's verse, thought to date from around his fiftieth year, describes a visit to his friend Shōji Rokubei's (Layman Yūsai, d. 1750) residence in Hara for an autumn moon viewing, during which he was treated to noodles made from newly harvested soba (buckwheat). As soba was said to be one of Hakuin's favorite foods, the gathering may have been held in his honor.

Shōji, a cousin of Hakuin, was an influential citizen of Hara. Like Hakuin's mother, he was an avid Nichiren Buddhist, yet he, his brother Yūtetsu, and his daughter O-Satsu (1714–89) all studied Zen under Hakuin. Satsu appears in a number of stories in Hakuin's records, all showing her to have been a formidable Zen laywoman (e.g., Precious Mirror Cave, *pp. 199–200; 236–38).*

In Japan, soba crops are harvested in summer and autumn. Although the noodles are eaten throughout the year, soba lovers esteem above all the fragrance and flavor of those made from the new, freshly ground autumn kernels. Soba appears as a theme in three other pieces in Poison Blossoms *(#136, #145, #170).*

I hadn't climbed into the hills and surveyed the autumn skies,
Knowing I'd visit Mr. Shōji's on the thirteenth of the month.
The Moon Lady's face was hidden, veiled by curtains of rain.
I hung a lamp, passed the time reading the poems of Po Chu-i.
Shōji served new soba—thinly sliced jade—the greatest of treats.
The eaves were still dripping, cries of delight—the bright full
    moon!
I got up, my bones transparent, and walked in the garden,
A white peak crowned with snow rose into the clearing sky!

. . . .

I hadn't climbed. The custom of autumn moon viewing was introduced from China in the Heian period. The Chinese custom of climbing a high hill on the Double Nine Festival (the ninth of the ninth month) and drinking chrysanthemum wine is alluded to in the first line of the verse. The beauty of the autumn moon on the thirteenth of the ninth month is reputed to be second only to that seen on the fifteenth of the eighth month.

Moon Lady. Lady Ch'ang, the Moon Lady, stole the elixir of immortality from her husband, drank it, and fled to the moon, where she changed into a frog, whose shape can be seen on its surface.

My bones transparent alludes to a famous line in a verse by the fourteenth-century Zen poet Jakushitsu Genkō: "As I grow older, a mountain retreat appeals all the more strongly to my feeling; / Even when I am buried, after death, underneath the rock, my bones will be as thoroughly transparent as ever" (trans. D.T. Suzuki's *Zen and Japanese Culture*, p. 357).

A white peak. An annotation attached to the final line apparently records Hakuin's own words: "Gazing up at the clearing skies, Mount Fuji was so sharp and distinct it seemed that you could reach out and take it in your hands."

:135. Verse with Preface Thanking Monks Chō and Tan for Their Help in Completing Construction of the New Meditation Hall

In the Chronological Biography *for Hakuin's fifty-first year (1736) we read, "There were now eight monks residing at Shōin-ji. In summer, the master lectured on the* Blue Cliff Record. *In autumn, thanks in large part to the efforts of Chō of Tango and Tan of Bungo, the construction of a new Monks' Hall was completed at Shōin-ji. The master composed a verse to express his gratitude." This is one year later than the date Hakuin gives here. Apart from the information Hakuin provides here, nothing is known about these two monks.*

IN RESPONSE TO REPEATED requests from friends of Shōin-ji, in autumn of 1735 we set about constructing a small Meditation Hall. From the very first hammer tap, the brothers in the assembly endured hardship and fatigue that is hard to express in words, and it will continue up until the work is finished. But with everyone pitching in and working together, the hall will soon be completed.

Yesterday, a priest who often comes and stays at Shōin-ji paid us a visit. He sat for a while, then got up to leave. I said, "Return tomorrow and stay over so you can lend the brothers a hand." With that he had a change of heart and said he would stay on. But later he slipped away and returned to his temple. It made me wonder, Is he is wise, or just half-baked? I couldn't understand why he should be afraid of a little work.

But he put me in mind of the men who had been working steadily and enduring bitter hardships for twenty or thirty days now. Certainly none of them balked at the difficulties. Among them, monks Chō and Tan stood out. They persevered from start to finish, their stalwart valor increasing the closer they approached the goal. Neither of them is particularly robust. Where did they acquire those constitutions of stone and steel? How were they able to put forth that unceasing effort?

Strive on, Brothers Chō and Tan. I have no doubt that the exemplary conduct you have shown throughout this project is merely the first indication of the many splendid things you will accomplish in the future.

Thirty days since we began work on a small Monks' Hall.
Many projects start out well; few reach final completion.
Brother Tan from Bungo and Brother Chō from Tango,
You've done your part, striving as if your karmic destiny.
You were the first to set out on frigid begging rounds,
You hauled water and fuel, you worked the rice-pounder,
Coated plaster on the walls, and took turns in the kitchen
Preparing the meals, never wasting a single grain of rice.
You carried mud from the hamlet with faces of steel,
Hopped mallets in hand over the roofs like monkeys.
Your straw sandals are broken, your *tabi* full of holes,
Robes frayed and ragged, workpants shabby and torn.
You never shirked chores or tasks whether large or small,
Never took a clean job and left foul ones for others.
At night you spread leaves and sit upright in zazen,
You are up before dawn picking greens in the frost.
I can't even offer a rice ball to reward your efforts.
I've given you no teachings, either prose or verse.
Stinging fists and angry glares are your daily fare,
Ramshackle dwellings with rickety floors your nights.

I regret I'm too old to see how you two turn out,
But work hard and vow never to seek profit or fame.
If you continue in this way to accumulate virtue,
Someday you'll be priests the whole world will admire.

334 : POISON BLOSSOMS FROM A THICKET OF THORN

. . . .

You carried mud. "The young monks went about their tasks, making their way back and forth to the village to haul mud for the walls, without any self-consciousness whatever" (annotation).
Rice ball. Rice flour and water kneaded into balls and boiled; simple fare.

136. RESPONDING TO AN INVITATION
TO THE NOGA RESIDENCE

A annotation inscribed on a draft manuscript of this verse tells us Hakuin wrote it in the middle of the tenth month of the nineteenth year of Kyōhō (1734), at the age of forty-nine. At the time he was apparently staying at Rinsen-an, a small temple in Shimizu village east of Hara. Mr. Noga (Noga Yoshisuke, also Gisuke, n.d.) was a local official (gon-dayu) of Suruga province whose residence was located next to Rinsen-an. Some of Hakuin's students served as priests of Rinsen-an, and he himself lectured there on numerous occasions. The temple figures in a number of verses in Poison Blossoms. *Mr. Noga makes one more appearance in* Poison Blossoms *(#138).*

> Mr. Noga is one who cherishes loyalty and uprightness.
> I've heard he is devoted to the common people as well.
> Yesterday, Mr. Noga came over and rapped at my gate,
> We passed a few hours discussing matters of the Way.
> He spoke earnestly of a desire his mother had expressed
> To treat me to some new soba from the autumn harvest.
> How could I possibly decline an invitation of this kind,
> Especially one issued from such a fine, elegant lady?
> Entering the tranquil atmosphere of the Noga home,
> The close, warm family ties were immediately evident.
> The bamboo basket, filled with red persimmons,
> The sparkling white hand-towel at the privy door.
> A dozen bookcases, stacked high with rare volumes,
> Two yellow chrysanthemums, like sisters in a vase.
> A sword gleaming on a stand, to dispel idle demons,
> The scroll in the alcove revealed a noble mind—
> Please do not say you've nothing to offer your guest.
> Hearts and minds like yours surpass the rarest delicacies.

. . . .

A fine, elegant lady. "Mr. Noga's wife came to Shōin-ji in person to issue the invitation" (annotation).

: 137. A Verse Answering Senior Priest Sai, Using His Rhymes

Senior priest Sai, later Ryōsai Genmyō (1706–86), was one of Hakuin's earliest students. After training and achieving an initial enlighten-ment under Kogetsu Zenzai in Kyushu, Ryōsai went to Shōin-ji and studied for several years with Hakuin. Hakuin eventually confirmed Ryōsai's attainment and designated him as a Dharma heir. Ryōsai served at Kagaku-ji in Mikawa prefecture (present Aichi prefecture), gaining a reputation for his Chinese kambun *verse, a collection of which he published under the title* Jishō-roku *(1793).*

Ryōsai has the distinction of being the first person Hakuin sanc-tioned to teach, yet in his later years Hakuin expressed regret at having mistakenly confirmed Ryōsai before he had completed his training: "If I had only waited another three years…no one in the country would have been able to touch him" (e.g., Stories from a Thicket of Thorn and Briar, *p. 120). Because of this, the fact that Ryōsai returned to Kogetsu's temple after leaving Hakuin, and Ryō-sai's penchant for literary Zen, he is sometimes regarded as belong-ing to the Kogetsu line.*

> On the day monk Sai returned from the east,
> Nervous as a farmer whose tax is overdue,
> He found I was out and went to wait at an inn.
> He returned at midnight and rapped at the gate.
> Sensing new resolve to see the matter through,
> I got up to inspect him in the light of the lamp.
> When I broached the matter of the Original Person,
> He set forth his views. I responded to them,
> Falling easily into kind, grandmotherly Zen.
> After an absence of some three or four years,
> Here he was, seeking instruction once again,
> When I probed at the center, his responses were adroit.
> Bore ahead, Ryōsai, with unflagging resolve!

Take this precious jewel of old Hakuin's,
Make it the treasure of your own house!

:138. A Verse at Rinsen-an, Following the Rhymes of Zen Man Ryōsai

(When we first arrived at the temple, Kyū and Yui were out on
a begging expedition, so we were entertained by Mr. Noga, a warm
and compassionate old gentleman who lives next door).

*All that is known about Kyū (Ekyū, n.d.), who was apparently
the resident priest at Rinsen-an at this time, is that he originally
received Dharma transmission from a teacher in the Suzuki Shōsan
(1579–1655) lineage after attaining enlightenment at the young age
of fifteen; and that at sixteen, he was appointed head of Rinsen-an,
which had originally been one of Shōsan's temples. As Kyū appears
together with Ryōsai in Hakuin's* Chronological Biography *(age
forty-nine) as a senior monk (jōza) studying at Shōin-ji, the present
verse probably dates from Hakuin's forties. Nothing is known of the
monk Yui. Mr. Noga appeared before, #136.*

Poking around in silence, fumbling for the latchkey,
We entered a hermitage cloistered by towering trees.
There was no fire burning in the brazier to welcome us,
On top of a desk, a single book lay open, half read.
Striking the bronze chime, we bowed before Buddha,
The sound reached cottages beyond the bamboo fence.
An old gentleman from the house next door
Came and offered us some cups of hot tea.

. . . .

Poking around...key. "The monk Kyū always hid the key in the bushes. Ryōsai
knew that because he had formerly resided at Rinsen-an" (annotation).

: 139. A Verse Describing a Previous Visit to Rinsen-an, Following the Same Rhymes as Before

A hot midsummer's day, how many years back?
We walked here together, visited this hermitage.
You composed a fine verse; you didn't jot it down.
I hummed one in response, now it too is forgotten.
The heavily wooded forest gave us merciful shade,
Cracks in the walls brought cooling drafts of breeze.
Mr. Noga came from Yukawa to treat us to noodles.
I now recall with great fondness those bygone days.

. . . .

Cracks in the wall. "Rinsen-an was small and ramshackle, but because of that the cooling summer breeze came right inside" (annotation).

Mr. Noga...noodles. Yukawa was a village located just south of the hermitage. An annotation identifies the noodles as *somen*, served cold.

: 140. Plum Rains Fall for Days on End, I Think of Zen Men Sai and Jō in Their Practice Retreat

Sai is Ryōsai Genmyō; Jō is unidentified. Hakuin seems to have composed his long verse (which runs to sixty-six lines) at Shōin-ji during the rainy season in the fifth lunar month while the two monks were engaged in a period of solitary practice at Rinsen-an. Ryōsai's study with Hakuin lasted several years, beginning in 1735, when Hakuin was fifty; this verse probably dates from that period. "[Yellow] plum rain" gets its name from the fact that the ripening of the plum tree's fruit coincides with the annual rainy season.

Pelting yellow plum rains day after day,
Beat the rice shoots down to the earth.
Spating torrents roar like angry dragons,
Roiling higher than waves in a stormy sea.
The firewood wet, floor planks yawning,
Oven cold, snails crawling everywhere.
Bridges are swept away in the violent flow,

Oxcarts gulped into its muddy maw.
Chestnut blossoms thrown and scattered,
Red pomegranate buds pummeled down.
I pity my two monks sitting and dozing
Till their legs beneath them molder away.
The walls of rain that shut them indoors
Keep them from leaving to beg for food.
But this is how Zen monks acquire strength.
Let's hear no prayers for the rain to cease.
If you were in a training hall anywhere else,
Everything you need would be provided.
What can possibly have entered your heads,
To take on adversity like this from choice?
Having had no news since the deluge began,
I sent a packet of tea leaves over in secret.
Brother Sai hails from Owari province,
Brother Jō from the capital, farther west.
Nagoya and Kyoto have their differences,
But the two monks share a single dream.
In Nan-shan, leopards hide in heavy rain
For fear their fur will lose its fine gloss.
At Hsi-ling, gentlemen lived on bracken
To stay free of the world's golden chains.
It is said someone who studies the Way
Should live apart, away from the world.
How noble is the monk who turns recluse,
Possessing nothing but a robe and bowl.
His age is the same as the great sky above;
He contains the entire universe within.
Under the protection of the Dragon Kings,
Neither fire nor flood can cause him harm.
If the Great Yu had not controlled the floods,
We'd all have turned into shrimps and clams.
While Yu succeeded in subduing the waters,
Not even he could stave off the river of lust.
Its waves rise and churn with raging force,
No rafts exist for either foolish or wise.
If you drown, you sink to the floors of Hell,
You are hauled before Lord Emma's court,

Condemned to be tossed for endless lives
On the boundless ocean of samsaric night.
How can you free yourself from such a fate?
There is a way, yielding miraculous results,
Within you, in the lining of your own robe!
Is there anyone who is not a living Buddha?
Each and every one of us is old Shaka himself,
But we blunder and seek him somewhere else.
Why do we suffer this terrible misfortune?
The serpents of fame and wealth and greed.
Be dauntless, dauntless and brave above all,
Learn to overcome these poisonous vermin.
The way that enables you to yank their fangs
Is yours upon grasping the nature of mind;
Boring in, discerning that impeccable nature,
You achieve oneness with fragments of mist.
Achieve satori, make the Four Wisdoms appear,
Elsewise you'll end up in an unfortunate place.
I composed this lengthy string of needless verses
To ease the tedium of these interminable rains.

. . . .

In Nan-shan...leopards hide. The reference appears in a passage in *Biographies of Famous Women (Lieh-nu chuan)*, ch. 2.

At Hsi-ling, gentlemen lived on bracken. A reference to Po I and Shu Ch'i, brother princes who renounced their claims on the throne, and fled into the mountains of Hsi-ling, where they subsisted on wild plants until they died of cold and hunger.

If the Great Yu...floods. Based on a well-known saying, "If it had not been for Emperor Yu [who drained the swamps and brought the rivers under control], we would all now be fish." Hakuin assumes this entirely Chinese myth as part of the Zen heritage.

Stave off the river of lust (aiga). "When the river of desire dries up, you will gain release from suffering" *(Heroic March Sutra, ch. 4).*

Emma's court. Where the dead are brought to receive their final judgment.

You achieve...fragments of mist. "It is not only your own body, but also the body of the mountains and rivers, self and others [and everything else in the universe] as well" (annotation).

:141. NINE VERSES WRITTEN ON A VISIT TO BUTSUJITSU RŌJIN, WITH PREFACE

Butsujitsu Rōjin (Old Man Buddha Sun) was a sobriquet adopted by Hakuin's longtime friend Unzan Sotai (1685–1747), taken from the "mountain name" of his temple, Butsujitsu-zan Kongō-ji. Unzan had recently turned Kongō-ji over to his Dharma successor Fūhō and retired to a small hermitage nearby. I have translated the first five of the nine verses.

Although these poems convey respect and fondness, they seem a bit perfunctory too, deploying well-worn Zen tropes in patently extravagant praise of Unzan. They were written in 1735, when both men were forty-nine. Previous references to Unzan (he also appears in #119, #126, and #127) mention his weak constitution. Did Hakuin dash them off in the course of an evening's visit in an attempt to cheer up his ailing friend?

[Hakuin's preface to the poems]

AT THE BEGINNING OF spring in the twentieth year of the Kyōhō era (1735), Butsujitsu Rōjin picked up his robe and bowl and retired to a secluded spot in the neighboring village. I immediately wanted to go and congratulate him, but being old and indolent, I never got around to doing it. On a fine day at the end of the third month, I took up my staff and set out to pay him a visit.

Gazing over a landscape of shady green trees through cherry blossoms scattering in the breeze, I could make out a small dwelling with a narrow peaked roof, but I was unable to find any path that would take me there. I walked down one lane, but it petered out, so I came back and tried another one. As I hesitated, undecided, with the sun dipping low in the sky, I began having second thoughts about the visit. Ah, a friend and boon companion of forty years, was living only a few miles away, yet I couldn't even find my way to his dwelling. It may be that this was simply because recluses tend naturally to conceal their whereabouts. Nonetheless, this made an inexplicably strong impression on me.

Presently a monk appeared and he led me to Unzan's dwelling. It was sparse and spartan, a fine place to leach the mundane from one's bones.

On meeting, host and guest both broke into spontaneous guffaws of laughter. That night, Master Unzan wrote a verse. I responded, using the same rhymes.

I

> No feasting on phoenix marrow or rare dragon livers,
> A gimp-legged old pot black with use will do just fine.
> Dharma successor secure, the heavy burden now lifted,
> You can coil up in your grass hut and doze like a dragon.
> Your pure words are astonishing, like a dog biting a pig.
> Your verses change a man's bones, like an old sage's elixir.
> People really shouldn't wonder that such a man exists:
> Among trees, the Ch'un, among grasses, the orchid.

. . . .

Like a dog biting a pig. Allusion to the sudden means a Zen teacher uses to destroy ignorance in students.

Your verses change. "Bone-transforming verses," a Taoist phrase. Hakuin borrows the language of the elixir from ancient Chinese sources, depicting it in many writings as a life-giving product of Zen's "inner alchemy," the refined cinnabar produced by concentrating the vital energy in the cinnabar field (*tanden*) below the navel during Zen meditation. The image in the original is of a precious substance kept in a jar of purest crystal, whose fragrance seeps out and pervades the entire world.

The Ch'un is a fabulous tree for which spring and autumn both last eight thousand years (*Chuang Tzu*, p. 30).

II

> For thirty years you sat inside your den at Kongō-ji
> Like a gimp-legged cat on the prowl for old rat livers.
> Your tiger-eyed glance made people tremble like leaves,
> A napping dragon, coiled peacefully like an old pine tree.
> Your skills as a thief would put even Hou Hei to shame,
> Your daily fare of vegetable broth beggars even Fan Tan.
> Retired from temple affairs, you live a life of seclusion,
> An orchid flowering by a hut amid the pond-side grasses.

. . . .

Gimp-legged cat. Descriptive of Unzan's Zen activity, "[This was] Unzan's everyday behavior in teaching his students" (annotation). Rats' livers stand for the worthlessly small; presumably the delusions of his disciples.

Hou Hei is a legendary Chinese thief. *Fan Tan* (d. 189 BCE) was so poor that as a youth was unable to leave the house because he lacked clothing, but he eventually rose to become a minister of state.

III

His pure talk never fails to purify one's bone and marrow,
His tiny garden embodies the hermit's most vital essence.
A snail-shell dwelling, pure and spare, to nurture his spirit,
Dragon pines, with ancient coils, to pray for his longevity.
He makes you tea with a few dippers from the water pipe,
Serves you a grain or two of pure cinnabar from his bag.
His desk is piled high with wonderfully wrought verses,
Just like those Su Hui stitched out for her husband.

. . . .

Su Hui (4th century). The wife of an official who was banished to the western desert regions, she passed her time by embroidering verses to send to her exiled husband.

IV

Less hope of apprehending this priest's quiet working
Than the turtle has of divesting the monkey of his liver.
Just when you think you have a carp, it becomes a dragon
Spiraling through a bottomless pool, impossible to find.
He might look like a tired old bull at his midday nap,
But try to get close, he's over the border like a peregrine.
He's like an Udumbara illuminating the dusty world,
A rare and splendid orchid flowering in a red-hot kiln.

. . . .

Turtle has of divesting...liver. This alludes to a story, found in the *Fo-pen hsing ching*, that Hakuin illustrated in one of his Zen paintings (*HZC*, #550).

The following version of the story is from *Tales of Past and Present* (*Konjaku Monogatari*, kan 5), a collection of tales from the late Heian period.

"Long ago, on a hill by the shores of the Indian sea, there was a monkey who lived on fruits he found. In the ocean nearby lived a turtle and his wife. The wife said to her husband, 'I am pregnant with your child, but my womb is unsound and I am certain to have a difficult birth. If you give me some medicine, I will be able to give birth easily.' When the husband asked what kind of medicine was best, his wife replied, 'I've heard that raw monkey liver is the finest medicine for afflictions of the abdomen.' The turtle went down to the seashore and got into conversation with a monkey. 'Do you have all the food that you need where you live?' he asked. 'I never have enough,' said the monkey. 'Near my house is a vast forest,' said the turtle. 'The trees and bushes are filled with fruit throughout the year. Let me take you there, and you can eat as much as you want.' Unaware that he was being tricked, the monkey joyfully agreed. 'Come, let's be off,' said the turtle, letting the monkey crawl up onto his carapace. Once out at sea, he said to the monkey, 'You do not know this, but I have a pregnant wife who is afflicted with an illness of the womb. We heard that a monkey's raw liver is the best medicine for such an ailment. I tricked you into coming with me so that I could get your liver.' 'How unfortunate,' said the monkey. 'I appreciate your being so truthful with me, but haven't you heard that we monkeys don't keep our livers in our bodies? We hang them in trees. If you had told me about this before we set out, I could have given you my liver, and the livers of the other monkeys as well. So even if you kill me here, I'm sorry, but it won't do you any good. I have no liver.' The turtle, believing what the monkey said, replied, 'All right. Let's go back. You can give me your liver when we get there.' 'Of course,' said the monkey. 'If we go back, I could do that with ease.' With the monkey still on his carapace, the turtle paddled his way back to the shore. As soon as they arrived, the turtle let the monkey down. The monkey immediately scampered up to the highest branches of the nearest tree. Looking down at the turtle far below, he said, 'How could you be so dumb? Who ever heard of anyone having a liver apart from his body?' The turtle, realizing he'd been tricked but powerless to do anything about it, looked up at the monkey and said, 'You're the stupid one, monkey. The bottom of the sea is filled with delicious fruits,' and he swam off and disappeared beneath the waves.

"Even in the past, the animals were lacking in wise judgment, but human foolishness is no different."

V

An old dragon has been seen lurking north of Kongō-ji,
He has sharp crocodile teeth and fearsome tiger stripes.
His lightning moves knock the chocks from people's minds.
His thunder flushes the dragons out from Arhats' nails.
His eloquence surges up like waves on the ocean deeps,
His fox-slobber verses spew bushels of pure cinnabar.
Most folks don't cotton to his withered, forthright look,
Bitter as yellow bark, more fragrant than purple orchids.

. . . .

Arhats' nails. "It is said that when dragons descend to earth, they conceal themselves under the Arhats' fingernails" (annotation). Here "dragons" seem to represent the advanced states of realization to which the Arhats attach.

   Fox slobber. "Fox slobber kills Buddhas and patriarchs alike" (annotation).

   Yellow bark. The bark of the *phellodendron amurense,* a bitter substance used in Chinese medicine.

:142. LAMENTING PRIEST YŌSHUN

Yōshun Shudaku (1666–1735) was the head priest of Seiken-ji, a large and important Zen temple at the Okitsu post stop, about thirty miles down the coast west of Hara. Yōshun died on the first of the fifth month of 1735, so this verse probably dates from Hakuin's fiftieth year. Twenty years senior to Hakuin, Yōshun had apparently been instrumental in installing Hakuin as head priest at Shōin-ji. Recognizing Hakuin's superior ability, Yōshun made frequent visits to Shōin-ji, a small branch temple of Seiken-ji, to receive his instruction.

An ugly face, light gleaming angrily from both his eyes,
He left kith and kin behind, yet still he spits cold frost.
Why is it, when night comes, the tears fall like rain?
In the Dharma homeland a ridgepole has been lost.

. . . .

Dharma homeland. The text has "lands to the south," that is, India and China.

:143. Untitled Verse

Written in Hakuin's fifty-sixth year, as he was preparing to leave for
Keirin-ji in Kai province to conduct a lecture meeting on the Blue
Cliff Record *(see #145). The verse is quoted in the* Chronological
Biography *(Precious Mirror Cave, p. 206).*

O N THE AFTERNOON OF the seventeenth of the first month of the first
year of Kampō (1741), I heard sounds of a commotion from the *kuri*
(the kitchen and priests' quarters). Upon inquiring, I was told that it was
the porters bundling and tying up my baggage. It was being sent ahead to
Kai province where I had been invited to deliver lectures. This perturbed
me. "I don't want them carrying all this heavy baggage up to Kai province,"
I said. "Get rid of some things to lighten their load. Then I won't have
as much as Hua-yen did, but I'll still have more than Yun-feng." All the
bundles were unpacked and search was made for articles that could be left
behind, but I don't think they came up with a single thing.

> Priestly paraphernalia all packed up for my Dharma show,
> I'm ashamed to be making men carry it all the way to Kai.
> If you happen to run into Master Ssu-ma along the way,
> Be sure you tell him that it's not Master Hakuin's baggage!

. . . .

I won't have as much as Hua-yen...more than Yun-feng. Allusions to two
anecdotes about priests and their baggage. The first, from *Ta-hui's Arsenal*,
tells how the official Ssu-ma Kuang discerned the true character of a Zen
priest from the amount of baggage he carried with him.

"Hua-yen was a disciple of Zen master Yuan-chao. He experienced a realization when he spilled a drink he was carrying. He wrote a verse:

> "This one mistake, this single mistake,
> Is worth more than thousands in gold.
> Sedge hat on my head, travel pouch at my waist,
> At the tip of my staff the pure breeze and full moon.

"Layman Fa-cheng [1019–1083; prominent official, scholar, and poet] constantly studied this verse. One day he had a sudden satori when he saw a Zen
master on the high seat glance quietly right and left. He composed a verse
and sent it to Master Yuan-chao.

> "One look at the master's gaze, I entered deep enlightenment,
> His teacher's mind conveyed to me the causes and conditions.
> Your rivers and hills, although a thousand leagues distant,
> Are wondrous sights and sounds beneath my very eyes.

"After Fa-cheng retired from his post as minister and went to live in the capital, he remembered Hua-yen's verse teaching and invited him to come and stay at his residence. When word reached him that Hua-yen had crossed into his province, he set out to meet him. As he was getting into his carriage, the official Ssu-ma Kuang (1019–86) happened by and asked where he was going. Fa-cheng replied that he had invited Zen master Hua-yen to stay at his home and he was going to meet him. 'Do you mind if I go along?' asked Ssu-ma. They rode side by side to the post station to await the master's arrival. Presently, ten loads of baggage suddenly passed by. When Ssu-ma asked whom the baggage belonged to, the porters replied that it belonged to Hua-yen. Ssu-ma got on his horse and began to leave. 'Why leave now? I thought you wanted to see Hua-yen,' said Fa-cheng. 'I've already seen as much as I need to,' replied Ssu-ma. Miao-hsi [Ta-hui] heard this story from Layman Li Yi-chung."

The second story is from *Precious Lessons of the Zen School:* The priest Huang-lung Hui-nan said, "Once when I was traveling to Hunan together with Wen-yueh, we saw a Zen monk on pilgrimage who was carrying a large basket. Wen-yueh made a face, expressing his surprise. I scolded him, 'Instead of ridding yourself of the baggage in your own mind, you add baggage by including what others are carrying as well. Don't you find that greatly fatiguing?'"

Be sure you tell him...baggage. 'Layman's sake, three pints,' an expression a priest might use to try to excuse himself when buying sake from a wine-seller: 'It's not for me. I'm buying it for a layman friend.' The attempt at evasion only reveals the fraud: Using an excuse like that reveals your guilt" (annotation).

:144. LAMENTING SENIOR MONK GU

According to an annotation, "Senior Monk Gu (Tōgu) was from Hachiman in Suruga province. He studied in Kyushu with Kogetsu and Kogetsu's heir, Zuigan, before arriving at Shōin-ji....Unfortu-

nately, he died at [nearby] Rinsen-an." His name appears in the Letter
to Senior Attendant Kō (#83), but we know nothing about him. He
was one of a number of monks who died while training at Shōin-ji,
whose gravestones can still be seen lining the temple cemetery.

Han-shan moved with great speed; but you left us too quickly.
When we met as teacher and student, neither yielded an inch.
The autumn wind swirls the dry leaves, threshes the reeds,
Snowflakes flutter into a glowing furnace and are gone.

. . . .

The reference to Han-shan's speed is found in the *Blue Cliff Record*, Case 34.
Apparently, it just means that Senior Monk Gu died much too young.

:145. FOR THE HEAD PRIEST AT KEIRIN-JI,
USING HIS RHYMES

This long verse was written for Rempō Chishō (d. 1770), the head
priest of Keirin-ji, a large Zen temple in the highlands of Kai province
north of Mount Fuji, an area Hakuin visited on numerous occasions
to conduct practice assemblies. Hakuin is responding to a verse letter
from Rempō, presumably the one he mentions in the opening lines.
　Like Ranshitsu Tōiku (1682–1743; see #28), his teacher and prede-
cessor at Keirin-ji, Rempō was a friend and student of Hakuin, one
of a number of priests in Suruga, Kai, Tōtōmi, and Izu provinces who
visited him at Shōin-ji to continue post-satori practice while training
students in their own temples. According to Tōrei, Rempō applied
himself "with the greatest determination to koan work under Hakuin,
studying with him for many years even after taking over Keirin-ji
from Ranshitsu" (Draft Biography). Two letters Hakuin sent Rempō
are translated above, #81 and #82. The previous abbot, Rempō's
teacher Ranshitsu, who was still alive in 1741, is not mentioned here.
After he turned Keirin-ji over to his student, Rempō had presumably
moved into a retirement temple, probably Jitoku-ji, a branch temple
of Keirin-ji (#28), also located in eastern Kai province.
　Keirin-ji figures in ten of the pieces in the Poison Blossoms *col-*
lection, more than any other temple except Shōin-ji itself. Like the
present verse, most of the pieces are related to the large meeting on the

Blue Cliff Record, *attended by over two hundred people, that Hakuin conducted at Keirin-ji in the winter of 1741.*

Although fascinating glimpses of Hakuin's travels are found in other of his letters (e.g. Beating the Cloth Drum, #22), *none of them is as detailed, or provides the same kind of insight into the day-to-day teaching activity he engaged in on these trips.*

Hakuin's narrative describes a night crossing of Kagosaka Pass (elevation 3500 feet) east of Mount Fuji, an important, but in winter sometimes perilous conduit that linked Kai with Suruga and Shinano provinces and other areas of eastern Japan. Rempō would also have used this route on his frequent trips to take sanzen *with Hakuin.* Hakuin's letter expresses his relief at hearing of Rempō's safe return, suggesting that after the meeting he had escorted Hakuin back to Shōin-ji.*

An annotation mentions another mishap that occurred, apparently on this trip, which would explain why Hakuin's party was late in reaching the pass. His palanquin broke down early in the day, and to get the necessary parts to fix it attendants Daikyū and Tetsu were obliged to dismantle a cart they found in a nearby temple.

As soon as I learned you were safe, I breathed a sigh of relief,
Then I rebuked my monks for not opening your letter sooner.
On remembering my inattentiveness, the sweat rose in shame;
On recalling your kindnesses, the tears rolled down my cheeks.
How many times have we braved the snows of Kagosaka Pass,
How often raised our teaching banners high over Ujō Castle?†
But nothing compares to that anxious night in mud and snow
When you hiked over twenty miles to guide us down to safety.
My litter bearers were struggling through thigh-deep drifts;
We were only halfway to our destination when darkness fell.
Men shouting support and encouragement to one another;
My attendants, unfed and haggard, nearly dead on their feet.
Inching along dark trails, jagged ice biting their straw sandals,
Frozen trees thrusting razor-sharp branches to block their way.

*There is mention of an alternate, more roundabout, route, but it had hazards of its own, since it involved taking a boat down the swift-flowing Fuji River west of Mount Fuji.
†The name *Ujō*, "Feather Castle," used for the region surrounding Yamura village, was the site of the "White Feather Castle" and Keirin-ji.

Then someone spied a light, a faint star far to the northwest.
It came closer, rising and falling, hesitating, and then stopping.
Was it a specter of some kind? Was it a dreaded tengu goblin?
We stood riveted to the spot, watching in wonderment and fear.
How could we know it was Rempō, the head priest of Keirin-ji,
Making his way up the mountain paths in person to meet us!
Straw-sandals, bamboo staff in one hand, firebrand in the other,
Behind him a man packing extra fuel to feed the burning torch.
We began gesticulating joyously at each other across the valley;
Our two parties joined, new friends and old, eyes wet with tears.
Before all had been spoken, we were headed northward again,
Rempō in the vanguard, lighting the way with his flaming torch.
It was midnight when we finally reached the Yoshida post stop
Where lodgings had been readied for us at Mr. Shioya's house.
Greatly relieved, I was asleep in no time, snorting like a horse.
Rempō alone, with much on his mind, passed a sleepless night.
Next morning, we proceeded in a group to Gekkō-ji in Yoshida,*
Then climbed the steps and entered Ichijō-ji's sacred precincts.†
The priest was at the gate waiting to meet us, beaming with joy,
He said a soba lunch was waiting; the prospect lifted our brows.
Treating us from the first as though we were old companions,
He engaged us in pure talk; we realized his deep love of the Way.
When we left, Rempō refused to allow me to quit my palanquin;
He walked slowly along beside it, never once abandoning his
     post,
A faithful samurai protecting his lord from any possible danger,
Or a truly dutiful son caring benevolently for an elderly father.
On the way priests appeared from local temples and trailed
     behind,
Not because of my virtue, but because Rempō sent out the word.
After a long march we reached the hermitage in Yamura village,
To find people frantically making preparations for the midday
     meal,
Young and old hurrying about, yelling and waving at one
     another.
On crossing a long bridge that spanned a precipitous chasm,

---

*It is nine miles from Gekkō-ji in Yoshida to Keirin-ji in Yamura village.
†*Ichijō-ji* is located between Yoshida and Keirin-ji; the priest is unidentified.

Elders gathered from a hundred hamlets were waiting to greet
us;
Villagers with cheerful smiles could be seen rushing in all
directions.
A great bell at the summit boomed out, announcing our arrival;
Before the temple gate black-robed priests stood in a solemn
row.
Entering the austere precincts, we emerged into another world;
From spots like this, watched over by gods, great men appear.
Shrine trees on the summit were crowned with auspicious
clouds,
A propitious mist mantled Kinsei and the surrounding
countryside.*
To the southwest, eternal snow capped the summit of Mount
Fuji;
To the northeast, behind Keirin-ji, rose a rampant hundred-foot
lion.†
Inside, both elder priests and acolytes received me as a father,
Training monks were queued thick as a hedgerow to give
welcome.
A perfect reception, everything ready, nothing overlooked.‡
I blew on my conch trumpet, pounded on my Dharma drum,
Imparting the teachings, showering down sweet Dharma rain.§
Whose courage and vision brought this sacred occasion about?
One who took little sleep, rose early, and never showed fatigue.
Had a man of such spirit served under a king or provincial lord,
He would rise to the heights, a head minister or chief councilor.
Had he turned such deep consideration to his parents' care,
He would undoubtedly accumulate tremendous stores of merit.
Instead, he blundered, wasted it all on a donkey priest like me.
Though honored indeed to receive such a splendid reception,

---

* *Kinsei* is a name given to the area around Yamura and Tsuru village.
†*Hyakushaku no shi*: the name of a crag-like cliff behind Keirin-ji.
‡The original has "all four necessities of a monk," i.e., sleeping quarters, clothing, food
and drink, and medicine.
§*Beating the drum and blowing the conch shell*, announcing Dharma talks and other
important events, are here metaphors for Hakuin's talks; Dharma rain, a metaphor for
his teachings, which benefit sentient beings.

I deeply regret the only means I possess for repaying the favor
Is a set of sharp teeth, more spiked and jagged than the Nine
Peaks.*
They make idle spirits flee in panic, demons howl off in fear;
The gods of poverty, hidden in darkness, are crippled with grief.
People today give Zen less regard than the dirt beneath their
feet,
Its life of transcendent wisdom hangs by a very thin thread.
When the fruit of Shao-lin lies moldering before our very eyes,
How praiseworthy one man works so tirelessly to master them!†

:146. Verse Inscribed on a Painting of Mount Fuji

The painting of Mount Fuji on which this was inscribed, probably dating from Hakuin's seventy-second year, was done at the request of his former student Sozan Sotai (d. 1771), the head priest of Jishō-ji ("Self-nature" temple) in Nakatsu on the northern coast of the island of Kyushu. Sozan had asked Hakuin for a painting of Daruma. Hakuin painted a large picture of Mount Fuji with a Daimyō procession passing beneath it, explaining in the verse that his painting has in fact depicted Daruma. The painting is reproduced in Religious Art of Zen Master Hakuin, *p. 24.*

Having successfully captured the old Indian's true face,
I can now send this along to the priest in far-off Jishō-ji.
If you have doubts about a Boys' Festival in December,
Whip the straw sheep forward. Go ask the wooden man.

. . . .

Old Indian's true face. "If you want to see Bodhidharma, look at Mount Fuji. What about this inscription on the painting of Mount Fuji? Everyone sitting in this room is Daruma's true face. If you don't know that, you're no Zen monk!" (annotation)

Nine Peaks (Chiu-yi shan): a range of jagged summits in Hunan province. An allusion to Hakuin's teaching style.
†*Shao-lin* is Bodhidharma, the name taken from the place where he lived. The "praiseworthy" man is Rempō.

"Some time ago I received some paper and a request for a portrait of Bodhidharma (the old Indian) from the head priest of Jishō-ji. I believe I have now captured the old patriarch's true features, and I am sending the results off to Jishō-ji. But if he or anyone else has trouble understanding this painting that I did on the Boys' Festival in December, they should spur forward the straw sheep and ask the wooden man about it" (annotation). The annual Boys' Festival is held in May, not December, so it, like straw sheep and wooden men, is an *impossibilia*, something that cannot possibly occur or exist.

:147. VERSE ON BONSEKI

One of a number of verses Hakuin wrote on the theme of Bonseki, Bonsan, *and spirit rocks of one kind or other. Here he describes a* Bonseki, *or miniature rock landscape, for which he seems to have had a particular fondness. It is probably the same one he writes about in #98 and #99. The subject is dealt with at some length in* The Religious Art of Zen Master Hakuin, *Chapter Three, "Rocks, Pumpkinhead, Toys, and Birds."*

> I was born with a powerful love for the rocks and streams,
> In this little stone I see an endless range of emerald peaks.
> Master Hsieh liked to roam the summits in special clogs,
> You do not need clogs to enjoy the mountains on this tray.
> Chih Tun is said to have purchased a mountain with gold,
> This one can be yours without such a lavish expenditure.
> Sumeru is very high, but Lord Indra dwells on its summit,
> Lanka steep and rugged, but Buddha climbed it to preach.
> The rock on this tray may be tiny, but no one can climb it,
> No celebrated peak on earth can surpass this little stone.

. . . .

Master Hsieh. The Chinese nature poet Hsieh Ling-yuan (384–433), known for his mountain climbing feats, devised a special studded sole which he attached to his footwear to facilitate his ascents. In his final years, the Buddhist priest Chih Tun (314–366) purchased an entire mountain in which to seclude himself.

Lanka. Mount Lanka, where the Buddha is said to have preached the *Lankavatara Sutra.*

:148. UNTITLED VERSE

Although Hakuin is known to have had more than a few nuns and laywomen among his students, this is one of the few pieces in Poison Blossoms *specifically addressed to one of them. The nun Eshō-ni (d. 1764), a student of Hakuin and friend of Tōrei, surfaces from time to time in both their records. Her most prominent appearance is the one in which she probes, in the manner of a teacher, or a wiser senior disciple, the satori that Yamanashi Harushige (Heishirō) experienced after a brief but intense period of solitary practice (*Beating the Cloth Drum, *p.159;* Precious Mirror Cave, *p. 215). When Tōrei fled to Kyoto to foil Hakuin's plans to install him as head priest of Shōin-ji, he stopped in at Eshō's hermitage before departing to express his gratitude to her. These episodes, and the present piece as well, show that both Hakuin and Tōrei deeply respected her.*

Eshō had taken religious vows after the death of her husband, being ordained by Yōshun Shudaku of Seiken-ji. According to an annotation, at the time Hakuin visited her, she was residing near Shōin-ji in a hermitage named Kanji-an, no doubt in order to receive Hakuin's instruction. Apparently she and six other nuns who were staying with her traveled to Kai province to attend the lectures Hakuin gave on the Blue Cliff Record *in 1741. They must have encountered the same difficult weather conditions Hakuin experienced on his trip a few days later, and no doubt with considerably less assistance than he received (see #145).*

SEVEN SAGE NUNS SET out ahead of me to make their way to Kei-rin-ji in Kai province. The day before they left, they invited me to their hermitage. In their devotion to the Dharma they had made great efforts, foraging far and near to obtain some tea and rice cakes to offer. Moved by their kindness and sincerity, I expressed my thanks to them by chanting out one of my rustic verses. Ah! You nuns are in love with your ears. Me, I'm in love with my mouth. *Ahahah!*

> Zen practice is like travel, more neighbors the farther you go,
> All the more for one who has seen the east wall strike the west.
> Before you were able to completely penetrate that koan,
> Everything was a silver mountain or towering iron cliff.
> But when the time came, and you bored right through it,
> You knew that you yourself are the mountains and cliffs.

You still have one final difficult barrier to pass through:
At sunrise, a thief burrows through the storehouse wall.

. . . .

Zen practice is like travel. Confucius said, "Virtue is not alone. It invariably has neighbors" (*Analects of Confucius*, p. 34).

East wall strike the west. "Cold Mountain has a house /Without beams or partitions / Six doors open left and right / A hall revealing emerald sky / All rooms completely vacant / East wall striking against west / And not a single thing inside" (*Kanzan-shi*, ed. Iritani, p. 167). "Hakuin wrote this because Eshō had already grasped those words" (annotation).

Silver mountain...cliff. From a saying by Po-yun Shou-tuan: "The ancients left behind a phrase or half phrase for you. Before you penetrate it, it is like a silver mountain or an iron wall. One day when you suddenly break through, you know for the first time that you yourself are the mountain and the wall" (*Compendium of the Five Lamps*, ch. 19; quoted in *Blue Cliff Record,* Case 57).

At sunrise...storehouse wall. "What a dumb thief, waiting until dawn to break in" (annotation). There is another annotation, attributed to Tōrei: "The first arrow was not so important. The second one was." It implies that the "burrowing" arrow was to help Eshō-ni achieve a second breakthrough even more important than the one she had experienced while working on Han-shan's words, "East wall striking against west."

:149. Ungaku (Cloud Peak)

Hakuin awarded this Dharma name to Akiyama Fumizō (n.d.) in autumn of 1739 during a meeting on Ta-hui's Letters (referred to here as the Letters of the Master of Ummon Hermitage) *he was conducting at the residence of his lay student Akiyama Michitomo in Izu province (Precious Mirror Cave, p. 204). We learn from an annotation that "Akiyama Fumizō was the former head of one of three branches of the influential Akiyama clan of northern Izu." The name Ungaku, "Cloud Peak," was no doubt suggested to Hakuin by the sobriquet Ummon, "Cloud Gate," which Ta-hui had used. This meeting also figures in #57 above.*

IN AUTUMN OF THE fourth year of Gembun (1739), I responded to a request from Mr. Akiyama and delivered Zen lectures for over two weeks on the *Letters of the Master of Ummon Hermitage.* An old man who lived next door to the Akiyama residence came every day to attend. Because he was hard of hearing, he always sat as close to my desk as he could get. One day when the meeting was nearing its end, he came to me and asked for a Dharma name. I gave him the name Ungaku Jimon Jōza. He was the father of Akiyama Masanaga.

Cloud Peak
Leaving not a single trace, it embraces the entire world.
As speculations run their course, it opens out on all sides.
A solitary peak, swallowing and spitting out frozen cloud.
Priests and laymen throng his gates, straining for a single
    word.

:150. ON SENDING DŌKA ZENNIN OFF TO VISIT HIS FATHER

Dōka is the name Hakuin's disciple Tōrei used until the age of thirty-four when he was installed as head priest of Muryō-ji. Although the records show Tōrei leaving Shōin-ji more than once during his training there to return to his home in Ōmi province to nurse his ailing mother (d. 1748), no visits are mentioned to his father, who died in 1749. This visit probably dates from around 1745, a few years after Tōrei's arrival at Shōin-ji.

Dōka put some paper before me, asking for a verse,
He is about to set out for home to visit his father.
Because he wants "phrases that are right to the point,"
I chew my writing brush, brow privately furrowed.

. . . .

I chew my . . . furrowed. "Is this line the one that is 'right to the point'? Anyone who has heard the sound of one hand will find this amusing" (annotation).

:151. VERSE IN REPLY TO A LETTER FROM SENIOR MONK DŌKA

Tōrei's Chronological Biography *for 1745 records that "in the tenth month he sequestered himself in a hermitage he called Yamato-ya in front of Hōkō-ji [the Hall of the Great Buddha, in the Higashiyama area of Kyoto] and began a solitary retreat, devoting himself to the most rigorous practice for one hundred and fifty days without shaving or bathing, and taking little food. On the fiftieth day, he suddenly smashed the one bright pearl. Fifty days later, he penetrated and clearly saw Master Hakuin's everyday Zen working....The following spring he sent a letter to Hakuin expressing the attainment he had achieved. Taking one look at it, Hakuin said, 'Dōka has passed through,' and joyfully composed a verse to answer him."*

Hakuin's Chronological Biography *for the following year (1746) has: "A letter arrived from Dōka, who was then residing in the eastern hills of Kyoto, informing Hakuin of his acceptance of the Dharma transmission Hakuin had offered him. The master responded with a verse [see below]. When Hakuin expressed a desire to make his sanction of Tōrei public, several senior disciples tried to dissuade him. 'If you can't bring yourself to believe in the man from reading what he writes,' Hakuin told them, 'how are you going to understand what is written in the books about the ancient Zen masters?'"* (Precious Mirror Cave, *pp. 210–11*).

> A golden carp tailing through the weeds of Ōmi's vast waters,
> Surmounting countless perils, has passed beyond the Dragon
>   Gate.
> Free at last to sport among the deadly waves of the Buddha
>   ocean,
> He performs the true charity—by giving not a drop to others.

. . . .

Ōmi's vast waters...Dragon Gate. Biwa-ko, the largest Japanese lake, is located in Tōrei's home province of Ōmi. According to Chinese legend, carp that scaled the formidable three-tiered waterfall at the Dragon Gate transformed into dragons.

The true charity. "Later, when you raise your Dharma standard [and begin teaching], don't sell the Buddha's Dharma cheaply" (annotation).

:152. THANKING NAKAI MASAATSU FOR CREATING AN ARTIFICIAL MOUNTAIN, WITH PREFACE

*This was written to commemorate the completion of a temple gar-
den at Shōin-ji, created thanks to a donation from Nakai Masaatsu
(also Zenzō, n.d.) of Yoshiwara village. The project was conceived
after Hakuin received the two large rocks from Ishii Gentōku
described in #130 above.*

I WAS BORN WITH A love for the simple and unadorned. I have less skill
in human affairs than a pigeon. I'm slower on my feet than any turtle.
Despite an innate love of rocks and streams, I have no high mountains
around here to climb, no flowing rivers to gaze upon. Fortunately, I am not
deficient in wonderful companions—Mr. Ishii, a physician celebrated for
his healing skills, and Mr. Nakai, a fine gentleman of great taste and refinement. Pitying my chronic illness, this weakness for the rocks and running
waters, Mr. Ishii put his young men to work, having them transport some
remarkable spirit rocks to Shōin-ji from a far distant spot. This inspired
Mr. Nakai to come and personally construct a range of mountains in the
temple gardens. Beautiful scenery burgeoned forth, creating splendid vis-
tas soothing and satisfying to the heart

On seeing what they had done, I thought to myself that for all Mr.
Nakai's wonderful landscaping skills, if Mr. Ishii had not sent the rocks,
this beautiful garden would not exist. And in spite of Mr. Ishii's effort
in transporting the rocks here, without Mr. Nakai's skills, those gemlike
rocks would probably still be lying among the weeds. Indeed, the two
most desired but difficult things to obtain had been obtained, but even
so, unless the monks training at Shōin-ji had lent a hand, Mr. Ishii and I
would have had no means of moving the rocks. And finally, even after all
that effort, had I not been blessed with some free time, how could I have
enjoyed this wonderful scenery? Seen in this way, it can be said that all the
four necessary elements have now been obtained. Hence I have written a
verse to thank all concerned for their effort.

> Thousand-foot waterfalls, purifying the mind to its depths,
> Make the soaring pine trees seem even greener to the eye.
> Mount Hua, soaring beside Mount Li's awesome peaks,
> The splendors of Mount Lu beside those of Mount Chiu-i.
> Old Huang, returning to the world once again, stands on

The cliff, his stick in hand, as though herding a white flock.
Gazing at my new garden, I have to laugh at old Chih Tun,
Begging funds for a hermitage to foster poetic thoughts
A soft breeze whispers in from the emerald pine boughs,
The rain brings out the tiger stripes on the rocks and stones.
Silver sand, like eternal snow, spreads from the cave mouth.
A mossy valley torrent keeps its frostlike gleam all year.
Sitting in my humble hut, deep creases furrow my brow—
This setting sun is one thing I could never put into verse.

. . . .

Two most desired but difficult things to obtain. In the preface to his poem "Ascending the Pavilion of King T'eng," the T'ang poet Wang Po (648–675) called fine weather, beautiful scenery, appreciative hearts, and enjoyable occupations the four excellent conditions; he also said that a worthy host and elegant guest were the two things most desirable but difficult to obtain. The terms "four excellent conditions" and "two rarities" became proverbial.

Master Huang (Huang Ch'u-p'ing). Born into a poor sheep herding family, at the age of fourteen Huang met a Taoist priest who discerned his capability and took him to study at Mount Chin-hua. For forty years his brother Ch'u-ch'i searched in vain for him. One day he met a Taoist who told him that a man named Ch'u-p'ing who tended sheep at Mount Chin-hua was surely his lost brother. He set out immediately with the priest and was finally reunited with Ch'u-p'ing. When asked about his sheep, Ch'u-p'ing said they were on the eastern side of the hill, but when Ch'u-ch'i went to see them he found only white rocks on the hillside. "There are no sheep there," said Ch'u-ch'i. "There are," said Ch'u-p'ing, "it's just that you are unable to see them." When they went together to the spot, Ch'u-p'ing shouted out, "Get up, sheep!" The white stones immediately transformed into tens of thousands of sheep. Ch'u-ch'i said, "You can do this because you have mastered the sages' arts, elder brother. Do you think I could master them too?" "If you practice diligently you can," he replied. Ch'u-ch'i left his home and family and devoted himself to the study of the Way under Ch'u-p'ing, and both men ended up living to be five hundred years old (*Biographies of Divine Sages*).

Chih Tun (314–366). An influential scholar and priest of the early period of Chinese Buddhism who is said to have purchased an entire mountain in which to spend his retirement. See #147.

:153. UNTITLED VERSE

Hakuin wrote this verse for a Sōtō monk named Ryōgo (n.d.) from Nagato province at the western tip of Honshu. This piece must be seen in the context of Hakuin's sharp criticism of contemporary Sōtō Zen for failing to use the koan to bring students to the breakthrough kenshō experience.

A MONK (RYŌGO) CAME AND said, "I penetrated to a wonderful understanding of the Buffalo Passes Through the Window. Whatever phrase I might give you would choke off any words either you or old Wu-tsu tried to spit out."

"Can you tell me what you have understood?" I said.

"I present you with the nose and tail that didn't make it through the window!"

My response was a burst of laughter. The monk bristled.

"In the future," I said, "if you really do grasp that koan, your face is going to be red with embarrassment when you recall those words, and you will have nowhere to hide."

Then I composed a verse:

> Fire is used to test gems, proofstones used to test gold,
> This koan shows how phony your understanding is.
> Giving the Buffalo Through the Window to a sightless monk
> Is like offering tea to a parrot, donating gold coins to a cat.

. . . .

The Buffalo through the Window. "Master Wu-tsu said, 'It is like a buffalo passing through a window. Its head, horns, and four legs have all passed through. Why can't the tail also pass through?'" (*Gateless Barrier,* Case 38.)

:154. UNTITLED VERSE

This verse was written for Senior Monk Teki (Benteki, n.d.), a monk from Ryōtan-ji in Tōtōmi province who was one of Hakuin's earliest students. He served as Hakuin's attendant at Shōin-ji from around 1717, Hakuin's thirty-second year, until the tenth year of Kyōhō

(1725) when this verse was written. He later resided as head priest at Kenchū-ji in Kai province. Two other stories in which he figures are given in the endnotes following the piece.

ZEN MAN TEKI OF Mino province has served as my attendant for eight years now, devoting himself with determination to his training. If he continues in this course without faltering, he will surely experience an immense joy of a kind he has never known before.

In autumn of the tenth year of Kyōhō (1725), a letter arrived from Teki's home urging him to return. On the day of his departure he came and asked me to write some words for the occasion. I'm not good at composing poems. I don't know much about Zen, either. But if Teki is after the matter of greatest importance to a Zen monk, then the horses and carts he will encounter on his way home, the tea he will drink at the roadside teahouses—they are all koans presenting themselves to him. What is there for me to add to that? Still, since I am not unmoved by feelings of sadness at his parting, perhaps I can set down a word or two for him direct from my vitals.

> Teki, you asked me for some words to take with you.
> Whatever I wrote would miss the mark by a country mile.
> But since you've ground ink and laid paper in front of me:
> "Beneath the falling leaves, a brow darkens in sadness."

. . . .

Teki Zōsu appears in the *Chronological Biography*, age thirty-eight. "The quality of provisions in the temple larder grew steadily worse. The monks made the rounds of nearby shops begging for shōyu that had gone off and was going to be thrown out. Once at mealtime the temple cook, Teki Zōsu, served some cold miso soup the surface of which was alive with wriggling maggots. "Pay more attention to your work," scolded Hakuin. "Maggots breed in rancid shōyu," said Teki. "I couldn't bring myself to kill them, so I just poured it all into the stock and made the soup without heating it" (*Precious Mirror Cave*, p. 196).

In a piece titled "Instructions to the Assembly at the Request of Benteki of Kenchū-ji" (untranslated here), written in 1757 when Hakuin was seventy-two, Hakuin cites the heroic practice of T'zu-ming, who kept himself awake during long sessions of zazen by jabbing himself in the thigh with a gimlet. Then he says, "In the seventh year of Hōreki (1757), when I went to visit

Kōzen-ji in Shinano and Nanshō-ji in Kai, I stopped the night at Kenchū-ji, where a former student of mine, Benteki Jōza, the master of Hoan Hermitage, readied a sheet of paper for me. He pressed me two or three times to write something for the benefit of future generations. So I licked my writing brush and wrote this." Hakuin's inscription goes on to exhort Benteki to continue to dedicate himself to his training, not to be satisfied with what he has attained so far, not to just "scamper around in the mud like a rat" enjoying his position as head of a large temple, but to work hard to fulfill his Bodhisattva vow to guide others to enlightenment (*Poison Blossoms, Book Two*).

:155. UNTITLED VERSE

This verse was written for Senior Monk Genkyoku (d. 1771, also known as Sojun), who came to Hakuin from his home temple Daihi-ji in Akita in the far north of Honshū. It apparently dates from 1743, the year Genkyoku was called back to his home temple because of the death of his teacher (annotation).

SENIOR MONK GENKYOKU CAME and joined the crew of frozen starvelings who dwell in this old reprobate's cave. Having endured the suffering there for a number of years, the blowing of the autumn wind suddenly made him nostalgic for his northern home. I wrote a poem to send him off.

> My Dharma cave's fangs and talons are not the skin or the
>   marrow,
> Before I even hold them up, demons begin to wail, gods to
>   lament.
> Three years you trained under me, weathering a great many
>   hardships.
> Return Genkyoku, return and lend this blundering old bonze
>   a hand.

. . . .

Old reprobate, Hakuin, a reference to his sobriquet Sendai-ō (Sk. *icchantika*).
    Not the skin or the marrow. An allusion to famous words Bodhidharma is said to have spoken on transmitting his Dharma to four disciples: "Tao-fu

has attained my skin, Tsung-chi my flesh, Tao-yu my bones. Hui-k'o (who became the second Zen Patriarch) has attained my marrow."

There is a lengthy annotation on this piece, apparently written by one of Tōrei's students: "Genkyoku studied with Kogetsu Zenzai in Kyushu for ten years, then with Daidō Bunka in Tamba west of Kyoto, before coming to Hakuin. His devotion to his practice was rigorous in the extreme. When master Tōrei first arrived at Shōin-ji at the age of twenty-two, Hakuin assigned Genkyoku to show him the ropes.... While studying at Shōin-ji, Genkyoku lived at Shinkō-in in Hara. Because he never had proper food or clothing, he was always sickly, suffering during the summer months from an intermittent fever....By nature a person of uncompromising integrity, he had a Zen style like that of Senior Monk Ting. He is said to have lived in a hut he fashioned next to Akita Castle, but he was such a formidable presence that monks avoided him, and he lived without an attendant. One day Morin, the head priest of Daihi-ji, asked Genkyoku to become his successor at the temple. Genkyoku said, "What are you saying? I wouldn't think of transmitting my Dharma to you. Why would I want to receive yours? Just leave, and don't ever ask me that again."

Senior Monk Ting (n.d.) is regarded as having faithfully transmitted the severe, uncompromising spirit of his master Lin-chi's Zen. Often depicted in Zen paintings, he is usually shown engaged in a violent assault on other monks. He once had to be stopped from throwing a monk off a bridge when the monk couldn't answer a question. Case 32 of the *Blue Cliff Record* relates an exchange Ting had with three monks. "What did your teacher Lin-chi say in teaching his monks?" one of them asked. Ting cited Lin-chi's: "You monks, there is a true man in this lump of red flesh with no rank or station. He is always going in and out through the gates of your senses. Those who have not proved this, look! look!" Another of the monks said, "Why didn't he say, 'There is no true man of no rank or station?'" Ting immediately grabbed him and began throttling him. "How is a true man of no rank different from an untrue man of no rank?" he demanded. "Speak quickly! Say something!" The monk was unable to open his mouth. His face turned yellow and green. Ting seemed on the verge of finishing him off then and there, but the other two monks separated them. "If you two hadn't been here," said Ting, "I would have choked the life from the piddling little imp."

Blundering old bonze. The original term, *mutenchi,* refers to a priest who is totally inactive and ineffective. When the term appeared earlier (#81), the annotations said, "No different from a stone Buddha," and "Completely and utterly useless!"

:156. VERSES ON READING THE WORDS OF NATIONAL MASTER DAIKYŪ, WITH PREFACE

Daikyū Sōkyū (1468–1549) was a Rinzai priest who lived during the Sengoku (Warring States) period. A student of Tokuhō Zenketsu at Ryōan-ji in Kyoto, he received Tokuhō's Dharma sanction and succeeded him as head priest at Ryōan-ji after the latter's death. Daikyū also served as abbot at the Myōshin-ji headquarters monastery, and it was at the Myōshin-ji subtemple Reiun-in, built for Daikyū's retirement, that Emperor Go-Nara (reigned 1526–57) is said to have visited him. Go-Nara awarded him the honorific "National Master" title Enman Honkō Kokushi.

In old age, Daikyū established Rinzai-ji in Suruga province at the behest of Imagawa Yoshimoto, an influential Daimyō and warlord, later killed by Oda Nobunaga. Daikyū's records, Kentō-roku ("Viewing the Peach Blossoms Record"), were divided into sections, each section devoted to the teachings he gave at the various temples where he had served. It was first published in Kyoto in 1748, at about the same time this piece was written. Hakuin mentions reading a manuscript version preserved at Rinzai-ji in his native Suruga, and also the newly printed version, both of which he praises highly. He pays tribute to Myōshin-ji priest Muchaku Dōchū for the deep understanding he showed in editing the text for publication. But he expresses concern about the completeness of Dōchū's edition, since it does not include the records of the teachings Daikyū delivered when he resided at Rinzai-ji. Hakuin says he himself has readied a complete manuscript of Daikyū's records that contains the omitted material as well, in hopes that it will one day be published.

IN WINTER, THE FIFTH of the eleventh month, first year of Kan'en (1748), a large meeting and vegetarian feast was held at Dairyū-zan Rinzaizen-ji in Sumpu to commemorate the two hundredth anniversary of National Master Enman Honkō's death. I attended the meeting together with a score or so monks from my temple. I asked head priest Kanjū to offer his comments on the deadly verses in *Hsu-t'ang's Comments on One Hundred Koans.* He refused, but I kept after him until finally he agreed. Ascending the Seat of the Dharma King, he taught with free, unhindered eloquence, using steep and lofty Zen means, striking fear deep into the hearts of those assembled.

After the ceremony, one of the monks came back and said, "I've kicked Lin-chi's Three Barriers over on their back. As for Ch'ang-sha's Seven Steps, what are they?*

Raising my hand, I stopped him and said, "Something isn't right. Those words don't match your attainment. Where did you get them?"

The monk said, "They're from the Dharma words Daikyū Kokushi spoke when he was installed as founder of Rinzai-ji."

Instinctively I rose, solemnly offered incense at the altar, and performed three prostrations. "I thought that after the passing of Daitō Kokushi and Kanzan Kokushi, founding fathers of Daitoku-ji and Myōshin-ji, the patriarchal groves had gone completely to seed," I said. "I never expected to discover this old priest (Daikyū) alive and teaching two hundred years after them. It's like talking about salted plums and finding your mouth watering, or like knowing the taste of everything in a cooking vessel by sampling a single morsel. What a shame we can't see the entire contents of that pot!"†

While I was in Sumpu on official business in the middle of the tenth month of this year, I had the good fortune to visit Rinzai-ji and have a look at Daikyū's records. As I had expected, they were not a bit different from the morsel I had already sampled. They were, to the last drop, as virulently poisonous as *Chen* feathers or wolf's fangs. They possessed the abundance of Tao Shu or I Tun, were expressed with the potent vigor of Hsiang Chi or Chao Yun, had stratagems as unconventional as Fei Ch'ang or Chang Hua, and subtle charms as seductive as those of Yang Kuei Fei or Chao Chun.‡ They yielded nothing whatever to Tz'u-ming's glorious utterance, Chen-ching's informal talk, Ling-yuan's general discourse, Hsi-keng's addresses from the high seat, or the long letters Ta-hui sent his students.§ Gooseflesh began rising all over my body. I slapped my knees in admiration and gratitude.

---

*The *Chronological Biography* account has Hsuan-sha for Ch'ang-sha. (*Precious Mirror Cave*, p. 214)
†That is, we can't read Daikyū's records in their entirety.
‡Tao Shu (Fan Li, 5th century BCE) and I Tun (Huan Tan, 1st century BCE) were both officials who amassed large fortunes, their names becoming synonymous with great wealth. Hsiang Chi and Chao Yun were great heroes of the wars of the Three Kingdoms, both possessed of Herculean strength. Fei Ch'ang was a Han dynasty necromancer. Chang Hua was a scholar and statesman under the first Ch'in emperor. Yang Kuei Fei and (Wang) Chao Chun are two of the great beauties of ancient China.
§This string of flattering comparisons ranks Daikyū's *Record* with the teachings of Zen predecessors Hakuin held in highest esteem: the utterance Tz'u-ming (Shih-shuang

While at Rinzai-ji I was shown a piece of silk brocade ten foot square which I was told Daikyū had received from Emperor Go-Nara. It was exceedingly beautiful, its lustrous colors dazzling to the eye. I said, "As rare and priceless as this is, it can't even compare to even half a word or a partial phrase from the National Master—it's a difference between mud and cloud."

I declared to a Rinzai-ji monk named Bon Zennin seated next to me, "We can be proud that our country produced a priest of Daikyū's caliber. This record of his is a true validation of Hsi-keng's prophecy that genuine Zen followers would increase daily in our country.* It is unique, a truly peerless treasure, unsurpassed in the annals of our school. It is in no way inferior to the *Blue Cliff Record* or *Record of Hsu-t'ang*. Its enduring radiance will shine forever, gloriously illuminating our land. To show my gratitude to the National Master, I want to make a fair copy of the records in their entirety to preserve them for posterity. In future, if a congenial spirit appears and offers to help, it might be published as well. What better way to make our school thrive and prosper!"

Bon was nodding his head in agreement, almost dancing with joy. I tried to remember how many times I had visited Rinzai-ji in Sumpu since I began teaching at Shōin-ji, but never once had I experienced a joy like this. On the trip back to Shōin-ji I was telling everyone I met about Daikyū's records.

Prior to a recent *rōhatsu* training session, a Zen man named Ryō†—a disciple of the head priest of Kaifuku-in at the Myōshin-ji headquarters monastery in Kyoto—who had accompanied me to the Rinzai-ji meeting, came to me with a packet of books. "These are the Zen records of National

---

Ch'u-yuan, 986–1039) made when he stuck a gimlet into his thigh to keep from dozing off during zazen, which he quotes frequently in his writings. Chen-ching K'o-wen's (1025–1102) informal talk (*shōsan*) is found in *Compendium of the Five Lamps*, ch. 17; Ling-yuan I-ching's (d. 1117) general discourse (*fusetsu*), in *Compendium*, ch. 17; Hsi-keng's (Hsu-t'ang Chih-yu, 1185–1269) talks from the high seat (*jōdō*) in *Record of Hsu-t'ang*; Ta-hui's letters in the *Ta-hui shu*.

*Hsi-keng's (Hsu-t'ang) prophecy is said to have been pronounced in a verse Hsi-keng gave his Japanese disciple Daiō Kokushi on the latter's departure to return to Japan (see page 46). Nothing seems to be known about Bon Zennin (Zennin means simply "Zen man").

†Later known as Shikyō Eryō (1722–1787), he was one of Hakuin's most important Dharma heirs, said to have been instrumental in spreading Hakuin Zen in the Kyoto area. Ordained at Kaifuku-in subtemple of Myōshin-ji in Kyoto, he studied with Hakuin for about ten years, returning to become head priest at Kaifuku-in in 1757.

Master [Daikyū] Honkō," he said. "They are called the *Kentō Records* and were compiled by Priest Ryūge of Myōshin-ji."*

I felt as though I had obtained a bright torch on a dark road. I offered incense, opened the book reverently, and began reading. I found it possessed a lofty Zen style, rich in profound and subtle principles, profound erudition marked by a sharp and thrusting discernment, a beautiful literary style, and truly extraordinary religious verses. It all shone out clearly, beyond any doubt, right under my very eyes. Ah, a book such as this is the face—the very eyebrows and eyes—of our Japanese Zen school.

If the priest of Ryūge-in had not possessed the true Dharma eye, Daikyū's records would have disappeared into the bellies of bookworms and been lost forever. But Ryūge's Dharma eye notwithstanding, unless old Daikyū had first achieved that profound attainment, how could these wonderful records ever have appeared? Still, these records must stand as one of the finest fruits of Ryūge's enlightened understanding.

I was surprised, however, that only three or four pages had been included from the record of Daikyū's teaching at Rinzai-ji. I wondered why the material that is preserved at Rinzai-ji had not all been incorporated into this edition of the *Kentō Records*. Was this a case of a priceless jade the experts had failed to recognize?†

I told Brother Ryō to write a letter to Bon at Rinzai-ji: "Tell him that he should not relax his efforts in transcribing a fair copy of the *Kentō Records* [including all the material in the Rinzai-ji manuscript] just because they have recently been published; and not to say that because the saltiness of the vast ocean can be known from tasting a single drop, the National Master's fundamental meaning can be known from this new edition alone. To believe a puddle made by a horse's hoof is sufficient is the view of a

<hr/>

Ryūge ("Dragon Flower"). A sobriquet used by Muchaku Dōchū, after the name of his retirement temple, Ryūge-in.

†Allusion to a story in the *Han-fei tzu*. A man named Pien Ho found a block of jade-stone in the mountains and presented it to the king. An expert pronounced it to be an ordinary stone, and for attempting to deceive the king, Pien Ho's left foot was cut off. When the next king ascended the throne, Pien Ho again presented the jade, but it was rejected again, and his right leg was chopped off. When the next king was enthroned, Pien Ho went before the gates of city and wailed out in lamentation for three days and nights. Hearing of this, the king asked the reason. Pien Ho told him, "I do not cry because of my mutilation, but because a true gem has been rejected as a false one, and a loyal subject branded as a deceiver." This time, the lapidary who tested the stone pronounced it to be jade of the finest quality. The story gave rise to the proverb, "Having eyes but not recognizing the jadestone of Mount Ch'ing."

clam or mussel. To believe the vast ocean is limited is the perspective of a whale or other monster of the deep. The men who long ago compiled the Buddhist canon in the Pippali Cave did not think it was sufficient to include the *Flower Garland Sutra* alone, and because of that today we have the Buddha's teaching in all its variety—both partial and full, sudden and gradual. Be sure that you tell Bon all of this."

I am old and lazy. I can't recite the poems I could when I was thirty. I am fully aware how disgraceful my talents are. So why do I go on composing rustic verses like these? In certain circumstances even Mother Mu was known to laugh. Even Hsi-shih was sometimes seen to break into a smile. The ugly woman of Wu-yen and the beauty Yang Kuei-fei had equally good reasons to weep. They laughed or wept not caring about what people thought. I wonder, though, will these verses of mine make Mother Mu laugh?*

I

I used to think no Dharma eye had opened in the eastern seas,
My troubles with the *Kentō Records* have proved I was wrong.
Its quiet words, perfectly expressed, laid bare my dim
　　perceptions.
What a truly extraordinary collection of Zen records these are!

. . . .

The eastern seas. Japan.

II

From the depths of *prajna* samadhi, a rich display of verbal
　　insights,
Dharma fangs and talons, striking to the truth of the seven schools.

*According to legend, Mother Mu (Mu Mu), the fourth of the Yellow Emperor's wives, was ugly but extremely sagacious. Lady Hsi-shih (one of the four great beauties of ancient China) would knit her brows as if in pain, thinking it enhanced her beauty. The woman of Wu-yen, who is said to have been repulsive in every feature, at the age of forty demanded an audience with the Emperor. Despite laughter from the surrounding courtiers, she so impressed him with her intelligence that he took her for a wife. The imperial consort Yang Kuei-fei (another of the four great beauties) was strangled to placate rebellious imperial troops.

368 : POISON BLOSSOMS FROM A THICKET OF THORN

A great priest, the kind who appears once in five hundred years,
A divine dragon that burst from the depths of our Dharma sea.

. . . .

Fangs and talons: metaphors for the trenchant working of Daikyū's Zen utterances.

Seven schools: the Kuei-yang, Lin-chi, Ts'ao-tung, Yun-men, Fa-yen, Yang-ch'i, and Huang-lung lines of Chinese Zen.

III

Each verse strikes like a thunderclap, throws my mind for a loop.
A profusion of peach flowers budding on a Dragon Flower Tree.
Struggling sheepishly in my dotage, lacking meditative strength,
Plagued by these complexities, I can't get a good night's sleep.

. . . .

Peach flowers alludes to the *Record of Kentō* (literally "seeing the peach blossoms") with a probable allusion to the story of the enlightenment Ling-yun had upon seeing peach blossoms.

Dragon Flower (Ryūge). A sobriquet used by Muchaku Dōchū, the Myōshin-ji priest who edited the *Record of Kentō*. The name Dragon Flower also refers to the Bodhisattva Maitreya, and to the place where he will teach as a Buddha when he appears in the world far in the future. The "complexities" (*kattō*) are those Hakuin struggled with in reading through the record.

IV

As springtime splendor is slowly fading from the Purple Fields,
Who could have imagined such a branch in Flower Garden?
As Ryūge has compiled and edited the *Peach Blossom Records*,
When Maitreya appears in the world, he'll be several hours late.

. . . .

Purple Fields (Murasakino) and *Flower Garden* (Hanazono) are the locations in Kyoto of Daitoku-ji and Myōshin-ji. Although Daitoku-ji was the older temple, by Hakuin's time the Myōshin-ji line, to which he belonged, had come to assume a growing dominance it would retain throughout the Edo period.

Ryūge (Dragon Flower) is also used as a name for Maitreya, a Bodhisattva who resides in the Tushita Heaven. It is said that Maitreya will descend into this world far in the future, become a Buddha, and teach and liberate beings at three assemblies under a Dragon Flower Tree.

Hakuin says that when Maitreya finally does appear in the world, he will find the work he appeared to accomplish, guiding beings to enlightenment, is already being carried out thanks to his namesake Daikyū's work.

V

Men with placid minds don't speak; water doesn't flow on level
    ground.
Which is why I can do nothing but shed a tear or break into a
    smile.
This old chuffer hasn't chanted a verse for over thirty years,
Since these records appeared, I've been warbling like a thrush.

VI

Ever since Master Daikyū's records arrived at my place,
I've been exhausted, my zazen cushion worn to shreds.
You could take some pages from it and send them to China,
I don't think folks there could grasp his meaning either.

. . . .

Worn to shreds because Hakuin had used it so much while meditating on Daikyū's records.

VII

If a person is really set on reading the *Kentō Records*,
He first must resolve the question of Chao-chou's Mu,
Next must penetrate the story of Nan-ch'uan's Death.
He'll have it rolling like a gem in the palm of his hand.

:157. Thoughts on a Winter Day

This verse, dating from the winter training period of 1744, Hakuin's fifty-ninth year, alludes to a lecture meeting on the Vimalakirti Sutra *he had scheduled for the following spring at Jitoku-ji in Kai province.*

> Over a hundred monks humming to themselves in the frigid
> cold,
> Not one of them complaining about the bitter frost and snow.
> Though the wonders of springtime will unfold in the Amra
> gardens,
> First enter the Snowy Mountains, ask about the hidden scent.

. . . .

Amra gardens, in the city of Vaishali. The site where the *Vimalakirti Sutra* was preached. The hidden scent is that of plum flowers, blossoming in the winter snow at the coldest time of the year.

:158. Matching the Rhymes of a Verse by Senior Monk Sai at the Beginning of the Year

Senior Monk Sai (Sai Shuso; Shuso is a title used for senior monks) is Ryōsai Genmyō, who has appeared a number of times before. This verse probably dates from around 1734, which is about the time Ryōsai first arrived at Shōin-ji to begin his study under Hakuin. According to an annotation, it was written during a ninety-day winter practice retreat that included the rōhatsu *training period.*

> Four or five monks are seated deep inside white cloud.
> A flaggy haired senior monk has shown special diligence.
> All ties cast aside, things flowed on as smoothly as water
> The full ninety days—their minds now chaster than ice.
> With the New Year drawing near, we have no polished rice;
> Come spring we'll still be seated dozing in the lamp light.
> I'm deeply grateful that you have chosen this rigorous life,
> Heedless of profit or fame—you are heroes indeed.

. . . .

Lines 1–2: "This dates from the time Kokurin [Hakuin] first raised his Dharma banners to teach" (annotation).

Flaggy haired senior monk. Ryōsai, according to an annotation, "left his head unshaved during the winter months."

:159. On a Visit to Konryū-ji the Temple Master Wrote a Verse. I Responded, Following his Rhymes

This seems to date from about the same time as the previous verse. Konryū-ji was a small temple under Shōin-ji's jurisdiction. It was located east of Hara near Mount Ashitaka, in the foothills of Mount Fuji. An annotation on the "Temple Master" has, "Perhaps Ryōsai (Genmyō)," the first student Hakuin gave permission to teach. There is nothing in Ryōsai's biography to connect him with Konryū-ji, though it is possible Hakuin may have installed him there to look after the temple for a time.

> Yen Hui spent his life in a hovel, savoring adversity.
> Ts'ao-chih could produce marvelous seven-pace verse.
> But the free, unfettered life you lead transcends them both,
> Like the green pine tree surpasses all the flowers on earth.

. . . .

Yen Hui. Confucius's favorite disciple, lived his life in extreme poverty while following the master's teachings.

Ts'ao Chih (192–232) was a prodigy who could produce poems easily on any given theme. At the bidding of his brother, the first Emperor of the Wei dynasty, he is said to have composed an impromptu verse in the time it took him to walk only seven steps.

BOOK TEN (SUPPLEMENT 1)
Capping Words for the Heart Sutra (*Shingyō Jakugo*)—Miscellaneous Writings (*Zatsubun*)—Inscriptions for Paintings (*San*)—Religious Verses (*Geju*)

. . . .

This one-volume supplement to Poison Blossoms, Keisō-dokuzui shūi, *contains material that was for some reason omitted— perhaps it had been unobtainable, perhaps just overlooked— at the time the original selection was compiled. It was published and financed separately, although the two works seem to have appeared at about the same time (see Introduction, pp. 10–13). The bulk of this supplement (which for convenience I call Book Ten), about three-fourths of the text, is taken up by the Shingyō Jakugo (Capping Words for the Heart Sutra), Hakuin's commentary on the* Heart Sutra.

I. Heart Sutra—
Commentary on the *Heart Sutra*

:160. Capping Words and Verses

Hakuin's Zen commentary on the Heart Sutra, *which later came to be known as* Dokugo Shingyō (Poison Words for the Heart Sutra), *is one of Hakuin's main contributions to Zen* jakugo (*capping word*) *literature, his other important work in that line being* Kaian-kokugo (Dream Words from a Land of Dreams). *Twenty years ago, I published an extensively annotated translation of this work under the title* Zen Words for the Heart. *Some (mostly) cosmetic changes have been made to the text for the present version.*

Hakuin addresses his first capping words to the capping words and verses themselves, which make up his Zen commentary on the sutra text. The opening sections deal with the individual words that make up the sutra title, Mahā-prajñā-paramita Hridaya Sūtra— Great Wisdom Perfection Heart Sutra.

Capping Words and Verses

A BLIND OLD GEEZER INSIDE a dark cave thick with a maze of vines and creepers. He returns stark naked and sits in the weeds. Poor Master Fu, a pity he's going to lose all those lovely mansions! And don't say these words are cold and indifferent, that they have no taste. One bellyful eliminates your hunger to the end of time.

> He casts a forest of thorns over the entire universe,
> Catching in its tangles every monk on earth;
> I pray you will recognize the Way to deliverance,
> And enjoy yourself hawking inside a lotus thread.

. . . .

The blind old geezer. The Bodhisattva Free and Unrestricted Seeing (Kanjizai; Kannon), who preaches the sutra, but refers as well to Hakuin himself, the author of the capping words and verses.

A maze of vines and creepers. Verbal complications and conceptual under-standing. Unable to stand on their own, they attach and constrict intrinsic wisdom and prevent it from working freely. Beneath the hard words is sug-gested the proper role of the Bodhisattva who leaves the naked suchness of his own enlightenment and, undisturbed by the obstructing senses, preaches to beings in the world of relativity (*the weeds*). Of his blindness, the modern Rinzai teacher Sugawara Jiho says, "Not being blind, we see mountains, riv-ers, men and women, and other things, and we think this gives us a kind of freedom, while in fact it is the cause of our unfreedom....The great Buddhist teachers of the past are people who went forward to become blind men" (*Kenchō Donge Shingyō*, p.3).

Poor Master Fu. Lines from Hsueh-tou's *Ancestral Heroes Collection*. Fu Ta-shih, a celebrated layman of early Chinese Buddhism, was regarded as an incarnation of Maitreya, Buddha of the future. Maitreya is depicted in the *Flower Garland Sutra* as dwelling in the splendidly bejeweled palaces of enlightenment he created in the Tushita Heaven. The wisdom expounded in the sutra, and at work in Hakuin's comments as well, negates all things; nothing can escape it, not the dwellings of sentient beings immured within their selfhood, not even Maitreya's enlightened universe.

A lotus thread is a fine, string-like filament that appears when the lotus root is cut, formed from the viscous substance that exudes from the sev-ered surface. Here it stands for something infinitesimally small and narrow. Hakuin exhorts students to free themselves from the entangling forest of discriminatory attachments and attain the perfect, unfettered activity that comes with total attainment.

MAHA

The Chinese translated this as "great." But what is it? There isn't anything in all the universe you can compare it to. Almost everyone thinks *maha* means "wide and vast"—they're wrong! Even a Superior Man has a love of wealth, but he knows the proper way to get it. Bring me a *small prajna*!

A million Sumerus in a dewdrop on a hair tip,
Three thousand worlds in a foam-fleck on the sea.

A pair of young lads in the eyes of a midge
Play games with the world; they never stop.

. . . .

Even a Superior Man...he knows the proper way to get it. To the Superior Man (a Confucian term here connoting the Bodhisattva), wisdom is the only true wealth, and the only proper way to get it is through the attainment of *kenshō.*

Sumeru is the mountain said to stand at the center of the world.

Three thousand worlds, constituting the universe in its entirety.

Midge translates *chiao-ming,* described as an infinitesimally small insect whose universe is a follicle of hair in a mosquito's eyebrow.

PRAJNA

The Chinese translated this as "wisdom." Everyone has it in consummate perfection. When is this fellow going to stop making these mud pies? You'll never see it until your fingers let go from the edge of the cliff. Why? Don't trim your nails at the foot of a lamp. You might get an inchworm to measure lengths, but don't ask a snail to plow a rocky field.

Ears like the dumb, eyes like the blind.
The empty sky losing itself to midnight.
Even Shariputra couldn't get a good look.
The clubfoot Persian crossed at a different ford.

. . . .

Mud pies. Words and phrases.

Don't trim your nails at the foot of a lamp. A popular Japanese saying, based on the belief that cutting one's nails at night was dangerous because it was then that spirits and demons came out. It is said to have been a favorite "turning word" of Hakuin's teacher Shōju Rojin *(Shōju Rōjin Shū, p. 33).* Here it apparently cautions students against relaxing their efforts as they strive toward realization.

You might get an inchworm to measure...rocky field. Even supposing an inchworm or "looper" is measuring lengths as it hunches along, a snail (with horns, somewhat resembling an ox) cannot plow a rocky field. Don't ask the impossible. "There is a sweetness in *prajna,* but without passing through many difficult spots, you'll never known its taste" (annotation).

Shariputra was foremost in wisdom among the Buddha's followers. The

Heart Sutra is preached at his request.

The clubfoot Persian crossed. Even as Kannon explains it, wisdom is long gone.

PARAMITA

The Chinese translation for this is "reach the other shore." But where is that? He's digging himself into a hole to get at the blue sky. Shrimps wriggle and jump, but they won't escape the dipper. The place where the Treasure lies is near at hand—*take one more step!* "Master Hsieh sits in his boat, wringing water from his line. Even the clearest-eyed monk is stricken with grief."

> Is there anyone on earth who's a "man of this shore"?
> How sad to stand mistaken on a wave-lashed quay!
> Pursuing practice with your roots to life unsevered
> Is a pointless struggle, however long it lasts.

. . . .

Shrimps wriggle...the dipper. The *paramitas* are the practices Bodhisattvas undertake to escape the suffering of "this shore" and reach the enlightened realm of Nirvana or Buddhahood on the "other shore." In fact, the other shore is this shore, which can only be attained by grasping the Buddha-nature within.

Master Hsieh sits in his boat...stricken with grief. Hsieh is the family name of the ninth-century Chinese monk Hsuan-sha Shih-pei, who was a fisherman before entering religious life. In *Hekigan Hishō*, Hakuin uses these two lines in a verse comment on the koan Hsuan-sha's Triple Invalid (*Blue Cliff Record*, Case 88). Since the fishing line is always in the water, it is futile to attempt to wring it dry. Hsuan-sha's attempts suggest the purposeless activity of the Bodhisattva in helping fellow beings to cross to the other shore, which is difficult even for a deeply enlightened monk to grasp.

Pursuing practice...long it lasts. "This zazen cushion discerns *prajna* wisdom. It is right here that the other shore is reached" (annotation).

HEART

For untold ages this didn't have a name. Then they blundered and gave it one. Even gold dust blinds when it gets into your eyes. A mani gem is just another blemish on the Dharma. What is *This*! Most people are like the fellow who confused a saddle remnant for his dead father's jawbone. People who study the Way are ignorant of the truth simply because at the start of their practice they confound it with their own discriminations. Those have been the very source of birth-and-death since the beginning of time, yet the fools take them for their original Self.

> Clearly, this is ungettable within the Three Worlds—
> An empty sky swept clean away. Not a particle left.
> On the zazen seat, in the dead of night, cold as steel.
> At the window, moonlight bright with plum shadows!

. . . .

Heart. "Also called Amida. Also called Hell. Even in the *Compendium of the Five Lamps* and *Records of the Lamp* [the two most important Zen collections], few priests are found who have grasped the truth of the Bodhi-mind [heart]. Lacking the Bodhi-mind, you will fall into hell even if you are a prince or a shōgun, not to mention ordinary men and women" (annotation, probably reporting Hakuin's own words).

Those have been the very source of…original Self. Ch'ang-sha Ching-ts'en's well-known saying.

Clearly…ungettable within the Three Worlds. Words from the *Diamond Sutra.* The Three Worlds are those of past, present, and future.

SUTRA

"Thus I have heard. The Buddha was once....." *Faugh!* Who wants to roll *that* open! Most people go fossicking inside piles of paper trash for yellow scripture scrolls with little red knobs. Just plucking another clove off a lily bulb.

> This is one sutra they didn't compile
> Inside that cave at Pippali.
> Kumarajiva had no words to translate it;
> Ananda himself couldn't get wind of it.
> At the north window, icy drafts whistle through cracks,
> At the south pond, a wild goose stands in snowy reeds.
> Above, the mountain is pinched thin with cold;
> Freezing clouds threaten to plunge from the sky.

> Buddhas might descend to this world by the thousands,
> They couldn't add or subtract one thing.

. . . .

Thus I have heard...was once... The traditional opening for Buddhist sutras.

Just plucking another clove. The bulb of a lily is composed of a number of smaller bulbs or cloves, and has no real core. Pluck them off one by one and you are left with nothing. To seek Wisdom by reading sutras one after another is like picking cloves off a lily bulb, looking for its center. An annotation adds, "When you are not yet enlightened, sutras are not really sutras. When you are enlightened, a lily bulb, even one clove, is a sutra of ultimate suchness."

Kumarajiva. The great Central Asian monk celebrated for his translations of Buddhist sutras into Chinese, among which is a translation of the *Heart Sutra*.

Ananda. A disciple of the Buddha who is reputed to have heard and memorized all the teachings the Buddha preached during his lifetime. He played an important role in the compilation of the first collection of sutras, said to have taken place inside the Pippali cave in central India.

At the north window...subtract one thing. "This is the true *Heart Sutra* and no one, not even a Buddha, can change that in any way" (annotation).

KANJIZAI (FREE AND UNOBSTRUCTED SEEING)

Why, it's the Bodhisattva of Butuoyan! The Great Fellow who's found in us all. Search the whole earth, you'll never find a single unfree person. You clear your throat. You spit. You move your arms. You don't need others' help. Who clapped chains on you? Who's holding you back? Lift up your left hand, you just may scratch a Buddha's head. Raise your right hand. When will you be able to avoid feeling a dog's head?

> Fingers clasp and feet walk on without the help of others,
> As thoughts and emotions pile up great stocks of Wrong.
> But cast aside pros and cons, and all likes and dislikes,
> I'll call you a Kanjizai right there where you snout!

. . . .

The sutra begins with the Bodhisattva entering deep meditation (samadhi) prior to preaching.

Kanjizai—Sanskrit, Avalokitesvara; Chinese, Kuanyin—is the embodiment of wisdom and compassion, the basic forces that inform all Bodhisattvas. In Japan he (or she) is more commonly known by the name Kanzeon (short form: Kannon). Kanjizai, meaning "free and unrestricted seeing," represents the student or religious seeker striving for the highest level of wisdom; Kanzeon, "perceiver of the sounds of the world's [suffering]," represents the role of compassionate teacher, one who has postponed final attainment in order to teach others, vowing never to rest until the last being has also crossed the sea of suffering to the other shore of enlightenment.

Butuoyan, "the mountain crag Butuo," (Butuo-shan), or Potalaka, is the mythical mountain dwelling place of the Bodhisattva. The Chinese associated Butuoyan with an island off the coast in the East China Sea. But, Hakuin says, don't look for him there; look within your own mind.

BODHISATTVA

To distinguish him from Shravakas and Solitary Buddhas, and from full-fledged Buddhas as well, he's given the provisional name of Bodhisattva. He's on the road but hasn't budged from home; he's away from home all the time but isn't on the road. I'll snatch the practice of the Four Universal Vows from you, Bodhisattva—that's the very thing to make you a Superior Man, able all eight ways.

> He has transcended the formless nest of personal emptiness,
> Gets tossed in the troubled waves of the sea of birth and death.
> Take refuge in the Great Merciful One who relieves all suffering
> In a hundred million different forms, through endless space
> and time.

. . . .

Shravakas and Solitary Buddhas. Buddhist practicers of the Two Vehicles who seek enlightenment for themselves but make no effort to teach others. To Hakuin, they represent a type of practice he regards as incomplete and inferior to that of the Mahayana Bodhisattva, who while striving toward Buddhahood attempts to assist others to enlightenment as well.

He's on the road...on the road. From the *Record of Lin-chi.*

I'll snatch from you...all eight ways. The truly Superior Man (Bodhisattva) lives in the world to respond to the needs of suffering beings, while at the same time dwelling always at home within the timeless realm of enlightenment.

This mode of being is reflected in his Universal Vows (*shigu seigan*): "Sentient beings are numberless, I vow to save them; the deluding passions are inexhaustible, I vow to destroy them; the Dharma gates are manifold, I vow to know them; the Buddha Way is supreme, I vow to master it."

Able all eight ways. In its original Confucian setting, this would refer to the eight Confucian virtues: benevolence, propriety, filiality, and so on. While difficult to explain fully in Hakuin's Zen context, the point of the statement as a whole seems to be that a Bodhisattva is not fully fledged until any taint of Bodhisattvahood is transcended as well.

PRACTICING

What's he prattling on about now! Stirring up trouble. You sleep at night, you're up and about during the day, pissing, passing shit. The clouds sail on, the streams flow along, leaves fall, flowers scatter. But when you hesitate or stop to think, Hell rears up in all its hellish forms. Practicing is like that, all right, but unless you penetrate by the sweat of your own brow and see it for yourself, there is trouble in store for you, and plenty of it!

> Who is the one that works your hands and feet?
> Eats and drinks when you're hungry and thirsty?
> If a hair of discrimination enters into these acts,
> You've killed off Chaos, boring holes for his eyes.

. . . .

You've killed off Chaos...eyes. Reference to a story in the *Chuang Tzu*. The gods, having finished creating a new world, decided to show their appreciation to Chaos, whose self-effacing help had been essential to their work, by supplying him with the same senses they themselves enjoyed. They began by boring holes in him to give him the sense of sight, but as they were congratulating themselves on the splendid results, Chaos died. Chaos is the state prior to the arising of discrimination.

DEEP *PRAJNA PARAMITA*

Yahh!! Gouging out good flesh. Creating fresh wounds. Queer thing, this "*prajna*" of his! What's it like? Deep? Shallow? Like river water? Tell me about a wisdom with deeps and shallows. Mistaken identity, I'm afraid. He's mistaken a pheasant for a phoenix.

Annulling form in the quest for emptiness is called shallow,
Seeing emptiness in the fullness of myriad forms called deep.
Blithering on about wisdom with form and emptiness in his
    hands,
Like a lame tortoise in a glass jug clumping after a flying bird.

. . . .

Mistaken a pheasant for a phoenix. This is based on an old Chinese tale. The
king of Ch'u was a great bird lover who filled his palace with feathered creatures of every kind. An enterprising merchant hoping to gain his favor went
to Mount Tan where the phoenix was said to nest and searched high and low
for the mythical bird. As he was about to give up and return home, he met a
man carrying a strange-looking fowl. It was actually a pheasant, but the man
told him it was a famous Mount Tan phoenix, so the merchant bought it
and took it to present to the king. The king thought it a rather poor-looking
phoenix, but it did have a long tail like a phoenix, and since a phoenix was
said to be an auspicious bird, he accepted it with great pleasure (*T'ai-p'ing
Kuang-chi*, ch. 461).

(At That) Time

He's done it again! Scraping out another piece of perfectly good flesh.
Before all the infinite kalpas in the past and after all those in the future, the
Feather Cutter Blade gleams cold in its sheath with a wonderful vibrant
radiance. A fabulous night-shining pearl brought forth on its tray.

Yesterday morning we swept out the soot of the old year.
Tonight we pound the rice for the New Year's goodies.
There's a pine tree with roots, oranges with green leaves.
Putting on a fresh new robe, I await the coming guests.

. . . .

The Feather Cutter Blade. A sword so sharp it would sever a feather blown
against it; a metaphor for the mind of wisdom.

The lecture meeting at which Hakuin delivered these comments on
the *Heart Sutra* was apparently held during the winter months, hence the
description of New Year's preparations at Shōin-ji. The verse expresses the
essential oneness of time and being in the ordinary activities of temple life.

He Clearly Sees

An immaculate Diamond Eye. It is free of even the finest dust. But don't go blinking it open over a bed of flying lime cinders! Where does this "seeing" take place? The entire earth is the eye of a Buddhist monk. It's exactly as Hsuan-sha said.

> An ant inside a mite's eye is walking around a mill.
> A tiny spider is spinning a web inside a midge's ear.
> Tushita Heaven, the world of man, the floors of hell,
> Clear and distinct as a mango in the palm of the hand.

. . . .

Where does this "seeing" take place? Seeing presumes a seer and something seen, but no such duality exists in the deep wisdom *paramita*, where, as a well-known Zen saying asserts, "The entire universe is the eye of a Buddhist monk."

It's exactly as Hsuan-sha said. Reference to words Hsuan-sha Shih-pei uttered on hearing that Ling-yun had attained enlightenment on seeing flowering peach blossoms: "All fine and good, fine and good. But I guarantee you brother Ling-yun still hadn't got it all." The words came to be known as "Hsuan-sha's utterance." Hakuin often uses them in the sense of something that is not yet fully achieved to stress the necessity of post-satori training. See notes to Book One, #37.

All Five Skandhas Are Empty

The sacred turtle's tail sweeps away her tracks, but how can the tail help leaving tracks of its own? Forms are like the towering Iron Mountains, sensation and perception like a trenchant Diamond Sword, conception and consciousness like a mani gem that fulfills the heart's desires. But you must realize how far there is to go. Before you know it, darkness will overtake you once again.

> You see another's five and you think that's you
> You cling to them with personal pride or shame.
> It's like a bubble of foam on the waves' surface,
> It's like a lightning bolt flashing across the sky.

. . . .

The five skandhas, *or aggregates*—form, perception, conception, volition, and consciousness—are the component elements of all sentient being.

How can the tail avoid leaving traces of its own? After having said "All things are empty," the words "all things are empty" still remain.

The Iron Hoop Mountains circle the outer limits of the world. Emptiness is far from being mere vacuity. Form (one of the *skandhas*) has a presence as undeniable as mountains; the functions of the mind (the other four *skandhas*) work like an invincible diamond sword to annihilate illusion, and like the fabulous mani gem to fulfill every wish. To grasp the true meaning of the *skandhas'* emptiness in this way takes years of hard training, and human life is all too brief.

And Is Delivered from All Distress and Suffering

The shadow in the guest's cup never was a snake. How clear, in a dream, the three worlds are. When you wake, all is empty, the myriad worlds *Mu*.

> The ogre outside shoves the door,
> The ogre inside holds it fast.
> Poring sweat from head to tail,
> Struggling for their very lives,
> Fighting on throughout the night,
> Until the dawn appears at last,
> Then laughter fills the early light—
> They were friends from the first!

. . . .

The shadow in the guest's cup never was a snake. An allusion to an old Chinese story. The Chinese official Yueh invited a friend to help him celebrate when he was appointed governor. He poured the friend a large cup of wine, but when he raised it up to drink he saw a snake wriggling on the surface of the wine. He closed his eyes and gulped it down but immediately begged to be excused and rushed home. Certain that he had swallowed the snake, he became ill and took to his bed. The governor, on learning what had happened, invited him over again. He set a wine cup before his friend and asked him if the snake was still there. When the friend nodded, Yueh pointed to a bow hanging on the wall, a reflection of which had been cast on the surface of the wine. We conjure up illusions such as the five *skandhas*, thus creating the cause of our suffering. Hakuin quotes the words from a verse in the *Lin-kuan lu*, ch.2.

The verse recasts a story from *Treatise on the Perfection of Great Wisdom*, ch. 92, about a pair of travelers who lost their way and became separated deep in the mountains. One of them wandered aimlessly until overtaken by darkness. He approached a small, lonely cottage and asked the householder for lodging. The householder refused, saying he was being haunted by night goblins, but the traveler persisted and the householder finally allowed him to stay. After supper, he heard a vigorous rattling at the door. He ran and put his shoulder against the door, holding it fast. All night long the banging and clawing continued outside the door, and inside the traveler held it secure just as tenaciously. But when daylight came, the traveler saw that the goblin he had been struggling against was the friend he had been separated from the previous day, who had also come to the cottage seeking shelter.

The ogre inside is the courageous and resolute heart of the Buddhist practicer; the ogre outside is his illusions and desires. Dawn is the opening of enlightenment, when it is realized that illusions are no other than enlightenment.

Shariputra

Huh! What could this pipsqueak of an Arhat have to offer, with his measly fruits! Around here, even Buddhas and Patriarchs have to beg for their lives. Where is he going to hide, with his Hinayana face and Mahayana heart? At Vimalakirti's, he couldn't even get his manhood back. He surely can't have forgotten the way he sweated and squirmed?

> In the Deer Park this man's wisdom surpassed all the rest.
> He startled Uncle Long Nails while still in the womb.
> He studied with the Great Man himself, took down his sutra,
> Was Rahula's private tutor, the clever Mynah Lady's kid.

. . . .

With his Hinayana face and Mahayana heart. Shariputra, a follower of the Hinayana, or Smaller Vehicle, tradition who lived prior to the appearance of the Mahayana teaching, was in heart already a follower of that teaching. In the *Lotus Sutra* the Buddha predicts that in the future disciples like Shariputra will surpass the stage of Arhatship and achieve Buddhahood.

In the *Vimalakirti Sutra,* when layman Vimalakirti and the Bodhisattva Manjusri discuss the role of the Bodhisattva, Shariputra is present along with a celestial maiden of Bodhisattvic attainments. Shariputra is resentful that a woman should be there, thinking she will defile the gathering. He engages her in debate on the possibility of enlightenment for women, intending to put her in her place. Instead, he reveals his inability to transcend the distinction of sex. She transforms him into a celestial maiden and challenges him to change himself back into a man, which he is unable to do because of the attachments that remain in his mind.

Uncle Long Nails was the brother of Shariputra's mother. Returning home after long and diligent study in great centers of learning, he found that his sister was pregnant. He was surprised to see that she had become extremely intelligent and eloquent, and was impossible to best in argument. Remembering that a woman carrying a child of great wisdom was said to acquire such wisdom herself, he resolved to study with greater diligence in order not to be overshadowed by his new nephew. From then on he even grudged the time to cut his fingernails, which grew to great length.

The Great Man is Kannon. *Rahula,* the son Shakamuni fathered prior to his entrance into religious life, was taught by Shariputra and later became one of the Buddha's disciples. *The Mynah Lady* is Shariputra's mother Shari (Shariputra means "son of Shari"), who received her name, meaning "mynah bird," because of her eloquence and piercing eyes.

FORM IS NO OTHER THAN EMPTINESS, EMPTINESS NO OTHER THAN FORM

A nice hot kettle of stew, and he ruins it by tossing a couple of rat turds in. It's no good pushing delicacies at someone with a full belly. Striking aside waves to look for water, when the waves *are* water!

> Forms don't hinder emptiness; emptiness is the tissue of form.
> Emptiness doesn't destroy forms; forms are the flesh
> of emptiness.
> Inside the Dharma gates where form and emptiness are not two,
> A lame turtle with painted eyebrows stands in the evening
> breeze.

. . . .

The rat turds *are form and emptiness.*

FORM IS EMPTINESS, EMPTINESS IS FORM

What utter rubbish! A useless collection of junk. Don't be teaching gibbons how to climb trees. These goods have been gathering dust on the shelves for two thousand years. Master Hsieh sits in his fishing boat wringing water from his line.

> A bush warbler pipes intermittently in the spring breeze.
> A thin mist hovers over the peach trees in the warm sun.
> A group of young girls, cicada heads and moth-eyebrows,
> Twirl sprays of blossom, one over each brocade shoulder.

. . . .

Master Hsieh sits in his fishing boat wringing water from his line. Earlier in the commentary, in the capping words for *Paramita* (p. 378), Hakuin used this same phrase in alluding to the apparently useless effort Bodhisattvas exert as they strive to lead others to enlightenment. Here he chides Kanjizai for repeating these needless assertions about form and emptiness.

The verse depicts forms from the actual world, which are, in themselves, no other than emptiness.

Cicada heads and moth eyebrows are stock descriptions of female beauty.

AND IT IS THE SAME FOR SENSATION, PERCEPTION, CONCEPTION, AND CONSCIOUSNESS

Now look at him—wallowing in the sow-grass! If you take no notice of these strange apparitions when they appear, they self-destruct. A snow Buddha is a terrible eyesore when the sun comes out. You certainly won't see funny things like that around here.

> Earth wind fire water—tracks left when a bird takes flight.
> Form sensation perception conception—sparks in the eye.
> A stone woman works a shuttle, her skinny elbows flying,
> A mud cow barrels through the surf baring her bicuspids.

. . . .

Hakuin's comment on *Snow Buddha:* "When the snow melts, all the horse shit appears" *(Hekigan Hishō, Case 44).*

Earth wind fire water are the four great elements of the material world. *Sparks* are spots that appear to your eyes when you rub them.

The final lines of the verse, exemplifying the principle that sensation, perception, conception, and consciousness are empty, caution against the error of falling into a passive state of "empty" emptiness. The twentieth-century Zen teacher Sugawara Jiho calls them "secret passwords that allow you to enter into the truth of 'all things are empty.'"

SHARIPUTRA, ALL THINGS ARE EMPTY APPEARANCES

It's like he's rubbing his eyes to make himself see flowers in the air. If all things don't exist to begin with, what do we want with "empty appearances"? He is defecating and spraying pee all over a spotlessly clean yard.

> Earth and all its hills and streams are a palace in the air,
> Heaven and hell are bogey bazaars atop the ocean waves.
> Pure lands and impure world are brushes of turtle-hair,
> Nirvana and samsara riding whips made from hare-horn.

. . . .

Flowers in the air. Spots seen by those with eye disease; they can also be made to appear by rubbing the eyes.

Turtle-hair and hare-horn. Stock metaphors for that which does not exist and, by extension, false notions and delusions.

The pure lands are the Buddhist paradise, or "other shore" of Nirvana; the impure world is the realm of transmigratory births and deaths in which we live.

THEY ARE NOT BORN, NOT DESTROYED, NOT STAINED, NOT PURE; THEY DO NOT INCREASE OR DECREASE

Real front-page news! But is that the way things really are? How did you find things weren't born or destroyed? Don't try to swindle us. An elbow doesn't bend outward.

> Two little chaps in your eyes are awaiting their guests.
> The Valley Spirit isn't dead, she is expecting your call.
> No one ever got dirty by residing in the human world;

Not a single clean face is seen in Buddha's pure lands.
Eighty thousand shares of Dharma—isn't that enough?
Billions of Buddha-lands, contained in next to nothing.
The pillow-prince of Hantan gains honor and respect,
The governor of Nanke gleefully rakes in all the taxes.

. . . .

Two little chaps are "eyebabies" reflected in the viewer's eye. Working freely and mindlessly, they show all things as they truly are. The *Valley Spirit* is the echo that, though void of any fixed substance or self, responds instantly to someone's call. These first two lines both illustrate the true principle of Not Born, Not Destroyed.

Eighty thousand shares of Dharma. There are said to be eighty-four-thousand Buddhist teachings, one for each of the eighty-four-thousand passions.

The pillow-prince of Hantan. This is based on a Chinese folktale. A young man who left home for a career in the capital stopped at a place called Hantan and, while waiting for his lunch to cook, took a nap and dreamed he had passed through an illustrious career, culminating in an appointment as chief minister of state. When he awoke and saw the food still cooking on the fire, he realized life was an empty dream and returned home. "The world is a dream within a dream" (annotation).

The governor of Nanke. Based on another folktale. A man fell asleep under a locust tree and dreamed he was summoned to the court of a king and asked to govern the difficult province of Nanke. Under his rule the people became wealthy enough to pay him taxes and make him a rich man. One day a messenger arrived to tell him the kingdom was in danger and the capital must be moved, and asked him to return to his original home until he was needed again. He woke up in the midst of a great storm. He later found a deserted anthill in the trunk of the locust tree; the ants had all left before the storm had struck.

THEREFORE, IN EMPTINESS

A regular jackal's den. A cave of shadowy ghosts. How many pilgrims have fallen in here! A deep, black pit. The unutterable darkness of the grave. What a terrifying place!

Over a hundred cold hungry men, phoenixes among monks,
Spread their winter fans and offer New Year's greetings.

On the wall hangs a blue-eyed, purple-bearded old man,
In a jar are the fragrant flowers of the chaste plum tree.
Cold to muffle even the bush warbler's bright clear notes,
Warmth rising up to the Zen seats from red-hot coals.
There are presents of wild yams, in plaits of straw,
And for old men, sugared sweets, laid in their wrappers.

. . . .

The verse describes the New Year's scene at the small rural temple where Hakuin resided. In the previous section he warned against attaching to empty emptiness; now he gives concrete descriptions of true emptiness.

Blue-eyed, purple-bearded old man. Bodhidharma, founder of the Zen school, whose picture is hung during the New Year period.

Bush warbler. The winter cold is still too severe for the *uguisu*, or bush warbler, whose familiar pipings herald the coming of spring.

In the Zen hall, a brazier is set out for the guests who will come to pay their respects. The yams and sweets, of which Hakuin was inordinately fond, are presents sent by members of the lay congregation.

No Form No Sensation Perception Conception Or Consciousness

Dreams. Delusions. Blossoms in the air. Why bother grasping at *them*? Profit and loss. Right and wrong. Toss all that out. You're being too scrupulous. Just stirring up trouble. What's the good of making everything an empty void?

A boundless, unencumbered place—empty, open, still.
Earth, its hills and rivers, are names, nothing more.
Splitting mind into four, bundling all form up into one,
No more than sounds echoing through an empty ravine.

. . . .

Splitting mind into four, into one. Dissecting mental function into sensation, perception, conception, and consciousness [representing the spiritual aspect of self], then adding form [the physical aspect]. These five make up the five *skandhas*, or aggregates, that together constitute the self. "Attaching names such as mind or form, but originally they don't exist" (annotation).

No Eyes, Ears, Nose, Tongue, Body, Mind; No Form, Sound, Scent, Taste, Touch, Dharmas; No Realm of Seeing, and So On to No Realm of Consciousness

Well I've got eyes and ears, a nose and tongue—a body and mind too! And forms, sounds, smells, tastes, touch and thoughts *do* exist! Beneath a clear autumn sky stretch endless wastes where no one goes. A horseman comes riding from the west? Who is he!

> When the six senses stir even slightly, the six dusts arise.
> When the mind root is quiet, the six dusts rest as well.
> The roots, dusts, and consciousnesses, eighteen realms—
> Foam bubbles forming on the waves of a shoreless sea.

. . . .

Beneath a clear autumn sky...Who is he? Hakuin uses these lines by the eighth-century Chinese poet Wang Ch'ang-ling to express the realm of absolute emptiness and the marvelous working of enlightenment that emerges from within it. He calls on students to affirm the sutra's negations for themselves. "Unless you have already grasped this, then whether you say it exists or doesn't is childish. Why is this verse used here? It has poisonous thorns and brambles that rise up into the very skies. But until you have heard the sound of one hand and made your way through their virulent poison, it is all completely useless" (annotation).

The six senses or roots (eyes, ears, nose, tongue, sense of touch, and faculty of mind), interact with the *six dusts* (shape and color, sound, odor, taste, touch, and mental objects or dharmas) producing the *six consciousnesses* (sight, hearing, smell, taste, touch, and mind), thus manifesting the external world to us. The first five roots and consciousnesses function in conjunction with the sixth, mind or faculty of mind, which is their source. When the mind root remains quiet and unattached, the six dusts do not arise.

No Ignorance, No End of Ignorance and So On Until No Old Age And Death, and No Ending of Old Age and Death

Bright pearls scattered inside a silken purple curtain. Pearls stuffed inside a beggar's filthy old bag—it takes a wise man to know *those* are jewels. The water a cow drinks turns to cream; the water a snake drinks turns to poison. The sages' twelve-storied mansions are perpetually wrapped in five-colored clouds beyond man's reach.

> Twelve causes are created, twelve causes extinguished,
> We call creators ordinary men and extinguishers sages.
> This is the universe as it is seen by a Solitary Buddha,
> The dusts in his eyes are spinning about in Emptiness.
> Who is it that can really see the dust flying in his eyes?
> O cherished Dharma Wheel, great, perfect, and sudden!
> Enter its radiance, grasp it and then make it your own,
> Free yourself from that mange-ridden wild fox carcass.

. . . .

Here the sutra text gives an abbreviated list of the twelve links in the chain of causation: ignorance, contact, consciousness, names and forms, sense organs, touch, feeling, desire, clinging, becoming, birth, old age and death. Ignorance (literally, "no light"), the first of these, is the cause of all the rest; each in turn causes and affects the other in an endless and unbroken chain. The chain of causation is associated with the Solitary Buddha, who gains enlightenment by contemplating it and going on to exhaust ignorance and the other links in the chain. It is also the fundamental Buddhist conception of human existence, based on a relation of causal origination and karmic transmigration. In the Mahayana tradition, when "no light" is replaced by "light," or wisdom, all the links of the chain become, as such, functions of wisdom.

Bright pearls...curtain. The pearls are a metaphor for the mind manifested in total perfection. Unable to see clearly the shining pearls (symbols of the original self) scattered out inside a silk curtain, an ignorant person can only wonder what they are; the enlightened know they are a treasure. "Ignorance is in and of itself a beautiful and splendid thing. To someone who truly understands, it is the precious treasure of the Bodhisattva's myriad virtues" (annotation).

The sages' twelve-storied mansions...are beyond man's reach. The five-colored clouds are the five *skandhas* or components that make up the material and mental aspects of the self. *Twelve-storied mansions* indicate the twelve-linked chain of causation within the self, seen and experienced by the enlightened as an abode of tranquility and bliss.

The dusts in his eyes are spinning about in Emptiness. The causes and effects in the twelve-linked chain are like flecks in the eye. Though the enlightenment of the Pratyeka-buddha allows him to realize tranquility and the emptiness and formlessness of all things, to the Mahayana Bodhisattva these too are no more than particles of dust floating in the eye.

Free yourself from…carcass. Allusion to a remark attributed to the Buddha that Hakuin frequently cites: "I'd rather you be transformed into the mangy old carcass of a wild fox than for you ever to accept the one-sided truths of the Shravaka and Solitary Buddha."

No Pain, Karma, Extinction, Way

Gems shining in the dawn light beyond the bamboo blind. The blockhead goes at them with an upraised sword. The salt in the seawater. The size in the paint. Egrets settling in a field—a thousand flakes of snow. Yellow warblers alighting on a tree—branches bursting into bloom.

> Four burning bullets, red-hot to the core, put on
> Straw sandals at midnight, soar beyond the clouds.
> The Four Truths (pain, karma, extinction, Way) aren't
> At the end or the beginning, aren't perfect or sudden.
> Kaundinya, Bhadrika, and Kulika, and the others too,
> Had their face gates burnt off before they even knew it.
> The Golden Sage wasn't netting shrimp in the Deer Park,
> He was secretly anticipating their Mahayana roots.

. . . .

Pain, karma, extinction, Way. The Four Noble Truths the Buddha used to explain the causes of suffering and path of deliverance.

Gems shining…bamboo blind. The gems are the Four Noble Truths. Not knowing the priceless worth of the Four Truths, ignorant people and those of partial attainment such as Shravakas and Solitary Buddhas regard them as undesirable and attempt to eliminate them.

Egrets settling…bursting into bloom. "Here is a realm where differences are so slight as to be indistinguishable" (annotation).

At the end or the beginning…perfect or sudden. The Buddha taught the Four Truths to followers of the Lesser Vehicle. They are not found among the Mahayana sutras, which are classified into these four types according to the periods in which the Buddha preached them.

Kaundinya, Bhadrika, Kulika. Three of five ascetics who heard the Buddha's first sermon in which he expounded the Four Noble Truths. They became his followers and later achieved the stage of Arhat.

Golden Sage is the Buddha; *shrimp* are the Arhats who were present in the Deer Park when the Buddha first preached his Dharma. Although they were apparently the object of the Buddha's teaching, the enlightened eye of the Bodhisattva sees that he was preaching the Mahayana Dharma all along. Shibayama Zenkei comments that everything depends on the person using the net. If he has great skill, he will come up not with shrimp but with people of great enlightenment.

No Wisdom, No Attaining

Setting up house in the grave again! So many misunderstand these words! A dead man peering bug-eyed from a coffin. Shout yourself hoarse at Prince Chang on the paper, you won't get a peep out of him!

> A black fire, burning with a dark gemlike brilliance,
> Vast heaven and earth drained of their native colors.
> Mountains and rivers don't appear in the mirror of mind,
> A hundred million worlds are agonizing, all for nothing.

. . . .

A dead man...coffin. A state between life and death in which one remains attached to empty emptiness, unable to deepen one's own attainment or to work for others' salvation. "Misunderstand these words and you're a dead man" (annotation).

Shout yourself hoarse at Prince Chang. Allusion to a story that is referred to in the preface of the *Blue Cliff Record*. A prince told his subjects that he would continue to protect them even after his death. All they had to do if they were ever in peril was to go before his portrait and invoke his name. He would come to their aid. When an enemy army threatened the country, people did as he had instructed, but to no avail. The county soon fell to the invaders.

"If you think this is satori, you will be like Prince Chang on the paper, of no use whatever" (annotation). "You must grasp it yourself" (Shibayama Zenkei).

A black fire...gemlike brilliance. A black fire, being virtually indiscernible, comes upon you unawares, destroying you and everything else in its path. (See "Black Fire," Book Four, #64.)

As He Has Nothing to Attain, He Is a Bodhisattva

Put that down! The thief is pleading innocence with the stolen goods in his hands. Responding freely to sentient beings according to circumstances wherever he may be, but never leaving the Bodhisattva seat. Unless you are clear about three and eight and nine, you'll have a lot to think about as you confront the world.

> Bodhisattva, Enlightened Person, Great Being,
> In Chinese, he's a "sentient being of great heart."
> Entering the three ways, he takes on our suffering,
> Unbidden, he appears joyfully throughout the world.
> Vowing not to accept the fruits of partial enlightenment,
> He deepens his attainment while working to save others.
> Even should the vastness of empty space be exhausted,
> His vow to save all sentient beings will never end.

. . . .

The thief is pleading innocence...his hands. Hakuin says to let go of non-attainment too.

Unless you are clear about three and eight and nine...world. One of many glosses on this phrase explains that three, eight, and nine add up to twenty, and that a Chinese character for the number twenty is sometimes used in place of the character *nien* (Japanese *nen*), thought or thinking.

The three ways. The realms of hell, hungry ghosts, and animals.

Even should...never end. These words, often quoted by Hakuin and others, appear originally in a vow composed by Zen master P'a-shan jan (*Admonitions for Buddhists*).

Because He Depends upon the Wisdom *Paramita*

What a choke-pear! He's gagging on it! If you see anything at all to depend on, spit it out at once! I can bear the northern wastes of Yu-chou, but the mildness of Chiang-nan is sheer agony.

> Tell us you found greed and anger among Arhats but
> Don't babble about a Bodhisattva depending on wisdom.
> If you catch sight of one depending on anything at all,
> He's not really unhindered, he's shackled up in chains.
> Bodhisattva and Wisdom are essentially not different,
> Pearls rolling on a tray; sudden, ready, uninhibited.
> He's neither worldly nor saintly, neither stupid nor wise.
> A crying shame, when you draw a snake, to paint on legs.

. . . .

I can bear the northern...sheer agony. Wisdom and Bodhisattva are one and the same. The first phrase refers to the previous: "As he has nothing to attain, he is a Bodhisattva," the second part to "Because he depends upon the wisdom *paramita*."

A crying shame...to paint on legs. The "legs" are dependence upon wisdom.

HIS MIND IS UNHINDERED; BEING UNHINDERED, HE KNOWS NO FEAR, AND IS FAR BEYOND ALL TOPSY TURVY THOUGHT

Nothing out of the ordinary there. Supernatural powers and marvelous activity—drawing water and carrying firewood. Raising my head, I see the sun setting over my old home in the west.

> It isn't mind or nature; it isn't Nirvana either.
> It's not the Buddha, the patriarchs, or Wisdom.
> The ten worlds are a red-hot iron mallet head
> That shatters empty space into eternal serenity.
> Just parting his lips, great lion roars come forth,
> Scaring the life from foxes, hares, and badgers.
> Wizard-like, taking the form of what's before him,
> Changing at will in response to situations at hand.
> When he hears Mother Li's left shoulder is ailing,
> He burns some moxa on Granny Chang's right leg.
> Delusive thoughts, fears, sorrows and all the rest,
> Like a drop of water flung into a bottomless gorge.
> When dispatched to Ch'i, Ch'ih was wrapped in fine furs,
> When Li succumbed, his coffin was plain and unsheathed.
> The priest in the hermitage is roused from his midday nap,
> Village boys have climbed the hedge and are stealing bamboo
>   shoots.

. . . .

Drawing water...firewood. Well-known words from a verse by Layman P'ang.

Raising my head...in the west. "When you reach your goal and look around, you find that things are no different from before" (annotation).

Each of the verse's four-line stanzas is keyed to one of the four clauses in the sutra passage.

The ten worlds. The Dharma universe in its entirety, including the six realms of illusion (hell, hungry ghosts, animals, fighting demons, human beings, and devas) and four realms of enlightenment (Shravaka, Solitary Buddha, Bodhisattva, and Buddha).

When he hears Mother Li's left shoulder is ailing. An old Taoist story tells of Mother Li, a rich woman with a painful growth on her left shoulder, being taken by Granny Chang to a Taoist healer. Knowing his patient disliked moxa-cautery, the healer cured her by burning moxa on Granny Chang's right leg.

When dispatched to Ch'i…plain and unsheathed. These two stories from the Confucian *Analects* are no doubt meant to exemplify the resourcefulness of superior adepts, who are able to adapt their means and methods at will. "These are the great dharani of Sendai's [Hakuin's] cave" (annotation).

When Confucius's disciple Ch'ih was dispatched on a mission, Master Jan requested an allowance of grain to support Ch'ih's mother. Confucius told him to give her a certain amount, but Jan actually gave her much more. When Confucius learned of it, he said, "When Ch'ih left on his mission, he drove sleek horses and was wrapped in fine furs. There is a saying, 'A Superior Man helps out the needy; he does not make the rich richer still.'"

After Yen Hui died, his father begged Confucius for his carriage so he could sell it to buy an outer casing for his son's coffin. Confucius refused, telling him that when his own son Li died, his coffin had no outer casing, and he had not given up his carriage to buy one for him because it was not proper that he walk on foot.

And Reaches Final Nirvana

This is the hole pilgrims all fall into. They fill it up year after year. He's gone off again to flit with the ghosts. It's worse than stinking socks! The upright men of our tribe are not like this. With us, the father conceals for the sake of the son, the son for the sake of the father.

> The mind of birth-and-death of all beings
> Is in and of itself the Buddhas' great Nirvana.
> A wooden hen warms an egg perching on a coffin.
> A clay mare sniffs the breeze and returns to the barn.

. . . .

The upright men of our tribe are not like this. Confucius, being told of a man in a neighboring country called Upright K'ung because he bore witness against his father when the latter made off with a sheep, said, "In my country, uprightness is somewhat different. The father shields the son, the son shields the father." Teaching students about "reaching final Nirvana" can only harm them.

BECAUSE ALL BUDDHAS OF PAST, PRESENT, AND FUTURE DEPEND UPON THE WISDOM *PARAMITA*

Holding a good person down only cheapens him. The bare skin and bones are fine as they are. They have a natural elegance and grace. There's no need to lard them with powder and rouge. There are no cold spots in a seething cauldron.

> Wisdom brings forth the Buddhas of the three worlds;
> The Buddhas of the three worlds all enact this wisdom.
> Inexhaustible reciprocity of host and guest—*Onsoro!*
> Cranes screech in an old nest banged about by the wind.

. . . .

"As a Buddha's wisdom is all-encompassing, there should be nothing left over for him to depend upon" (annotation).

Inexhaustible reciprocity of host and guest. Allusion to the interrelation that exists between all Buddhas and the wisdom *paramita*. Shibayama suggests the comparison of Indra's Net, the infinite variety of interrelation and inclusiveness of all things in the universe: to the Buddha's enlightened eye, each of those things is a manifestation of ultimate truth.

Onsoro. A dharani, or magic spell, said to contain mystic power. Here it may be seen as a spontaneous affirmation of the ultimately inexpressible truth of Wisdom. One commentator describes it as "the voice of the Buddhas of past, present, and future preaching and enacting wisdom." "Wisdom and Buddhas exist in an inexhaustible relation, with Buddhas the body and Wisdom the function, or with Wisdom the body and Buddhas the function" (annotation).

Cranes screech...in the wind. "Can this mean *Onsorosoro*? What ever *does* it mean?" (annotation).

They Attain The Highest Enlightenment

Stop hammering spikes into empty space! A steer may give birth to a calf, but no Buddha was ever enlightened by relying on Wisdom. Why? Because from the first *prajna* and enlightenment are not two. Besides, if a Buddha has anything at all left to attain, he is no Buddha. This is like a blazing conflagration. If Buddhas and patriarchs get too close, they get burned to death like everyone else.

> Otters will be catching fish in trees long before
> Buddhas are enlightened by relying on something.
> And declaring a Buddha has something to attain!
> Next he'll blither about an Arhat's marital bliss.

. . . .

Next he'll blither about an Arhat's marital bliss. Arhats are celibate.

Know Therefore that the Wisdom *Paramita* Is the Great Mantra

Hauling water to sell beside a river. Don't drag that beat-up old lacquer bowl out here! Transcribe a word three times and a crow becomes a how, and then ends up a horse. He's trying to palm off shoddy goods on us again, like some shady little shopkeeper. When walking at night, don't tread on anything white—if it's not water, it's usually a stone.

> Cherish the great mantra of your own self-nature,
> It turns a red-hot iron ball to finest, sweetest nectar.
> Heaven, hell, and the world right here on earth—
> A snowflake disappearing into a glowing furnace.

. . . .

Don't drag that beat-up old lacquer bowl out here! At mountain shrines in China, lacquer bowls that had been used for Taoist rites were cast into a rushing torrent. They were badly damaged by the time they reached the village in the valley below, and utterly useless to the villagers.

Transcribe a word three times... The characters for "crow," "how," and "horse" are similar in form. When texts were copied and recopied by hand, scribes often mistook one character for another, and the mistake would sometimes change the original meaning completely. After all his explanations of wisdom, Kanjizai ends up with something altogether different from what he intended. He would be better off keeping his mouth shut.

When walking at night, don't tread on anything white. In the pitch blackness of night (Emptiness), you are moving in a realm where "not one thing exists." Anything you might see is sure to be an illusion. Ignore it, it can only harm you.

Cherish the great mantra of your own self-nature. When you grasp the wisdom within you through the experience known as *kenshō* ("seeing into your own nature"), all the entangling passions and the suffering they cause transform into perfect freedom and bliss.

THE GREAT AND GLORIOUS MANTRA

Don't give us "great and glorious" mantras! Break that rough-hewn mountain staff and the great earth's Indigenous Black stretches out in all directions. Heaven and earth lose all their shapes and colors. Sun and moon swallow up their light. Black ink pouring into a black lacquer tub.

> Great, glorious mantra of our primal being in absolute
> perfection
> Casts a calm radiance over the world's hills and streams.
> All the vast ocean of karmic hindrance from infinite ages past—
> Like a bubble rising on the waves, like a spark before the eyes.

. . . .

Rough-hewn mountain staff. A staff that has been broken off a mountain tree and used just as it is. A metaphor for the self in its natural state; the Buddha-nature. Hakuin tells students to forget about words such as "great and glorious mantra." Concentrate on the urgent business of realizing the great and glorious mantra (wisdom) in themselves. If they do, everything in the universe, self included, will be destroyed, and they will find themselves in the total blackness of the undifferentiated realm of enlightenment—where not one thing exists.

All the vast ocean...past. "If the great and glorious mantra is manifested in the dawn of *kenshō*, then you will see that the vast ocean of your karmic hindrances from the beginningless beginning are bubbles rising on the waves, sparks appearing before your eyes...and they will disappear without a trace" (annotation).

THE HIGHEST MANTRA

What about down around your feet? Bring me the lowest mantra! Autumn leaves falling amid pattering drops of rain evoke deep feelings, but how can it compare to the intimate richness of sunset clouds glowing over fields of yellowing grain?

> The Finest, the Noblest, the First,
> Enthralling even Shaka and Maitreya,
> Though each person has it at birth,
> Each must die and then be reborn.

. . . .

What about down…feet? "If coming to the highest mantra you look up, there's no way you can avoid stepping in tengu shit" (annotation). Tengu are winged, long-nosed demons that inhabit the mountains and forests. "Becoming a tengu" has connotations of overweening self-assurance and arrogance.

Autumn leaves falling…yellowing grain. "This is old Hakuin's highest mantra" (annotation). One modern commentator has suggested that the melancholy autumn scene depicted in the first line evokes the impermanence of life, while the second line evokes the joy and splendor of life's fullness, which can be known only by proceeding through impermanence and death into the enlightened realm of ultimate Wisdom, the highest mantra. This theme is repeated in the final line of Hakuin's verse, "Each must die and then be reborn." In Zen writings the word "intimate" usually connotes the idea of oneness rather than closeness. See p. 34 for a different translation of the lines.

THE SUPREME MANTRA

Gabble gabble! His talking makes two stakes appear. What became of the Single Stake? Where is it? Who said, "There is nothing to equal it anywhere, above or below or in the four quarters"? He's broken it all up. Ripped it into tiny bits. Pieces are strewn all over. Te-yun, you blunt old gimlet, how many times are you going descend from the summit of Wonder Peak and get a foolish old sage to help you fill up the well with snow?

> Last winter the plum was bitter cold.
> A dash of rain—a burst of bloom!
> Its shadows move in the pale moonlight,

Its subtle scent wafts in the spring breeze.
Yesterday you were a snow-covered tree,
Today your boughs are starred with blossoms!
What cold and privation have you weathered,
Venerable queen of the flower realm!

. . . .

His talking makes two stakes appear. "What is prior to the uttering of a single word—that is splendid. When you start talking about things like Emptiness and Mu, you make two stakes appear" (annotation).

Te-yun...well with snow. An allusion to lines from Hsueh-tou's *Ancestral Heroes Collection* (see p. 113): "How many times has the idle old gimlet Te-yun / Made his way down from his Marvelous Peak! / He hires other foolish wise men and together / They keep filling the well with snow."

Hakuin chides Kanjizai for attempting to reduce the wisdom *paramita* to the level of ordinary discrimination. As Hakuin's verse implies, it is only after years of arduous training that it can be grasped and its marvelous results enjoyed.

WHICH IS CAPABLE OF REMOVING ALL SUFFERING

Picking a lily bulb apart to find a core. Shaving a square bamboo staff to make it round. Using a Persian carpet for a drumhead. Nine times nine is now and always eighty-one. Nineteen and twenty-nine meet, but neither offers its hand.

When you pass the test of Mind and Emptiness,
Your *skandhas* and elements turn to instant ash,
Heavens and hells are broken-down old furniture,
Buddha-worlds and demon-realms blasted to bits.
A yellow bird chortles ecstatic strains of "White Snow."
A black turtle clambers up a lighthouse, sword in belt.
If anyone has a mind to participate in their samadhi,
They must once shed rivers of white-beaded sweat.

. . . .

A lily bulb has no real center; it is the cloves that make it up.

Shaving a square bamboo...a drumhead. "Taking things of great value and turning them into objects of little consequence" (annotation). Square bamboo is extremely difficult to grow; to shave it round would be to ruin it.

Kanjizai speaks of attaining Nirvana by removing suffering. Attempting to do that, Hakuin says, would be to throw out the baby with the bathwater, since suffering and Nirvana are inseparable.

A yellow bird...sword in belt. "This is the vital, life-giving samadhi of all the Buddhas of the three worlds" (annotation).

"White Snow." A tune with an unsurpassed melody but which is exceedingly difficult to perform.

It Is True, It Is Not False

A falsehood! He's lying through his teeth! The arrow has already flown the China coast. You rub elbows with him all day long. How do you resemble him?

> Master Yen of Ch'i bumped off three valiant men.
> Szechuan Chiang subdued a brace of bold generals.
> A cockcrow let a man give fierce tigers the slip.
> A sheep's head was dangled to peddle dog flesh.
> A man pointed to a deer to see who'd submit.
> A stepmother's bee dashed a father's fond hopes.
> T'ao Chu led the beauty of Yueh to her death.
> Chi-hsin surrendered himself to the ruler of Ch'u.
> A man slept under a bridge, supping on charcoal;
> A girl wept at a well for a clasp she's thrown in.
> A king's corpse got away in a load of ripe fish.
> A father's chipped tooth gnawed off a son's ear.
> Burning by day a log road along the river cliffs,
> Crossing at nightfall by the Ch'eng-ts'ang ford
> When your gaze penetrates to the center of these
> A yard of cold steel glints like frost in its sheath.

. . . .

Each of the first fourteen lines of the verse alludes to an episode from Chinese legend or history in which falsehood or deception, prompted in most cases by loyalty and devotion, plays a central role. Presumably, Hakuin uses them to allude to the often baffling and outrageous methods Zen teachers employ in pushing students across the threshold into enlightenment.

Master Yen was minister of the state of Ch'i. He contrived a plan to dispose of three faithful retainers whose obstinacy and self-righteousness were the cause of constant unrest. Calling them together, he presented them with two peaches, but they had difficulty accepting them, since taking one would mean denying it to another. They deferred back and forth until finally, to solve the dilemma, one of them committed suicide. The others, not to be outdone, killed themselves as well.

Led by generals Chung-hui and Teng-ai, the armies of Wei launched a surprise attack on the kingdom of Shu (Szechuan) and, despite the valiant efforts of wily General Chiang, subdued the Shu forces. The lord of Shu surrendered, and Chiang was captured as well. Recognizing Chiang's ability, Chung-hui made him a counselor. When Teng-ai was ennobled for his service, Chiang, sensing Chung-hui's deep resentment, persuaded him to slander his rival to the lord of Wei. The lord of Wei believed the charges and had Teng-ai imprisoned. Learning that Chung-hui aspired to become ruler of Shu, Chiang incited him to insurrection. During the ensuing battles between the lord of Wei and the rebel forces, Chiang killed Teng-ai in his prison cell, and later both he and Chung-hui perished in the losing rebel cause. Though unable to defeat Wei as commander of the Shu forces, Chiang thus brought about the deaths of its two valiant generals.

Because of its aggressive policies, Ch'in's neighbors feared it as "a land of fierce tigers." The Ch'in emperor, after inviting the wise and courageous Meng Ch'ang-chun to serve at his court, decided he could not trust him, and would have had him executed had not Meng bribed the king's favorite to intercede on his behalf, promising her a precious robe of white fox. Meng had presented the robe to the emperor on his arrival at court and to give it to the lady he was now obliged to steal it back. Allowed to leave, Meng set out immediately before the theft could be discovered. He reached the border in the middle of the night with the king's men not far behind. The barrier would not open until first cockcrow, so one of Meng's followers who was an expert at imitating birdcalls made a sound like a crowing cock. The barrier was raised and Meng escaped to safety.

The fifth line refers to the powerful chief eunuch Chao-kao. Aware of the ill will some of his officials bore him, Chao determined to test their loyalty. He presented a deer to the king and told him it was a horse. The king just laughed, but Chao kept insisting it was a horse and asked the officials present their opinions. Some agreed it was a horse, some remained silent, and a few said it was a deer. Chao promoted those who agreed with him and punished the others.

A stepmother wanted her husband's favorite son out of the way. She caught a large bee, pulled out its stinger, and placed the bee on the lapel of her robe, aware that her husband was watching from a distance. Seeing the bee, the son tried to brush it away. His father, thinking he was making improper advances toward his stepmother, reprimanded him angrily. The son's protestations of innocence were to no avail, and he was at last driven to suicide.

T'ao Chu (Chu of T'ao) was a sobriquet used by the famous minister Fan-li. When Yueh was defeated by the lord of Wu, the Yueh forces were captured and put to death. The lord of Yueh begged for clemency, and despite warnings from advisers that he might later prove dangerous, the lord of Wu spared his life. The lord of Yueh was finally able to convince the lord of Wu of his fealty and was allowed to return to his own country, where he faithfully served the Wu interests and sent frequent offerings of tribute. The lord of Wu, his mind now at rest, gave himself up to a life of decadence, and he asked Yueh to send him fifty beautiful maidens for his seraglio. Among them was Hsi-shih, the lady of Yueh, one of the celebrated beauties of Chinese history. The lord of Wu spent all his time with her, neglecting the government, which fell into turmoil. At this point the faithful retainer T'ao Chu convinced the lord of Yueh that the time was ripe to avenge the earlier defeat. The Yueh forces marched and defeated Wu handily. The lord of Yueh took Hsi-shih as his concubine, disregarding the examples T'ao Chu recited to him of beautiful women who had been the ruin of a country. On their way back to Yueh, at a spot called Stone Lake, Tao Chu put Hsi-shih in a boat, took her to the middle of the lake, and explained that he would have to kill her for the sake of the country. Before he could, however, she flung herself into the water and drowned.

When the first Han emperor was besieged by the forces of Ch'u and had no hope of escape, a captain in his army named Chi-hsin told the king of Ch'u that his lord had decided to surrender and would proceed to the Ch'u headquarters through the eastern gates of the city. The soldiers of Ch'u all gathered at the gates to catch sight of the emperor, but Chi-hsin took his master's place in a covered palanquin, allowing him to escape from the western gates. When the Ch'u king discovered the ruse, he had Chi-hsin roasted on a burning pyre.

The man who slept under a bridge was Yu-jang. He served as a vassal of Fan Chung-hang, but he was not highly esteemed by his master, so when Fan was overthrown by Chih-po, Yu-jang offered Chih-po his services. Chih-po took a liking to him and Yu-jang became a trusted retainer. When Chih-po was killed by Hsiang-tzu, ruler of Chao, Yu-jang tried again and again, without success, to avenge his death. Finally, swallowing charcoal and daubing his body with lacquer, he disguised himself as a leper and took up residence with other outcasts under a bridge, awaiting the day when Hsiang-tzu would pass over it. When Hsiang-tzu finally did come, however, his horse sensed Yu-jang's presence as it approached the bridge and refused to cross. Yu, discovered lying in wait, was apprehended. Hsiang-tzu asked him why, having served the murderer of his first master, he was now so strongly bent on revenge. Yu-jang replied that while his first master had treated him like an ordinary man, Chih-po had always treated him with honor, and he wanted to requite him in kind. He begged Hsiang-tzu for a piece of his clothing so that he could fulfill his vow before he was executed. Upon being given Hsiang-tzu's coat, Yu-jang thrust into it three times with his sword, saying, "I can report this to Chih-po when I meet him in the next world." He then fell on his sword and died.

The notorious thief Houpai saw a young girl weeping beside a well as he was making off with an armful of valuables, and stopped to ask what was wrong. She told him she had dropped a precious hair clasp into the well and was certain to be punished for losing it when she returned home. Feeling sorry for her, Houpai stripped off his clothes and climbed down to retrieve the clasp. But while Houpai was down the well, the girl, who was really Houhei, a famous thief in her own right, made off with the booty and Houpai's clothes as well.

Chao-kao, the tyrannical minister who appeared before in the story about the horse and the deer, was accompanying the king of Ch'in on a hunting excursion far from the capital when the king suddenly died. Wanting to control the selection of the king's successor, Chao-kao kept the death a secret and took the king's body back to the capital in the royal palanquin as if he were alive. Afraid that the smell of the decaying corpse would be noticed on the long journey, he disguised it by having a large quantity of fermented fish placed over the body. His strategy worked, and the new king appointed him chief minister.

An eldest son in the west of China struck his father and broke two of his teeth. The father, incensed at this unfilial act, decided to prosecute him. If convicted, the penalty was death. The son sought the advice of a clever acquaintance who, after a moment's thought, suddenly bit the son on the ear. He told him that when he was called before the magistrate and asked to explain his action, he should say his father had broken his teeth when he bit his ear in a fit of rage. Using this ploy, the son managed to escape the executioner's block, but on his way home he was struck dead by a bolt of lightning.

Burning by day....Ch'eng-ts'ang ford. This refers to an intrigue at the beginning of the Han dynasty. After leading a revolt against the lord of Ch'in,

Hsiang-yu emerged as the most powerful force in the country. He proclaimed himself king of Western Ch'u and appointed Liu-pang governor of the Han. Aware that Liu-pang had great ambitions of his own, and feeling uneasy having him near, Hsiang-yu sent him to the land of Shu in the remote western regions and kept his troops battle ready just in case. Chang-liang, a retainer of Hsiang-yu who was secretly working for Liu-pang, assured Hsiang-yu that Liu-pang no long presented a threat. He advised him to make doubly sure by having the plank road over which Liu-pang would have to pass were he to attack burned and rendered impassable. Now that his rival was effectively bottled up within the mountainous borders of Shu, and with Hsiang-yu finally feeling secure, Chang-liang sent word to Liu-pang that the time for attack had come. Using a secret road that crossed the river at a place called Ch'en-ts'ang, Liu-pang surprised and destroyed Hsiang-yu's armies and went on to establish the Han empire.

THEREFORE I PREACH THE *PRAJNA PARAMITA* MANTRA

Well what have you been doing up till now? It's like a teetotaler trying to force wine down your throat. You don't get the real taste by swilling it cup after cup. Unable to return for ten full years, you forget the Way you came.

> He preached it before, and now he trots it out again!
> Snowdrifts accumulating over accumulated snowdrifts.
> There isn't a single place you can hide or escape it,
> So who's the wine for? We're all drunk to the gills!

. . . .

Unable to return for ten full years, you forget the way you came. A line from the poems of Han-shan (Cold Mountain). With years of practice, enlightenment deepens until it is free of any trace or odor of enlightenment. "Ten years stands for ten worlds or realms of living beings; the universe. To detach oneself from these realms is to become a Buddha and be no longer affected by the karmic influences of the ten worlds. This is the real meaning of the wisdom *paramita*" (annotation).

Preach The Mantra That Goes

He's at it again! Over and over! What about woodcutters' songs? Fishermen's chanteys? Where do they come in? What about warbling thrushes and twittering swallows? When you enter the waves, don't start culling bubbles from the surf!

These weed-choked fields with seven-word furrows,
Great castles of verbiage wrought in five-word lines,
Were not written for the eyes of old veteran priests,
I wrote them for you monks, cold and hungry in your huts.
For if you can't find the Way and transform your self,
You stay trapped, entangled down a bottomless pit.
And don't try to tell me that my poems are too hard,
Face it, the problem is your own eyeless state.
When you come on a word you don't understand,
Quick, bite it at once. Chew it down to the pith!
Once soaked to the bone in a cold sweat of death,
All the koans Zen has are yanked up a root and stem.
With toil and trouble, I too once glimpsed the Edge,
I smashed the scale that moves with a blind arm.
Once that tool of unknowing is shattered for good,
You fill with the fierceness and courage of lions.
Zen is blessed with a power to bring this about,
Why not use it, bore through to Perfect Integrity?
Today people turn away from Zen as if it were dirt,
Who will then carry on the life-thread of Wisdom?
I'm not just an old man with an itch to write verse,
I want to rouse stalwart seekers wherever they are.
The superior know at a glance where the arrow flies,
Others will just prattle about the rhythm and rhyme.
Ssu-ma Kuang of the Sung was a prince among men,
What a shame eyes of such worth remained unopened!
When he came upon difficult, "hard-to-pass" koans,
He said they were riddles made to vex young monks.
For gravest crimes man must always be repentant,
Surely slander of the Dharma is no minor offense!
Crowds of such miscreants are at large in the world,

The Zen landscape is barren almost beyond belief.
If the mind of the Buddha-patriarchs is in your grasp,
How could you possibly remain blind to their words?
To determine how authentic your own attainment is,
The words of the patriarchs serve as bright mirrors.
Today Zen is practiced in a lax, half-assed fashion,
Men following others' words, fancies of their own.
If hearsay and book learning can satisfy your needs,
The patriarchal gardens are still a million miles off.
So I beseech you, great men, forget your own welfare,
Make Zen's five-petaled flower blossom once more!

. . . .

What about woodcutters' songs? Fishermen's chanteys? To the enlightened eye, all things are preaching the wonderful wisdom mantra. In creating distinctions Kanjizai also creates the causes of delusion.

The scale that weighs with a blind arm. A scale with no markings or calibrations on the balance arm. A symbol for the mind or self, the fundamental source of ignorance, which is incapable of accurate measurement, yet which the unenlightened make the basis of their discriminations. Here it may refer to the mind that has broken through into the undifferentiated realm of emptiness but that now must also transcend that realm as well.

Ssu-ma of the Sung was a true prince among men. The famous eleventh-century Confucian scholar Ssu-ma Kuang was not actually anti-Buddhist. Hakuin criticizes him for misleading students by misunderstanding or misrepresenting the Zen teaching in his writings.

The five-petaled Zen flower. A reference to the five schools that appeared during Zen's golden age in the T'ang dynasty.

GATE GATE PARAGATE PARASAMGATE BODHI SVAHA

Serving a Superior Man is easy; pleasing him an impossible task. Sunset clouds sail together with a lone wild duck; the autumn waters are a single color with the clear autumn sky. Rainsqualls sweep from the hamlet in the south to the hamlet in the north. A young wife carries a box lunch to her mother-in-law in the fields. A grandchild is fed with morsels from grandfather's mouth.

It is now midwinter, the first year of Enkyō.
My students got together and had these words

Carved on wood (each character cost ten *mon*,
more than two thousand in all!), from a desire
To preserve all these dream-babblings of mine.
I have added on this final verse for them,
As a tribute of thanks for their kindness.

The verses are finished. I clasp my hands and pray:
"Empty space may cease but my vow will never end.
Any merit my praising of wisdom brings, I transfer
To others, that they may gain the realm of suchness.
Trusting myself to the Buddhas of the three worlds,
To Zen patriarchs and all sages in the ten directions,
To every deva, naga, and demon guarding the Law,
And all the gods in this Land of the Mulberry Tree,
I pray that all the brethren that reside with me here
Will with steadfast resolve and diamond-hard minds,
Move with all dispatch to break through the Barrier,
And keeping the precepts gem ever perfectly bright
In mind, and sweeping clear all demons of delusion,
Benefit without rest the vast suffering multitudes."

. . . .

The sutra ends with this mantra or mystic spell, usually rendered, "O Wisdom, gone, gone, gone to the other shore, landed at the other shore!" D. T. Suzuki has described it as the spontaneous affirmation of enlightenment emerging from Kanjizai's inner being. The seventeenth-century Sōtō teacher Tenkei Denson says, "any attempt to apply reason or logic here only reduces the mantra to a dead and lifeless utterance."

Serving a Superior Man is easy. To please him, an impossible task. Hakuin applies this saying from the Confucian *Analects* to the fully achieved Bodhisattva or Zen teacher. Because he treats people with compassion according to their capacities, he is easy to serve, but because he is also completely impartial, it is impossible to please him unless you are in accord with the Way.

Sunset clouds sail together with a lone wild duck; the autumn water is a single color with the clear autumn sky. Hakuin uses these lines by the T'ang poet Wang Po describing a landscape where distinctions are difficult to make out to express the essential oneness of identity and difference, which is also the relation of the final esoteric mantra to the exoteric portion in the rest of the sutra.

Rainsqualls sweep...morsels from grandfather's mouth. Hakuin uses these lines from a poem by the Sung poet and Zen layman Huang T'ing-chien to express the daily reality of the wisdom *paramita*'s marvelous working. "Not even a veteran monk can grasp this without passing through a thicket of briar. This old priest [Hakuin] suffered through thirty years of trials and tribulations to spit out these words. If someone wants to know what they mean, I haven't the slightest idea. It's for him to undertake great exertions and grasp them for himself" (annotation). Sugawara Jiho calls this "the farthest reaches of Zen attainment, Hakuin's own wisdom *paramita* mantra."

The first year of Enkyō. 1744. Hakuin was sixty years old.

The Land of the Mulberry Tree. A poetical name for Japan.

II. Miscellaneous Writings (*Zatsubun*)

:161. Reading *Jinja-kō Bengi* (*Resolving Doubts about a Study of Our Shintō Shrines*)

This long piece, dating from Hakuin's forty-eighth year, was provoked by the anti-Buddhist writings of the prominent Confucian scholar Hayashi Razan (1583–1657), in particular, Razan's Honchō Jinja-kō (A Study of Our Shintō Shrines), *published in six volumes between 1638 and 1645. As the above title indicates, Hakuin was not reading* A Study of Our Shintō Shrines *itself, but passages from that work which were included in* Jinja-kō Bengi, Resolving Doubts about Jinja-kō, *a work by the Shingon priest Jakuhon (1631–1701) of Mount Kōya published in 1686, which critiques Razan's work from a Buddhist perspective. Hakuin makes no more than passing reference to the* Bengi *or its author, whom he refers to here by the sobriquet Unseki-dō, devoting his response almost exclusively to Razan's animadversions against Buddhism.*

A trusted advisor to Tokugawa Ieyasu and one of the most influential scholars of the Tokugawa period, Razan, also known as Hayashi Dōshun, was founder of the important Hayashi clan of Confucian scholars that played a leading role in establishing Neo-Confucianism as the orthodox creed of Tokugawa governance. Consisting largely of a survey of Shintō shrines and legends, A Study of Our Shintō Shrines *may be seen as part Razan's overall program of curtailing Buddhist influence in the country. In doing this he used Shintō as an ally, much as his great Chinese mentor Chu Hsi had used Taoism in a campaign to suppress Buddhist influence in Sung China.*

Attacking such an important figure, especially with such intemperate language, might have landed Hakuin in hot water with government authorities. Several years earlier, government censors had already placed one of his books, Snake Strawberries, *on its list of proscribed works for violating the taboo of mentioning the name of Ieyasu, the first Tokugawa Shōgun, in print.*

It was no doubt out of such concerns that the well-known Confucian teacher Yanada Zeigan (1672–1757), after reading Poison Blossoms *in manuscript, recommended to Hakuin that he consider deleting the diatribe from his collection. This unsolicited advice drew a furious reaction from Hakuin, who immediately told his student Daishū, who was in charge of editing* Poison Blossoms, *that he was no longer interested in using the preface he had asked Zeigan to write for the collection, since it was now obvious that "Zeigan had no understanding of Zen" (see Introduction, p. 9). A series of letters Hakuin wrote Daishū at the time (see* Beating the Cloth Drum, *pp. 122–25) make clear his outrage at Zeigan's suggestion, but also reveal the steps he took after reflecting over the matter. These included hedging his bets—"just to be on the safe side"—by telling Daishū to move the piece to the end of collection, where it could be lopped off, should that become necessary, without disturbing the rest of the text. In the end, however, he decided to shift the piece from the main part of the text and insert it in the one-volume* Supplement. *The reason for this is unstated, but is no doubt related to the fact that the* Supplement *was funded, and published, separately from the rest of the collection.*

ONE AUTUMN NIGHT IN the eighteenth year of the Kyōhō era (1733), I had taken time off from my zazen and was having a good nap propped in my chair. I was awakened by Attendant Boku. He was holding a small book. "You have always told me that Hayashi Razan was an outstanding scholar and wise retainer, a man with a fine literary style who had revived Confucian learning in Japan," he said. "But I am not so sure about that. On my way here yesterday I stopped at Kōgen-ji. There was a book there he had written. I brought it back with me to disturb your slumber." I looked and saw that the title was *Jinja-kō Bengi*. It contained Hayashi Razan's *Jinja-kō* and comments *(Bengi)* added by Unseki-dō of Kii province.

I had long heard of Razan's illustrious reputation, and I was aware that he had written this work. After reading the first three or four pages, Razan's outstanding talent and Unseki's erudition both became clear to me. This promised to be a wonderful occasion for me, so I adjusted my robe, sat up straight, rubbed the sleep from my eyes, and began to read it out loud.

Both men advanced lofty arguments. It seemed as though I were sitting together with them and listening to them speak. After reading it through, however, I found myself both surprised and puzzled, saddened and fearful at the same time.

My notion that Hayashi was an outstanding Confucian scholar with a fine literary style was not without reason. Although insignificant in size, our country does not yield to any in her long line of emperors or great worth of her people, not to mention her wealth of Buddhist teachers. Tendai prelates of great virtue, eminent Shingon priests, profound teachers of the Pure Land and Zen traditions and of the Precepts school as well appear in our nation's history like the stars in the firmament, like the stones on a *go* board.

Why had such a large number of wise and virtuous people appeared? They were vastly superior to their counterparts in China. Was it not because our country is the pure and undefiled land of the *kami*? Was it not because it is a place where Buddhahood is perfectly realized? I had long wondered why such men had emerged only within the Buddhist tradition. Surely people of similar caliber must also exist among the Confucians. I had supposed Hayashi Razan to be one of their most outstanding teachers.

Tonight, as I read Razan's book, any reasons I had for praising him abruptly vanished. By the time I was finished, I was very unhappy with it indeed. How could I have imagined it would be so shameless and contemptible, so virulent? I was amazed. I only regretted that in the past I had so easily and mistakenly approved of this book without looking into the quality of its arguments or aptness of its methods. I had moreover made the same mistake that Hayashi did when, unable to plumb the secrets of Buddhism's sublime Way, he recklessly condemned it without deeply examining its teachings.

Long ago, outstanding men such as Confucius's disciples Yuan Hsien and Yan Hui cast aside all thought of fame or profit, left the dust of worldly life behind them, and happily spent their lives in broken-down shacks in the hinterlands in order to realize the Way of virtue. Today those who call themselves scholars read a couple of dozen books, listen to several months of lectures, and then suddenly, consumed by flames of jealousy and envy, take it into their heads that their most urgent business is to attack Buddhism. In them, the "correct mind and sincere purpose" that Confucians talk about plays second fiddle to enmity. Elderly scholars who preach the cardinal virtues of morality, charity, and justice are pressed by the exigencies of providing for wives and families to follow in the wake of power and influence. Essential notions such as Confucius's "the Great Way I teach is the same throughout," or Mencius's "vast and unyielding *ch'i* [that unites rightness and the Way]," end up being no more than artifacts lying forgotten on the back shelves. No wonder a person who has truly attained the Way has not appeared from among them. It is unreasonable to expect a hawk or kite to produce a cry like a phoenix, or to seek leopard spots on the back of a pig.

There is no way you can equate them with monks and nuns who turn from fame and wealth, cut all ties to the world, make their minds tranquil through meditation, drink from valley streams, and sleep in rude dwellings as they seek the marvelous and unsurpassed Way with rigorous practice and with singleminded devotion. Human beings are all born with a wonderfully clear, mirror-like wisdom, a gemlike mind that is perfectly empty. Whether it shines forth or becomes dark and murky depends solely on the diligence with which it is polished. Why is it that, instead of being ashamed that they lack the strength to muster the necessary resolve, they envy the success the Buddha Dharma enjoys and feel enmity towards those with lofty aspirations?

In the interest of wise governance, when rulers and sage ministers of the past learned of words or deeds they felt they could profit from, even if they came from women or young children, from cowherds or servants, woodcutters or fishermen, they would accept them and put them to use in the affairs of state. They only feared that they would hear of them too late, or that they would not profit from them enough. Not to mention the marvelous teachings left behind by Shakamuni, the compassionate father of the three worlds. How many kings, emperors, and lesser rulers as well have benefited from his teaching? How can anyone lightly dismiss that? [As Chu Hsi said,] "A superior man should seek to remain blameless while living among those who deserve blame." Why do these people do the opposite and try to find fault among those who are blameless?

Attempting to achieve dominance in the country by disparaging blameless people is not the conduct of the superior man. Not to mention that what they are attacking are the teachings of the World-Honored One, a sage of unsurpassed wisdom who is venerated in all countries throughout the world. With sheep-like discernment and fox-like cunning, they may recklessly disparage him, but they cannot succeed. It is like a shrimp or sardine envying the great ocean, a mayfly resenting the sky overhead. They are just wasting their effort.

Razan, you and your colleagues are quick to deny the fundamental Buddhist principle of karma in the three worlds, calling it a delusion having no basis in reality. Ah! Even if you denied it until the oceans dried up, you would be unable to do away with the principle of cause and effect. It is an inexorable natural law. That you are unable to grasp this can only mean that you have been bewitched by foxes. What did Buddhism ever do to you that would make you so resentful?

The patriarchs in all the Buddhist sects and temples have been possessed of talent rarely encountered in the world. Their mirror-like wisdom shines forth like the sun, their observance of the discipline has a gemlike purity that glows as chastely as the moon. The heavenly gods have protected them, the earth gods have treated them with reverence. The legacy of their customs and meritorious deeds is clearly set forth in the biographies and other records that have been passed down. Yet people like you want to tar such people with same brush as the tengu demons! When I read that in your book, tears ran down my cheeks. And if my Dharma progeny far in the future read those words, they too will surely grit their teeth with resentment. Are these the thoughts of a "man of virtue"? Are these the designs of a "superior man"?

Dōshun, you took some delirious words spoken by a yamabushi priest named Gyōshin, a fantastic tale by another yamabushi named Unkei, and made that the main thrust of your anti-Buddhist rant. How could someone regarded as a great Confucian teacher behave in such a despicable and underhanded way? Just who were those yamabushi? Even supposing they were not demented or talking in their sleep, to cite villainous characters like them to substantiate your accusations is meaningless. Not to say fraudulent or make-believe. Not to say ravings in a dream world.*

---

*The reference to the yamabushi Gyōshin appears in the sixth part of the final volume (*gekan*) of Razan's work: "Moreover many priests who are arrogant and prideful, envious or bad-tempered, are transformed into tengu goblins. Dengyō, Kōbō, Jikaku, and

Divulging matters without basis in fact are what people call dreams, visions, or fantasies, yet you make a special point of asserting such delusions in hopes of destroying the reputations of good and virtuous Buddhist priests. Are those the aspirations of a man of great stature? Your recklessness is scandalous, your dreams utterly disgraceful. Only a madman could discover value in these wild ravings, find anything to admire in these absurd hallucinations. He would indeed be living in a dream.

You Confucians always make a point of asserting that there is no afterlife, but here, in order to support your allegations, you tell a tale about someone turning into a tengu after he dies. The confusion of your logic, as Priest Jakuhon's investigations have pointed out, can only provoke our laughter.

Ah! It is in his words and deeds that that a superior man shows great prudence. It is in governing his speech that a Buddhist sage is particularly careful. Long ago there lived a demon with a golden body and a head like a pig. Millions of foul-smelling maggots poured from his mouth, causing him indescribable suffering. The Buddha said, "He is undergoing this terrible retribution because when he was monk, upholding the pure precepts, he was unable to control his speech."*

For vilifying an elderly monk, a senior priest fell into hell for endless kalpas and was then born into a family of the ignoble *candhala* caste. For reviling a monk, a farmer was transformed on the spot into a venomous

---

Chishō are examples of this. One of those who became a tengu was Gyōshin of Yamato province. He declared to the priest Kyōen: 'I was formerly a ranking priest (Sōzu) of the Naka-no-in. How can Buddhist priests or temple maidens exorcise me? My mind is filled with notions of abusing and slandering, reviling and disdaining. I have over three hundred followers, all possessed of miraculous powers, who seek people at the end of their lives to haunt and oppress them. From long in the past, when eminent and erudite priests approaching death were beset upon by evil demons, that was all my doing." Unkei appears in the same section: "In the fifth year of the Jōwa period (1349) a yamabushi named Unkei from Mount Haguro in Dewa province was on his way to visit Tenryū-ji in Kyoto. When he reached the western outskirts of the capital he encountered an elderly yamabushi priest, and accompanied him up to the temple on nearby Mount Atago. He noticed a strange-looking priest among the assembly there. The priest declared, 'These are Gembō, Shinsai, Kanchō, Jie, Raigō, Ninkai [eminent priests of former times].'" After listing a number of former emperors and empresses who were present as well, the text continues, "As Unkei was getting ready to leave, the elderly priest declared, 'This is the dwelling place of Tarōbō,' and he awoke as if from a dream. Dazed, he found himself seated under a *muku* tree at the site of the ancient capital."

*From the *Fa-yuan chu-lin*, ch. 76. The story appears on p. 121.

evil dragon. For uttering an offensive remark, an old woman was struck dead by a bolt of lightning. The intemperate speech of the nun Wei-miao, the pernicious words of the monk Shan-hsing, the retribution suffered by Hui-t'iao and Sung-yu might also be cited*—I don't have space to cite them all. I have heard it said that it is unenlightened men and women possessed of a certain amount of intelligence who create the kind of evil karma that sends them into the lowest realms of hell.

You Confucians are fond of stating loudly that when a person dies, the *kon* part of the soul flies off and the *haku* part disperses, leaving not even a particle of dust behind. If you are correct, then that is that. If, on the other hand, the Court of Hell with its stern, unsmiling judges and lictors does indeed exist, then when you die you will be presented with a full accounting of your evil deeds, omitting none, and you will have no time to cover up your deceitful speech. When that happens, you will fear the many tortures awaiting you in the Screaming Hells. There is no doubt that the loud assertions and facile declarations you make today will send you straight into those Screaming Hells. On that account, I must feel the greatest pity for you.

In the past the Confucian Chang Wu-chin, envious of Buddhism's large and splendid monasteries, questioned whether Chinese should place such value on a foreign religion. He made up his mind to reduce their influence by writing an anti-Buddhist tract. Words of caution from his wise wife made him have second thoughts.† Happening to read the *Vimala-kirti Sutra*, all the envy and resentment in his heart suddenly vanished, and he wrote *Hu-fa lun*, a splendid treatise that advocates defending the Dharma. Isn't that a wonderful story, one that should be told again and again through the years? Chang later rose to become Prime Minister, lived to be over eighty, and worked to protect and preserve the Dharma to the end of his days. He is a fine example of "the superior man willing to rectify his mistakes." He is entirely different from those anti-Buddhist crusaders who are destined to become laughingstocks to later generations.

---

*When the priest Hui-t'iao made intemperate remarks against Buddhism during a sermon, his tongue suddenly popped three feet out of his mouth and blood began appearing from his eyes and nose and ears (*Hsu-kao-seng chuan,* ch. 15). Sung-yu burned Buddhist statues to keep himself warm, and when Hui-tang sent him a letter of reproach, he used it as toilet paper (*Hsu-kao-seng chuan,* ch. 25).

†Chang Wu-chin (Chang Shang-ying, 1043–1121). His wife is reported to have said: "From the very first, no Buddha exists. Why write about that? You should write about the Buddha that exists" (*Compendium of the Five Lamps,* ch.11).

A genuine spiritual nature is innate in every person. How can they fail to grasp the workings of cause and effect that are clearly taking place before their very eyes? They can through their actions acquire the four Buddha-wisdoms. How can they fail to understand the clear and obvious principles of cause and effect at work within the three worlds? Buddhism is clearly an unrivalled teaching. There is no doubt that it aids in governing the country, in meting out proper punishments, and, in destroying the cycle of suffering, extends even into the darkness of the next world. Lowly hunters and trappers, woodcutters and fuel gatherers can understand this. Why are you unable to believe it? But no, because of a single envious thought and in order to gain a mere temporary advantage, you doggedly insist on launching attacks on Buddhism.

This morbid habit of attacking Buddhism began long ago with Han Yu (768–824), was nurtured and kept alive by Chu Hsi (1130–1200), and its lingering toxins have trickled down to Hayashi Razan and his ilk. The causes of the malady are extremely obscure and difficult to recognize. Even the greatest physician can easily overlook them. Works such as K'ung-ku's *Shang-chih p'ien*, Fo-Jih's *Fu-chiao pien*, Shang-ying's *Hu-fa lun*, and T'ien-le's *Chin-yu p'ien* have gone into minute detail, with masterly skill, in attempting to diagnose them. Nonetheless, I do not think they have succeeded in grasping the root cause of the ailment. I know where these deep-seated roots are found. They are not in vital areas, ones that are impossible to treat. I will now try to examine them without overlooking even the smallest, most minute clues and symptoms.

Ever since the sun of Buddhism began to illuminate our land with its rays, the heavenly gods Indra and Brahma embraced and worshipped it; the nagas protected it; kings and nobles worshipped it; samurai and ordinary people were devoted to it. Owing to this, Buddhist students receiving alms from the lay community are able to undergo Buddhist training freely and without reserve. With minds free of mundane thoughts and worries, provided with the four essentials, they can devote themselves wholeheartedly and with unflagging zeal to the three learnings.* As a result of this they can achieve a rich harvest within, while the light from their observance of the precepts and their good works shines forth without. Splendid Buddhist temples have been erected, rules and regulations established governing the Buddhist community's behavior. Statesman and government officials

---

*Four essentials (*shishu seiku*): food and drink, clothing, bedding, and medicine); three learnings (*sangaku*): meditation, study of the precepts and sutras.

cannot treat them as vassals. Not even their fathers and their mothers can address them as children. As their practice continues, they become able to provide great help and guidance to others, and the merits they attain extend even to the gods and demons. Having received in their person the seal of the Dharma King, they are truly the jewels of the human world. This describes what is means to be a Buddhist.

Observe those who call themselves Confucians. They inure themselves to the rigors of cold weather, are oblivious of the summer heat, spending the whole year teaching and preaching assiduously. Yet despite their best efforts, not ten of them are able to secure teaching positions. Even if one of them succeeds in obtaining a stipend as someone's retainer, it never exceeds two hundred *koku* of rice. Didn't a scholar as celebrated at Han Yu write: "It is warm this winter; why do my children weep from the cold? There was a bountiful harvest; why does my wife lament the scarcity of food?" It is even truer for all the penurious scholars of lesser standing.

This kindles secret feelings of envy in their hearts, and they abruptly set about honing their verbal weapons to slander and revile Buddhists, thinking, "All of us, gods, lords, and retainers alike must work together and find a way to rid the country of this foreign creed. We must topple the Buddhist images, burn their scriptures, destroy their temples, and appropriate their lands so we can expand our own schools around the country and make our teachings prosper. If we succeed in establishing Confucianism as the only teaching in the land, our achievement will rival that of the Great Yu and his assistants Yi and Ch'i in subjugating the rivers and swamps. In the actual world in which men live, the Confucian teaching is the one that should be cherished and made to flourish. How regrettable that a foreign teaching has been allowed to achieve such success."

It is like the pig that out of enmity for a hill of gold spent all its time rooting away at it. The pig succeeded only in polishing the gold and giving it a more splendid luster. Hence the unhappiness and anger of these perpetually frowning Confucians only increases, and it continues, suppressed and smoldering, until they grow old and die.

I think that in Han Yu's case the fever from this sickness was rather weak, and only affected his limbs. In time it would probably have cleared up of itself. In Chu Hsi, however, the fever was an internal one, so that he seemed perfectly well and displayed few outward symptoms. In Hayashi Razan, the malady took hold internally and externally as well, so that each word he utters—rantings about the three worlds, about no afterlife, about Buddhist priests—it all comes out perverted and confused. His is a truly pitiful ailment. How can it be cured? The cure is high rank, prosperity, and authority, and a successful career—and they must be present in equal measures. But a mediocre person of indolent habits finds these extremely difficult to acquire. Not to mention that such benefits are heaven-sent and the gods and demons are not at all generous in imparting them. But these men think that all they need to enjoy heaven's backing is a good moral sense and a sympathy for others, and that they do not have to accumulate virtue in themselves. As a result, they proceed to persecute good people and revile what is lofty and virtuous. How could they be so mistaken?

The true Buddha-body pervades the entire Dharma universe. It does not perish in the world-ending kalpa fire and does not disappear when the great Vairambha wind disperses the universe. It is bright and clear within all phenomena and in the minds of all sentient beings. No matter how much it is praised or exalted, it does not increase. No matter how much it is reviled, it does not decrease. Much less could it be affected by the envy or spite of a run-of-the-mill Confucian. What is sad is that men like these, in whom the eye of wisdom is neither lofty nor bright, whose knowledge is neither great nor far reaching, who just cling doggedly to their own mean and petty views, constantly whip up the raging flames of the hell of interminable pain by teaching things that harm simple and honest people.

In the past, great figures like Prince Shōtoku, Hōdō Shinsen, Sugawara Michizane, and En no Gyōja,* who made themselves conversant with both this world and the next—something totally beyond the ken of ignorant, unenlightened people—worshipped both *kami* and the Buddhas unceasingly. It is clear from records that are found in ancient writings that the Japanese *kami* were not at all averse to the Buddhist teachings. Just look at the stories of Zōga at the Ise Shrine, Gedatsu at the Iwashimizu Hachiman Shrine, Myōe at the Kasuga Shrine, Taichō at the Hakusan Shrine, Gyōgi at the Shirahige Shrine, Kanshun at the Hiyoshi Shrine, Jōkan at the Yoshino Shrine, or Shōren at the Atsuta Shrine.† Why didn't Hayashi quote those stories? Why did he consider only the deluded ravings of Gyōshin and

---

*Hōdō Shinsen is a legendary figure who is said to have flown to Japan from India at the time of the Emperor Kōtoku (7th century) and established temples in Harima province. En no Gyōja (7th century) is regarded as the founder of the Shugendō tradition of ascetic "mountain" Buddhism.

†Zōga, a Buddhist monk from Mount Hiei, received an oracle from the deity of the Ise Shrine telling him to give his clothing to a beggar and did so, returning naked to Mount Hiei (*Zoku Honchō Ōjō-den*, 12). The other eminent priests mentioned here also received communications from the deities of the Shintō shrines they visited (or from their intermediaries). The stories appear in the *Collection of Sand and Pebbles*, vol. 1, except those of Taichō Hosshi (*Honchō Kōsō-den*, 6) and Gyōgi (source unknown).

Unkei and cite them in his writings? Is that the extent of an outstanding scholar's discernment? Is that the measure of a wise man's knowledge? If he is willing to believe such farcical accounts, why doesn't he believe Shōen's account of the miracle wrought by the deity of Kasuga as well? Or, since he prefers to place his trust in dream stories, why doesn't he accept the divine revelations the priest Shōshin received from the deity Jōzenji at the Hiyoshi Shrine or those the great deity of Sekizan imparted to the monk of Miidera when that temple was burned down?*

Over eighty thousand *kami* are enshrined throughout the sixty provinces of our country, all of them possessing sublime virtues and manifesting themselves with marvelous power. In the thousand years since Buddhism was first introduced, have not Buddhist images in numbers well in excess of eighty thousand been enshrined throughout the country? Are not millions of fascicles of Buddhist scripture in existence as well? The Shintō *kami* are manifestations of Buddhas and Bodhisattvas. Buddhas and Bodhisattvas are their original forms. The relation between the two is essentially nondual, like water and waves. If the Japanese *kami* had considered Buddhism harmful to the country and without benefit to its people, they would hardly have tolerated even one Buddhist image or one book of its scriptures. This is the land of the *kami*. We are subjects of the *kami*. Had they opposed Buddhism, they would have no need to sit idly by and allow it to spread.

Saying the kami were unaware at the beginning that Buddhism had no value would be to call them ignorant. Saying they despised Buddhism but were unable to restrain its spread would likewise show contempt for them. Or would you suggest that the *kami*, being unable to prevent Buddhism from spreading, have waited a thousand years, until now, so they could recruit you Confucians to do the job for them? Utterly ridiculous!

Ah, the mind of a person who would find satisfaction in beating down others is no different from that of a treacherous minister who sets his sights on his prince's throne. Such a man will never be satisfied until he has it all. "If a family gets a hundred chariots, it will soon harbor secret ambitions to acquire a state with a thousand."†

---

*The three stories referred to here are also found in the *Collection of Sand and Pebbles*, vol. 1.

†On a visit to the Liang state, Mencius was asked by the king what he should do to profit his kingdom. Mencius replied he had only counsels of benevolence and virtuousness to give, and cautioned the king against speaking of profit. "If a king asks what can be done to profit his kingdom, ministers will ask what can be done to profit their families, superiors and inferiors of all ranks will try to profit from one another, thus endangering

For Shintōists now to ally themselves with Confucians and attempt to stamp out Buddhism would be like supporting usurper Wang Mang in his plot to overthrow the Han or coddling Ssu-ma I.* If Confucians and Shintōists could set their anti-Buddhist habits aside for the time being and investigate their own ideals of morality, humanity, and justice until they grasped the divine principle that lies at the heart of both teachings, they would both find that their virtue increased by the day, and they would pass on their teachings to their followers and their good fortune to their descendants. How splendid that would be. Why be so vindictive, like a spiteful mother-in-law thinking up ways to vent her jealousy on her daughter-in-law? How could they act in such a mean and shameful manner?

A Shintō scholar named Tatsuno Hirochika has discussed the similarities and differences between Confucianism and Buddhism in some detail in his *Shinkoku Kaigi-hen*.† It is a fair and just assessment, so it is unnecessary for me to revisit the issues here.

It should be clear from what has been said that Buddhist priests themselves must take measures to protect and preserve their teachings. It is their mission to take the true teachings on their shoulders and defend the Dharma fortress. If they merely pride themselves on the success the teachings enjoy and rely on the benefits of government patronage, then write worthless screeds and amuse themselves in the composition of clumsy verses, they are no different from the profligate son of a wealthy family who lives a life of lavish extravagance and abandons himself to the pleasures of the flesh, who is oblivious of the money he wastes, and fails even to learn proper etiquette. Can such men regard themselves as children of the compassionate Buddha, people worthy to receive donations from the lay community?

Autumn is deepening in the halls of Zen, bitter frost forms in its groves. Priests attach to worldly divertissements like an autumn cicada clinging

---

the kingdom. In a kingdom of ten thousand war chariots, a usurper who murders a king will become head of a state of a thousand chariots; in a state of a thousand chariots, the murderer of its prince will become head of a clan of a hundred chariots. Although to have a thousand chariots out of ten thousand, or a hundred out of a thousand, is not an insignificant gain, if virtuousness is put last, and profit put first, people will not be content until they attempt to usurp it all" (*Mencius*, p. 49).

*Wang Mang (c.45 BC–23 AD), known infamously as "the Usurper," plotted to overthrow the Han dynasty. Ssu-ma I (178–251) hid his ambitions while serving the Wei dynasty, but finally betrayed his masters; he was later was regarded as founder of the Chin dynasty.

†*Resolving Doubts About the Land of the Kami* by the Shintō priest Tatsuno Hirochika (1616–1693), published in 1673, uses Buddhist concepts to explain basic Shintō principles.

to a leaf. They maintain the donations and other emoluments they receive like a rooster guarding the nest eggs. No wonder the Confucians regard us as their mortal enemies, despise us as though we were clods of dirt. And it is not only the Confucians that feel this way. If an uprising should take place in the Dharma citadel and the Buddhas were threatened with defeat, what power do we have to defend them? What strategies do we possess to support and maintain them? We have now reached a time when we must be deeply concerned and truly vigilant.

Zen teachers have recently appeared around the country who, feeling compassion for their students, use expedient means to encourage them and spur them on in their practice. Among these students are some true patricians of the hidden depths, monks who make it seem that spring-time may be returning to the Zen gardens. I fervently hope that each of them will seize this auspicious moment and continue their struggle with renewed vigor. But I also worry that the radiance they have produced may be only a short but brilliant flash of light given out by the Dharma lamp before it sputters out altogether.

The Buddha Way is actualized when a true person appears. In attaining the Way, he becomes a precious treasure. Marvelous blades like the fabled Ryōsen or Taia swords have a frosty glint that can reflect a person's very vitals, a cold flame that seems to glow from their precious sheath. But unless someone appears who is capable of using them, they are unable to cut even an earthworm in half and they fail to achieve their true potential of cutting through steel.

When Buddhism was first transmitted to China, Taoist adepts such as Fei Shu-ya and Ch'u Shan-hsin attempted to repel it using secret arts, but the Buddhist monks Kashyapa-Matanga and Chu Fa-lan, armed with the Buddhas' latent power and manifesting eighteen miraculous powers of their own, thwarted them. It was like the elephant king gazing down at a herd of sheep, and the Taoists meekly submitted. They ended up taking the tonsure and were received into the sangha.*

At the time of the T'ang emperor T'ai-tsung (600–649), a Taoist named Shih-hua schemed to demean and discredit Buddhists by fashioning a lad-der made of sword blades for spiritual adepts to climb. The monk Ch'ung-hui frustrated this attempt by ascending the ladder with ease, and was

---

*Shih-shih tzu-chien, ch. 1.

awarded a purple robe from the emperor.* During the reign of the T'ang emperor Hsien-tsung, the official Han Yu, hoping to curb Buddhism's influence on the emperor, offered a memorial to the throne protesting the worship of a Buddha relic. The emperor was furious and had him exiled to the frontier province of Chao-chou. There he became friends with Zen master Ta-tien, who conquered him with laughter and cheerful conversation.† During the T'ai-ping era of the Northern Wei dynasty (440–445), the scholar Ts'ui-hao, a favorite of Emperor T'ai Wu, advised him to destroy Buddhist temples and execute its priests. When the executioner's blade miraculously failed to injure the monk Tan-shih, he was thrown into the tigers' den, but the animals cowered back in fear. Astounded by these events, T'ai Wu repented his actions and converted to Buddhism. Ts'ui-hao was soon after deposed by the five clans, and in the fourteenth year of Shao-pei (450), the emperor was assassinated.‡

During the Chia-yu era of the Northern Sung (1056–1063) when Ou-yang Hsiu, Li T'ai-pai, Chief Minister Han-ch'i and others were promulgating anti-Buddhist tracts, Zen master Ch'i-sung wrote *Treatise to Assist the Teachings,* preaching the unity of Confucianism, Taoism, and Buddhism. Even the Confucians were impressed by this work and obliged to accept it.§

During the Ch'un-hsi era of the Southern Sung (1174–89), Chu Hsi engaged in a campaign against Buddhism, but the ideas and arguments he used were all taken from Buddhist scripture. In the Cheng-t'ung era (1436–1549) of the Ming dynasty, K'ung-ku Ching-lung preached the unity of the three traditions in the *Shang-chih pien,* an outstanding work that corrected Chu Hsi's errors and left him no place wherever to hide.

Shih-shih tzu-chien, ch. 7.

†In 819 the Emperor Hsien-tsung placed in his palace a finger bone of the Buddha said to possess miraculous powers. Han Yu, a well-known scholar and statesman of the time, presented a written protest, for which he was exiled (*Shih-shih tzu-chien,* ch. 7). The story of Han Yu's encounters with Zen master Ta-tien Pao-tsung (732–824) appears in *Compendium of the Five Lamps,* ch. 20.

‡Ts'ui-hao (d. 450) was a scholar who served under the Emperor T'ai Wu of the Northern Wei (440–451). Discovering stores of arms and wine in a Buddhist temple at Ch'ang-an, he advised the emperor to have the priests put to death (*Shih-shih tzu-chien,* ch. 3).

§*Shih-shih tzu-chien,* ch. 9.

The Zen patriarchs were all inspired by the great wheel of their Bodhisattva vow to undertake the most rigorous practice, putting their very lives
at risk, as they sought to penetrate the deep source of the Buddha's truth.
Their minds had the capacity to hold entire oceans, the wisdom in their
faces shone like the sun or moon. With their lofty virtue and the purity
that comes from constantly upholding the precepts, they protected and
preserved the Dharma for the sake of their Dharma heirs. They are models to be held up for ten thousand generations. Is there anyone like them
today? Confucians, Taoists, and Shintōists may pool their efforts and try
to force Buddhists into submission, but they will be no more successful
than a sparrow fluttering up at a hawk, or a starving dog baring its teeth
at a lion.

What is most frightening, however, is the decline of Buddhism itself.
Why has it happened? Try to find a monk who is truly engaged in Zen
practice. You won't be able to come up with a single one. Most of them
are caught up in literary pursuits. They take great pleasure in just ambling
along humming worthless verses. They're no different from stray dogs
chasing after a clod of dirt.

Some of them succeed in hoodwinking laymen and -women into giving
them donations by twittering off half-baked teachings like this: "There's
nothing special about satori. Each person is furnished from the first with
an immaculately pure self-nature. It's not as if you can't eat rice if you
aren't enlightened. It's not as if you can't relieve your bowels without satori.
Satori is perfectly complete and freely functioning from the very first. A
person who hasn't experienced satori doesn't mistake a crow for a heron.
He doesn't refer to fire as water. He goes on living his life, eating his rice
and drinking his tea, without any trouble whatever. That is the way a true
and authentic Zen monk conducts himself."

They couldn't be more mistaken. They're like a man trying to peel a
melon with a long spear. It is so featherbrained and downright silly that
you can hardly bear to watch.

Others offer teachings like this: "The delusions of birth-and-death are
profound, the karmic hindrances that arise from them severe. Do as many
daily sutra recitations as you can. Perform endless prostrations before
Buddhist images. Repeat these and other practices over and over and over
until you grow old and death brings deliverance." Idle nonsense! If that
were the extent of the Zen teaching, why would Bodhidharma have taken
the trouble of traveling to China to transmit his teaching of *kenshō*? He

might just as well have scribbled down a few lines in a letter and told them, "Do the Nembutsu." *Kenshō* is like a poisonous lacquer drum, like the vast conflagrations in Hell.* It is far beyond the reach of the weak-willed or half-hearted.

Still others say: "The Buddha Dharma is something that proceeds from shallow to deep, from what is close to what is distant." They assemble some koans and assign them to students, saying, "When you finish this, I'll give you another one to solve. When you're through with that, there's this one," guiding students to illusory realizations and false understandings. It becomes like puzzle solving. What hindrances they create for them! They should be classed down there with the Maras, the evil demons! It is perverse notions like theirs that has corrupted the Buddha's Dharma and destroyed the ancestral teachings. One cannot direct criticism at Hayashi Razan alone. My worry, what keeps constantly freezing my liver, is the state of present-day Zen itself.

To those students engaged in negotiating the hidden depths, I respectfully say: Do not stray into the citadel of evil demons I have just described to you. Just take a genuine koan and bore into it. "A monk asked Chao-chou, 'Does a dog have the Buddha-nature, or not?' Chao-chou said, 'Mu.'" This is a precious Dharma juggernaut that crushes the demon citadel beneath its wheels, an invincible sword that cuts down discrimination and delusions of every kind. Chao-chou just said "Mu." Bore steadily into it. Whether you are in a quiet place or a noisy one, whether you are moving or standing or sitting or lying down, bore into it from the sides, from the front and the back, when breathing in and breathing out, sleeping and awaking, steadily becoming one with this "Mu," and continuing to bore in.

At the beginning, various delusory thoughts and mental projections will rise up one after another to lead you astray. It will seem as though you are on a field of battle, amid a great confusion of struggle and flight. Or as though you are standing in the crowded pit of a raucous kabuki performance. Your mind will be much more unsettled than it normally is, and will be jumping and japing around like a monkey, or suddenly darting off like a startled horse. But if you do not strike the drum of retreat and carry steadily on, those delusory thoughts and perceptions will eventually come to an end. It will seem to you as though you have fallen into an enormous

*The sound of the drum and the conflagrations kill all who come into contact with them: allusion to the great death experienced in *kenshō*.

demon cave soaring up a thousand miles, or have entered an enclosure with walls of steel countless layers thick. Unable to go forward, unable to retreat, with nothing but an impenetrable blackness on all sides, there will no place at all you can put either hand or foot. If at that time you continue to forge ahead without fear, all of a sudden the world in all ten directions will become like a great sheet of ice, like an enormous crystal of blue glass. All your principles and words will be exhausted, all your mental operations will cease. Now, without giving rise to thoughts or emotions, the more satoris you experience, the deeper your understanding becomes, and the more diligently you must apply yourself to your koan. All at once, when you become one with the mind that has been boring into the koan, the sheet of ice and everything else will abruptly vanish, and you will experience the indescribable joy of dying and being reborn.

When you reach this point, not even the Buddhas and patriarchs themselves can touch you. You find that just by leisurely turning your head, koans you had not encountered before—Tsui-yen's Eyebrows or Chien-feng's Three Kinds of Infirmity—are now perfectly in your grasp. And when you take this attainment with you to a true Zen master and have him examine it, he will grasp your hand and break into a smile. Then all the hogwash Kokurin [Hakuin] has been eagerly dishing out to you in these pages will become just another of his embarrassing performances.

III. Inscriptions for Paintings (*San*)

162. Inscription for a Painting of Clam Kannon

Hakuin painted many examples of this Kannon, which depicts the Bodhisattva emerging from the shell of a clam, though none with this particular inscription is known.

> Conchs, clams, and other shellfish of their ilk
> Are said to doze soundly for a thousand years.
> If they fail to encounter a Buddha when he appears,
> There's always the venerable old sage of Potalaka.

. . . .

In admonishing his disciple Aniruddha for constantly succumbing to the sleep demon during his sermons, the Buddha pointed out that conchs, clams, and other shellfish, which doze off into naps of a thousand years, lose any chance to encounter a Buddha, who appears only rarely in the human world (*Heroic March Sutra*, ch. 5).

Potalaka is the island in the southern seas where Kannon is said to dwell.

Kannon is said to manifest herself in an infinite number of forms in response to the needs of sentient beings. The clam Kannon originated in China, where stories about it appear in the Zen records of the Sung dynasty. The version found in the *Records of the Lamp*, ch. 4, is as follows: The T'ang emperor Wen Tsung was extremely fond of clams, and everyone in the kingdom was aware of the fact. Government officials stationed near the seashore competed to provide clams for the Emperor's table. One day in the fifth year of T'ai-hu (831) a chef in the imperial kitchens came upon a clam that he was unable to open, despite his best efforts. Thinking it somewhat unusual, he mentioned it to the emperor. On placing the clam on the altar and offering incense and prayers, the clam suddenly opened and the Bodhisattva Kannon appeared from within. None of the emperor's ministers were able to tell him what this meant, so he wrapped the clam in brocade, placed it in a precious sandalwood box, and presented it to the Hsing-shan temple, instructing the monks to perform ceremonies for it. An eminent Zen priest, summoned to explain, told the emperor that Bodhisattvas did not appear without reason, and this one had no doubt appeared in hopes of deepening the emperor's faith in the Buddha Dharma. To explain himself, the Zen master quoted some lines from the *Kannon Sutra* that tell how the Bodhisattva saves people by manifesting himself and preaching the Dharma. The emperor replied that while the Bodhisattva had indeed appeared, he had still not heard him preach the Dharma. The priest asked the emperor whether he thought what he had seen was usual or unusual, and whether or not he believed what he had seen. The emperor said that it was definitely unusual and that he deeply believed in what he had seen. "Then you have heard his Dharma preaching," replied the priest. With that, the emperor experienced a sudden realization and grasped the meaning of the incident. He is said to have ordered images of the Bodhisattva to be enshrined in temples throughout the empire. See *Precious Mirror Cave*, pp. 273–4.

Although this account was known in Japan from Kamakura times, and Clam Kannon appears in a work on Buddhist iconography published in the

Genroku period (1688–1704), Hakuin seems to have been the first to use it in Zen painting.

:163. Inscription for a Painting of Hotei

> Behaving like a small child,
> Japing about like a monkey.
> Watch out, Zen patriarchs!
> Watch out for this bubblehead!

:164. Inscription for a Painting of Zen Master Takusui

The Zen priest Takusui Chōmo is a shadowy figure who no doubt would have been forgotten were it not for the Dharma Words of Priest Takusui, *a work in* kana *script that appeared in 1740, not long before this inscription was written. According to an annotation in* Poison Blossoms, *"Takusui was from Echigo province. On entering the priesthood he always had a liking for Bassui Tokushō's brand of Zen. He continued his practice, keeping his distance from the world and living among the forests and hills until he reached old age.... When over one hundred years old he traveled to Enzan in Kai province in hopes of reviving the traditions of master Bassui. When that plan did not pan out, he left and lived in a hermitage in Edo."*

This inscription was written in Chinese verse (translated into prose here) on a portrait of Takusui at the request of Yamanashi Harushige (1707–62), a man Hakuin apparently regarded as one of his most accomplished lay students. The basic facts surrounding Yamanashi's request, no doubt more or less accurate, are told in a local history titled Annals of Ihara (Ihara Gunshi). *"Yamanashi acquired the painting of Takusui while he was stopping at a temple called Jigen-an on a trip through Musashi province. He joyfully took it to Suruga and showed it to Master Hakuin, who praised Yamanashi's strong spiritual resolve, and inscribed a colophon over the painting...that he dated the third year of Hōreki [1753, when Hakuin was 68]). The painting is still preserved in the Yamanashi home as a family treasure." There is a record of the painting being*

shown in an exhibition of Hakuin's works held in Shizuoka in 1944,
but it is said to have subsequently been destroyed in the war.

The son of a wealthy family of sake brewers, Yamanashi became
head of the business at the age of thirty-seven. He began his study
of Zen under Hakuin four years later, following the death of his
brother. The most detailed account of Yamanashi is that in Akiyama
Kanji's Buddhist Monk Hakuin, "Hakuin Oshō and Ryōtetsu Kōji."

The incredible story of the satori Yamanashi attained in his first
attempt at zazen appears in various forms in Hakuin's records and
has become one of the staples of Hakuin Zen. The most widely
known versions of the story are found in Hakuin's Chronological
Biography *(Precious Mirror Cave, pp. 213–15), in a long letter to*
*Yamanashi written by Hakuin himself (*Beating the Cloth Drum,
pp. 61–77), and in Stories from a Thicket of Thorn and Briar, *a*
nineteenth-century collection of anecdotes about Hakuin's followers.
These versions all differ in significant ways from the briefer account
Hakuin gives here.

L IVING IN IHARA IN Suruga, Mr. Yamanashi Harushige doesn't read
or recite sutras, much less engage in Zen practice, but for the past six
years he has been performing hidden charity, taking care of the sick and
elderly, and doing what he can to relieve their suffering.

As he was visiting a friend's residence one day, he heard someone reading out a passage from a book: "If a man desires to master the Buddha Way,
he must above all achieve *kenshō. Kenshō* is attained by the uninterrupted
application of concentrated effort. If you practice with undivided effort,
kenshō will surely come. For sentient beings with great courage, Buddhahood comes in an instant of thought. For sentient beings who are lax and
indolent, Nirvana will not come even after endless kalpas."

These words filled Yamanashi with joy. He plucked up his courage, saying, "If this is what the practice of the Way entails, I see no reason why I
can't rouse myself up and have a go at it myself." Returning to his home,
he shut himself up in a room, clenched his teeth, and began to sit in an
utterly motionless state. He battled constantly against intruding thoughts,
refusing adamantly to submit to them. His entire body was drenched in
nervous sweat. That night, before the fifth watch (3–5 a.m.), he gave up his
life and perished into the great death. When dawn came and he gradually
returned to his senses, he got up and immediately set out for my temple.
When he arrived and knocked at my gate, I ushered him in and tested

him with several koan stories. He passed through them all without the least hesitation.

Reading through the old Zen histories, it is rare indeed to find a story such as this one. The Japanese book Yamanashi heard being recited was the *Dharma Words of Priest Takusui*. Deeply conscious of the debt he owed Master Takusui, Yamanashi traveled to Jigen-an in Edo, where he obtained a *chinsō* portrait of Takusui. Mounting the painting himself, he brought it to me and asked me to write some words on it. I felt so happy for him that I could not refuse. I ended up summarizing his story and inscribing it over the painting.

Yamanashi had often asked me for a Dharma name, but for a long time I did not give much thought to his request. Now I have decided to give him the Dharma name Ryōtetsu (Completely Penetrated), and the lay sobriquet Jiun (Compassionate Cloud). I hope that a relentless determination arises in him that will inspire him to undertake the great Bodhisattva practice, and enable him to perfect the seed of Buddha wisdom together with all other beings throughout the Dharma universe.

. . . .

In an earlier version of the story, Hakuin portrays Yamanashi as a pleasure-seeking voluptuary who had a sudden change of heart and achieved an overnight satori. In this, his latest version, Yamanashi's profligacy is unmentioned, and he is described as someone who had given charitable contributions to the needy even before he encountered Takusui's teaching and resolved to try zazen practice.

The following chronology can be pieced together. Yamanashi visits the waterfall near his home and experiences the transience of human life in the fifth month of 1748. On the twenty-first of the same month, he hears Takusui's book being recited and on an unspecified day in the same month visits Hakuin to have his satori confirmed. Five years later, in 1753, Yamanashi procures the portrait of Takusui at Jigen-an in Edo, and on the twenty-fifth of the sixth month visits Hakuin (perhaps at a temple in Kai province where he was lecturing) to request a colophon for the portrait.

165. Inscription for a Painting of Two Mice Doing Sumo

Hakuin painted several works on this theme. In two examples of mouse sumo reproduced in HZB (#556 and #557), a mouse also acts as referee; a white mouse in one painting, a black mouse in the other, and the deity Daikoku, the god of wealth, is a spectator, represented in abbreviated form by his rice bale, his mallet of good fortune (uchide no kozuchi), and straw raincoat. For their significance and reproductions of the paintings, which have inscriptions similar to this one, see Religious Art of Zen Master Hakuin, *pp. 181–85.*

From the descriptions in the verse below, as well as from annotations attached to the piece, we know that the painting on which Hakuin wrote the present inscription portrayed the Sumo match in a slightly different form: "two mice are engaged in sumo, with Daikoku in the center of the picture acting as referee." In Japan, mice (or rats) came to be regarded as Daikoku's messenger animal, a relationship which is traced to a story of mice saving the god Ōkuninushi (whose name can also be read Daikoku) from being burned alive by the violent deity Susano-o.

*We learn from another annotation that "When Hakuin was lecturing in Bizen province, Ikeda Iyo-no-kami, the Daimyō of Okayama castle, brought out this painting and asked him to inscribe a colophon for it." Ōta Junsensai, identified by Hakuin as the painter of the picture, was a retainer of Lord Ikeda. Hakuin's inscription can be dated to 1751, his sixty-sixth year, when he lectured at Shōrin-ji in Okayama, Bizen province (*Precious Mirror Cave, *p. 217). It is hard to say whether Hakuin's own mouse sumo paintings were inspired by Ōta's work, but judging from the calligraphy of the colophons he inscribed on them, an earlier date seems more likely.*

Two mice dwell in everyone's mind,
One of them black, one of them white.
They are forever engaged in sumo,
The outcome always touch and go.
If the black one comes out on top,
Good fortune transforms into bad,

And not in the present life alone;
You enter the evil ways for good.
If the white one comes out on top,
Bad fortune transforms into good,
And not in the present life alone;
A favorable rebirth is also gained.
Shame, honor, success and failure,
It all starts off with these two mice.
Even a deity of Daikoku's power
Is unable to overthrow the black mouse.
His magic mallet, rendered useless,
Lies entirely forgotten at his side.
So he grabs a fan, raises it high,
Rooting for the white mouse to win.
Once you subdue the black rebel,
You *become* a god of good fortune.
How sad that in this decadent age
The black mice have such strength,
Madly striving for the upper hand,
Bellies fired by cravings and fears.
What does the white mouse represent?
A mind of kindness and compassion.
What does the black one represent?
A mind of greed (or an evil land tax).
Gnawing away at the Bodhi sprouts,
Devouring the seeds of *prajna* wisdom.

Who painted this strange picture?
The artist is named Ōta Junsensai.

. . . .

God of god fortune. Fukurokuju, one of the Seven Gods of Good Luck, is said
to bestow longevity and good fortune, which for Hakuin means the timeless
life of enlightenment and the good fortune that enlightenment brings.

   So he grabs a fan. In Sumo, the referee holds an open ceremonial war fan
like those that were used by military commanders, who would raise and
lower the fan in various ways to issue commands to soldiers on the battlefield.

166. Inscription for a Painting of Ants Walking Around a Mill

> Plodding ants on the rim of an iron mill
> Moving idly on and on, never stopping,
> Like sentient beings revolving endlessly
> Through the six paths of transmigration,
> Being born here, then dying over there,
> Becoming a hungry ghost, or an animal.
> If you want to escape this round of suffering
> You must hear the sound of the single hand.

. . . .

The painting is reproduced in Religious Art of Zen Master Hakuin, *p. 36.*

167. Praising Myself

Hakuin inscribed this verse over most of his self-portraits.

> At the ground of a thousand Buddhas, hated by a thousand
> Buddhas,
> Among a troop of myriad demons, hated by the troop of
> demons.
> He unnerves today's perverse gangs of silent illumination
> Zennists,
> He exterminates the bat-blind bonzes that deny cause and effect.
> This broken-down old shavepate, unseemly and uncouth,
> By adding on this one more ugliness, makes himself still uglier.

IV. RELIGIOUS VERSES (*GEJU*)

:168. INSTRUCTIONS FOR STUDENTS

Bury your self-nature alive inside in a cave of briars,
Stab your inmost spirit to death inside a thicket of thorn.
Greens and yellow mushrooms, great white radishes,
Oven glowing hot—yet still you cry for golden leaves.

. . . .

The final line alludes to a well-known metaphor: giving a young child some yellow leaves and telling him they are gold to coax him to stop crying, which is used to describe a master descending from the ultimate principle and using expedient means *(upaya)* to make his teaching more accessible to a student.

:169. A POEM OF THANKS FOR A RUG AND TOBACCO

A splendid rug, suddenly delivered to my little temple,
Covered with green dragons asleep in deep blue pools.
I mustn't forget the tobacco, just right for the quiet here.
Filling my *kiseru*, I puff auspicious five-colored clouds.

. . . .

Smoking is said to have been introduced to Japan by Portuguese sailors in the sixteenth century. Thanks in part to the use of the metal *kiseru*, or long-handled smoking pipe, it had spread throughout Japan well before Hakuin's day. Monks on pilgrimage used tobacco seeds to pay for their food and lodging. Hakuin's fondness for his *kiseru* is well documented in his life records. Perhaps the most interesting episode is the one that describes his attendant Tōrei, a stickler for upholding the precepts, entering Hakuin's chambers and finding him trying to conceal a smoking pipe behind his back. Out of feelings of filial devotion, and to avoid embarrassing his teacher, Tōrei, without showing the least bit of displeasure, sat down, took Hakuin's *kiseru*, filled it with tobacco, and handed it back to him. Hakuin happily proceeded to receive his student in a "relaxed and happy manner" (*Chronological Biography of Zen Priest Tōrei*, age 32).

:170. A Poem of Thanks for a Soba Feast

We learn from verses on the subject in Poison Blossoms *that Hakuin was a great lover of soba (buckwheat) noodles. It was apparently during Hakuin's lifetime that soba started being sold in special shops in Edo, but even before that, at least as early as the sixteenth century, they were being made and eaten at home. Soba is an autumn crop, and noodles and dumplings made from soba flour milled from newly harvested kernels and eaten with a dipping sauce or in a hot broth are considered a special delicacy.*

The first of the verses, dating probably from Hakuin's forties or fifties, describes the making of the noodles by the same procedure used today. The soba flour is carefully combined with water and kneaded into a heavy dough, then flattened with a long rolling pin into a thin sheet. During this process the entire sheet of dough is furled onto the rolling pin, pounded sharply on the cutting board, and then unrolled. This is repeated over and over until the dough has reached the desired thickness. It is then folded over into numerous layers and cut with a special knife into long noodle-like strings. The "unfurled mirror" describes the smooth, flattened sheet of soba dough unrolled on the cutting board.

> Soba flour, soft and white, sifted through a silken skein,
> Is transformed into finest soba noodles for the invited guest.
> Furled on the pin, pounded with sharp thundering claps,
> Furled, unfurled, flattened until round and mirror smooth,
> Then folded in many layers and carefully cut into long thin
>   threads.
> Boiled and set in silver bowls, as pure as new fallen snow.
> I ate them with bitter grated daikon, a boon companion,
> Now sit stuffed and bloated, enjoying the autumn breeze.

BOOK ELEVEN
Supplement 2

:171. Gudō's Lingering Radiance

Hakuin's intention to include this work in his Zen records is clearly stated on the cover of the printed edition of Gudō's Lingering Radiance, where the words "Supplement to Poison Blossoms from a Thicket of Thorn" appear next to the title. As it happened, however, he published it independently. He had been promised a donation to cover the cost of publishing the entire Poison Blossoms collection, but this promise had become doubtful, so when laymen who were attending a meeting he was conducting in Takayama, Hida province, offered to donate the necessary funds to publish the newly completed manuscript, Hakuin promptly accepted and sent it to the bookseller in Kyoto with instructions that it be printed as a single volume titled Gudō's Lingering Radiance (Hōkan Ishō). It proceeded through the printing process in a very short time and appeared only a few months later (for particulars, see the Introduction, p. 6).

The Japanese title Hōkan Ishō, literally "Precious Mirror's Lingering Radiance," uses the name Precious Mirror (Hōkan), taken from the National Master title Daien Hōkan that the emperor had awarded to Gudō Tōshoku (1579–1661). A leading figure in Rinzai Zen of the first half of the seventeenth century, Gudō numbered among his many Dharma heirs such well known priests as Suzuki Shōsan, Shidō Munan, and Isshi Bunshu. From Hakuin's perspective, the most important of these was Shidō Munan, the teacher of Shōju Rōjin. Hakuin traced his Dharma lineage through Shōju, Munan, and Gudō, to the Kamakura priests Daiō, Daitō, and Kanzan, who founded the Japanese line of Rinzai Zen to which he belonged, and from them even further back to Daiō's Chinese teacher Hsu-t'ang Chih-yu.

In Gudō's Lingering Radiance, Hakuin praises Gudō for keeping alive the authentic tradition of koan Zen when it had fallen to a low ebb amid the various new approaches to Zen study that had appeared in the seventeenth century in response to the new realities

that emerged during the first century of Tokugawa rule. Among
these new teachings were Bankei Yōtaku's Unborn Zen, and various
forms of Nembutsu Zen, promulgated first by Ungo Kiyō and later
by émigré Chinese Ōbaku priests. Hakuin vigorously attacks all of
these teachings for undermining students' spiritual determination
and subverting what he viewed as the true traditions of koan Zen
as exemplified by Gudō, Daitō, and Hsu-t'ang.

Hakuin's reasons for writing Gudō's Lingering Radiance are
explained in the Chronological Biography:

> In spring [of 1758] the master was invited to lecture at Rurikō-ji
> in Mino province [where Gudō had formerly served as head
> priest]. He decided to use the meeting to celebrate in advance
> the one hundredth death anniversary of National Master Gudō
> with a series of lectures on the Blue Cliff Record. The monks
> living at Shōin-ji showed scant interest in the idea, but that
> made him all the more determined to proceed...and eventu-
> ally they came around and lent their support as well....Upon
> arriving at Rurikō-ji the master composed a letter which he had
> distributed to temples far and wide. He wrote: "As we reach the
> one hundredth anniversary of Master Gudō's death, I propose to
> deliver a series of lectures on the Blue Cliff Record. Anyone who
> feels a debt of Dharma gratitude to the National Master should
> come to Rurikō-ji to offer incense and make their bows to him."
>
> He also sent letters to senior priests in Gudō's teaching line
> urging them to arrange for Gudō's Zen records, now in manu-
> script, to be published. Discussions were held and various opin-
> ions were voiced, but in the end they were unable to reach any
> decision on the matter. The master was incensed by their lack
> of enthusiasm.
>
> At the end of the Rurikō-ji meeting, he received invitations
> from other temples in Mino province. After visiting each of
> them, he headed for Sōyū-ji in Takayama, Hida province, for
> talks on the Blue Cliff Record. On route to Sōyū-ji his exas-
> peration at the failure of his fellow priests to support the print-
> ing of Gudō's records prompted him to compose a work titled
> Gudō's Lingering Radiance. When he arrived at Sōyū-ji he
> wrote out a fair copy of the text and showed it to the monks.
> (Precious Mirror Cave, pp. 223–4)

THE GREAT ZEN MASTER Daien Hōkan [Gudō] has thousands of Dharma heirs. He established over a score of temples. His virtue is incomparably great. Several fascicles of Zen records containing his words and deeds have been compiled, and manuscripts of the work are preserved today at Shinshō-ji in Mino province and Chūzan-ji in Ise province. Filled with steep and lofty words and phrases unmatched in other records past or present, they constitute a great treasure and Dharma asset for all schools of Buddhism.

A priest, fearing that the master's records might be lost, could be seen moping about with furrowed brow. He lamented: "Is not this record a wonderful glowing torch on a midnight path? Is it not like a compass on a foggy sea? If we continue to neglect it like this, leave it buried away among piles of old papers, before long it will disappear into the bellies of the silverfish and not a single word will be transmitted to future generations. How could anyone who regards himself as a descendant of the National Teacher bear to sit idly by and watch that happen? It must be printed to make sure it will be preserved for later generations of students."

Elder priests in Master Gudō's lineage gathered and vigorously debated the proposal. One ignorant fellow, who was allied to the shameful "withered sitting" school of Zen, pulled a difficult face and speaking in a smarmy, bantering tone, said:

"No, no. Wait just a minute. To do as you propose would be no easy matter. We must not carelessly allow the fearless, uplifting words of the National Master to fall into vulgar, worldly hands. Even if we did imprudently have them published, few people would be able to appreciate the hidden pleasures they contain. No one would purchase it or read a single page of it. It is much better that his records remain hidden away and preserved in a safe place."

With that the discussion abruptly ended, and this unprecedented project was abandoned.

To whose house, and what lineage, does a rascal such as you belong? You can only be one of those benighted reprobates the Buddha said was beyond saving. Have you no fear of the retribution you will receive for the terrible sin you have committed? Your actions are sure to anger the gods Brahma and Indra and all the guardian protectors of Buddhas and patriarchs in the ten directions. They will surely expunge your name from the rolls of the priesthood. Those words from your mouth are a karmic act that will be engraved on the Lord of Hell's iron slate as a sin greater than causing blood to flow from a Buddha's body. You will sink forever into the depths of the Tongue-pulling Hell with no respite from its horrible sufferings for tens of thousands of kalpas. Even if a million Buddhas were to appear in the world, they would be unable to grant absolution for a sin of such magnitude. You are destined to sink into cauldrons overflowing with poisonous flames and molten lead, to be beaten with the merciless iron whips of cow-headed lictors.

Your everyday life has been motivated by foolish hopes, thoughts of fame and worldly fortune, and you have looked on with narrowed eyes at the good deeds performed by others. Even if you happened to see a Buddhist sutra or a Zen record, you would be as clueless as a fisherman gazing at a battle-axe or a kitten at a piece of brocade. Why do you suppose priests are numbered among the Three Treasures of Buddha, Dharma, and Priesthood? It is because they are supposed to disperse and transmit the Dharma treasure in the latter day, to employ the power of sutra recitation and words and letters to lead people to liberation. The Dharma that the Buddha expounded is a priceless treasure, but it was not possible for him to transmit it entirely on his own. It has been kept alive to the present day thanks to the precious treasure of the priesthood.

How can we number the gangs of skin-headed miscreants that infest the land today, people who cannot read the sutras or write about the Dharma, among the Three Treasures? To them, profit and wealth are the very life-source itself. They spend their lives without giving a thought to the Buddha's teaching. When they see the son of a rich family, they fawn over him as though he were more important than the Buddhas or Zen patriarchs themselves. All the gods of heaven and earth, and the many other deities that protect the Dharma, even those enshrined in the smallest, most remote hamlets, must regard these miserable creatures with the deepest loathing.

Long ago, after Shakamuni entered Nirvana, his disciples Mahakashapa, Shariputra, Maudgalyayana, Ananda, and five hundred great Arhats gathered for a conference in the Pippali cave. They began assembling the palm leaves on which Buddha's teachings of sudden and gradual attainment and the greater and lesser vehicles were inscribed, until they finally had one hundred thousand leaves filled with his preaching. Why weren't they concerned about letting them "fall carelessly into the clutches of the worldly and vulgar?" Why weren't they afraid that no one would buy them? Thanks to their efforts, the Dharma has enjoyed unending prosperity, helping both men and devas to attain enlightenment. Later, Nagarjuna wrote his *Treatise on the Perfection of Great Wisdom*, Asanga his *Thirty Stanzas*,

Bodhidharma the *Collection of the Six Gates*, the Third Patriarch Seng-ts'an *Verses on Belief in Mind*, Huang-po *The Essentials of Mind Transmission*, and Zen master Po-chang compiled his *Pure Regulations*. Collections of Yun-men's and Lin-chi's recorded sayings were made; both Fen-yang and Hsueh-tou composed verses on one hundred koans, and Yuan-wu added his detailed comments to the latter. In Japan, recorded sayings were compiled for National Masters Daiō and Daitō; also for Daikyū Sōkyū. In each of these works, the teacher has set forth the hidden keys to the upward striving of his house. Why did no one worry about allowing these teachings to fall into vulgar, worldly hands? They have become great and precious lamps that illuminate the world's darkness. We must bow reverently to the disciples of master Yun-men, who wrote down their teacher's precious instructions on their paper robes.* In preserving such teachings so they could later be printed, they have transmitted Dharma gifts of priceless and timeless significance.

In this latter day when the Dharma is in a state of degeneration, what a great pity it is to find these phony "silent illumination" bonzes vying with one another for prominence by constantly filling their followers' heads with nonsense like this:

"Pledge that you will never look at words or letters—they will most surely bury your spirits under. You must never make the mistake of opening the records of the Zen patriarchs—they will inflict irreparable damage to your self-nature. Just remain as you are, in a state of absolute nondoing (*buji*), in Zen's ultimate state of no-thought, no-mind. When even a flicker of thought attaches to this primal state, it creates karma that will send you directly into the three evil paths of existence. If you are hungry, eat something. If you feel out of sorts, lie down and sleep it off. Move naturally, with the course of things, freely and joyfully. Don't exert any effort. There's no Buddha for you to seek, there's no Dharma for you to preach. It is this secret that allows you to lead an artless and completely natural way of life."

Shiftless, headstrong rascals hear this shameless drivel and go waltzing about, wagging their tails with joy. They proceed to seek out warm and comfortable temples where they will have plenty to eat, where they can indulge in long sessions of blissful sleep. They can't read Buddhist texts. They are unable to write. It would be hard to find ignorance and dull-wittedness of this order in a horse and a cow. On the day their parents

---

*They did this in secret because Yun-men forbade any transcription of his teachings.

allowed them to leave home and enter the Buddhist priesthood, how could they have dreamed they would turn into such baldheaded morons?

Using the method of teaching by expedient means that he had devised, the Buddha said in a preaching at the Deer Park that the state of no thought, no striving, no practice, and no realization was supreme and ultimate enlightenment. Those who believe that these expedient teachings are the Buddha's essential teaching are Shravakas and others belonging to the Two Vehicles, who cannot remotely approach even the Arhats' meager attainment.

In fact, the Buddha's essential teaching is this: "I would rather you were reborn as a mangy old fox than for you to become a follower of the Two Vehicles." If by placing your trust in this false teaching you sink below the level of a suppurating fox, what possible help can you be to others? Seeking the truth of Nirvana by trying to sweep away suffering and its causes is like trying to flail the clouds and mist from the sky with a long pole. You will keep sweeping until you grow old and die. Your suffering will continue for three lives, sixty long kalpas, and since throughout those rebirths you will be unable to gain the strength that comes from *kenshō*, you will be destined to move through a series of purposeless, empty lives and purposeless, empty deaths.

Some of today's silent illumination Zennists may have experienced a limited *kenshō* such as the Pratyeka-buddhas achieve. But they then attach mulishly to the truth they have grasped and are unable to proceed beyond it. They cling to an empty emptiness, and they deny the principle of cause and effect and future existence. Angulimalya scorned the Buddha's disciple Shariputra, saying, "You have no more wisdom than an earthworm buried in the mud. It gazes up but is unable to see a single thing."*

A fully attained Bodhisattva is not like that. He undergoes untold difficulties and suffering as he bores completely through the great Way's profoundest source. Even then he refuses to remain in the final abode of highest enlightenment. Instead he investigates extensively through the sutras and commentaries, through works of the Lesser and Greater Vehicles, accumulating an immeasurable store of superlative Dharma assets. Vigorously spurring forward the wheel of the four great vows, he works to extend salvation to all sentient beings, endeavoring constantly to practice the great Dharma

---

*Angulimalya, a ruthless killer, vowed he would kill a thousand people and make a wreath with their fingers. Buddha stopped him from making his own mother his one thousandth victim and converted him to Buddhism.

giving, his efforts never faltering over timeless kalpas—"even should the great void itself end, his universal vow would never be exhausted."

Recently, one of the blind, false priests who advocate "withered sitting," silent illumination Zen brought a group of monks all the way from Harima province and took up temporary residence in an old temple in western Mino province.* After ringing the temple bell and gathering people to the temple, the priest gave them a muddled teaching that denied the principle of cause and effect, not a single word of it worth hearing. "Heaven and Hell do not exist. Birth and death and Nirvana are illusions. After you die, the *kon* spirit returns to the heavens and the *haku* spirit returns to the Yellow Springs.† What could remain once your body is cremated? For whom are those offerings of tea, incense, and flowers made?"

His teaching deeply confused upstanding members of the lay community. Glaring angrily, their teeth tightly clenched, they said, "For years we have believed in the teachings Buddhist priests gave us. We have held annual memorial services to worship the Buddhas. But it was all completely mistaken." They immediately set about destroying the altar rooms in their houses. They cast out all the wooden and clay Buddhist images that were enshrined in them. They turned the gravesites of their parents into farmland. In market and field they sang songs that poured scorn on Buddhist priests.

In order to learn for himself what this man was preaching, a priest of Gudō's Zen lineage attended one of his lecture meetings. When he was afterward introduced to the man, the priest spoke frankly. "It is said that unless you have something beneficial to say, you should hold your tongue. Nonetheless, I feel compelled to ask why you refute what other priests have always taught about the spirits of the dead?"

"I have never seen a dead person's spirit. That is my basis for refuting those teachings," he replied.

"Have you been to China or India and seen them for yourself? If you believe only what you see, India and China should not exist either. Don't you realize that everyone who does not experience *kenshō*, whether he is a priest or a layman, becomes a ghost or spirit when he dies?"

---

*As Harima was Bankei Yōtaku's home province, this can be taken as a reference to one of his successors.

†*Kon* is the soul or spirit's yang aspect, *haku* the yin aspect. It was believed that at death the *kon* part returned to the heavens and the *haku* part to the netherworld, or Yellow Springs.

The priest's head sunk on his chest, his face assuming a pallid, claylike hue.

"Why do you continue to deceive laymen and -women with such false teachings? I am going to return here tomorrow and ask you about a certain matter. If you are unable to answer, a terrifying fate lies in store for you."

Although the lecture meeting was still only several days old, the priest stole away that night and fled to Ōgaki. He took a room there in a layman's house and soon began spreading his irresponsible notions once again. Citizens of western Mino province who lived within five leagues of Ōgaki all fell under the spell of the nonsense the blind priest fed them. Rumor has it that they stopped holding memorial services for their parents and ceased observing the traditional Urabon festival for the spirits of the dead.

The preaching of the Buddhist Dharma is not to be treated lightly. It must be undertaken only with the utmost care and prudence. Anyone who preaches an impure Dharma is destined to fall into Hell. A man once heard a priest speak just two words—"Does not fall"—and descended for five hundred lives into existence as a fox.* For leading his followers astray, this priest has committed a sin that is certain to land him in the deepest part of the Hell of Interminable Pain.

Among the villages surrounding Kyoto and Edo one sometimes encounters those phony roadside blowhards known as *dangi* priests.†
These roadside preachers sit on thick cushions, raising themselves high above their audience, and deliver bantering monologue that is coarse and vulgar from beginning to end. Their primary aim is to get people to give them donations. They push a dipper in people's faces, urging them to drop some money into it, or pass a basket around for the same purpose. They will on occasion even leave their teaching perch and descend into the audience, imploring them loudly for their help. "Money! Please. I want your money!" It's just like the beggars you see down around the Uji Bridge. People with any sense narrow their eyes when they see this and get up and leave.

Not only the landed gentry but wealthy citizens as well will tell you that preachings to spread the Buddhist teaching are designed for the ears of ignorant old men and women, not for people of refined discernment.

Careful reflection shows how true this is. With a deep sigh and furrowed brow I am obliged to report that the great majority of those called

---

*Reference to the story "Po-chang's Fox," found in the *Gateless Barrier,* Case 2.
†These were Buddhist priests, or people posing as such, who received money from people by preaching to them in a humorous style at the roadside.

priests today are no better than these roadside beggars. Respect and reverence for Buddha's Dharma is steadily being undermined, and the sangha's reputation decreases by the hour. How deplorable it is to witness the decline of the Dharma in this Latter Day.

Although what these fellows teach is not worth a proper refutation, how could a person who has even the smallest desire to protect the Dharma shrink from even that small effort? Though these shameless priests possess mouths—they'd have to in order to take in food*—they should starve to death rather than open them to expound a bogus teaching. For having committed the sin of slandering the true Dharma, they are indeed to be pitied. For their transgression and for disgracing the priesthood, they are headed for a retribution of endless torment.

Some years ago, during the Shōhō era (1644–48), if I remember correctly, there lived in eastern Mino province an ignorant priest who persisted in totally deluding lay followers with a teaching that denied the working of karma. It was much the same as the teaching preached by the priest from Harima province just mentioned. His lay followers threw out the Buddhist images in their shrine rooms. They destroyed their ancestors' graves. Not long after, the god of pestilence visited the homes of people who had converted to the perverse views of this priest. Enlisting the help of a shrine maiden, they prayed for assistance. The deity of the shrine delivered an oracle through the maiden, revealing that the false teachings they were following had brought on the epidemic.

Enraged and burning with resentment, young and old assembled and began laying plans to waylay the sham priest in the night and beat the life out of him. The priest, beside himself with fear, stole out of his temple under cover of darkness with seven or eight of his followers and fled eastward in the direction of Edo. But before they had reached the Ōda crossing they were suddenly enveloped in thick, muscular black clouds as dark as ink. Rain poured down on them as if from inverted buckets. Lightning flashes, accompanied by deafening claps of thunder, split the earth around them. Terrified, the priests collapsed to the ground. They recovered and prostrated themselves, only to once again fall to the ground unconscious.

When the thunder had ceased and the skies had cleared, astonished

---

*Hakuin uses the saying, *kuchi areba, kui; kata areba, kiru*: "As long as you have a mouth you can eat; as long as you have shoulders you can wear a robe," meaning: no one need worry about sustaining life; he will be able to manage somehow or other.

villagers from the nearby hamlets gathered around the priests. Pitying them, they gave them water and medicine. The priests gradually regained their senses, but when they were able to get up and move about, they were surprised to find that their teacher was nowhere to be seen. He had totally vanished. They ran this way and that, calling out his name. Who could have imagined? His head, arms, legs, and other parts of his body were found scattered in seven different places along the river levee! A Buddhist priest must be extremely careful not to expound teachings that deny cause and effect.

Another elder priest belonging to this karma-denying, Dharma-destroying fraternity appeared in western Mino province during the Genroku era (1688–1704). The fellow obviously had no experience of *kenshō* whatever, and yet he still he tirelessly spread his noxious teachings among the lay community. But as we learned from the story of the Harima priest, if there is anything you want to avoid at all costs, it is the accumulation of evil karma by expounding a false teaching.

This priest fell afoul of some baseless accusations that were directed at him out of the blue. The accusations were traced to their source, and some truly abhorrent facts came to light. It seems there was a layman attached to his temple who was especially skilled in the devious methods of deceitful argument. Fired by a grudge he harbored against the priest, the layman worked up a fabric of groundless allegations and together with his confederates drafted a written complaint. They affixed their seals to it and presented it on at least ten occasions to officials at the castle. As many of the officials were receptive to bribes, the layman finally succeeded in having an obscure and unfair judgment issued. The priest was sentenced to death and executed.

Not long after that, one of the officials who had delivered the judgment suddenly began raving like a lunatic. He was in great agony and seemed to be suffocating. At this point the spirit of the priest appeared to the official. "I was innocent," he said. "But in a most villainous manner you and your confederates had me put to death. Your crime extends beyond the limits of the universe. When you die, you will fall into the Hell of Interminable Suffering." Three days later, pop-eyed and grinding his teeth, the official died.

The priest's spirit now visited the official's confederates one by one, haunting them with his accusations until they were all petrified with fear. Hardly a day passed without a funeral being held for one of them. Those who still survived fled in broad daylight with their hair hanging loose around their necks and shoulders. They could be seen dodging and darting at great speed this way and that like wild hares. Some died raging with anger, cursing and reviling, shrieking and spitting blood. Others argued boundary disputes or water rights for their fields, hurled abuse at one another, and finally took up their mattocks and sickles, wielding them in open conflict. The fierce fighting left rows of bodies lining the village streets. With farmlands and villages filled with murderous cries, you would have thought you had fallen into one of the Shrieking Hells. And all of this was caused by the priest's vengeful spirit. Entering people's vitals, he would have them cursing angrily, or shrieking bitterly, or gnashing their teeth in a wrathful frenzy.

The priest had a young disciple in his early thirties. Unable to just sit back and witness these terrible acts of violence, he put on his surplice, made three deep bows, and offered a stick of incense. Weeping mournfully, and with great trepidation, he fearfully addressed his teacher's funeral tablet (*ihai*) on the altar:

"My teacher was a fine Buddhist priest, a person deeply committed to the Way. How could such a man have become involved in this terrible business? What transgression was it that got him involved in these awful and misfortunate events?"

A spirit appeared and answered. "I am indeed sad to hear you ask such questions. If you yourself should break through into *kenshō*, you must never rest satisfied with that small attainment. It would be a sin of such magnitude as to fill the vast heavens. In the past I myself engaged in arduous training. I was focused solely on investigating the hidden depths. I believed that I had acquired the power that comes from *kenshō*. But because I left my teacher too soon, I lapsed into believing the nihilistic teaching that existence ends with death.* I regret that I did not push forward the wheel of the four great vows and work to save others. How precious is the ocean-like vastness of the four universal vows, which can free people from attachment to a one-sided, empty emptiness. You must never place your trust in false doctrines preached by false teachers."

By the time the spirit had finished speaking, sorrowful tears were flowing like blood down his cheeks. The disciple, also in tears, made a deep bow and left. He now realized for the first time what a truly fearful

---

*Literally, the *danmu* (or *danken*) heresy, which denies that one is rewarded or punished in a subsequent existence for deeds committed in the present life.

undertaking it is to preach the Dharma, and that now he must above all dedicate his efforts to seeking the Bodhi mind.

In the Shōtoku era (1711–15) there was a priest in Edo who called himself Zenkai. He is said to have been a nephew of Butchō Rōjin.* He began his Zen practice at the age of twenty-three and experienced a *kenshō*. Unfortunately, however, he did not encounter a real teacher and never learned about post-satori practice. Attached to the understanding he had attained, he continued to practice "withered tree" sitting. But he lamented how difficult it still was for him to control the workings of his mind. He decided to enter the mountains of Kumano on the Kii peninsula, cut himself off from the outside world, and devote himself to an austere training regimen. On his way, he passed through Awano in Mino province, thinking to stop for a while with several priests of his acquaintance who were residing there. Meeting Zenkai and seeing the strength he had attained in his pursuit of the Way, his friends were more than glad to take him in when he arrived. But they were dismayed when they heard of his plan to proceed into the forests of Kumano. They urged him to find a quiet hermitage in Mino. Zenkai agreed, and gave up his idea of going to Kumano altogether.

It is a thousand pities that because a student fails to encounter a genuine teacher at the beginning of his training and remains ignorant of the practice that continues after satori, he will delight in immersing himself in a pure existence of this kind, cut off from the world. Engaged in such profitless silent meditation, he focuses intently on ridding his mind of thoughts and attaining a state of no-mind, constantly sweeping thoughts from his mind and doing everything he can to keep it empty and pure.

For forty years Zenkai continued to reside in the hermitage he built in Mino. With growing age, his resolve began to falter. His heart grew weary. He found that the more he tried to sweep thoughts from his mind, the more confused his mind became. Although having lived to a considerable age as a Buddhist priest, as death approached his fears of the sufferings that lay ahead in the next world remained. He began quietly to recite the Nembutsu. When in time he came to regard this as a rather roundabout way of reaching awakening, he started repeating his own name instead, "Zenkai, Zenkai," over and over.

Where had the original attainment he had experienced as a young

---

*Butchō Ka'nan (1642–1716). A Sōtō priest perhaps best known as the teacher of the haiku poets Bashō and Kikaku.

monk gone? Now his nights were plagued by bad dreams, his days tormented by troubling thoughts. He visited various Buddhist teachers seeking their advice on how to break through this impasse. They told him he was suffering from "Zen sickness" and could offer him no help. He took to moping about, and doing zazen with tears in his eyes.

One priest, feeling pity for him, said, "Why don't you go to Suruga province and see Master Kokurin [Hakuin]. I am sure he will be able to help you."

With considerable difficulty owing to his great age, the priest made his way to my temple in Suruga and earnestly requested an interview. The monk who received him came to my chambers with a smile on his face. "A grubby old priest with a broken-down old pilgrim's case on his back just showed up," he reported. "His hair is tangled like a mugwort ball, he has a filthy face, and his robe and sedge hat are in tatters. He requested an interview with you in the gruff accent of the Bandō region. Will you see him?"

I said, "Tell him I'm sick. Give him something to eat and then send him on his way." Then I heard a voice shouting loudly from outside the gate, "I'm an old man. I'm over eighty years old. I had a very long trip to come here. Are you going to pretend you're sick and just send me away! Where is your compassion?" I had little choice but to grant his request. He came into my chambers. "I have suffered for years from Zen sickness," he blustered. "Please, master, in your great compassion, do something for me. Help me!"

"Tell me about your Zen sickness—what is it like?" I asked.

"I'm troubled by thoughts in the daytime. At night I have bad dreams," he replied.

"Do you know what is having those troubling thoughts?" I asked.

"Stop, please. I can't bear to think about emptiness," he said.

"What's wrong with thinking about emptiness?" I asked.

"If a person attaches to emptiness, he will surely fall into hell."

"Come a little closer, I'm going to free you from your suffering."

"I'm certainly glad to hear that," he said, and drew towards me.

"Do you know how many hells exist for someone attached to emptiness?" I asked him.

"No, I don't know that," he replied.

"There are eighty-six. I want you to go down into hell right now and distribute yourself among all eighty-six."

Wordless, the priest stared pie-eyed at me.

"Come on! Get down into them!"

"Priests are supposed to save you from hell. What kind of teacher would try to send a student there?" he cried.

"You say you're from Kantō, but it seems you've never heard what Suzuki Shōsan said: 'The direct, rough-hewn spirit of Kantō is very close to Zen.'* If you were really a Kantō priest, you should be able to jump into hell without a second thought."

"Could you?" he said.

"Get down there and explore those hells, one by one! There's not a single hell I haven't fallen into!"

He abruptly prostrated himself before me. His eyes had filled with tears. "What a great and wonderful teacher you are, master Hakuin," he said. "Your compassion has liberated me. Allowed me to break completely free from my delusions. I feel as though I have suddenly awakened from a terrible dream. There is no way I can describe the joy I now feel!" He prostrated himself twenty or thirty times, crying and laughing all the while. He then left, returned to the guests' quarters, latched the door shut, and went to sleep.

The next morning Zenkai approached me with a broad smile on his face. I asked him whether he had seen any bad dreams during the night. "I hadn't enjoyed a sound sleep for over forty years," he said. "But last night I slept like a log. It's the difference between a mediocre physician, who always doles out the same medicine to his patients, and a great one, who prescribes a purgative at just the right time. If you had not applied that purgative just when you did, how could you have saved me from that terrible sickness?"†

When he finished speaking, he performed I don't know how many prostrations before me. I myself was overcome with joy. I spelled out to him, in slow and deliberate terms, the importance of the practice that comes after satori. I also gave him a piece of paper inscribed with the four universal vows. He came to me a few days later, made his parting bows and, with a mixed feeling of joy and sorrow, went on his way.

From Shōin-ji he traveled to Edo, where he took up residence in a hermitage. He formed the habit of facing toward the west [the direction of

---

*The words Hakuin uses here, *Kantō rappa*, are not recorded in the dictionary. They are used by the Zen teacher Suzuki Shōsan (1579–1655) to describe the rugged and direct character of the samurai of the Kantō region (around Edo), in contrast to the elegance and refinement of those in the more cultured home provinces around Kyoto.

†Hakuin uses the name *konren-zai*, a well-known Chinese herbal medicine, used at the time as a purgative.

Hakuin's temple], making his bows, and mournfully weeping: "How fortunate I was to encounter a venerable priest who pushed me down into the great hells. I trod the karmic roots tying me to birth and death into the dust. I kicked over the mill churning out evil passions in that old den. And I attained the wonderful joy and peace of the great deliverance. Yet if I become satisfied with this, I'll turn out to be just like Mokuami.* How wonderful that old priest's great mercy and compassion was, teaching me about post-satori training and the four universal vows. How wonderful the wheel of the four vows, which smashes the perverse notion that death is the end of all things. Its virtue surpasses all the secrets of the three worlds.

"Throughout the past there have been those who sank into the morass of this empty emptiness after attaining enlightenment because they trusted in their own arbitrary views. Fond of citing phrases such as 'a man with no matters in his mind is truly noble,' preaching notions like those of Taoist hermits in the tradition of Chuang Tzu and Lao Tzu, they declared that true happiness is found in the total detachment of empty emptiness. They squandered their precious time on earth leading a shameless life in accord with their own self-centered lights, and as a result they piled up incalculable stores of evil karma, unaware that they were destined to fall into the evil paths forever.

"One of these priests, a man who greatly revered Shakamuni Buddha, died and was reborn as a fine horse named Shōgetsu. It had this priest's name emblazoned on its lower left flank. Then he was reborn as an ox-demon pulling a cart of fire in hell. Another priest died and was born as a large turtle that paddled in the Nagara River. Yet another priest turned into a plague demon who brought death and suffering to countless men and women. Another was ripped apart by lightning for preaching that all things end with death.

"All of them came to these unfortunate ends because they were ignorant of post-satori training. If I had not received the teaching of an enlightened master, I would have ended up exactly as they did. I would have fallen into

---

*From the proverb "*moto no Mokuami*" ("the same Mokuami as before"), which is based on an episode in Japanese history. The sixteenth-century warlord Tsutsui Junshō, suffering from a fatal illness and wanting to conceal the fact of his death until his son and heir came of age, ordered his followers to use a poor blind monk named Mokuami, whose voice resembled his, as his double. After carrying out this role and living in extreme luxury for over a year, the son attained his majority, and Mokuami was abruptly returned to his former indigence.

the evil destinations when I died and suffered indescribable torments. I must honor and value above all else the debt, so impossible to repay, that I owe my teacher.

"I have recently been greatly puzzled as to why none of the fine Buddhist teachers of the past has spoken of the practice that comes after satori. I searched through the *Records of the Lamp, Compendium of the Five Lamps, Extensive Records of the Lamp, Sequel to the Records of the Lamp,* the *Blue Cliff Record, Record of Hsu-t'ang,* and *Records of the Essential Mirror.* I combed the records of other Zen masters as well. But I never found any mention of this very important matter. How wonderful it is that my teacher Kokurin has devoted his life to making this great truth known, to teaching people that post-satori practice invariably gives rise to the Bodhi-mind and enables people to avoid the awful fate that awaits them in the evil paths. He is indeed an Udumbara flower, blossoming in the degenerate latter day of the Dharma, the kind of priest who appears only once every five hundred years! How fortunate someone as unworthy as me was able to encounter him. If I had not, I never would have avoided that terrible calamity. No matter what I do, no matter how hard I try, I will never be able to repay even one tenth of the debt I owe him.

"There have been numberless people throughout the past who despite having attained satori sank into the view that death is the end of all existence by relying on their own confused notions. Some of them have preached that 'doing nothing is the true man of nobility.' Some have claimed, 'we are Buddhas just as we are,' pointing out that a wooden bowl left in its original state and receiving no lacquer will never chip or lose its color. Notions like these are the dregs of thoroughly fatuous assumptions. You could coat them with sticky rice and throw them out under the trees, but not even the crows would show the least interest in them.

"These people have simply confounded the fundamental source of their illusions for their original face, their true self, when it is in fact the eighth or store consciousness. This is the reason the great teacher Ch'ang-sha said, 'practicers fail to grasp the truth because they continue to seek it in the workings of their minds. Those workings have been the source of samsaric rebirth from the beginning of time, yet still they refer to it foolishly as "the original person."'*

"Anyone who believes these heretical views is a fool of the first order. He brings suffering and destruction on himself. Many people think this

---

Records of the Lamp, ch. 10.

nondiscriminatory consciousness is the true mind, that true Buddhist practice consists of assiduously sweeping away deluded thoughts. But even if they swept thoughts away nonstop for three billion kalpas, they would never attain the Buddha Way, and their chances would be even worse if they also held the perverse views of 'do-nothing' Zen and empty, one-sided emptiness. Such people are sure to fall into one of the three evil destinations of rebirth—Hell, Hungry Ghosts, or Animals—when they die. The prevalence of these views is a dire omen that the Buddha Dharma is dying out.

"These errors are due entirely to the lack of the Bodhi-mind. You should concentrate all your efforts on preaching the Dharma. Apart from this, there is no Bodhi-mind. The supreme Bodhi-mind is a jewel beyond all price. Anyone who calls himself a Buddhist priest must be aware of this peerless and inestimable path.

"Long ago the World-Honored One expounded this verse teaching:*

"Were all the rarest treasures throughout the three worlds
Distributed as alms, the merit obtained from doing that
Would be far exceeded by one phrase of Dharma preaching.
Were all essential things in the three worlds given as alms,
Its merit would be greatly surpassed by one Dharma utterance.
Were gems as numerous as Ganges sand offered as alms
At services performed for Tathagatas in all ten directions,
Its merit would be far exceeded by one word of Dharma
    preaching.

"Why does no one expound such a preaching in this period of the latter day? I have heard from Kokurin that this verse well describes National Master Gudō's style of Zen. Imagine how joyful Master Gudō must be, dwelling within the great samadhi, at having acquired such a Dharma son, a Dharma son who excels his Dharma father! It is for this reason that even when I sleep I never allow my feet to face west [the direction of Hakuin's temple]."

After uttering words like these, old Zenkai always prostrated himself in tears. When I heard how he was always praising me in this way, I held my nose a little higher, in spite of myself.

---

*Similar verses are found in the Lotus and Flower Garland sutras.

How could I have conceived that by conducting a lecture meeting on the *Blue Cliff Record,* I would penetrate the secret of Tung-shan's Five Ranks? I was so exceedingly happy, my tongue inadvertently poked out of my mouth. Who understands the tremendous power that the Five Ranks possess? They are a great and unsurpassed Dharma treasure that could rescue today's muddled, karma-denying Zennists from the terrible fate awaiting them in the evil paths. A precious torch whose brightness can illuminate the darkness of this degenerate day. Although the Sōtō sect possesses this truly wonderful asset, its priests remain attached to zazen and give no consideration to it. Priests of the Rinzai sect reject it because they regard it as different from their own brand of Zen. This is like concealing the fabulous, night-gleaming pearl inside a box.* They have rejected it like a shard left and forgotten in an old shed. They are like a blind man who discards his walking stick.

The secrets of the Five Ranks have been transmitted through the ages in the *Precious Mirror Samadhi.* The author of the *Precious Mirror Samadhi* is unknown. Zen patriarchs Shih-t'ou, Yueh-shan, and Yun-yen imparted the secrets of the Five Ranks personally from one to another in the privacy of the teaching room. Tung-shan Liang-chieh took great care in composing his verses on the Five Ranks, setting forth with clarity the Five Ranks' gradual progression. Tung-shan's work is like a brilliant torch on a dark night path, like a ferry that appears at a difficult ford to take you across to the other shore.†

Master Shōju said, "The patriarchal teachers in their great compassion devised the principles of the Five Ranks in order to save students who had attained satori from the danger of entering the evil paths. If a student devotes himself assiduously to the Five Ranks, he will surely succeed in realizing the Four Wisdoms. Sadly, the Zen gardens have fallen into their present state of decay because priests who prided themselves on attaining a partial enlightenment remained ignorant of the true essentials of Buddhist practice. Unwittingly they entered the stagnant water of meager attainment, fell forever into a black pit filled with hard, dry seeds. And all because they did not know the secrets of the Five Ranks.

"The Five Ranks appear in the *Precious Mirror Samadhi*:

> In the six lines of the Double Li hexagram,
> Phenomenal and Universal are interdependent:

---

*See above, p. 132.
†Hakuin explains the Five Ranks in greater detail in Book Three, #51, #52.

When folded, they become three,
When their permutations end, they are five.

"'Universal' is the embodiment of the true formless form. 'Phenomenal' describes the function of the myriad dharmas in their particularity. When a practicer in pursuit of awakening kindles a fire in his vitals and presses forward through a thousand trials and ten thousand tribulations, he will, as a result of the dauntless courage he has exerted, smash the eighth storehouse consciousness. As the eighth consciousness shatters, his heart and liver will shatter as well, and he will immediately experience the great death. He will be astonished to discover that the eighth consciousness is itself the radiant Great Mirror Wisdom, and he will note that its radiance is the color of black lacquer. When he attains this point, he will understand for the first time that heaven and earth and empty space in all directions do not exist. There is for him no seer or seen, here or there, this or that, and yet he embraces all the myriad things in the universe. This is the first of the Five Ranks, called Phenomenal within Universal. Tung-shan's verse has:

At the third watch of the night, before the moon comes up.

The pitch darkness of the third night watch is the Rank of the Absolute or Universal. Embraced within it are all the myriad dharmas—the Rank of the Relative or Phenomenal. At this point, the practicer's discernment is still not fully clear. He moves as though in the shadow of a lamp—"the old suspicions still remain."

If the student remains satisfied and does not proceed beyond this, he will unfortunately fall forever into the poisonous seas of empty, one-sided emptiness. If he continues beyond it, he will enter the Precious Mirror Samadhi, in which self and objects reflect each other like facing mirrors. This is also known as contemplation of the true form of all dharmas. Here the relativities and differences of the actual world (all dharmas) are grasped as such, as the true form of sameness or identity (true forms).

Although the two mirrors illuminate each other, no image is reflected in either of them. Mind and its environment are in a state of oneness, self and things in a state of nonduality. The self that views and the objects viewed fuse perfectly into one. This is the Five Ranks' Universal within Phenomenal.

Here the practicer attains the Wisdom of Sameness in which, unattached to distinctions of this and that, he discerns the sameness or identity of all things. Yet if he stops and resides in this Wisdom, he becomes like a demon keeping watch over a corpse in a coffin. If he does not leave this Rank, he will find himself seated in a sea of virulent poison. The Rank of Coming from Within the Universal was devised to free students from this deadly sea. Tung-shan's verse says, "Within nothingness is a way beyond the worldly dust." Today, the Sōtō school calls this "coming from the realm of absolute identity into the realm of relativity and difference."

In the Wisdom of Sameness, where all things are seen as identical, with no attachment to differences of any kind, there is no self or other, no inner or outer, no entering or departing. It is like a round lump of iron or steel. It is here that "the way within nothingness" is to be sought. What is this "way within nothingness"? It is the path that great and unconditional compassion opens up within nothingness. It is not a narrow trail, like those used by woodcutters. It is a great royal way, which leads directly to the capital of ultimate nondoing.

Thanks to unconditional great compassion, the student learns the comportment of the Bodhisattva and works constantly to create the conditions of a Buddha-land on earth. This practice is the function of the Bodhi-mind itself. How wonderful, the arousing of the Bodhi-mind! Without the Bodhi-mind, we would all of us fall into the evil ways.

If a person wishes to attain the Bodhi-mind, he must whip forward the wheel of the four universal vows, working to deepen his own enlightenment while helping sentient beings still left behind in illusion. Foremost among all the ways of doing this is preaching the Dharma—the great Dharma gift.

The Dharma gift is not imparted to all students in the same way. It is imparted in response to their differing capacities—superior, average, and inferior. To teach students of superior capacity, the teacher must himself possess superior capacity. The best way to achieve that capacity is through the attainment of *kenshō*, seeing into your true nature. Unless you have clarified your own self-nature, you can hardly expect to clarify it for others. You must achieve a clear *kenshō*, as clear as though you are looking down at it in the palm of your hand.

Next, you must penetrate koan stories filled with deadliest poison—Su-shan's Memorial Tower and Nan-ch'uan's Flower in the Garden. You must make your way through impenetrable thorn thickets that stretch for ten thousand leagues, boring into the great matter that is impossible to understand, impossible to enter. Then you must throw yourself into the study of the sutras and commentaries and assemble a boundless store of priceless Dharma assets. When you have done that, you will have attained the Wisdom of Marvelous Observation.

But even when you have assembled an infinite store of Dharma assets, if you just bundle them up and forget about them, they will be no more use to you than discarded tools in an empty shed. You must gird yourself up and devote yourself with fierce determination to putting these assets to work in liberating all the numberless sentient beings. Such is the conduct of the Bodhisattva who strives to establish a Buddha-land on earth. This is called the Wisdom of Benefiting Others. It is Arriving at Mutual Integration, the fourth of the Five Ranks. Recently, some have said that this is the rank of Arriving within the Phenomenal, but such a statement is ludicrous.* Tung-shan's verse says, "Two blades cross, no need for either to draw back."

In a previous verse Tung-shan also said, "Don't break the taboo of using names that cannot be spoken." You must not put ultimate things into words. If you speak of such things as "mind" or "nature," or anything relating to the true self, you will break the taboo. "Grandmotherly compassion," chewing up rice before feeding it to your child, would also fall under this taboo. It is like dragging an ox into the weeds and trying to force it to eat.

You must vow that you will never teach or preach "grandmotherly" Zen. It is a great impediment to a student striving to attain enlightenment. It is like feeding poison to a favorite daughter. Once the poison enters her body, it destroys her womb so that she will be incapable of giving birth. "Cutting open the chrysalis to free a cicada" is also grandmotherly Zen. Such an act hinders the development of the great doubt, and unless a student is able to form a great doubt, he cannot achieve a great satori. Silent illumination, withered sitting, do-nothing Zen, with its "unvarnished bowls just as they are," shuts the gates of enlightenment fast. It takes a valiant hero, a young boy who has left his home and parents to seek the Way, and turns him into a blind and ignorant oaf.

Today, at a time when the true Zen traditions have fallen to earth and the true Dharma headed for extinction, it is terrifying to see these false priests promulgating such pernicious teachings. Why can't they just teach

---

*Hakuin presumably refers to some contemporary Sōtō work on the Five Ranks, though Tung-shan himself uses a phrase similar to this, Coming from within the Phenomenal (*Henchūshi*). It was later emended by the Sung dynasty Lin-chi priest Fen-yang Shan-chao (947–1024) to Arriving at Integration (*Kenchūshi*), a change Hakuin embraces.

the true Dharma? A Dharma teaching can be extraordinarily beneficial or extraordinarily harmful. If the Dharma is taught for monetary gain or reputation, it is an impure teaching. Someone who preaches an impure Dharma will fall directly into Hell when he dies. Praising oneself and deprecating others violates the Buddhist precepts. You should regard all people as though they were your only child. Whether court noble or peasant, the self-nature at the depths of their being is one and the same. If there is the slightest discrimination in the way you view them, that also is contrary to the Buddha Way. But among all teachings, the most perverse and abhorrent is one that denies the principle of karma and karmic rebirth.

On the occasion of National Master Gudō's one hundredth death anniversary, I visited Rurikō-ji in Mino province and lectured on a score of cases in the *Blue Cliff Record*. During my stay I heard stories about the Zen teaching in the Mino area. It seems that successors of the sham priests I have been mentioning have won over clerics and lay people in various places in the province by preaching the heresy that everything ends with death.*

To refute the perverse and nebulous empty emptiness of these men, I scribbled off a rude series of verses as I was being carried by palanquin from Mino to Hida province. Words like "servant," "vassal," and even "slave" have been applied to people who merely follow in the ruts of the ancients when composing poetry. Although I have emulated the verses in the Buddha's sutras and disregarded such poetic niceties as meter and rhyme, I will still no doubt be censured as "a slave of religious verse."

There once was a priest, proficient in both wisdom and practice, who resolved to seek out a peaceful sanctuary where he could engage in a retreat.† After considerable effort, he finally located a cave deep in the mountains. He was extremely happy with the site. There was a large flat rock in front and a large tree towering above it. He did zazen all day long on the flat rock. But when night came, a flock of herons, several hundred strong, flew in and perched in the tree overhead. They squawked and squabbled all through the night. The priest looked up, performed *gasshō*, and addressed them in a loud voice, "There are many large trees in the world. With your wings you herons could fly and perch in any of them.

*The *danmu* heresy, which teaches that the self has no future existence after death, thus denying the Buddhist principle of cause and effect.
†This story is told in the *Commentary on the Great Wisdom Sutra*, ch. 17; also *Horse Thistles*, p. 225.

It took me a long time and much hard travel to find a quiet spot where I could meditate. Leave this tree and allow me to do my zazen. You make so much noise that it is impossible for me to concentrate on my practice."

At first light the herons flew off again, but at dusk they returned and assumed their perches in the tree. Angered, the priest was unable to get any sleep that night, and as the herons flew off the next morning, he glared up at them and yelled at the top of his lungs, "Why do you insist on flying in here and disturbing my meditation! If you keep coming here, I'll have to leave this cave and find another one somewhere else. If I end up wandering aimlessly around the country and am unable to complete my practice, I will be reborn as a great and powerful hawk. I will grab you, rip you to pieces, and devour you all!"

When night came, the herons returned once again, and the priest set out with tears in his eyes for other parts. After much travel he came to a cave among the cliffs. It overlooked a deep lake ten thousand yards across, and was large enough for him to make into his living quarters. It was a spot of great beauty and tranquility totally cut off from the world, so the priest was elated, and unpacked his travel pouch to stay. He spent the entire day sitting upright in zazen, immersed in the profound realm of no-mind.

Unfortunately, the lake was inhabited by a great many fish and turtles, and their sporting and splashing through the waves day and night created considerable noise. This troubled and angered the priest as much as the squawking herons had. When they too ignored all his pleas and attempts to reason with them, he went to the lakeside and hollered out, "You are obstructing my zazen. What did I ever do to you to deserve this? I'm going to leave this cave, but if I fail to attain the Way, I'm going to be reborn as an otter. I'm going to tear all of you to shreds and eat you!"

The priest left the cave in tears the next morning, but as he walked along he was no longer able to endure the resentment burning inside him. "I'll no doubt find similar obstacles wherever I go. I'll never be free of this anger. I'll be better off ending my life right here. Then I won't have to endure this anger and resentment any longer."

In this fit of rage he threw himself into the lake and sank beneath the waves. He was soon reborn as an otter, and began sporting freely through the water, turning and twisting a hundred different ways, catching the denizens of the lake one by one. He ripped off their heads, he crushed them in his teeth, until the lake was crimson with their blood. Exhausted, the otter fell back in a daze. Just then a noisy flock of squawking herons flew overhead. Taking one look at them, the otter's eyes filled with hate. Gnashing his teeth, he yelled up at the birds, "I've been waiting for you herons. I made a promise on that flat rock under the large tree. I've been waiting for a chance to carry it out ever since I became an otter. Not a single bird is going to leave here alive." Two great hawk-like wings suddenly sprouted from his sides and he rose out of the lake and began flapping his way through the sky. He moved like a lightning bolt, seizing the herons in midair, ripping them apart and devouring them. Heron wings and feathers wafted on the wind like willow fluff. Their blood fell like crimson rain from the sky. The clear pure waters of the bottomless lake once again turned crimson.

How many lives had he taken? He belonged to the fraternity of Buddhist priests, but because he never learned about the practice that must continue after *kenshō*, he ended up inflicting these terrible calamities. He is truly to be pitied.

Long ago there was a priest of great erudition named Gedatsu at Mount Kasagi.* He often accompanied Myōe Shōnin to visit the Kasuga Shrine in Nara. When Myōe entered the shrine, the deity opened the inner doors and revealed his entire form to him. They engaged in pure spiritual discourse extending over all the sutras and commentaries. When Gedatsu went in, he could see only the deity's back, and he was never accorded the privilege of spiritual discourse. Once day, he tearfully addressed the deity, "What is it the deity finds lacking in me? How do I differ from Myōe? When Myōe comes you engage in long dialogues. But you never have a single word for me. Why do you not treat us the same? In rejecting me, it would seem that you are acting against your great vow to save all beings equally."

The deity spoke. "It is because of your achievements in learning that you are able to see my back. My only regret is that you lack the Bodhi-mind."

Gedatsu performed his bows, retired with tears in his eyes, and departed. From that time on, he constantly sought to understand why the deity had said that he lacked the Bodhi-mind.

One night, as he hung up the lamp and began to read, he heard a commotion outside, and the sounds of angry voices. Carefully opening a hole in the paper window, he peered fearfully outside. Throngs of evil demons in monstrous shapes were milling about. Some had long noses that curved up to their foreheads, others had mouths that gaped from ear to ear. They lashed out at one another, their eyes filled with hate, hurtling about with

*Hakuin tells this story in somewhat more detail in *Wild Ivy*, pp. 39–45.

lightning speed, snapping and biting with murderous intent, spattering blood everywhere—it was a scene from the realm of the fighting demons, the bloodcurdling yells from one of the Shrieking Hells.

One look had Gedatsu shaking in terror. His hair stood on end. He was on the verge of losing consciousness when he noticed an old priest, perhaps eighty years old, standing next to him. He was wearing a robe the color of yellow incense with a purple surplice over his shoulders. He was holding a rosary of crystal beads in one hand, a staff in the other. He quietly approached Gedatsu and said,

"I am a priest who lives near the fields of Kasuga. I came here when I saw that you were in imminent danger. Those unearthly beings you see come from realm of the tengu. Ever since the time of the very first Buddha, even wise and eminent priests, if they lack the Bodhi-mind and teach others the withered sitting of silent illumination, have all fallen into the paths of Mara. These beings have come here with the sole intent of making you a member of their group. But because you have in the past often provided guidance to younger monks, it is difficult for them to succeed. However, one way or another, they will before long accomplish their end and draw you in with them."

Astounded, Gedatsu made a bow and said, "Please, explain the teaching of the Bodhi-mind to me."

The priest said, "Anyone who wants to realize the Bodhi-mind must never give credence to bogus silent illumination Zen. Those who would tell you that "no-thought, no-mind" is Zen, or "He who has nothing to do is truly noble," will never master the Buddha Way. You should before everything else gird the loins of your mind and achieve a *kenshō* that is as clear as a fruit in the palm of your hand. Constantly put all the four great vows into practice. Assemble boundless Dharma assets and practice the great Dharma giving to benefit sentient beings. How truly wonderful this Bodhi-mind is!"

When the priest finished speaking, he vanished. So did the infernal shapes outside the room. It is said that this priest was a manifestation of the Kasuga deity. Would he not be deeply saddened if he saw today's withered Zennists? Priests who have not experienced *kenshō*, who do not engage in koan practice, who do not read the sutras or uphold the precepts? Priests who call themselves "upward strivers who do nothing at all," who after eating their fill of rice every day, go sit and doze on their zazen seats, yawning away, totally wasting their lives? Such people, who have learned nothing from the bitter experience of their past lives, are destined to return to their old haunts in the three evil paths when they die. Do you imagine that the deities are pleased to see this? Or does it sadden them?

Long ago, a priest named Ronshiki built a small hermitage on Mount Ikoma south of the city of Nara. He led a spartan existence, constantly engaged in the study of the *Lotus Sutra*. By cultivating a small field he was able to eke out enough food to sustain himself. He refused all visitors, fearing the attachments that would ensue from receiving their alms. He had a disciple named Sanuki who placed his faith in a teaching that denied future existence and the principle of cause and effect. Refraining from doing either good or evil, Sanuki passed a life of unprecedented idleness and indolence. When Ronshiki died, he left the hermitage to Sanuki.

Sanuki passed away four or five years later, falling directly into the evil paths of existence. He moved from one hell to another, experiencing the full measure of their terrors. In one of these hells, off in a corner, he saw a small dwelling. Its desolate tranquility reminded him of his former hermitage. Peering inside, he saw the frail, gaunt figure of his teacher Ronshiki reciting the *Lotus Sutra*. Saddened and surprised, Sanuki approached his teacher but held back from speaking to him. "My teacher performed meritorious deeds throughout his life. Everyone praised him as a man of deep faith, someone who led a strict and austere life," he thought. "I always assumed he would be residing blissfully in one of the Pure Lands. How is it possible that he is here in this terrible place of suffering?" Struggling with feelings of sadness and fear, Sanuki drew nearer and said,

"Master, you performed many virtuous acts during your lifetime. You were extremely devout. You engaged in religious practice, earned universal praise. I was sure that you had been reborn into the Pure Land."

Ronshiki, half in joy, half in sorrow, replied, "It is true that I performed good acts in my lifetime. But unfortunately I was utterly lacking in the Bodhi-mind."

"You always recited the *Lotus Sutra*, even in the bitterest cold of winter or sweltering summer heat. Surely that must show you possessed the Bodhi-mind," said Sanuki.

"No," said Ronshiki. "This is something you don't know about. A person can perform tens of thousands of virtuous acts, but if he lacks the Bodhi-mind, he will fall into the evil regions when he dies. It is true that I was very diligent in reciting the *Lotus Sutra* and always held the sutra in mind. But that was done merely for my own sake. It is the kind of practice undertaken by adherents of the Two Vehicles. I didn't engage in the greater practice that is directed toward others. Because of that, I ended up here together with followers of the Two Vehicles, those who acquire only a small attainment. I live alone in this isolated corner of hell, a realm filled with the most terrible perils, but thanks to the virtue inherent in the *Lotus Sutra* I have suffered no torment whatever. I nonetheless find it unbearable, never being able to avoid the constant cries and shrieks of victims. There is never any relief from this. The experience has broken my heart and spirit, and the sounds have rendered me deaf. I deeply regret the narrow, meager effort I put forth in my former life. Because I strove only for my own benefit, without giving a thought to others, I must accept the consequences of my actions. I have no one to blame but myself.

"There are priests today who pride themselves on teaching the doctrine of silent illumination, do-nothing Zen. They dispense with all acts that benefit either themselves or others. They preach the doctrine of no-mind with their minds filled with thought, they seek formlessness while still clutching tightly to forms. They are content when they have located a temple where they will have comfortable quarters and plenty to eat, and there they sleep their lives vainly away in a state of ignorance. This is all the result of the teachings propagated by false teachers. Because of them, priests and monks more numerous than Ganges sand have fallen into hell.

"A person who aspires to give rise to the Bodhi-mind must once experience a thoroughgoing *kenshō*. Then he must proceed to rip the divine, death-dealing koans to shreds, yank out the claws and fangs of the Dharma cave, make his way through impenetrable thickets, thousands of leagues of thorn and briar, and trample over thousands of secret, firmly shut barriers. He must carefully investigate the sutras and commentaries, both partial and complete, and master the scriptures and sacred writings of other traditions as well, acquiring a boundless store of great Dharma assets. He must then extend the great gift of Dharma to all beings, benefiting and liberating them, so they can all perfect the Buddha wisdom within. This is the practice of the perfectly achieved Bodhisattva. But Sanuki, your life in the human world is still not complete. You should return as quickly as possible."

"If only I could," said Sanuki. "But I doubt if there is any way in the ten directions that would lead me out of here."

"Wait until the reverend Jizō appears," Ronshiki said. "Ask him to help you."

Sanuki prostrated himself in gratitude. Not long after that they heard the sound of the metal rings rattling in Jizō's staff. It grew steadily louder, and suddenly the great Bodhisattva passed right in front of them. Teacher and student both prostrated themselves. Sanuki said, "Please, great Bodhisattva, have pity on me and show me the way back to the human world."

The Bodhisattva smiled and led Sanuki away with him. They entered a vast plain. Sanuki saw noxious fumes rising everywhere, fire flying through the air like sleet, and blackened, charcoal-like objects littering the ground. Here young and old, rich and poor, all dwelled together. There were merchants and peasants, kings and warriors, teachers, scholars, and priests, as well as those of the untouchable castes. There were also figures with shaved pates and surplices on their shoulders. An inordinate number of them were the sham priests of silent illumination Zen. With bloated, drum-like bellies and throats so narrowed that a needle could not pass through them, they were unable to swallow a single grain of rice, or a drop of water. They sobbed and cried out piteously:

"How deeply we regret the mistaken notions we held when we lived in the human world! We thought that after we died and were cremated, nothing remained, that heaven and hell were only empty words. We thought that making offerings to the Buddhas and the priesthood was meaningless. We said whatever we wanted to say, did whatever we pleased, unbound by any rules, and feared nothing. How could we have imagined that we would be subjected to these unspeakable torments!"

The sight of these beings, weeping pitifully, screaming and wailing, was beyond description. One old female ghost, completely naked, her body severely emaciated and blackened like a piece of charcoal, her eyes filled with anger, came up and began waving her arms and screaming at the top of her voice.

"Aren't you my son? Aren't you Sanuki? Those karma-denying notions of yours caused me to fall into this terrible place. You accepted the teachings of your evil teacher and his doctrine of no-thought, no-mind, and you persisted in saying that 'silent illumination' and 'withered sitting' is Buddhahood. You were happy to seek out places where you had lots of food and could live in comfort, then you deceived others as well, people with genuine roots of goodness, and you caused them to fall into the black pit of ignorance together with you. Now these wrongheaded teachers are found throughout the land, glibly parroting these same mistaken teachings. How will anyone be able to attain true salvation? Their crimes are so great and vast that heaven itself cannot contain them. Your own mother, your first victim, fell into the realm of hungry ghosts. If it weren't for you, I would not have to undergo this suffering! People say that a family that gives its son to the priesthood will be reborn into the heavenly realms for nine generations—hogwash! I'm going to rip you to pieces and devour you! It will give me some solace for all these years I've being suffering from this terrible hunger and thirst." Her hair stood up on her head, and she began flitting about like an evil demon.

Jizō Bodhisattva addressed her courteously and attempted to console her. "This person may resemble your son, but he isn't. He is another's person's child. Even if you did rip him to pieces and devour him, it would not bring you any benefit. It would be better for you to work for the peace of your own spirit." The Bodhisattva concealed Sanuki under the sleeve of his robe to protect him and they quickly made their escape. Sanuki then fell into a deep, dark pit. When he finally came to, he found himself [back in the human world], bathed in sweat.

Sanuki told everyone he encountered about the sufferings he had seen people experiencing in hell. Listening to him, they began shaking in panic fear, their bodies covered thickly with sweat. Conferring among themselves in secret with narrowed brows, they said, "For a long time now we've been hoodwinked by the deluded notions this evil priest has peddled to us. Shamelessly feeding us his wicked opinions, he would tell us, 'Don't worry about those teachings describing the terrors of Hell. All you need do is to remain free from seeking, free from all attachments. I want you to be like an incense burner inside an old shrine, in a constant state of no-self, no-mind. To do that is to be an old Buddha. What need is there beyond that to experience *kenshō* or attain satori? Cast all words and verbal complications aside. The old Zen stories and koans are a pack of nonsense. The teaching I give you is the best one that the Zen school has to offer. Even a menial servant can follow it. Hell and heaven are fictions. As long as you don't murder someone, or commit arson, nothing you could do will cause you to fall into Hell. And even if you do commit such grave transgressions, then we will enter the evil regions together. We'll just accept our fate, without harboring any doubts or concerns about it at all.'

"Such teachings took a great burden from our minds. We had no fears of the afterlife at all. We simply followed our desires, eating when we were hungry and drinking when we were thirsty. We could never have imagined that we would hear those experiences that Sanuki brought back with him. We fell into a terrible state of fear, not knowing what to do or where to turn.

"We deeply regret that, having been so fortunate as to receive human rebirth, which is so difficult to attain, we are now in danger of falling once again into the depths of the shrieking hells. Our teacher is already there, undergoing retribution for his evil doctrines. Who can we blame? What in the world could he have been thinking? Leading people into the evil destinations like that?"

Years ago, a woman from Hamamatsu turned into an evil demon when she died.* Taking possession of her own sister, she described to her the terrors of hell and begged her to help save her from its torments. A person who heard about this, finding her story hard to believe, asked the demon, "Didn't a virtuous Zen priest come and offer incense at your funeral? How could you have suffered such an unfortunate fate?" "Virtuous priest?" the demon replied. "What a lame joke that is. For preaching all those endless sermons that denied karmic cause and effect, he became a cow demon. He is now down in hell pulling a cart of flames. It is because he came and offered incense at my funeral that I fell into hell with him. Far from being a true priest and teacher, he was totally untrustworthy, a thoroughly disreputable character. Without having achieved *kenshō*, possessing no Dharma assets whatever, he continued to preach his pernicious, karma-denying doctrines. He would say, 'When you walk under the willow trees, won't they be green even without *kenshō*? Cherry blossoms will be pink. If you are of a mind to walk around, then walk around. If you want to sit down, sit down. Your utterly free and independent self is a precious thing! It is the natural, intrinsic body of all the Buddhas of the past. Do not go chasing about amid constantly changing circumstances trying to attain it on your own. When the mind ceases its seeking, the self is naturally at peace.' He hoodwinked a great many men and women with this teaching. It is a yawning, bottomless pit that lies in wait for people who are striving to attain liberation. Doing nothing, remaining just as you are,† is the golden chain that brings about their undoing. The worthy cause of satori thus ends in an evil result."

When the demon finished speaking, he began wailing piteously and screaming for help, filling everyone who heard him with terror and draining them of courage. "We are also destined for the evil regions when we die," they said. "What kind of religious practice did those sham priests

---

*A longer version of this story appears in *Wild Ivy* (p. 5), where Hakuin says it comes from Suzuki Shōsan's *Tales of Cause and Effect* (Inga Monogatari). A somewhat similar story is found in chapter five of that work.

†*Kinsa no nan*, literally, the "golden chain calamity." A teaching promising the ultimate prize of total freedom but which, causing you to attach to a partial attainment, should end up hindering you.

perform? What kind of attainment did they achieve? In the present day it is people like them and their false doctrines that has brought the Dharma to ruin and blasted the seeds that give rise to Buddhahood. Where are the deities who stand guard over the Dharma? Why doesn't Heaven punish these scoundrels?"

It is said that when the Dharma prospers, devils and demons prosper as well. Then why is it that today, when the Dharma is so weak, the demons alone are enjoying such prosperity? Even if Master Gudō were to reappear in the world once again, it would not be easy for him to overcome them. Our only hope is that a redoubtable generation of young monks will appear that will devote themselves assiduously to their training and go on to protect the true Dharma. Unless people of outstanding capacity acquire the kind of strength that will enable them to ascend the very heavens, it will be impossible to redeem the conditions that prevail in this latter day. Now everyone lives in fear of the horrible torments that await them in the three evil destinations of karmic existence. It is all because of these ignorant teachers and their pernicious teachings.

After the death of Master Gudō, the world was without any genuine teacher, and entered a period of great peril. A person who has not achieved *kenshō* should never put himself forward as a Zen teacher. He will hinder the attainment of genuine satori in younger generations of students and unwittingly harm the Dharma-body's lifeblood of wisdom. All those who regard themselves as descendants of the National Master should strive to revive and revitalize his style of Zen, which now lies in the dust. Anyone who desires to return the school to these true traditions should take to heart the teachings left behind by Master Shōju.

Shōju was a Dharma grandson of Master Gudō. He had a mind that was unequalled in its loftiness, rigor, and harshness. He was always teaching people with words like this:*

"Once you have experienced the breakthrough into *kenshō*, you are a fool to remain content with that small attainment. My ancestor the venerable Daien Hōkan [Gudō], gripping death-dealing talismans in his hands, brought enormous benefit to people. In his dealings with Zen students he always had power to spare.

"Long ago, seven wise women declared to the god Indra, 'If you don't

---

*As Hakuin tends to add elements of his own teaching when he quotes Shōju, sometimes, as here, it is difficult to know where a quotation ends.

have them, how can you expect to help others?"* [When Indra reported this to the Buddha,] the Buddha replied, "None of my great Arhats could understand this meaning. It is only the great Bodhisattvas who can fully grasp its significance."

What is "this meaning"? It is that which I call the poison claws and fangs of the Dharma cave.†

One day, it was before I was even nine years old, I heard someone describe the terrors of Hell. It terrified me, and I began moping about, unhappy and despondent, my eyes always wet with tears. When I turned twelve, I went in secret to my mother and begged her to allow me to enter the Buddhist priesthood. I prayed to the Bodhisattva Kannon, I worshipped the deity Tenjin, imploring them for their help. When I reached twenty-three, I traveled to the training hall of Eigan-ji in Echigo province. I worked on penetrating the source of my self-nature, keeping at it without rest, pushing myself mercilessly, dying ten times over. When I moved about I was unaware of what I was doing; when I sat I was unaware I was sitting. I was unseeing and unhearing, deaf and dumb, oblivious to all things. I felt as if I had become, as the Zen people say, "just like a dead man." One night as I was doing zazen, I suddenly heard the sound of a temple bell and my body and mind dropped completely away—I was free of even the finest dust. I experienced for the first time the truth of the saying, "not a speck of ground exists on the great earth." It was as though a thick veil of cloud and mist had suddenly opened up and I was gazing a brilliant sunrise. I shouted in spite of myself, "Old Yen-t'ou is alive!" Startled, my fellow monks came running to find out what had happened, thinking I had lost my mind. From that time on, the banners of self-esteem soared up higher than the mountain peaks. I kept crowing to myself, "No one in the past two or three hundred years has achieved such a profound enlightenment!" A constant smile on my face, I was heedless of everyone I saw—they all seemed to be enveloped in thick mist. What ecstatic joy I felt!

I must have been receiving the unseen help of the Buddha-patriarchs, for then, by chance, I encountered Shōju Rōjin and continued my study

---

*"Them" are three things the women had requested of Indra: a tree without roots, a piece of land where there is neither light nor shade, and a mountain valley where a shout does not echo. A fuller version of this story appears in *Essential Teachings of Zen Master Hakuin*, pp. 31–32.
†In a manuscript copy of *Oradegama*, Hakuin adds to this: "It is the final, ultimate word" (*matsugo no ikku*).

under him. He was a direct lineal descendent of National Master Gudō. What a priceless treasure such a great and authentic Zen teacher is!

Shōju took my pride and arrogance and crushed it like an eggshell in his hand. He looked down and laughed at me as though I was an earthworm wriggling in the mud. It seemed as though I had tumbled into a black pit thousands of feet deep. All my former joy and elation was now transformed into so much sorrow and woe. My eyes were constantly filled with tears, as though I had just lost my father or mother.

Seeing me in this pitiful state aroused grandmotherly concern in the old teacher. In his compassion he assigned me one of the venomous Zen stories to work on. [After that he gave me] Su-shan's Memorial Tower, The Water Buffalo Comes Through the Window, Nan-ch'uan's Death, Nan-ch'uan's Flower in the Garden, Chien-feng's Three Kinds of Sickness, A Thousand Snowy Peaks,* Rhinoceros Fan, Willow-fluff Blowing in the Wind,† Huang-po's Gobbler of Dregs, and The Old Woman Burns Down the Hut. As he did, he told me:

"These are the deadly old amulets of our school. After National Master Gudō passed away, people began to reject this 'small matter' that had been transmitted through generations of patriarchal teachers in India, China, and Japan as though it were dirt.‡ What we have left are priests of the Two Vehicle persuasion, groups that are content with a small, partial attainment. Locating true descendants of the authentic Zen way is like seeking the North Star in the midday sun. I am the only one left in the entire country. What I keenly regret is that I have not yet been able to find anyone to whom I can hand on this transmission. The great life-thread of wisdom is hanging by this one thin strand. You must work very hard, grinding your flesh and bone to powder if you must, to instill vital life in these genuine traditions. You must crush those devilish groups who would deny the working of karma. Become like a great and glorious minister who restores his country to prosperity. If you want to crush the devils who are destroying the true Dharma, you must struggle through a thicket of thorn

---

*Ts'ao-shan's Thousand Peaks: "When the thousand peaks are covered with snow, why is it one peak has none?"
†Koan based on a verse comment by Ta-hui on the Mu koan: "Lotus leaves, perfect discs, rounder than mirrors; / Water chestnuts, spiked needles, sharper than gimlets. / Wind blows through the willow flowers, fluff-balls sail; / Rain striking the pear blossoms, dragonflies dart."
‡"Small matter" (*shashi*)—the true essence of the authentic Zen transmission.

that extends for thousands of leagues, knocking over as you do the dark, tightly secured barriers that lead to higher attainment.

As the Zen teacher Huang-po said, "The great teacher Niu-t'ou preaches the Dharma with great freedom, but he doesn't yet understand about the barriers of our school that lead to higher attainment. Unless he obtains the key to unlock those barriers, how will he be able to overcome the devil legions that would destroy the true Dharma."*

I took up the koan that Shōju gave me and tried to penetrate it. It was like trying to work myself up a sheet of thick steel ten thousand feet high, or like climbing a treacherous mountain peak carrying an enormous weight on my back. In time, my conscious mind and its distracting thoughts disappeared; all my arts and skills, all my words and principles, were completely exhausted. I was like an utter simpleton, someone who knows nothing at all.

One day I went into the village on a begging expedition. I was standing in front of a house, just like a wooden statue, when suddenly a crazy person ran out and began pummeling me about the head, smashing my sedge hat to pieces. I fell to the ground unconscious, and as I did, the jade pavilion toppled over, the sheet of thickly layered ice that surrounded me shattered. I gave up the ghost, perishing into the Great Death. Passersby gathered round with looks of pity on their faces. When I gradually returned to my senses and got up, I found my entire body was bathed in cold sweat. I also discovered that I could penetrate all the difficult-to-pass koans I had been struggling with to their very roots. I burst into great peals of laughter in spite of myself, and began clapping my hands together. In all my twenty-five years on earth I had never experienced such joy before. I was dancing on air, waving my arms wildly about.

I walked back to Shōju's hermitage and told him what I had experienced. One look at me filled him with joy as well. He took his fan and began stroking my back with it. I bid farewell to Shōju not long after that and set out alone for my home province. Shōju accompanied me halfway down the mountain. When it finally came time to part, he took my hand in his and gave me the parting words, "In the future you must devote yourself to producing one or two students who can penetrate through the barriers as you have. You will in that way pay back the profound debt you owe the Buddha-patriarchs." I bowed to him and departed. Ever since that

*Records of the Lamp, ch. 9.

time, for over thirty or forty years, for the Dharma's sake I have been tire-lessly teaching students who have come to me from all over the country. Among them there are now a score or more who can give good accounts of themselves. Who knows, perhaps one or two of them are the kind of monk Shōju was talking about.

Thirty, forty years ago I used to assign people Chao-chou's Mu to work on. In time I came to realize how difficult it was for students to attain ken-shō using the Mu koan. Many of them wrestled with it until their dying day without ever gaining the power to penetrate it.

More recently, I have been telling them to hear the sound of one hand. After they hear the sound, I test them with other koans. I tell them to produce Mount Fuji from an inrō seal-case, to erect Tōji pagoda inside a water vase, to fatten the workhorse in I-chou by feeding the pet cow in Huai-chou grain, to grind a tea-mill inside a goose egg. I will not confirm that they have attained the Perfect Great Mirror Wisdom until they can penetrate these and see them as clearly as if they are in the palm of their hand. Next I have them put a stop to all sounds—birds and animals, flutes and bells and drums—whatever. Or I might tell them to stop the sailboats far out at sea.* After they have passed these one by one, they are ready to enter the Precious Mirror Samadhi. This is also called the con-templation of all things as forms of truth. It is the same as the Five Ranks' samadhi of Universal and Phenomenal, in which there is no self that sees and no objects to be seen; difference is identity, identity is difference. Lin-chi called it being at home yet on the road; being on the road yet at home. When a person reaches this point, he has attained the Wisdom of Sameness.

If he regards this sameness as a precious state and dwells in it, he will become like a fox or badger sleeping comfortably in an old lair, or a demon guarding a corpse in a coffin. How wonderful it is that a dragon will never look twice at a pond of such stagnant water.† I then have them take up and doubt some koan stories like the ones Shōju first assigned me: Su-shan's Memorial Tower, The Water Buffalo Comes Through the Window, Nan-ch'uan's Death, Nan-ch'uan's Flower in the Garden. Not until they have

---

*All these koans, except the one about fattening the workhorse, which is found in the *Lin-kuan lu*, were created by Hakuin himself.
†"A dragon that would be content to sleep at the bottom of a stagnant pool would never be able to soar up into the heavens [as he should]" (annotation).

passed through each of these will I confirm their attainment of the Wisdom of Marvelous Observation.

After that they must engage even more vigorously in gathering Dharma assets from a wide variety of sources so they can preach the great Dharma and bring benefit to countless living beings. Such is the true meaning of the Bodhisattva's vow. How wonderful is this vow that the Bodhisattva practices constantly and unflaggingly for infinite kalpas, to achieve deeper attainment himself while helping others to achieve it as well. It is the great Zen function, responding with perfect, marvelous freedom to all things according to their needs and capacities. This is called the Wisdom of Benefiting Others.

How wonderful to finally possess all Four Wisdoms! When the Four Wisdoms are bright and clear, you will also be armed with the four virtues that define the practice of a fully attained Bodhisattva.* This is the style of Zen National Master Gudō advocated and embodied in himself.

I wrote this work in a period of a few days. An old priest came around to serve as my attendant, grinding ink and setting out writing paper for me. By the time I had finished the draft and starting writing out a fair copy, the old priest seemed to have memorized. He could recite five to ten lines at a time. This surprised me, and puzzled me as well.

One day he came and bowed quietly in front of me. "When you have finished writing this out, and the book is complete," he said, "would you give me the draft? I am ignorant and weak-minded. In my heart I have always performed *gasshō*, thinking that today the Buddha's Dharma was vigorous and prospering. But reading what you have written in *Gudō's Lingering Radiance*, I have learned to my great regret that the true and authentic form of our Zen school's treasury of the true Dharma eye and wondrous mind of Nirvana, our greatest and most essential matter, is now on the verge of dying out altogether. And I also know who is responsible for this calamity. It is karma-denying priests with their perverse notions of silent illumination Zen who have undermined the true Dharma and obstructed later generations of students from attaining it. What a hateful and deplorable group they and their minions are! They are mortal enemies of all followers of Buddha. Even a king or prime minister would be unable

---

*The four virtues (*shi-toku*) that come with the attainment of Nirvana, or satori: permanency, joy, freedom, and purity.

to sweep them aside. They could not be removed by armed force. So there is no chance that someone of my meager abilities and intelligence could overcome them.

"But if you give me this manuscript, I will gather young men of great promise. We will band together and pledge a great and sacred oath: no matter what difficulties we encounter we will penetrate every koan, including those final ones so hard to pass, and we will spur ourselves forward until the old traditions that now lie in the dust have been revived. In the past, the great Chang Liang devised superlative strategies that repelled the enemy and protected the kingdoms of Pa and Chu. Yu Jang swallowed charcoal and lay in wait under a bridge in order to avenge his master's death. If we can muster our efforts as they did, it should not be too difficult for us to requite our debt to the Buddhas by overthrowing these pernicious priests who deny cause and effect."

On hearing that, I handed him the manuscript, telling him, "How splendid! Such loyalty and courageous spirit are altogether extraordinary!"

The old priest then sat up straight and correct and asked, "Who are those shameful priests? What enmity or resentment could make them want to destroy the true Dharma? What do they hope to gain by hindering later generations of students from seeking to achieve enlightenment? Even if you beat four or five of them to death every day, no one would reproach you!"

"No," I replied. "These men are not consciously trying to harm the true Dharma. It is just that they started their practice under an incompetent teacher. They merely followed his instructions, trying to remain thoughtless and mindless. Because a great doubt never arose in their minds, they never attained great enlightenment. Because they ignored the sutras and records of the Zen patriarchs, they acquired no Dharma assets, and so to the end of their lives they remained ignorant, dull-witted ignoramuses. Growing old, they began calling themselves Zen masters, saying they are your 'good friend.' But they can teach only the commonplace notions that happen to pop into their minds. Ignorant of the inner secrets that would enable them to produce a true Zen person, they just go on repeating phrases like, 'I am a Buddha just as I am!' If they are incapable of producing a student to carry on the Zen transmission, how can the true Dharma expect to survive in this latter day? That is the reason the Dharma is teetering on the brink of ruin.

"What, then, is the inner secret for producing a genuine Zen person? If you want to produce a genuine Zen disciple, nothing surpasses the dark and difficult koan barriers. In order to obtain true students to pass on the Dharma transmission, the Zen patriarchs of India, China, and Japan have laid down these thickets of thorn and briar, extending out for thousands of leagues. Without these barriers, the Zen groves would be like a pool of stagnant water. Its inmates would look like the herds of cranes you see standing around in the rice fields.

"When a new monk comes to my temple, I ask, 'Do you hear the sound of one hand?' This koan is like an iron stake. It drives him into a corner. He must gnaw away at it from all sides. Hold it up and examine it from every angle. No matter how much he suffers, no matter how tired he becomes, even if he seems to be on the brink of death, he will get no help from me at all. He exhausts his skills, runs out of words and rational means. [Suddenly, the time will come when] the phoenix breaks free of the golden net, when the crane escapes from the enclosure.

"Now he cannot hesitate for a split second. Ten thousand more tightly closed barriers lie ahead of him. Not until he has negotiated his way through that barrier forest of thorn and briar will I teach him about the practice that comes after satori, teach him about the Bodhi-mind, and send him out to begin putting the four great vows into practice, an activity that will engage him until the end of time."

Now, I have not written all these words down because I want to record the events of my own foolish life. My sole aim is to make the Zen school's methods for penetrating the secret koan barriers known to students so they will be able to forge on and acquire the strength that comes from attaining satori. My desire for them to achieve this strength is in no way different from my eagerness to have them raise up once again the traditions of National Master Gudō, which now lie forgotten in the dust.

I am not pridefully waving my own teaching banners. At the present time, publishing the *Record of Gudō* is the only idea I can come up with to help revive these withering traditions. To the venerable Zen teachers who share my concerns I say with great respect: Let us benefit future generations of Zen students by publishing these Zen records. There could be no greater or more fitting memorial to the National Master on this one hundredth anniversary of his death.

. . . .

[Colophon] The printing of this work was made possible by
donations from members of the lay community of Sōyū-ji in
Takayama, Hida province
The eighth month of the eighth year of Hōreki (1758)
Printed by Ogawa Gembei of Teramachi Street in Kyoto
And Funatsu Shinuemon of Shinsaibashi in Osaka

Select Glossary List of Terms and Proper Names

Alaya consciousness: Eighth Consciousness

Amida Buddha. The central Buddha in Chinese and Japanese Pure Land Buddhism

Arhat. One who has attained the highest rank in the Hinayana tradition

Bankei Yōtaku (1622–1693). Zen master best known for his teaching of "Unborn" (*fushō*) Zen, which Hakuin ceaselessly attacked in his writings

Bandō. The region of east-central Honshū around the city of Edo

Bodhi-mind (Sanskrit *Bodhichitta*). The "mind of enlightenment"; the aspiration to carry out the Four Great Vows (deepening self-awakening while working to help others reach liberation) that arises in the mind after attainment of *kenshō;* characteristic of post-satori practice

Bodhidharma. The First Patriarch of Chinese Zen, who brought Zen's mind-to-mind transmission to China from India

Bodhisattva. One who aspires to attain Buddhahood and carries out various practices to achieve that goal. Compassion is the outstanding characteristic of the Bodhisattva, who postpones his or her own entry into nirvana in order to assist others. Particularly important in Mahayana Buddhism (see Two Vehicles)

Chen feathers. A deadly poison

cinnabar field. *Tanden*; the center of breathing located below the navel; often used in the combined form *kikai tanden*, the cinnabar field located in the ocean of *ki*

claws and fangs of the Dharma cave (*hokkutsu no sōge*). An expression, originally from the *Records from the Groves of Zen* (*Lin-kuan lu*), descriptive of a koan's power to bring students to experience the "great death" (*taishi ichiban*), or satori; also that power embodied in an enlightened teacher. Usually used together with "divine death-dealing amulets"

closed barrier Zen (*kansa Zen*). Hakuin's term for koan practice, in which students must pass through numerous koan "barriers" deva realms. Highest of the six realms of unenlightened existence; in the ten realms they are below the four enlightened realms of Shravaka, Pratyeka-buddha, Bodhisattva, and Buddha

difficult-to-pass koans: hard-to-pass koans

divine death-dealing amulets. (*Datsumyō no shimpu*; also life-destroying charms). Originally, Taoist charms said to give the possessor the power to take life at will. Used similarly to "claws and fangs of the Dharma cave," with which it is generally paired, in Hakuin's works

Draft Biography. Tōrei's original, unpublished manuscript of the Hakuin *Chronological Biography,* containing much material deleted from the published text

Dragon Gate *(Ryūmon).* A three-tiered waterfall cut through the mountains of Lung-men to open up a passage for the Yellow River. It was said that on the third day of the third month, when peach trees are in flower, carp that succeeded in scaling this waterfall turned into dragons

Dragon staff certificate. A certificate, consisting of a painting of a priest's staff transforming into a dragon, which Hakuin awarded to students who attained *kenshō* (An account of these is given in *Precious Mirror Cave,* Chapter Two)

eighth "storehouse" consciousness (Sanskrit *ālaya-vijñāna*). The fundamental consciousness. in which all karma past and present existence is stored. Hakuin often refers to it as pitch-blackness, or describes it as a pitch-dark cave; when broken through or "inverted" in the attainment of enlightenment, it transforms suddenly into the all-illuminating Great Perfect Mirror Wisdom

Emma (Yama). King of Realm of the Dead

evil paths (of existence). The three lowest of the six paths or worlds in which unenlightened beings transmigrate: the realms of hell, hungry ghosts, and beasts.

Five Cardinal Sins. Patricide, matricide, killing an enlightened being, creating a schism within the sangha, shedding the blood of a Buddha

Five Chinese Zen Schools. Schools or teaching lineages, named after their founders, that developed in Chinese Zen between the T'ang and Sung dynasties: Kuei-yang, Lin-chi, Ts'ao-tung, Yun-men, and Fa-yen

Five Ranks. A teaching device attributed to the T'ang priest Tung-shan that was used in Japanese Sōtō Zen but was generally ignored in the Rinzai school. Hakuin gave it an important role in his program of post-satori training

Fivefold Eye. The human eye, the eye of the gods that sees all things at all times, the eye of wisdom that discerns the true forms of all things, the Dharma eye that is able to save others using skillful means, and the Buddha eye that knows all things, reflecting them as they are in themselves

Four Great (also Universal; Bodhisattva) Vows (*shigu seigan*). Vows Mahayana Buddhists take upon their entrance into religious life: To save all sentient beings; to end the inexhaustible delusive passions; to study all the infinite Dharma teachings; to master the unsurpassable Buddha Way

Four Wisdoms (*shi-chi*) attained in enlightenment: the great perfect mirror wisdom that reflects all things in their suchness; the wisdom that discerns the ultimate sameness of all things; the wisdom that discerns the distinctive features of all phenomena; the wisdom that promotes the work of Buddhahood

Fox slobber (*koen*; also *yako enda*, wild fox slobber) is a deadly poison; used as a metaphor for Zen teachings

fusetsu: General Discourse

gasshō. Pressing the palms of the hands together, fingers pointing upwards, in an expression of thankfulness, reverence, or prayer

General Discourse (*Fusetsu*). Described as teachings setting forth the essential matter of Zen; given in less informal circumstances than the *Jōdō*, without the need for offering incense or wearing the Dharma robe

Great Perfect Mirror Wisdom. See Four Wisdoms

hard-to-pass koans (*nantō*; literally, "hard to pass through"). Hakuin gives varying lists of hard-to-pass koans in his writings. In the system of koan study that developed after Hakuin's death, a type of koan used for advanced students

Hell of Incessant Suffering (Sanskrit, *Avichi*). The lowest level in the realm of hell, reserved for those who have committed one of the Five Cardinal Sins

inka (*inka-shōmei*). The certification or sanction of spiritual attainment (*kenshō*) awarded to students by a Rinzai teacher

Jōdō. "Ascending the high seat." Done when the teacher delivers a formal lecture from the high seat in the Dharma Hall

Ka! Shout uttered on entering satori; often synonymous with enlightenment itself

kalpa. An incalculably long period of time; an aeon

kami. Deities that are the central objects of worship in Japanese Shintō

kenshō. "Seeing into one's own self-nature"; approximate synonym for satori; normally limited to the initial breakthrough experience

ki. The vital energy or "breath," said to be located below the navel, that circulates through the body and is essential to health and the sustenance of life

kinhin. "Walking meditation," practiced between long periods of zazen

koku. One *koku* of rice, about 280 liters, weighing about 150 kilograms; enough, it was said, to feed one person for one year

Kokurin ("Crane Grove"). The *sangō* or "mountain name" of Hakuin's temple Shōin-ji; also referring, by extension, to Hakuin himself

Kokushi: National Master or Teacher. An honorific title traditionally bestowed by the emperor

Latter-Day Dharma. The age of the Dharma's destruction, the last of three periods a Buddha's teaching passes through after his death as it gradually loses its power to guide people to enlightenment

mon. Coins used in Hakuin's time; they were holed, allowing them to be strung together

Mu koan (*Gateless Barrier*, Case 1). Famous koan traditionally assigned to beginning students: A monk asked master Chao-chou, "Does a dog have a Buddha-nature, or not?" Chao-chou answered, "Mu" [literally, "Nothing" or "Not"]

Naikan meditation ("introspective meditation"). Hakuin's method for *Naikan* meditation is found in *Idle Talk on a Night Boat (Yasen-kanna). Precious Mirror Cave*, Chapter Three

Nembutsu. The practice used in Pure Land Buddhism of repeating the name of Amida Buddha in the formula "*Namu Amida Butsu*" (I entrust myself to Amida Buddha)

Oshō. A term of respect commonly used for a senior priest, usually, but not always, indicating he is head priest of a temple

Po I: see Shu Ch'i

post-satori training (*gogo no shūgyō*). The practice that begins after attainment of *kenshō*, defined by Hakuin as working for deeper self-awakening while helping others to reach liberation

Pratyeka-buddha ("Private" Buddha). See Two Vehicles

raksha demons. Originally, malignant spirits possessing supernatural power and the ability to move a great speed; they also appear in Mahayana literature as guardians of Buddhism

ri. The Japanese mile, about 4 kilometers (2.44 miles)

rōhatsu training session (*rōhatsu sesshin*). The period of concentrated zazen practice held in Japanese Rinzai monasteries from the first day of the twelfth month and ending on the morning of the eighth day

ryō. A standard gold piece in use in Edo, Japan weighing about 18 grams, a large percent gold

sanzen. Literally, to study Zen. In Hakuin's works it normally refers to koan study as well as to the Zen teacher's private interview with his students

satori. Enlightenment

segaki (*segaki-e*). A ceremony at which services are held and food and drink offered to beings in the hungry ghost existence as well as those in the other realms of samsaric rebirth.

shippei. A bamboo staff two feet or more in length bound with wisteria vine and covered with black lacquer used by Zen teachers

Shōbutsuji. Minor Buddhist Observances. This includes funeral services, ceremonies consecrating Buddhist images, etc.

Shōin-ji. Hakuin's temple in Hara, Suruga province

Shōsan. Informal talks given at any time and on any occasion

Shravaka. See Two Vehicles

Shu Ch'i and Po I. Celebrated pair of brother princes renowned for integrity and faithfulness. When their father made known his intention to leave the throne to Shu Ch'i, the latter declared that he could not deprive his elder brother Po I of his birthright and they both fled into the mountains, supporting themselves on wild plants until they finally perished of cold and hunger

silent illumination (*mokushō*) Zen. A term usually associated with practices of the Sōtō school, as contrasted with the koan Zen of the Rinzai school. Hakuin uses it for all types of Zen practice, including those of his own Rinzai school, that do not force the student to focus on the breakthrough to satori

Six Paths. The six ways of unenlightened existence: (1) hell, (2) the realm of hungry ghosts, (3) beasts, (4) asuras, (5) human beings, and (6) devas (heavenly beings)

Sound of One Hand koan (*sekishu no onjō*). A two-part koan Hakuin devised in his mid-sixties for beginning students: first, Hear the sound of one hand clapping; then, Put a stop to all sounds.

storehouse consciousness: eighth consciousness

Suiriku (Suiriku-e). Similar to the segaki-e; a ceremony at which food and drink is offered for the repose of the dead and the liberation of all beings in the water (sui) and on land (riku)

talisman, life-destroying: See divine death-dealing amulets

tanden: See cinnabar field

Ten Evil Acts (jū-aku; also Transgressions): taking life, stealing, illicit sexual conduct, lying, harsh words, defaming, duplicity, greed, anger, and holding mistaken views

tengu; tengu demon. Winged, long-nosed goblin-like beings. They appear in both benevolent and malicious forms, as protectors and as opponents of the Buddhist Dharma

Tenjin. Deified form of the court scholar, statesman, and poet Sugawara Michizane enshrined at the main Kitano Tenmangu in Kyoto

three Buddha bodies. The three kinds of body a Buddha may possess: the eternal and absolute Dharma-body, indescribable and inconceivable; the Reward- or Recompense-body, obtained as a result of practicing the Bodhisattva way, in which the Buddha preached to the great assemblies described in the sutras; and the Transformation-body, the body he manifests to human beings

Three Poisons. The major evil passions: greed, anger, stupidity

Three Worlds or Realms; also Triple World (sangai). The realms of desire, form, and formlessness inhabited by unenlightened beings who transmigrate within the six paths of existence. Those in the realm of desire are governed by desires; those in the world of form have physical form but no desires; those in the realm of formlessness are free from both desire and form

Two Vehicles: the Shravaka, a disciple who achieves liberation upon listening to the Buddhist teachings, and the Pratyeka-buddha, who achieves liberation but does not undertake to teach others. Hakuin regarded them as inferior to the Bodhisattva, whose life is devoted to saving other beings as well

Udumbara. A plant said to bloom only once every three thousand years; used to described the rare appearance of a Buddha in the world

Unborn Zen. The Zen teaching of the seventeenth century Zen master Bankei Yōtaku, which retained considerable popularity into the eighteenth century. Hakuin uses the term, as he does silent illumination Zen, do-nothing Zen, and dead- [withered-] sitting Zen, in a more general sense to indicate a type of Zen practice that does not focus the student on the breakthrough into *kenshō,* or satori

Vimalakirti. The central figure of the *Vimalakirti Sutra;* regarded in the Zen school as the ideal of the lay practicer

yamabushi. "Mountain ascetic" of the Shugendō tradition.

Select Bibliography

ABBREVIATIONS

HHZ *Hakuin Zenji Hōgo Zenshū (Zen Master Hakuin's Complete Dharma Writings)*. 14 volumes. Edited by Yoshizawa Katsuhiro. Kyoto: Zenbunka kenkyūsho, 2000–2006

HON *Hakuin Oshō Nempu (Chronological Biography of Priest Hakuin)*. Edited by Katō Shōshun. Shibunkaku, 1985

HOS *Hakuin Oshō Shōden (Detailed Biography of Priest Hakuin)*. Rikugawa Taiun. Sankibō, 1965

HOZ *Hakuin Oshō Zenshū (Complete Works of Priest Hakuin)*. 8 volumes. Tokyo, 1935

HZB *Hakuin Zenga Bokusei (Hakuin's Zen Painting and Calligraphy)*. 3 volumes. Nigensha, 2011

SH *Shamon Hakuin (Buddhist Monk Hakuin)*. Shizuoka, 1983

Admonitions for Buddhists (Hsi-men ching-hsun) T48.

Analects of Confucius, The. Translated by Burton Watson. Columbia, 2007.

Ancestral Heroes Collection (Tsu-ying-chi). An anthology of religious verse by the Sung master Hsueh-tou Ch'ung-hsien.

Beating the Cloth Drum: The Letters of Zen Master Hakuin. Translated by Norman Waddell. Shambhala, 2012.

Biographies of Divine Sages (Shen-hsien chuan). Edited by Sawada Zuihō, Heibonsha, 1993.

Biographies of Famous Women (Lieh-nu chuan). By Liu Hsiang.

Biographies of Zen Priests of Modern Times (Kinsei Zenrin Sōbō-den). 2 vols. Edited by Nōnin Kōdō. Zen Bunka kenkyūsho, 2002 .

Blue Cliff Record (Pi-yen lu) T48. Translated by Thomas and J.C. Cleary. Boston: Shambhala, 1977.

Bodhidharma's Six Gates (Shao-shih liu-men) T48. Collection of six short treatises attributed to Bodhidharma.

Book of Changes (I Ching).

Book of Equanimity (Ts'ung-jung lu) T48. Important koan collection used in Sōtō Zen. Translated *Book of Serenity*, Thomas Cleary, Shambhala, 1998.

Book of Lieh Tzu. Translated by A. C. Graham. John Murray, 1960.

Buddhist Monk Hakuin (Shamon Hakuin). Akiyama Kanji. Shizuoka, 1983.

Ch'an-lin lei-chu (Classified Collection of the Zen Forest) ZZ67. Largest classified collection of Zen koan .

Chronicles of the Buddha-patriarchs (Fo-tsu t'ung-chi) T49.

Chronological Biography: full title *Chronological Biography of Zen Master Shinki Dokumyō, Founder of Ryūtaku-ji (Ryūtaku-kaiso Shinki Dokumyō Zenji Nempu).* Edited by Katō Shōshun. Shibunkaku, 1985.

Chronological Biography of Zen Priest Tōrei (Tōrei Oshō Nempu). Edited by Nishimura Eshin. Shibunkaku, 1982.

Ch'uan-lao's Comments on the Diamond Sutra (Ch'uan-lao Chin-kang ching) ZZ38–4.

Chuang Tzu, The Complete Works. Translated by Burton Watson. Columbia University Press, 1968.

Classified Collection of the Zen Forest: see *Ch'an-lin lei-chu.*

Collection of Sand and Pebbles (Shaseki-shū). Tokyo: Iwanami bunko, 1943.

Commentary on the Daruma Zen-kyō (Daruma Zen-kyō settsū-kōsho). Work by Tōrei, published in 1784.

Commentary on the Great Wisdom Sutra (Ta-chih-tu-lun; Daichidoron). Attributed to *Nagarjuna.*

Compendium of the Five Lamps (Wu-teng hui-yuan) ZZ2B:10–11. A comprehensive collection of Zen records compiled in the Sung dynasty.

Comprehensive Records of Yun-men (Yun-men kuang-lu) T47.

Detailed Biography of Zen Master Hakuin (Hakuin Oshō Shōden). Rikugawa Taiun. Sankibō, 1963.

Detailed Study of the Fundamental Principles of the Five Houses of Zen (Goke sanshō yōro mon HOZ7). A work by Tōrei Enji.

Dharma Words of Priest Takusui (Takusui Oshō Hōgo). Zenmon Hōgo Shū vol. 3. Kōyōkan. 1921.

Dharma Words in Japanese on Cause and Effect: Kana Innen Hōgo

Diamond Sutra (Chin-kan ching) T8.

Dictionary of Buddhist Terms and Concepts. Tokyo: Nichiren International, 1983.

Divergent Concepts in Sutra and Vinaya Texts (Ching-lu I-hsiang) T53.

Dokugo Shingyō. Shibayama Zenkei's annotated edition of Hakuin's comments on the *Heart Sutra.* Kichūdō, 1978.

Draft Biography. Tōrei's manuscript version of Hakuin's *Chronological Biography.* A fairly complete text is found in *Detailed Biography of Zen Priest Hakuin.*

Dream Words from a Land of Dreams (Kaian-kokugo). Hakuin's Zen commentary on the *Record of Daitō.* The best edition is *Kaian-kokugo,* edited by Dōmae Sōkan. Zenbunka kenkyūsho, 2003.

Essential Teachings of Zen Master Hakuin. Norman Waddell. Boston: Shambhala, 1994. Translation of Hakuin's *Sokkō-roku kaien-fusetsu (Talks Introductory to Lectures on the Record of Hsu-t'ang).*

Essentials of Mind Transmission (Ch'uan-hsin fa-yao) T48.

Essentials of Successive Records of the Lamp (Tsung-men Lien-teng hui-yao) ZZ2.2–9.3–5.

Extensive Records of Zen Priest Po-yun (Po-yun ch'an-shih kuang-lu) ZZ2.25.3.

Eye of Men and Gods (Jen-t'ien yen-mu) T48. Sayings and verses by priests of the Five Chinese Zen Schools. Compiled by Hui-yen Chih-chao.

Flower Garland Sutra (Hua-yen ching) T9.

Four Part Record (Shibu-roku) T48. A composite work published in Japan containing *Verses on Belief in Mind (Hsin-hsin-ming), Verses on Realizing the Way (Cheng-tao ke), The Ten Ox-herding Pictures (Shih-niu t'u),* and *Principles of Zazen (Tso-ch'an-i).*

Fu-chiao pien: Treatise to Assist the Teachings.

Gateless Barrier (Wu-men kuan) T48. Important koan collection.

General Commentary on the Vimalakirti Sutra (Wei-mo ching lueh-shu) T1778.

Genkō Shakusho (Chronicle of Buddhism of the Genkō Era). By Kokan Shiren. Early history of Japanese Buddhism. Nihon Bukkyō Zensho 101.

Great Cessation and Insight (Mo-ho chih-kuan) T46. Treatise on Mahayana theory and practice by T'ien-t'ai founder Chih-i.

Gudō's Lingering Radiance (Hōkan Ishō) HOZ1.

Hakuin. Takeuchi Naotsugi. Chikuma, 1965. A large compilation of Hakuin's Zenga and calligraphy.

Hakuin Kōroku (Hakuin's Extensive Zen Records). 2 volumes. Tokyo, 1902.

Hakuin Oshō Nempu. Edited by Katō Shōshun. Shibunkaku, 1985.

Hakuin's Zen Painting and Calligraphy (Hakuin Zenga-bokuseki). 3 vols. Nigensha, 2011.

Han-shan shih (Cold Mountain Poems). All page references are to the *Zen no goroku* edition edited by Matsumura and Iritani. Chikuma, 1970.

Hekigan Hishō (Hakuin's Secret Comments on the Blue Cliff Record). Seikō-zasshi-sha, 1916.

Heroic March Sutra (Shurangama Sutra; C. Leng-yen ching) T642. Mahayana sutra widely read and quoted in Zen texts.

Hōkyō-ki (Diary of the Hōkyō Era). Practice diary kept by Dōgen during his study in China. "*Dōgen's Hōkyō-ki*" *(Eastern Buddhist* x 1; xi 2, 1977–78).

Honchō Kōsō-den (Lives of Eminent Japanese Priests). 75 vols. Compiled by Mangan Shiban. Dainihon Bukkyō Zensho, 103.

Horse Thistles (Oniazami). Work by Hakuin. *HHZ2.*

Hsu-kao-seng chuan (Further Biographies of Eminent Monks) T50.

Hsu-t'ang's Verse Comments on One Hundred Koans (Hsu-t'ang po-tse sung-ku). Found in *Record of Hsu-t'ang, ch. 5.*

Hu-fa lun (Essay in Defense of the Dharma) T52. Sung dynasty compilation by Chang Wu-chin.

I Ching, The. Translation by Cary Baynes. Pantheon Books, 1961.

Idle Talk on a Night Boat (Yasen-kanna) HHZ4. Translated in *Precious Mirror Cave,* pp. 83–115.

Jinja-kō Bengi (Resolving Doubts about A Study of Our Shintō Shrines). Work by the Shingon priest Jakugon.

Kana Innen Hōgo (Dharma Words in Japanese on Cause and Effect) HHZ11. Hakuin work.

Kao-shih chuan (Biographies of Noble Sages). By Huang Fu-mi (2nd century)

Keisō dokuzui (Poison Blossoms from a Thicket of Thorn) HOZ 2.

Kenchō Donge Shingyō (Kenchō Donge's Shingyō). Privately printed, 1935. A commentary on Hakuin's *Dokugo Shingyō* by Sugawara Jiho.

Kentō-roku (Record of Kentō: Viewing the Peach Blossoms Record). Zen records of Daikyū Sōkyū. Kokuyaku Zengaku Taisei, vol. 25.

Talks Introductory to Lectures on the Record of Hsu-t'ang (Sokkō-roku kaien-fusetsu). See *Essential Teachings of Zen Master Hakuin.*

Ling-yuan pi-yu. Zen master Ling-yuan's (d. 1117) letters to his students. *Kokuyaku Zenshū Sōsho 2.*

Lotus Sutra, The. Translated by Burton Watson. Columbia University Press, 1993.

Manjusri's Preaching of the Great Wisdom Sutra (Monjushiri-shosetsu maka-hannya-haramitta-kyō) T23.

Mencius. Translated by D.C. Lau. Penguin Books, 1970.

Moshio-shū. HHZ13. Collection of Hakuin's Japanese poetry.

Mutterings to the Wall (Kabe Sōsho) HHZ1. Work by Hakuin.

Nirvana Sutra (Ta-pan nieh-p'an ching) T12.

Old Granny's Tea-Grinding Songs (Obaba-dono no Kohiki Uta) HHZ 13. Translated in *Precious Mirror Cave.*

Oradegama. HHZ9. Work by Hakuin. Translated in *Zen Master Hakuin, Selected Writings.*

Poison Words for the Heart (Dokugo Shingyō). Hakuin commentary translated as *Zen Words for the Heart.* Norman Waddell. Boston: Shambhala, 1996.

Praise of the Five Houses of the True School (Wu-chia cheng-tsung-tsan) ZZ 2B–8. Biographies of important priests of the Five Chinese Zen schools, compiled by the thirteenth-century priest Hsi-sou Shao-t'an.

Precious Lessons of the Zen School (Ch'an-lin pao-tsun) T48. Twelfth-century collection of anecdotes and teachings taken from the lives and sayings of Sung Zen teachers.

Precious Mirror Cave, Hakuin's. A Zen Miscellany. Translated by Norman Waddell. Translations of Hakuin's autobiography *Sakushin osana monogatari, Takayama Yūkichi monogatari, Yasenkanna, Obaba-dono no Kohiki Uta, Hōkyōkutsu no ki,* and Hakuin's *Chronological Biography.* Berkeley: Counterpoint Press, 2009.

Precious Mirror Samadhi (Pao-ching san-mei) T47. Zen poem traditionally ascribed to Tung-shan Liang-chieh.

Pure Regulations, Po-chang's (Po-chang ch'ing-kuei) T48.

Record of Bukkō (Bukkō-roku) T80–2.

Record of National Master Daiō (Daiō Kokushi goroku). Zen records of Nampo Jōmyō (Daiō Kokushi). Edited by Yanagida Seizan. Kichūdo, 1957.

Record of Daitō (Daitō-roku) T81. Zen records of Shūhō Myōchō (Daitō Kokushi).

Record of Hsu-t'ang (Hsu-t'ang yu-lu) T47. Zen records of the Sung priest Hsu-t'ang Chih-yu.

Record of Lin-chi (Lin-chi lu) T47.

Record of Yun-an (Yun-an Tan-hua yu-lu) ZZ2.26.4.

Recorded Sayings of Layman P'ang. Translated by Ruth Sasaki, Iriya Yoshitaka, and Dana Fraser. Tokyo: Weatherhill, 1971.

Records of National Master Ryūhō: Record of Daitō.

Records of Sung-yuan (Sung-yuan lu) ZZ2.26.3.

Records of the Authentic Lamp (Shūmon Shōtō-roku). Compilation of the records of Japanese Zen Myōshin-ji priests by Tōyō Eichō. First published in the early 17th century.

Records of the Essential Mirror (Tsung-ching lu) T48.

Records of the Grand Historian (Shih-chi). 2 vols. Translated by Burton Watson. Columbia University Press, 1958.

Records of the Lamp [of the Ching-te Era] (Ching-te ch'uang-teng lu) T51. By Tao-yuan. Standard collection of Chinese Zen records.

Records of the Old Worthies (Ku-tsun-su yu-lu). ZZ 2.24–1.

Redolence from the Cold Forest (Kanrin Ihō) HOZ4. A selection of Zen and Buddhist texts Hakuin made for students; first published in 1769.

Religious Art of Zen Master Hakuin. Yoshizawa Katsuhiro with Norman Waddell. Berkeley: Counterpoint Press, 2009.

Resolving Doubts About the Land of the Kami (Shinkoku Kaigi-hen). Work by the Shintō priest Tatsuno Hirochika (1616–1693); published in 1673.

San-t'i-shih (Poetry in Three Styles). 13th-century collection of T'ang poetry influential in Japanese Zen circles.

Sendai's Comments on the Poems of Han-shan (Kanzan-shi Sendai-kimon) HOZ4. Work by Hakuin.

Sentinel at the Gates (Mikaki mori) HHZ8. Work by Hakuin.

Shan-hai ching (The Classic of Mountains and Seas). Translated by Anne Birrell. Penguin, 2000.

Shang-chih pien. Work in two volumes by the Ming priest K'ung-ku Chinglung criticizing the anti-Buddhist thought of Chu Hsi and promoting the unity of Confucianism, Taoism and Buddhism.

Shih-shih tzu-chien. A glossary of Buddhist words and terms compiled at the beginning of the 12th century. *Kokuyaku issai-kyō,* 123.

Shōju Dōkyō Etan Anju Anroku. A short religious biography of Hakuin's teacher Shōju Rōjin; first published in Abe Hōshun's *Shōju Rōjin.* Gagetsu-an, Nagano, 1931.

Shurangama Sutra: Heroic March Sutra.

Snake Legs for Kaien-fusetsu (Kaien-futsetsu Dasoku). Tōrei's annotations for Hakuin's *Sokkō-roku kaien-fusetsu;* published 1752.

Snake Strawberries (Hebiichigo) HHZ1. Work by Hakuin. Translated in *Zen Master Hakuin, Selected Writings.*

Soin-shō (Soin's Annotations). Japanese commentary on *San-t'i-shih* by Sesshin Soin. First published at the beginning of the 17th century.

Sokkō-roku kaien-fusetsu: Essential Teachings of Zen Master Hakuin.

Spurring Students Through the Zen Barriers (Ch'an-kuan tse-hsin) T48. Compiled by the Ming priest Yun-ch'i Chu-hung. *Zenkan-sakushin,* edited by Fujiyoshi Jikai. Chikuma, 1970.

Stories from a Thicket of Thorn and Briar (Keikyoku sōdan) HOZ1. A collection of stories about Hakuin and his students, compiled by Myōki Sōseki and published in the 19th century.

Stories Recorded at Yun-wo Hermitage (Yun-wo chi-t'an) ZZ2.21.

Sutra of Forty-two Sections (Ssu-shih-erh chang ching) T17.

Sutra on Creating Images of Buddha (Tso-fo hsing-hsiang ching) T692.

Sutra of the Bequeathed Teaching (Fo-i chueh-ching) T389.

Ta-hui's Arsenal (Ta-hui wu-k'u) T47. A collection of koans and anecdotes with Ta-hui's comments.

Ta-hui's General Discourses (Ta-hui p'u-shuo). Dainihon kōtei zōkyō, 31.

Tai-hui's Letters (Ta-hui shu) T47. A collection of Ta-hui's letters of religious instruction to lay followers.

Tale of My Childhood (Sakushin Osana monogatari). Work by Hakuin. *III1Z7.* Translated in *Precious Mirror Cave,* pp. 3–37.

Tales of Cause and Effect (Inga Monogatari). Compiled by the Zen teacher Suzuki Shōsan; first published in the second half of the 17th century.

Three Teachings of the Buddha-patriarchs (Fo-tsu san-ching) ZZ59–1. Consisting of *Kuei-shan ching-ts'e, Ssu-shih-erh chang ching,* and *I-chueh ching*

Treatise in Thirty Stanzas (San-shih sung) T31. By Vasubandhu.

Treatise on the Adornments of the Mahayana (Ta-ch'eng chuan-yen ching lun) T31.

Treatise on the Perfection of Great Wisdom (Ta-chih-tu-lun) T1509. Kumarajiva's Chinese translation of a commentary on the *Mahāprajñāpāramitā Sūtra* attributed to Nagarjuna.

Treatise to Assist the Teachings (Fu-chiao pien). By the Rinzai teacher Fo-jih Ch'i-sung. *Hogyō-hen,* edited by Araki Kengo. Chikuma, 1981.

Tso-chuan (Tso's Narrative). Tso Chuan; Selections from China's Oldest Narrative History. Translated by Burton Watson. Columbia University Press, 1989.

Unborn: The Life and Teachings of Zen Master Bankei. Translated by Norman Waddell. North Point Press, 1980.

Vimalakirti Sutra (Wei-mo ching) T14.

Vimalakirti Sutra, The. Translated by Burton Watson. Columbia University Press, 1997.

Wake-up for Sleepyheads (Neboke no mezamashi) HOZ6. Hakuin work.

Wild Ivy (Itsumadegusa) HHZ3. Hakuin autobiography. Translated by Norman Waddell. Boston: Shambhala, 1999.

Yanada Zeigan Zenshū. 2 vols. Akashi-shi kyōiku-iinkai, 1934.

Zen Dust. Miura Isshu and Ruth Sasaki. Kyoto, 1966.

Zen Master Hakuin; Selected Writings. Translated by Philip Yampolsky. Columbia University Press, 1971.

Zen Teachings of Master Lin-chi. Translated by Burton Watson. Columbia University Press, 1993.

Zen Words for the Heart. Translation of *Dokugo Shingyō.* Norman Waddell. Boston: Shambhala, 1996.

Zengo Ji-i. Nakagawa Shibuan. Tokyo, 1969.

Zenrinkushū. Edited by Shibayama Zenkei. Kyoto, Kichūdō, 1964. Book of Zen phrases.

Index